Crime, Deviance, and Social Control in the 21st Century

Crime, Deviance, and Social Control in the 21st Century

A Justice and Rights Perspective

Edited by Claudio Colaguori

CANADIAN
SCHOLARS

Toronto | Vancouver

Crime, Deviance, and Social Control in the 21st Century: A Justice and Rights Perspective
Edited by Claudio Colaguori

First published in 2023 by
Canadian Scholars, an imprint of CSP Books Inc.
425 Adelaide Street West, Suite 200
Toronto, Ontario
M5V 3C1

www.canadianscholars.ca

Library and Archives Canada Cataloguing in Publication

Title: Crime, deviance, and social control in the 21st century : a justice and rights perspective /
    edited by Claudio Colaguori.
Names: Colaguori, Claudio, 1964- editor.
Description: Includes bibliographical references.
Identifiers: Canadiana (print) 20220420610 | Canadiana (ebook) 20220420661 | ISBN
    9781773383330 (softcover) | ISBN 9781773383354 (EPUB) | ISBN 9781773383347 (PDF)
Subjects: LCSH: Crime. | LCSH: Deviant behavior. | LCSH: Social control. | LCSH: Social
    justice.
Classification: LCC HV6025 .C725 2022 | DDC 364—dc23

Page layout by S4Carlisle Publishing Services
Cover design by Rafael Chimicatti

Printed and bound in Ontario, Canada

Canadä

Contents

Detailed Contents

CHAPTER 1

Understanding Crime, Deviance, and Social Control

Claudio Colaguori

LEARNING OBJECTIVES

In this chapter, you will

- understand how crime, deviance, and social control are related to power relations;
- begin to familiarize yourself with some of the main concepts involved in the study of crime, deviance, and social control;
- learn about the history of the study of criminal and deviant behaviour that formed modern criminology;
- develop critical thinking tools that will help you understand the controversies and complexities of studying crime; and
- learn how criminology offers a unique perspective to examining prevailing harms, risks, and controversies in our global society.

INTRODUCTION

The history of human society is replete with acts of wrongdoing, **crime**, and injustice. People have inflicted harms on one another in various ways, from the denial of basic freedoms to the deliberate killing of innocents in the name of some higher authority. At the beginning of the 21st century, the serious issues of *crime*, *corruption*, and *violence* continue to disrupt the civil order that is essential for a peaceful and just society. Fears and worries about social disorder continue to form part of our daily lives. Whether we hear about criminal victimization in the news or have personal experiences with such problems, it is apparent to many that injustice is a common and problematic part of our modern society. Acts of human wrongdoing disturb us, and yet *they often also intrigue and fascinate us.* Forms of human conflict have long captivated the human imagination and are so much a part of our shared social history that they form the basis of the great dramas of classical antiquity from the ancient Greeks through to Shakespeare right up to the present day, where the large number of crime-themed television programs, books, comics, movies, and popular news media continue to capture the public imagination. Crime is both a compelling topic and an important social concern. The discipline of **criminology** aims to understand the issues of harm and criminal wrongdoing, as well as the consequences of attempts to control these behaviours.

The realities of crime, illegal activity, and wrongdoing raise a number of important questions. What does the continuing occurrence of criminal activity and ongoing victimization say about the nature and progress of our society? Is the persistence of crime and social disorder a reflection of an innately deviant human nature? Do people learn to become criminals? Are crime, violence, and disorder the result of our society not having progressed beyond the social problems of the past? Is the presence of crime and disorder symptomatic of an unequal political and economic order? These questions may be straightforward, but the answers are often not.

The study of crime and society involves engaging with numerous controversial and complex issues. There are many different types of crime and many different causes for it as well. Despite this complexity, matters of crime and **justice** are often presented in the news media in a simplistic way that contributes to public misperceptions. Issues involving crime also invoke strong personal emotions such as fear, grief, hatred, and vengeance.

There is no doubt that crime and deviance is both a fascinating and a challenging area of study. Students of criminology come to learn that issues regarding deviant and criminal behaviour, law-breaking, and justice are best understood within the context of powerful social forces in our society. Some social issues that pertain to the study of crime and its control involve:

- the antagonistic nature of interpersonal relations;
- the difficulties of achieving the aims and goals of the justice system;
- racial, cultural, and gender inequalities;
- the unequal distribution of economic opportunity, wealth, and resources; and
- the history of discrimination against marginalized peoples.

All of these factors deal with the issue of **power**. The study of crime, **deviance**, and **social control** is, to a large extent, the study of power relations. It involves understanding how certain individuals and groups exercise considerable influence over others. Some examples include the following:

- The power that a criminal has over the fate of their victim.
- The power that the law and the criminal justice system have over those who are accused of a crime and hence the power of the **state** to punish.
- The power that the popular communications media has in circulating ideas, assumptions, and myths about crime, criminals, and justice officials.
- The power that an influential group has over claiming that someone's behaviour is immoral and therefore punishable.
- The power that technology such as firearms and the internet has over intensifying the capacity for criminals to inflict harm and victimization on others.
- The power that police forces have over members of the public who can be apprehended or charged or killed in unlawful circumstances.
- The power that corporations have to engage in forms of wrongdoing such as breaking environmental or labour laws if it serves their interests in the pursuit of profits.
- The power of the use of violent force to destroy property or to inflict physical injury and death on people.

Power relations are evident when examining matters of crime and social control, but understanding how subtle power relations shape our lives in other ways is not always obvious or easy to recognize. As Michel Foucault (1926–1984) observed, power is often hidden in the midst of our social interactions with others and in the ways we engage with social institutions like the family, the communications media, and the state, all of which have a substantial influence over us.

In the words of scholars ...

Power is tolerable only on condition that it masks a substantial part of itself.... Its success is proportional to its ability to hide its own mechanisms.

Michel Foucault, *The History of Sexuality Volume 1: An Introduction.* 1980

Box 1.1: Crime Myths vs. Realities: What Are the Most Dangerous Types of Crime?

What comes to mind when you hear the word *criminal*? Many people think of a typical "street criminal," someone who engages in theft, assault, and gun violence, for example. It is a widely held myth that street crime represents the most imminent criminal threat to the well-being of citizens (Box, 1983). Such perceptions are not surprising given that the mainstream news media often reports on such crimes to the exclusion of other, more substantial types of illegalities. Although the destructive acts of street criminals are certainly a matter of public concern, what is less known is that the types of crime that do the most overall damage are the crimes of the powerful. Take note of the following list of examples of crime and wrongdoing perpetrated by powerful criminal organizations, business enterprises, and nation-states.

- The illegal poaching and sale of wild animals, which includes gorilla parts, shark finning, and ivory tusk poaching from elephants and rhinos, among many other examples, are viewed by **Interpol** as among the worst environmental crimes the world currently faces. As a result of the killing of wild animals for their parts, many species are facing near extinction.
- The 2010 Deepwater Horizon oil disaster, which was the largest accidental oil spill in history; the addition of tetraethyl lead, a notorious neurotoxin, to gasoline for almost a century, and which is still being added to vehicle fuel in some countries; and the 2015 Volkswagen diesel fuel emission "scandal," where the company deliberately concealed that its vehicles were emitting 40 times the legally allowable amount of nitrogen oxide emissions, are just some examples of the petrochemical crimes that have caused massive harm, contributing to habitat destruction and the emission of carcinogenic and other disease-causing substances into the environment.
- The 2008 financial crisis caused by the illegal activities of mortgage lenders eventually led to a global recession that cost people worldwide trillions of dollars in lost savings and, for many, the loss of home ownership. Banking fraud and deceptive monetary practices continue to be an ongoing problem across the globe.

- The ongoing problem of human enslavement and trafficking is believed to generate upwards of $12 billion annually for organized crime cartels. This type of crime involves the illegal captivity, sale, and control of an estimated 30 million persons, primarily as forced labourers and sex workers.

- From 1831 until the last residential school closed in 1996, Indigenous people in Canada were subject to the heinous practice of "aggressive assimilation" whereby approximately 150,000 children were forcibly removed from their own families to be indoctrinated in a repressive institutional system. Forced to live in substandard conditions, often for years, they suffered physical deprivation, sexual abuse, and emotional trauma as the state sought to deny them their culture, language, and identity.

- In February 2014, General Motors (GM) finally issued a recall for approximately 30 million vehicles worldwide due to a faulty ignition switch that would turn off the vehicle while it was being driven, causing the driver to lose steering control and crash. The problem caused at least 124 avoidable deaths, since GM knew of the problem at least 10 years before issuing the recall, yet failed to take action.

- From the mislabelling of foreign-grown vegetables as "product of Canada" to health supplements containing virtually none of the herbal ingredients stated on the label, as well as food products that have been knowingly adulterated with toxic ingredients, the case of *food fraud* is an ongoing concern that directly affects the health safety of consumers.

Large-scale criminal activity perpetrated by those with power negatively impacts the lives of millions of people annually and yet, in the public eye, the term *criminal* still tends to evoke traditional categories of street thugs. For criminologist Steven Box (1983), the process of deflecting attention away from the criminal harms perpetrated by powerful organizations is part of the misleading process of **mystification**. In focusing on the crimes of the relatively powerless as the most "dangerous," the existing hierarchical order of society is maintained and the interests of the powerful are more easily protected.

EXPLAINING CRIME

Crime is a virtually universal phenomenon in human societies, and rule-making and rule-breaking are normal aspects of human behaviour. In the previous section, you were introduced to the idea that the issues of crime, deviance, and control are interrelated and involve different types of power relations. But what about *crime* itself? What does the concept actually mean? *Crime* is a broad term that can refer to a few different things, making it difficult to define in a straightforward way.

Crime as a Legal Concept

In the most technical sense, a *crime* is defined as an act or behaviour that is prohibited by criminal law, and which authorities attempt to control through punishment. Simply put, a crime is an *illegal* act. In this strict technical sense, *crime* is a legal concept. Yet, even in the strict legal sense, there is a vast range of different acts that are officially classified as criminal and many of these are completely unrelated to each other. Furthermore, acts that are classified as "illegal" and "criminal" change with time and place. Those in positions of authority who have the power to determine what remains legal and what is deemed illegal possess a substantial amount of power. But defining something as illegal does not mean it is inherently wrong or unjust. For this reason and others, criminal law has changed continually over time to reflect the greater good and improve justice.

Crime as a Type of Wrongdoing

Upon closer examination, we begin to see that *criminality* often goes beyond legal conceptions of reality to include actions that upset social standards of safety and order that form the basis of peace and security. Crime in this broader sense is understood as a type of social harm, wrongdoing, or improper activity. The term *crime* is also used metaphorically to refer to a wide range of acts perceived to be wrong. Take, for example, the phrase "the price of that cauliflower is criminal!" In that sense, the term *criminal* invokes a sense of outrage against something seen to be *unfair*.

A non-legal conception of "crime" also conveys the idea that an act or behaviour is harmful in some way to the larger social group and thus should be restricted, not necessarily by law and police but through disapproval from others. This conception of crime as wrongdoing or "something bad" is significantly influenced by shared *ethical* and *moral* judgments that define cultural codes of right and wrong.

Crime as a Social Event Involving Numerous Factors

The term *crime* is broad and can refer, variously, to murder, an employer violating safety regulations, someone stealing a chocolate bar, a person being in possession of a restricted drug, or the procurement of sexual relations in exchange for money. A crime is not always an individual act but can also involve other social factors. Thus, the third conception of crime emphasizes how a number of different elements need to converge in order to produce a **criminal event**. For researchers Cohen and Felson (1979), the three main elements required for crime to occur include: 1) a motivated offender, 2) a target or victim, and 3) the absence of controls to prevent the crime. Each of these three components is in and of itself a complex element influenced by many individual and social factors.

Box 1.2: The Changing Nature of Crime and Criminal Law: Drugs and Alcohol

What is legally defined as a crime can change with time and place, as well as across political and historical contexts. A clear illustration of the shifting meaning of criminality is evident when a new government comes into power and has ideas about what should be legal and what should be illegal. This new government may implement changes to existing criminal law and policy to reflect its view of what is right and what is wrong. Due to this regular political renewal, criminal justice policies are in a process of constant change. Take, for example, the case of drug laws in Canada. For almost a century, the personal use and sale of certain narcotic drugs, many of which were freely available in tonics and other personal items prior to 1908, have been severely prohibited by law. In fact, drug laws and their enforcement by police and the courts have made up a very large portion of criminal justice activity in many nations around the world. There has been a widespread social control campaign known as the **war on drugs** whereby the governments of many nations have made the sale and possession of prohibited drugs subject to severe punishment, have engaged in environmentally destructive crop eradication methods, and state agents have colluded with criminal organizations (Paley, 2014). Furthermore, the immense law enforcement resources directed at the problem of drug control have failed to curb the use and sale of narcotic and other prohibited drugs worldwide, and the problem of drug-related deaths is a growing epidemic. The war on drugs has done little to reduce illicit drug use or help those who are dangerously addicted to narcotics. It has, however, been the occasion for widespread corruption and abuse of power among people on both sides of the law involving guns, organized criminal gangs, murder, and **corruption**. As a result of changing attitudes and newly formed laws, drug policies in Canada have undergone dramatic change.

Some people claim that drug laws are unfair and hypocritical since legal drugs such as alcohol and tobacco, which cause a substantial number of deaths on an annual basis, are freely consumed while other less dangerous drugs are illegal. Some claim that the drug criminalization campaign is rooted in **institutional racism** and corporate power interests, and not the well-being of the public. Others claim that drug use causes increased street crime and life-shattering forms of drug addiction, and for these reasons illicit drugs need to be controlled by law. Who has the right to decide if a person should be free to use mind-altering substances? Alcohol is at the root of alcoholism, traffic fatalities, violence, birth defects, and liver disease to such an extent that it is arguably a major component of harm in our society. Should its sale and consumption be made illegal as once was the case? Does the fact that some people abuse alcohol mean that responsible consumers should be denied the freedom to enjoy wine with dinner? Why did the alcohol prohibition movement fail so quickly but the ban on other intoxicating substances last for so long? These examples involving drugs and crime serve to further illustrate the complex and changing nature of crime and the power relations involved.

EXPLAINING DEVIANCE AND NON-CONFORMITY

So far you have read some ideas about crime, but what about *deviance*? What is the difference? The concepts of crime and deviance are interrelated but differ from each other in important ways. One could say that virtually *all crimes are expressions of deviance, but not all forms of deviance are necessarily criminal.* While crime is a type of illegal wrongdoing, deviant behaviour is not necessarily illegal or even harmful. Behaviour can be designated as deviant simply because it is uncommon, unusual, or rare. Behaviour that violates or challenges social norms is defined as an expression of non-conformity, a concept that exists in relation to deviance. Sometimes what is considered normal behaviour is a matter of courtesy, etiquette, and respect (such as not coughing in a person's face), or proper interpersonal conduct (for example, when one is sharing an elevator with others).

What is considered normal versus deviant is often defined by power relations. Think of romantic relationships as an example. What is considered normal in that realm, and how has this changed over time? Is it "normal" or "deviant" to date someone of the same sex? Why is it considered normal in some cultures for men to have more than one wife, but a woman cannot have more than one husband? The rules, cultural codes, and customs that define deviance and normalcy are not neutral or objective; they are shaped by dominant values that are reflections of power relations designed to maintain and protect a particular version of society.

When it comes to romance and sexual relations, the **patriarchal order** is the system of power that heavily influences values, codes, and judgments about the right and wrong ways to love another person, including what is acceptable and what is deviant in such matters. Judgments about what is considered deviant are difficult to determine in a precise or objective way, because they are *relative* to the cultural or social group that makes such a determination. An objective definition of deviance is also elusive because what is considered deviant changes across culture, time, and place, and adapts with changes in social attitudes.

Let's look at more examples. The excessive consumption of alcohol is not a rare thing, even though such behaviour is very harmful to oneself and one's social relationships. Alcohol abuse (once a prohibited activity) is itself legal, often tolerated,

Box 1.3: Think About It: *Are You a Criminal?*

Have you ever broken the law? Have you ever stolen something, purchased a stolen item, or used illegal drugs? Have you ever engaged in willful, harmful wrongdoing knowing full well that you shouldn't be doing it? It is tempting to see criminality in an "us versus them" way where we see ourselves as innocent of all violations and the behaviour of others as the problem, but criminality in its different forms runs through almost everyone's lives, as perpetrators or as victims. As Jock Young (1942–2013) wrote, "for although it may be true that all people commit crime, it is palpably obvious that they do not commit the same kinds of crime or to the same extent" (1988, p. 246). Challenge yourself to go beyond simplistic viewpoints and see how various acts of crime and wrongdoing are woven into the daily practices of people in everyday life.

and even encouraged in some social settings such as a house party, where the sober non-drinker may be considered deviant by others. While the excessive consumption of alcohol is not criminal in and of itself, certain actions that may be undertaken while drunk, such as driving a vehicle and engaging in non-consensual sex, are. In Canada, drunk driving has been a crime since the 1920s. It has taken decades of active campaigning and increasing law enforcement activities to raise public awareness of the collective responsibility of citizens, and yet Canada continues to face the problem of road accidents caused by impaired drivers.

Deviance is a concept with broad meaning. It can refer to behaviour that is odd, abnormal, weird, unusual, taboo, unpopular, or unconventional. Although not exclusively, *deviance* can be defined as practices, beliefs, or behaviours that are:

- frowned upon by the majority, such as ignoring standards of personal hygiene;
- defined as unacceptable by those who have the power to make moral judgments over others, such as when parents dictate who their children can marry;
- in violation of or not conforming to common social or cultural norms and practices, such as being a member of a cult;
- viewed as radical forms of self-expression that deviate from the standards of acceptability as defined by the mainstream of society, such as a person who has body piercings and tattoos deemed to be excessive;
- viewed as an unconscionable act that is not necessarily illegal, such as suicide;
- viewed as an abuse of power relations by those who use their positions of authority over others, such as a cruel or corrupt manager in the workplace;
- a challenge to established institutional authorities, such as environmental activism or critical journalism.

The concept of *deviance* is often paired with the concept of *social control*. Social order, which forms part of harmonious social relations, is in all societies maintained by various forms of social control, which can be voluntary or externally imposed. In some cases, forms of social control are excessive and unjust. Throughout this book, you will read examples of how people have resisted attempts at being controlled because they disagree with what is being demanded of them. In other cases, people deliberately violate rules because they desire a different social order, and, in such cases, deviant, non-conforming behaviour may serve a higher purpose. Deviant behaviour can be odd or heroic, and it is often controversial.

EXPLAINING SOCIAL ORDER AND SOCIAL CONTROL

Humans are social creatures who live in groups and depend on a *cooperative* social order. When a society has a relatively small population, it is easier to establish a stable order among members, but cooperation is much more difficult in large social groups, like those that inhabit modern cities. When collected together in very large numbers, people can behave in troublesome ways, often without being noticed. So, how do we go about ensuring that people refrain from acting in ways that disrupt the order and stability of a society in a modern, urban context? What sorts of *control mechanisms* and *systems of regulation* are used to maintain a stable, peaceful social order? *Social control* is a concept that refers to a wide range of practices that aim to maintain an ordered pattern of conduct among people in a society. It is important to note that because some forms of social order maintenance use forceful means, they are often considered *repressive* and, because they are imposed on people, can be considered forms of *domination*. Other forms of social control are *regulative* and function to ensure stability; these are considered mostly consensual and are thus generally welcomed by the public. While issues of social control are complex and involve ethical questions about freedom, most people would agree that individuals should not be so free as to do whatever they please: the behaviour of a few can have disruptive effects on the lives of others, and thus certain limits on freedom are seen as reasonable. There are a number of different ways that the behaviour of people is limited, regulated, and ordered. We can refer to two basic forms of social control as *hard* and *soft* as indicated in box 1.4.

Box 1.4: Hard and Soft Forms of Social Control

Hard Control	Soft Control
formal control through coercive force or action	*informal control through ideas and norms*
• state use of tyrannical force/ military violence	• conformity and consent to rules
• punishment and incarceration	• cultural norms, values, and taboos
• police use of lethal force	• ideological hegemony
• intrusive forms of surveillance	• moral regulation through shaming, dishonour, and social rejection

The concept of control has been central to the study of human social behaviour as far back as Émile Durkheim's (1858–1917) idea that freedom is limited by the external constraints that are "imposed on the individual by the surrounding society" (Coser, 1982, p. 13). Social norms, codes, and rules of behaviour are "internalized into the personality" of people to such an extent that individuals engage in the "voluntary acceptance of social rules" (p. 15). *Normative control* is contrasted with *coercive control* where the latter relies on the "threat of the use of force" (p. 15). The concept of **moral regulation** lies somewhere in between normative and coercive controls because it can be voluntary if one accepts the moral values of the group but may take repressive form if moral constraints are imposed upon the individual against their will. **Crime control** practices, including policing and incarceration, remain an important aspect of the study of crime and deviance because they are the most powerful aspects of overall social control (Garland, 2001).

Despite the presence of crime and other forms of social disruption, most people in Canadian society go about their daily lives relatively free of disruption from serious crimes. The stable order of modern society arises from the combined effectiveness of *voluntary* and *involuntary* social controls. Think about how a society is ordered by imagining the sorts of mundane human activities that take place on a regular day. Most people get up to go to school or work, and they usually get dressed in a socially acceptable manner, have something to eat, interact with communications media that inform them of things and maintain social connections, and they attend to their errands, duties, and schedules. When they leave the house, their behaviour is regulated by signs, roadways, and transportation systems, and by other people who may speak out if a person misbehaves. If people are driving improperly or being unruly, the police can be involved. For the most part, the majority of people follow the basic rules and codes of conduct that *softly* regulate social behaviour. Most people generally don't erupt into temper tantrums when they arrive to the bank and see a line-up of people waiting to be served. Nor do people cut in line, and if they do, they are often met with various forms of angry disapproval and are told to take their place by others waiting their turn in line.

Most Canadians consent to the established civil order of society and the rules and limitations it places on each of us. People willingly consent to being ordered because they generally agree with the order of things. This form of voluntary, *consensual* self-regulation that most people engage in is part of what the social theorist

Antonio Gramsci (1891–1937) termed **hegemony**. After the day is done, instead of strategizing on how to revolutionize the order of society, most people unwind by having food and engaging in leisure behaviour like watching television, shopping, or interacting with others in person or through electronic media. For the most part, these mundane activities and the ideas that surround them work to pacify people into conformity and keep deviant tendencies in check.

If you think about the level of conformity to order that exists in modern society, the success of control is quite remarkable! Despite the occurrence of crime and deviance, the vast majority of people *do* conform and act according to the established rules and norms of society. As you shall see throughout this book, there are always exceptions, and some people engage in willful wrongdoing with socially disruptive results. When soft forms of control fail to regulate people, hard controls such as the lethal force of the state and the threat of punishment are utilized.

THREATS TO SOCIAL ORDER AND THE PROCESS OF CRIMINALIZATION

Throughout modern history those who possess the strongest forms of power, referred to as the ruling classes, have used their power to maintain a form of society that secures their own interests and limits or punishes the behaviour of those seen as a threat to the established social order. Some historical examples of threats to order include people whose morals, beliefs, or lifestyles conflict with the values of the ruling classes; these include workers who go on strike or members of political parties that are outside of mainstream politics. In 2015, animal rights activist Anita Krajnc was criminally charged after she gave water to pigs on their way to slaughter (Cragg, 2017). How did her act represent a threat to the established social order? Sometimes the threat to order affects all social groups and comes in the form of what we see to be typical criminal activity like robbery, assault, rape, fraud, and murder. Historically, the largest threats to the established social order have come from people who think in ways that challenge the dominant order and are thus seen as deviant and dangerous. The process of **criminalization** has often been invoked to control the thoughts and actions of individuals and groups perceived to be a threat to the order established by those who hold power.

Where unequal power relations exist, people inevitably emerge who want to challenge and change society to produce a better, more just social order. Those who are often seen as a threat to the existing order include members of radical or non-mainstream political groups; critical intellectuals and journalists; marginalized groups of persons often made up of immigrants, sexual and gender minorities, the homeless, girls and women, workers, Indigenous groups, and racial and ethnic minorities; and people who have broken certain laws and who are designated as "criminals."

In the early part of the 20th century, people believed to represent a threat to the established order were referred to as the **dangerous classes** and were looked upon with suspicion by the dominant groups, who used the criminal law to control and punish transgressions. Although times have changed, the situation that configures relations between the powerful and the powerless in terms of deviance and social control is still a matter of serious concern. Throughout this book, you will see examples of the conflict between attempts to regulate certain behaviours and attempts at resisting what many people see as *repressive* social control.

Attempts to maintain social order have long been a part of human civilization. Many would agree that a stable and peaceful social order is a real need for a truly humane and civil society. Disagreements arise over such questions as: What particular order is the best one for all the members of society? Whose economic and cultural interests are served by a particular social order? What sorts of injustices take place in the very attempt to maintain a particular order? Central to these questions is the power of the law and of criminal law in particular.

LAW, POWER, ORDER, AND THE CRIMINAL JUSTICE SYSTEM

What often comes to mind when we think of formal social controls are the agents and institutions of the **criminal justice system**, which include the police, lawyers, judges, and prisons. Their task is the maintenance of order through the application of legal sanctions. The phrase *law and order* conveys how the two concepts often go hand in hand, with law as the means of regulating social order.

The criminal justice system has been one of the most controversial institutions in modern society. While it is relied upon to control crime and wrongdoing, it is also expected to deliver justice. Yet the criminal justice system has itself been criticized for being an *instrument of injustice* for various reasons, including the bias of the law in favour of people with monetary power. The police have also been criticized for their use of lethal force against suspects from marginalized and racialized groups in society. Additionally, the criminal justice system is poorly equipped to protect citizens from future occurrences of criminal harm because it generally deals with crimes after they have already occurred. The criminal justice system is thus *reactive* rather than *proactive*, which means it is not particularly effective at crime prevention. For these and other reasons, criminal justice matters remain central issues of public concern.

Whether it is a case of **systemic discrimination** or abuses of discretionary power, there are many incidences of the justice system itself becoming the source of injustice. Take, for example, cases of **wrongful convictions** where innocent people are imprisoned for crimes they did not commit. In such cases, administrative errors and sometimes deliberate wrongdoing by justice system officials occur because the police and the courts are under tremendous pressure by the public to convict and punish those thought to be responsible for serious crimes. In the efforts to achieve the goal of justice, sometimes things can go very wrong and the innocent are punished by the justice system, while those who are actually guilty of the crime go unpunished.

The example of systemic discrimination is another significant criticism of the criminal justice system. Why do prisons in Canada not accurately reflect the cultural, economic, and racial composition of the society at large? How is it that some social groups have a disproportionate number of their members in prison? Critical criminology would argue, for example, that the overrepresentation of Indigenous people in Canadian prisons is not because that particular group has an inherent tendency towards criminality; rather, there exists a systemic problem where Indigenous people are more likely to be the targets of police activity and less likely to have access to justice system resources as a way of defending themselves from criminal charges.

Not only are those with power in the form of money and social resources better able to escape legal complications and evade criminal charges than those who lack such resources, they are also better able to use the power of law to sue those they see as a threat to their elite position in society. To some extent, the law has always benefitted those with power and privilege. Not only is this legal bias in favour of the rich apparent in modern analyses of law and society but it was also noted in classical times by thinkers such as Anacharsis.

In the words of scholars ...

Laws are like spiders' webs, and will, like them, only entangle and hold the weak and the poor, while the rich and powerful will easily break through them.

Anacharsis, Circa 6th century BCE

CRIMINAL JUSTICE, SOCIAL JUSTICE, AND HUMAN RIGHTS

The **law** is arguably the most powerful social force in modern society and is widely seen as the primary mechanism to attain justice. When a criminal deliberately victimizes another person, this is generally understood to be among the highest forms of injustice, and the *power* of the law is relied upon as a way of addressing this *violation*. While the principles of *law* and *justice* are often paired together, they are two different things. The *law* is a system of formal rules whose aim is to regulate the conduct of citizens, whereas the concept of *justice* refers to an outcome of a dispute that is just, fair, and ethical in response to a wrongdoing, injury, or mistreatment inflicted on a person or group.

The concept of justice is an ancient one. *Justice* can refer to a social condition that ensures the rights of people are upheld and that the fair treatment of people accused of wrongdoing prevails. *Justice* also refers to the fairness of outcomes in cases of conflict or dispute. The concept of justice applies to both perpetrator and victim in cases of criminal wrongdoing. *Justice* can also refer to the righteousness of punishments meted out against those who have perpetrated crimes against persons or property.

According to Herbert I. Packer (1964), there are two competing models of justice that form the foundations of criminal law and procedure: the **crime control model** and the **due process model**. The crime control model believes that justice is based primarily on public safety and on the efficient conviction and strict punishment of criminals. Crime control advocates side with law enforcement agents in assuming that most people charged with a crime are factually guilty. The crime control philosophy of justice is widely associated with a *law and order* perspective and *zero tolerance* policies. In contrast, the due process model is based on the rights of the accused and on the *presumption of innocence* (the idea that a person must be considered innocent of charges until proven guilty in a court of law). Those accused of a crime should be entitled to full legal representation and a fair trial. The justice system must adhere to fair and open procedures to safeguard against abuses of power by justice system officials, which can result in horrific forms of injustice, such as the wrongful conviction of innocent people. Advocates of the crime control model believe that the criminal justice system is "too soft" on criminals, whereas proponents of due process believe that the system does not uphold the ideal of rights and thus produces systemic discrimination and injustice (Goff, 2004).

The concept of justice goes beyond criminal matters. It is also relevant in a broader sense in referring to the fair treatment of social groups who have suffered some form of collective injustice, for example, people who have been forcibly removed from their own homeland or discriminated against by their own government or by other groups simply because of their race, culture, personal characteristics, or beliefs. This latter conception of justice is explored primarily through the concept of **human rights**, which is defined as the basic freedoms that uphold the dignity and equality of all people by virtue of their being human and thus deserving of respect and protection from oppression and persecution.

Of growing importance in many countries around the world is the idea of **social justice**, which refers to creating social conditions where people are given equal chances to prosper socially and economically and to be included in positions of status and power regardless of their personal characteristics. People designated as "different" in terms of their race, culture, gender, age, disability, sexuality, and/ or body shape, for example, have been subjected to decades of serious forms of social discrimination and have had little or no protection under the law. The concept of deviance is especially relevant to those who have been victims of such forms of injustice; people designated as "deviant types" have been punished through social exclusion from full participation in social life despite not having done anything to be punished for (i.e., not having broken any laws). Similarly, crimes against these groups have not always been prosecuted to the full extent of the law even when the law did include them under its protection (which it has not always done). As you shall see throughout this book, contemporary criminology is expanding its scope of concerns to include violations of human rights and social justice.

THE SOCIAL CONSTRUCTION OF CRIME AND DEVIANCE

A major thesis in the social sciences is that humans create the worlds they live in; put another way, they engage in the **social construction of reality**. Let's look at some examples. If a person takes another person's life, is it a crime? You may have immediately thought about murder or homicide, but what about a person accidentally killing someone in self-defence, or a medical doctor assisting a person in ending their own life, or the state executing a prisoner in the act of **capital punishment**, or a soldier killing an enemy soldier in battle? All of these acts result in death, but the circumstances and the meanings that surround them are quite different. Since the meanings we ascribe to an act are as significant as the act itself, this illustrates that crime and criminality are *socially constructed categories* rather than objective or naturally occurring phenomena. By attaching specific, shared meanings to the taking of a life, we are in effect agreeing upon the *reality* of that act. The definition we give to a certain behaviour *applies* simply because the majority of people agree to it. The concept of *social construction* thus has to do with the power of numerous social forces, including the consent of the public, to shape and define what is accepted as reality.

People tend to think of crime as an either/or issue, resorting to binaries such as good vs. evil or guilty vs. innocent. However, crime, deviance, and control are complex, multifaceted issues that have been dealt with in different ways over time. Both the criminal act and the responses to criminal acts are interpreted by meanings and judgments decided on by people, not by laws of nature. These shared meanings of an act are conveyed in the *label* used to name a particular act. The process by which a person is designated as a "criminal" is not only a legal determination but is also shaped by moral and cultural biases that influence the reality of crime and its control. While some acts of wrongdoing such as murder are almost universally defined as criminal, other acts like consuming drugs and alcohol are defined differently by different societies and by groups of people.

The labels we use to make sense of certain behaviours form a part of the social construction of reality. For example, if a person is labelled as a "drug user" or "prostitute" or "ex-con" or "homeless person," what sort of moral judgments about the person come to mind? Generally, people tend to think of such individuals in a negative way. They develop a prejudiced view of them and may perhaps socially reject them. Now what if you are told that the drug user is a person who takes medical marijuana for cancer treatment? What if you were told that the person labelled a prostitute was actually kidnapped from their town by people they trusted, sold into sexual enslavement against their will, and has been enslaved for so long that they are now unable to rebuild their life? Or what if the so-called prostitute personally identifies as a "sexual surrogate" who provides sexual services of their own free will to people who do not have access to sexual partners? What if we are told that the "ex-con" spent time in prison for a crime that they did not even commit because they were wrongly imprisoned, and even though they are out of prison, their life is now ruined? Do these circumstances change the way such people are seen? Do they change how you might treat these people if you were to meet them?

As you can see, understandings of crime and deviance are difficult and complicated because they are bound up with common assumptions, biases, and taken-for-granted ideas about right and wrong. All of these beliefs are socially constructed. Sometimes our assumptions are so powerful that they have an effect on how we respond to people even though these individuals may have done nothing wrong or harmful. It is important to note that even though the meaning we attach to criminal or deviant behaviour is socially constructed, this does not mean that criminality is not real. The act of ending a person's life is objectively real; it is the meaning we attach to the death that is socially defined in different ways.

When we hear of people referred to as a "criminal," we often do not challenge the validity of that label, even though it is used in a wide variety of ways. Criminal can mean "enemy of society" and "outlaw" or "rebel" and "hero." Crime and criminality are also socially constructed, because what the law defines as a legally punishable criminal offence changes with time, place, and historical circumstance. An act that was once defined as criminal can one day be defined as normal and acceptable, even heroic.

Tattoos and leather jackets once symbolized an undesirable non-conformist or outlaw; today they are fashionable forms of self-expression. The historically recent changed status of marijuana use in Canada is another prime example of how laws and public attitudes involving criminal wrongdoing can vary. There is not much about crime and the law that is fixed and permanent across time and place; change depends on who has the power to decide on the rules. When members of the public feel a law is unjust, often it will be challenged. Sometimes people break the law deliberately to demonstrate against what they see as its unfairness. This is known as **civil disobedience**. The law, as Zinn (1997) reminds us, does not always equal justice, and what is deemed criminal is constantly under challenge by civil society and from legal professionals. Protest groups, social movements, and activist organizations have often challenged the power of legal authorities to decide what is criminal and what is legally acceptable.

In the words of scholars …

Are we not more obligated to achieve justice than to obey the law? The law may serve justice, as when it forbids rape and murder or requires a school to admit all students regardless of race or nationality. But when it sends young men to war, when it protects the rich and punishes the poor, then law and justice are opposed to one another. In that case where is our greater obligation: to law or to justice?

Howard Zinn, "Law and Justice." 1997

Box 1.5: The Law and Civil Disobedience

When it comes to understanding the relation between law, power, and justice, the historic case of Viola Desmond (1914–1965) is noteworthy. On November 8, 1946, Viola, a 32-year-old African-Canadian resident of Nova Scotia, went to the Roseland Theatre to see a movie. She refused to sit in the balcony section designated for Black people and instead deliberately sat in the white-only section, which had better seating. Desmond was not allowed to remain; she was forcibly removed, arrested, jailed overnight, and fined. She was also charged with defrauding the government for the difference in the taxes on the upstairs ticket versus the downstairs ticket, which was one cent. Although she tried to fight the charge in court, she was unsuccessful. Her case brought public attention to the issue of segregation and, in 1954, Nova Scotia repealed its segregation laws. In April 2010, the Lieutenant Governor of Nova Scotia granted Viola Desmond a posthumous pardon, the first of its kind to be granted in Canada. Today she is hailed as a hero for standing up for what is just. Her example shows us how deliberate acts of law-breaking legally defined as criminal can actually be heroic acts of justice. The Desmond case demonstrates the socially constructed nature of criminality and how it is based not on universal ethical categories of right and wrong but on subjective moral judgments that support the power interests and worldviews of the dominant social group over and above the interests and the rights of others (Colley, 2016; Williams, 2018).

THE DISCIPLINE OF CRIMINOLOGY AND ITS HISTORICAL ORIGINS

The study of criminal and deviant behaviour is a fascinating topic. Both as an academic area of inquiry and as a matter of concern for citizens who desire a safer, more just, and peaceful society, criminology responds to our longstanding desire to gain insight into the "dark side" of human nature. The study of crime and wrongdoing raises many questions: Why do so many people find the nasty side of human behaviour compelling? Why are there so many television programs and movies that deal with crime, violence, law, and policing? Why is there so much crime, disorder, and injustice in the world?

Issues of right and wrong, disorder and deviance, and punishment and justice are fundamental to all human societies. In ancient societies, rulers made attempts to establish civil order by passing laws and codes of conduct to give citizens clear guidelines about what was acceptable conduct and what was not. We are generally familiar with the organizing role of social rules. As discussed earlier, our social systems contain both informal and formal rules of conduct. Most of us are familiar with the Ten Commandments as a set of formal rules from the ancient world that attempted to place limits on behaviour and establish a moral order. Approximately 3,700 years ago, the **Code of Hammurabi** (1792–1750 BCE) was established to set out rules of behaviour designed to maintain social order and also included the repercussions of breaking these tenets. At that time, the rulers recognized that human behaviour needed to be regulated or some people would take advantage of others, create conflict, and disrupt the balance of the community. The famous code of justice known as "an eye for an eye, a tooth for a tooth," otherwise known as *lex talionis* or the *law of retaliation*, comes to us from the Code of Hammurabi. It forms the basis of many of the attempts to create an ordered and just society using the power of legal authority.

In ancient societies, there was not yet any highly developed theory of crime and deviance except for scattered references to proper conduct and remedies for rule-breaking in works of theology, law, and philosophy. In the ancient world, the authority of law was based on the authority of deities. In modern society, religious authority has given way to the civil authority of the political state. Criminology began to become established as a formal discipline in the Western world with the decline of religious authority and the rise of the **secular state** around the time of the **Age of Enlightenment** in the 18th century. During that time, momentous changes were taking place that altered the nature and organization of human societies. New ideas of **humanism** and individual freedom began to emerge amidst momentous social change. Vast numbers of people migrated from a rural existence to densely populated industrial cities. New types of social and economic relations developed between people. Modern forms of progress existed alongside new forms of misery, poverty, and destitution. In this context of social inequality, many types of behaviour were designated as illegal. The new industrial capitalist society posed many challenges for those in charge, who aimed to maintain the new order of society. Towards this end, researchers in disciplines including **sociology** and **psychology** began to study the new society and its effects on human behaviour.

Since the 18th century, criminological ideas have developed into a body of knowledge intent on establishing a scientific understanding of criminal and deviant behaviour, along with practical measures through which wrongdoing should be controlled. The rise of modern industrial urban societies not only failed to reduce substantial historical problems such as slavery, poverty, and discrimination, it prompted the following:

- new fears associated with people designated as *dangerous classes*
- mass urban migration and people seeking refuge
- unemployment and **dispossession**
- new state laws regulating "disorderly behaviour"
- the creation of modern police forces and complex criminal justice systems
- the creation of many new social control institutions, such as asylums and prisons, on a large scale
- new threats and risks of victimization from criminal predation and state-corporate corruption due to the loss of community associated with city life

Crime rates increased in the new industrial society, and new types of legally defined crimes were created, mostly to control the behaviour of the poor and powerless and to protect the authority of those who owned property. Crime was not necessarily caused by the new society but emerged in **correlation** with its features, especially the inequalities between the wealthy and the poor. Many new laws were implemented to regulate social unrest, especially among the working class. The court system was often corrupt and unjustly biased in favour of the wealthy. Punishments were harsh, inhumane, and often took *cruel and unusual* forms such as torture, hanging, and/or public flogging. Despite the attempts of modern industrial society to move beyond the injustices of the past, new abuses of power emerged.

Social scientific thought aimed to address human social problems associated with modern industrial society. Attempts were made to understand criminal behaviour from a rigorous scientific perspective. Rather than seeing criminals as people possessed by evil forces, investigators began to look for more rational explanations. The emerging fields of **evolutionary biology** and **rational philosophy** had an influence on how researchers began to understand criminality. As we shall see in Chapter 2, in the early days of criminology numerous different theories of crime causation were proposed, many of which were limited and dangerously flawed.

Not only were researchers concerned with the scientific understanding of criminal behaviour, they were also motivated by another aspect of the Enlightenment: the ethics of humanism. The concern for human well-being and the problem of rampant injustice influenced how some early criminologists such as Cesare Beccaria (1738–1794) thought about punishment and the rehabilitation of criminals. Many who studied crime and justice were also concerned about the rise of abuses of power that were associated with corrupt state officials within the legal system. Over the course of time, progressive ideas and practices were implemented to substantially improve the operation of the criminal justice system. For example, the **rights of the accused** were established, persons accused of a crime were allowed legal representation, and other measures aimed at establishing legal fairness such as the **presumption of innocence** were created.

What eventually became clear to early researchers is that the complexities of human social behaviour were not as clearly understood as, for example, the workings of mechanical systems or microbial infections in the body. Many researchers realized that human society does not follow the laws of nature but operates on the basis of human-made/socially constructed laws. It became evident to researchers that complex social phenomena such as crime required multiple explanations and diverse approaches.

The study of crime and deviance today continues to be concerned with the broader question of social order and the use of just measures to control crime. In Chapters 2 and 3, we shall examine a number of theoretical explanations for why crime and deviance occur and what social forces exist to keep these tendencies in check. The combination of a wide range of *theories* about why people behave the way they do in relation to rule-breaking has furnished the intellectual foundations of criminology. All forms of scholarly inquiry begin by asking basic, fundamental questions, and criminology is no different. It asks a range of questions about deviant human behaviour, including:

- Why do some people conform to the established rules, norms, and laws of society while others violate these standards without regard for punishment or concern for how their actions may affect the lives of others?
- What is the best way to deal with a person who intentionally engages in criminal wrongdoing?
- Are criminals less intelligent or more intelligent than those who do not break the law?
- How can criminal wrongdoing be controlled in a way that balances justice, human rights, and public safety?

These questions are among the many that have made the discipline of criminology central to the well-being of human societies.

How we understand criminal activity can determine the ways we attempt to control it from a **criminal justice policy** perspective. For example, if we feel that criminal behaviour is rooted in a person's biology, we may believe that it is mostly beyond a person's control and cannot be changed. In this case, rather than try to rehabilitate a criminal offender, we may opt to segregate them from others so that they can do no more harm. On the other hand, if we feel that an offender's criminal tendencies are brought about through the emotional impact of their difficult life experiences, then we may opt to offer counselling and emotional support with the aim to rehabilitate the offender and *correct* their behaviour. Thus, how we make sense of and understand criminality has direct *policy implications* such as the creation of new laws, different types of punishments, and specialized policing practices to maximize public safety and limit the social harms associated with crime.

In another example, if our theory tells us that people commit crimes because they have few economic options in life and thus commit the crime of theft for the sake of economic survival, then it stands to reason that in order to reduce that type of crime, policies should be implemented to give people the economic opportunities they need to survive so that they don't have to take from others. On the other hand, the theory may indicate that a person commits theft not because they are in need but because they hang out with people who think it is exciting and fun to break into places and steal things that don't belong to them. What policy might prevent or discourage people from stealing things from others, using this theoretical approach? As you can see from these hypothetical scenarios, understanding why people commit crime and how to deter them from doing so can be quite challenging. You will see throughout this book that there are many types of crime and many theories of criminality that can be used to explain wrongdoing.

Box 1.6: Criminology as a Window on the World

What would it mean if someone were to claim that we live in a *criminal society*? When we hear the daily news and are told about the wrongdoing going on in the world, we see that the extent of criminality is so vast that it forms part of every sector of society and affects virtually every person's life in some way. In no particular order, we have to contend with theft and robbery, terrorism and hate crimes, corporate crime, tax evasion, sexual abuse and sexual assault, murder, civil war, corruption, bribery, environmental destruction, animal poaching and whale slaughter, bullying, arson, identity theft, computer hacking and malware scams, vandalism, Ponzi schemes and investment fraud, abuses of power and corruption, human rights violations, illegal drug and alcohol abuse, the use of performance enhancing drugs in sport, hijacking, animal abuse, dangerous and impaired driving traffic deaths, home invasions, suicide bombing, organized crime and gang activity, gun-related crime, child soldiers, child brides, pedophilia, tainted foods, counterfeit products, human trafficking and enslavement, mass incarceration, whistleblowing, civil disobedience, the arrest of people engaged in lawful protest, war crimes, firearms and weapons crime, pickpocketing, kidnapping, abduction, gay bashing, road rage, domestic abuse, state repression, illegal detentions, torture, toxic dumping and pollution, illegal laser pointing, the murder of journalists, counterfeit money, violence, data theft, price-fixing … the list goes on.

It would not be an exaggeration to say that the global society we face in the 21st century is replete with multiple forms of criminality and destructive wrongdoing. Criminology is a unique interdisciplinary field of study because it is ideally suited to drawing attention to the ways in which criminal harm is interwoven with everyday life and how crime is in the background of the regular functioning of our global society. In this sense criminology serves as a *window on the world* by equipping us with the understanding to make sense of, and hopefully address, the criminal harms that put life at risk.

Although there have been remarkable advances in the quality of life for many people in terms of increased lifespan, greater access to goods and services, and greater legal protections for basic and fundamental freedoms, among others, many of these advances are not shared by all. Many people worldwide remain at risk. Struggles for continuing advances for human freedom and justice take numerous forms. Whether we are speaking of the right to safe streets where a citizen can walk freely without fear of attack, or the right of citizens to be fully protected by their government agencies from the threat posed by dangerous products and the criminal activities of corporations, addressing criminal wrongdoing is an essential part of progress and justice.

Generally speaking, criminology is growing into the broad study of social harm; however, as a traditional field of study, it often has failed to examine the many threats to safety in the world beyond those that fit within the strict definition of a legally defined *criminal act*. The failure to focus on the many other significant threats to human life is a shortcoming of criminology and a reason why the field is constantly expanding to examine a variety of harms and threats such as corporate wrongdoing, the violation of human rights, growing forms of social conflict such as bullying and cyberbullying, and the rise of hatred and violence. **Peacemaking criminology** is one perspective within criminology that is oriented against "war on crime" perspectives and towards practices aimed at promoting justice, peace, and security through the reduction of social disadvantages including exclusion and discrimination on the basis of gender identity, sexual orientation, race, ethnicity, disability, income, age, or lifestyle (Pepinsky & Quinney, 1991).

A criminology oriented towards public safety, quality of life, and general harm reduction is also concerned with studying the prevalent causes of harm and the possibilities of eliminating major causes of preventable deaths, which include poverty, infectious and chronic diseases, traffic-related deaths, suicide, lethal violence, warfare, famine and malnutrition, alcohol and substance abuse, pollution toxicity, and gender selective female infanticide, as well as miscellaneous deaths such as medical errors and deadly accidents and poisonings, just to name a few. While crime is a particularly pernicious form of harm because it is often willful and deliberate, it is useful to consider how criminal harm ranks in relation to other often overlooked and preventable threats to human life and safety.

Crime is a complex problem that is difficult to control. It often requires multiple explanations, and thus the ways in which it is managed are also complicated. This "complexity" of crime is typical of most human social behaviour. Different disciplinary perspectives can help us begin to understand the various dimensions of human behaviour. Humans can be understood as complex individuals (psychology); as creatures influenced by their social environment (sociology); as agents who engage in relations of exchange (**economics**); as beings with strong biological drive forces (**sociobiology**); as people who relate to one another through cultural and symbolic meanings (**anthropology**); and as individuals who often violate rules and norms (**criminology** and law). Criminology examines human behaviour in a social context but from a unique perspective that draws on a variety of disciplines of study and thus criminology is considered to be an *interdisciplinary* field of study.

Box 1.7: The Subfields of Criminology

Criminology has numerous subfields and areas of research interest that continue to develop. Students of criminology often go on to conduct research or do policy work in a criminological subfield pertaining to any of the following:

- criminal behaviour and criminal profiling
- criminal psychology, antisocial behaviour, and psychopathy
- crime control and crime prevention
- law and society, criminal law, and legal and justice policy
- the sociology of deviance, including deviant subcultures and cults
- forensic psychology and psychiatry
- penology, which includes punishment and prisons, rehabilitation, parole, and corrections
- policing, law enforcement, and security
- cultural criminology, including the study of representations of crime in news, social media, and entertainment media
- economic and financial crime
- victimology
- violence and violent crime such as gun crime, domestic violence, rape, and murder
- criminal statistics and the measurement of different crimes by rate and type, and by their association with varieties of demographic factors

- criminalistics, investigations, and the study of forensic evidence in detecting and prosecuting crime
- criminological theory and the study of crime causation
- green criminology and environmental crimes
- global espionage, security, and surveillance studies
- the sale, use, and abuse of narcotic drugs and controlled substances and reforms in this area
- global cybercrime including online attacks, cyberbullying, internet fraud, and computer scams
- transnational crime including organized crime, human trafficking, and smuggling
- moral regulation and vice crimes, including the ethics of personal drug use, sex-trade work, and gender-based discrimination
- deviance, non-conformity, and the regulation of alternative forms of personal expression including the criminalization of dissent, activist social movements, and whistleblowing
- crimes of the state and official corruption
- war crimes, atrocity, and crimes against humanity
- crime, deviance, and justice issues affecting Indigenous communities and other historically marginalized groups

CONCLUSION

Crime is a complex phenomenon and is defined in a number of different ways. While it is technically a legal concept, it can also refer to harms, violations, and types of wrongdoing that are not technically illegal. The concept of crime is related to the terms *deviance* and *social control* and all three of these play an important role in the history and development of modern criminology.

Although crime, deviance, and social control are extremely important social issues and interesting to study, they are complex phenomena that are not always simple to understand. A critical perspective of crime, deviance, and social control encourages us to view wrongdoing beyond the limited binary of good versus evil and to recognize the complex of factors that combine to produce criminal realities.

It is important to recognize the role that power plays in the commission of crime and victimization. Power influences social relations and is evident in meaningful designations such as "deviant" versus "law-abiding citizen" that serve to maintain boundaries of dominance and subordination among people. Later in this book, you will learn about *moral regulation* and how the subjective judgments of those with power can influence the law and other social forces to regulate the behaviour of others and construct criminality. Power also figures into the processes of crime and control because these are inextricably bound with the system of law and the struggle for justice and human rights.

Criminology is a broad, interdisciplinary field of study that has changed substantially with time. As society becomes more technologically and socially complex and new opportunities for crime emerge, the discipline of criminology expands with additional subfields of study, many of which are explored in this book. Criminological insights offer detailed explanations for many social problems in global societies today, and thus criminology can serve as a *window on the world*.

REVIEW QUESTIONS

1. How can crime be understood as an expression of power relations?
2. Explain why social control is an important concept for understandings of crime and deviance. What are the differences between *hard* and *soft* forms of control?
3. What aspects of the study of crime, deviance, and social control do you find particularly interesting and why?

GLOSSARY

Age of Enlightenment: A period in 18th-century Europe characterized by unprecedented advancements in science and philosophy that gave rise to the progressive changes of the modern era, against the backwardness and superstition of the previous age.

anthropology: The academic discipline that studies human social behaviour and the diversity of human culture past and present.

capital punishment (also known as the *death penalty*): The most extreme form of punishment whereby the state exercises its right to take the life of a person accused of a crime.

civil disobedience: A conscientious type of social resistance involving the deliberate violation of the law as an expression of protest or dissent against a perceived injustice.

Code of Hammurabi: An ancient (1754 BCE) Mesopotamian legal code, created by the Babylonian king Hammurabi, that set out laws and punishments in matters ranging from fraud and theft to slavery, contracts, and divorce, among others, and is widely regarded as one of the oldest surviving records of an attempt to establish a legal order.

correlation: A measurable relationship between two or more variable phenomena that can be seen to go together but in which one element does not necessarily cause the other.

corruption: The unfair abuse of one's position of power or authority for the purpose of professional or private gain through the manipulation of others through coercive means.

crime: Technically, an act or behaviour prohibited by law, but the term is also used broadly to refer to acts of injustice, grievous wrongdoing, or harmful behaviour.

crime control: The various techniques that are employed to reduce crime such as policing, the incapacitation of offenders, and the use of crime prevention strategies.

crime control model: A philosophy of criminal justice that emphasizes a tough-on-crime approach and the strength of police and prosecutorial power as the basis of public safety.

criminal event: As defined by Cohen and Felson (1979), a criminal event consists of three main elements: 1) a motivated offender, 2) a target or victim, and 3) the absence of controls to prevent the crime.

criminal justice policy: The changing set of practices and laws that guide the operation of the criminal justice system. Policies can include the treatment of offenders during arrest through to incarceration and probation.

criminal justice system: The institution tasked with the control of crime and the treatment of offenders, and whose primary elements are the police, lawyers, the prison system, and the correction and rehabilitation of offenders.

criminalization: The process whereby an act or behaviour is designated as a criminal offence and which may reflect the bias of those who control criminal justice policy.

criminology: The academic discipline that studies crime, the causes of criminal behaviour, and crime control, along with related issues such as deviance and policing, among others.

dangerous classes: A historical term used to refer to people (such as racial and ethnic immigrants, striking workers, vagrants, or prostitutes) believed to represent a threat to the established order and who were looked upon with suspicion by those in power who used the criminal law to control and punish them.

deviance: A sociological concept that refers to deviation from socially acceptable norms and standards of behaviour, conduct, or lifestyle.

dispossession: A type of socially oppressive practice whereby people are deprived of the elements required for dignified survival, such as housing, land, and access to natural resources.

due process model: A philosophy of criminal justice that emphasizes the rights of the accused to a fair trial and legal representation and upholds the value that a person is innocent unless proven guilty beyond a reasonable doubt.

economics: The academic discipline that studies the exchange of goods and services in a social context, as well as the nature and operation of the financial system.

evolutionary biology: A subfield of the academic discipline of biology that examines the role of the evolutionary process of natural selection in living organisms.

hegemony: A type of political domination or control of people that is based on their voluntary submission or public consent to the established values and beliefs that support an existing social arrangement.

human rights: The basic freedoms that uphold the dignity and equality of all people by virtue of their being human and thus deserving of respect and protection from oppression and persecution as guaranteed by law.

humanism: An ethical system of thought expressed in philosophy and art that emphasizes the concern for human well-being as the guiding principle of life (as opposed to religious or deistic principles that focused on otherworldly matters such as the afterlife).

institutional racism: A type of racial discrimination that disadvantages specific groups of people by virtue of the inequitable bureaucratic rules and operation of a particular institution.

Interpol: The International Criminal Police Organization, a global policing institution that consists of members from numerous countries and cooperates primarily on transnational organized crime, human trafficking, illicit drug sales, war crimes, and other forms of complex illegal activities that require policing efforts across various jurisdictions.

justice: An outcome of a dispute that is just, fair, and ethical in response to a wrongdoing, injury, or mistreatment inflicted on a person or group.

law: The state-run system of official rules that govern the conduct of members in a given nation or territory, regulate wrongdoing, and maintain stable social relations in civil and financial matters, and whose violation is subject to sanction, penalty, or punishment.

moral regulation: A traditional form of social control whereby moral values and judgments involving shaming and social exclusion regulate social solidarity and personal conduct.

mystification: The process whereby the meaning of a cultural message is deliberately misdirected to create confusion or to influence its interpretation.

patriarchal order: A type of hierarchical social organization privileging male power that emerged in human civilization approximately 5,000 years ago and is reproduced in numerous institutions such as the family, the state, and religion, where males generally hold dominant status.

peacemaking criminology: A criminological orientation that stands against punitive justice and affirms practices aimed at the humane rehabilitation of offenders and the promotion of social justice, peace, security, and crime reduction through the mitigation of social systemic disadvantages.

power: A social scientific concept that refers to the capacity to control the fate of, or exert influence over, the behaviour or the decision-making ability of others.

presumption of innocence: A legal concept that affirms the principle that a person accused of a crime is considered to be innocent of all charges until they can be proven to be guilty.

psychology: The academic discipline that studies individual human and social behaviour, the human mind, and cognitive processes.

rational philosophy: A branch of philosophy that privileges logical reason over speculation and faith as a way of arriving at valid conclusions about the nature of reality.

rights of the accused: A legal concept that affirms the principle that a person accused of a crime is guaranteed basic rights, such as the right to a fair trial, that need to be upheld in order for a fair and just outcome.

secular state: The political institutions of a government that operate independent of the influence of any religious authority or religious doctrine, based on modern secular values and laws.

social construction of reality: A sociological concept that refers to how human realities are the product of shared meanings about what is real, which holds that human social forces, as opposed to natural laws, determine the nature of social reality.

social control: A sociological concept that refers to the large-scale organization and regulation of human conduct through shared norms and values, as well as through laws and violent force.

social justice: A condition of fairness where people are given equal chances to prosper socially and economically and to be included in positions of status and power regardless of their personal characteristics.

sociobiology: The academic discipline that studies the biological basis of human behaviour and emphasizes evolutionary processes.

sociology: The academic discipline that studies modern human societies, social institutions, and social problems.

state (also known as the *nation-state*): The political apparatus that forms government and has legal power over the people and resources in a given geographical territory.

systemic discrimination: A type of racial, gender, or cultural discrimination perpetuated by unfair institutional practices or policies that are a part of the way the social system functions.

war on drugs: An American-led policing and military campaign aimed at halting the manufacture, sale, and use of illicit drugs globally, which has been heavily criticized as ineffective, oppressive, and unjust.

wrongful convictions: Cases where factually innocent people are deemed guilty and convicted for crimes they did not commit.

REFERENCES

Box. S. (1983). *Power, crime, and mystification*. Tavistock Publications.

Cohen, L. E., & Felson, M. (1979). Social change and crime rate trends: A routine activity approach. *American Sociological Review*, *44*(4), 588–608.

Colley, S. B. (2016, November 9). Viola Desmond was arrested at the Roseland Theatre 70 years ago. *CBC News Online*. Retrieved from https://www.cbc.ca/news/canada/nova-scotia/viola-desmond-roseland-theatre-nova-scotia-1.3842359

Coser, L. (1982). The notion of control in sociological theory. In J. Gibbs (Ed.), *Social control: Views from the social sciences* (pp. 13–22). SAGE Publications.

Cragg, S. (2017, May 4). Pig trial: Anita Krajnc found not guilty of mischief charge for giving water to pigs. *CBC News Online*. Retrieved from https://www.cbc.ca/news/canada/hamilton/pig-trial-verdict-1.4098046

Foucault, M. (1980). *The history of sexuality*. Volume 1: *An introduction*. Vintage Books.

Garland, D. (2001). *The culture of control: Crime and social order in contemporary society*. University of Chicago Press.

Goff, C. (2004). *Criminal justice in Canada* (3rd ed.). Nelson.

Packer, H. L. (1964). Two models of the criminal process. *University of Pennsylvania Law Review, 113*(1), 1–68. Retrieved from https://scholarship.law.upenn.edu/penn_law_review/vol113/iss1/1

Paley, D. (2014). *Drug war capitalism.* AK Press.

Pepinsky, H. E., & Quinney, R. (Eds.). (1991). *Criminology as peacemaking.* University of Indiana Press.

Williams, C. (2018, March 8). New $10 bill featuring civil rights activist Viola Desmond unveiled. *CBC.* Retrieved from https://www.cbc.ca/news/canada/nova-scotia/viola-desmond-10-unveiled-1.4567290

Young, J. (1988). Thinking seriously about crime: Some models of criminology. In M. Fitzgerald, G. McLennan, & J. Pawson (Eds.), *Crime and society: Readings in history and theory* (pp. 206–260). Routledge.

Zinn, H. (1997). Law and justice. In *The Zinn reader: Writings on disobedience and democracy* (pp. 367–402). Seven Stories Press.

CHAPTER 2

The Origins of Criminological Theory and Legacy Theories in the Study of Crime, Deviance, and Social Control

Claudio Colaguori

LEARNING OBJECTIVES

In this chapter, you will

- gain an understanding of what is meant by *theory* and how theorizing criminological issues is a process that has changed over time;
- understand how the history of criminological theory has a troubled past, and in some cases was used to justify social discrimination and human atrocity;
- understand how the study of crime, deviance, and social control takes place through a variety of complimentary and contrasting theoretical perspectives;
- learn how criminological concepts and theories play a role in the formation of crime control and criminal justice policies; and
- become familiar with the foundational theories in criminology that have left a lasting legacy on the discipline that continues in the present.

INTRODUCTION

One of the most engaging yet challenging aspects of studying crime, deviance, and social control is the field of **criminological theory**. The range of theories within criminology is extensive, and they represent various attempts at explaining criminal and deviant behaviour. This chapter will provide an overview of traditional theories of crime that have formed the foundation of criminology. Since these theories continue to inform research today, they can be considered *legacy* theories. They include biological, psychological, sociological, and social control perspectives, as well as pre-scientific perspectives.

Criminological theories present us with a remarkable history of changing conceptions of human wrongdoing and ideas regarding social control strategies over time. Each **theory** sets out a perspective that explains and defines crime and deviance from a unique point of view, and each has its own biases and specific points of emphasis. In the course of explaining some of the main theories of crime, deviance, and social control, this chapter also examines how ideas associated with the history of criminological thought are connected to social policy formation, including those which produced injustice and violations of human rights.

In the words of scholars ...

Hostility to theory usually means an opposition to other people's theories and an oblivion of one's own.

Terry Eagleton, *Literary Theory: An Introduction.* 1983

WHAT IS A THEORY?

It is likely that you are familiar with the term *theory*. We all engage in the informal practice of theorizing when we try to make sense of the world in which we live. How we understand the realities of our lives is influenced by the dominant ideas, assumptions, and beliefs that prevail in a given time and place. Whenever we hold an opinion about something, we are basing it on assumptions we believe to be factually valid and therefore true. For example, if you were to ask a friend the question "Why did that drunk driver go the wrong way on the road and kill people in another car?", imagine the sorts of responses you would get. Perhaps your friend would say "the laws against drunk driving aren't tough enough" or "alcohol impairs driving skills and judgment" or "it was dark and the road signs were not clearly visible, so it is easy for a driver to make a mistake" or "people are risk takers and sometimes the innocent suffer the consequences." Each response contains a *theoretical premise* that seems to make sense or is partly correct and may be worth exploring further. This is what theorizing is all about—making sense of the complexities of crime for the purpose of trying to control, prevent, and otherwise manage the narrative in some way. As Young (1981) indicates below, conversations "about crime" inevitably involve some form of theorizing.

The term *theory* is often used in everyday language to mean conjecture or speculation about how to explain something. Some people take exception to "theory" and claim that they are only interested in "facts." As Eagleton (1983) observes, such a view is shortsighted since every truth claim is in essence based on a theory. Often the term is used in a pejorative way to dismiss particular interpretations of reality put forth by others, as in the phrase "Oh, that's just a theory!" This sort of usage is not necessarily what is meant by the term *theory* in the sciences. In the technical sense, a theory is a formal analytic model that furnishes explanations or interpretations of a particular natural or social phenomenon. Theories are expressed through **concepts**, which comprise the scientific terminology used to identify and name specific phenomena revealed through research and analysis. A theory is not necessarily to be understood as something opposed to a fact—rather, theories often help researchers determine facts. *Theorization* is an analytic process that researchers use to arrive at general understandings of the phenomenon being studied. Within criminology, the term *theory* refers to a framework of understanding that offers a general explanation for why crime occurs.

In the words of scholars ...

We are likely to encounter the "conversation about crime" wherever we turn—in conversations at a bus stop, or in the pub, reading the news ... or listening to a phone-in on the radio. These conversations will not only reflect the concern with what is commonly perceived as the ever-rising rate of crime, our feelings about what this means, and what ought to be done about it. They will also draw on a range of implicit explanations as to what causes crime and a range of implications as to how to deal with it, even though we are not aware that we are using criminological theories and explanations of crime at all.

Jock Young, *Thinking Seriously About Crime*. 1981

Theories as Paradigms of Thought

The theories that inform scientific research in each discipline undergo transformations over time. They are updated with changing historical conditions or corrected based on new evidence, or they are discarded and replaced with different, more valid theories. The philosopher of science Thomas Kuhn (1922–1966) wrote about the process of how certain theories rise to prominence, while other theories taper off and get replaced. For Kuhn, the fundamental theories within a scientific discipline of study undergo dramatic shifts because of changes in factual evidence, as well as other non-scientific influences. A criminological theory develops validity and gains prominence when it is based on some form of proof or evidence that is gathered through **empirical research methods** such as observation, measurement, and other ways of gathering real-world facts. When a theoretical perspective becomes dominant, it is established as the leading **paradigm** within a discipline of study. Criminological thinking has had a number of *paradigm shifts* from the 1800s to the present, but unlike many of the other sciences where one or two large paradigms of thought tend to displace most of the others, criminological research is often informed by multiple paradigms simultaneously, depending on the preference of the criminologist and on the type of crime being researched.

Although many theories of human activity are useful in the attempt to understand crime and deviance, no single theory can provide a full and complete understanding of all criminal phenomena. Since there are so many varieties of crime and deviant behaviour, it makes sense that criminologists depend on a wide range of theories in their research. Certain types of crime are better understood through particular theories that are more properly suited to them, and different researchers may have their own preferential biases for working with one theory over another. For example, studying serial murderers is perhaps best understood through theories that focus on individual explanations of criminal behaviour rather than through the influence of society on criminality, whereas cybercrime might best be understood through theories that emphasize technological and economic factors. In many cases, a single type of crime can be examined from a number of different theories simultaneously. This makes criminological theory a dynamic branch of knowledge about human behaviour and wrongdoing.

THE DAZZLING AND DISTURBING HISTORY OF CRIMINOLOGICAL THEORY

"Degenerate," "imbecile," "idiot," "feeble-minded," "moron," "born criminal." It is likely that you have heard such terms before. It may interest you to know that before they became derogatory labels used in everyday language they originated as concepts from early researchers who attempted to classify "deviant" humans on the basis of their presumed "natural inferiority." Classification has always been a part of scientific study, and it certainly played a role in early criminology.

Criminology as a specialized discipline did not form until scientific research began to flourish in the 1800s. Prior to the rise of modern scientific criminological theories, researchers and specialists from law, medicine, psychiatry, and other fields developed theories to try and understand and control deviant and criminal behaviour. However, it would be misleading to suggest that the development of criminological theory was a smooth and gradual transition from strange ideas to valid scientific theories, or even that there was consensus among theorists once the transition did take place. Indeed, the story of criminology is full of bizarre, brilliant, daring, and controversial ideas that often contrast with each other. As you shall see in what follows, many of the early attempts at theorizing criminality were rife with problematic assumptions about criminality being related to a person's body type, intelligence levels, sexuality and gender, and even culture and race as causes of criminality.

The Demonic Perspective: Seeing People as Good or Evil

During the Middle Ages in Europe, people generally understood natural phenomena and human behaviour as guided by supernatural forces. There existed a widely shared belief in the powers of evil spirits, and the world was seen as a battleground between forces of "good" versus "evil." People who engaged in odd behaviour or succumbed to illness were believed to be under the influence of demonic forces. As Stephen J. Pfohl states, "the demonic perspective is the oldest of all known perspectives on deviance. It suggests that we look for the cause and cure of deviant behaviour in the realm of the supernatural" (1985, p. 20). You might think that the rise of scientific perspectives would have made superstitious beliefs about demonic possession a thing of the past, but even in the present day many believe that supernatural forces have an influence on human affairs, and terms like *good* and *evil* are regularly invoked in matters of crime and wrongdoing. According to a 2018 news report, one Sicilian priest claims that "requests by Italians who want an exorcism has tripled to about 500,000 cases in the last few years ... [he] believes the high numbers of reported exorcisms over the last few years are linked to a rise in people visiting fortune tellers and Tarot card readers, which he said, 'let in the devil'" (Dangerfield, 2018).

Box 2.1: Media Coverage of Demonic Fraud: When Old Ideas Conflict with Modern Law

In 2018, a Toronto woman was "charged with fraud and pretending to practise witchcraft after she allegedly convinced a man that he needed to sell his house and transfer the money to her account in order to get rid of evil spirits.... [She] convinced the man that in order to get rid of evil spirits in his home, he had to sell the house and transfer the money to her account, where it would remain until the spirits were gone.... The man sold his car and home and lost more than $600,000 in the alleged scheme, police said" (CTV News, 2018).

In the 1st session of the 42nd Parliament that part of the law that "makes it an offence to fraudulently pretend to practise witchcraft, sorcery, enchantment, or conjuration, to tell fortunes for money, and to pretend to discover, through the use of the occult. This offence has likely been deemed obsolete and redundant, [since] the general offence of defrauding the public of property or money by deceit, falsehood, or other fraudulent means" can be used to prosecute such offences (Casavant et al., 2018).

This case is an interesting example of how criminal law has changed across time. In the past, the law was founded on superstitious principles and supported the reality of witchcraft. Then the law changed and viewed witchcraft practice as a type of fraud. Now the law is changing once again to remove such language from the legal code altogether.

In the era of the "demonic perspective," which peaked for a few hundred years starting in the 15th century, it was a common belief that those who engaged in wrongdoing or odd and unusual behaviour were not in full control of their actions but rather were possessed by evil spirits who compelled them to behave in evil ways. People born with physical irregularities, unique attributes, or disabilities were often labelled as "cursed" and thought to be in league with the devil. Based on this terminal way of thinking, there was little hope for those accused of evil deeds.

Those in power who promoted a demonic worldview perpetuated supernatural beliefs as a way to maintain control over others to further their own personal interests and to destroy anyone seen as a threat. The power of authorities was based mostly on distorted interpretations of religious dogma, and it helped to maintain a strict **patriarchal order** that protected the authority of men and dominated females in virtually all aspects of social life. Anyone who challenged the authority of the Church in Europe often did so at their own peril. By many accounts, thousands of people were put to death by inquisitions and tribunals where no sense of fairness, justice, or presumption of innocence existed for the accused. Officials in Europe conducted "witch hunts" against religious minorities and anyone who challenged the authority of the Church under the charge of **heresy**. Women and girls in particular were often persecuted as the victims of witch trials and thus the era was marked by widespread **misogyny**—the hatred of females—and **femicide**—the deliberate killing of females. It is estimated that hundreds of thousands of females were accused of witchcraft and were charged with sorcery and tortured to death in the most gruesome of manners with the excuse being that they had caused plagues, famines, and illness with their magic spells (Davis & Stasz, 1990).

Theoretical Concepts Regarding Modern-Era Persecutions

In the modern era, and the 20th century in particular, organized campaigns of hatred and the targeted persecution of specific groups of people are notorious historical occurrences considered some of the worst atrocities humanity has witnessed. Collectivities of people have been targeted and persecuted on the basis of their cultural, religious, racial, sexual and gender identities, and on the basis of their political beliefs. This phenomenon, which is often associated with the injustices of warfare, is known as **collective punishment**. Such pernicious forms of mass persecution have in some cases led to large-scale atrocities such as **genocide** and **war crimes**. Among the most infamous example of the mass-scale demonization and destruction of a targeted group of people is the Holocaust of World War II, where upwards of "6 million Jews were among the more than 20 million people annihilated at Hitler's behest [where] only the Jews were marked for total destruction" (Bauman, 1989, p. x). Such wholesale acts of mass criminality are only possible with the consent of the general population driven by a propaganda campaign of fear and hatred directed against the targeted group. It is a strategy of political power to create the perception of an enemy who is defined as "different" and is seen to pose a threat to the well-being and security of society. Thus in criminological theorizations of persecution, the concept of the *other*, as one who is deemed inferior, subhuman, and therefore expendable, is central to understanding many modern **crimes against humanity**. One of the theories that makes substantial contributions to the ongoing problem of persecution on the basis of identity is **critical race theory**, which contributes to criminological understandings of the problem of the unusually high incarceration rates for racial and cultural minorities in many parts of the world including Canada and the USA and is seen by many as a form of collective punishment.

The political theorist Carl Schmitt (1888–1985) identified the "friend–enemy distinction" as one of the main features of political relations. Individuals who hold political power in times of crisis will often generate an "us versus them" situation, where the enemy "other" is blamed for existing social problems and becomes the target of **human rights** violations and other forms of discriminatory abuse, persecution, and even annihilation.

The era of communism versus capitalism which marked much of the second half of the 20th century was a "cold war" period where a political persecution known as "The Red Scare" was evident. Fears of a communist invasion or nuclear annihilation by the foreign enemy was part of everyday life in North America. People accused of having "communist sympathies" including professors, writers, journalists, activists, singers, actors, and artists in the USA and Canada became the target of both open interrogations and secret government investigations. The 1950s era of **McCarthyism**, as it was called, represented a typical state-sponsored persecution insofar as people accused of being a "communist" were "blacklisted" and officials in power actively sought to destroy their lives. Many political states around the world today continue to compile secret files on citizens they see as a threat to their power, and in some countries, this involves the corrupt abuse of the criminal justice system for the detention and incarceration of **political prisoners**.

Persecutions of targeted people are more likely to flourish when a *culture of suspicion* is promoted in the news media and by political figures (Visano, 1998). Today we are living in the **post-9/11 era**, which is marked by the global "war on terror" that commenced shortly after the attacks on the World Trade Center high-rise towers in New York City on September 11th, 2001. The American-led military response to the attacks has drastically transformed the nature of social life in a manner that has given rise to a new type of **asymmetrical warfare** where the enemy, in the name of religious fundamentalism, poses a threat to civilians in public spaces and is thus more difficult to engage and restrain. Attempts to control the terrorist enemy threat have had a number of serious social consequences, including a rise in forms of hatred and mistrust directed against Islamic, Arabic, and numerous other racialized groups in what is known as **Islamophobia**. The situation is one that has created more open forms of racial and cultural fears that threaten the stability of **civil society**.

The "war on terror" has caused various nations in the world to amplify their military, surveillance, and police powers alongside the reduction of typical legal protections, rights, and freedoms that are normally afforded to all citizens in peace times. This post-9/11 condition of reduced freedoms for the sake of security and protection is termed a **state of exception**, and critics have raised concerns about the exception becoming the new normal as human rights violations; the persecution and murder of journalists; the use of torture, illegal detentions, and interrogations; and the widespread practice of mass surveillance and illegal espionage are now common occurrences around the world. As we shall see in the next section, mass atrocities have often been justified on the basis of targeted groups of people being designated as biologically inferior and thus unworthy of humane treatment.

Box 2.2: When Critical Thinking Is Deemed a Criminal Activity: Thought Crimes from Giordano Bruno to Antonio Gramsci

During the medieval period in Europe, when the good versus evil worldview prevailed, religious state authorities maintained power through various means including violence, torture, judicial inquisitions, and the suppression of freedom of speech and independent thought. In such a context, putting forth new ideas and scientific discoveries was a dangerous activity, and many thinkers who offered new ideas were brutally punished by the authorities. Giordano Bruno (1548–1600), a philosopher and mathematician, was charged with heresy for his ideas about astronomy and Christianity. Even though many of his ideas, such as his theorizing that the stars in the night sky were actually distant suns, eventually proved to be true, no deviation from Church doctrine was tolerated, and for his crimes he was tried, imprisoned, and eventually burned at the stake (Rowland, 2008).

Much later in Italian history, the critical theorist Antonio Gramsci (1891–1937), upon whose ideas **cultural criminology** is heavily based, was severely punished by the Fascist regime in Italy in 1926 by 5 years of internment plus 20 years of imprisonment. The prosecutor at Gramsci's trial stated, "we must stop this brain working for twenty years!" (Gramsci, 1971, p. xviii). Imprisonment did not stop Gramsci's mind, however. He wrote thousands of pages of political theory that were smuggled out of prison, some of which were eventually published in the 1950s as *Selections from the Prison Notebooks*.

Gramsci theorized that those in ruling positions of power will attempt to dominate the population at large through *ideological hegemony*—a social control strategy involving the constant promotion of ideas that aim to generate public consent to the established order. It is ironic that while the Italian Fascist state sought to suppress and silence Gramsci, he was formulating a theory of the very process of social control he was being subjected to.

Are we living in a time where freedom of expression is promoted or controlled? Are there any authorities in your life that try to control what you think and believe?

EARLY BIOLOGICAL DETERMINISM AND SCIENTIFIC RACISM

As religious authority and the power of superstition declined, the rise of scientific methods of inquiry based on factual evidence became the dominant paradigm. Scientific methods of inquiry meant that ideas needed to be verified with experimentation, testing, and *adequate* proof before being accepted as valid. However, that didn't mean that all of the new theories that claimed to follow the principles of scientific inquiry were accurate and unproblematic. It is important to note the extent to which racism, sexism, body-typing, and other forms of *pseudo-science* were an integral part of many early theories of crime and deviance. Many early "scientific" theories were based on presumed natural differences and were often used by those in power to justify brutality against people of difference and to maintain their hold on power.

A large number of researchers began to apply misconstrued ideas based on the evolutionary theory of Charles Darwin (1809–1882) to criminological issues. For example, William Sheldon (1898–1977) and Ernst Kretschmer (1888–1964) theorized that a person's body size and shape determined one's personality type, which in turn had an influence on a person's capacity for deviant behaviour. Such theorists were working within the primitive form of a theoretical perspective that is still dominant today known as **biological determinism**. You may note that biological determinism provides a "scientific" argument to support many of the practices and underlying beliefs that were previously supported by the demonic perspective, and thus problematic bias persists despite paradigmatic change. Many biological theorists worked under the troubling assumption that different races of people were naturally inferior in terms of innate intelligence, ability, and level of humanity, and they tried to prove such assumptions through the use of flawed examples of people designated as "born criminals" or "degenerates."

Are some people more biologically inferior to others and thus prone to criminal behaviour? Can you tell if a person is a criminal just by looking at their physical features? These were some of the basic assumptions in the infamous theory of Cesare Lombroso (1835–1909), perhaps the most noteworthy of the early criminological theorists working from a biological—Darwinian—perspective. He based his ideas on the physical features of prison inmates to develop a theory that classified humans into normal and *criminal* types. He posited that some people were under-evolved, primitive, and thus "caveman" like in comparison to "normal" humans. These people could be identified by distinctive physical features such as their excessive hairiness, unique skull shape, and darker skin in comparison to other prison inmates. Such people were considered **atavistic**, "evolutionary throwbacks" with a propensity for criminality. Lombroso and his many followers, including Enrico Ferri (1856–1929), studied prison inmates to theorize that the worst of the atavistic criminals were *born criminals*—a term that survives into the present, which implies that their negative behaviour cannot be corrected because it is part of their biological nature.

Lombroso did attempt to adhere to scientific methods of research insofar as he based his findings on the empirical measurement of the physical features of actual prison inmates, but his conclusion that such men were lower on the scale of evolutionary development was flawed. Lombroso's interpretation of his findings was a misapplication of Darwin's insights about human evolution. Further, Lombroso did not consider the social and political reasons why such people ended up in prison in the first place. We can presume that many of the men who ended up in the prisons he studied were not necessarily guilty of terrible crimes but may have ended up there for other reasons.

The theories of early scientific criminologists like Lombroso, although quite problematic, are not completely useless to the advancement of criminological theory. By challenging such theories and finding faults in them, certain insights were gained and flawed ideas were discarded and avoided in subsequent theories. Testing whether or not a theory holds up to scrutiny is an important part of the progressive process of theorizing that helps to expand the discipline of criminology and create better policies to deal with criminality as an ongoing social problem. With the passage of time, Lombroso's theory of criminal atavism did not measure up and was eventually discarded. However, his method of identifying criminal patterns and types was an idea taken up by others to influence the criminal investigation practice of **criminal profiling**. Today, theories that aim to identify certain people as biologically inferior have not completely disappeared but are dismissed as forms of **scientific racism**. As Jalava and colleagues (2015) remark, theories often become widely recognized not because of their truth and accuracy but because they affirm popular fears and biases about good and evil.

In the words of scholars ...

A core requirement for the born criminal theory's popularity is fear, and so the theory's acceptance as common sense tracks closely with the way we assess threats.... The way we think about evil is a particular type of thinking— impressionistic, wishful, and uncritical. [Our era has] the right mix of fear, politics, and technologies to elevate born criminality into received wisdom.

Jarkko Jalava, Stephanie Griffiths, and Michael Maraun. *The Myth of the Born Criminal: Psychopathy, Neurobiology, and the Creation of the Modern Degenerate.* 2015

Contemporary Biological Explanations

Biological theories of human behaviour may have a troubled past, but they have persisted to become a dominant and important paradigm of theorizing. Although the problems of racism (Gould, 1981; Rose et al., 1984) and sexism (Bleier, 1984) rooted in biological theory are not far behind us historically, that doesn't mean biological explanations have no value for criminological theory today. The focus today, however, has shifted beyond examining external physical features such as body type and "race" to internal biological factors that can exert influence on human behaviour. These internal factors include brain injuries; emotional, hormonal, and toxic environmental influences on gene expression; and emotional temperament (Richerson & Boyd, 2005; Rosen, 2005). For example, research indicates that developmental fetal exposure to toxic substances like tobacco and alcohol can result in individuals who are born with genetic variances that can impair one's capacity to engage in socially acceptable levels of emotional control, and thus can have a tendency towards aggressive and antisocial behaviour (McGloin et al., 2006). Biological, along with psychological, theories of crime, which comprise an extensive area of criminological research, are discussed in greater detail in Chapter 7.

Biological Theories of Human Inferiority and Their Relation to Human Rights Violations

Theories of born criminality and biological inferiority have historically been used to justify social injustices of the worst kind. Such theories are based on the idea that some people are naturally superior to others. *Eugenics*, a term coined by Francis Galton (1822–1911), is a concept that refers to the selective breeding of humans with the goal of producing genetically superior offspring. Galton believed that social problems like crime are the result of biologically inferior people and that selective breeding to produce superior humans and restricting the birth of genetically inferior humans was the key to addressing many of the problems of early industrial societies, such as rising poverty and so-called *moral crimes* like alcohol consumption and the existence of unwed, pregnant young women. Ideas concerning the control of human breeding have proliferated throughout the modern era, and birth control policies were implemented to control the reproduction of targeted groups based on their presumed biological inferiority and their presumed threat to the genetic health of the human group.

Those deemed unfit to reproduce by authorities have historically been subject to compulsory sterilization programs by the state. In some provinces in Canada, people targeted for sterilization included Indigenous peoples; many poor, unwed young women; those deemed mentally ill; non-English-speaking immigrants; and various others who were selected by government agents. The control of people on the basis of their presumed biological inferiority has taken other forms beyond sexual sterilization; the term *ethnocide*, for example, refers to the targeted persecution of select racial or cultural groups and has involved attempts to eliminate the distinctive cultural identity of a group by outlawing their native language, beliefs, and practices. The purpose of ethnocide is to force the assimilation of the dominated group into the culture and religion of the dominating group.

Genocide is a more extreme form of attempts to eliminate or "exterminate" specific groups of people deemed undesirable by those with the power to do so. Genocidal atrocities often occur in the context of civil war or armed conflict. The modern era has been witness to a number of mass killings, including the Armenian (1915–1916), Ukrainian (1932–1933), and Cambodian (1975–1979) genocides among numerous others. Late 20th-century examples of targeted mass killings involve the Balkan war of Eastern Europe and the Hutu versus Tutsi conflict in Rwanda, both of which occurred in the early 1990s, and the more recent Rohingya genocide in Myanmar that began in 2016. The odious term *ethnic cleansing*, which is often used to refer to campaigns of mass killing of targeted groups, contains the same underlying eugenic idea that certain types of people are lesser beings whose presence will "stain" the society and need to be "cleansed" out of it. Such examples illustrate in stark terms how the ideas we use to understand reality can have powerful social consequences when they become the basis for social control policies.

Box 2.3: State-Sponsored Involuntary Sexual Sterilization: The Case of Leilani Muir

The attempt to prevent people from producing offspring has been a primary strategy used by state authorities to control disadvantaged individuals and groups in many parts of the world. A noteworthy Canadian case is that of Leilani Muir (1944–2016), who, in 1955, at the request of her unfit mother, was sent to an Alberta Provincial Training School for Mental Defectives, where she scored low on intelligence quotient (IQ) testing and was subsequently designated a "moron." On these grounds, Leilani was selected for sexual sterilization surgery without her consent and had her fallopian tubes tied, thereby rendering her unable to bear children. After spending approximately 10 years in the institution, Leilani left to begin life on the outside. Suffering many life difficulties, including failed relationships, depression, and trauma, and after having learned that she was surgically sterilized, she eventually initiated a lawsuit for damages against the Alberta government for its abuse of authority under the *Sexual Sterilization Act* of Alberta, which was enacted in 1928 and not repealed until 1972. In 1996, Alberta court judge Madam Justice Joanne B. Veit awarded Muir damages and costs amounting to approximately $970,000. The judge ruled that "the damage inflicted by the operation was catastrophic" and the "wrongful stigmatization of Ms. Muir as a moron ... has humiliated Ms. Muir every day of her life" (Wahlsten, 1997).

How does the case of Leilani Muir help to illustrate the criminological ideas discussed in this chapter so far? As you continue to read, try to make connections between problematic criminological ideas and the potential consequences of social control policies.

FROM CLASSICAL RATIONAL THEORIES TO MODERN CRIMINAL JUSTICE POLICY: CRIME AS RISK-TAKING AND INDIVIDUAL CHOICE

Alongside the development of theories of "criminal types," a number of early *classical* researchers were intent on humanizing the system of criminal justice in an attempt to address ongoing corruption, injustice, and the inhumane treatment of those accused of crime. Justice systems were failing to progress in a manner in accordance with the humanistic principles of the Enlightenment, and they continued to serve the interests of corrupt officials in power. One significant early classical theorist to address the problem of how to control criminal behaviour in a rational manner was Cesare Beccaria, who was very critical of the widespread use of cruel punishments, which he saw as unjust, such as torture and the death penalty. Beccaria's contribution to ideas on the reform of crime control and the ethics of punishment marked a major shift in the trend towards humanizing the criminal justice system. His ideas initiated a process of positive transformations in the legal system that continues up to today.

In the words of scholars ...

This vain profusion of punishments, which has never made men better, has moved me to inquire whether capital punishment is truly useful and just in a well-organized state.

Cesare Beccaria, *On Crimes and Punishments*. 1764

Another theorist who contributed to the development of classical theories of crime and justice is Jeremy Bentham (1748–1832). Bentham was interested in the individual motivations that compelled people to engage in willful rule-breaking and how deliberate wrongdoing could be effectively controlled. Bentham thought that human behaviour was guided by the fulfilment of *desire*—he theorized that people were driven to seek pleasure and avoid pain, a view of human nature termed **hedonism**. The fundamental premise is that humans are motivated by pain and pleasure. Rewards and punishments, Bentham thought, should form the basis of strategy aimed at controlling criminality (Bentham, 2007 [1789]). The entire system of criminal law is predicated on the assumption that people will obey the law for fear of punishment and will thus be *deterred* from engaging in criminal activity—this *rational aversion to risk* is the basis of the theory of **deterrence,** and it still informs the system of legal sanction that is in place throughout much of the world today.

Jeremy Bentham is also noted for his architectural design for the ultimate prison: the **panopticon**. *Pan-optic* means all-seeing. Bentham's design for the ideal prison would enable prison guards to view and thus monitor the behaviour of inmates from an ideal vantage point. The idea that prisons should be constructed so as to maximize the surveillance of inmates has had a significant influence on the design of prisons around the world. According to deterrence theory, if inmates were aware that their behaviour was being monitored, this would encourage them to behave *correctly*. The idea of the *panoptic surveillance*—the all-seeing eye—was revived much later by Michel Foucault as a metaphor for the present system of widespread surveillance that has become one of the primary techniques of social control in modern "disciplinary" societies, which shall be discussed further in Chapter 3.

The classical perspective of criminal justice that laid the foundations for modern systems of crime prevention policy in its contemporary formulation is known as **rational choice theory**. In their development of the theory, Cornish and Clarke (1986) studied the choices people make and the possible risks and rewards one contemplates prior to committing a criminal act. The theory supposes that criminals make deliberate decisions about whether to engage in rule-breaking based on *whether they think they can get away with it*. Thus, criminal behaviour is not merely impulsive behaviour but is rationally calculated. Rational behaviour theories of crime are based on a number of general assumptions, which include the following:

- Criminal behaviour is the product of rational choice exercised through free will, and people choose to conform, or deviate, based on the rewards, incentives, and punishments for doing so.

- Since people are free to act based on rational calculations of their actions, they should be held responsible for the choices they make and the consequences of their actions.
- Criminal wrongdoing should result in swift and timely punishment to serve the primary goal of deterring future wrongdoing and to serve as an example to others.

Researchers today generally recognize that criminal behaviour is more complicated than rational calculation theories would imply. Criminals are aware that the law prohibits their illegal actions, but they engage in criminal wrongdoing anyway. Consider the following statement:

> It's not about knowing the difference between right and wrong. Some people will do bad things for the thrill of it or just because they just want to.

Perhaps most people, criminals included, are not motivated by logical, rational decision making but by irrational choices based on the pursuit of selfish desires. Maybe, for some people, doing bad things is in itself pleasurable. This assumption is the basis of the (perhaps irrational) choice theory proposed by Katz, who in *Seductions of Crime* identified how some criminals are seduced by the feelings of pleasure they get from committing a crime—by "what it means, feels, sounds, tastes, or looks like to commit a particular crime" (1988, p. 3). The idea that criminals are driven by irrational desires is familiar, as in the phrase "a crime of passion," but it also applies to the thrill some people get simply from being mischievous or "evil" and getting away with doing something wrong.

In the words of scholars ...

The description of "cold-blooded, senseless murders" has been left to writers outside of the social sciences. Neither academic methods or academic theories seem to be able to grasp why such killers may have been courteous to their victims just moments before the killing, why they often wait until they have dominated victims in sealed-off environments before coldly executing them, or how it makes sense to kill them when only petty cash is at stake.

Jack Katz, *Seductions of Crime*. 1988

In debating basic questions such as the true aim and purpose of restrictive laws, the real reasons for incarceration, and how best to deter and control crime, policymakers still work under the general assumption that individuals are to be held responsible for the conscious choices they make. The motivations people have to commit crimes, rational or nefarious, are often influenced by the psychological state of mind of the individual, and it is the topic of psychological theories of crime to which we now turn.

PSYCHOLOGICAL THEORIES OF CRIMINAL AND DEVIANT BEHAVIOUR

From early in the development of criminological theory, characteristics of the human mind and the motivations behind bad or wrong behaviour have been assessed as factors in understanding deviance and crime. As such, psychological theories have made substantial contributions to understanding the complexities of individual factors affecting potential criminality by focusing on a number of factors that include the following:

- antisocial emotional motivations, including the pleasures and thrills experienced when committing acts of wrongdoing
- low levels of intelligence, cognitive development, and capacity for moral judgment
- disordered, distorted, or impaired patterns of thought and behaviour
- individual emotional temperament and dominant personality traits that predispose a person towards callousness and wrongdoing
- impaired capacities for coping with stress, frustration, trauma, and abuse
- pronounced and debilitating psychiatric/mental impairments known as **psychopathologies**

For many people, the very idea of a "criminal" evokes the image of a *deranged* person with a "sick mind" that is more *devious* than the typical law-abiding person. The idea of the "criminal mind" remains a popular theme in studies of criminal behaviour and is a source of particular fascination to the general public, so much so that it forms the basis for many popular crime-themed entertainment programs and movies—which shall be discussed in Chapter 4.

Are devious thoughts inherently pathological, or is it normal for people to have them? Why are some people able to restrain their aggression in times of stress and conflict while others can't help but lash out? Psychological theorists of crime have attempted to provide answers to these types of questions in a variety of ways to better understand the link between individual thought patterns, unsound states of mind, and criminal behaviour.

Classical psychologists like Sigmund Freud (1865–1939), B. F. Skinner (1904–1990), and Jean Piaget (1896–1980) emphasized the extent to which humans are fundamentally defined by their psychological natures, which can falter. The varieties of psychological research that followed after early pioneering work in psychology indicates that individual behaviour results from a complex interrelation between:

- innate personality traits and emotional temperament;
- influences from the social environment that shape learning; and
- the subjective emotional responses one has to personal experiences, especially during the formative period of childhood.

The history of the early psychological "treatments" inflicted upon those deemed mentally infirm seems sordid and bereft of compassion, and includes lobotomies, electroshock therapy, and prolonged straight-jacketing. As discussed in box 2.4, the use and abuse of psychiatric labels as a form of repressive social control continues in various contexts today.

Early theorists working within a psychological paradigm such as Charles Goring (1870–1919), Alfred Binet (1857–1911), and H. H. Goddard (1866–1957) focused on factors that aim to measure *quality of mind* such as "insanity" and **Intelligence Quotient** (IQ) as factors that can lead to criminality. IQ performance scores and their relation to criminality is problematic for a number of reasons. The assumption that those who score low on intelligence tests are necessarily more prone to criminal wrongdoing is questionable, especially if we consider that some forms of criminal activity require high levels of cognitive and analytic ability. Ted Kaczynski, the "Unabomber," was often touted in the news media as being a criminal genius (Oleson, 2016).

IQ testing is also problematic on the basis of cultural bias since it assumes that a standardized test can accurately measure different types of intelligence across diverse cultures. What is disturbing about theories that aim to link intelligence with crime and deviance are the types of social policies that emerged from intelligence testing and from Goddard's work in particular. In the early 1900s in the USA, Goddard and his research team deliberately increased the number of immigrant deportations by claiming that such people were "feeble-minded" and thus deemed inadmissible. In addition to eugenicist policies, psychological theories were also used for other unethical forms of social exclusion and population control.

Despite the disturbing historical use of psychological theories to enforce repressive social control policies, psychological research has developed much useful knowledge that relates directly to certain forms of deviance and criminality such as bullying, violent offenders, and organizational and corporate criminality. In the next subsection, we shall briefly overview how psychological behaviour leading to criminality is not necessarily an illness or innate factor but is something that can be learned.

Learning Theory, Aggression, and Criminality

The basic idea of **learning theory** is that human social and psychological development from infancy onwards is based on behaviours learned through meaningful interactions with others. Learning occurs in numerous ways, including through mimicry or imitation and a system of rewards and punishments known as *conditioning*. Conditioned learning takes place primarily in a social context of interaction with others. In general, *prosocial* or positive behaviour is reinforced by social acceptance from others, and *antisocial* or negative behaviour is met with social rejection.

The pioneering work of Albert Bandura (1925–2021) has also influenced criminological understandings of violence and aggression. Bandura's (1973) *social learning theory* is relevant to criminology insofar as interpersonal violence and aggression are examined as behaviours that can be learned through *modelling* or imitation of others. Alternatively, such behaviours can be discouraged through interactions with *significant others* such as family, peer group, and cultural influences where it is treated as inappropriate and combined with social rejection.

Aside from learned aggression, there are other individual factors in temperament and cultural codes of honour that can influence whether an individual will display aggressive behaviour in particular circumstances. For example, Cohen and colleagues (1996) found that men raised in the Southern US showed higher spikes in testosterone and more behavioural aggression after being insulted than Northerners; if not insulted, they were less behaviourally aggressive than Northerners. This example reinforces the idea that antisocial behavioural aggression can be simultaneously individual, contextual, and cultural.

Studies that examine the processes through which non-violent, prosocial forms of behaviour are reinforced are especially relevant to criminology insofar as high levels of physical aggression in childhood are often related to violence in adulthood. Thus, Richard E. Tremblay and his co-authors' (2004) study of aggression in toddler-age children seems to reinforce Bandura's theory insofar as some studies indicate that childhood aggressive behaviour peaks at around age two and declines afterwards if there is substantial negative reinforcement by parents and by other children who choose not to play with peers unwilling or unable to restrain their aggressive behaviour.

Personality Type and Criminality

Another significant psychological theory applied to criminal behaviour focuses on the type of character or personality that defines an individual. Personality theorists measure elements of personality known as "traits" that identify prominent features of a person's temperament, such as whether one is an "introvert" or an "extrovert," "assertive" or "submissive." Yochelson and Samenow's study entitled *The Criminal Personality*, which spanned three volumes from 1976 to 1986, theorizes that "the criminal" is someone who makes *errors in thinking* to such an extent that they are "a different breed of person ... [who have a] different ... mental makeup" (2004, p. 31). Such assertions support the concept of the *criminal mind*, which opens up policy options for treatment of criminal offenders with psychological abnormalities. Yet it has also been criticized as reducing the complexities of criminal behaviour to individual personality factors that largely ignore social, cultural, and historical forces and the power relations that influence a person's psychological well-being (Smail, 1999). Nevertheless, social factors alone cannot account for extreme forms of *heinous* and violent criminality evident in the acts of **psychopaths** and serial killers, and thus psychological theories of criminality extend upon theories of *abnormal psychology* and *personality disorders* such as *narcissism*. Of course, not all cases of narcissism or other personality disorders produce criminal behaviour. Furthermore, out of the many people who have been subject to victimization, trauma, and abuse, and are thus subject to the same "tainted origins and thwarted ambitions, only a tiny minority of them become killers" (Leyton, 2005, p. 323).

Criminal–psychopathic behaviour, such as in the case of *serial killers* and *multiple murderers*, is not only a psychological phenomenon but such violent behaviour is often *socially and culturally directed*, which makes the fact of multiple and mass murderers a sociological phenomenon. As Leyton indicates, the psychopathic violence of *multiple murderers* often reveals "the cultural origins of their motives" (2005, p. 7). Think of the current media coverage of terrorist violence—many so-called lone-wolf terrorists claim to have acted on behalf of a terrorist organization. Had they perpetrated their violence in another time and place, would such individuals make the same claims about their motives and affiliations?

Also note the following: perpetrators of gross acts of murderous violence will often justify their heinous acts on the basis of political radicalism or racial and/or gendered hatred. For example, the murderer Marc Lepine, who grew up with family violence, at the age of 25 used a semi-automatic rifle to kill 14 women and wound 10 others in 1989 in what is infamously known as the Montreal Massacre. Lepine deliberately targeted women and blamed "feminists" for the troubles in his life. While domestic violence does appear more socially directed and potentially amplified and/or fostered by a culture of misogyny and is thus a *gendered* phenomenon, victims of serial murderers are about evenly distributed by gender, where 48 percent are male, and 52 percent are female (Aamodt, 2016).

Perhaps the most popularized criminal personality is the psychopath. It is important to emphasize that *psychopathy* is not the same as *psychosis*, the latter being a state of psychological impairment to the point where one is unable to accurately understand reality. Psychosis is not necessarily associated with criminal behaviour. Theorists have also distinguished between psychopaths and those with **antisocial personality** disorder. Psychopaths generally have social skills that allow them to easily penetrate the lives of others, such as charm and false confidence along with authoritarian qualities and aggression. They are often chronic liars and experts at manipulation who do not feel guilt or shame about the control they exert over the lives of others and the trouble they cause in their efforts to fulfil their own ambitions and desires. *Antisocial* personality types, on the contrary, are characterized by shortcomings with regards to basic social interaction skills such as ease of conversation, a lack of familiarity with social cues, and with reclusiveness. They are often easily frustrated and prone to aggression and paranoid thoughts. It is important to remind readers that just because a person may have personality traits that are associated with psychopathy or antisocial personality disorder does not mean that they will engage in crime. Nor do all types of violent criminality necessarily involve forms of mental incapacitation. The relation between personality type and criminality is complex, and one should always exercise caution when drawing facile conclusions and applying clinical labels to complex actions.

Although it is common to associate psychopathic personality types with crimes involving violence and murder, it should be noted that such psychopathic people also penetrate organizational bureaucracies to senior management positions in attempts to further their personal goals. The research of C. R. Boddy (2006) suggests that "organisational psychopaths may be responsible for more than their fair share of organisational misbehaviour including accounting fraud, stock manipulation, unnecessarily high job losses, and corporately induced environmental damage." In a similar line of analysis, Joel Bakan's (2004) study in *The Corporation* makes interesting connections between psychopathic individuals and the operational logic of business enterprises engaged in "the pathological pursuit of profit and power." It should be noted that claims of psychopathic individuals penetrating the ranks of institutions and leading to criminal wrongdoing is often an exaggerated one. A critique of such claims is explored in Jalava and colleagues' (2015) book *The Myth of the Born Criminal: Psychopathy, Neurobiology, and the Creation of the Modern Degenerate*.

Stress, Frustration, Aggression, and Coping

Psychological theories are also important to understanding the *consequences of victimization*, as well as criminality in terms of subjective consequences to emotional frustration. People have differing *thresholds* for stress tolerance, and in some cases people who get excessively frustrated will respond with aggression. This stimulus-response reaction was first theorized in 1939 through the research of Dollard and Miller and their associates as the **frustration–aggression hypothesis**. The theory remains useful in understanding certain types of criminal and interpersonal violence and aggression.

There are different types of responses to trauma and stress that serve as examples of deviant behaviour rather than criminal behaviour. Although there is a wide range of differences between individual capacities for coping with stress and trauma, some who have suffered traumatic emotional difficulty, victimization, or abuse can develop thoughts or *ideations* that compel them to behave dangerously towards others and themselves. Examples of ill-fated coping strategies in response to stress, victimization, or abuse can include addictive behaviours such as alcoholism, nicotine addiction, and narcotic drug abuse—responses that span definitions of both criminal and deviant behaviours. In some cases, maladaptive coping behaviours are associated with expressions of violence to oneself. The phenomenon of non-suicidal self-injury (such as the deliberate cutting of the skin with sharp objects), where individuals will harm themselves in an attempt to appease deep emotional pain, shock, or guilt, is a case in point. Self-injury is an example of non-criminal deviant behaviour with a strong psychological component (Cawood & Huprich, 2011; Connors, 1996; Klonsky, 2007).

PSYCHOLOGICAL DISORDERS AND CRIMINAL JUSTICE

It is important to note that psychological theories have also been used to exonerate perpetrators of criminal activity. In Britain in 1844, one Daniel M'Naghten was charged with murdering a government official. His defence was that he suffered from mental "delusions" and was thus not in control of his actions and, therefore, was *not criminally responsible*. The courts accepted this plea and absolved him of the crime. Known as the **M'Naghten rule**, this case established a **legal precedent** whereby an accused can be found not legally guilty because their impaired psychological state caused them to be unaware of their wrongdoing and thus not consciously in control of their actions. Psychological theories of crime pertain directly to a category of research dealing with the "criminally insane" and with the policy challenges posed by such a category of offender.

The issue of criminal insanity came to light in a Canadian context through the 2008 case of Vince Li, who brutally hacked to death 22-year-old Tim McLean, another passenger on the bus they were travelling on. At Li's trial, his defence team argued that Li is a schizophrenic and was in the midst of a psychotic episode at the time of the murder. The court found him not criminally responsible on account of mental disorder. Such cases often cause great public uproar about the inadequacies of the justice system, as many do not accept the idea that criminal behaviour should be treated differently depending of the mental state of the offender (Urback, 2017). Psychiatrist Thomas Szasz (1920–2012), author of *The Myth of Mental Illness* (1961/2010), often appeared before the courts as an expert witness against offenders pleading insanity. Szasz's was not an argument against the M'Naghten rule specifically but a broad-based opposition to the reality of any psychiatric diagnoses anywhere, and he was especially critical of the reliance of criminal courts upon psychiatrists as expert witnesses.

The matter of criminality and psychological disorders is complex, controversial, and poses serious challenges to criminal justice practice. The treatment of criminal offenders with psychiatric disorders challenges the justice system in terms of how they are handled before the legal courts and in the court of public opinion. Their incarceration in facilities without adequate provisions for people with clinical psychological difficulties is a growing concern, as "more mentally ill persons are in jails and prisons than in hospitals" (Torrey et al., 2010).

Box 2.4: How the State Criminalizes Dissent through the Application of Powerful Psychiatric Labels

A glaring example of how certain political state actors will engage in multifaceted forms of wrongdoing that they attempt to justify on the basis of scientific authority is the 2017 case of Ugandan Professor Stella Nyanzi. Professor Nyanzi, motivated by her activist desire to improve political conditions in her country, saw fit to criticize the president of her country on Facebook. She wrote that the president was "a pair of buttocks"—and for this "crime," she served a five-week sentence in a "maximum security prison on charges of offensive communication and cyber harassment." As the CBC News (2017) coverage of this issue reported, she continued to be the subject of surveillance and her "children [were] subject to police interrogations at school." Upon being released on bail state, authorities "demanded she be subject to psychiatric evaluation, claiming she must be insane for criticizing the president." Nyanzi stated, "the accusations, the suggestions that I could be mentally ill or of unsound mind, I think that is a ploy, a scheme, a trick, a strategy to intimidate, to silence."

Nyanzi is exercising her rights as a citizen to express dissent against a president who has held power since 1989 and has been accused of corruption, broken promises, and tyranny. What sort of society is created when citizens fear their governments and are jailed for engaging in freedom of speech? Do you have similar fears when you post something on social media?

Stella Nyanzi's treatment by the Ugandan government illustrates how, in many cases, different criminological concepts complement one another in highlighting the complex practices of power involved in the *criminalization* process. As you continue to read through this chapter, think about how this case involves the criminalization of dissent, labelling theory, stigma, the misapplication of psychopathological diagnoses, the authority of state power, political corruption, and the construction of political prisoners. Can you think of any more criminological theories that pertain to Professor Nyanzi's case?

LEGACY THEORIES IN THE SOCIOLOGY OF CRIME, DEVIANCE, AND SOCIAL CONTROL

Thus far in this chapter, you have read about theories of criminality and deviance that largely examine individual characteristics related to criminal behaviour. Sociological theories of crime and deviance emphasize that humans are *social beings* who exist primarily in relation to others. People in society form a part of and are influenced by larger *social structures* and *social forces* that exert powerful influences on the conduct of people and on the options available to them in life. Sociological theories are also distinctive in their scientific methodology as they make use of statistical data and other empirical measures. Sociological explanations examine the role of the following:

Social Structures—the patterns of interactions and personal investments that form and maintain institutions like the family, the workplace, religious organizations, the state, education systems, peer and cultural groups, for example,

and

Social Forces—the shared norms, values, morals, beliefs, cultural ideals, and compulsions that organize social activity, such as competition, pride, honour, success and ambition, patriotism, and the desire for social and political change, as examples.

Sociological theories examine how various features of society exert an influence on or limit criminal and deviant behaviour. Like the psychology of crime, the sociology of crime is a very broad field of study, so the focus here will be limited to only a few major theorists who have made substantial contributions to the study of crime and deviance and who have influenced the theories of others who came after. The ideas of Émile Durkheim, Edwin Sutherland (1883–1950), and Robert Merton (1910–2003) are among those sociologists who can be considered *legacy theorists* because their ideas helped establish criminology as a formal academic discipline. Furthermore, their ideas have stood the test of time and continue to furnish models of research for contemporary criminologists.

The Normal and the Pathological—The Deviance Theory of Émile Durkheim

Is crime normal or is it a pathological *illness*, as suggested by some psychological theories? Émile Durkheim established the importance of sociological explanations for deviant behaviour through his classic study of suicide, written in 1897. Although suicide is generally regarded as a purely individualistic act, Durkheim theorized that a person can be compelled to take their own life for social reasons, especially feelings of social exclusion. Durkheim theorized that the connections or **social bonds** that exist between people not only keep them integrated with others in society, they also give people a sense of meaning and purpose. To lack this sense of social *solidarity* with others is to potentially suffer a type of meaninglessness or *loss of self* that Durkheim termed **anomie**. For Durkheim, anomie exists along a spectrum of individuals being *under-* or *over*-included in the bonds of society. Those who are socially excluded or rejected by others can become *anomic* and more likely to commit suicide. Sometimes people take their own lives in the exact opposite situation, where they are overly immersed in a social group and thus willingly sacrifice themselves for a shared cause. The kamikaze bombers of World

War II who took their own lives by crashing their airplanes into enemy ships, or current-day adult suicide bombers who blow themselves up for a cause they believe in are examples of the latter type of *anomic* suicide. Durkheim developed an entire theory of society by exploring the complexities of the deviant act of suicide.

Durkheim's theory of anomie is based on his premise that for a society to function in a stable and meaningful way, there must be cohesive social relations. Members of a society should willingly cooperate with one another by regulating themselves and obeying right and wrong conduct because it is in the best interest of everyone and thus the moral choice. This process of **moral regulation** identified by Durkheim is a fundamental aspect of social order maintenance. He did not mean that forms of social regulation should be imposed on people in a repressive manner by an external authority, but that the moral values that guide personal conduct should be formed by consensus. People regulate and restrain themselves when they consent to the shared *norms*, *values*, and *morals* of their society. Chapter 5 examines how morality is also tied to social control and how it has historically influenced the formation of law.

Durkheim also made another significant contribution to criminological theory when he claimed that acts of deviance and criminality should not be understood as inherently pathological, dysfunctional, or abnormal. He theorized that "crime is normal because a society exempt from it is utterly impossible" (1938/2010, p. 35). "Crime," Durkheim asserted, "is then, necessary"; it is bound up with the fundamental conditions of all social life, and by that very fact it is useful ... to the normal evolution of morality and law" (1938/2010, p. 36). The claim that criminal and deviant behaviour is somehow useful or *functional* was explored further by others, including Robert Merton.

Anomie and Strain Theory—Robert K. Merton

Robert Merton theorized that some forms of deviant and even criminal behaviour actually help stabilize and regulate the social order by either reinforcing the boundaries of acceptable and unacceptable behaviour or changing them. For example, if the law prohibits the use of marijuana and yet thousands of citizens continue to use it, then new laws may be passed to decriminalize marijuana. This is exactly what has occurred in Canada and other places around the world. A formerly criminal, illegal behaviour has become legal because people refused to accept the existing legal and the moral restrictions such a law created.

An example of how the ongoing commission of crime actually reinforces an illegal and socially unacceptable status is evident with **cybercrime**. As we shall see in Chapter 11, the internet has created new freedoms for people alongside new opportunities for criminality. Online bullying and "sextortion" are examples of cybercrimes that the Canadian public has clearly spoken out against, and thus the moral and legal boundaries that place limits on internet conduct are reinforced by the continued commission of such forms of cybercrime.

Merton also expanded on ideas from Durkheim by applying the concept of anomie to specific social situations. Recall that for Durkheim, anomie involves a type of individual disconnectedness from a social group or a lack of solidarity with the larger norms, values, and morals of society. Researchers who study criminal gang membership often remark that young people are "more vulnerable to street gang membership" if they lack strong familial bonds or have no family bonds (Maxson et al., 1998). Merton is, however, noted for his unique contribution to criminology known as **strain theory**, which explains deviance as the result of particular kinds of social pressures and *strains* one faces in achieving success in life. According to Merton, most members of our goal-driven society accept the idea that success and personal freedom is achieved through monetary wealth—the strain emerges because not every person has the same access to the means to achieve success. Why do some people accept the normative standards of achieving economic success through the pursuit of education and by embracing a strong work ethic while others resort to criminal activity, rule-breaking, and wrongdoing to achieve monetary success? For Merton, there is a disjuncture between the

a. widely accepted *cultural end goal* of achieving financial success, and
b. the available *institutional means* for achieving it.

The conflict between these means and ends causes personal *strain.*

A person can respond to the strain between societal goals and institutional means through various *modes of individual adaptation* ranging on a scale from *innovation* to *rebellion* among other possible responses, as outlined in his *anomie as strain* theory (see table 2.1). Criminals who break the law for monetary gain

Table 2.1: Merton's Typology of Modes of Individual Adaptation

Modes of adaptation	Cultural goals	Institutional means
i. Conformity	+	+
ii. Innovation	+	−
iii. Ritualism	−	+
iv. Retreatism	−	−
v. Rebellion	+/−	+/−

+ = acceptance; − = rejection; +/− = rejection of prevailing values and substitution of new values.
(Adapted from Lee & Newby, 1986)

would be classified as "innovators." Strain theory is a clear example of a socio-logical theory of crime since it involves consideration of both social structures and social forces on personal conduct that can lead to deviance and crime.

Differential Association Theory and White-Collar Crime—Edwin H. Sutherland

Another notable criminological theorist whose legacy helped establish the sociological perspective in criminology was Edwin Sutherland. In his later 1939 work, *Principles of Criminology*, co-authored with Donald Cressey (1919–1987), the theory of **differential association** combined insights of psychological pat-terns of learning within a social context. However, the theory did not emphasize psychopathology or abnormality but focused on normal patterns of socializa-tion whereby people acquire the norms, values, beliefs, and behaviours of the groups of people with whom one regularly associates and interacts. Differential association emphasizes how criminal patterns of behaviour are acquired in an interactive process whereby one learns the "techniques of committing the crime ... the specific direction of motives, drives, rationalizations, and attitudes" of criminal conduct (Sutherland, 2010, p. 472). If one internalizes the attitudes and behaviours of an intimate social group, then one is likely to adopt their lifestyle. We can see how influential associations with others can create a **deviant subcul-ture** such as criminal gangs, cults, and organized crime groups where a shared mentality and strong social bonds maintain criminality.

Differential association theory can also explain how people are influenced by others they identify with to such an extent that they engage in wrongdoing to "fit in" and gain social approval. The example of soccer hooliganism, in which crowds of predominantly rowdy young males engage in aggression directed against prop-erty and fans of the opposing team, illustrates how strong associations can dra-matically influence people to engage in criminal behaviour.

Beyond sharing an interest in differential association theory, Sutherland and Cressey were among the first to study **corporate crime** and **white-collar crime**. Sutherland's seminal 1949 text *White Collar Crime* broke new ground with its shift in focus away from the typical poor "street crime" and working-class "blue collar" offenders, to the criminality of those who occupy positions of *privilege* and *power*. Sutherland reminded criminologists that although poverty and crime are inter-related, so are wealth and crime.

In his 1940 address to the American Sociological Association, Sutherland stated "that 'white-collar crime' was indeed a *serious* crime, whose absence from discussion in conventional criminology was a scandal" (cited in Taylor, 1999,

p. 157). White-collar crime, "crime committed by a person of respectability and high status in the course of his occupation ... had enormous consequences ... in terms of financial costs [that] were very nearly always passed on by corporations or businesses to the rest of the citizenry" (cited in Taylor, 1999, p. 157) and thus "the financial cost of white-collar crime is probably several times as great as the financial cost of all the crimes which are customarily regarded as 'the crime problem'" (Sutherland, 1949, p. 12). This insight is especially valid today in our globalized society insofar as the **2008 financial crisis**, resulting from the criminal wrongdoing of banking executives around the world, serves as an example of how lives can be destroyed just as easily by corporate criminality as by violent criminal victimization. In *White Collar Crime*, Sutherland examines how the social forces of "free enterprise" and "free competition" in the marketplace stimulate professional ambition and manipulative practices that are learned and mutually reinforced through collegial alliances (1949).

Sutherland's study brought a new range of criminal wrongdoings more squarely into focus for future criminological inquiry. He listed "price-fixing, anti-trust violations, violations of workers' safety legislation, bank frauds, infringement of patents, trademarks and copyrights, financial manipulations, war crimes, and very many other instances of corporate and individual 'malfeasance'" (Taylor, 1999, p. 157). As a result of his pioneering work in the field, corporate crime has become an established field in criminology that influences policy formation in the area of consumer protection legislation, environmental protection law, and labour law among others.

Subcultural Theory

Another significant criminological theory focuses on the formation of deviant and criminal *subcultures* such as outlaw biker gangs, youth street gangs (Chaskin, 2010), organized crime cartels (Schneider, 2017), and religious and political cults (Lalich, 2004). **Subcultural theory**, which was developed extensively by the **Chicago School** in the 1930s, emerged out of the study of juvenile delinquency in the inner city. Wolfgang and Ferracuti's 1967 book *The Subculture of Violence* offered an encyclopedic account of *violent subcultures* and the group norms that perpetuate violence but has been criticized for linking violence with specific ethnic and racialized groups—a problematic tendency that runs through numerous early studies of criminal violence. In contrast, Anderson's (1999) account of street gang violence is a respected study of how inner-city violence is often the typical reaction to *interpersonal acts of disrespect* among rival street gang members (Brezina et al., 2004).

The criminology of deviant subcultures has expanded substantially and examines the ways in which numerous subcultural groups maintain exclusive microsocieties through the use of selective membership, distrust of outsiders, specific styles of dress, codes of honour, and the use of specialized language known as an *argot*. Deviant subcultures develop secretive methods and engage in limited interactions to conceal their lifestyles. Of course, not all subcultures are criminal. Howard Becker's (1963) influential study *Outsiders* helped establish new theoretical categories such as "rule creators" and "rule enforcers" in the study of groups such as drug users and musicians, who were examined as deviants of moral scorn and rejection by mainstream society. Subcultural theories of criminology also focus on the formation of group subculture identity and codes of behaviour among police officers and other specialized groups who share common lifestyles (Herbert, 1998).

While early criminology generally focused on the study of deviant and criminal subcultures such as criminal street gangs, subcultural theory now also examines the rise of terrorist organizations (Griset & Mahan, 2012), as well as the formation of subcultures of criminality among economic and political elites (Simon, 2006). Another area of theorizing deviant subcultures examines "hippies," "punk rockers," and "ravers" as deviant expressions of resistance to mainstream society expressed through lifestyles guided by radical musical styles (Williams, 2011).

Control Theory and Crime Prevention

Control theory is another example of a sociological explanation of crime with a practical focus on policy formation in terms of *crime prevention strategies* (Schneider, 2015). In many cases, criminals are quite aware that what they are doing is wrong. What, then, is the deciding factor behind the decision to commit a crime? Have you ever heard the phrase "What have you got to lose?" Jackson Toby (1957) theorized that individuals who have a **stake in conformity**—meaning if they have significant social investments such as a career, a house, children, and many other societal connections to normalcy that keep them grounded—they will be dissuaded from rule-breaking and taking risks that can land them in prison and are thus more likely to conform. Similarly, conforming, law-abiding individuals according to Hirschi's (1969) **social bond theory** have pre-existing *attachments*, *commitments*, *involvements*, and shared *beliefs* with the lives of others that they do not want to risk by committing a crime.

Gottfredson and Hirschi (1990) also offered a theory of control that combined insights from psychological and sociological perspectives to suggest that crime results from the impulsivity of persons with low levels of self-control. According to this theory, people do bad things because "they just can't help themselves" and thus need to be prevented from doing crime through explicit formal control mechanisms. Just as a toddler should be prevented from accessing the top of an open staircase, so a would-be burglar should be prevented from entering someone else's home through secure locks and barred windows.

Even though at some level wrongdoers are quite aware of their indiscretions, they still attempt to justify their actions through twisted reasoning, denials, and excuses in the attempt to *neutralize* the culpability of their wrongdoing. Sykes and Matza (1957) outlined various **techniques of neutralization** invoked by the wrongdoer. These include the following:

- *Denial of responsibility*: "I really didn't mean to steal the bicycle."
- *Denial of injury*: "They can afford to buy another bike."
- *Denial of victim*: "They deserved it because they left the garage open."
- *Condemning the condemners*: "These rich people steal from the rest of us every day, so why blame me for taking a little something back?!"
- *Appeal to higher loyalties*: "My little brother doesn't have a bicycle because it got stolen, so I felt justified replacing it for him by taking one from someone else."

People who engage in various rationalizations for their wrongdoing are attempting to navigate the difficult path between personal guilt, the social consequences of their actions, and poor self-control. Sykes and Matza's elaboration of how wrongdoers attempt to neutralize their actions stands in contrast to rational-choice perspectives because it reminds us that people are not always able to control themselves, and thus secondary crime control measures are often required for public safety.

Crime control perspectives raise a number of important ethical issues. For example, do you think that public spaces should have surveillance cameras installed? Should personal cellular devices be blocked from accessing certain websites? As with many criminological theories, deriving the most effective policies to control crime is not always an easy task.

CONCLUSION

This chapter has explained the practice of *theorization* and *conceptualization* and presented an overview of the traditional criminological paradigms. The ways that crime, deviance, and social control have been theorized over time has changed substantially and did not always follow a straightforward path from confusion towards growing accuracy and focus. Instead, different theories were developed to account for the variety and complexity of crimes. A critical perspective emphasizes how early criminological thought was connected to attempts by authorities to engage in social control. As such, it is important to recognize how the history of criminology is bound up with some dangerous and troubling ideas that historically have served to legitimize unjust and disturbing practices.

Criminology deals with some of the most controversial human issues involving justice and freedom, and for this reason it continually expands its critical focus as society changes. In the next chapter, you shall be introduced to explicitly critical criminological theories along with some policy-oriented conservative theories—both of which emphasize the role of power in understanding crime, deviance, and social control.

REVIEW QUESTIONS

1. Define and explain the term *theory*. How do criminological theories explain real-world realities of crime and controls?
2. Why do the origins of criminology have a somewhat "disturbing history"?
3. What are "legacy" theories in criminology and why are they still relevant?

GLOSSARY

2008 financial crisis: An economic upheaval of global proportion that created massive financial losses caused by financial markets collapsing due to the impact of predatory mortgage lending practices and undisclosed risks to borrowers, as well as wrongdoing and failure to act on the part of government and financial organizations.

anomie: A sociological concept coined by Emile Durkheim referring to an alienating loss of self that arises from a lack of solidarity with the members, norms, or morals of society, or, conversely, the individual overinvestment in a social cause.

antisocial personality: A personality type characterized by shortcomings with regards to basic social interaction skills, such as ease of conversation, and a lack of familiarity with social cues and a tendency towards reclusiveness, frustration, aggression, and paranoid thoughts.

asymmetrical warfare: A type of warfare where combat does not occur in established fields of battle, and where surprise attacks by non-traditional, often individual or small groups of combatants can strike at any place, including civilian spaces.

atavism: Cesare Lombroso's conceptual classification for a type of criminal he hypothesized to be born in a more primitive evolutionary state, lacking the voluntary self-control of a civilized person, and who is thus more prone to criminal behaviour.

biological determinism: A school of thought that emphasizes biological factors from body type to genetics as the most influential factors that determine human behaviour.

Chicago School: A diverse body of criminological scholarship developed by numerous researchers at the University of Chicago in the early 20th century that examined how some urban neighbourhoods with greater amounts of social disorganization have higher rates of crime.

civil society: A society where norms of civility, mutual respect, and cooperation prevail through the combined efforts of individuals and collective groups.

collective punishment: A type of maltreatment that targets a collective or group based on their racial, cultural, or political identity that can range from discrimination to more severe punishments such as detention.

concept: A scientific or analytic term that identifies and names specific natural or social phenomenon revealed through research findings or analysis.

corporate crime: Criminal activity engaged in by business corporations in the course of conducting business.

crimes against humanity: Large-scale atrocities inflicted on mostly civilian populations by those in power or those seeking to attain power that is so unconscionable that it is viewed as a crime against the entire human community.

criminal profiling: A technique of investigation based on gathering typically behavioural or geographical information with the aim of identifying a criminal perpetrator.

criminological theory: The broad range of interdisciplinary ideas and concepts that combine to form the analytic models used by researchers to understand and explain different types of crime and criminal phenomena.

critical race theory: A social theory based on law and power relations that critically analyzes social hierarchies of exclusion, discrimination, and domination that categorize people on the basis of their racial identity.

cultural criminology: The study of how narratives about crime have become products for public consumption that influence cultural conceptions of crime, criminal justice, and how crime plays a significant role in contemporary media culture.

cybercrime: Criminal wrongdoings that are perpetrated through computers and computer networks including the internet and social media that target individuals, groups, or technology and information systems.

deterrence: To deter, inhibit, or de-incentivize against the commission of crime or wrongdoing through the threat of negative repercussions such as punishment.

deviant subculture: A social group distinguished from the larger society by virtue of their members having cultural values, norms, and practices that depart substantially from the mainstream and defines their identity. Deviant subcultures can range from groups who practice alternative lifestyles to more extreme examples such as fanatical cults.

differential association: Edwin Sutherland's theory of criminal behaviour that emphasizes how criminal conduct and ways of thinking are learned through interactions with others who engage in criminal lifestyles.

empirical research methods: Methods of research aimed at verifying the validity of theoretical claims or hypotheses based on the analysis of measurable evidence gathered by experimentation or observation as proof.

ethnocide: Also known as "cultural genocide," the attempt to control and subjugate a particular social group through the systematic elimination of their cultural identity, language, and cultural practices.

eugenics: The selective breeding of humans with the goal of producing genetically superior offspring.

femicide: The deliberate killing of females, and in particular female fetuses and infants, for the purpose of gender selection in favour of male births.

frustration–aggression hypothesis: The observation that some people will respond with aggression when they are faced with frustration.

genocide: The systematic murder of a large number of people targeted on the basis of their belonging to a particular race, ethnicity, or creed.

hedonism: A lifestyle or view of human nature based upon the pursuit of pleasure and the avoidance of pain.

heresy: Beliefs, opinions, or teachings that violate religious dogma or orthodoxy as defined by authorities which are punishable.

human rights: The basic freedoms that uphold the dignity and equality of all people by virtue of their being human and thus deserving of respect and protection from oppression and persecution as guaranteed by law.

Intelligence Quotient (IQ): A number derived from testing that is purported to be a measure of a person's intelligence with a classification range from feeble-minded to genius.

Islamophobia: The fear and hatred of, and prejudice against, Muslims, especially the form that arose after the events of September 11th, 2001, and which links followers of Islam with the threat of terrorism and hatred of the West.

learning theory: A branch of psychology that studies how human behaviour is learned in a variety of ways from conditioned responses and rewarded behaviour to social learning from others.

legal precedent: A principle in the practice of law where the ruling in a particular case establishes a new benchmark for future cases of a similar nature.

McCarthyism: A state-sponsored campaign of persecution led by Senator Joseph McCarthy that took place in early-1950s America, which targeted individuals accused of being communists or communist sympathizers and were subsequently "blacklisted," lost their jobs, and had their lives destroyed in various ways purely on the basis of accusations and political viewpoints.

M'Naghten rule: A legal ruling in a criminal case where the accused is found not responsible for a crime because they were determined to be of unsound mind at the time the crime was committed.

misogyny: Hatred of or contempt for women.

moral regulation: The process of regulating individuals and social relations through the application of moral judgments that may elicit guilt, shame, and dishonour to control and sanction people into conforming with the dominant moral order.

panopticon: A late 18th-century prison with architectural features designed to maximize the surveillance of inmates by guards who are placed at a central vantage point.

paradigm: In the philosophy of science, a paradigm is a model of analysis that comes to dominate study and research within a particular discipline of study for a particular period of time.

patriarchal order: A type of hierarchical social organization that privileges male power, which emerged in human civilization approximately 5,000 years ago, and is reproduced in numerous institutions such as the family, the state, and religion, where males generally hold dominant status.

political prisoner: An individual who is incarcerated for their political or ideological beliefs by a government or other ruling authority who feels threatened by such beliefs.

post-9/11 era: The historical period following the events of September 11th, 2001, characterized by intensified forms of anti-terrorist governmental policies, revived warfare, and subsequent new security measures restricting individual rights and freedoms.

psychopath: A psychological diagnosis often associated with criminal and deviant behaviour, where the individual exhibits cunning, false confidence, authoritarian qualities, manipulation, and aggression in their attempts to exert control over others.

psychopathology: A generic term for a broad range of psychological disorders characterized by a pronounced and debilitating psychiatric or mental impairment that substantially affects one's quality of life.

rational choice theory: A theory of human behaviour that examines the motivating factors and rational decision-making processes or choices individuals make, including the risks and rewards one contemplates before acting in a specific set of circumstances.

scientific racism: A theory that uses the authority of science to make the claim that certain groups of humans are biologically inferior to others.

social bond theory: The theory that people with strong social bonds to others based on mutual attachments, commitments, involvements, and shared beliefs will compel such people to conform to a law-abiding lifestyle.

social bonds: The meaningful social relations that create solidarity and support among people and lead to the formation of human societies.

stake in conformity: The theory that the more a person conforms to conventional lifestyle goals, such as gainful employment, dependent social relations, and financial commitments, the greater the likelihood they will not deviate into criminal activities because they have too much to lose if they get caught.

state of exception: A concept from political theory referring to a condition where the governmental state temporarily suspends legal protections and maximizes its powers in response to a crisis or emergency situation that threatens public safety.

strain theory: Robert Merton's theory that explains crime and deviance as the result of particular kinds of social pressures and strains that one faces in achieving economic success in life and subsequently compels them to violate normative and legal codes of conduct.

subcultural theory: A theory that emphasizes how deviant or criminal lifestyles and patterns of behaviour develop in the context of a person's affiliation with a subculture that embraces non-conformist norms.

techniques of neutralization: The criminological theory outlined by Sykes and Matza that explains how wrongdoers attempt to justify their behaviour and neutralize or minimize the extent of their wrongdoing through various rationalizations.

theory: A formal analytic model that aims to hypothesize about, explain, understand, or interpret a particular natural or social phenomenon.

war crime: A horrific act perpetrated in the context of warfare that violates acceptable standards of military combat, such as the murder of captured enemy soldiers, targeting of civilians, rape of women and girls, torture, and beheading, among other atrocities.

white-collar crime: Criminal activities committed by high-status or well-to-do individuals who occupy positions of privilege and power.

REFERENCES

Aamodt, M. G. (2016, September 4). *Serial killer statistics.* Retrieved from http://maamodt.asp.radford.edu/Serial%20Killer%20Information%20Center/Serial%20Killer%20Statistics.pdf

Anderson, E. (1999). *Code of the street: Decency, violence, and the moral life of the inner city.* W. W. Norton & Company.

As It Happens. (2017, September 8). Woman faces psych evaluation for calling Uganda's president "a pair of buttocks." *CBC Radio.* Retrieved from https://www.cbc.ca/radio/asithappens/as-it-happens-friday-edition-1.4143260/woman-faces-psych-evaluation-for-calling-uganda-s-president-a-pair-of-buttocks-1.4143263

Bakan, J. (2004). *The corporation: The pathological pursuit of profit and power.* Penguin Canada.

Bandura, A. (1973). *Aggression: A social learning analysis.* Prentice-Hall.

Bauman, Z. (1989). *Modernity and the Holocaust.* Cornell University Press.

Beccaria, C. (1986). *On crimes and punishments.* Hackett. (Original work published 1764)

Becker, H. (1963). *Outsiders: Studies in the sociology of deviance.* The Free Press.

Bentham, J. (2007 [1789]). *An introduction to the principles of morals and legislation.* Dover Publications.

Bleier, R. (1984). *Science and gender: A critique of biology and its theories on women.* Pergamon Press.

Boddy, C. R. (2006). The dark side of management decisions: Organisational psychopaths. *Management Decision, 44*(10), 1461–1475. https://doi.org/10.1108/00251740610715759

Brezina, T., Agnew, R., Cullen, F. T., & Wright, J. P. (2004). The code of the street: A quantitative assessment of Elijah Anderson's subculture of violence thesis and its contribution to youth violence research. *Youth Violence and Juvenile Justice, 2*(4), 303–328. https://doi.org/10.1177/1541204004267780

Casavant, L., Charron-Tousignant, M., MacKay, R., Nicol, J., & Shaw, E. (2018, December 18). *Legislative summary of Bill C-51: An Act to amend the Criminal Code and the Department of Justice Act and to make consequential amendments to another Act.* Parliament of Canada. Library of Parliament—Research Publications. Retrieved from https://lop.parl.ca/sites/PublicWebsite/default/en_CA/ResearchPublications/ LegislativeSummaries/421C51E

Cawood, C. D., & Huprich, S. K. (2011). Late adolescent nonsuicidal self-injury: The roles of coping style, self-esteem, and personality pathology. *Journal of Personality Disorders, 25*(6), 765–781. https://doi.org/10.1521/pedi.2011.25.6.765

Chaskin, R. J. (Ed.). (2010). *Youth gangs and community intervention: Research, practice, and evidence.* Columbia University Press.

Cohen, D., Nisbett, R. E., Bowdle, B. F., & Schwarz, N. (1996). Insult, aggression, and the southern culture of honor: An "experimental ethnography." *Journal of Personality and Social Psychology, 70*, 945–959.

Connors, R. (1996). Self-injury in trauma survivors: 1. Functions and meanings. *American Journal of Orthopsychiatry, 66*(2), 197–206. https://doi.org/10.1037/ h0080171

Cornish, D. B., & Clarke, R. V. (1986). *The reasoning criminal: Rational choice perspectives on offending.* Transaction Publishers.

Coser, L. (1982). The notion of control in sociological theory. In J. Gibbs (Ed.), *Social control: Views from the social sciences* (pp. 13–22). SAGE Publications.

CTV News. (2018, October 26). Woman charged with pretending to practice witchcraft after allegedly bilking man out of $600k. *CTV News.* Retrieved from https://www. ctvnews.ca/canada/woman-charged-with-pretending-to-practice-witchcraft-after- allegedly-bilking-man-out-of-600k-1.4149336

Dangerfield, K. (2018, February 26). Vatican launching new exorcism course as demand for it soars. *Global News.* Retrieved from https://globalnews.ca/news/4047582/ vatican-exorcism-training-course/

Davis, N. J., & Stasz, C. (1990). *Social control of deviance: A critical perspective.* McGraw-Hill.

Durkheim, E. (2010). The normal and the pathological. In H. N. Pontell (Ed.), *Social deviance: Readings in theory and research* (5th ed.). Pearson Prentice Hall. (Original work published 1938)

Eagleton, T. (1983). *Literary theory: An introduction.* Verso.

Gottfredson, M. R., & Hirschi, T. (1990). *A general theory of crime.* Stanford University Press.

Gould, S. J. (1981). *The mismeasure of man.* W. W. Norton & Company.

Gramsci, A. (1971). *Selections from the prison notebooks.* International Publishers.

Griset, P. L., & Mahan, S. (2012). *Terrorism in perspective.* SAGE Publications.

Herbert, S. (1998). Police subculture reconsidered. *Criminology, 36*(2), 343–370. https:// doi.org/10.1111/j.1745-9125.1998.tb01251.x

Hirschi, T. (1969). *Causes of delinquency.* University of California Press.

Jalava, J., Griffiths, S., & Maraun, M. (2015). *The myth of the born criminal: Psychopathy, neurobiology, and the creation of the modern degenerate*. University of Toronto Press.

Katz, J. (1988). *Seductions of crime*. Basic Books.

Klonsky, D. E. (2007). The functions of deliberate self-injury: A review of the evidence. *Clinical Psychology Review, 27*(2), 226–239. https://doi.org/10.1016/j.cpr.2006.08.002

Lalich, J. (2004). *Bounded choice: True believers and charismatic cults*. University of California Press.

Lee, D., & Newby, H. (1986). *The problem of sociology*. Century Hutchinson.

Leyton, E. (2005). *Hunting humans: The rise of the modern multiple murder*. McClelland & Stewart.

Maxson, C. L., Whitlock, M. L., & Klein, M. W. (1998). Vulnerability to street gang membership: Implications for practice. *Social Service Review, 72*(1), 70–91. https://doi.org/10.1086/515746

McGloin, J. M., Pratt, T. C., & Piquero, A. R. (2006). A life-course analysis of the criminogenic effects of maternal cigarette smoking during pregnancy: A research note on the mediating impact of neuropsychological deficit. *Journal of Research in Crime and Delinquency, 43*(4), 412–426.

Oleson, J. C. (2016). *Criminal genius: A portrait of high-IQ offenders*. University of California Press.

Pfohl, S. J. (1985). *Images of deviance and social control: A sociological history*. McGraw-Hill.

Richerson, P. J., & Boyd, R. (2005). *Not by genes alone: How culture transformed human evolution*. University of Chicago Press.

Rose, S., Lewontin, R. C., & Kamin, L. J. (1984). *Not in our genes: Biology, ideology and human nature*. Penguin Books.

Rosen, S. P. (2005). *War and human nature*. Princeton University Press.

Rowland, I. D. (2008). *Giordano Bruno: Philosopher/heretic*. University of Chicago Press.

Smail, D. (1999). *The origins of unhappiness: A new understanding of personal distress*. Constable and Company.

Schneider, S. (2015). *Crime prevention: Theory and practice* (2nd ed.). CRC Press.

Schneider, S. (2017). *Canadian organized crime*. Canadian Scholars.

Simon, D. (2006). *Elite deviance* (8th ed.). Pearson Education.

Sutherland, E. H. (1949). *White collar crime*. Holt, Rinehart and Winston.

Sutherland, E. H. (2010). A sociological theory of criminal behavior. In S. G. Tibbetts & C. Hemmens (Eds.), *Criminological theory: A text/reader*. SAGE Publications.

Sutherland, E., & Cressey, D. (1939). *Principles of criminology* (3rd ed.). J. B. Lippincott Company.

Sutherland, E. H. & Cressey, D. R. (1924). *Principles of criminology*. University of Chicago Press.

Sykes, G. M., & Matza, D. (1957). Techniques of neutralization: A theory of delinquency. *American Sociological Review, 22*(46), 664–670.

Szasz, T. S. (2010). *The myth of mental illness: Foundations of a theory of personal conduct.* Harper Collins. (Original work published 1961)

Taylor, I. (1999). *Crime in context: A critical criminology of market societies.* Westview Press.

Toby, J. (1957). Social disorganization and stake in conformity: Complementary factors in the predatory behaviour of hoodlums. *Journal of Criminal Law & Criminology, 48,* 12–17.

Torrey E. F., Kennard, A. D., Eslinger, D., Lamb, R., & Pavle, J. (2010). *More mentally ill persons are in jails and prisons than hospitals: A survey of the states.* Treatment Advocacy Center. Retrieved from http://tulare.networkofcare.org/library/final_jails_v_hospitals_study1.pdf

Tremblay R. E., Nagin, D. S., Séguin, J. R., Zoccolillo, M., Zelazo, P. D., Boivin, M., Pérusse, D., & Japel, C. (2004). Physical aggression during early childhood: Trajectories and predictors. *Pediatrics, 114*(1), e43–e50. Retrieved from https://pediatrics.aappublications.org/content/114/1/e43

Urback, R. (2017, February 13). Vince Li is not evil; he's sick. But the justice system is treating him like he's cured. *CBC News.* Retrieved from http://www.cbc.ca/news/opinion/vince-li-discharge-1.3979861

Visano, L. A. (Ed.). (1998). *Crime and culture: Refining the traditions.* Canadian Scholars.

Wahlsten, D. (1997). Leilani Muir versus the philosopher king: Eugenics on trial in Alberta. *Genetica,* 99, 185. https://doi.org/10.1007/BF02259522

Wolfgang, M E. & Ferracuti, F. (1982 [1967]). *The subculture of violence: towards an integrated theory in criminology.* Sage Publishing.

Williams, J. P. (2011). *Subcultural theory: Traditions and concepts.* Polity Press.

Yochelson, S., & Samenow, S. (2004). *The criminal personality: A profile for change.* Rowman and Littlefield.

Young, J. (1981). Thinking seriously about crime: Some models of criminology. In M. Fitzgerald, G. McLennan, & J. Pawson (Eds.), *Crime and society: Readings in history and theory.* Routledge & Kegan Paul.

CHAPTER 3

Critical and Contemporary Theories of Crime, Deviance, and Social Control

Claudio Colaguori

LEARNING OBJECTIVES

In this chapter, you will

- understand how some contemporary theories of crime, deviance, and social control focus specifically on power relations and social inequality;
- learn about cultural criminology and explore why crime-themed programs and news are so compelling for viewers;
- discover the ways criminological theory has changed to reflect new social problems and social control issues in the 21st century;
- explore more recent work on environmental crimes and feminist and queer criminological theory; and
- learn about geographical theories of crime, as well as the *zero tolerance* and crime control policies they inspire.

INTRODUCTION

In Chapter 2, you were introduced to some important issues that shaped the early history of theories about crime, deviance, and control, along with a brief overview of *legacy theories* in criminology. This chapter introduces some critical and contemporary theories that focus squarely on issues of power and control, along with more recent theories that explain some of the difficult criminological issues facing the world at present. As our modern technological society changes with time, some crimes are reduced while new types of crime emerge. Social conditions that have transformed criminological theories include the continuing problem of social and economic inequality, the expansion of communications media into everyday life, the persistence of warfare, new technologies of mass surveillance, and global net-works of organized crime. Next-generation criminological theory has moved be-yond a focus on criminal justice towards a concern with issues of *social* justice, such as prisoners' rights and discriminatory law enforcement, the violation of gender and sexual rights and freedoms, the destruction of the ecological environment, and the ethics of animal rights. New directions in criminology emerged as a result of the dramatic social changes that started in the 1960s and have expanded the terrain of theory to include political power and popular cultural reactions to crime and injustice.

LABELLING THEORY: DEVIANT DESIGNATIONS, STIGMA, AND MORAL PANIC

Some argue that what constitutes a crime is a matter of interpretation. The *inter-pretive perspective* formally known as **symbolic interactionism** furnishes one of the theoretical foundations of **labelling theory**. Labelling theory is a unique para-digm in relation to other theoretical perspectives because, rather than focusing on the criminal *act*, it examines the *meanings* ascribed to such acts. Labelling theory thus has a distinct focus on the *social construction* of criminality. Furthermore, it examines how those with the *power* to do so are able to successfully apply deviant designations to the conduct of others, and the consequences that arise from doing so (Becker, 1963).

Labelling theory introduced the concept of power squarely into criminological theory and was the forerunner of many critical theories of crime, deviance, and control. It finds its origins in the work of early sociologists such as G. H. Mead (1863–1931), Max Weber (1864–1920), and Charles Horton Cooley (1864–1929), who each theorized that a person's perception of reality develops through our *interactions* with others with whom we share *symbolic* meanings and *interpretations* of the world. As a criminological theory, labelling is about how we collectively interpret and judge the behaviour of others as normal or abnormal, deviant or conformist. The premise is as follows: if enough people start using negative names to *label* a person and *describe* them, then it is quite possible for the label to stick and have a defining influence on that person's identity. Not only will others begin to see the person and their behaviour in a way that is defined by the negative label but the person who is so labelled may come to internalize the label to such an extent that, in the case of crime, they may begin to see themselves as *criminal*, thereby giving them further licence to do wrong things.

Erving Goffman (1922–1982) theorized that if a negative label is success-fully applied to a person, then their identity can be *tarnished* or *spoiled* to the point where a **stigma** is formed. The application of *stigmatizing* labels has long been a part of the *naming and shaming* process that is an ancient type of social control. Shaming is not just about making people feel bad; it is a way of influencing their behaviour through eliciting guilt, feelings of dishonour, and social rejection. Authoritative labels play an important role in the process of assigning *deviant designations* to those who can then be socially excluded and deemed *outsiders*.

Labelling theory is a broad area of criminology. It developed over time through contributions from numerous theorists including Frank Tannenbaum (1893–1969), who studied identity formation in juvenile gang members; Howard Becker (1928–), who studied the subcultures of musicians and marijuana users (1963); and Edwin Lemert (1912–1996), whose work critiqued studies of deviance based in pathological and functionalist perspectives (Pfohl 1985, p. 285). The impetus behind the growth of early labelling theory was dissatisfaction with traditional academic explanations of crime and deviance. Later-generation labelling theory was influenced by the critical social consciousness of the 1960s, which called upon people to *question authority*, to challenge the mainstream values of North American **culture**, and to rethink the ethics of the Vietnam war, including the decisions of governments to use their power indiscriminately against those with less power (Pfohl, 1985, p. 286).

In the words of scholars ...

Deviance is not a quality of the act a person commits, but rather a consequence of the application by others of rules and sanctions to an "offender." The deviant is one to whom that label has been successfully applied; deviant behaviour is behaviour that people so label.

Howard Becker, *Outsiders.* 1963

Labelling theory also explains the process by which powerful agents of social control, such as the state and the news media, are able to influence the *societal reaction* to certain forms of behaviour and conduct. The central concept that relates to this creation of an intense public reaction to crime is **moral panic**. Stanley Cohen (1942–2013) developed the concept to refer to a widespread overreaction to a perceived criminal or moral threat to society that calls for some sort of extreme response or severe social control measure. Moral panics are often started by certain individuals or groups, referred to as **moral entrepreneurs**, who hope to gain some sort of benefit by capitalizing on the crisis produced. Moral entrepreneurs are usually those with the power to engage in **claims making**. Spector and Kitsuse have theorized how social problems are often *constructed* using collective definitions put forth by those who actively make *claims*, *assertions*, or *grievances* about controversies, such as *crime waves* or the legalization of recreational drugs (1987, p. 73–77). Moral panics are further sensationalized through popular media representations of a situation that promulgate alarmist claims. Such alarmism can have a substantial influence on public perceptions and fears about crime and can also influence crime control policy.

While some moral panics are small in scale, short-lived, and generated by special interest groups who seek personal attention for their cause, there are cases of large-scale moral panics that have occurred for long periods of time. Many of these incidents have had serious and costly social consequences, such as the witch hunts and McCarthyism that were discussed in Chapter 2.

The concept of moral panic also relates to the larger process of *hegemonic* social control discussed previously. For example, Stuart Hall and colleagues (1978), in *Policing the Crisis: Mugging, the State, and Law and Order*, examined how crime panics sensationalized in the popular news media work to enrage the public about the threat of criminals rather than the threat posed by other social problems. Moral panics about the growing menace of crime deflect public attention *away* from other significant threats to public safety and security, such as increasing social and economic inequality, political corruption, and the decline of public services. For Hall et al., the state needs to maintain legitimacy in an effort to avert a *crisis in hegemony* (1978, p. 196). Moral panics reported in the media thus support the state in its propagandistic efforts to maintain public support and conceal the contradictions and shortcomings of government. Getting the public to worry about the immediate threat of criminal victimization means they may be less concerned with the bigger political problems in society.

It should be noted that not all expressions of moral outrage or the raising of awareness about crime constitute an unjustified moral panic. If no particular interest group stands to benefit financially or politically, then public outrage against wrongdoing may be genuine. For example, do you think that police baiting of those who frequent sex trade websites represents a legitimate effort to counter online pedophiles and the sexual trafficking of minors, or are such efforts part of a moral panic that benefits anti-prostitution groups and increased police powers?

The premises of labelling theory have concrete policy implications, especially in terms of public shaming and stigmatization. Publicly advertised lists of registered sex offenders and naming people charged with driving under the influence of drugs or alcohol are examples of shaming designed to both deter the offender and protect the public safety. John Braithwaite's (1989) theory of **reintegrative shaming** is a type of labelling perspective relevant to both youth and Indigenous conceptions of justice and corrections. Reintegrative shaming emphasizes the social control and recuperative functions of shame and self-esteem in cultures with strong "communitarian and interdependent" social bonds (Braithwaite, 1989). Braithwaite emphasizes the importance of reintegrating offenders back into meaningful non-criminal roles in society after they have been shamed; otherwise, there is a risk of stigmatizing them, which can lead to the formation of a criminal identity. In this approach, shaming the wrongdoer serves as a form of **moral regulation**; the dishonour associated with the transgression is intended to deter the individual from committing future offences.

CRITICAL AND CONFLICT THEORIES OF CRIME AND CONTROL

Many critical theories in the social sciences, criminology included, owe a debt to the sociology of Karl Marx (1818–1883) and Friedrich Engels (1820–1895), who theorized that capitalist societies exist in a state of constant tension and conflict of interests between the two main economic classes of people in society:

- those who own, control, and generate financial profit from the resources of society, such as the banks, the manufacturing and sales industries, and the communications systems, and who thus monopolize political and economic power (known as the *bourgeoisie* or the elite ruling class)

versus

- those who work for others as wage earners with minimal social power in the economic system and who constitute the majority of the population (known as the *proletariat* or working class).

Although Marx and Engels wrote relatively little about crime, and much more about law, many subsequent theorists expanded on their theory of *class conflict* to develop the **conflict perspective** as a way of explaining crime, criminalization, and injustice in societies characterized by economic inequality. While many critical criminological theories approach the study of crime and deviance by examining the role of social forces and the *power relations* that exist in society,

Marxist-oriented criminologists focus on the power of the ruling class to make the law and benefit from the laws that are enforced. Critical conflict theories raise questions such as the following:

- "How does economic inequality and limited economic opportunity promote criminality?"
- "How does the political state and ruling class perpetuate violence and inequality?"
- "What gives those who hold political power the right to decide that a particular act is illegal while other, similar acts are legal?"
- "Why are the crimes of the powerless heavily publicized and prosecuted over the crimes of the powerful?"
- "Why are prison inmate populations in North America disproportionately made up of cultural and racial groups who have historically been marginalized and discriminated against?"

Willem Bonger (1876–1940) is noteworthy as one of the early Marxist theorists to apply a conflict perspective to crime. For Bonger, criminal thoughts and motivations are generated from the exploitative social relations that emerge from the competitive, selfish, and egoistic forms of conflicted interactions that exist within a capitalist society, where political and economic power is monopolized by a small but dominant class of the population (1916/2015). According to Bonger, if economic resources were more equally distributed—for instance, people were given fair wages, access to affordable housing, food, healthcare, education, and the other necessities of life—then people would not need to resort to crime. A non-competitive society based on social relations of altruism and community would have minimal amounts of the selfishness and greed that Bonger sees as the source of most criminal motivation. Bonger asserts that capitalist systems of competition also create hierarchies of dominance within groups of the poor and working classes that further stimulate criminal rivalries and pit the downtrodden against each other.

Is Bonger correct that eliminating economic inequalities will virtually eliminate crime? Bonger's theory may not provide a full answer to the question of crime causation, but it raises a number of issues about how crime can be stimulated by social and economic deprivation. For example, a number of researchers, including Elliot Currie (1985), suggest that crime rates go down in times of economic prosperity when more employment opportunities abound.

It is important to note that at the time of Bonger's writings in the age of early 20th-century industrial capitalism many new laws were specifically directed against the poor, unemployed, homeless, and immigrants, and the punishments for breaking them were severe. As indicated in Chapter 1, many downtrodden people were designated as *dangerous classes* and suffered from a lack of basic labour rights and social security. If workers did pose a threat to the capitalist order, it was through the formation of trade unions and social movement activities that revealed the rampant injustices and power imbalances of what Marx referred to as *vampire capitalism*: how the capitalist system sucks the lifeblood out of those who toil for the benefit of the bourgeois ruling class. Seeing these organized threats to the social order that benefitted them, the ruling classes enacted numerous laws to control the behaviour and conduct of the so-called dangerous classes, while striking workers were often brutally put down by police forces working on behalf of business owners.

Punishing the Poor as Penal Policy

Conflict theories also posit that ruling elites view crime as a form of *dissident action* against the capitalist system. For elites during the rapid industrialization of the early 20th century, crime was seen as a threat to the economic order, and those who disrupted that order in any way (for instance, the poor, the unemployed, orphans, vagrants, or the mentally ill or physically infirm through practices such as begging) were deemed *surplus populations* in need of institutionalization in an asylum or prison or other type of *confinement institution* (Davis & Stasz, 1990).

An early and ground-breaking critical analysis of the use of punishment as an extension of ruling class domination was the 1939 joint study by Georg Rusche and Otto Kirchheimer entitled *Punishment and Social Structure*. The authors argue that "punishment [is] a social phenomenon, which has a set of determinants and a social significance which go well beyond the technical requirements of crime control" (Garland, 1990, p. 91). For Rusche and Kirchheimer, the capitalist class struggle is played out in the penal system since it is one element "within a wider strategy of controlling the poor, in which factories, workhouses, the poor laws [and] the labour market all play corresponding parts" (Garland, 1990, p. 91). In his 1933 essay, Rusche stated, "the criminal law and the daily work of criminal courts are directed almost exclusively against those people whose class background, poverty, neglected education, or demoralization drove them to crime" (as cited in Garland, 1990, p. 91). Rusche and Kirchheimer's analysis examined the relation between a surplus of workers in the labour market and the use of penal practices to manage and control the unemployed surplus populations that are more likely to end up in conflict with the law and caught up in the system of criminalization and incarceration.

Various other theorists have examined the ways in which penal policies such as sentencing and incarceration have a relation to the overall functioning of the social system that extends beyond crime control and reflects social divisions and economic conflicts that exist in the larger society. Prison theorist Nils Christie (1928–2015) in *Crime Control as Industry* (1993) made a substantial contribution to the study of how incarceration practices form a part of the larger system of increasingly punitive crime control measures taking place in many industrial societies that target the poor and working class.

After being largely ignored for many years, the work of Rusche and Kirchheimer gained renewed prominence among criminologists towards the end of the 20th century with the rise of the **prison–industrial complex** and the phenomenon of **mass incarceration** becoming a distinctive and troubling outcome of punitive crime control systems (Colaguori, 2005). The practice of building many new prisons to house increasing numbers of convicted offenders became a profit-based enterprise, especially in the United States where young Black males are significantly overrepresented in prison populations (Herivel & Wright, 2003). In many prisons in Canada, the number of Indigenous persons is out of proportion with their numbers within the general population (La Prairie, 2002). Such disparities have long been criticized as evidence of systemic racial and cultural discrimination by legal authorities and by the criminal justice system in general. Clearly the relation between criminological theory, crime control policy, and power is a complex one, and you will be encouraged to think more about the difficulties crime control poses for different groups in society as you read through this book.

Law, Conflict, and the Power to Criminalize

A number of other noted criminological theorists developed Marxist, class conflict–oriented analyses of crime emerging from social inequalities. These scholars include Thorsten Sellin (1896–1994), who examined how different *cultural* (rather than economic) groups can conflict with each other. George Vold (1896–1967) examined how different social groups pursue their own interests by influencing the creation of laws that benefit their positions of power and subsequently reduce the ability of competing groups to advance their own interests through the law. Another criminological theorist working within a legal–conflict perspective that also analyzed the role of law as a social force in the production of criminality was Austin Turk (1934–2014), author of *Criminality and Legal Order* (1969). Livy Visano summarizes Turk's view of criminality as a type of "social status defined by the way in which an individual is perceived, evaluated and treated by legal authorities" (1998, p. 121). Richard Quinney, in *Critique of Legal Order* (1974), theorized how the nature and application of criminal law serves those in power through the creation of a specific *legal order*, a type of societal arrangement that benefits the ruling class by formulating and applying legal definitions of crime biased in their favour. For Quinney, criminal law is used not only for controlling crime but as "an instrument of the state and ruling class to maintain and perpetuate the existing social and economic order" (2000, p. 107).

Class-based differences in the application of criminal law have significant consequences for the lives of people who live within the social order that law creates. Thus, what unites legal–conflict theorists is the view that laws are a reflection of the power interests of elite groups insofar as laws are selectively enforced, resulting in groups with less power being disproportionately criminalized.

Critical criminologists working within a legal power paradigm follow in the tradition of Max Weber, whose sociology of power theory emphasized how the law of the state represents the highest expression of authority in society. For Weber, the system of law is a type of *rational–legal authority* that sets out a "legal code which claims the obedience of all members of the society" (as cited in Lee & Newby, 1986, p. 182). Those with elite status who make and control the law use it to govern in a variety of ways: they influence the expiration of old laws and the creation of new laws that benefit them directly; they hire the best legal representation; and they wield influence over the punitive application of law through privileged relations with the police and the court system. Furthermore, many elite members of society possess the power of law directly because they work in the legal profession or have close contacts within it.

Weber's critical theory of society also emphasized the power of the state and its governmental apparatus as that which maintains order through direct force. When officials who govern through the state feel their economic or political power is threatened, they often resort to repression and violence against their adversaries. As Weber indicated, the ultimate power of the state is evident in the fact that it maintains the exclusive legal authority to use violence. He wrote, "a state is a human community that claims the monopoly of the legitimate use of physical force within a given territory" (1946, p. 78). We shall now turn to theories of state power, **state crime**, and state violence, which have all become important areas of study within 21st century criminology.

In the words of scholars ...

Criminal law is used by the state and the ruling class to secure the survival of the capitalist system, and, as capitalist society is further threatened by its own contradictions, criminal law will be increasingly used in the attempt to maintain domestic order.

Richard Quinney, *Bearing Witness to Crime and Social Justice.* 2000

THEORIES OF STATE POWER, STATE CRIME, AND STATE VIOLENCE

When we hear about crime and criminals, we typically do not think about the criminal acts perpetrated by the *political state*. Crimes committed by the state, such as official corruption, abuse of the power of political office, the tyrannical use of force, illegal espionage, the harassment and murder of journalists, and war crimes, among many others, have been the cause of significant harm and injustice worldwide, and yet crimes committed by state officials have long been ignored by mainstream criminology. State crime is a type of criminal conduct involving "acts defined by law as criminal and committed by state officials in the pursuit of their job as representatives of the state" (Chambliss, 1989, p. 184).

In his 1988 address to the American Criminology Society, entitled *State-Organized Crime*, critical criminologist William Chambliss (1933–2014) pointed out that criminal activities have long been a regular part of state practices. He cited the brutal conquering of the Americas as a process whereby the Spanish and the Portuguese engaged in rape, murder, open piracy, and looting of gold and other riches as examples of historically documented state wrongdoing. Chambliss (1989) further lists the following examples of American state crimes from the 20th century: the smuggling of drugs and weapons, assassinations and murders, and the illegal wiretapping and surveillance of citizens and foreign subjects. While we might prefer to think that such practices are a part of the horrific histories of past eras, many political states today continue to engage in wide range of criminal wrongdoing (Ross, 2000; Rothe & Mullins, 2011).

The state is a paradoxical entity. At one level, it is obligated to protect the public good by ensuring the smooth operation of the social institutions under its management (such as education, healthcare, finance, and various civil services). It also has to maintain law and order to help ensure the peace and security of its citizens. Yet those who hold political office are often unwilling to relinquish the powers they have, even at the expense of the lives of the citizens they are obligated to protect.

In the words of scholars ...

There is a form of crime that has heretofore escaped criminological inquiry, yet its persistence and omnipresence raise theoretical and methodological issues crucial to the development of criminology as a science. I am referring to what I call "state-organized crime."

William Chambliss, *Presidential Address to the American Society of Criminology.* 1989

As we saw in the discussion of *hard control* in Chapter 1, the state uses force to maintain order through the violent use of legal punishment (including the right to kill through capital punishment), policing, and weaponized military force. While most civil states aim to minimize the use of violent force in their attempts to secure order, violence is a regular part of state governance in both wartime and peacetime. Davis and Stasz write that for "critical theorists ... it is the modern state that is the most instrumental in creating and sustaining a violent social environment" (1990, p. 277). The state maintains and *normalizes* violence in a number of ways that include implementing social policies that disadvantage certain groups of people, reducing social services, promoting job loss and unemployment, increasing security and military expenditures, and promoting a **criminogenic** social environment, including declarations of war on other states and, in some cases, against its own citizens.

Violent force is often seen as the means through which societal changes can be made, with the popular ideology that violence is an effective way of addressing problems; subsequently, there are numerous campaigns that openly promote and valorize state violence such as the *war on drugs* and *war on crime*. Violent force is often glamourized as a form of power and regularly celebrated in media entertainment spectacles that feature themes of heroism, strength, and power based on the ability to wield violence.

The study of violence has often been a side note within traditional criminology, where scholars tend to focus on forms of interpersonal violence such as rape, murder, assault, and gun violence, rather than on violence as an issue in and of itself. However, the recent rise of concern over terrorist violence since the attacks of September 11, 2001, has renewed intellectual interest in the development of broad-ranging theories of violence. According to Sylvia Walby (2013), violence has been a fundamental element in the organization of social life in modernity and is bound up with practices of colonization, warfare/militarization, gender relations, securitization, and the continuation of patriarchal norms and values.

Violence is an activity with contradictory meanings. At one level, it is seen as a destructive force to be avoided, and at another level, it is seen as a way to produce positive results. Violence, thus, is primarily a technique of *social control* used by individuals and by the state to coerce the behaviour of others to abide by their will (Colaguori, 2010). The use of lethal violence has often been employed by state actors in the course of attempting to attain political goals. Note the following brief examples:

- From 1974 to 1983, the Argentinean state hunted down and murdered approximately 30,000 people deemed to be enemies of the state in what was called the "Dirty War," where state terrorism against presumed enemies included murder, kidnappings, torture, and rape (Wright, 2007).
- From approximately 1884 to 1996, the Canadian state took at least 150,000 Indigenous (First Nations, Inuit, and Métis) children from their families to be culturally assimilated in a residential school system that banned the use of Indigenous languages and customs and occasioned children to suffer physical, sexual, and mental abuse, resulting in death for approximately 6,000 of those children (Schwartz, 2015). (With the recent and ongoing discovery of unmarked graves at former residential school sites, this number may be even higher than previously estimated.) The loss of Indigenous culture, along with the theft of lands and violations of treaties, forms part of the complex and long-standing program of genocide and ethnocide (also known as "cultural genocide") suffered by First Nations people that has been cast as a Canadian state crime against humanity (Monchalin, 2016).
- As of 2011, the Syrian state has been engaged in a civil war with its own citizens, which began when a 14-year-old boy's graffiti suggested it was time for the leader to step down from power. Since then, approximately 500,000 have died, including 55,000 children, and chemical weapons have been used in contravention of international law, and yet all sides in the war deny responsibility for atrocities committed (Bakke & Kuypers, 2016).

Despite modern progress, armed conflicts and wars have killed and continue to kill many millions of civilians in numerous regions around the world (Slim, 2008).

The problem of violence is one of many pressing concerns characterizing the **new world order** that has emerged to shape social life and change the realities of crime, disorder, and social control in the 21st century. A number of theoretical concepts have been applied to new areas of analysis in the study of crime and control that mark the convergence between criminological theory and concepts from social, philosophical, and political theory. It is to these contemporary areas of criminological theorization that we now turn.

THE LEFT-REALIST CRITIQUE OF LEFT-IDEALIST THEORIES OF CRIME

The theoretical criminology developed by earlier Marxist-oriented conflict theorists who embraced a left-wing perspective established new critical directions in criminological theory, and yet conflict theory left many questions about crime unanswered. The development of the **left-realism** theoretical perspective introduced by Taylor, Walton, and Young in their book *The New Criminology* (1973) set out to address the shortcomings of previous articulations of conflict theory. According to left-realist criminologists, old-school leftist/Marxist types of conflict theories of crime and social control were based on a set of unquestioned *idealized* assumptions, such as:

- a belief that the social forces that create the conditions for crime predominantly criminalize the innocent;
- the view that most of the criminal problems of society are a result of ruling-class oppression and the ruling-class monopoly over the legal system; and
- the understanding that certain forms of criminal activity are authentic acts of social resistance and represent a *revolt* against the capitalist system (Lea & Young, 1984/1996).

Perhaps most significantly, the left realists argue that old leftist theories of crime overlook the fact that crime itself is a real harm, a serious form of injustice, and a real threat to public safety that needs to be controlled regardless of whether or not it is a symptom of an unequal social order. Left realists also emphasize that very little crime takes the form of revolutionary activity directed against the established system; rather, the working class, the poor, the powerless, the marginalized, and racialized peoples are most often the targets of predatory crime as well as the primary subjects of repressive street-level policing. What left realism shares with old left/Marxist theories is a deep concern for the marginalized and the powerless. In that regard, it has an *activist* dimension to it as expressed in its concern with the formation of policies that focus on those whose lives are regularly impacted by different forms of criminal victimization at work, school, or at home and those who are less able to create safe spaces and communities for themselves.

In addition to offering critical revisions to early left-wing theories of crime and control, Jock Young (2007) suggests that poverty and/or a lack of full or meaningful employment are *not* direct causes of crime; otherwise, crime rates would reduce substantially in good economic times, which they do not. Instead, "relative deprivation" (Lea & Young, 1984/1996) and "social exclusion" (Young, 2007) are the factors that motivate criminality. Thus, new-left criminology blends dimensions of sociological theories from Durkheim and Merton (legacy theories discussed in Chapter 2) into their criminology but retain the Marxist premise that people "make history ... not in circumstances of their own choosing" but under the circumstances of "the class nature of society ... [and] the extraordinary inequalities of wealth and power ... [that exist] in modern capitalist societies" (Young, 2011, p. 213).

Left-realist theories of crime can also apply to criminal wrongdoings in non-capitalist societies where different types of power imbalances exist and thus social exclusion occurs. Young (2007) theorized that social exclusion is a type of "othering" that is becoming more prominent in contemporary societies. He explores the concept of social "disembeddedness" as a type of vertigo, or disorienting uncertainty, about one's life that creates the human potential for both inventiveness, insecurity, and deviance (2007, p. 3). Within these contexts, many potential responses, including crime, can occur.

Young states, "on a substantive level *The New Criminology* demanded that an adequate theory should first address the problem of human nature and social order and to take cognizance of the human predicament," thereby considering the "totality" of society and its numerous social harms beyond criminal victimization (2011, p. 213). Thus, for Taylor, Walton, and Young, new critical directions in criminology should be fully critical theories of society where crime is both a significant form of injustice in society and a reflection of systemic power imbalances within that society.

In the words of scholars ...

The criminalization of vast numbers of middle-class youth (for "offences" of a hedonistic, or specifically oppositional nature) ... the "master institutions" of the state, and of the political economy are unable to disguise their own inability to adhere to their own rules and regulations.... A criminology which is to be adequate to an understanding of these developments, and which will be able to bring politics back into the discussion of what were previously technical issues, will need to deal with the society as a totality.

Ian Taylor, Paul Walton, and Jock Young, *The New Criminology: For a Social Theory of Deviance.* 1973

Neoliberal Market Society, Crime, and Incivility

Ian Taylor's work *Crime in Context: A Critical Criminology of Market Societies* (1999) revisits the theory of social conflicts, including criminal activity, that emerge in a society marked by economic inequality. Rather than performing a class-conflict analysis, Taylor expands on the "new criminology" he developed with Walton and Young (1973) and examines how forms of conflict arise between members of the working class themselves (rather than between the working class and the ruling class). He theorizes that new kinds of growing social tensions are among the troubles created in so-called developed societies, which have been "fundamentally transformed by the demise of mass manufacturing industry"; this, in turn, contributes to "the ever-intrusive fear and reality of crime" (1999, p. 4). The substantial loss of stable jobs as a result of what Taylor referred to as a post-Fordist society, where the transfer of mass manufacturing jobs in the United Kingdom and North America to so-called developing low-wage nations, has intensified the pre-existing social divisions and conflicts created by market pressures. What is nowadays referred to as economic **neoliberalism** creates unemployment, underemployment, and rising costs of living, as well as the erosion of social services. As a result, people are classified as "winners and losers" in relation to the economic hierarchy created by the market system (Taylor 1999, p. 5). Taylor theorizes that such social conditions generate forms of competition characterized by a type of "defensive/aggressive individualism" that pits people against each other in everyday situations. The values of the competitive "market culture" are transferred onto social relations to create a widespread *cultural* phenomenon that is expressed in antisocial outbursts like "road rage" and other "uncivil *in-your-face* types of public encounters" that occur in everyday exchanges of "discontent" among people who are increasingly at odds with one another (1999, p. 5).

Taylor's (1999) analysis of a competitive us-versus-them culture lends insight into how social conflict can become criminogenic. In the context of job scarcity, the loss of social safety nets, and increasingly precarious life circumstances, those who are disaffected can be prompted to engage in uncivil, antisocial activities ranging from the violent hatred directed at others, as expressed in soccer hooliganism, racist behaviours, and anti-immigrant rallies, to various types of predatory crimes against persons and property. All of these activities are criminal expressions of rage by those who feel the lived effects of social insecurity caused by competitive market forces. Taylor's work helps explain the rise of *neo-tribalism*, which is an element of cultural conflict in the current global condition of neoliberalism, where different identity groups are compelled to compete for jobs, social status, rights, and recognition.

In the words of scholars ...

I want ... to explain ... burglaries, car thefts, the use of guns, the sale of drugs ... as a product of the competitive individualism ... [and] "in-your-face" incivility ... [that is] an essential feature of "market culture" itself [and] is at the core of the defensive/aggressive individualism which many young people exhibit in a "winner–loser culture."

Ian Taylor, *Crime in Context: A Critical Criminology of Market Societies.* 1999

Left-realist criminology is in essence a reaction to technical studies of crime and an attempt to expand the scope of criminology beyond crime causation towards a theory of societal conflict as a whole. In addition to being a critique of former criminological paradigms, the insights of left realism help explain contemporary challenges. As Lea suggests, "the renewal of the Left realist tradition in criminology is vital for an understanding of crime and criminal justice in the context of a dominant neoliberalism" (2016, p. 53). Left realism thus serves as a useful lens through which to analyze contemporary crime

Box 3.1: Social Issues That Influence 21st-Century Criminological Theory

As you have read in this book so far, criminological thought is often informed by the historical context in which it is produced. With the advent of the new millennium, a substantial number of geopolitical changes have occurred that influenced the trajectory of criminological theory. Some of the significant historical changes affecting the scope of 21st-century criminology include:

- the globalization of neoliberal capitalism that developed in part from the 1989 fall of the Berlin Wall and the collapse of the Soviet Union, along with the establishment of unprecedented legal rights for corporations, resulting in significant economic crises, acts of corporate crime in the financial sector, and a growing gap between rich and poor on a global scale;
- the expansion of the world wide web, the spread of social media, and the invention of cryptocurrencies, thus creating cyberspace;
- the terrorist attacks of September 11, 2001, on American soil and the subsequent American-led *war on terror*, as well as the renewed use of torture as an interrogation technique in many nations;
- public backlash against post-9/11 policies that threatened civil liberties through mass surveillance and a subsequent resurgence of debates and activism surrounding human rights and social justice;
- the continuing popularity and proliferation of crime-themed entertainment programs, films, and video games as a mainstay of popular culture;
- the growing environmental crisis that includes global warming, climate disruption, and major energy industry pollution catastrophes;
- the establishment of transnational organized crime networks that profit from human trafficking, new forms of enslavement, sexual exploitation, and the traffic in illegal goods and illicit drugs;
- ongoing wars and a refugee crisis from people fleeing civil wars and armed conflicts in various parts of the world moving to the global South, Western Europe, and North America, movements which are often met with expressions of racism, hatred, and xenophobia;
- a growing shift in criminal justice policies that previously upheld the so-called war on drugs, marked by the unprecedented legalization of cannabis in many parts of the world, and the attendant new social and economic formations that are occurring from drug law reform.

and justice issues. Taylor (1999) and Lea (2016) suggest that such topics include the following:

- economic and financial crimes reflective of the conflicts of the global marketplace, such as money laundering and financial fraud;
- predatory crimes, including new forms of cybercrime and professional crimes;
- illegal arms and weapons sales, along with the gun violence that these activities encourage;
- terrorism;
- environmental pollution;
- the increasing militarization of law enforcement and the rise of private prisons, private police forces, and private militias;
- differential patterns of incarceration rates that reflect systemic discrimination.

THE DISCIPLINARY SOCIETY: SURVEILLANCE AND HYPERSECURITY IN THE POST–9/11 ERA

Michel Foucault is a theorist who has had a profound influence on contemporary criminology and across the social sciences. While his major works were published in the 1970s, a new generation of theorists are finding direct relevance between his ideas and problems of the current era. Foucault's analysis centres on the concept of power and provides a critique of social control through a number of concepts that have direct application to the study of crime and society. Heavily influenced by major thinkers such as Friedrich Nietzsche (1844–1900) and Max Weber, Foucault sought to delve deep into the workings of society by examining the specific ways in which forms of social *power* are transmitted to shape human conduct. For Foucault, *power* refers to the social forces that make society take the shape that it does through forces of domination. Power is predominantly found in the workings of institutions such as hospitals, schools, prisons, families, governments, and so on, but it is also a characteristic of the individuals who make up such institutions. People reflect power relations when they submit to forms of domination and become *docile* or subservient subjects, and they also reflect power when they *resist* forms of social control and become *active agents* of social change. This complex orchestration of back-and-forth power relations is what constitutes society and serves as a model through which crime and social control can be understood.

For Foucault, institutions try to maintain power by producing official forms of knowledge such as scientific theories, religious treatises, or laws that are written down and guide how an institution operates. This type of formal, institutional knowledge is what Foucault refers to as **discourse**, and it has authority over the conduct of people, especially when experts draw upon the discourses of their professions. For criminological theory, Foucault's study of the prison system is of particular relevance. In his book *Discipline and Punish: The Birth of the Prison* (1979), Foucault revisits Bentham's idea of the panopticon by theorizing how the prison system of surveillance and control of inmates was increasingly becoming a model for the regulation of public bodies in society at large. He likened modern society itself to a giant panopticon where systems of institutional power attempt to regulate people through the ceaseless shaping and monitoring of their lives. Foucault argued that "this surveillance is based on a system of permanent registration" and observed that "the gaze is alert everywhere" (1979, pp. 195–196). The aim of constant surveillance is to compel people to obey systems of power and become *disciplined subjects*, and hence Foucault's concept of the **disciplinary society** has been adopted by criminological theorists to describe the rise of the **hypersecurity state**, with its intensified penal policies and the increased surveillance monitoring of citizens, all of whom are suspect in an age of post-9/11 terror alerts and other risks and threats.

Another of Foucault's concepts that has applications for criminology and social control theory is **governmentality**. Governmentality, in Foucauldian terms, does not refer to statecraft, leadership, or the practice of politics. It refers to the widespread and differentiated minute routines, thoughts, and behaviours citizens engage in, which bind them to the existing political order and thus extends and *normalizes* bureaucratic control over their lives. Governmentality has a more sinister dimension that allows top-down systems of power to exert control over human bodies, including control over the *life and death process*, a concept called **biopower** (Colaguori, 2013; Foucault, 1980). Biopower is defined as the right of the *sovereign*, the state institution that has claimed the authority to rule, to "*take* life or *let* live, to *foster* life or *disallow* it to the point of death" (Foucault, 1980, p. 138). In the past in Europe, the Church authorities maintained biopower, for example, by killing those deemed heretics and by allowing others to live as long as they abided by Church doctrine or official discourse. Foucault also identified biopower in relation to control by religious or state authorities over human sexuality, for example, by decreeing what sexual acts are allowed and what forms of sexual expression are forbidden and criminalized. Biopower thus relates to so-called moral crimes, deviance, and vices, such as recreational drug use, prostitution, and prohibitions against homosexuality, all of which are explored in Chapter 5.

In the modern era, biopower and governmentality are also exercised via the **criminalization of dissent** where the social change initiatives of environmental, anti-violence, and anti-hate activists, among others, are punished, with participants often deemed enemies of the state. The application of criminal labels to dissident people is an increasing phenomenon post-9/11, where new anti-terror laws have been created to extend the power of the state through its lethal authority over the lives of people, even though in many cases such laws are applied to acts that have virtually nothing to do with actual terrorist activities.

Foucault was by no means the only thinker to write at length about the significance of institutional power and social control. George Orwell's sociological dystopian novel *Nineteen Eighty-Four* (1949) captured the repressive dimension of what was later elaborated on by Foucault. In *Asylums*, Erving Goffman also wrote about the *total institution* using the example of asylums for people with mental illness to outline how such institutions regulate behaviour in coordinated and regimented ways. Giorgio Agamben (2003) revived the notion of a *state of exception*, first developed by Carl Schmitt (1888–1985), to address the normalization of authoritarian political powers, associated primarily with repressive regimes, which have now become a regular part of political life in many nations, including heightened surveillance, securitization, and the tampering with due process procedures for suspects, among other limitations placed upon the liberty of citizens.

These concepts from Foucault and Agamben relate to contemporary criminology because they help to explain how the law is applied to specific forms of conduct that are criminalized. These theories also refer to acts of wrongdoing engaged in by state authorities that are contraventions of international law, such as illegal detention and torture of suspects, ethnic profiling, discrimination based on racial and cultural categories such as systemic Islamophobia, the use of anti-terror legislation to criminalize dissent and political opposition, and the severe limitations of freedom in terms of restrictions on movement and travel, which has in turn created new criminal opportunities for human traffickers and the illegal market in firearms and weaponry.

CULTURAL CRIMINOLOGY: THEORIZING NEWS AND ENTERTAINMENT MEDIA REPRESENTATIONS OF CRIME

Crime is an aspect of our culture. It is a major theme in the stories and concerns we share as a society. Crime is a regular component of the daily news broadcasts and is one of the most popular entertainment genres among television programs, books, and movies. What accounts for the enduring popular fascination with crime, law, and policing? How do viewing audiences make sense of and react to entertainment programs and news about crime? According to Jeff Ferrell, **cultural criminology**, a field of inquiry that attempts to answer such questions, "emphasizes the role of *culture*—that is, the shared styles and symbols, subcultures of crime, mass media dynamics, and related factors—in shaping the nature of criminals, criminal actions, and even criminal justice" (Ferrell, 2009, p. 219). For cultural criminologists, *culture* does not refer to ethnicity but to *popular media culture*, and thus cultural criminology uses concepts from a variety of disciplines including cultural studies, sociology, film studies, political science, and communication studies to theorize the ways that popular crime-themed media and news broadcasts represent particular images and narratives of crime. In addition, cultural criminologists seek to understand how audiences who *consume* crime-themed news and programs are entertained and influenced by them. Cultural criminologists recognize how mass media content has a profound influence on public perceptions of crime and justice and thus research the ways in which popular culture can serve as the medium through which social control takes place. Numerous theories have been advanced that examine the ways in which consumers of crime stories subjectively respond to them.

Researchers note that people who watch a lot of crime shows often fancy themselves minor experts on the topic of criminal investigations and criminal minds. Ian Taylor developed the concept of **commonsense criminology** to refer to how the "cinematic and televisual representations [of crime], and the accompanying forensic and socio-biological literature, are helping to construct and legitimize a form of populist criminology" (1999, p. 2). We see evidence of this "commonsense criminology" when fans of crime programs display their assumed knowledge of practices such as the use of DNA evidence in criminal investigations, blood spatter analysis, or serial killer profiling, or with criminal justice procedures such as the reading of Miranda rights ("You have the right to remain silent. Anything you say can be used against you," etc.) by a police officer to a detained suspect. One manifestation of commonsense criminology has been referred to as the **CSI** (crime scene investigation) **effect**, a phenomenon whereby the widespread popularity of crime-themed entertainment programs has influenced public understandings of criminal investigations and proceedings to such an extent that viewers feel they have developed a degree of expertise on such matters as forensic investigations. The CSI effect has also been demonstrated in the influence that popular crime dramas have on the deliberations of juries in criminal trial proceedings (Lawson, 2009).

While public understandings of crime, criminals, and justice procedures are strongly influenced by messages disseminated by the popular media, this can occur in different ways. George Gerbner (1919–2005) developed a **cultivation model** of media analysis indicating that heavy viewing of television tends to *cultivate* attitudes among viewers that make them supportive of mainstream political values. Carlson (1985) applied Gerbner's cultivation theory to crime-themed programming and found that heavy viewers are more likely to develop a *scary world syndrome* and thus be supportive of harsh and punitive criminal justice policies. The process whereby cultural messages draw people into conformity with the established order of society has been referred to as the *hegemonic process* (Gitlin, 1979). As discussed in previous chapters, **ideological hegemony** (Gramsci, 1971) is the theory that common sense ideas about power and social hierarchies that are embedded in mass media messages are more effective than the use of force at getting people to consent to the established political order. *Ideology* is defined as set of ideas that is used to justify and legitimate a social system based on unequal power relations. Ideologies are culturally shared commonsense beliefs that obscure and mask the power dynamics in society by tampering with people's ability to perceive the material conditions of society as they actually are, a process termed **mystification** (Barthes, 1973; Eagleton, 1991). Dominant ideologies and the process of mystification are largely maintained by popular communications media as a dimension of cultural control that profoundly shapes public perceptions of crime through systematic misrepresentations of reality.

The process of media misrepresentations of crime was further theorized by Steven Box (1937–1987), who also employed the concept of mystification to examine how media representations of crime and criminalization perpetuate deceptive myths. Box stated that crime-themed representations generally mislead the public about the realities of criminal harm insofar as they promote the perception that crime is caused primarily by disadvantaged members of society who are deemed *dangerous classes*, and the "vast amount of avoidable harm, injury and deprivation imposed on the ordinary population by the state, transnational and other corporations" and other crimes of the powerful are substantially underplayed in popular media narratives about crime (1983, p. 14). The problematic result of media-generated crime myths and *moral panics* may be that people begin to fear serial killers, satanic cults, and underworld conspiracies rather than more realistic threats to human well-being such as environmental destruction, political and corporate wrongdoing, and institutional forms of social injustice.

Cultural criminology has continued to develop concepts that highlight the ways in which consumers of popular media crime messages are influenced by, and react to, such messages. The concept of **transgression** appears regularly in the work of cultural criminologists. Although a transgression is literally an act that violates a rule or code, in the context of scholarly literature on criminology, the term has been used to refer to the feelings of dangerous adventure and escape experienced by the viewer of crime programs and movies or by those who enjoy crime-themed video games who are free to transgress without legal consequence. Insofar as *media reality* is an artificial reality and a distorted representation of the real world, it lends itself to the ambitions of the viewer/player, who can immerse themselves in the vicarious enjoyment of revenge over their criminal adversary. Alternatively, the viewer may identify with those being pursued by law enforcement characters and may even enjoy the consequence-free guilty pleasure of being a rule-breaking, violent offender. Transgression has also been researched as a type of excitement sought by crime program viewers as an antidote to their boredom with the alienating conditions of modern life (Ferrell, 2004). Deriving pleasure and excitement from identifying with the characters featured in graphic crime programs can be seen as a type of "deviant leisure" activity, akin to engaging in extreme thrill activities, violent sports, "graffiti writing," and "street racing," which, in "an era of 'cool individualism' … [recognizes that it is] culturally imperative to form a unique identity that is distinct from 'the herd,' to transgress" even though such attempts draw the alienated individual back into conformity with the images of mainstream pop culture (Smith & Raymen, 2018, p. 64).

Cultural criminology offers a fascinating interpretation of the enduring popularity of crime-themed programs. Its insights help us see how media messages can operate as forms of social control while remaining entertaining and how individual viewer identities are negotiated with and against the dramas and characters brought to life in popular representations of crime.

FEMINIST, TRANSNATIONAL FEMINIST, AND QUEER CRIMINOLOGY

As with the history of almost all scientific disciplines, the foundations of criminological theory have been the product of the ideas of men; the voices and input of women have been virtually excluded. Only with recent shifts towards more inclusive knowledge production have women and scholars from other underrepresented groups been able to make substantial contributions to criminology worldwide, thereby adding to its shifting areas of focus.

When women were mentioned in early criminology, they were often treated as aberrations, the victims (and perpetrators) of moral transgressions, or as under-evolved criminal specimens. For example, when confronted with the statistical fact that virtually all prison inmates were males, Lombroso and Ferrero (1893/2004), instead of drawing on their evolutionary atavistic theory to argue that female rates of criminality were so low that they must therefore be more highly evolved than men, reverted to the sexist bias of the times. They concluded that women were actually *less* evolved than men but that their inherent criminal tendencies were kept in check by fulfillment of their maternal roles and by the repression of their sexuality (Deutschmann, 2002, p. 142). According to Lombroso and Ferrero, "for the conception and execution of evil, it is clear that the innocuous semi-criminal present in the normal woman must be transformed into a born criminal more terrible than any man" (1895, p. 151). Otto Pollack's (1908–1998) book *The Criminality of Women* (1950), which appeared half a century after Lombroso and Ferrero's, did not claim that women were less criminal than men but that their crimes were of a different nature and perhaps less violent. Nevertheless, Pollack maintained sexist stereotypes and believed women were deceitful by nature, supporting his claim by drawing on female biological factors. The biological justification of gendered stereotypes has long been a problem in the sciences and, as Ruth Bleier (1923–1988) wrote, science has played a role "in the creation of an elaborate mythology of women's biological inferiority as an explanation for their subordinate position in the cultures of western civilizations" (1984, p. vii). **Feminist criminology** arose in part, then, as a reaction against the sexist claims of early patriarchal criminology and as a critique of sociobiological explanations of gender differences in criminality. Davis and Stasz emphasized how in traditional literature, religion, philosophy, and the sciences "women as an order are considered deviant" (1990, p. 217) and noted that woman and girls have been subject to repressive moral judgments that have not historically been applied to males. Such moral prejudices continue to influence the ways that females are processed and treated by state authorities and justice systems.

Recent work on women and crime has done much to challenge the sexist biases in criminology, but there is still work to be done. As Gavigan wrote, "feminist criminologists now must do more than denounce mainstream criminology for its failure to acknowledge the significance of female crime" (1987, p. 215). Important areas of analysis include addressing how the criminality of women and girls is correlated with gender and economic exclusion, as well as exploring the ways in which criminology has historically ignored the extent to which females are the primary victims of domestic violence and sexual assault. These issues, while always a factor in women's lives, gained traction thanks to the consciousness-raising movements of the 1960s; by the 1970s, "feminist criminology began focusing on the ways in which patriarchal society enabled the abuse of women" (Sharp, 2009, p. 246). The work of Chesney-Lind (1989) has contributed to the field of feminist criminology, examining how females are subject to a system of "gender stratification" in which they are offered less power and fewer opportunities than males. This, in turn, restricts their life options and subjects them to harsher forms of victimization and social control.

Feminist criminology has also exposed the fact that young women and girls are more likely to be abused and leave home with few resources. They often run into trouble because of vulnerability or are compelled out of desperation to marry early (often to inadequate, unsupportive partners), and the cycle of victimization and potential criminalization can ensue in an attempt to survive. Feminist perspectives on crime also examine how female youth offenders are treated more harshly in comparison to male youths by the criminal justice system, from sentencing to incarceration, and how the institution and practice of criminal law have been inadequate at addressing violence against women (DeKeseredy, 2000; Stevens et al., 2011). Moreover, the criminal justice system engages in systemic discrimination against racialized and Indigenous women (Comack & Balfour, 2004). Another significant area of feminist criminological research pertains to violence against women. In Canada, this is a growing public concern, especially in relation to the problem of missing and murdered Indigenous women and girls (MMIWG) and the inability of courts of law to adequately address cases of sexual assault.

The problem of violence against women is by no means confined to Canada. Various types of violence against women takes different forms in different countries. **Transnational feminist criminology** is a growing theoretical perspective that combines the critique of patriarchal practices predominant in nations outside of North America with a human rights perspective to focus on rampant rates of rape, sexual abuse, acid attacks, female genital mutilation, forced marriage, honour killings, the infanticide of female fetuses and infants, and the deliberate sale and trafficking of girls into the illicit sex trade. The transnational feminist perspective also takes into account the systematic exclusion of girls from education and schooling as well as the exclusion of women from active participation in economic and financial institutions (Ehrenreich & Hochschild, 2002; Maidment, 2006).

The gender selective determination of sexual practices, sexual preferences, and sexual orientations by religious institutions and the state have been fundamental aspects of social control for centuries. Michel Foucault's concept of biopower, described earlier in this chapter, pertains to ways in which forms of control over the bodies of people are exercised through the dictation of sexuality and procreation. Official categories of sexual normalcy and sexual deviancy have long been associated with *repressive moral regulation* and with the policing of so-called **moral crimes** (also known as vice crimes) such as gambling, illicit drug use, prostitution/sex-trade work, and, until recently, sodomy and homosexuality. The rise of a renewed human rights and social justice awareness have occasioned criminologists to focus on the ways in which people who do not fit into the heteronormative social order, or how those whose gender identity does not conform to the binary categories of male and female, have historically been ignored by criminology. Thus, **queer criminology**, "a theoretical and practical approach that highlights ... the stigmatization, the criminalization, and ... the rejection of the Queer community which is to say the LGBTQ+ (lesbian, gay, bisexual, transgender, and queer) population, as both victims and offenders by academe and the criminal legal system" is an area of growing criminological research (Buist & Lenning, 2016, p. 2). This contemporary interest is due, in part, to the fact that in the West homosexuality was, up until recently, considered a psychiatric disorder and deemed illegal. Expressions of gender variation and homosexuality continue to remain illegal and/or intolerable in many nations and in some cases are punishable by death (Tin, 2008).

In North America, attempts at controlling non-heteronormative social difference were initiated through various means including psychobiologically through hormonal manipulation, politically through state repressive practices of police raids of gay and lesbian social establishments, and via religious-based conversion therapies. Social rejection of LGTBQ+ teens by parents and guardians remains a significant social problem that can lead to homelessness and a drift into deviant lifestyles, substance abuse, and suicide. Queer criminology is an essential component of the *human rights turn* within contemporary criminology as it addresses ongoing concerns with the quest for justice and social equity.

GREEN CRIMINOLOGY AND ENVIRONMENTAL CRIME

Acts of plunder, violence, and destruction against the *environment*, the shared ecological spaces where people, along with flora and fauna, live in a delicate natural balance with each other, are increasingly recognized by criminological theorists as an under-researched area of grievous wrongdoing. The deliberate toxic pollution of the air and waterways, such as the addition of tetraethyllead to gasoline or the leaching of toxic tailing refuse from mining operations into rivers (as in the case of the Ok Tedi mining disaster), have long been presented as types of corporate wrongdoing, excused on the basis of managerial oversight and, in some cases, were actually legally allowed forms of pollution. Many other acts of corporate wrongdoing against the environment, such as over-fishing or massive oil spills, have been understood by criminologists as types of *corporate crime*. However, because some acts of violence against the environment escape legal definitions of criminality, and because the harms are often the result of diffuse actions over long periods of time, blame and intent is difficult to prove in a court of law. As a result, a new perspective of crimes against the environment has emerged named **green criminology**. As Burns writes, "annually far more people are killed from environmental crimes than from traditional homicides and millions more suffer ill effects from environmental harms. Yet, the study of environmental crime is largely absent from the criminal justice and criminology research literatures" (Burns, 2009, p. 481).

Societal awareness about environmental harm is not something new, but the extent of public interest often depends on the occurrence and reporting of ecologically destructive events. The 1962 publication of Rachel Carson's (1907–1964) groundbreaking work *Silent Spring*, which raised the alarm about the devastating effects of synthetic chemicals, marked the beginning of the modern environmental movement. Since that time, there have been numerous disasters involving nuclear, petrochemical, military–industrial, and natural resource–extraction industries. Since the 1960s, there have been widespread efforts to implement responsible environmental policies, but global progress on many issues (such as global climate disruption) has been slow in coming, and environmental crimes remain a regular occurrence.

The threat of looming global catastrophe occasioned theorist Ulrich Beck (1944–2015) to develop the concept of the **risk society**. This idea refers to the rapidly forming conditions of modern society whereby human industrial activity via resource extraction has been so significant that it has created a new planetary reality that poses a risk to life which threatens to become larger than the human capacity to contain it. A substantial part of the *risk* is environmental and thus Beck's work is an important theoretical paradigm for green criminologists.

Green criminological theory explores the causes of, and public reactions to, environmental crimes, as well as the challenges faced in classifying environmental wrongdoing as *crimes*. It also attempts to account for the ways in which environmental crimes present problems for legal prosecution and practical deterrence. Green criminology intersects with the criminalization of dissent and *eco-piracy* insofar as environmental and animal rights activists have been subject to severe sanctions and repression by state officials and private security forces protecting corporate interests against environmental responsibility (see South & Brisman, 2013).

CONSERVATIVE PERSPECTIVES: LAW AND ORDER AND ZERO-TOLERANCE CRIME CONTROL POLICIES

As this book has been emphasizing, the theories developed to understand the causes of crime often have a direct relation to the types of policies implemented to control crime. This relation between theory and policy is evident in the American criminology that emerged in reaction to abstract leftist theories of crime from the United Kingdom that did not easily lend themselves to realistic crime control policy changes. Around the mid-1970s, a number of pessimistic critiques of criminal justice practices began to appear. Robert Martinson (1927–1979), in a 1974 study, expressed discontent with efforts at rehabilitating prisoners by infamously claiming that "nothing works" at reducing crime. Although he would later modify his stance, Martinson set in motion a framework of questioning that would eventually come to form the theoretical and practical basis for the conservative **law and order** or **zero-tolerance perspectives** of crime control that gave rise to new strategies of policing and harsher punishments. While some claim that stricter criminal justice policies helped to reduce crime rates, others charge that these more severe approaches led to increases of **racial profiling** and contributed to the phenomenon of mass incarceration.

In 1975, James Q. Wilson (1931–2012) made the critical claim that research into the causes of crime was a waste of effort, "not because crime has no root causes, but because a free society can do so little about attacking these causes that a concern for their elimination becomes little more than an excuse for doing nothing" (2013, p. xxiv). Wilson's ideas, along with those of his collaborator Richard J. Herrnstein (1930–1994), would lend criminological support to the conservative law and order turn in criminal justice policy in North America. While conservative theories of crime and control tend to focus on individual offenders and left-realist theories tend to focus on social and economic forces, both perspectives share the idea that "disadvantaged persons ... are the principal victims of crime" (Wilson, 2013, p. xxii).

Conservative theories of crime are to a large extent rooted in some basic ideas from Durkheim; a stable social order that effectively contains destructive forms of criminality and controls other disorderly threats to peace and social solidarity is best established through combined *informal* (shared norms and values) and *formal* controls (laws, policing, and punishment). For Wilson, "predatory crime violates the social contract" (2013, p. xxiii), and so zero-tolerance policies assuage populist sentiments surrounding fears of criminal victimization and the need to maintain public safety. Such goals do not necessarily require detailed knowledge about the deep causes of crime, and thus rather than attempting to figure out the root causes of crime, Wilson and Herrnstein, in their 1985 tome *Crime and Human Nature: The Definitive Study of the Causes of Crime*, shifted theoretical investigation onto what is referred to in criminology as the **correlates of crime**. This type of criminological theorizing steps back from claiming that something specific is the *cause* of crime and instead makes a less definitive claim: that a certain type of crime is often *connected, associated with,* or *linked to* some demographic factor in particular. For example, Wilson and Herrnstein (1985) list gender, age, family, labour, community, television and media, school, drugs, and race as factors that can help to explain rates of crime. Research into the correlates of crime continues in mainstream criminology in the exploration of many factors, including citizenship, weather, guns, immigration, victimization, mental illness, religion, social class, and intelligence (Miller, 2009). The premise of this type of criminology is that although we may not be able to affect changes in crime rates by going after the deep root causes in each individual, crime can be controlled to some extent if law enforcement agents know where to look for it.

In the words of scholars ...

I believe ... that our society does not need to choose between helping the disadvantaged and fighting crime; to the contrary, helping the disadvantaged is desirable in its own right, and reducing crime is in itself a major source of assistance to those disadvantaged persons who are the principal victims of crime.

James Q. Wilson, *Thinking About Crime*. 2013

Another conservative criminological theory with a distinct focus on crime control, put forth by James Q. Wilson and George L. Kelling, is known as the **broken windows theory**. The theory posits that "the fear of being bothered by disorderly people" and the presence of "panhandlers, drunks, addicts, rowdy teenagers, prostitutes, loiterers, and the mentally disturbed" are signs that incivility is flourishing and the neighbourhood is in decay (1982/2005, p. 461). According to Wilson and Kelling, the conventional view that sees petty disturbances as mere nuisances of city life is shortsighted. They write that "social psychologists and police officers tend to agree that if a window on a building is broken and is left un-repaired, all the rest of the windows will soon be broken" (p. 462). Unattended property damage is a sign that no one cares and can create an environment that invites more crime, wrongdoing, and property damage. If members in such a neighbourhood maintain proper standards and quickly replace any broken window, then other members of the community would respect both public space and other people's homes and property. The theory resonates with the ideas of Oscar Newman, who put forth a theory of "defensible space" (1972). Newman theorized that crime rates in an area will be reduced if residents claim their homes and adjacent properties as their own personal *territory* so as to give the impression that they will defend it against those who may be thinking of violating it. Manicured lawns, well-kept homes, active playgrounds, and other signs of vitality signify to would-be criminals that such places are secured because they belong to people who care about them and will protect them against criminal activity. Another related geographical approach is that of C. Ray Jeffery is his 1971 *Crime Prevention through Environmental Design*, which offered the theory that urban spaces should be designed to discourage criminal activity by making it easier to monitor potential wrongdoers, on the one hand, and limiting opportunities for loitering and vandalism on the other. This notion of prioritizing the secure design of lived spaces even went so far as to make park benches difficult to sleep on. Such theories have had a significant influence on neighbourhood revitalization plans, crime control, and law enforcement policies in numerous cities.

The regulation and surveillance of public spaces has long been the basis of crime control. In the era before organized police forces, community members would regulate the activity of people on the streets by taking matters into their own hands and forcibly ejecting troublemakers and undesirables. In modern times, public order maintenance has largely become the onerous task of the police. Thus, zero-tolerance policies, when followed through to their logical conclusion, mean that not even minute acts of civil disruption are to be tolerated. If the police let one person get away with sleeping drunk on the sidewalk or allow one squeegee kid to rush out into vehicular traffic to beg for change, then multiple acts of wrongdoing by others will follow. Zero tolerance means making sure no pattern of criminality is allowed to begin. As Wilson and Kelling state, "arresting a single drunk or a single vagrant who has harmed no identifiable person seems unjust, and in a sense it is. But failing to do anything about a score of drunks or a hundred vagrants may destroy an entire community" (1982/2005, p. 467).

The world of theory and the world of practice do not always mesh so neatly; although zero-tolerance policies have been praised by some as effective in cleaning up many cities in North America, significant problems have arisen. Wilson and Kelling ask, "How do we ensure that the police do not become agents of neighborhood bigotry?" (1982/2005, p. 467). A new generation of social justice–oriented criminologists have the same concern, citing as evidence the rise of discriminatory carding practices, racial profiling, and the abuse of lethal force in numerous cities

Box 3.2: Rising or Falling Crime Rates: What Is the Reality?

If we consider the barrage of daily reports about crime and victimization occurring in the world today, we are likely to believe that crime is always on the rise, living conditions have become more dangerous, and people are more unsafe. This is not an unreasonable belief given that reports of crime make up a substantial portion of media content, and many new types of crimes are now occurring in our globalized, computerized, and conflicted world. Furthermore, the growing gap between rich and poor means that many people are living in conditions of desperation, making them more vulnerable to victimization. But is it true that overall crime is on the rise, or have crime rates steadily decreased since the 1990s, as many criminologists posit? How do we weigh such claims against specific types of crime, such as homicide, which has steadily increased in Canada since 2014 (Statistics Canada, 2021)? How can we trust claims that crime rates are declining when so many new forms of fraud, victimization, and predation, which did not even exist 20 years ago, now take place? Can official crime statistics be trusted to give us an accurate picture of crime, victimization, and harm occurring in the world today? Do crime statistics provide an accurate measure of the range of actual threats to life affecting human life globally? Consider the following headline: "Pollution causing more deaths worldwide than war or smoking" (Associated Press, 2017). Why do crime statistics not take into account such large-scale forms of organized human wrongdoing? The mythology that criminal victimization remains the major threat to human life is a longstanding public belief that continues to be regularly promoted in the news and entertainment broadcasts to the exclusion of other threats to human life. How can the insights from critical criminology work to challenge myths and misconceptions and promote a broader conception of injustice?

When it comes to criminal harm, what is myth and what is reality? As Kappeler and Potter write, "crime myths are real in the minds of their believers and have definite social consequences ... they provide us with a conceptual framework from which to identify certain social issues as crime related, to develop our personal opinions on issues of justice, and to apply ready-made solutions to social problems" (2005, pp. 2–3). How have the many theories covered in this chapter challenged your views about the causes of crime and the effectiveness of crime control? When reading the rest of this book, you are encouraged to expand your understanding of the complex realities and broad scope of human wrongdoing in an attempt to dispel myths and misconceptions about crime and justice.

across North America where uneasy relations exist between police forces and some of the communities they serve. Backlash against discriminatory and deadly law enforcement practices has given rise to prominent social movements such as **Black Lives Matter** (BLM). The BLM movement arose circa 2013 in the United States as a response to the racist bias inherent in broken windows–based community policing efforts that led to numerous unjust police killings of Black people (Camp & Heatherton, 2016).

CONCLUSION

This chapter presented an overview of some contemporary critical theories of crime and their origins in sociological theories of the interpretation of social meaning and social conflict. It also covered new areas of theorizing crime that go beyond typical conceptions of *the criminal* to examine crimes committed by state officials, crimes against the environment, and crimes that target people who do not self-identify along heteronormative lines of affiliation. As the globalized world continues to change economically and technologically, criminal activity also changes, and new ways of theorizing crimes of the 21st century are emerging. As Ian Taylor reminds us, criminology remains "a form of social and cultural analysis in which there are no agreed foundations" (1999, p. 4). Criminology, as an interdisciplinary body of thought, deals with crime, deviance, and social control, arguably some of the most complex and controversial human issues, and for this reason examines its subject matter from several different angles. In the rest of this book, you will see how theory illuminates various criminological issues involving injustice and power. Keep these theories in mind when reading through the remaining chapters and when you try to make sense of the criminal realities you encounter in your day-to-day life.

REVIEW QUESTIONS

1. Some criminological theories are traditional while others are critical. What makes a theory "critical"?
2. Explain how changes in social life in the 21st century have influenced the nature of criminal activity.
3. Explain some aspects of law and order and zero-tolerance theories of crime control. What are some of the problems associated with these approaches to criminal justice?

GLOSSARY

biopower: A concept coined by Michel Foucault that refers to the power exercised by state authorities to control human bodies, including the power to take life or determine the conditions under which people live.

Black Lives Matter: An activist social movement originating in the USA that aims to raise awareness and policy changes against racial profiling and the abuse of lethal force by police officers against Black people.

broken windows theory: A crime prevention and control theory based on the idea that public and police tolerance for minor acts of crime and wrongdoing has a tendency to encourage the commission of more serious crimes.

claims making: A process by which social problems are constructed by claims made by those who are active in their assertions or grievances about particular social problems, such as the claim that there is a rise in a particular type of criminal activity.

commonsense criminology: A popular way of talking about criminality typically revealed in public conversations that reflect simplistic understandings of criminology. Commonsense criminology is informed by the content and focus of popular crime-themed entertainment programming, including topics such as the criminal mind, serial killers, dramatic portrayals of policing street criminals, and law and order perspectives of justice.

conflict perspective: A theory of society based on Marx and Engels's analysis of the conflict between economic classes in capitalism that has been used by criminologists to explain the causes of crime and criminalization as the result of economic inequality.

correlates of crime: Demographic factors such as age, race, location, alcohol use, gender, or income level as social factors that are connected to, associated with, or linked to a particular type of crime but do not necessarily cause it.

criminalization of dissent: The criminalization and punishment of individuals and groups who express dissent against established social and political realities and whose interest is the active pursuit of social change, including environmental, anti-violence, and anti-hate activism.

criminogenic: To generate, stimulate, or cause crime and/or criminal behaviour.

CSI effect: A phenomenon whereby avid viewer interest in, and knowledge gained from, criminal investigation–type television programs has influenced both the assumptions and expectations about how criminal cases are able to be solved.

cultivation model: A theory that concludes that heavy television viewing tends to cultivate attitudes among viewers that make them supportive of mainstream political values.

cultural criminology: The study of how media narratives about crime have become popular products for public consumption that in turn influence cultural ideas about crime, criminality, and criminal justice.

culture: The system of values, beliefs, and practices that characterize a specific human group and define its identity.

disciplinary society: Michel Foucault's concept used to identify how modern society is characterized by excessive forms of social control, both external (such as surveillance systems and punishment) and internal (such as docile obedience) that discipline, regulate, and govern populations.

discourse: The formal knowledge disseminated by institutional and professional authorities that regulates the conduct of people.

feminist criminology: An anti-patriarchal criminology that developed as a critique of the tendency within traditional mainstream criminology and among justice system officials to reproduce sexist stereotypes and to ignore the differential treatment of female crime and wrongdoing.

governmentality: The normalized routines and practices citizens engage in that bind them to the existing political order and thus extend bureaucratic governmental control over their lives.

green criminology: An emerging branch of criminology that examines harms and crimes against the natural environment such as pollution, toxic emissions, illegal fishing, whaling, forest depletion, and human-made disasters, among others, that pose a risk to planetary life.

hypersecurity state: A concept that refers to the political state's practice of intensifying security policies, increasing the surveillance and monitoring of citizens, and enforcing the criminalization of dissent, all under the auspices of fighting terror and maintaining security.

ideological hegemony: A theory of social control that emphasizes how dominant ideologies and widely shared beliefs are used to get people to consent to the established political order.

ideology: A set of ideas or belief systems used to justify, legitimate, and normalize social arrangements based on unequal power relations.

labelling theory: A criminological theory that focuses on the meanings ascribed to an act that is labelled deviant or criminal, rather than on the act itself.

law and order perspective: A crime control perspective that emphasizes a tough-on-crime, public safety approach based on increased policing, zero tolerance for illegal acts, and strict criminal justice sentencing practices.

left realism: A theory of crime that questions idealized assumptions inherent in earlier 20th-century left/Marxist theories of crime that similarly emphasizes the role of social and economic disadvantage in the creation of crime, but which also explains that crime disproportionally victimizes the poor and powerless and that crime is a real social problem that needs to be controlled regardless of its causes.

mass incarceration: A term that refers to the overuse of imprisonment as a crime control strategy, and which results in a high proportion of the population serving prison sentences.

moral crimes: A category of illegal activity such as gambling, prostitution/sex-trade work, illicit drug use, and, until recently, sodomy and homosexuality, that have historically been viewed as morally reprehensible vices that may corrupt the values of society.

moral entrepreneurs: Individuals or groups who hope to gain some sort of benefit by capitalizing on the crisis or moral panic generated by the occurrence of a sensationalized crime trend.

moral panic: A sensationalized, exaggerated response to a crime trend based on fears that the moral fabric of society is under threat unless something is done to stop it.

moral regulation: A traditional form of social control whereby moral values and judgments serve to regulate social behaviour and personal conduct and is reflected informally in codes of conduct and more formally in law.

mystification: An ideological process, usually generated by communications media, that masks the power dynamics of a social issue by obscuring and influencing the way it is perceived by the public.

neoliberalism: A political and economic trend based on the decline of social services and the promotion of competition, individualism, corporate rights, and the globalization of the free-market capitalist system.

new world order: A term that refers to the geopolitical configuration of military and economic power relations that began to form at the start of the 21st century, characterized by American military hegemony and ongoing civil conflict and warfare.

prison–industrial complex: A configuration of the prison system, especially in the United States in the late 20th century, whereby the mass incarceration of inmates was overseen by private companies contracted to operate prisons for profit.

queer criminology: A subfield of criminology that focuses on the historic and current criminalization of LGBTQ+ (lesbian, gay, bisexual, transgender, and queer) people subjected to discriminatory practices by the justice system and other social institutions.

racial profiling: The police apprehension of crime suspects on the basis of their racial characteristics.

reintegrative shaming: A type of crime control method that shames the offender into being reintegrated into their community group by appealing to the offender's non-criminal sense of self-esteem.

risk society: Ulrich Beck's concept whereby human industrial activity via resource extraction has been so significant that it has created a new planetary reality that poses a risk to life, which threatens to become larger than the human capacity to contain it.

state crime: A type of criminal conduct committed by state officials and governments, ranging from political corruption to war crimes.

stigma: In labelling theory, the tarnishing or spoiling of a person's identity due to the successful application of a negative label onto them.

symbolic interactionism: A branch of sociology that emphasizes the shared meanings and interpretations of social reality that guide people in their interactions with others.

transgression: The willful and pleasurable violation of a rule, law, or social code of conduct, as well as the entertainment experienced at the symbolic/emotional level by those who watch crime dramas or play violent video games.

transnational feminist criminology: A theoretical perspective in criminology that combines the critique of patriarchal practices predominant in nations outside of North America with a human-rights focus on rape, sexual abuse, acid attacks, female genital mutilation, forced marriage, honour killings, the infanticide of female fetuses and infants, and the deliberate sale and trafficking of girls into the illicit sex trade.

zero-tolerance perspective: A law and order perspective on policing and crime control based on the premise that tolerance of small infractions will encourage offenders towards the commission of greater violations; thus, even seemingly minor acts of lawbreaking need to be prosecuted.

REFERENCES

Agamben, G. (2003). *State of exception*. University of Chicago Press.

Associated Press. (2017, October 20). Pollution causing more deaths worldwide than war or smoking. *CBC News*. Retrieved from http://www.cbc.ca/news/health/pollution-worldwide-deaths-1.4363613

Bakke, P. C., & Kuypers, J. A. (2016). The Syrian civil war, international outreach, and a clash of worldviews. *KB Journal, 11*(2), 1.

Barthes, R. (1973). *Mythologies*. Paladin Books.

Becker, H. (1963). *Outsiders: Studies in the sociology of deviance*. The Free Press.

Bleier, R. (1984). *Science and gender: A critique of biology and its theories on women*. Pergamon Press.

Bonger, W. A. (2015). *Criminality and economic conditions*. Forgotten Books. (Original work published 1916)

Box, S. (1983). *Power, crime, and mystification*. Tavistock Publications.

Braithwaite, J. (1989). *Crime, shame, and reintegration*. Cambridge University Press.

Buist, C . L., & Lenning, E. (2016). *Queer criminology*. Routledge.

Burns, R. G. (2009). Environmental crime. In J. M. Miller (Ed.), *21st century criminology: A reference handbook* (Vol. 2; pp. 481–489). SAGE Publications.

Camp, J. T., & Heatherton, C. (Eds.). (2016). *Policing the planet: Why the policing crisis led to Black Lives Matter*. Verso.

Carlson, J. M. (1985). *Prime time law enforcement: Crime show viewing and attitudes toward the criminal justice system*. Praeger.

Carson, R. (1962). *Silent Spring*. Houghton Mifflin.

Chambliss, W. J. (1989). State-organized crime—The American Society of Criminology, 1988 Presidential Address. *Criminology, 27*(2), 183–208. https://doi.org/10.1111/j .1745-9125.1989.tb01028.x

Chesney-Lind, M. (1989). Feminist theory. In P. A. Adler & P. Adler (Eds.), *Constructions of deviance: Social power, context, and interaction* (7th ed.). Wadsworth Publishing.

Christie, N. (1993). *Crime control as industry*. Routledge.

Colaguori, C. (2005). The prison industrial complex and social division in market societies: The hyper-security state, crime and expendable populations. In L. A. Visano (Ed.), *Law and criminal justice: A critical inquiry* (pp. 353–370). The Athenian Policy Forum.

Colaguori, C. (2010). Symbolic violence and the violation of human rights: Continuing the sociological critique of domination. *International Journal of Criminology and Sociological Theory, 3*(2).

Colaguori, C. (Ed.). (2013). *Security, life and death: Governmentality and biopower in the post 9/11 era*. de Sitter Publications.

Comack, E., & Balfour, G. (2004). *The power to criminalize: Violence, inequality and the law*. Fernwood Publishing.

Currie, E. (1985). *Confronting crime*. Pantheon Books.

Davis, N. J., & Stasz, C. (1990). *Social control of deviance: A critical perspective*. McGraw-Hill.

DeKeseredy, W. S. (2000). *Women, crime, and the Canadian criminal justice system*. Anderson Publishing.

Deutschmann, L. B. (2002). *Deviance and social control* (3rd ed.). Nelson Thomson.

Eagleton, T. (1991). *Ideology: An introduction*. Verso.

Ehrenreich, B., & Hochschild, A. R. (Eds.). (2002). *Global woman: Nannies, maids, and sex workers in the new economy*. Henry Holt & Co.

Ferrell, J. (2004). Boredom, crime and criminology. *Theoretical Criminology, 8*(3), 287–302.

Ferrell, J. (2009). Cultural criminology. In J. M. Miller (Ed.), *21st century criminology: A reference handbook* (Vol. 2; pp. 219–227). SAGE Publications.

Foucault, M. (1979). *Discipline and punish: The birth of the prison*. Penguin.

Foucault, M. (1980). *Power/knowledge*. Penguin.

Garland, D. (1990). *Punishment and modern society: A study in social theory*. University of Chicago Press.

Gavigan, S. (1987). Women's crime: New perspectives and old theories. In E. Adelberg & C. Currie (Eds.), *Too few to count: Canadian women in conflict with the law* (pp. 47–66). Press Gang Publishers.

Gitlin, T. (1979). Prime time ideology: The hegemonic process in television entertainment. *Social Problems, 26*(3), 251–266.

Goffman, E. (1961). *Asylums: Essays on the condition of the social situation of mental patients and other inmates*. Anchor Books.

Gramsci, A. (1971). *Selections from the prison notebooks*. (G. N. Smith & Q. Hoare, Trans.). International Publishing Company.

Hall, S., Critcher, C., Jefferson, T., Clarke, J., & Roberts, B. (1978). *Policing the crisis: Mugging, the state, and law and order*. Macmillan.

Herivel, T., & Wright, P. (2003). *Prison nation: The warehousing of America's poor*. Routledge.

Jeffery, C. R. (1971). *Crime prevention through environmental design*. SAGE Publications.

Kappeler, V. E., & Potter, G. W. (2005). *The mythology of crime and criminal justice*. Waveland Press.

La Prairie, C. (2002). Aboriginal over-representation in the criminal justice system: A tale of nine cities. *Canadian Journal of Criminology / Revue Canadienne de criminology, 44*(2), 181–208.

Lawson, T. F. (2009, November 3). Before the verdict and beyond the verdict: The CSI infection within modern criminal jury trials. *Loyola University Chicago Law Journal, 41*, 132, 142. Retrieved from https://lawcommons.luc.edu/luclj/vol41/iss1/4/

Lea, J. (2016). Left realism: A radical criminology for the current crisis. *International Journal for Crime, Justice and Social Democracy, 5*(3), 53–65.

Lea, J., & Young, J. (1996). Relative deprivation. In J. Muncie, E. MacLaughlin, & M. Langan (Eds.), *Criminological perspectives: A reader* (pp. 136–144). SAGE Publications. (Original work published 1984)

Lee, D., & Newby, H. (1986). *The problem of sociology*. Routledge.

Lombroso, C., & Ferrero, G. (1895). *The female offender.* D. Appleton & Company.

Lombroso, C., & Ferrero, G. (2004). *Criminal woman, the prostitute, and the normal woman.* (N. Hahn Rafter & M. Gibson, Trans.). Duke University Press. (Original work published 1893)

Maidment, M. (2006). Transgressing boundaries: Feminist perspectives in criminology. In W. S. DeKeseredy & B. Perry (Eds.), *Advancing critical criminology: Theory and application* (pp. 43–62). Lexington Books.

Martinson, R. (1974). What works?—questions and answers about prison reform. *The Public Interest* (Spring), 22–54.

Miller, J. M. (Ed.). (2009). *21st century criminology: A reference handbook.* SAGE Publications.

Monchalin, L. (2016). *The colonial problem: An Indigenous perspective on crime and injustice in Canada.* University of Toronto Press.

Newman, O. (1972). *Defensible space: Crime prevention through urban design.* Macmillan.

Orwell, G. (1949). *Nineteen eighty-four.* Strecker & Warburg.

Pfohl, S.J. (1985). *Images of deviance & social control: A sociological history.* McGraw-Hill Book Company.

Pollack, O. (1950). *The criminality of women.* University of Pennsylvania Press.

Quinney, R. (1974). *Critique of legal order: Crime control in capitalist society.* Little, Brown and Company.

Quinney, R. (2000). *Bearing witness to crime and social justice.* State University of New York Press.

Ross, J. I. (2000). *Varieties of state crime and its control.* Criminal Justice Press.

Rothe, D. L., & Mullins, C. W. (Eds.). (2011). *State crime: Current perspectives.* Rutgers University Press.

Rusche, G., & Kirchheimer, O. (1939). *Punishment and social structure.* Russell & Russell.

Schwartz, D. (2015, June 3). Truth and Reconciliation Commission: By the numbers. *CBC News.* Retrieved from https://www.cbc.ca/news/indigenous/truth-and-reconciliation-commission-by-the-numbers-1.3096185

Sharp, S. F. (2009). Feminist criminology. In J. M. Miller (Ed.), *21st century criminology: A reference handbook* (Vol. 2, pp. 245–251). SAGE Publications.

Slim, H. (2008). *Killing civilians: Method, madness and morality in war.* Columbia University Press.

Smith, O., & Raymen, T. (2018). Deviant leisure: A criminological perspective. *Theoretical Criminology, 22*(1), 63–82.

Spector, M., & Kitsuse, J. I. (1987). *Constructing social problems.* Transaction Publishers.

South, N., & Brisman, A. (Eds.). (2013). *Routledge international handbook of green criminology*. Routledge.

Statistics Canada. (2021, November 25). *Homicide in Canada, 2020*. Government of Canada. Retrieved from https://www150.statcan.gc.ca/n1/daily-quotidien/211125/dq211125b-eng.htm

Stevens, T., Morash, M., & Chesney-Lind, M. (2011). Are girls getting tougher, or are we tougher on girls? Probability of arrest and juvenile court oversight in 1980 and 2000. *Justice Quarterly, 28*(5), 719–744. https://doi.org/10.1080/07418825.2010.532146

Taylor, I. (1999). *Crime in context: A critical criminology of market societies*. Polity Press.

Taylor, I., Walton, P., & Young, J. (1973). *The new criminology: For a social theory of deviance*. Routledge & Kegan Paul.

Tin, L.-G. (Ed.). (2008). *The dictionary of homophobia: A global history of gay & lesbian experience* (M. Redburn, Trans.). Arsenal Pulp Press.

Turk, A. (1969). *Criminality and legal order*. Rand McNally.

Visano, L. A. (1998). *Crime and culture: Refining the traditions*. Canadian Scholars.

Walby, S. (2013). Violence and society: Introduction to an emerging field of sociology. *Current Sociology, 61*(2), 95–111.

Weber, M. (1946). *From Max Weber: Essays in sociology*. Oxford University Press.

Wilson, J. Q. (Ed.). (2013). *Thinking about crime* (rev. ed.). Basic Books.

Wilson, J. Q., & Herrnstein, R. L. (1985). *Crime and human nature: The definitive study of the causes of crime*. Simon & Schuster.

Wilson, J. Q., & Kelling, G. L. (2005). Broken windows: The police and neighborhood safety. In T. Newburn (Ed.), *Policing: Key readings* (pp. 460–471). Routledge. (Original work published 1982)

Wright, T. C. (2007). *State terrorism in Latin America: Chile, Argentina, and international human rights*. Rowman & Littlefield.

Young, J. (2007). *The vertigo of late modernity*. SAGE Publications.

Young, J. (2011). *The criminological imagination*. Wiley.

CHAPTER 4

Cultural Criminology and Popular Media Representations of Crime

Stephen Muzzatti, Claudio Colaguori, and Emma Smith

LEARNING OBJECTIVES

In this chapter, you will

- discover how crime-themed media draws on widely held views about criminality that create a type of *commonsense criminology*;
- learn about the history of crime-themed news and entertainment and how the topic of crime became a commodity for popular consumption;
- review different theories that explain how popular media representations of crime influence public perceptions of crime and criminal justice;
- explore how crime programs function as forms of social control by perpetuating dominant ideologies and distorting the reality of crime and control;
- learn about cultural criminology, the postmodern celebration of violence, and the so-called "carnival of crime"; and
- consider how crime-themed programming is arguably the most popular and versatile genre of entertainment that continually changes to reflect new social dynamics.

INTRODUCTION: COMMONSENSE CRIMINOLOGY AND CULTURAL CRIMINOLOGY

The issue of crime has long been a central topic of interest for people. It is not surprising that crime, law, and policing have been featured themes in popular media from pulp-fiction novels and comics of the early 1900s onwards to the crime columns of the daily newspapers and in the popular dramas that appeared with the rise of television in the 1950s. The public consumption of stories and images about crime remains as popular as ever. Today, crime-themed entertainment forms a major part of Hollywood blockbuster movies, television, and the content of on-line video streaming services. Crime-themed programming, from entertainment to news, is a powerful element in the *social construction* of public perceptions about crime and justice. This makes it an important subject of consideration for crimin-ologists. Why is entertainment programming based on crime, law, and policing so popular? Why do producers and broadcasters of entertainment programs release so many new crime shows each and every year?

It is likely that before studying criminology you had some ideas about matters relating to crime, such as policing, criminal investigations, trial procedures, and the drama of prison life. You may have strong views about punishment and the criminal mind. You probably know what DNA evidence and lie detector testing are. It is likely that people who watch a lot of crime-themed programming can talk about crime at a far greater length than they can about astronomy or zoology, even though there are many programs about outer space and animals on television. Why do so many people claim to know so much about crime? Where did they get all this knowledge about crime and society? Is what they know accurate? The ideas presented to the public through crime-themed communications media, from news, reality television programs, and prime-time dramas to social media sites, Hollywood films, and video games, have considerable influence on common-sense understandings about matters pertaining to crime, justice, and society.

Criminologist Ian Taylor (1999) employed the concept of **commonsense criminology** to identify the extent to which members of the public esteem them-selves as minor experts on crime and society. The ideas presented to viewers in the ever-expanding list of crime-themed programs, from daily news broadcasts to shows about police, espionage, and forensic investigations, to documentaries about true crime, serial killers, and mafia shows, among many others, combine to give viewers the impression that they have some sort of expertise on criminality and crime control. For Taylor and other criminologists, popular crime **discourse** shapes public perceptions. The communications media is arguably one of the most powerful of all social institutions because it is extremely effective at disseminat-ing influential messages about how our society presumably works. It entertains us and informs us; yet, often it *mis*informs us. Within the process of depicting crime, various forms of bias and distortion form part of the ways in which crime issues are represented. Certain themes about crime, justice, and power are emphasized while others are almost completely ignored. The relationship between media mes-sages and audience response to them is complex and interesting and is explored through the theories and concepts of **cultural criminology**, some of which were introduced in Chapter 3.

Box 4.1: Popular Conceptions of Crime and Commonsense Criminology

Commonsense criminology refers to a popular discourse reflected in a layperson's simplistic understanding of crime that results from the influence of crime-themed entertainment programming and its typical themes (Taylor, 1999). Themes may include the criminal mind, serial killers, dramatic portrayals of policing street criminals and crimes of the downtrodden, law and order perspectives of justice, and violent dramas of good versus evil. Commonsense criminology is further informed by sociobiological explanations of criminal behaviour, the belief in forensic precision, and predictive criminal psychology. It generally excludes the social, political, and economic causes of crime, and it tends to ignore crimes of the powerful, such as corporate crime. As Taylor writes, "commonsense criminology [is] organized around 'the criminal' and, particularly, 'the criminal mind' as an 'object of analysis' ... it is closely associated with what sociologists would call 'a discourse' ... that is concerned with the 'dangerous offender' ... new ways of surveillance [and] the minimization of personal risk" (1999, p. 2). By selecting certain graphic and sensationalized themes over others, commonsense criminology focuses on individual causes of crime and specific types of heinous and violent criminals, thereby obscuring the larger, systemic power relations involved in the generation of crime in society.

Cultural criminologists study the history of how narratives about crime have become products of consumption; *crime* is thus a type of **commodity** produced by the **culture industry** that consists of television, news media outlets, and other corporately owned media providers. Cultural criminologists also conceptualize how audience members who *consume* crime-themed news and programs are entertained and influenced by them. Numerous theories attempt to explain the effects that media messages have on people. Some theories emphasize how media messages shape public perceptions of crime while others explore how individuals develop subjective interpretations of what is presented to them. Media messages about crime are unique insofar as they are often fictional representations about the actual social problem of crime and the actual social institution of the criminal justice system. For these reasons, such messages are scrutinized closely by criminologists who attempt to understand the persuasive influence of crime-themed media and how it can be both compelling and misleading.

Box 4.2: Media-Generated Crime Myths and Commonsense Criminology

Look at this *Life* magazine cover image from 1968. It is an example of
how popular news media cultivates crime myths that contribute to the
formation of *commonsense criminology*. It features a sensationalized story
that captures the attention of the reader. The stark formatting of the
image presents us with mugshots of two accused killers. One is James Earl
Ray, the man who assassinated Martin Luther King, Jr., on April 4, 1968,
and the other is Sirhan Sirhan, the man who shot Robert F. Kennedy on
June 5, 1968. The subheading below the main title leaves little room for
criminological interpretation of the murders; the reader is simply referred
to "the psychobiology of violence." Once readers delve into the actual story
in the magazine, they find a discussion of the psychological and biological
roots of violence and the mention of laboratory research of monkeys
engaged in so-called rage experiments as the preferred theory of criminal
violence. There is virtually no discussion of the fact that the targets of the
murderers were not randomly selected but were progressives who promised
social change and offered hope in politically turbulent times. This biological

determinist explanation steers the fascinated reader away from other interpretations of how violence is socially and culturally directed, and not just the expression of a deranged mind malfunctioning because of faulty biology. Have you come across any other examples of media myths that present a common sense, biological explanation of criminal violence?

(*LIFE.* "The Accused: Ray and Sirhan," pp. 24–34, and "The Psychobiology of Violence," *64*(25): 67–71).

A HISTORICAL OVERVIEW OF POPULAR MEDIA'S FASCINATION WITH CRIME

The portrayal of crime, both real and fictional, has been a central theme in many mass media narratives. Crime is not only central to the production of news in Canadian society but it also constitutes what is arguably the largest and oldest genre of entertainment (Colaguori, 2011; Dowler et. al., 2006; Muzzatti, 2010). As members of a technologically advanced society, we are major consumers of popular media stories. These mediated *cultural* narratives are tremendously influential in the way we think about ourselves, the world around us, and our stance on controversial issues involving crime. This may include topics like how much crime we think there is in our society, what kind of crimes are being committed (as well as where and by whom), and the likelihood of our own victimization. Cultural narratives also influence our opinions of, and faith in, the police and other agents of the criminal justice system and shape our views on criminal justice policies, such as drug legalization, harm-reduction strategies, trolling and cyberbullying, workplace safety, Sharia law, traditional Indigenous justice practices, online privacy, sexual consent, and border security, to name just a few.

Although the concept of a crime has been with us for as long as we have had criminal law, crime in the media is a much more recent (but by no means new) phenomenon. Some of the earliest media narratives of crime took the form of news. Indeed, two millennia ago, the Roman senator Cicero lamented the too-frequent reports of criminal violence that filled ancient Rome's newspaper (the *acta diurnal populi Romani*). While actual accounts of crime in early news were relatively rare, some attention was devoted to issues of justice as a retributive response to wrongdoing by the authorities. News-like accounts of executions can be found in historical records throughout the world. Accounts of executions were recounted for public audiences in gruesome detail, serving as both a source of vicarious titillation and, ideally, as a general deterrent. We must realize that low levels of literacy and the technical difficulties of reproducing the written word meant that these presentations of crime were not nearly as widely disseminated for most of human history as they have been in the 20th and 21st centuries.

By the middle of the 17th century in England, *newsbooks* (an early form of broadsheet newspapers) began to include sensational accounts of crime. In North America, the publication of crime narratives goes back to the earliest days of settler-colonialism. News accounts of American colonists convicted of public drunkenness, inappropriate behaviour between men and women, or using profanity were common, as were stories of people being punished by lashings or with time in the stocks or the pillory. For example, in 1656, a newspaper in Boston reported that a naval officer, Captain Kemble, was placed in the stocks for having engaged in lewd behaviour on the Sabbath, while a Salem paper recounted the fines imposed on John Smith and Mrs. John Kitchin for their frequent absences from church. Crime news coverage heavily emphasized the shaming and punishment of offenders, ranging from clipping ears and branding to public lashings and executions (Muzzatti, 2012).

While crime clearly was included in the early news media, it was not until the 19th century that it became a standard component of news narratives. Growing populations, increased literacy, and technological advancements during the early decades of the Industrial Revolution fundamentally changed the ways in which people acquired information about crime. The regular portrayal of crime as a **newsworthy** topic blossomed in early 19th-century newspapers. During the 1830s, bizarre and provocative crime news coverage under the auspices of the *astonishingly real* became standard fare. Some of these early incarnations were seen in France, where the press fuelled a desire for atrocious spectacles among the public the through its focus on *faits divers*—bizarre and fear-laden crime news coverage (Carney, 2010).

Fledgling North American newspapers such as the *New York Herald* and *The Sun* boosted their circulation considerably with long, drawn-out crime stories that served as a venue for debates about policing, private security, and gang activity (Miller, 1975). By the mid-1840s, the penny presses in the United States began to publish lurid accounts and photos of the dead and dying. These frequently related to street crime, but also featured images of death resulting from what was often termed *industrial accidents* (what we today know as corporate violence). While this decade began with a clear distinction between the treatment of crime in exploitative newspapers versus their more serious counterparts, it was not long before all papers were including sensationalized stories and photographs of heinous crimes as part of their staple offerings.

Although newspapers were regularly covering a host of crime and criminal justice issues in connection with city politics, industry, labour movements, and immigration by the mid-19th century, the entertainment media were only just beginning to look at crime as a thematic source. Some of the earliest instances of crime as entertainment came in the form of serialized fiction in newspapers and magazines. For example, tales of the world's most famous detectives, Sherlock Holmes and Dr. Watson, first appeared in a British magazine in the late 1880s, and North American readers were introduced to a series of tough lawmen and desperate criminals in nickel weeklies and dime-store novels in the ensuing decades. And although English-language novels about detectives have arguably existed since the 18th century, as a popular genre, detective fiction is a product of Depression-era America (Muzzatti, 2013). Today, "the crime genre is now more popular than ever before—in fact crime novels and thrillers are now outselling all other fiction genres" (*The Telegraph*, 2018).

By the turn of the 20th century, crime took on the character of the truly saleable media commodity it is today. During this time, large police departments hosted crime reporters whose focus it was to report on the major activities of the department. This epoch also saw the rise of sensational and graphic *yellow journalism*, exemplified by *New York World*. These periodicals ran features on atrocious (though statistically rare) criminal violence, including bank robbery, kidnapping, white slavery, and gangland murders. The *San Francisco Examiner* similarly entertained readers, devoting a quarter of the paper to coverage of crime. Stories about *lewd* and *lascivious* behaviour and sardonic coverage of arrestees brought into lower courts were also standard fare.

By the 1920s, crime news coverage took on an increasingly lurid, sensational flavour. A growing number of mediated depictions of crime, particularly visual representations of dead crime victims, were regularly published in newspapers. News audiences were inundated with photographs of spectacular death moments brought on by criminal violence on the streets of urban metropolises. During this decade, news coverage of crime also harkened back to an earlier age with respect to the punishment of criminals. News accounts of trials abounded, as did exposés on hard labour in prison and executions of convicted felons. In 1928, newspaper photographer Tom Howard smuggled a small camera into the press viewing gallery of New York's Sing Sing Prison during the execution of convicted murderer Ruth Snyder. Howard snapped a photo as the electricity surged through Snyder's body. The blurry full-page photo of Snyder's jolting body, captioned "DEAD!," appeared on the front of New York's *Daily News* the following morning. By the end of the day, the paper had sold more than 1.5 million copies, the highest sale of any paper in history at the time.

The general public's social desire to consume crime through the news coalesced with newspaper visuals and media loops by the 1930s. From fatal bar brawls and car chases to brothel raids and mobster gangland warfare, the mediated reality of crime swelled in the 1930s and 1940s. New York photojournalist Arthur Fellig built his early career on capturing explicit photos of crime scenes that he sold to newspapers and magazines. The work of Fellig and journalists like him not only generated substantial profits for newspapers and magazines but perhaps, even more importantly, helped to establish crime as the primary topic of media reporting and public interest.

In the words of scholars ...

Crime has moved from being a subspecies of tabloid journalism to the very heart of our electronic media culture and there it more and more centrally generates narratives about our social order and social pathology.

Richard Osborne, *Crime and the Media: The Post-Modern Spectacle*. 1995

The 1930s through to the 1950s also saw an explosion in crime fiction publishing and the birth of radio crime dramas featuring programs such as *Calling All Cars* (1933–1939), *Crime Doesn't Pay* (1935–1952), and *Police Headquarters* (1932). These and other similar dramas were explicitly and unapologetically about *law and order*, presenting entertaining (though one-dimensional) images of desperate criminals and noble criminal justice officials. In the United States, the director of the Federal Bureau of Investigation (FBI), J. Edgar Hoover, designed a media campaign that portrayed his agents as crime fighters and the suspects as dangerous criminals who were difficult to apprehend. By the mid-1950s, higher standards of living and a strong economy resulted in lower crime rates, but ironically, greater media attention on crime.

According to Surette (2015), the mid-20th century was a watershed moment for crime in the media, with increasingly aggressive marketing of crime news through specialized *crime beat reporting*. The result was more sensationalistic presentations of crime that relied even more heavily upon the police, crown prosecutors, and other criminal justice officials for commentary and analysis. The 1950s and 1960s saw a marked increase in these types of narratives, as well as more direct involvement by criminal justice personnel and agencies in crafting them, first through news, but later in Hollywood films and television programs. Both *The Man from U.N.C.L.E* (1964–1968) and *The FBI* (1965–1974) were TV shows produced with the support and endorsement of the FBI. Hoover himself served as a consultant on the latter series until his death, although he never appeared on camera, and many episodes ended with a segment profiling an actual fugitive from the FBI's Most Wanted list (Van Veeren, 2009). It is interesting to note that this program was one of the earliest examples of intertextual storytelling about the work of criminal justice agencies. Premised on a comingling of the real and the fictional, this strategy eventually became the touchstone of much of the televisual crime entertainment in the 1990s and first decade of the 21st century. This so-called "torn from the headlines" marketing of scripted programming was evident in some of the most popular programs of the time, including the multiple incarnations of the *Law and Order* (1990–2010) and *CSI* franchises (2000–2015), and has recently re-emerged in miniseries such as *Bad Blood* (2017), *The Murder of Laci Peterson* (2017), and *Law and Order True Crime: The Menendez Brothers* (2017; Smith & Muzzatti, 2018).

The last quarter of the 20th century saw an explosion in the growth of crime-themed television programming. For most of the 1970s and 1980s, television crime shows were action-packed but relatively light hour-long dramas featuring patrol-level police officers, detective partners, or private investigators. Popular options included *cHiPs* (1977–1983), *Cagney & Lacey* (1981–1988), *Starsky & Hutch* (1975–1979), *Miami Vice* (1984–1989), *Charlie's Angels* (1976–1981), *Magnum P.I.* (1980–1988), and *Simon & Simon* (1981–1989). First airing in 1981, *Hill Street Blues* proved to be a notable exception to typically formulaic crime dramas and heralded many of the medium's more progressive offerings. Set in the "Hill Street" division of an unnamed American city, the program dealt with grittier themes in a more nuanced fashion than did its predecessors. Themes such as poverty, urban blight, police use of force, political corruption, police–community relations, substance abuse, and others were explored through a large cast of characters including police officers, civilian police employees, community activists, gang members, prosecutors, legal aid counsels, city officials, and municipal politicians. Over the course of the past three decades the genre has expanded exponentially. Immensely popular and often graphic programs such as *Chicago P.D.* (2014–), *Criminal Minds* (2005–2020), the *NCIS* franchise (2003–), *19-2* (2014–2017), and the multiple incarnations of *CSI* (2000–) and *Law & Order* (1990–2010, 2022–) enthrall audiences by celebrating the investigative, scientific, and retributive components of the criminal justice system. Meanwhile, programs such as *The Sopranos* (1999–2007), *Dexter* (2006–2013), *Sons of Anarchy* (2008–2014), *The Shield* (2002–2008), and *White Collar* (2009–2014) titillate by presenting the decadent pleasures revolving around crime, vigilantism, and sweet revenge.

The current epoch also spawned the now ubiquitous **infotainment** format, which presented exposés of deviant lifestyles and sordid activities. Taking cues from more established infotainment programs, a glut of so-called trash TV came onto the market, including daytime talk shows such as *Maury* (1991–2022) and *Jerry Springer* (1991–2018), which focused on salacious, scandalous topics ranging from out-of-control teens and marital infidelity through to illegal acts such as drug use and incest. A slightly more muted sensationalism, coupled with a more openly retributive theme, was evident on *America's Most Wanted* (1988–2012). Interspersing the host's presentation of the facts of a case with dramatic recreations, the program solicited information from viewers in apprehending suspects believed to be responsible for heinous crimes.

The blending of these genres produced what Gregg Barak astutely referred to as "crime-infotainment" (1994, p. 271). Focusing first on particularly heinous criminal cases, such as that of the abduction and murder of toddler Jeremy Bulger by two minors in England, the O.J. Simpson case in the USA, and the crimes of Paul Bernardo and Karla Homolka in Canada, the media created what Soothill and his colleagues (2004) were to later conceptualize as **mega-cases**. This term refers to crimes that, as a result of some combination of rarity, severity, complexity, and brutality elicit powerful responses from public audiences and enjoy great longevity. For example, the cultural resonance of such atrocities as the Manson Family murders in suburban Los Angeles in 1969 or the shoeshine boy murder in downtown Toronto in 1977 attest to the retrospective power of the mega-case phenomenon even though these crimes occurred long before media strategies had been fully developed. Indeed, the aforementioned revisiting of the Menendez brothers murders, as well as the murder of Lacey Peterson, in recent TV miniseries (21 years and 13 years after the conclusion of the respective cases) speaks to the rapacity of the crime-infotainment business.

The narratives that inform much of crime infotainment trivialize human suffering and reinforce simplistic images of crime and criminality as an enterprise monopolized by marginalized, poor, and racialized people. The final decade of the 20th century also saw the proliferation of crime-based reality TV. Possibly the most well-known crime program of this era was the Fox network's program *COPS*. Debuting in 1989, *COPS* was one of the first forays into crime *vérité*, drawing on footage from dashboard-mounted and portable, handheld cameras to (re)present the experiences of patrol officers as they pursued and arrested suspects (Muzzatti, 2012). Immensely popular, the program inspired numerous 21st-century imitations such as *To Serve and Protect* (1993–2003), *Police Women* (2009–2013), *Dallas SWAT* (2006–2007) (and its spinoffs *Detroit SWAT* [2016] and *Kansas City SWAT* [2006–2007]), and variations on the theme, such as *Dog the Bounty Hunter* (2002–2012) and *Dog and Beth on the Hunt* (2013–2015). Today, more technically sophisticated (though no less problematic) variations on these programs exist in the forms of *Live P.D.* (2016–2020) with Dan Abrams.

The 21st-century confluence of expanding media outlets (including, in particular, the rapid ascension of the internet), increasingly oligopolistic ownership patterns, and the concomitant pressure to maximize profit by reducing production costs led to a scramble for inexpensive and readily available content. Surveillance footage, much of which originated from police vehicles' dashboard cameras and private security recordings from shopping malls and convenience stores, soon augmented hidden camera footage. This was itself recently surpassed by smartphone recordings as the raw material for a host of outrageous television specials, ongoing series, and websites such as *World's Wildest Police Videos* (1998–2001) and *America's Dumbest Criminals* (1996–2000), along with any number of YouTube or other social media sites featuring *owned* or *failed* crime-themed uploads.

The crime genre has stood the test of time with audiences because its formula of protagonist versus antagonist repeats, innovates, and capitalizes on the ancient, dynamic theme of good versus evil. This focus has a versatility that lends itself well to the shifting world of political realities and the propagandistic needs of power systems. Indeed, so much of crime-themed programming has historically served as part of a political strategy that capitalizes on tragedy and fear. As Visano notes, "crime stories have become the new circus, a public spectacle parading tragic events as advertised entertainment" (2006, p. 117). Since ancient times, the mass public has been attracted to spectacle, especially displays involving violence, vengeance, and scandal. It is not surprising, then, that crime narratives in movies, television, or print have become primary commodities within contemporary media culture. As Osborne writes, crime is at the "heart of our electronic media culture"; it is the main story (1995, p. 30). While it is generally accepted that crime-themed media has an established history in the way we frame social problems, the meanings that are made of the crime stories people consume is a productive area of research within modern criminology to which we shall now turn.

POPULAR MEDIA MESSAGES AND THEIR INFLUENCE ON AUDIENCE BELIEFS ABOUT CRIME AND JUSTICE

Long ago, the philosopher Plato (circa 400 BCE) wrote a parable about how images can shape our perceptions of reality to such an extent that they can be highly deceptive. The parable is about people who were imprisoned in a cave since birth and were shown nothing but puppet-show images projected on a wall they were faced towards. Let us presume that the cave prisoners had never left the cave to behold that another reality (the truth of the real world) existed outside of the cave. "In every way ... such prisoners would recognize as reality nothing but the shadows of those artificial objects" (Plato, quoted in O'Neill, 1991, p. 4). For the cave dwellers, the illusions would be real to such an extent that if they were escorted out of the cave to the light of day, they would believe the actual, real world was a falsehood, a grand illusion. Plato's parable of the cave dwellers serves as a metaphor for the power of illusion that engulfs those of us who live in a world composed of distorted and deceptive media image representations of reality, and for those who forego critical judgment and often mistake the simulated *spectacle* of media messages for the real world. The power that mediated images, messages, and representations of reality have over those who consume them has been a substantial area of study. As previous sections of this chapter have indicated, the theme of crime is a dominant one in our media culture. What effects do the myriad images, stories, and news messages about crime have on public perceptions of reality? How do people interpret, consume, and respond to crime-themed dramas and news broadcasts? Numerous theories have been developed to address these illuminating questions. These theories include the direct effects model, the limited effects model, cultivation analysis, the ideological deception model, and reception theory, all of which are discussed next.

The Direct Effects Model and Limited Effects Model of Media Messaging

The direct effects model (also referred to as the magic bullet or hypodermic needle theory) is an early (circa 1930s) theory that claims mass mediated messages have a direct, powerful influence on the shaping of public perceptions of reality. It presumes that audiences are, for the most part, gullible, passive consumers of media messages who absorb the meanings intended by the producers of media messages. The direct effects model is akin to the **propaganda** theory of communications where people exercise very little critical thinking in relation to what is presented to them. The result is that they are susceptible to mass persuasion and readily conform to what the media presents as truth.

The direct effects model would argue that the stories of crime presented through the mass media have a direct influence on the beliefs and perceptions that audience members develop in relation to crime and criminal justice. Premised on the view that the spectator holds virtually no **agency** or free will, this theory highlights the looming power of media agencies to manipulate the minds of the masses. According to direct effects theories, crime-themed shows are not made-to-order because the viewing audience requests them; rather, producers make specific *types* of shows and public tastes are shaped into wanting more of those particular viewing options. Direct effects are also implied in claims that violent entertainment programming and violent video games tend to promote violence among consumers.

Contrasting the direct effects model is the limited effects model, which claims that media messages are not particularly effective at public persuasion and cannot alter deep desires or change a person's strongly held political beliefs. Sociologist Paul Lazarsfeld's (1901–1976) research on media effects indicated that people's core values and beliefs remain consistent despite exposure to a diversity of media messages (1940). According to a limited effects model, crime-themed programs have a limited capacity to change the previously held beliefs or tastes of viewing audiences. Viewers who hold values supportive of punitive crime control measures will be attracted to watching shows that feature crime control as a central theme, such as in *Law and Order*. Thus, people generally prefer and select media messages that already conform to their own subjective tastes, and they ignore those that do not. Similarly, if a person with an inherently non-violent temperament watches violent crime shows and plays violent video games, they will not become violent in their actual lives, regardless of the amount of their exposure to violence.

Both direct effects and limited effects theories seem to make reasonable arguments, so which of them is valid? Or can it be that both of them are just too one-sided, and the truth about the effects of media messages on audiences lies somewhere in between? Many theories of media influence build on the early tradition of effects research. Other perspectives examine variables such as economic interests, culture, subjective interpretation, and the expansion of technological society into everyday life.

The Frankfurt School of Critical Theory: The Culture Industry and Mass Deception

One of the earliest theories that examines how entertainment media operate as a system of social control that shapes consciousness and public perception is the Frankfurt School's critical theory of mass deception. In the 1940s, two scholars of the Frankfurt School, Max Horkheimer (1895–1973) and Theodor Adorno (1903–1969), developed the concept of the **culture industry** to explain how corporately produced cultural texts disseminated via radio, television programs, books, and movies form the foundation of modern mass culture, monopolizing artistic expression in consumer society and serving as a powerful instrument of deception and social control. The industry that makes movies, television content, and popular music is interested primarily in making profit and thus all of its products are to be seen as commodities, not public services. If a television series makes a high profit it is celebrated as a success; if it does not, it is deemed a failure and cancelled.

Horkheimer and Adorno believed that the movies and television shows produced by the culture industry follow uniform, predictable, and standardized formulas. Drawing often on clichés, these cultural commodities employ repetitive and simplistic themes, which lack the sophistication, diversity, authenticity, and transformative power of independent art forms, thus promoting mass conformity. Critical cultural expressions that raise social awareness are displaced by the monopolizing volume of endless corporate productions. As Horkheimer and Adorno write,

> Under monopoly all mass culture is identical, and the lines of its artificial framework begin to show through. The people at the top are no longer so interested in concealing monopoly: as its violence becomes more open, so its power grows. Movies and radio need no longer pretend to be art. The truth that they are just business is made into an ideology in order to justify the rubbish they deliberately produce. They call themselves industries; and when their directors' incomes are published, any doubt about the social utility of the finished products is removed (1944/1972, p. 121).

While the culture industry is primarily a business for making profit, it is also a system whose product popularity depends on how well products appeal to the public. Thus, entertainment programs need to align with so-called commonsense social attitudes and popular opinion, and in doing so they reproduce the dominant *ideologies of consumerism* and the *political values of capitalism*. This process of mass conformity to the order of society involves a process Horkheimer and Adorno (1944/1972) identify as the **reification** of consciousness, where the individual is shaped into a consumer object for the functioning of the established political and economic order. The analysis of how mass media and popular entertainment products pacify and deceive the mass public was developed most forcefully by the Frankfurt School and almost all other critical theories elaborate on these theorists' model of cultural domination.

Have you ever contemplated how your favourite television show is a product, a mere commodity designed to lure audiences and sell commercial time to advertisers? Do you feel like you are being manipulated when you watch television? Do crime-themed programs generally follow standardized formulas of good versus evil, or are they highly diverse and artistic? Critical theories of entertainment media engage with these sorts of analytic questions.

In the words of scholars ...

The messages transmitted through television are not accurate reflections of reality, nor are they neutral with regard to social and political values ... there is a "television reality" that is quite distinct from the "real world."

James M. Carlson, *Prime Time Law Enforcement: Crime Show Viewing and Attitudes toward the Criminal Justice System.* 1985

Cultivation Analysis

Perhaps most crime shows are simple-minded, formulaic, and predictable, but isn't that part of what makes them fun to watch? Maybe people who enjoy watching their favourite crime shows are not directly affected by the underlying messages in them, but what about long-term exposure? George Gerbner's **cultivation theory** addresses the shortcomings of media effects research and claims that long-term exposure to the *symbolic environment* of the mass media tends to *cultivate* commonly shared mainstream values and worldviews among viewers through a process termed **mainstreaming** (Gerbner et al., 2002, p. 311). As Carlson summarizes, Gerbner and his colleagues "have argued that there is a strong relationship between heavy television viewing and the cultivation of a television-biased conception of reality. Television presents a distorted image of reality, which is reflected in the viewpoints of heavy viewers [who] tend to give 'television answers' in response to a wide variety of survey questions" (Carlson, 1985, p. 7). Perhaps you are familiar with this phenomenon: You are having a conversation with a friend about a controversial topic, and they begin to make all sorts of claims and arguments, telling you that they know something to be true because they have been following this issue in the news. Maybe they will tell you that the justice system is "too soft" on crime or that "immigrants commit too much crime." Where did they get such information? Why do they seem so convinced? According to Gerbner and his colleagues, repeated exposure to specific political themes on television "cultivates" responses in people that reflect "mainstream" traditional social and conservative political values (Carlson, 1985). The cultural influence of media messages is pervasive, so even people who do not watch much television may receive second-hand exposure to mainstream messages when they interact with those who do watch a lot of television.

Carlson applies cultivation theory to examine the "distorted world of TV criminal justice," what he calls "prime time criminal justice" (1985, p. 29). He notes that heavy viewers of crime-themed television programs feel strongly that they live in an unsafe and "mean world," and the "television world is a dangerous place where every citizen must use extreme caution to avoid becoming a victim of some terrible crime" (p. 48). Carlson stresses how the typical crime drama will most often emphasize a **crime control model** of justice over a **due process model** (Packer, 1964). As discussed in Chapter 1, the crime control model emphasizes a *tough on crime*, pro-police and prosecutor approach, whereas the due process model emphasizes procedural fairness, the rights of the accused, and the criminalization process from the perspective of the accused. Numerous crime-themed television dramas engage the viewer's interest by eliciting an emotional appeal based on vengeance against the so-called bad guys. In many crime and law dramas such as *Law and Order*, the police and prosecuting agents are certain that a suspect is factually guilty, but they are blocked from moving towards a conviction because evidence is deemed inadmissible or the presiding judge disallows a motion. In such programs, law enforcement agents express frustration that the legal system unfairly restricts their ability to gain a conviction. The viewer shares in the frustration that restrictive procedural rules need to be followed, and the guilty often go free as a result. Such sentiments cultivate a hostility against due process and a preference for the values of crime control, and thus they form the basis of the viewer's emotional investment in the drama (Colaguori, 2011). Is it true that the criminal justice system is soft on crime? Do you agree that heavy viewers of crime programs believe they live in a *scary world* and are thus more supportive of harsh and punitive criminal justice policies than people who do not watch crime shows? What about people who watch a lot of television and are not cultivated into mainstream thinking on social issues like crime? How can we explain such anomalies?

Audience Reception Theory and the Encoding/Decoding Model

Stuart Hall (1932–2014) proposed a theory of media messaging that is based on **semiotics**, the science of signs, signification, and message systems. Hall's model begins with the premise that the sender of a message (which can be the producer of an advertisement or a television show) intentionally *encodes* it with a specific meaning, and the receiver of that message *decodes* or interprets that meaning (1973/1980) in a variety of possible ways. Whether or not the intended meaning is accurately conveyed remains a central question of semiotics. Messages must have some sort of meaning in order to be of significance to the person receiving that message or they will be ignored. Some messages have simple direct meaning, such as a red, octagonal stop sign, while other sign systems, such as television crime dramas, are far more complex. The ways that people understand messages can vary substantially. Just because someone is sending a propaganda message does not mean the receiver will absorb the propagandistic message at face value. One may simply enjoy the colours on the propaganda poster and completely ignore the intended message! The interpretation of messages is subjective. No one can dictate with exactitude how a person receiving a complex message will interpret it. How television messages are consumed or *decoded* and made meaningful is what matters most in Hall's theory. So, what are the possible ways that viewers of crime programs will interpret them?

As you may recall from Chapter 3, the process whereby cultural messages draw people into conformity with the order of society has been referred to as the *hegemonic process* (Gitlin, 1979). **Ideological hegemony** (Gramsci, 1971) is the theory that common sense, taken-for-granted ideas about power and hierarchy embedded in mass media messages are effective at getting people to *consent* to and defend the established political order. Crime shows are complex messages composed of numerous scenes, dialogue, and plotlines. They have a surface meaning and an underlying meaning; the latter often conveys the so-called moral of the story. Although crime shows may not be deliberately encoded with hegemonic ideas, conformist values are often present in the underlying subtext of the story because they are part of the ideological framework of the writers and the thematic structure of popular stories. Nevertheless, even blatantly hegemonic texts do not guarantee viewer conformity to the established order. Hall suggests that while the most common response to a televisual text is a hegemonic one, there are two other possible ways in which televisual messages can be interpreted by audience members.

The Dominant–Hegemonic Position

In the dominant–hegemonic type of response, the receiver of the message affirms and accepts its intended meaning and is thus "operating inside the dominant code" of meaning and established ideologies of society (Hall, 1973/1980, p. 126). This is the most common way that crime shows are decoded or understood by audiences. For example, *good* is represented by law enforcement agents, while *evil* is represented by criminals, and the justice system needs to be clever and strong to fight the scourge of crime. Viewers who accept dominant encoded meanings support taken-for-granted views, such as the idea that *might is right* or that justice officials are *true heroes*. The message they may take away is that there is nothing wrong with the hierarchical order of society; the problem of crime is the fault of bad people.

The Negotiated Code

With this response, the viewer's decoded meaning varies somewhat from the dominant ideological meaning and is influenced by the situational context of the reader (Hall, 1973/1980). In this case, the viewer accepts some elements of the intended message but twists its meaning to accord with their own biases and interpretive point of view. For example, the viewer may have personal experience with the justice system and so they can see that some of what is presented in a crime show is questionable; nevertheless, they find the program entertaining.

The Oppositional Code

In this response, the viewer fully perceives the intended meaning of the message but consciously opposes and rejects this as false and misleading (Hall, 1973/1980). An example in this case would be a viewer who exercises critical judgment because they have studied criminology and know the difference between media *representations* and actual *realities* of crime. They take exception to what is presented and simply cannot identify with its content or be entertained by it because they see through its artificial construction. In this case, the crime show is not successful as a tool of hegemonic control.

Box 4.3: Ideologies of Justice, Race, Ethnicity, and Gender in Crime-Themed News and Entertainment Programs

Are crime-themed entertainment programs merely leisurely escapes, or is our way of thinking being influenced when we watch them? How do the underlying ideologies embedded in crime programs serve to legitimize hierarchies of social inequality as natural and inevitable? Do crime dramas actually serve to generate support for the prevailing social system and thus serve a *hegemonic* function? To begin to answer such questions, we must first understand that a crime program is a type of symbolic *text* similar to a book, advertisement, or piece of artwork. A crime program is a complex *message* that tells a story and conveys multiple meanings, and it has at least two basic levels of content:

1. The manifest content, which is the explicit, self-evident story on the surface; and
2. The latent content, which is the underlying meaning that the story implies or infers.

Sigmund Freud's method of interpreting dreams explains that what we remember of our dreams is merely their manifest content. This serves as a symbolic camouflage of the true deeper meaning of the dream, which is only revealed when we figure out what each element in the dream actually means. Crime dramas similarly have various levels of meaning. What we are presented with on the manifest level is a story, generally based on an adversarial conflict between a protagonist and an antagonist, that features the ways these characters attempt to defeat each other through clever strategy and violence. In many recent crime dramas, there are variations on the theme, and sometimes even the good people are bad and vice versa. In the course of being entertained by the drama, viewers receive explicit and implicit messages about justice, politics, and right and wrong.

In order to be compelling, crime programs need to resonate with the ideological biases and sentiments of the viewer. Such ideas are *ideological* because they represent commonsense ways of thinking that make power relations seem natural and inevitable, rather than socially constructed. As we saw in Chapter 3, the critical concept of **ideology** developed by Marx and later by Gramsci refers to a deceptive type of knowledge that creates a type of false consciousness, which aims to generate mass consent to the prevailing social order. Ideological hegemony operates across *all* spaces of cultural production, including fictional dramas as well as news coverage of crime. Some of the ideological myths inherent in law and order types of crime dramas and news broadcasts are:

- crime is the number one social problem
- crime is perpetrated primarily by certain types of people
- the justice system is too soft on criminals
- the solution to crime is to catch law-breakers, lock them up, and throw away the key
- criminals and prisoners have too many rights
- law enforcement and justice system officials rarely make mistakes because they have the backing of scientific expertise and investigational precision to ensure accuracy
- the crime- and enemy-fighting protagonists of popular culture who fight evil with violence are iconic representations of heroism, honour, and the good
- heinous violence is the result of an individual's sick mind, rather than something that is socially and culturally produced

What makes such beliefs *ideological* is the extent to which they function as forms of social control by creating *necessary illusions* (Chomsky, 1989) that *manufacture consent* through the manipulation of public opinion (Lippmann, 1922/2004). Crime and action-based popular entertainment can also be ideological because the drama often centres around explicitly political themes like patriotism, imperialism, terrorism, duty, and honour. Loyalty to the prevailing order is reinforced when the viewer is drawn into siding with the protagonist hero and despising the enemy/criminal antagonist. Crime-themed programming lends itself exceedingly well to the perpetuation of ideological myths because it is based on simplistic moral categories like right and wrong and good and evil (Box, 1983; Garcia & Arkerson, 2018; Lenz, 2017; Potter & Kappeler, 1998).

Crime-themed entertainment and news programs are also ideological insofar as they perpetuate widely held negative stereotypes and beliefs about criminalized groups (Russell-Brown, 2009). Potter and Kappeler, remarking on stereotyping in crime-themed media, state, "the audience remains uninformed and ignorant about the reality of crime and preconceived racist, sexist, and classist stereotypes are reinforced, building support for the criminalization of groups along the lines of race, class, and gender" (2012, p. 8). Discriminatory ideologies in crime-themed media often produce prejudicial hatred and differential criminalization by resorting to well-worn stereotypes:

- Racialized representations of Black males as criminals, gang members, and drug dealers remain consistent elements in crime-themed media. They are significantly overreported in the news and overrepresented in crime dramas involving conflicts with police (Rome, 2004).
- The persistent ethnic stereotype of the Italian mafia gangster continues to be a mainstay theme of numerous crime dramas (for example, *The Sopranos*) and even in children's movies (*Shark Tale*), as well as in news broadcasts of organized crime (Connell & Gardaphé, 2010).
- Indigenous people are repeatedly represented in news media as victims of crime, and in action and Western movies as primitive savages (*The Revenant*), while the viewer is often ideologically drawn into siding with the white man in dramatic fictional conflicts between natives and settlers (see the documentary *Reel Injun*; Diamond, 2009).

- The portrayal of Arabic, Middle Eastern, and Afghan people as criminals and terrorists in a vast array of news broadcasts and crime-action dramas is one ideological manifestation of the widespread **Islamophobic** discriminatory trend that began prior to 9/11 and intensified sharply thereafter (Alsultany, 2012).
- Reality policing programs like *COPS* and *Southern Justice* regularly depict police encounters with downtrodden and marginalized people, who are often presented stereotypically as "white trash" (Newitz & Ray, 1996).
- Reinforcing biblical myths of woman as the original sinner, films such as *Monster* and *Basic Instinct* often represent women who transgress or kill as hysterical, evil *monsters* (Jewkes, 2015; Whiteley, 2012).
- Male crime-fighting superheroes, detectives, and police officers are often depicted as hypermasculine characters (such as James Bond, Rambo, Dirty Harry, Iron Man) who use weaponized violence to solve problems, thereby perpetuating problematic conceptions of male identity.

In both its manifest and latent content, crime-themed media reproduces crime myths, problematic ideologies of justice, and stereotypical depictions of people who have already suffered historical oppression and remain the subjects of discriminatory forms of media representation. To what extent do problematic racial, ethnic, and gender depictions continue to form part of crime-themed entertainment? Do you think that times are changing and negative stereotypes in crime programming are becoming less common?

CRITICAL CONCEPTS IN THE STUDY OF CRIME-THEMED NEWS AND ENTERTAINMENT MEDIA

Although the study of media and crime borrows analytic concepts from other disciplines, criminologists have also developed concepts specific to understanding the relationship between representations of crime in the popular media and the range of public responses to them. The concept of **moral panic** focuses on the production of fear as a strategy of social control. Another significant concept is the **CSI effect,** which refers to how viewers of investigative crime programs develop a type of amateur skillset about solving crimes and prosecuting criminals.

Moral Panic

The promotion of fear among the populace is an ancient strategy of social control. Public fear can be produced through the use of tyrannical force or through panic spread by alarmist messages. The analysis of fear spread by the media builds on a number of concepts including promotional culture (Wernick, 1991), the relation between public issues and personal troubles (Mills, 1959), the social construction of crime problems (Surette, 2015), the **scary world syndrome** (Gerbner & Gross, 1976), and the **problem frame** (Altheide, 1997), among others. Altheide suggests,

> Fear is pervasive in American society and it has been produced through the interaction of commercial media, entertainment formats and programming, and the rise of "the problem frame." *Frames* are the focus, a parameter or boundary, for discussing a particular event.... [Framing] illegal drug use as a "public health issue" as opposed to a "criminal justice issue" will shape the way it is discussed and responded to. (Altheide, 1997, pp. 648–651)

Recall that in Chapter 3 the concept of moral panic was introduced to refer to the generation of an intense public reaction to criminal or deviant behaviour perceived to be a moral threat to society, one that calls for some sort of extreme response or drastic social control measure. Stanley Cohen's (1972) notion of moral panic has been a core concept in the work of many who study crime and the media. Cohen contends that moral panics do not happen spontaneously or by accident; while he does not place all the blame on the media, he does point out that sensationalized media coverage of an issue can produce a moral panic.

Cohen's (1972) original study focused on the public reaction to clashes between members of two youth gangs in late-1960s England. Many subsequent scholars have similarly applied the concept of a moral panic to members of *youth tribes* (online gamers, tag artists, goths, chavs, hip-hop fans, street racers, emo kids, etc.), and some have gone beyond the original focus to apply it to other groups and activities (e.g., Syrian refugees, fentanyl users, G20 protestors, Satanists, pedophiles, panhandlers, serial killers, terrorists, etc.).

While moral panics are far more common in our media culture than in previous generations (Hall & Winlow, 2015; Young, 2011), they are not phenomena that happen automatically. Rather, they result from of an interplay of behaviours and responses involving several actors, including 1) folk devils, 2) rule enforcers, 3) the media, 4) politicians, 5) the public, and 6) action groups (Muzzatti, 2006). Folk devils are the individuals responsible for the behaviour designated as morally repugnant. Unlike ostensibly normal deviants or criminals, these folks are "unambiguously unfavourable symbols" (Cohen, 1972, p. 41). While, as noted above, it is often members of youth subcultures who are designated as folk devils, the label is not solely restricted to them. Folk devils are highly stylized images of despised and marginalized people. In short, folk devils are demonized groups that are all that *we* (i.e., honest, law-abiding folks) are not.

The media is the single most influential actor in the orchestration and promulgation of a moral panic (Critcher, 2003). Media coverage of certain kinds of criminal behaviour, particularly those involving youth perpetrators, is usually distorted. It serves to inflate the seriousness of the incidents, making them appear more heinous and frequent than they truly are. Public anxiety and fear are whipped up through the use of journalistic and linguistic devices. "Special cover story," "in-depth exposé," or "investigative report" style coverage employs dramatic photos, video, and soundbites, along with highly moralistic editorializing. In such instances, terms and phrases such as *plague* and *scourge* serve to make the occurrences appear dire and more rampant than they really are. In such instances, small cohorts of young people are easily transformed into "rampaging mobs," minor property damage swells to "wholesale destruction," and scuffles are termed "riots."

Crime dramas and news reporting not only frame criminal issues in a sensationalized manner; they employ repetitive themes and media tropes that help construct a discourse of fear that is often reflected in public conversations about social problems. For example, in the post-9/11 era, news reporting has become increasingly *terrorist-centric*; it features regular coverage of the threat of terrorism and terrorist acts worldwide over and above other types of significant threats to life (Colaguori & Torres, 2012). Words like *Taliban* and *ISIS* are now familiar to viewing audiences just as they have become terms familiar to the public more generally. Thus, the criminal–enemy antagonist is no longer confined to the typical gangster/criminal but now includes the "terrorist" as featured in numerous films including *True Lies* (1994), *Iron Man* (2008), and *American Sniper* (2014). The concept of the criminal has thus expanded beyond domestic dangerous persons to include foreign enemies who also pose a threat to public safety. Boggs and Pollard (2007) in *The Hollywood War Machine* examine how war movies function as mass propaganda by criminalizing and generating public fear of foreign *others*, subsequently helping to generate public support for foreign invasions and war.

Studying how the media generates fear and moral panic allows researchers to make sense of the strategies by which certain forms of behaviour and certain individuals, groups, and communities come to be defined as criminal and subjected to mechanisms of social control and moral regulation. While it was only in the late 20th century that such phenomena started to be studied as moral panics, collective overreaction to behaviour designated as deviant or threatening is by no means a recent phenomenon. As indicated in Chapter 1, history is rife with examples of distorted views of social problems, which not only exaggerated the threat and targeted disenfranchised and powerless groups as the cause but also resulted in the creation of punitive laws and social policies to solve them. Pogroms, witch hunts, McCarthyism, the *Chinese Exclusion Act*, alcohol prohibition, and Indian residential schools are all examples of the consequences of moral panics that occurred long before the term was coined and the criminological study of them as such began. Will the concept of a moral panic continue as a useful tool in our understanding of crime, and more importantly, will moral panics continue to rage? The answer to both questions is a resounding yes. As Cohen asserted in 1972, moral panics will continue to be generated and new "folk devils" will be created. The process will continue if politicians and other leaders are rewarded for advancing simplistic and punitive solutions to crime problems, if criminal justice agencies advance a shortsighted, and ultimately detrimental, *war on crime*, and if the media continue to monopolize public understandings of crime with their sensationalistic interpretations.

The CSI Effect

One prominent instance of *commonsense criminology* perpetuated by crime-themed media is known as the CSI effect. The concept references the popular investigative crime drama *CSI: Crime Scene Investigation*, which originally aired in 2000 on the CBS Network. The focus on forensic investigation is also the primary theme on documentary-style crime shows like *Forensic Files* (1996–2001) and *F2: Forensic Factor* (2006–2010), among others. The CSI effect is a phenomenon whereby avid viewer interest in, and knowledge gained from, criminal investigation–type television programs influence public assumptions and expectations about how criminal cases are able to be solved. The CSI effect is not concerned with the *ideological* influence crime dramas have on audience members but with the extent to which crime dramas actually impart *practical* knowledge and crime skills to viewers of *CSI*-type crime shows. Furthermore, as Holmgren and Fordham write, "this so-called CSI effect includes the increased and unrealistic expectation that crime scenes will yield plentiful forensic samples that can be analyzed by near-infallible forensic science techniques and will be presented as such in the courtroom" (2011, p. s63). Criminal forensics involves the collection and laboratory analysis of crime scene evidence such as objects found at the crime scene, including insect larvae in corpses; stages of bodily decay and dental evidence in corpses; blood spatter analysis; fingerprints; DNA in saliva, semen, and hair; and soil imprints, among others. Mirroring what they see on television, viewers are quick to assert the importance of forensic evidence and expertise when crimes are investigated in the real world. People will say, "We need solid evidence!", or repeat the line about glove evidence from the O. J. Simpson mega-case: "If it doesn't fit, you must acquit!"

Some studies seem to indicate that the CSI effect has a profound influence on the opinions and deliberations of jurists, on jury selection, and in overall criminal trial proceedings that is akin to a CSI *infection* (Lawson, 2009). Other studies claim a CSI effect cannot be fully supported, and "that while jurors may question why such [forensic] evidence was not introduced, they would still carefully weigh all other evidence" (Holmgren & Fordham, 2011, p. s68).

The CSI effect is one example of how crime-themed entertainment programming has an influence on the way actual crimes are prosecuted. The relation between television crime and real crime raises other questions about the potential influence of crime-themed media: To what extent does the popularization of criminal investigative techniques serve to empower would-be criminals who learn to avoid detection through employing the knowledge they have gained from investigative crime shows? Does crime television serve as a how-to guide that serves to educate and inspire criminals towards the commission of violent crimes? Do crime shows promote **copycat crime**? These questions beg further research; however, the actual occurrence of copycat criminality is rare and certainly difficult to measure, and thus it is fair to say that in the multifaceted relationship between crime programs and their audiences, viewer entertainment is the main incentive, rather than the acquisition of criminal skills (Surette, 2016).

CULTURAL CRIMINOLOGY AND THE TRANSGRESSIVE SPECTACLE OF VIOLENCE

Perhaps the most provocative of media theories is that of **postmodernism,** which emphasizes the power of spectacle and takes the idea of the media's proliferation of images to the extreme. From the perspective of postmodernism, media messages don't just influence cultural realities; they *are* reality. Let us return to Plato's parable of the cave, which furnishes us with a "remarkable allegory of the mass age of television whose extreme tendencies are identified with postmodern culture" (O'Neill, 1991, p. 4). For Plato's cave dwellers, the imagistic representations of the world have become the actual world. The idea that we now live in a cave world of illusions that has taken over reality has been explored at length by the semiotician Jean Baudrillard (1929–2007), who claims that in the technological age, we are so immersed in a world of images and representations that we can no longer distinguish between what is real and what is illusion, that the world of false images and messages have become the new reality. The *simulation* of reality (images via television, advertisements, social media, consumer objects, fashion, bodies, cityscapes, etc.) has become so pervasive that we now live in a new *hyperreal* world of representations (Baudrillard, 1983). Additionally, those in power who try to monopolize the postmodern machine of technological communications and images can no longer control people through manipulative strategies of power because the system of illusions has taken on a life of its own. The film *The Matrix* (1999), which was loosely based on Baudrillard's theory, exemplifies the extent to which people are so immersed in a world of illusory realities that they no longer have a solid reference point for what is real.

Such insights about how representations make up our reality have implications for how the public understands the volume of images of crime that form our news and entertainment media environments. As Hayward observes, "the true meaning of crime [is] to be found not in the essential (and essentially false) factuality of crime rates, but in the contested processes of symbolic display ... images of crime ... [are] becoming as 'real' as crime and criminal justice itself" (Hayward, 2010, p. 1). The postmodern world that surrounds us with images is the *society of the spectacle* (Debord, 1994), which includes images of violence and destruction. This abundance of images is not external to us; as Debord writes, "the spectacle is not a collection of images; rather it is a social relationship between people that is mediated by images" (1994, p. 12).

Cultural criminology draws directly on ideas from postmodern theories of spectacle and hyperreality and the seductive power of violence. Violence has become a fundamental part of the symbolic life of images and is something both feared and celebrated. Those who desire an escape from the stress and meaninglessness of life in the antisocial world of hyperreality often embrace the thrill of violence. Violence has become the medium for power, self-expression, leisure, and fun. The myriad violent video games, graphic crime shows, superhero comic book crime (Phillips & Strobl, 2013), and military/war themed entertainment items (Boggs & Pollard, 2007) that explicitly feature violent forms of expression provide the means for visual adventure, escape, and cathartic release of frustration. In cultural criminology, this escapism is theorized as a type of sensual self-abandon, known as **transgression**. The literal meaning of *transgression* is a violation, sin, vice, or wrongdoing. Cultural criminologists broaden the meaning of *transgression* to refer to transcending the boundaries of acceptable behaviour or deviating from social norms with a deliberate degree of recklessness, disorder, or revelry. Think of the sorts of extreme leisure activities many people now find exhilarating, such as bungee jumping, skydiving, mixed martial arts fighting, escape rooms, BASE jumping, storm chasing, and the dangerous foolishness of mostly young males that forms the content of ultimate fail videos—all of which play on the thrill of taking risks. For those unwilling to commit actual transgression, there is the option of consuming visual transgression in the form of crime stories and images.

Cultural criminologist Mike Presdee (2000) argues that transgressive escapism is to be found in many new trends of extreme deviant and criminal behaviour. There is a relationship between real acts of transgressive violence, such as soccer hooliganism, hockey riots, and acts of hate and humiliation, and the increasing popularity of visual transgressive commodities such as zombie and vampire programs, sadomasochistic novels and movies, and Goth culture, which are ritualized forms of transgressive expression that *normalize violence* and *celebrate death* (Colaguori, 2012; Presdee, 2000). For Presdee, the transgressive dimension of *crime culture* "anticipates the ability to destroy, disrupt and dissent" that is also reflected in the leisure and pleasure that people seek in crime and violence entertainment programs (2000, p. 8). Presdee's theory of the **carnival of crime** applies to how individuals and groups commit crime, wrongdoing, dangerous foolishness, and radical rule-breaking to express pent-up frustration and as an outlet for unmet desires. Take note of the following August 16, 2018, CBC news story:

Police have charged a 34-year-old woman who climbed and damaged a construction crane in downtown Toronto on Thursday morning, before being rescued by fire department workers. Police and firefighters negotiated with the woman, who appeared to be topless, for about an hour before she descended. It took crews about two hours to get the woman—who was 14 storeys up, in the crane operator's compartment—back to the ground. It wasn't immediately clear how long she had been there.... It's the second such incident in 16 months in Toronto. In April 2017, a 23-year-old woman was rescued, and in January plead guilty to two mischief counts. (CBC News, 2018)

And in February 2019, CTV news reported that

Police are investigating after a video surfaced online of a woman throwing a chair and other objects off a Toronto condo balcony.... [The 19-year-old] Toronto resident, briefly appeared in court on Wednesday to face charges of common nuisance, mischief endangering life and damage to property over $5,000. (Nersessian & Cousins, 2019)

Through social media, we see an example of the spread of risk-taking challenges among youth in the following story:

> Parental warnings about the Momo Challenge have swept Facebook and other social media in recent days. Parents have expressed concern about purported videos allegedly circulating online that feature a grinning creature with matted hair and bulging eyes encouraging children to hurt themselves or engage in other dangerous actions, such as turning on stoves without telling their parents. (Gollom, 2019)

What compels some people to engage in these sorts of reckless behaviours? What makes these forms of criminal activities uniquely transgressive? Presdee's analysis of illicit, reckless, hyperviolent, and death-centric transgressive crimes and deviant pleasures helps us make sense of how social anxieties get reflected in the cultural carnival of crime. Presdee builds upon semiotician Mikhail Bakhtin's (1895–1975) concept of the *carnival* to describe features of transgressive, excessive behaviours that have long formed a part of cultural festivals. For Bakhtin (1965/1984), the town carnival of previous times was a bacchanal event that provided an occasion for celebration, a release from order, and a symbolic festival that mocked societal authority. Today, carnivalesque forms of transgression (like hockey fan street riots and wanton vandalism) are distorted, destructive caricatures of authentic carnivals that aimed to violate certain cultural taboos in a display of social resistance.

In the words of scholars ...

We need a criminology that can comment on how culture kills. That death by dancing or death by media can and does happen.

Mike Presdee, *Cultural Criminology and the Carnival of Crime*. 2000

The Carnival of Crime: Violence and Violation

Notions of carnival and transgression have long been associated with popular culture and public entertainment (Danesi, 2019). From a criminological perspective, Presdee (2000) critically examines the complex intersections of consumer culture and transgressive performances in his book *Cultural Criminology and the Carnival of Crime*. Affirming Taylor's (1999) observation about the rise of "in-your-face incivility" as an emerging feature of social relations, Presdee highlights accounts of callousness, flamboyant cruelty, and violence, including references to school shootings in the United States and rural Canada, a series of nail-bomb attacks in London, and the execution of a popular female television presenter. Serving as a theoretical basis for the non-conventional research of cultural criminologists, the *carnival* model emphasizes the appropriation and transformation of crime into mass-market and personal pleasures. Like moths gravitating towards the bright light of an open flame, crime viewing audiences are understood as active chasers of violent, humiliating, destructive, and exhilarating criminal images through this perspective.

Presdee (2000) highlights the carnivalesque elements of excess and the grotesque to make sense of the forms of transgressive criminality that are emerging themes in contemporary popular culture. Participants in transgressive revelries abandon any commitment to order and momentarily suspend their responsibilities. Consumers of transgressive crime narratives also engage in a similar process of temporary, transitory freedom from societal constraints where they can enjoy a sort of *second life* that lies outside of their normal routine behaviour. Bakhtin (1965/1984) identified a "second life of the people," which is the irrational, secretive, dark side of existence that is not shared with everyone because it is often "immoral, uncivilised, obscene, and unfathomable social behaviour ... [an] unofficial life where we express our fears of rational life ... and law loses its power" (Presdee, 2000, p. 8).

The viewing audience's endless fascination with the violence and crime of their favourite televisual dramas reflects a lust for transgression. Audiences simultaneously strive to escape their real social commitments and surrender to their wild imaginations and deviant desires as a remedy for the *boredom of everyday life* (Ferrell, 2004). Viewers opt for crime dramas as safe options to experience "rage, anger, and hatred" (Presdee, 2000, p. 5). Captivating storylines and alluring characters are developed so that viewers can engage in the pleasure of vicarious vengeance and transgression, a reflection of "the buzz and excitement of the act of doing wrong itself" (p. 5).

Postmodern society now includes the hyperreal world of the internet and social media, which is part active reality and part illusion. For those who seek to engage in violation under the cover of virtual anonymity, Presdee writes, "the internet is fast becoming the safe site of the second life of the people" (2000, p. 54). The internet and social media furnish a worldwide arena of transgressive options that allow people to troll, shame, harass, bombast, humiliate, malign, gossip, steal, cheat, embezzle, bully, post revenge porn, and otherwise violate social norms in various manners, all in the difficult-to-police and relatively anonymous realm of cyberspace.

Violation and *violence* remain predominant transgressive themes in the carnival of crime. The definition of *acceptable* violence within media culture keeps expanding. In competitive-themed entertainment, in sports, and often in public interactions with others, conflict and violence serve as the media to express transgressive disdain. Entertainment now takes shape as a forum for conflict, exemplified in the concept of the **mediagon**, the modern coliseum of violent spectacle where adversarial contest is played out in the arena of combat, and victory is achieved through the destruction of the other. The themes of violence and death in the mediagon are evident in the numerous animal predator programs, imperialist and war history programs, crime dramas, and competitive sports features (Colaguori, 2012). The expanding enterprises of the World Wrestling Empire (WWE) and the action and horror genres of the film industry all depend on narratives of violent demolition and fighting in order to attract viewership. The formulaic production of these representations appeals to the thrills of spectatorship, including the direct humiliation of bodies placed in moments of danger. Presdee maintains: "In its consumption, violence is simplified and reduced to a trivial act of instant enjoyment; it thereby becomes no different from, say, the eating of a chocolate biscuit or the drinking of a can of Coke" (2000, p. 65).

It is important to note that, in addition to the media-fuelled carnivals, there exist everyday acts and establishments that are commodified into sites of transgressive pleasure and rebellion. The organization (formal or unauthorized) of raves and bar parties fuelled by mind-altering substances, the street racing of modified and stolen cars and motorcycles, internet bondage sites, and even the hazing and initiation processes affiliated with some fraternity/sorority and junior sports organizations all encompass characteristics of transgressive liberation and excitement. The ongoing existence of these transgressive rituals can link directly to the social need for escape from the rigid cycles of conformity within our modern world, but at some level merely reproduce the underlying order of domination, violence, and destruction in society.

Within our socially fragmented world, moderated through global trade practices, perpetual war, the violence of everyday life, and the machinery of manipulation that is popular culture, individuals are also consistently motivated by personal insecurity and fear. We turn to the consumption of images, goods, and adventurous experiences as an exercise to express our self-control, social status, and identity. Although the carnival of crime emphasizes the commodification of violence and transgression within our contemporary world, our modern realities of instability and anxiety propel many of us to embrace pseudo-carnivals at any expense.

CONCLUSION: INNOVATIONS IN THE CRIME GENRE

This chapter has discussed how crime-themed media has a long and diverse history and remains an extremely popular genre of entertainment and news programming. Although there are different explanations about the ways in which media messages about crime influence audiences, it is generally understood that crime programming is not neutral in its content or meaning. While crime programs both entertain and inform audiences, they simultaneously disseminate misleading mythologies about crime and reproduce ideologies of discrimination.

Crime dramas are based upon the time-honoured formula of good-versus-evil, which has provided the foundation for most crime shows. Police dramas of the 1970s and 1980s were based on simplistic cop-versus-criminal rivalries that maintained the good-versus-evil formula, as in Clint Eastwood's *Dirty Harry* (1971). Yet even in the 1970s, Eastwood's movie *Magnum Force* (1973) blurred the boundary between good and evil when police officers themselves went beyond the law to achieve justice. Variations on the theme are normal for the crime genre, which is highly versatile and continually changes to reflect new social dynamics. Simplistic formulas are changing to reflect multidimensional realities that present more complex portrayals of crime and criminality. Boundaries between good and evil are blurred, and the potential for transgressive viewer adventure is multiplied by innovative protagonists like Steven Avery in *Making a Murderer* (2015–2018), Dexter Morgan in *Dexter*, Marty Byrde in *Ozark* (2017–2022), Nasir Khan in *The Night Of* (2016), and Christopher Jeffries in *The Lost Honour of Christopher Jeffries* (2014), all of whom transcend simple, formulaic characters and allow for deeper levels of viewer identification. Complex plotlines that go beyond good and evil are evident in some highly literary crime series, such as *True Detective* (2014–2019), which expand the sophistication of the crime genre while leaving intact traditional elements of macabre and mystery. Dramatic films such as *Atanarjuat: The Fast Runner* (2001) further expand the diversity of the crime genre and reveal its capacity for artistic innovation and cultural complexity.

Innovations in the crime genre notwithstanding, the bulk of crime-themed media items remain culture industry commodities for public consumption. They are designed to appeal to those seeking the carnivalesque pleasures of visual transgression, yet, in doing so, they do nothing to disrupt or challenge the blatant reproduction of mainstream ideologies. Violence, vengeance, and adversarial conflict remain essential elements of most crime-themed entertainment. The genre continually produces seemingly endless versions of sensationalized true-crime programs like *Vengeance: Killer Lovers* (2019), *Very Scary People* (2019–), *Someone You*

Thought You Knew (2018–2019), *Primal Instinct* (2018–2019), and *Fear Thy Neighbor* (2014–). Content based on criminal minds, forensic investigations, and public fears of criminal victimization combine to give avid viewers of crime programs an emotionally charged sense that they are well informed about criminological issues. If we consider how crime-themed media powerfully influences public perceptions, which in turn can have an influence on politics and the formation of criminal justice policies, then the fictions on the screen have indeed merged with reality.

REVIEW QUESTIONS

1. What is "commonsense criminology"?
2. Which theory of media effects do you feel best explains how crime programs influence audiences? Explain why.
3. What is the "carnival of crime" and how does it relate to transgressive behaviours?

GLOSSARY

agency: The capacity of individuals to make decisions freely and in a way that represents their own best interests, in the context of social restraints and imposed limitations.

carnival of crime: A theory of criminal transgression that examines how some criminal acts and forms of wrongdoing are experienced by their perpetrators as radical rule-breaking and exciting expressions of disrespect that fulfil unmet desires and break through the restraints of social conformity.

commodity: A consumer product that is manufactured and offered for sale.

commonsense criminology: A layperson's simplistic understanding of crime that results from the consumption of popular crime-themed entertainment programming and its typical themes, such as the criminal mind, serial killers, dramatic portrayals of policing street criminals and crimes of the downtrodden, and law and order perspectives of justice.

copycat crime: A crime that is inspired, planned, or executed by copying a criminal act represented in the media.

crime control model: A philosophy of criminal justice that emphasizes a tough-on-crime approach and the strength of police and prosecutorial power as the basis of public safety.

CSI effect: A phenomenon whereby avid viewer interest in and knowledge gained from criminal investigation–type television programs has influenced both the assumptions and expectations about how criminal cases are able to be solved.

cultivation theory: A theory of media analysis that measures influence and indicates that heavy viewing of television tends to cultivate attitudes among viewers that make them supportive of mainstream political values.

cultural criminology: The study of how narratives about crime have become products for public consumption that influence cultural conceptions of crime and criminal justice and how crime plays a significant role in contemporary media culture.

culture industry: The industry that consists of corporately owned media including television, news media, fashion, and entertainment that produces a vast proportion of popular culture content within consumer society.

discourse: The official knowledge, concepts, and themes that are produced by a particular institution and form the basis of its ideological power.

due process model: A philosophy of criminal justice that emphasizes the rights of the accused to a fair trial and legal representation and upholds the value that a person is innocent unless proven guilty beyond a reasonable doubt.

ideological hegemony: A theory of social control where taken-for-granted ideas about power and hierarchy are embedded in media messages in order to get people to *consent* to and defend the established political order.

ideology: A deceptive type of popular knowledge that generates public consent to the prevailing social order and is used to make socially constructed hierarchies seem natural and inevitable.

infotainment: A genre of news broadcasting that informs and entertains and usually consists of content such as crime and celebrity gossip that is deliberately sensationalized for dramatic effect.

Islamophobia: Discrimination or prejudice directed against Arabic people and Muslims that is based on fear and misunderstanding.

mainstreaming: The process whereby viewer exposure to the *symbolic environment* of mass media messages and themes *cultivates* commonly shared, mainstream values.

mediagon: A concept describing the tendency within entertainment media offerings to depict violence, adversarial contest, combat, competition, and predation as dominant program themes, making such programs akin to a modern coliseum that provides viewer pleasure on the basis of consuming agony, victory, and defeat.

mega-cases: Crimes that, as a result of some combination of rarity, severity, complexity, and brutality, elicit powerful responses from public audiences and enjoy great longevity.

moral panic: The generation of an intense public reaction to criminal or deviant behaviour perceived to be a moral threat to society, which calls for some sort of extreme response or drastic social control measure.

newsworthy: An occurrence deemed significant or interesting enough to be worthy of coverage in the news reports.

postmodernism: The theory that contemporary popular culture, art, and design has departed significantly from the modern era and its claims to truth, and that media representations of reality create a world of illusions grounded in previous representations of reality such as art and photography.

problem frame: In media theory, the focus, parameter, or boundary for discussing a particular event that determines the way it is discussed and responded to.

propaganda: A type of mass communicated message, common in times of war, that is deliberately designed to promote a particular view or opinion for political purposes.

reification: A type of alienating loss of self whereby the individual is shaped into a consumer object to perpetuate the functioning of the established political and economic order.

scary world syndrome: The theory that heavy viewers of crime programs come to believe that they live in a scary world full of threats and dangers and are thus more supportive of harsh and punitive criminal justice policies than people who do not watch and are thus not influenced by crime programs.

semiotics: The study of symbols and signs and how they communicate meaning.

transgression: A violation, vice, or wrongdoing that, for cultural criminologists, also refers to acts that transcend the boundaries of acceptable behaviour or deviate from social norms with a deliberate degree of recklessness, disorder, or revelry.

REFERENCES

Alsultany, E. (2012). *Arabs and Muslims in the media: Race and representation after 9/11.* New York University Press.

Altheide, D. L. (1997). The news media, the problem frame, and the production of fear. *The Sociological Quarterly, 38*(4), 647–668.

Bakhtin, M. (1984). *Rabelais and his world.* Indiana University Press. (Original work published 1965)

Barak, G. (1994). Newsmaking criminology: Reflections on the media, intellectuals, and crime. In G. Barak (Ed.). *Media, process, and the social construction of crime* (pp. 237–264). Garland Publishing.

Baudrillard, J. (1983). *Simulations*. Semiotext(e).

Boggs, C., & Pollard, T. (2007). *The Hollywood war machine: U.S. militarism and popular culture*. Paradigm Publishers.

Box, S. (1983). *Power, crime, and mystification*. Tavistock Publications.

Carlson, J. M. (1985). *Prime time law enforcement: Crime show viewing and attitudes toward the criminal justice system*. Praeger Publishers.

Carney, P. (2010). Crime, punishment and the force of photographic spectacle. In K. Hayward & M. Presdee (Eds.), *Framing crime: Cultural criminology and the image* (pp. 17–35). Routledge.

CBC News. (2018, August 16). Woman charged after climbing, damaging crane in downtown Toronto. *CBC News*. Retrieved from https://www.cbc.ca/news/canada/toronto/woman-climbs-toronto-crane-1.4787270

Chomsky, N. (1989). *Necessary illusions: Thought control in democratic societies*. House of Anansi Press.

Cohen, S. (1972). *Folk devils and moral panics: The creation of the mods and rockers*. Basil Blackwell.

Colaguori, C. (2011). Prime time crime programming and the formation of authoritarian attitudes among viewers. *The Critical Criminologist, 20*(1). Retrieved from http://divisiononcriticalcriminology.com/wp-content/uploads/Critical-Criminology-20-1.pdf

Colaguori, C. (2012). *Agon culture: Competition, conflict and the problem of domination*. de Sitter Publications.

Colaguori, C., & Torres, C. (2012). Policing terrorism in the post 9/11 era: Critical concerns in an age of hypersecurity. In L. Tepperman & A. Kalyta (Eds.), *Reading sociology: Canadian perspectives* (2nd ed., pp. 291–294). Oxford University Press.

Connell, W. J., & Gardaphé, F. (Eds.). (2010). *Anti-Italianism: Essays on a prejudice*. Palgrave Macmillan.

Critcher, C. (2003). *Moral panics and the media*. Open University Press.

Danesi, M. (2019). *Popular culture: Introductory perspectives* (4th ed.). Rowman & Littlefield.

Debord, G. (1994). *The society of the spectacle*. Zone Books.

Diamond, N. (2009). *Reel Injuns* [Video]. Ottawa, Ontario, Canada: National Film Board. Retrieved from https://www.nfb.ca/distribution/film/reel_injun

Dowler, K., Fleming, T., & Muzzatti, S. L. (2006). Constructing crime: Media, crime and popular culture. *Canadian Journal of Criminology and Criminal Justice, 48*(6), 837–850.

Ferrell, J. (2004). Boredom, crime and criminology. *Theoretical Criminology, 8*(3), 287–302.

Garcia, V., & Arkerson, S. G. (2018). *Crime, media, and reality: Examining mixed messages about crime and justice in popular media*. Rowman & Littlefield.

Gerbner, G., & Gross, G. (1976, April). The scary world of TV's heavy viewer. *Psychology Today*, 89–91.

Gerbner, G., Gross, L., Morgan, M., & Signorielli, N. (2002). Charting the mainstream: Television's contributions to political orientations. In M. Morgan (Ed.), *Against the mainstream: The selected works of George Gerbner* (pp. 305–331). Peter Lang.

Gitlin, T. (1979). Prime time ideology: The hegemonic process in television entertainment. *Social Problems, 26*(3), 251–266.

Gollom, M. (2019, March 16). Parents "spreading the fear" to their kids over Momo Challenge. *CBC News*. Retrieved from https://www.cbc.ca/news/momo-challenge-parents-social-media-video-hoax-1.5039579

Gramsci, A. (1971). *Selections from the prison notebooks* (G. N. Smith & Q. Hoare, Trans.) International Publishers.

Hall, S. (1980). Encoding/decoding. In Centre for Contemporary Cultural Studies (Ed.), *Culture, media, language: Working papers in cultural studies, 1972–79* (pp. 128–138). Hutchinson. (Original work published 1973)

Hall, S., & Winlow, S. (2015). *Revitalizing criminological theory: Towards a new ultra-realism*. Routledge.

Hayward, K. J. (2010). Opening the lens: Cultural criminology and the image. In K. J. Hayward & M. Presdee (Eds.), *Framing crime: Cultural criminology and the image* (pp. 1–16). Routledge.

Holmgren, J. A., & Fordham, J. (2011). The CSI effect and the Canadian and the Australian jury. *Journal of Forensic Sciences, 56*(S1), S63(1).

Horkheimer, M., & Adorno, T. (1972). The culture industry: Enlightenment as mass deception. In *Dialectic of Enlightenment* (pp. 120–167). Continuum. (Original work published 1944)

Jewkes, Y. (2015). *Media and crime* (3rd ed.). SAGE Publications.

Lawson, T. F. (2009, November 3). Before the verdict and beyond the verdict: The CSI infection within modern criminal jury trials. *Loyola University Chicago Law Journal, 41*, 119.

Lazarsfeld, P. F. (1940). *Radio and the printed page: An introduction to the study of radio and its role in the communication of ideas*. Duell, Sloan, and Pearce.

Lenz, T. O. (2017). Ideology in the crime genre. *Crime, Media, and Popular Culture*. https://doi.org/10.1093/acrefore/9780190264079.013.168

LIFE. (1968a, June 21). The accused: Ray and Sirhan. *64*(25), 24–34.

LIFE. (1968b, June 21). The psycho-biology of violence. *64*(25), 67–71.

Lippmann, W. (2004). *Public opinion.* Dover Publications. (Original work published 1922)

Miller, W. R. (1975). Police authority in London and New York City, 1830–1870. *Journal of Social History, 8*(2), 81–101.

Mills, C. W. (1959). *The sociological imagination.* Oxford University Press.

Muzzatti, S. (2006). Cultural criminology: A decade and counting criminological chaos. In W. S. DeKeseredy & B. Perry (Eds.), *Advancing critical criminology: Theory and application* (pp. 63–82). Lexington Books.

Muzzatti, S. L. (2010). Drive it like you stole it: A cultural criminology of car commercials. In K. J. Hayward & M. Presdee (Eds.), *Framing crime: Cultural criminology and the image* (pp. 138–155). Routledge.

Muzzatti, S. L. (2012). Crime in the news media. In W. R. Miller (Ed.), *Social history of crime and punishment in America* (pp. 1242–1248). SAGE Publications.

Muzzatti, S. L. (2013). Popular portrayals of street crime. In J. I. Ross (Ed.), *Encyclopedia of street crime in America.* SAGE Publications.

Nersessian, M., & Cousins, B . (2019, February 13). Woman accused in Toronto balcony chair-tossing incident released on bail. *CTV News.*

Newitz, A., & Wray, M. (1996). What is "white trash"?: Stereotypes and economic conditions of poor whites in the U.S. *Minnesota Review, 47,* 57–72.

O'Neill, J. (1991). Plato's cave: Desire, power and the specular functions of the media. Ablex Publishing Corporation.

Osborne, R. (1995). Crime and the media: From media studies to post-modernism. In Kidd-Hewitt & R. Osborne (Eds.), *Crime and the media: The post-modern spectacle* (pp. 25–48). Pluto Press.

Packer, H. L. (1964). *Two models of the criminal process. University of Pennsylvania Law Review, 113*(1), 1–68.

Phillips, N. D., & Strobl, S. (2013). *Comic book crime: Truth, justice, and the American way.* New York University Press.

Potter, G. W., & Kappeler, V. E. (1998). *Constructing crime: Perspectives on making news and social problems.* Waveland Press.

Potter, G. W., & Kappeler, V. E. (2012). Introduction: Media, crime and hegemony. In D. L. Bissler & J. L. Conners (Eds.), *The harms of crime media: Essays on the perpetuation of racism, sexism and class stereotypes* (pp. 3–17). McFarland & Company.

Presdee, M. (2000). *Cultural criminology and the carnival of crime.* Routledge.

Rome, D. (2004). *Black demons: The media's depiction of the African American male criminal stereotype.* Praeger.

Russell-Brown, K. (2009). *The color of crime* (2nd ed.). New York University Press.

Smith, E., & Muzzatti, S. L. (2018). Sleeping with the fishes: A Canadian spectacle of ethnicity and crime in dramatic television. Paper presented at the XIX World Congress of Sociology, Toronto, Ontario, Canada, July 2018.

Soothill, K., Peelo, M., Pearson, J., & Francis, B. (2004). The reporting trajectories of top homicide cases in the media: A case study of the *Times*. *The Howard Journal of Criminal Justice, 43*(1), 1–14.

Surette, R. (2015). *Media, crime, and criminal justice: Images, realities and policies* (5th ed.). Wadsworth.

Surette, R. (2016). Measuring copycat crime. *Crime, Media, Culture: An International Journal, 12*(1), 37–64.

Taylor, I. (1999). *Crime in context: A critical criminology of market societies*. Westview Press.

The Telegraph. (2018, September 17). The 20 best crime novels of all time. Retrieved from https://www.telegraph.co.uk/books/what-to-read/20-best-crime-novels-time/

Van Veeren, E. (2009). Interrogating 24: Making sense of US counter-terrorism in the global war on terrorism. *New Political Science, 31*(3), 361–384. https://doi.org/10.1080/07393140903105991

Visano, L. A. (2006). *What do they know? Youth, culture and crime*. de Sitter Publications.

Wernick, A. (1991). *Promotional culture: Advertising, ideology, and symbolic expression*. SAGE Publications.

Whiteley, K. (2012). Monstrous, demonic and evil: Media constructs of women who kill. In D. L. Bissler, & J. L. Conners (Eds.), *The harms of crime media: Essays on the perpetuation of racism, sexism and class stereotypes* (pp. 91–110). McFarland & Company.

Young, J. (2011). *The criminological imagination*. Polity Press.

CHAPTER 5

Moral Regulation, Vice Crimes, and Social Control

Claudio Colaguori, Juliette Jarvis, Jennifer Kusz, Richard Jochelson, David Ireland, Maggie Quirt, and Brandon Trask

LEARNING OBJECTIVES

In this chapter, you will

- learn about the concept of moral regulation and how it relates to specific types of behaviour designated as deviant and criminal;
- understand some of the history concerning so-called victimless crimes, such as recreational drug and alcohol use, sex-trade work, and gambling;
- learn more about how the system of patriarchy establishes the moral underpinnings of forms of oppression that target females;
- think critically about how subjective moral values influence what our society accepts as right and wrong; and
- develop an understanding of how challenges to moral categories of behaviour inform human rights struggles.

INTRODUCTION

It is difficult to understand crime, law, and social control without acknowledging the moral premises upon which they, and the public reactions to them, are based. The concept of **morality** does not seem particularly problematic. To most people, morals exist as a sort of guide to the proper ways of conducting oneself as a member of a society. What is morality? What does the concept mean, and what is **moral regulation**? Why are some acts considered immoral? What premises underlie the judgment that a person is immoral? Strange and Loo write, "morality is a difficult concept to define because it is largely an abstract concept … [however] it is a strategy of evaluation or a means of distinguishing between goodness and badness" (1997, p. 4). The concept of morality generally has a positive connotation and so it is not likely that people take issue with the idea of moral correctness. The problem arises when people with power attempt to impose their own set of moral standards onto others who may starkly disagree with them and may be punished for doing so. Take the following examples:

- Hunt writes, "In 1911 the Chicago Vice Commission called for the regulation of the city's ice-cream parlours, which it judged to be locations in which scores of girls took their first steps towards immorality and prostitution" (1999, p. 1);
- in 1991, the musical group The Barenaked Ladies was banned from performing in Toronto's Nathan Phillips Square for New Year's Eve because the City's protocol office took moral exception to the group's name, claiming it "objectified women" (Friend, 2018); and
- in 1936, a **moral panic** campaign known as "reefer madness," based on the propaganda film of the same name, warned that marijuana use would lead the user down a path of "drug-crazed abandon," immorality, madness, and self-destruction.

Moral claims are often promoted in the name of protecting health, honour, and the public good, and although the field of moral regulation comprises a broad range of social issues this chapter is mostly concerned with the relation between morality, crime, and social control.

In the words of scholars ...

Law's connection with morality is ancient. Originally expressed in religious codes, laws relating to morality were packaged with regulations governing a wide range of prohibited behaviour ... the current Canadian *Criminal Code* ... is similar to that ancient code and it pronounces certain breaches of morality illegal.

Carolyn Strange and Tina Loo, *Making Good: Law and Moral Regulation in Canada, 1867–1939.* 1997

When the behaviours and life choices people make as individuals are designated as immoral, deviant, criminal, or illegal, these punitive judgments reflect a unique type of ancient power—a primitive form of social control that works its way into social relations even in the present day. As indicated in Chapter 1, moral judgment is a fundamental form of social control that exists alongside other types of regulation. Moral judgment is often at the basis of social order–maintenance that attempts to regulate the behaviour of individuals through condemnation, shaming, and social exclusion. The moral values within human cultures are often devised as an attempt to secure a social order that maximizes the higher social goal of order. However, oftentimes the imposition of moral values on people who do not subscribe to them is experienced as repressive, and such moral judgment is used by those with authority to exercise control. For much of human history, those with the power to decide what sort of order should shape society have determined what defines good and bad, as well as right and wrong. This type of social control, which is based on the invocation and imposition of a dominant set of moral values on the population at large, is the focus of the criminological subfield known as *moral regulation theory*. Moral regulation is a traditional form of social control whereby moral values and judgments serve to regulate social behaviour and personal conduct. Moral regulation exists in both informal codes that regulate social behaviour, such as social etiquette, manners, and other norms that define so-called respectable behaviour; and in *formal* codes of behaviour such as the law. The law has been described as a system of governing populations that is historically based on moral values and is thus one of the primary institutions involved in moral regulation (Strange & Loo, 1997). Other institutions regulate people through the promotion and enforcement of moral codes as well. Such institutions include religion, the family, and the state. As we saw in Chapter 2, European history provides stark examples of such regulation: individuals who expressed ideas contrary to church and state doctrine were charged with heresy and punished, often to death. In contemporary times, moral crimes can, in a sense, be understood as forms of modern secular heresy.

When we try to make sense of so-called moral crimes (which are officially classified as **vice crimes**), such as gambling, drug use, unconventional sexual behaviour, and sex-trade work, we are faced with a series of fundamental questions:

- Why are vice crimes sometimes referred to as victimless crimes, and are they truly so?
- How does designating certain activities as illegal end up supporting the moral and cultural values of the dominant group over and against the individual rights and freedoms of others?
- How can law become an impediment to justice, freedom, and **human rights**?
- How is regulating the conduct and lifestyle choices of certain people justified in the name of moral righteousness and protecting the greater good?

The last question is particularly relevant for issues of power relations in terms of the repression of women, girls, and youth, as well as people with non-conforming gender and sexual identities. The history of the criminalization of homosexuality through rendering same-sex attraction as illegal and punishable, the use of invasive **gay conversion therapy** to "correct" sexual behaviour deemed immoral, and how women have historically been subject to invasive therapies and medical procedures such as unnecessary sterilization and hysterectomies, among other examples, represent some deeply troubling examples of the traditional moral bias that has long been inherent in law. Equally troubling is the fact that such bias remains in place in many countries around the world. Perhaps you are familiar with the experience of living in a society where attending movie theatres was outlawed or where women were not legally allowed to drive or where playing music, accessing the internet, and posting on social media are illegal. How do such restrictions affect quality of life for people who live in morally repressive societies? Morality figures into crime, deviance, and social control in numerous other ways, including:

- the imposition of patriarchal cultural values of dishonour, shame, and violence on females;
- laws that prohibit or censor music, dancing, and forms of artistic expression;
- laws banning or controlling contraception and abortion;
- laws governing medically assisted suicide;
- laws that restrict gambling to state-run operations;
- laws governing the purchase and sale of sexual services;
- laws that criminalize the sale and use of consciousness-altering substances such as psychedelic mushrooms and other prohibited, "illicit" drugs;
- behavioural restrictions on holy days such as bans on Sunday shopping (which was the case in Canada for many years);
- laws against same-sex marriage and homosexuality and against the expression of transgender identities; and
- the inability of justice systems to adequately deal with sexualized violence.

Moral claims have often been mobilized to create and justify particular social policies as well as the continuation of traditional patriarchal institutions such as the nuclear family, heteronormative marriage, and organized religion. Moral claims are often raised in an attempt to preserve a particular type of dominant order that benefits certain groups over others. Thus, moral regulation is a significant form of power. For example, in times of moral panics, such as during crime waves, pandemics, or social upheaval, self-appointed moral crusaders often call for a return to traditional values and may blame social problems (such as crime) on the breakdown of the family structure. Such efforts are often a reaction against the opposing efforts of progressives who, in their attempt to reach ahead into a future with a more open society, will assert moral claims based on the need for human rights, equitable social inclusion, and individual freedom. The unending debate over how to create the best society is often underpinned by moral claims.

In the global East, moral regulation takes the form of authoritative claims, as expressed in the following media report.

> New Islamic criminal laws that took effect in Brunei ... punishing gay sex and adultery by stoning offenders to death, have triggered an outcry from countries, rights groups and celebrities far beyond the tiny Southeast Asian nation's shores ... "I want to see Islamic teachings in this country grow stronger," said Sultan Hassanal Bolkiah (Liang, 2019).

In the global West, moral regulation could take other forms that involve attempts at asserting the morals of one group over and above the rights of others. The historic Canadian example regarding the treatment of homosexuals being seen as a threat to national security during the Cold War is a case in point.

> In the 1950s and '60s, homosexuality is considered by many to be a horrible, shameful defect. With the Cold War in full swing, the Canadian government fears that closeted gays in the civil service, military or RCMP are a security risk—if their homosexuality was to be discovered by the enemy, they could be blackmailed into giving up government secrets. So the RCMP embarks on a mission to find and remove all gays from the civil service. They even have a so-called "fruit machine" to test for homosexuality (CBC News, 2005).

Box 5.1: Theories of Moral Regulation from Émile Durkheim to Michel Foucault

In Chapters 1 and 2, you were introduced to the concept of moral regulation as a social process theorized by Émile Durkheim, who explained how the stable functioning of society requires that the majority of people voluntarily consent to the shared values and morals of their society. In doing so, people agree as a group to regulate and restrain their conduct so that there is cohesive social solidarity and a more stable social order based on conformity to established communal norms. Since Durkheim, the field of moral regulation studies has developed into a unique area of research within criminology and beyond (Brock et al., 2014; Drahos, 2017). However, there has been substantial debate within the field as not all theorists of morality understand it as a unifying social force.

The critique of morality as an instrument of domination extends back to at least the philosophy of Friedrich Nietzsche, who maintained that "morality is the best of all devices for leading mankind by the nose!" (1895/2010, p. 57), adding to his earlier observation that "fear is again the mother of morals" (1886/1989, p. 113). For Nietzsche, the moral values imposed on European Christians in the early modern era served to weaken the population into subservience under the rule of hypocritical authorities who used guilt, moral shame, and fear to regulate the populations they ruled. Nietzsche identified religion as the primary institution that furnished the authoritative claims about what is good and what is evil. He examined how those in positions of political office would use religious categories of good versus evil to further their own agendas and increase their powers. Such ideas about morality and institutional control as the basis of modern power relations would later be developed by Michel Foucault, who owed his intellectual debt to Nietzsche and to Max Weber. Foucault would later go on to develop his own analysis of social regulation through the development of various concepts such as **biopower** and the **disciplinary society**—all of which remain central to contemporary criminology and legal theory and to the study of social and moral regulation.

Moral regulation often conflicts with the pursuit of human rights. When the morally based rules for how to live one's life come into conflict with the moral imperatives of another group, we see a typical example of competing human rights claims. Not every member of society is able or willing to conform to the established, traditional moral codes of the dominant group, nor does one single set of moral values promote individual freedom for all types of people. As they have done throughout history, people will deviate from prescribed morals, norms, and codes of behaviour. People will consume illegal drugs, drive a vehicle under the influence of alcohol, sell or purchase sexual services, or engage in extra-marital affairs, knowing full well that such behaviours may be forbidden. Certain examples of moral transgression illustrate that some moral regulations are generally accepted because violating them can present potential harm to others. What you have read thus far in this chapter should tell you that while there is public consensus on *some* morally based restrictions (such as prohibitions against murder and pedophilia), there is a lack of consensus on others (such as recreational drug use, abortion, and the sale and purchase sexual services).

Many people disagree with the dominant moral values of society, and those in power often pass laws that reflect and protect their own sets of moral values, which can and has historically resulted in the criminalization of difference. Moral regulation can move from something intended to produce social cohesion to something that operates as a form of repressive social control. What is relevant for criminology is how prejudicial moral values, such as a disdain for premarital sex or the stigma against those who engage in the recreational use of certain consciousness-altering substances (among other issues discussed in this chapter), move beyond *soft* forms of social control, such as shaming and social exclusion, to become regulated through *hard* forms of control such as criminal law sanctions and formal punishment. It is also important to note that moral judgments are not objective ideals. They can vary widely among cultures and places and can change with historical circumstances. For example, just over a century ago, many people believed it was morally acceptable to own and trade other human beings as property in the form of slaves. That practice is now widely seen as reprehensible and immoral (although it continues in different forms currently), and laws are in place that forbid it. Today there are problematic practices that are being challenged collectively, such as sexual assault, racism, caste systems, and other forms of oppressive discrimination that continue despite laws in place against them. Moral standards change, but some moral ideals run deep, and they continue to influence the categories of crime and deviance.

In the words of scholars ...

Moral regulation projects are an interesting and significant form of politics in which some people act to problematize the conduct, values, or culture of others and seek to impose regulation upon them.

Alan Hunt, *Governing Morals: A Social History of Moral Regulation.* 1999

VARIETIES OF VICE: THE REGULATION OF MORALITY AND CRIME

How have law and policing been used to reinforce a repressive moral order? What is a morality squad? Why are some so-called victimless crimes prosecuted while other harmful activities are not? What do these contradictions reveal about the nature of power relations in our society? Such questions continue to inform the ongoing activist struggle to address systemic harms and wrongdoings in our society. The next section of this chapter will examine some of the history and developments that have marked changes in vice crimes, as well as the ongoing struggle to address forms of injustice that emerge when the rigid moral values and laws of the dominant group are forcibly imposed on those who reject them.

SEXUAL REGULATION, PROSTITUTION, AND SEX-TRADE WORK

Although in Canada prostitution has never been a crime in and of itself, the moral regulation of this activity dates back prior to Confederation (Brock, 2000). A Nova Scotia Act of 1759 regarding houses of corrections and workhouses was the first legislation allowing imprisonment for what was deemed *lewd* behaviour. Despite social norms discouraging extra-marital sexual relations, early laws dealing with this type of behaviour initially aimed to curtail disorderly conduct more generally and limit its effects on the population (i.e., public nuisance and diseases). These laws included different aspects of the sex trade, such as operating brothels, procuring and living on the avails of prostitution, or soliciting. However, most regulations have been centred on the latter due, in part, to negative judgment about people engaging in sex-trade work against accepted codes of sexual conduct and gender roles. As a result, people selling sexual services, particularly women, have suffered greater legal repercussions despite the declared intent from legislators to punish exploiters. In recent years, prostitution laws have been challenged, including under the *Charter of Rights and Freedoms* in Canada, while there has been a growing movement to recognize the rights of sexual workers through policy and societal change.

A Brief History of Prostitution Laws in Canada

Prostitution practices expanded in Canada in the 1800s with the establishment of brothels, but repression at the time mainly occurred in relation to other criminal or socially reproved activities, often linked to drinking and gambling. Nevertheless, arbitrary enforcement of provisions designed to remove indigents and undesirables under the British 1824 *Vagrancy Act* meant people who ran, frequented, or worked in brothels or street walked could be detained. Police sporadically took action to quell concern or outrage when prostitution was seen more as a threat to morality than necessary to local economic and social conditions (McLaren, 1986). Yet pressure for stronger control grew as Victorian mores influenced campaigns for *social purity* and *sexual continence*—both of which are reflective of moral correctness. In view of the perceived moral dangers brought on by urbanization and industrialization in Western countries, attitudes towards children and women started to change, focusing in particular on protecting female sexual passivity from male impulses in order to uphold a righteous social code. The spectre of white slavery was used to induce support around anecdotes of youths being coerced or deceived into a life of wickedness. But men in power opposed further regulation of prostitution, which they regarded as a necessary evil protecting middle-class female virtue as well as their own class' privileges (Parker, 1983). Thus, reform was primarily concerned with the "fallen" woman whose individual character was blamed for their downfall. As Harrison writes,

> The knowledge that enormous numbers of people were compelled by sheer poverty to sell themselves was understandably unacceptable to that class which profited by their very deprivation and which relied on their availability as an outlet for its illicit sexuality. The myths were therefore required to serve two causes: they had to disguise the disturbing economic facts of prostitution by providing plausible causes for its existence other than bald penury, and they had to ensure that the blame and punishment for the moral delinquency involved were seen to rebound not on the client but on the prostitute (1977, pp. 250–251).

After Confederation, what was termed *defilement* of women under the age of 21 became prohibited in 1867, and vagrancy provisions were extended to include men living on the avails of prostitution in 1869. These provisions were integrated into the *Criminal Code* in 1892, making it also an offence to procure women "for unlawful carnal connection." The laws relating to procuring and living on the avails of prostitution continued to be amended over the next decades, supported by social purists, the temperance movement, and religious organizations. However, these legal objectives were not heavily enforced as only a few men were prosecuted under the avails and procurement laws, and historical records show far more convictions registered against women in relation to brothels (Lacasse, 1994; McLaren, 1986).

This contributed to moving prostitution activities towards the streets, in a cycle repeated many times over.

From the 1960s through the 1980s, changing values and the **sexual revolution** led to changes in moral regulations. In 1967, *The Criminal Law Amendment Act* or C-195 significantly modified the *Criminal Code* of Canada, in particular by decriminalizing homosexual acts performed in private. Although Justice Minister Pierre Trudeau then famously said, "there's no place for the state in the bedrooms of the nation," this view about relations between adults did not apply to visible signs of sexual activities still considered as deviant (CBC News, 1967). The sex industry and the gay community continued to experience repression, especially following actions such as the so-called clean-up of downtown Montreal in the 1970s, which targeted gay bars where men were arrested on charges of being found in a common bawdyhouse. In Toronto, the sexual assault and murder of a young boy by three men in a massage parlour on Yonge Street in July 1977 triggered a severe crackdown through police raids on massage parlours and strip clubs, which resulted in the arrests of owners, employees, and some patrons on charges related to prostitution or operating brothels (although most of the charges did not proceed). The continued pressure of police action and the application of municipal regulations previously ignored meant many businesses closed and relocated to less visible areas. Sex workers turning to the streets then became targets of policing activity. Some members of the gay community also became targets of morality-based policing, leading to the bathhouse raids of 1981, in which hundreds of men were arrested (Gollom, 2016).

The Debate around Sex-Trade Work

During the social upheaval of the 1960s and in the following decades, different views prompted public debate on prostitution. Complaints about public nuisances related to street-based activities called for a strengthening of the laws on soliciting for prostitution. Conversely, **second-wave feminism** pushed forward social reforms to fight sexual exploitation and violence and avoid the criminalization of women working in the sex industry. Discrimination in Canada's vagrancy laws was criticized, notably in the 1970 Report of the Royal Commission on the Status of Women, as these laws criminalized the status of "being a common prostitute" (rather than the behaviours associated with prostitution) and were applied overwhelmingly to women. This vagrancy provision was amended in 1972 to soliciting, defined as a gender-neutral offence based on an act; nevertheless, it rapidly came under scrutiny. Reviewing its interpretation, the Supreme Court declared in

1978 that such an activity must be importuning or "pressing or persistent," rather than simply based on indications that a person is willing to engage in prostitution (*R v Hutt*, 1978). In 1985, the federal government appointed a Special Committee on Pornography and Prostitution (the Fraser Committee), which recommended broad social and legal reforms but still favoured strong criminal sanctions against street prostitution. The vagrancy provision was repealed in 1985, replaced by a law barring communicating in public for the purposes of prostitution. This law was also challenged on several grounds, in particular freedom of expression under the Canadian *Charter of Rights and Freedoms*. Yet the Supreme Court found in 1990 that eliminating prostitution was a valid social goal justifying such a violation. Throughout the 1990s, multiple cities enacted zoning and licensing bylaws to limit local sex industries (e.g., escort services, exotic entertainers, and massage parlours), while also trying to control streetwalking, directly or indirectly, by using jaywalking and loitering bylaws (Robertson, 2003; van der Meulen & Valverde, 2013). While recognizing that the sex trade was the result of a patriarchal order, these measures nevertheless maintained the perception of this industry as a social evil, stigmatizing sex-trade workers in the process.

The debate thus endured as new advocacy groups were formed in the early 1980s, including the Canadian Organization for the Rights of Prostitutes (CORP) in Toronto and the Alliance for the Safety of Prostitutes (ASP) in Vancouver. These groups brought attention to the surge of cases related to prostitution offences, which went from 5 to 40 per 100,000 after the implementation of the 1985 law barring communication and pointed out that enforcement practices continued to penalize women more often and more severely (Rotenberg, 2016). These organizations were part of the emerging **sex-positive movement**, bringing together sex workers and members of the LGBTQ+ community, among others, to oppose legal or social control over the sexual activities of consenting adults. These activists questioned the vision born out of second-wave feminism of people engaging in sex work as solely victims; rather, they posed that prostitution, or pornography, can be a choice rather than a form of sexual exploitation (which can never be considered a voluntary act). Furthermore, the influence of **third-wave feminism** encouraged people to recognize diverse racial, cultural, and gender identities, as well as experiences marked by discrimination and inequality on different levels, such as for First Nations and LGBTQ+ people.

As actions were taken to promote sex workers' rights and agency, health and safety issues came to the forefront. Violence, particularly against street-based workers, grew dramatically in the 1990s due to the marginalization and displacement of sex work activities (van der Meulen et al., 2013). The media reported on a situation in the Downtown Eastside of Vancouver, where more than 60 women went missing. The case of Robert Pickton, who was arrested in 2002 and charged with the murders of 26 women, highlighted the issue of violence against sex-trade workers. A Vancouver advocacy group, Pivot, documented the harms associated with the criminalization of sex work (Pivot Legal Society Sex Work Subcommittee, 2004). It claimed that such criminalization made those laws unconstitutional and recommended repealing them to improve sex workers' safety. A sub-committee of the federal Standing Committee on Justice and Human rights was mandated in 2003 to review the laws to improve sex workers' and communities' safety. But no changes occurred, and two legal cases emerged in the next decade launched by sex workers in Toronto and Vancouver. These challenges were successful in 2013 when a unanimous Supreme Court ruling struck down the three provisions at issue: prohibitions against living off the avails of prostitution, keeping a bawdyhouse, and communication. All of these provisions were considered to be overbroad and prevented prostitutes from taking measures to ensure their own protection. As such, the court found that the provisions contributed to the risks to the health, safety, and lives of prostitutes and therefore violated sex workers' rights to security of the person under the *Charter of Rights and Freedoms*. Here, a distinction was established between objective measurable damage and subjective disapproval, known as **legal moralism**, and the legislative objectives of reducing nuisance and harm were determined to be largely exceeded by the detrimental effects of these provisions.

Although the decision to invalidate these provisions constituted a victory for some sex-trade workers, opposition remained. The federal authorities, rather than decriminalize activities surrounding sex-trade work, reframed the issue as a form of sexual exploitation that disproportionately and negatively impacts women and girls. The Harper government introduced *The Protection of Communities and Exploited Persons Act* in 2014, inspired by the **Nordic model** of *asymmetrical criminalization*, which targets the purchase but not the sale of sexual services. The act declares that "exploitation is inherent in prostitution" and prohibits promoting or advertising for the sale of sexual services, receiving a financial or material benefit from the prostitution of others, and procuring or buying sexual services. Provisions also include a prohibition on communicating for the purpose of buying sexual services and doing so for selling such services when in a public place or in any place open to public view. This change of paradigm, again focused on *exploiters*, aligned with conservative moral values (and, ironically, radical feminism) in its overall aim to eradicate prostitution. However, according to several advocacy groups, the new law did not resolve the situation and even exacerbated it. It is important to note the paradox of provisions that make the legal practise of prostitution virtually impossible, and therefore more clandestine, contrary to the objective of making social support services more accessible to victims of exploitation. According to another Pivot report, the legislation has resulted in the sweeping criminalization of the sex industry replicating risks to sex workers' health and safety and violating their constitutional rights (Pivot Legal Society, 2016). The death of Marylène Lévesque, killed in a hotel room in January 2020, was denounced by Stella, a Montreal-based organization, as an example of the harms of sex workers being pushed to compromise safety to avoid detection, effectively becoming "invisible." Under the new legislation, then, sex workers again bear the brunt of legal moralism.

Security and Equity for Sex Workers as a Human Rights Issue

Due to activism, sex-trade work is now well entrenched in human rights debates, even as the distinction with sex trafficking remains an issue. Moral entrepreneurs who equate sex work to trafficking contribute to moral panic about the recruitment of minors as sexually enslaved persons, which is far from the reality. Although most victims of sex trafficking are youths and migrants, they do not represent most of the sex-trade industry. In Canada, police statistics indicate that a small percentage of those charged with prostitution activities are youths (2% in 2014), while studies show a majority of women work for themselves in more tolerant cities (Toronto, Vancouver, Montreal) compared to the Maritimes and the Prairies where organized crime and pimps have more influence (Rotenberg, 2016; Shaver, 2005). Furthermore, limited resources of law agencies have led to varied enforcement across the country. In Quebec, for example, practices have maintained the previous focus on protection of minors (through denunciations) and on prostitution rings, rather than on individual exchanges of services: 233 clients were arrested between 2014 and 2017, as opposed to 314 in Edmonton in 2017 alone (Bilodeau, 2019). Rather than conflating sex work and trafficking, it is argued that actions should aim to prosecute cases of violence and coercive labour with existing laws (i.e., offences against the person and human trafficking provisions in the *Criminal Code* and the *Immigration and Refugee Protection Act*). Rather than helping sex workers, this conflation between the nature of sex work and its operating conditions serves as a strategy to advance a neo-abolitionist agenda, which obfuscates aspects of sex work organization and migration work that have to do with different labour and human rights issues (Toupin, 2006; Wijers & Lap-Chew, 1997). This is observed even in countries with more tolerant legislation, such as the Netherlands, with regulations and repression making it more difficult for sex workers to work independently.

From a moral standpoint, the question of access to sexual services is still contentious. Normative codes related to sex and gender continue to influence authorities and public responses to old and new practices. For instance, companies offering sex dolls for rent were deemed to contravene bylaws in Western Canada, while an effort to open a sex doll brothel in Texas in 2018 was also reproved (Martin, 2018). Pro sex-trade activists ask whether access to sexual services should be considered a right, as in the case of *sexual surrogates* for those without access to sexual partners due to certain conditions or disabilities. Some scholars and advocates have been seeking to demonstrate that legalizing prostitution does not necessarily mean reinforcing exploitation and may in fact be a better way to recognize and protect sex workers' rights. The cases of Germany, New Zealand, and Switzerland, among others, where barriers to access health and social services, workplace protection regimes and unionization, and the justice system have been removed, do not reveal an increase in criminality relating to sex work. This can prove essential in crisis situations, as it was for New Zealand sex workers, who, during lockdowns due to the COVID-19 pandemic, had access to emergency wage subsidy and job seekers' benefits, while those relegated to the informal economy in other countries struggled for survival.

In many nations around the world, exploitation is present in sex-trade work and requires efforts to address specific challenges in areas ranging from power and gender relations to immigration and access to justice. It is possible to ask whether the continued exclusion or marginalization of the sex-trade sector, as with others in which workers are mostly women and racial and sexual minorities, is a form of indirect discrimination and domination (Toupin, 2006). Rather than being understood as a moral issue, sex-trade work needs to be seen as shaped by multiple political, legal, economic, and social forces. Shifting the emphasis from morality-based law enforcement to community intervention would help develop sex-trade work policy based on an intersectional approach that addresses issues at the root of social inequalities affecting women and minorities without further marginalizing, disenfranchising, and endangering them. A human rights framework has the potential to provide choice and safety for all sex workers and include their perspectives in future law and policy reform.

SEXUAL ASSAULT, MORAL SHAMING, AND BACKWARDS RAPE LAWS AROUND THE WORLD

Sexualized violence against women and girls remains pervasive worldwide. Feminist scholars and other activists have advanced the concept of a *rape culture* to draw attention to the global prevalence of **sexual assault** as well as the lack of meaningful action from criminal justice systems to adequately prosecute perpetrators of violence against women and girls. Although the concept of rape culture has often been disputed as too encompassing in the sense that society as a whole does not enable a few individual rapists, critics such as Parenti point out that nevertheless "in many parts of the world, rape is accepted as an everyday occurrence and even a male prerogative" (2006, p. 71). Seen from this perspective, rape is an extension of patriarchal hegemony. Recent developments such as the #MeToo movement (circa 2017) have called attention to the extent of the phenomena of sexualized violence and harassment.

Academic research on rape, sexual assault, and women's rights have often focused on the Western world; however, more recently there has been growing awareness and activism regarding rape in South Asia since the 2010s. A CTV News article reports, "India has been shaken by a series of sexual assaults since 2012, when a student was gang-raped and murdered on a moving New Delhi bus. That attack galvanized a country where widespread violence against women had long been quietly accepted" (Associated Press, 2018). Notable cases in which calls for justice intensified include the arrest of 14 people allegedly involved in the kidnapping, rape, and burning to death of a teenage girl in 2018. In September 2020 in Lahore, Pakistan, a woman accompanied by her two children ran out of gas in her car and while phoning for help was pulled by two men from her vehicle to a nearby field, where she was gang-raped (Farooq, 2020). A BBC News article reports,

> when a top police official, charged with finding the attackers, implied the victim had been partly to blame for being out after dark alone, it ignited fury. Comments that previously may not have been publicly questioned are now being called out as victim-blaming: "Blaming the victim, judging a woman's character to determine whether she was a victim; these are rooted in our society for decades," says Moneeza Ahmed, who is part of a feminist collective (2020b).

Several countries in the region have outlawed virginity tests, a contested medical examination of a woman's hymen used with or without consent in rape cases or when a woman is accused of a moral crime such as premarital sex; however, the World Health Organization (WHO, 2018) indicated that the practice was still in place in 20 countries. These tests are "part of a larger structure of patriarchy that hinges victimhood on women's characters and perpetuates the myth of the 'perfect victim,'" notes Nighat Dad, a lawyer and rights activist (Janjua, 2021).

Within a culture of rape, erroneous beliefs regarding sex and gender are perpetuated (Burt, 1980), including *rape myths*, defined as "an inaccurate and/or stereotypical attitude or belief regarding sexual violence and victims of sexual violence" (Lyon & Welsh, 2017, p. 297). Rape myths are often legitimized not only within the family, culture, education, or media but also within the operations of criminal justice systems. Rape myths manifest in various forms of victim blaming, such as claims that women lie about being victims of sexual assault, women "ask for it" by wearing revealing clothing or wearing red nail polish, women say no and mean yes, and through the perception that only certain types of sexual activity (e.g., sexual acts with penetration) constitute rape, or that sexual assault is about sexual attraction (Benedict, 1992; Burt, 1980; Lyon & Welsh, 2017). Rape myths can also influence the perception of consent (Kilimnik & Humphreys 2018); for instance, the falsehood that a sexual act would not constitute rape unless a woman fights back contributes to misunderstandings of what sexual assault—and consent—looks like. Coercion-based rape legislation (which requires coercion, violence, physical force, or threat of violence or physical force to be a feature of the assault) is still in force in many countries, as opposed to a consent-based model. Problematically, the permeation of rape myths within our society has "led to a public misunderstanding of what constitutes rape and sexual assault" (p. 197). If a sexual assault does not meet the social expectation of what sexual assault should look like, as identified within the rape myth scripts, the victim is less likely to define their sexual assault as such and to self-identify as a victim. These sorts of misperceptions create legal system complications that make the prosecution of those who perpetrate sexual assault difficult. The 2016 Canadian trial of Jian Ghomeshi, a prominent radio personality charged with sexual assault and subsequently found not guilty, presented misconceptions regarding the relationships between him and the three complainants and offers a clear example of how the adversarial legal system is ill-equipped to address cases of sexual assault (CBC News, 2016b). A 2016 CBC News article reports that there are "460,000 sex assaults annually; for every 1,000 incidents, 33 are reported, 12 result in charges, 6 go to trial, and 3 lead to a conviction" (2016a). Although there has been a small increase in the reporting rate since then, there has been increased advocacy to explore other processes to address sexual assault, such as restorative justice (Wemmers, 2020).

Other examples of sexual assault cases nevertheless serve to illustrate the persistence of a global rape culture, which promotes rape myths and affects victims' standing in legal proceedings. In Italy, judges found two men not guilty in a case of rape as they agreed that the woman was "too masculine" and therefore too unattractive to have been a victim of sexual assault (Tamkin, 2019). Winfield (2019) pointed out that the victim's credibility as a witness was questioned because of her appearance; the judges could not accept that she was a victim of sexual assault because she did not fit with the typical sexual assault script that rape is about sex with attractive women. In Canada, a federal court judge faced consequences from the Canadian Justice Council after making inappropriate comments to a victim of sexual assault. As a provincial court judge, he questioned the credibility of the victim, whom he often referred to as the accused, and told the woman "pain and sex sometimes go together," in addition to asking her "Why couldn't you just keep your knees together?" (Associated Press, 2016). The judge did not believe the woman was sexually assaulted because she did not fight back. In this and the Italian case examples, the judges incorrectly equated sexual assault with sex and pleasure, as opposed to violence and power over another person. Furthermore, the blame for the sexual assault and the management of victimization was shifted away from the offender and onto the victim, ignoring the abundance of research evidence that suggests such an approach results in further victimization by the court process itself (Johnson, 2017; Larcombe et al., 2016).

Blame-shifting was also apparent in one of the first major Canadian cases since the #MeToo movement, when Matthew McKnight was charged with 13 counts of sexual assault against 13 women (Pruden, 2020). Challenges for the criminal justice system in this case included the lack of forensic evidence and the fact that the victims had been drinking and had poor recall of the events, with some believing they had been drugged and others indicating that they may have been flirting with or accepted drinks from McKnight. Benedict pointed out how some of these characteristics construct the victim as a "vamp," which impacts their credibility in the eyes of the criminal justice system. The woman is likely to be labelled as such if she knows the assailant, if they are of the same race/class/ethic group, if no weapon is used, if she is young/pretty, and if she in any way deviated from the traditional female role of modesty and moral virtue (1992, p. 19). Defence lawyer Bottos used these rape myths, suggesting that the women were lying or that they had "buyer's remorse" about their sexual encounter with McKnight (Pruden, 2020). Similar arguments were used by defence lawyers in the cases of Jian Ghomeshi in 2016 and Harvey Weinstein in 2020 (BBC News, 2020a). These proceedings resulted in acquittal or partial guilty verdicts due to the perception of the evidence provided by the victims as unreliable.

Another deeply troubling criminal justice system response to sexual assault has been "marry-your-rapist" laws, which allow perpetrators to avoid prosecution if they marry the rape victim. While these laws became increasingly uncommon in the 1970s, they still exist in several countries in Africa, Latin America, the Middle East, and Asia. Such provisions continue to shield perpetrators in cases of statutory rape (relations with minors). The practice also persists in places where it is not recognized by law but remains as a cultural tradition associated with honour. For example, Gowen (2015) describes how a judge advised a sexual assault victim to "mediate" with their offender, in a case that reflected historical Indian laws requiring women to marry their offenders, particularly if the victim becomes pregnant. There has been support in other countries, such as Turkey, Jordan, Tunisia, and Lebanon, for women to marry their offenders as a means to "save them" and their child from the shame and stigma of sexual assault (Gupta, 2020; Krishnan, 2020). These practices have been linked to moral values regarding female virginity and family honour and are often representative of a patriarchal culture (Gowen, 2015; Gupta, 2020; Krishnan, 2020).

While awareness of the effects of a global rape culture is increasing, moral attitudes regarding sexuality and gender perpetuate biases against victims of sexual assaults. These attitudes impact criminal justice processes at every level. In Canada, the "Unfounded" series by the *Globe and Mail* focused on sexual assault cases that were dismissed as supposedly unsubstantiated. The series revealed the varying consideration given to victims' allegations by police forces, noting a trend towards lesser charges and sentences, despite Canada having one of the most progressive sexual assault laws in the developed world (Doolittle, 2017, 2019). Beyond the understanding of consent, it is essential that gender relations and social inequalities be addressed outside of courts to bring about change.

Sexualized violence against women and girls is firmly entrenched in cultures of honour and shame. As Parenti notes, "in some places rape is considered a crime not by a man against a woman but by a woman against her family's honor" (2006, p. 73). In many instances around the world, women are assaulted and raped as punishment for something one of their relatives is alleged to have done, for other social and economic purposes such as land ownership, or simply because they are women and therefore not granted the same moral and legal standing as men. It is important to note how both the act of sexual assault and the social and legal responses to it are influenced by a tradition of moral regulation and patriarchal attitudes that come to influence justice system outcomes.

Moral Regulation as Violence and Misogyny

Female genital mutilation (BBC News, 2019; Rahman & Toubia, 2000), **honour killing** (Barmaki, 2019; Sev'er & Yurdakul, 2001), in-the-face **acid attacks** against females (Ahmad, 2012; Canadian Press, 2017), female infanticide

(DTE Staff, 2016), and the deliberate gender-selective femicide of female fetuses (Holmes, 2016) are just some examples of violent actions perpetrated against females under the guise of moral righteousness and cultural **misogyny**. Violent forms of control over the lives and bodies of women and girls have long been a fundamental aspect of female oppression in patriarchal societies. Aside from direct forms of physical violence, the use of moral codes of right and wrong has also justified various forms of gender-based violations of rights and freedoms, such as social shaming, forced marriage, child brides, and patriarchal divorce customs that restrict the rights of women to leave their abusive husbands. In this chapter thus far, we have seen that moral regulation is often centred on the control over a person's freedoms, which includes the sexual freedom of women. As Foucault noted, the regulation of sexuality is a fundamental strategy that institutions use as part of an overall strategy of social control. Under normative conditions, "sex is placed by power in a binary system: licit and illicit, permitted and forbidden" (1980/1990, p. 83); further, "sexuality … is involved … [in] the most varied strategies [including] … a hysterization of women's bodies" (p. 103–104). Since patriarchal society privileges the power, status, and sexual dominance of heterosexual males, it is predominantly females who suffer the pains of repressive moral regulation, especially in the realm of sexuality.

The moral regulation of females has historically been justified primarily through the cultural values of shame, (dis)honour, respect, reputation, and social status. In numerous traditionally patriarchal societies, women are expected to maintain their sexual honour for the duration of their lives. They are also expected to protect the honour of other women and girls related to them, as are the men (husbands and brothers in particular) who are tasked with sanctioning female relatives who deviate from prescribed moral standards, since that deviation will reflect shamefully on men's status (Sev'er & Yurdakul, 2001). A violation of the strict moral codes that govern women's honour can become the basis for violent retribution or banishment, often directly supported by custom or law (Schmidt, 2017).

In times of war, women who are raped by enemy soldiers are often abandoned by their families for bearing the seeds of the enemy and bringing shame to the family. Commenting on the fate of women raped in the Russian–Chechen war of 1999–2009, a Geneva Centre report quotes, "a sullied daughter is worse than a dead one to her father. It's a terrible disgrace. She'll never get married and no one will say a kind word to her, even though it is not her own fault that she was dishonoured" (Prochazkova, as cited in Slim, 2008, p. 66). Another heinous example of punishing females for moral code violations is the practice of honour killing. As Sev'er and Yurdakul note, drawing on the work of Amnesty International and Pervizat, "an *honor killing* is a generic term used to refer to the premeditated murder of preadolescent, adolescent, or adult women by one or more male members of the immediate or extended family. These killings are often undertaken when a family council decides on the time and form of execution due to an allegation, suspicion, or proof of sexual impropriety by the victim" (2001, p. 297).

As Sev'er and Yurdakul write, "Honor killings are one extreme in the worldwide patriarchal violence against women. They also occur in better established, developing, democratic, and secular states, and regretfully the incidence of such killings may be on the rise" (2001, p. 298). Honour killings take a number of forms beyond the typical example of killing women for code violations. The United Nations Office on Drugs and Crime (UNODC) notes data on honour killings are scarce, as such crimes often go unrecorded and unreported (2018, p. 31). Common examples of honour killings are "raped women who kill their rapists; mothers who kill infants that they conceived or gave birth to out of wedlock; and families (females included) who kill their daughters because they had sexual relations out of wedlock (in some cases even if they were forcefully raped)" (Barmaki, 2019, pp. 2–3).

Throughout history, women who failed to conform to the strict moral codes of patriarchy have often been the subject of severe sanctions that have been used to regulate their life choices and options (Lerner, 1986). The legacy of female shaming on the basis of sexual impropriety continues today in the many sexist slurs that are used to stigmatize and guilt women who fail to conform to restrictive patriarchal codes of behaviour. Terms like *whore*, *slut*, *witch*, and *bitch* are commonly used to denigrate women's character, yet one would be hard pressed to find similar terms that refer to male sexual impropriety as a measure of their character.

The conception of the powerful woman as a dangerous threat to the social order has a long history to it—one that emerged approximately 5,000 years ago with the campaign to suppress the status of women alongside the advance of the patriarchal order (Lerner, 1986). In the mythologies of many patriarchal cultures, women have been cast as monstrous beings, as evil temptresses and witches. In the biblical context, the female character is charged with being the source of *original sin* through the figure of Eve who, in her quest for knowledge, was held responsible for the downfall of humankind and cursed by God. Classical Western mythology also reproduces a narrative of feminine evil where many of the dangerous monsters (such as Medusa and the Sirens) are female figures. Citing historical examples, Davis and Stasz suggest the category of female has been designated as the *deviant gender* (1990, p. 217). Subsequently, women have been characterized as deceitful, as temptresses and seducers, and thus in need of especially strict regulation and control. Despite progress on women's rights, the ancient categories of madonna/virgin (emphasizing sexual modesty and virginal purity) and whore/slut (characterized by shameful, dishonourable, or dangerous behaviour) remain active in modern society—"a woman's *moral* violations … more upset society than her criminal ones" (Davis & Stasz, 1990, p. 213). This has greatly influenced perceptions of female deviance by the justice system, from witchcraft bans to the regulation of prostitution to cases of infanticide or spousal homicide where postpartum depression and battered woman syndrome are still not always recognized as valid legal defences. Various forms of social shaming are inflicted upon non-conforming females, and patriarchal values persist in law and cultural custom, from various forms of restriction and criminalization of abortion to discriminating dress codes. These serve as examples of the types of repressive moral regulation that continue to inform the basis of activist change and progressive policy formation towards greater gender equity and the promotion of women's rights (Nicholson, 2019).

In the words of scholars …

The system of patriarchy can function only with the cooperation of women. This cooperation is secured by a variety of means: gender indoctrination; educational deprivation; the denial to women of knowledge of their history; the dividing of women, one from the other, by defining "respectability" and "deviance" according to women's sexual activities; by restraints and outright coercion; by discrimination in access to economic resources and political power; and by awarding class privileges to conforming women.

Gerda Lerner, *The Creation of Patriarchy.* 1986

GAMBLING: FROM MORAL VICE TO STATE MONOPOLY

Gambling in casinos and buying lottery tickets are examples of how moral categories of right and wrong are directly tied to legal constructs of crime. Gambling was once considered a *moral **sin*** or **vice**; now it has become into a normal entertainment practice and legitimate source of profit generation by the state and other selected groups. How has this transformation come about? What social forces have led to the redefinition of gambling as acceptable leisure behaviour? Why do some forms of gambling remain illegal while other forms are allowed to prosper and are even promoted? Why is gambling now referred to in Canada as "gaming"?

The varying legal status of gambling throughout Canadian history is a fascinating—and very revealing—case study. The earliest gambling-related legislation prior to Confederation was derived from English law. It focused on the criminalization of dice games and gaming houses and also prohibited gambling by particular groups, such as servants (Smith, 2012, p. 289). Around the time of Confederation in 1867, English gambling law continued to apply in Canada (Smith, 2012, p. 289); notably, by this time, lotteries were frowned upon in England and therefore were prohibited in Canada.

The originally enacted version of the *Criminal Code of Canada*, from 1892, included a number of gambling offences under a section entitled "Offenses against Religion, Morals, and Public Convenience" (Campbell et al., 2005, p. 13). Over time, many changes were made to the *Criminal Code* in relation to aspects of gambling. For instance, in 1910, legal betting was limited to horse racetracks, though in 1917, in the midst of World War I, an order-in-council suspended betting because it was "incommensurate" with the war effort (p. 14). Horse-race betting was permitted again beginning in 1920, though in 1922 a criminal prohibition on betting on dice games, shell games, and other games was introduced (p. 14). By 1925, however, certain games of chance played for money were allowed at agricultural fairs and exhibitions (p. 14). In 1954, a confidence game referred to as "three-card Monte" (which is essentially a card-game equivalent to a shell game) was criminalized and remains prohibited to the present day (p. 14).

A significant change occurred in 1969, when the *Criminal Code* was amended by the Liberal government of Pierre Trudeau to allow federal and provincial governments to conduct lotteries (Campbell et al., 2005, p. 14). Charitable gambling using provincial licences was also expanded (p. 14). For the next decade and a half, the federal government and provincial governments competed for lottery revenues (pp. 15–16). Finally, in 1985, the Canadian Conservative government announced that it had reached an agreement with the provinces; in exchange for a one-time payment from the provinces to the federal government of $100 million (which was ultimately used to fund the Calgary Olympics) plus $24 million annually after that, indexed in order to account for inflation (p. 17), the federal government agreed to amend the *Criminal Code* to grant the provinces (and their partners or other parties that are granted provincial licences) exclusive authority over lotteries as well as electronic gambling, which is itself now a thriving field and includes online gambling (Campbell, 2009, p. 79).

Most types of gambling in Canada were considered vices prior to the 1969 and 1985 *Criminal Code* amendments (Campbell et al., 2005, p. 14). Since these amendments, there has been a dramatic expansion of gambling, to the point that net government revenues from gambling amount to several billion dollars annually (Campbell et al., 2005, p. 14; Cosgrave & Klassen, 2009, p. 3). Between 1992 and 2006, the gambling industry was the fastest growing sector in the Canadian economy (Cosgrave & Klassen, 2009, p. 3). In 1998, the criminal prohibition on dice-games wagering was lifted, further broadening the scope of offerings at casinos (Campbell et al., 2005, p. 14).

The changing legal status of gambling is illustrative of the fact that moral definitions of right and wrong are **sociolegal constructs**. The ability to label particular behaviours as criminal is a reflection of power. Whereas gambling was once outlawed and considered to be a moral sin, it is now encouraged as "gaming," advertised and facilitated by the state.

The criminal law now operates in Canada to protect the provincial and territorial government **monopoly** on gambling, obtained through negotiations with the federal government, given Parliament's exclusive ability to make criminal law (Cosgrave & Klassen, 2009, p. 7). Since "legalized gambling in Canada is organized as a state monopoly … in effect Canadian gamblers gamble against—or for—the state" (p. 7). The main difficulty with this arrangement is that "the state is in a conflict of interest: it is both the regulator and the beneficiary of gambling enterprises" (p. 11), and it is using the power of criminal law to its economic advantage.

While the use of criminal law in the prohibition of gambling was once justified because gambling was seen as a social ill, in large part originally stemming from the 16th-century Protestant view of gambling as a sin (Ramp & Badgley, 2009, p. 26), in light of "the decline of Protestant value hegemony in Canada" (Cosgrave & Klassen, 2009, p. 12), it is increasingly difficult for governments to justify the use of criminal law in this area. Given these shifting social attitudes, the state can no longer point to the need to protect against moral corruption with regard to gambling. However, there are other potential justifications for legislative restrictions on gambling, such as guarding against addiction and excessive risk-taking by citizens (Mathen, 2013, pp. 361–362). These rationalizations are undermined by government's actions in promoting (and significantly benefitting from) gambling. Provincial governments have come to rely heavily on the money generated from gambling, turning this into a "*de facto* form of taxation …[which] is regressive, with the poor spending a greater percentage of their income on gambling than … the wealthy" (Cosgrave & Klassen, 2009, p. 10). Thus, despite efforts to separate gambling from perceptions of vice and harmfulness, the practice continues to have a detrimental effect primarily on those who can least afford to lose money.

While the various levels of government in Canada are also aware of **problem gambling** (stemming from addiction), it is estimated that under 3 percent of revenue generated from "problem gamblers" is spent on the prevention and treatment of gambling addiction (Cosgrave & Klassen, 2009, p. 9). Government advertisements entreating people to "play responsibly" are reminiscent of tobacco companies' anti-smoking ads or alcohol firms' "drink responsibly" ads; of course, provincial governments, tobacco companies, and alcohol companies all stand to benefit from people behaving opposite to what these ads purport to request. Moreover, gambling, tobacco, and alcohol are all potentially addictive products.

The case of gambling is an excellent reminder that crimes are legal constructions, varying considerably through time and by location, and that "there is nothing inherent in any act that makes it unlawful" (Linden, 2009, p. 18). The ability to define what is criminal behaviour is a unique power. It is legitimate to question whether using Canadian criminal law to "consolidate provincial authority over gambling as a revenue-raising instrument and to expand its availability rather than restrict it in any meaningful sense" is "an appropriate use of the criminal law function in a democratic society" (Campbell, 2009, p. 89). However, governments would likely prefer that you simply "play on!"

Box 5.2: Moral Regulation, Colonialism, and the Settler State

While moral regulation tends to enforce a patriarchal order, it also supports systems of colonial domination. *Colonialism* is defined by the *Canadian Oxford Dictionary* as "a policy of acquiring or maintaining colonies" that includes "the exploitation or subjugation of a people by a larger or wealthier power" (Barber, 2006). As Kahnawà:ke Mohawk scholar Taiaiake Alfred notes, "the basic substance of the problem of colonialism is the belief in the superiority and universality of Euroamerican culture" (2005, p. 109). This comes at a significant cost to Indigenous peoples.

In Canada, as in a handful of other countries around the world, including the US, New Zealand, and Australia, a particular subset of colonialism has endured: settler colonialism. A settler state is generally defined by "the coexistence of diverse Indigenous and migrant collectivities" (Stasiulis & Yuval-Davis, 1995, p. 1). While colonization, and the violence it brings, has been a feature of many nations the world over, the defining feature of *settler* colonialism is that the colonial powers never leave. The result is a contemporary society in which both Indigenous peoples and settlers exist, sometimes in uneasy relationship with one another, and often with a distinctive demographic imbalance. In the case of Canada, where Indigenous people make up just under 5 percent of the total population (Statistics Canada, 2017), this coexistence is also marked by a violent history of cultural genocide (Truth and Reconciliation Commission of Canada, 2015). As Stasiulis and Jhappan note, the "short history of European settler colonization" in the land now known as Canada "includes the suppression of the land, civil, political, cultural and religious rights of Aboriginal peoples whose ancestors have inhabited the land 'since time immemorial'" (1995, p. 96).

Moral regulation has played a significant role in the violence perpetrated against Indigenous peoples in Canada. The *Indian Liquor Ordinance Act* (1867) made it illegal for anyone to sell liquor to an Indigenous person in the newly formed Dominion of Canada (Mawani, 2009, p. 191), and by 1874 "for an Indian to be found in a state of intoxication became an offence punishable by imprisonment of no more than one month" (Moss & Gardner-O'Toole, 1991). Moral regulation reached into other areas of activity when, in 1876, the *Indian Act* was passed as a means of consolidating the various pieces of colonial policy related to Indigenous peoples. With the passing of the *Indian Act*, "most First Nations games as well as any form of wagering by Indigenous peoples were outlawed"; gambling was, after all, viewed as a "moral issue" by British colonizers (Smith, 2012, p. 289). Less than a decade later, the colonial government of Sir John A. Macdonald initiated a series of amendments to the *Indian Act* to ban potlatches, a ceremonial practice carried out by west coast Indigenous peoples in Canada, as well as other cultural, spiritual, and religious practices (Pettipas, 2014, p. 3). As Pettipas notes, "government officials and missionaries contended that certain Indigenous religious practices were immoral and seriously undermined the assimilative objectives of Canadian Indian policy" (p. 3). Indigenous peoples were also prohibited from purchasing and consuming alcohol.

Moral regulation extended into the 20th century, and particularly in the 1970s, with the targeting of Indigenous women by healthcare officials for coercive sterilization, abortions, and birth control at a rate higher than the non-Indigenous population (Stote, 2017, p.112). In Alberta, for instance, where a provincial *Sexual Sterilization Act* was in force from 1929 to 1972, Indigenous women made up 2 to 3 percent of the population but comprised 6 percent of all women sterilized during this timeframe (Grekul et al., 2004, p. 375).

HIGH/DRY: THE LEGAL STATUS OF DRUGS AND ALCOHOL IN CANADIAN HISTORY

Alcohol, tobacco, cannabis, caffeine, acetaminophen, ecstasy, ibuprofen, cocaine, opium, crystal methamphetamine, magic mushrooms, and heroin are just some examples of **drugs** often associated with crime. As many Canadians know, these drugs do not all have the same legal status. While the use of caffeine is extremely common, socially acceptable, and completely legal (without any requirement for a medical prescription), possession of cocaine is a significant violation of Canadian criminal law, especially if it is being possessed in order for it to be sold to others. Moral judgments about particular drugs have led to the development of laws governing the access and use of these drugs (Boyd et al., 2017, pp. 344–345). But why and how did these notions originate and spread? Why have repressive drug laws persisted despite expert advice calling for reform? And why, in certain cases (such as recent changes governing marijuana use in Canada), have laws relating to substances changed over time?

For centuries, governments have instituted laws in order to regulate the behaviour of their citizens and subjects, with a view to establishing and maintaining law and order (Kowalchuk, 1989, p. 12). Critical criminologists argue that the origins of Canadian drug laws are "based on **class conflict** and **prejudice**" (Schweighofer, 1988, p. 176). This reflects the idea that actions engaged in or deemed acceptable "to those occupying society's 'moral centre' or those speaking for its 'moral majority'" (Kowalchuk, 1989, p. 12) are considered entirely decent and legal, whereas the equivalent behaviour engaged in by those of different classes and/or racial backgrounds is often targeted and labelled as immoral and criminal by those in power (p. 12). This is an inherent contradiction, and a study of the history of Canadian drug control is indeed a study in *hypocrisy* and *contradictions* (Hackler, 2003, p. 184; Kowalchuk, 1989, p. 12).

As a result of lobbying by the highly influential **temperance movement**, the first target of drug control in Canada was alcohol, in large part because of the supposed criminality caused by alcohol consumption among members of the working class (Schweighofer, 1988, p. 175). Originally, when the first temperance society in Canada was founded in 1828, the goal of this movement was to encourage a "tempering" (rather than elimination) of alcohol consumption (p. 176). However, temperance soon became focused on "total prohibition rather than moderation" and propaganda-based moral panic spread throughout society, sowing concern that alcohol was to blame for many of society's ills, such as acts of theft and violence, as well as mental illness (p. 176). Temperance advocates were driven by a "utilitarian view that individuals had to be forced to give up pleasures and vices alike, apparently to ennoble society" (Kowalchuk, 1989, p. 12). While alcohol prohibition was briefly enacted in Canada, it lost the support of the Canadian public shortly thereafter. This was due to the fact that alcohol was, even during prohibition, a "widely used drug and it was therefore possible for most people eventually to see through the exaggerations which supported prohibition" (Schweighofer, 1988, p. 185). However, temperance ideology and the prohibition movement also targeted other drugs, particularly ones that were less commonly used by the Caucasian majority of Canada at the time (p. 186). One of Canada's first laws directed at prohibiting recreational drugs outlawed opium in 1908 (MacFarlane et al., 2018, pp. 1–3). This overtly racist legislation was "explicitly crafted to target Chinese labourers rather than to address pharmacological evidence of harm" (Maynard, 2017, p. 47). From there, drug legislation expanded "as a social consensus began to emerge about the dangers of many substances" (MacFarlane et al., 2018, pp. 1–3).

One particularly influential person in the moral crusade against drugs was Emily Murphy (1868–1933), a *moral reformer* and an Edmonton Juvenile Court judge (in fact, the first female judge in the Commonwealth). Under the pseudonym of "Janey Canuck," Judge Murphy wrote a number of sensationalist articles about substance use that were published in *Maclean's* magazine (Kowalchuk, 1989, p. 13; MacFarlane et al., 2018, pp. 1–3; Maynard, 2017, p. 47). Judge Murphy's writings culminated in the publication of the impactful 1922 text entitled *The Black Candle*, which "was instrumental in the creation of subsequent federal drug laws" (Maynard, 2017, p. 47). This book "linked drugs to the destruction of the white race," and blamed the proliferation of drugs on "Chinese men, Mexicans, and Greeks … [and furthermore,] a significant portion of the photos exhibited in the text feature[d] Black men and women" (p. 47). A chapter about marijuana, for instance, claimed that cannabis "addicts … become raving maniacs and are liable to kill or indulge in any forms of violence to other persons using the most savage methods of cruelty without … any sense of moral responsibility" (Kowalchuk, 1989, p. 13). The equating of drug use with "crime, depravity and dissolution came to monopolize middle class information and moral sentiments" (p. 13) and had a significant impact on lawmakers. In 1923, the year following the publication of Judge Murphy's book, cannabis, "hasheesh" (as it was spelled in the legislation), cocaine, and heroin were outlawed (MacFarlane et al., 2018, pp. 1–3). Drug laws became "a mechanism of legally mandated, racially motivated surveillance, harassment and incarceration for racialized persons" (Maynard, 2017, p. 47).

In the early 20th century, particularly post–World War II, corporate power interests also had a hand in the legal control of drugs; hemp (a durable fabric made from the marijuana plant) was seen as a competitive threat to other products such as nylon, which is made from petroleum (Moberly & Hartsig, 2014). The promotion of nylon depended in part on the restriction and criminalization of hemp. Pharmaceutical companies around that same time also began successful lobbying for control over the production and sale of opiates thereby initiating, in part, a campaign criminalizing herbalists who traditionally sold opioids. Opioid drugs are currently recognized as an indispensable (although potentially addictive) item in medical pharmacology (Lammers, 2011).

With one exception (cannabis), these drug prohibitions have persisted to this day. On October 17, 2018, 95 years after it first prohibited the substance, Canada "legalized" cannabis, becoming only the second country in the world to do so (MacFarlane et al., 2018, p. 1). However, "legalization is something of a relative term; what was legalized was possession and distribution of some quantities of cannabis in some places by some people and for some purposes" (p. 1).

Prohibitions related to other drugs have largely persisted because of a "self-generating lobby for maintenance of drug laws since [the system] creates employment for police, jail guards, court administrators, government departments, Crown prosecutors, defence lawyers, and judges" (Kowalchuk, 1989, p. 12). Drug control is thus an essential part of the crime control industry. The decades-long and virtually global **war on drugs** has been a crucial element of the hegemonic practice by which dominant nations exercise territorial control over impoverished nations. As Paley writes, "the creation of anti-drug police forces and army units and spending on the drug war must be understood within the context of global capitalism and global warfare. In this context, the acquisition of territory and resources, including increased control over social worlds and labour power, is a crucial motivating factor" (2014, p. 19). Special-interest groups like doctors, pharmacists, pharmaceutical companies, and petrochemical companies also potentially would stand to lose money and power if most drug prohibitions were to be eliminated (Schweighofer, 1988, p. 176). Additionally, in contrast to alcohol, the remaining prohibited drugs are not as widely consumed, so "exaggerations of the dangers of heroin, cocaine, and other illicit drugs are much harder to expose since the majority of the public have only media sensationalism to provide knowledge of today's illicit drugs" (pp. 185–186).

It is clear that prohibition-focused policies tend to generate *criminal opportunities* (and subsequently significant profits) for organized crime, lessen government revenues (through lost taxation), result in significant government expenditures (particularly on law enforcement), and create a deregulated—and consequently unsafe—drug market (Boyd et al., 2017, pp. 358–359; Kowalchuk, 1989, p. 14). When governments prohibit certain drugs, yet allow, endorse, and profit off of the consumption of other types of drugs, the credibility of not only the information being provided by government about these substances but also the criminal justice system as a whole is undermined (Kowalchuk, 1989, p. 14).

Importantly, drug addiction can have a significant negative impact on individuals and communities (Britto et al., 2018, pp. 382–383). However, there is a significant push towards a change in perception, with growing recognition that drug use may be more appropriately viewed as a public health issue rather than criminal behaviour to be policed and prosecuted (p. 383; Kowalchuk, 1989, p. 14). Canada has recently permitted the use of safe-injection sites, which focus on mitigating the harm of drug consumption and protecting users of drugs (Britto et al., 2018, p. 383). Some jurisdictions (including Portugal) have recently decriminalized most or all drug possession for personal use; tellingly, this has not led to appreciable increases in rates of drug consumption (Boyd et al., 2017, p. 360). There is some potential for this approach to be taken in North America in the coming decades. Nevertheless, the study of the history of Canadian drug legislation is a powerful reminder of the oppression and hazards stemming from popularly held notions that are grounded in moral prejudice rather than objective science and data (p. 370).

CONCLUSION

Although the subject of morality and discussions regarding *proper conduct* have long been topics of concern in philosophy and sociology, the study of how morality is regulated by law to create forms of injustice is a relatively new area of study that has come to form part of contemporary criminology. The traditional criminological concern with criminal behaviour and the identification of criminal types has transformed over time to broader concerns of issues of justice and injustice based on questioning the very analytic categories that designated certain people as criminal and others as law-abiding. Individuals who broke laws aimed at regulating sex-trade work, gambling, non-heteronormative sexual orientations, and the use of prohibited substances began, by the 1960s, to be understood not as people plagued with criminal vices that threatened the moral fabric of society and "family values" but as individuals labelled as deviant due to the prejudicial focus of criminal law. Subsequently, such categories of rule-breaking began to be studied as modes of victimization and social exclusion.

With the rise of human rights progress and social justice and equity activism in the late 20th century, criminologists with a scholarly bias in favour of social progress began to understand how moral regulation is fundamentally about social control. Such scholars consider the ways in which morality can be imposed on others as a strategy of power and as a way of designating as deviant people who embrace non-conformist lifestyles that violate traditional morality norms and laws. While in some nations substantial progress has been made and new freedoms recognized that initiated changes in restrictive laws and oppressive policing practices, the repressive regulation of morality in various ways worldwide continues to be a social problem in conflict with the larger global goal of egalitarian justice, cosmopolitanism, and the quest for universal human rights.

REVIEW QUESTIONS

1. What is meant by the concept of moral regulation and how does morality influence the history of law and crime?
2. What types of vice crimes do you think present the greatest challenges from a justice and human rights perspective and why?
3. What role does patriarchy play in the regulation of morality?

GLOSSARY

acid attacks: A type of violent attack characterized by the throwing of a corrosive substance usually on the face of the victim that results in extreme physical damage such as disfiguration, blindness, and potential death, and is usually perpetrated with the intent to shame the victim for retribution or non-compliance.

biopower: The power exercised by state authorities to control human bodies, including the power to take life or determine the conditions under which people live.

class conflict: The struggle between groups comprised of individuals of different socioeconomic statuses.

disciplinary society: Michel Foucault's concept, used to identify how modern society is characterized by excessive forms of social control, both external (such as surveillance systems and punishment) and internal (such as docile obedience), that discipline, regulate, and govern populations.

drugs: Substances that change the biochemical operation of the operation of the body and/or the mind.

female genital mutilation: The deliberate excision of the external female genitals that can lead to potentially serious physical and psychological complications that is performed for cultural reasons and is recognized by the World Health Organization as a violation of the rights of women and girls.

gay conversion therapy: The practice of attempting to change a person's homosexual or bisexual orientation through the use of invasive hormonal treatments, religious indoctrination, or coercive psychotherapeutic intervention. Conversion therapy is not to be confused with hormone replacement therapy or with the legitimate use of hormones in gender affirming care.

honour killing: The premeditated murder of a female family member by one or more family members due to an allegation of sexual impropriety or the alleged casting of shame onto the family by the victim.

hormonal conversion therapy: The practice of attempting to change a person's homosexual or bisexual orientation, biological sex, or gender identity through the use of hormonal treatments. Note that HCT is not to be confused with the use of hormonal treatments for legitimate medical use, given with the full consent of an informed patient.

human rights: The basic freedoms that uphold the dignity and equality of all people by virtue of their being human and thus deserving of respect and protection from oppression and persecution as guaranteed by law.

legal moralism: A theory of jurisprudence and/or a philosophy of law that supports the use of laws to control behaviour according to society's moral values by prohibiting or mandating certain acts.

misogyny: Prejudicial discrimination against or hatred of women.

monopoly: An economic market configuration that is the opposite of free-market competition, where one economic entity is the only supplier/provider of goods and/or services in an industry in a particular jurisdiction.

moral panic: A sensationalized, exaggerated response to a crime trend based on fears that the moral fabric of society is under threat unless something is done to stop it.

moral regulation: A form of social control, reflected informally in codes of conduct and more formally in law, whereby moral values and judgments serve to regulate social behaviour and personal conduct.

morality: An abstract concept of good and bad (and by implication right and wrong) that prescribes a guide to the ways one ought to conduct oneself as a member of a society or social group and through which a particular type of social order is maintained.

Nordic model: An approach to prostitution (also known as the Sex Buyer Law, the Swedish Model, or neo-abolitionism) that criminalizes the buying of sex services, but not the people selling their services, with the objective of decreasing the demand for sex services by targeting soliciting and trafficking, and, over time, eradicating prostitution.

prejudice: Bias against individuals or groups, often targeting perceptible characteristics that differ from the person holding or demonstrating the bias.

problem gambling: A potentially harmful addiction to monetary betting on the outcome of games (sports, cards, games of chance, etc.).

second-wave feminism: A women's rights activist movement that emerged in the United States in the 1960s and grew globally until the late 1980s; it moved beyond suffrage (which had been central to first-wave feminism) to critique patriarchal institutions and social and cultural norms more generally, focusing on gender equality in both public and private areas, including family and the workplace.

sex-positive movement: A social justice movement that aims to promote more open attitudes and inclusive norms that recognize the natural and diversified experience of sexuality, female sexual freedom, and sexual identity including gender expression and orientation, and is supportive of body-positivity, sexual choice, safer sex practices, and LGBTQ+ and reproductive rights.

sexual assault: Any non-consensual sexual act, from unwanted touching and kissing to forcing the victim to touch the perpetrator in sexual ways and rape. According to sections 271–273 of the *Criminal Code of Canada* (R.S., 1985, c. C-46), sexual assault occurs if a person is touched in any way that interferes with their sexual integrity. The provisions, adopted in 1983, replace the offence of rape and tier sexual assault in three levels parallel to assault offences, according to the degree of force used. Other changes include the abrogation of spousal immunity, limits to the admissibility of past sexual history of the victim, and specifications regarding situations when someone cannot legally give consent, for example while being unconscious or incapacitated or because of their age. Canadian laws thus follow a consent-based model that is replacing coercion-based legislations in a growing number of countries.

sexual revolution: A sexual liberation social movement from the 1960s to the 1980s that formed part of broader challenges against repressive and traditional societal norms and gave rise to greater acceptance of various sex practices and identities outside of heteronormative relationships; the movement contributed to the legalization of contraception and abortion, as well as the normalization of nudism, pornography, and homosexuality.

sin: From a religious perspective, something that is viewed as being egregious behaviour, a transgression or wrongdoing against the teachings of God.

sociolegal constructs: Ideas that are created by social norms and reinforced through the passing of laws and other formal regulations.

temperance movement: An influential lobbying effort of the 19th and early 20th century that advocated first for the limiting of alcohol consumption and later for the outright prohibition of alcohol and non-medicinal drugs.

third-wave feminism: A shift in feminism that arose from the limits and dissentions within second-wave feminism, characterized by recognizing the intersection of different aspects of one's identity such as race, gender, class, education, and culture as levels through which prejudicial discrimination and oppression operate.

vice: An act or behaviour that is typically seen as a socially undesirable lifestyle choice; often, having a vice is seen as a moral failing of that particular individual.

vice crimes: A category of criminal classification (sometimes also referred to as victimless crimes) that refers to acts, habits, or lifestyle choices that are deemed harmful because of their presumed immorality rather than because of the harm they do to others, and include things such as gambling, illicit drug use, unconventional sexual behaviour, and sex-trade work.

war on drugs: A globally coordinated campaign aimed at curbing the use and sale of illicit drugs that emerged as a state reaction to student protests in the late 1960s and then became an American-led set of foreign and domestic policy initiatives peaking in the 1980s that involved severely punitive anti-drug laws as well as crop eradication on foreign soil.

REFERENCES

Ahmad, N. (2012). Weak laws against acid attacks on women: An Indian perspective. *Medico-Legal Journal, 80*(3), 110–120. https://doi.org/10.1258/mlj.2012.012020

Alfred, T. (2005). *Wasáse: Indigenous pathways of action and freedom.* University of Toronto Press.

Associated Press. (2016, September 10). Canadian judge to rape accuser: "Why couldn't you just keep your knees together?" *The Guardian.* Police arrest 14 in rape, killing of girl. *CTV.* Retrieved from https://www.ctvnews.ca/world/indian-police-arrest-14-in-rape-killing-of-girl-1.3916559

Associated Press. (2018, May 5). Indian police arrest 14 in rape, killing of girl. *CTV.* Retrieved from https://www.ctvnews.ca/world/indian-police-arrest-14-in-rapekilling-of-girl-1.3916559

Barber, K. (2006). Colonialism. In *Canadian Oxford dictionary* (2nd ed., p. 302). Oxford University Press.

Barmaki, R. (2019). Sex, honor, murder: A psychology of "honor killing." *Deviant Behavior, 42*(4), 373–491. https://doi.org/10.1080/01639625.2019.1695456

BBC News. (2019, December 19). Sudanese brides under pressure to have FGM—again. *BBC*. Retrieved from https://www.bbc.com/news/world-africa-49580860

BBC News. (2020a, March 12). Harvey Weinstein jailed for 23 years in rape trial. *BBC*. Retrieved from https://www.bbc.com/news/world-us-canada-51840532

BBC News. (2020b, September 19). Pakistan outcry over police victim-blaming of gang-raped mother. *BBC*. Retrieved from https://www.bbc.com/news/world-asia-54186609

Benedict, H. (1992). *Virgin or vamp: How the press covers sex crimes*. Oxford University Press.

Bilodeau, E. (2019, July 5). Prostitution: seulement 233 clients accusés depuis 2014. *La presse*. Retrieved from https://www.lapresse.ca/actualites/justice-et-faits-divers/2019-07-05/prostitution-seulement-233-clients-accuses-depuis-2014

Boyd, S., Carter, C., & MacPherson, D. (2017). Making drug use into a problem: The politics of drug policy in Canada. In W. Antony, J. Antony, & L. Samuelson (Eds.), *Power and resistance: Critical thinking about Canadian social issues* (6th ed., pp. 344–379). Fernwood Publishing.

Britto, S., Jones, N. A., & Ruddell, R. (2018). The criminal justice system. In M. A. Hurlbert (Ed.), *Pursuing justice: An introduction to justice studies* (2nd ed., pp. 362–401). Fernwood Publishing.

Brock, D. (2000). Victim, nuisance, fallen woman, outlaw, worker? Making the identity "prostitute" in Canadian criminal law. In D. E. Chunn & D. Lacombe (Eds.), *Law as a gendering practice* (pp. 79–99). Oxford University Press.

Brock, D., Glasbeek, A., & Murdocca, C. (Eds.). (2014). *Criminalization, representation, regulation: Thinking differently about crime*. University of Toronto Press.

Burt, M. R. (1980). Cultural myths and supports for rape. *Journal of Personality and Social Psychology, 38*(2), 217–230. https://doi.org/10.1037/0022-3514.38.2.217

Campbell, C. S. (2009). Canadian gambling policies. In J. F. Cosgrave & T. R. Klassen (Eds.), *Casino state: Legalized gambling in Canada* (pp. 69–90). University of Toronto Press.

Campbell, C. S., Hartnagel, T. F., & Smith, G. J. (2005). *The legalization of gambling in Canada*. Law Commission of Canada.

Canadian Press. (2017, August 14). Acid attacks are on the rise and toxic masculinity is the cause. *National Post*. Retrieved from https://nationalpost.com/pmn/news-pmn/theconversation-acid-attacks

CBC News. (1967, December 21). Trudeau: "There's no place for the state in the bedrooms of the nation." *CBC*. Retrieved from https://www.cbc.ca/archives/no-place-for-the-state-in-the-bedrooms-of-the-nation-1.4681298

CBC News. (2005, May 9). RCMP uses "fruit machine" to detect gays. *CBC*. Retrieved from https://www.cbc.ca/player/play/1402923309

CBC News. (2016a, February 20). How should Canada's court system deal with sexual assault cases? *CBC*. Retrieved from https://www.cbc.ca/news/canada/alternatives-to-sexual-assault-trials-forum-1.3456873

CBC News. (2016b, March 24). Jian Ghomeshi trial: Read highlights and judge's full decision. *CBC*. Retrieved from https://www.cbc.ca/news/canada/toronto/horkins-decision-ghomeshi-1.3505808

Cosgrave, J. F., & Klassen, T. R. (2009). Introduction: The shape of legalized gambling in Canada. In J. F. Cosgrave & T. R. Klassen (Eds.), *Casino state: Legalized gambling in Canada* (pp. 3–16). University of Toronto Press.

Davis, N. J., & Stasz, C. (1990). *Social control of deviance: A critical perspective*. McGraw-Hill.

Doolittle, R. (2017, December 8). The unfounded effect. *The Globe and Mail*. Retrieved from https://www.theglobeandmail.com/news/investigations/unfounded-37272-sexual-assault-cases-being-reviewed-402-unfounded-cases-reopened-so-far/article37245525/

Doolittle, R. (2019). *Had it coming: What's fair in the age of #MeToo?* Allen Lane.

Drahos, P. (2017). *Regulation theory: Foundations and applications*. Australian National University Press.

DTE Staff. (2016, July 8). India witnesses one of the highest female infanticide incidents in the world: Study. *DownToEarth*. Retrieved from https://www.downtoearth.org.in/news/health/amp/india-witnesses-one-of-the-highest-female-infanticide-incidents-in-the-world-54803

Farooq, U. (2020, September 10). Pakistanis outraged by gang rape of mother along major highway. *Thomson Reuters*. Retrieved from https://www.reuters.com/article/pakistan-rape/pakistanis-outraged-by-gang-rape-of-mother-along-major-highway-idINKBN2620AB

Foucault, M. (1990). *The history of sexuality: Vol. 1: An introduction*. Vintage. (Original work published 1980)

Friend, D. (2018, January 19). Let's hear it for the banned. *Toronto Star*. Retrieved from https://www.pressreader.com/canada/toronto-star/20180119/281483571797370

Gollom, M. (2016). Toronto bathhouse raids: How the arrests galvanized the gay community. *CBC*. Retrieved from https://www.cbc.ca/news/canada/toronto/bathhouse-raids-toronto-police-gay-community-arrests-apology-1.3645926

Gowen, A. (2015, July 9). Why an Indian judge thinks rapists should marry their victims. *The Washington Post*. Retrieved from https://www.washingtonpost.com/world/asia_pacific/why-an-indian-judge-thinks-rapists-should-marry-their-victims/2015/07/08/606f8998-23e5-11e5-b621-b55e495e9b78_story.html

Grekul, J., Krahn, A., & Odynak, D. (2004). Sterilizing the "feeble-minded": Eugenics in Alberta, Canada, 1929–1972. *Journal of Historical Sociology, 17*(4), 358–384. https://doi.org/10.1111/j.1467-6443.2004.00237.x

Gupta, P. (2020, August 24). How India's rape-survivors end up marrying their rapists. *Article 14*. Retrieved from https://www.article-14.com/post/how-india-s-rape-survivors-end-up-marrying-their-rapists

Hackler, J. C. (2003). Drug crime: The consequences of hypocrisy. In *Canadian criminology: Strategies and perspectives* (3rd ed., pp. 184–202). Prentice Hall.

Harrison, F. (1977). *The dark angel: Aspects of Victorian sexuality*. Sheldon Press.

Holmes, B. (2016, April 11). Records reveal gender-selective abortion taking place in Canada. *New Scientist*. Retrieved from https://www.newscientist.com/article/2083801-records-reveal-gender-selective-abortion-taking-place-in-canada/

Hunt, A. (1999). *Governing morals: A social history of moral regulation*. Cambridge University Press.

Janjua, H. (2021, January 6). Virginity tests for female rape survivors outlawed by Pakistani court. *The Guardian*. Retrieved from https://www.theguardian.com/global-development/2021/jan/06/virginity-tests-for-female-survivors-outlawed-by-pakistani-court

Johnson, H. (2017). Why doesn't she just report it? Apprehensions and contradictions for women who report sexual violence to the police. *Canadian Journal of Women and the Law, 29*(1), 36–59. https://doi.org/10.3138/cjwl.29.1.36

Kilimnik, C. D., & Humphreys, T. P. (2018). Understanding sexual consent and nonconsensual sexual experiences in undergraduate women: The role of identification and rape myth acceptance. *The Canadian Journal of Human Sexuality, 27*(3), 195–206. Retrieved from https://www.muse.jhu.edu/article/711713

Kowalchuk, J. J. (1989). Why control: The limits of temperance intervention. *Law Now, 14*(2), 12–14.

Krishnan, R. (2020, July 18). Kerala rape convict priest's plea to marry survivor not new—here are similar cases from past. *ThePrint*. Retrieved from https://theprint.in/judiciary/kerala-rape-convict-priests-plea-to-marry-survivor-not-new-here-are-similar-cases-from-past/463458/

Lacasse, D. (1994). *La prostitution féminine à Montréal: 1945–1970*. Éditions du Boréal.

Lammers, K., Jr. (2011). Rise of the pills. *University of the District of Columbia Law Review, 15*(1), 91–112.

Larcombe, W., Fileborn, B., Powell, A., Hanley, N., & Henry, N. (2016). "I think it's rape and I think he would be found not guilty: Focus group perceptions of (un)reasonable belief in consent in rape law. *Social & Legal Studies, 25*(5), 611–629. https://doi.org/10.1177/0964663916647442

Lerner, G. (1986). *The creation of patriarchy*. Oxford University Press.

Liang, A. (2019, April 3). Brunei defies growing censure to make gay sex and adultery punishable by stoning. *National Post*. Retrieved from https://nationalpost.com/news/world/brunei-invokes-laws-allow-stoning-for-gay-sex-adultery/

Linden, R. (2009). Crime, criminals, and criminology. In R. Linden (Ed.), *Criminology: A Canadian perspective* (6th ed., pp. 3–28). Nelson.

Lyon, D. R., & Welsh, A. (2017). *The psychology of criminal and violent behaviour*. Oxford University Press.

MacFarlane, B. A., Frater, R. J., & Michaelson, C. (2018). *Cannabis law: Quebec English edition*. Thomson Reuters.

Martin, F. (2018, October 17). Is this the end for a sex robot brothel in Houston? *Houston Public Media*. Retrieved from https://www.houstonpublicmedia.org/articles/news/in-depth/2018/10/17/308292/is-this-the-end-for-a-sex-robot-brothel-in-houston/

Mathen, C. (2013). "A precarious chancy situation": Aboriginal gaming rights in Canada. *University of British Columbia Law Review, 46*, 349–395.

Mawani, R. (2009). *Colonial proximities: Crossracial encounters and juridical truths in British Columbia, 1871–1921*. UBC Press.

Maynard, R. (2017). *Policing Black lives: State violence in Canada from slavery to the present*. Fernwood Publishing.

McLaren, J. P. S. (1986). Chasing the social evil: Moral fervour and the evolution of Canada's prostitution laws, 1867–1917. *Canadian Journal of Law and Society / Revue canadienne Droit et Société, 1*, 125–165.

Moberly, M. D., & Hartsig, C. L. (2014). Reaching the end of our rope? An appraisal of the movement to legalize industrial hemp. *Accord: Legal Journal for Practitioners, 3*(1), 1–42.

Moss. W., & Gardner-O'Toole, E. (1991). *Aboriginal People: History of discriminatory laws*. Law & Government Division, Government of Canada.

Nicholson, K. (2019, July 16). "Life after shame": Hidden camera victim lifts publication ban to empower other women. *CBC*. Retrieved from https://www.cbc.ca/news/canada/manitoba/shameless-circle-group-1.5212808

Nietzsche, F. (1989). *Beyond good and evil: Prelude to a philosophy of the future*. Vintage Books. (Original work published 1886)

Nietzsche, F. (2010). *The anti-Christ*. SoHo Books. (Original work published 1895)

Paley, D. (2014). *Drug war capitalism*. AK Press.

Parenti, M. (2006). *The culture struggle*. Seven Stories Press.

Parker, G. (1983). The legal regulation of sexual activity and the protection of females. *Osgoode Hall Law Journal, 21*(2), 187–244.

Pettipas, K. (2014). *Severing the ties that bind: Government repression of Indigenous religious ceremonies on the prairies*. University of Manitoba Press.

Pivot Legal Society. (2016). Evaluating Canada's sex work laws: The case for repeal. Pivot Legal Society.

Pivot Legal Society Sex Work Subcommittee. (2004). *Voices for dignity: A call to end the harms caused by Canada's sex trade laws*. Pivot Legal Society.

Pruden, J. G. (2020, July 4). He said, they said: Inside the trial of Matthew McKnight. *The Globe and Mail*. Retrieved from https://www.theglobeandmail.com/canada/article-he-said-they-said-inside-the-trial-of-matthew-mcknight/

Rahman, A., & Toubia, N. (2000). *Female genital mutilation: A guide to laws and policies worldwide*. Zed Books.

Ramp, W. & Badgley, K. (2009). "Blood money": Gambling and the formation of civic morality. In J. F. Cosgrave & T. R. Klassen (Eds.), *Casino state: Legalized gambling in Canada* (pp. 19–45). University of Toronto Press.

Robertson, J. R. (2003). *Prostitution*. Library of Parliament.

Rotenberg, C. (2016). *Prostitution offences in Canada: Statistical trends*. Catalogue no. 85-002-X. Statistics Canada.

Schmidt, S. (2017, October 25). No jail for Portuguese man who beat ex-wife—because her adultery assaulted his "honour." *National Post*. Retrieved from https://nationalpost.com/news/world/no-jail-for-portuguese-man-who-beat-ex-wife-because-her-adultery-assaulted-his-honour

Schweighofer, A. R. F. (1988). The Canadian temperance movement: Contemporary parallels. *Canadian Journal of Law and Society, 3*, 175–194.

Sev'er, A., & Yurdakul, G. (2001). Culture of honor, culture of change: A feminist analysis of honor killings in rural Turkey. *Violence Against Women, 7*(9), 964–998. https://doi.org/10.1177/10778010122182866

Shaver, F. M. (2005). Sex work research: Methodological and ethical challenges. *Journal of Interpersonal Violence, 20*(3), 296–319.

Slim, H. (2008). *Killing civilians: Method, madness, and morality in war*. Columbia University Press.

Smith, G. J. (2012). Sports betting in Canada. In P. M. Anderson, I. S. Blackshaw, R. C. R. Siekmann, & J. Soek (Eds.), *Sports betting: Law and policy* (pp. 288–303). TMC Asser Press.

Stasiulis, D., & Jhappan, R. (1995). The fractious politics of a settler society: Canada. In D. Stasiulis & N. Yuval-Davis (Eds.), *Unsettling settler societies: Articulations of gender, race, ethnicity and class* (pp. 95–131). SAGE Publications.

Stasiulis, D., & Yuval-Davis, N. (1995). Introduction: Beyond dichotomies—gender, race, ethnicity and class in settler societies. In D. Stasiulis & N. Yuval-Davis (Eds.), *Unsettling settler societies: Articulations of gender, race, ethnicity and class* (pp. 1–38). SAGE Publications.

Statistics Canada. (2017, October 25). *Aboriginal peoples in Canada: Key results from the 2016 Census.* Government of Canada. Retrieved from https://www150.statcan.gc.ca/n1/daily-quotidien/171025/dq171025a-eng.htm?indid=14430-1&indgeo=0

Stote, K. (2017). Decolonizing feminism: From reproductive abuse to reproductive justice. *Atlantis: Critical Studies in Gender, Culture, and Social Justice, 38*(1), 110–124.

Strange, C., & Loo, T. (1997). *Making good: Law and moral regulation in Canada, 1867–1939.* University of Toronto Press.

Tamkin, E. (2019, March 13). Italian men acquitted of rape because judges agreed that victim looked "too masculine" will face new trial. *National Post.* Retrieved from https://nationalpost.com/news/world/three-female-jurists-acquitted-two-men-because-the-woman-looked-too-masculine-to-be-raped

Toupin, L. (2006). Analyser autrement la « prostitution » et la « traite des femmes ». *Recherches féministes, 19*(1), 153–176.

Truth and Reconciliation Commission of Canada. (2015). *Honouring the truth, reconciling for the future: Summary of the final report of the Truth and Reconciliation Commission of Canada.*

United Nations Office on Drugs and Crime (UNODC). (2018). *Global study on homicide: Gender-related killing of women and girls.* Retrieved from https://www.unodc.org/documents/data-and-analysis/GSH2018/GSH18_Gender-related_killing_of_women_and_girls.pdf

van der Meulen, E., Durisin, E. M., & Love, V. (Eds.). (2013). *Selling sex: Experience, advocacy, and research on sex work in Canada.* UBC Press.

van der Meulen, E., & Valverde, M. (2013). Beyond the criminal code: Municipal licensing and zoning bylaws. In E. van der Meulen, E. M. Durisin, & V. Love (Eds.), *Selling sex: Experience, advocacy, and research on sex work in Canada* (pp. 314–322). UBC Press.

Wemmers, J. (2020). Restorative justice: How responsive to the victim is it? *The International Journal of Restorative Justice, 3*(1), 30–37.

Wijers, M., & Lap-Chew, L. (Directors). (1997). *Trafficking in women, Forced labour and slavery-like practices in marriage, domestic labour and prostitution.* STV.

Winfield, N. (2019, March 13). Italy outraged as court finds victim too ugly to be raped. *AP News*. Retrieved from https://apnews.com/article/6361b8de2200469d8f423b8fe cdee771

World Health Organization (WHO). (2018). *United Nations agencies call for ban on virginity testing*. Retrieved from https://www.who.int/news/item/17-10-2018- united-nations-agencies-call-for-ban-on-virginity-testing

Laws and Decisions

An Act for the Punishment of Idle and Disorderly Persons, and Rogues and Vagabonds, in That Part of Great Britain Called England (5 Geo. 4, c 83) [The "Vagrancy Act"].

Canada (Attorney General) v. Bedford, 2013 SCC 72, [2013] 3 S.C.R. 1101

Criminal Code, 1892, SC 1892, c 29, s 185

R v Hutt, [1978] 2 S.C.R. 476

Reference re ss 193 and 195.1(1)(c) of the *Criminal Code* (Man.), [1990] 1 S.C.R. 1123

R.S.C. 1985 (1st), c 51. *An Act to amend the Criminal Code (prostitution)*.

S.C. 2014, c 25. *Protection of Communities and Exploited Persons Act*

S.N.S. 1759 (1st) c 1 *An Act for Regulating and Maintaining a House of Correction or Work- House within the Town of Halifax, and for Binding out of Poor Children*

CHAPTER 6

The Criminalization of Dissent

Claudio Colaguori and Honor Brabazon

LEARNING OBJECTIVES

In this chapter, you will

- discover how people who engage in political dissent or express concerns about unjust social issues can become the targets of the criminalization process;
- learn about the different types of dissent and forms of social activism;
- begin to familiarize yourself with some important historical as well as recent examples of dissent and how they represent significant forms of progress for greater freedom and human rights;
- learn how criminology has contributed to our understanding of the criminalization of dissent; and
- explore why the practice of dissent is essential for democracy and social progress.

INTRODUCTION: PROGRESS, FREEDOM, AND DISSENT

All freedom begins with the freedom of thought. The right to think beyond convention, to challenge traditional practices that produce inequality and injustice, to question those in power who make laws that benefit their own interests, and to raise awareness about the problems that impede the egalitarian progress of society—all of these are essential for social freedom. Indeed, modern, cosmopolitan, democratic societies in the West were founded on a number of fundamental rights and freedoms that helped to establish a more just society distinct from the repressive, hierarchical societies that existed in the historical past. Maintaining freedom of speech, freedom of assembly, freedom of association, and "freedom of thought, belief, opinion, and expression" (Government of Canada, n.d.), among other **human rights** and freedoms, depends on the actions of citizens who mobilize change to create a more egalitarian, open, and just society.

Maintaining existing freedoms and gaining more types of social progress requires the active questioning of ruling elites. The right to question, critique, and express social and political **dissent** are fundamental dimensions of democracy, yet, in many cases, when citizens engage in critical questioning or challenge those in power through expressions of dissent, they often face serious reprisals ranging from discriminatory policing to detainment, to surveillance and espionage, and to criminal prosecution. As Watts states, "the fact that liberal–democratic states not only seem to disapprove of dissent but also regularly and routinely criminalize it points to a basic puzzle about the legitimacy of dissent in liberal–democratic states" (2020, p. 9). Dissent can be defined in simple terms as the public expression of opposition to a particular practice or policy. In **authoritarian societies,** public displays of dissent are perceived by those in power as acts of open defiance and are often met with serious reprisals such as imprisonment, torture, and death.

The fundamental freedoms that underpin democratic societies are not mere ideals. They are essential action items that are necessary to maintain social freedom and ward against the rise of tyrannical, oppressive governments. Despite the transition into the 21st century and the abundant social progress that has been made, there is a growing trend towards authoritarianism in many nations, as evidenced in the abandonment of democratic principles and associated civil liberties. As one report states, "globally, the past decade has been marked by the twin advances of authoritarianism and populism. The two are not always linked, but in situations ranging from the Philippines and Cambodia to Hungary and Poland, politicians have leveraged populist movements to seize power. Once in office, they have begun the process of dismantling the institutions designed to check their authority and protect human rights, particularly the judiciary and the media" (The Editors, 2020). Thus, current social and political freedoms are always at risk of being curtailed or eliminated.

Social progress often develops through collective action known as **social movements**. Many of us are familiar with the environmental movement or the civil rights movement, but as shall be mentioned further on in this chapter, not all social movements are expressions of *progressive* dissent. Collective social action such as marches, demonstrations, and protests can come from all sides of the political and ideological spectrum. Some public demonstrations are deemed *regressive* insofar as they stand against the implementation of progressive social change and are in support of restrictive laws, inequitable social practices, or oppressive cultural traditions:

- Social action that supports traditional, often patriarchal social systems, is considered *reactionary* because it is reacting to a perceived threat to the existing social order.
- Dissent that challenges traditional cultural and political ideas and policies and aims to promote social change to address problems of injustice, economic power imbalances, and social inequalities is considered *revolutionary* or *progressive*.

It is important to understand that modern societies consist of a complex dynamic of conflicting social forces that shape the course of history, and that, despite increased freedoms over time, there is always the risk of losing the freedoms gained. Dissent, as one form of political expression, is therefore essential to the vibrancy of any modern society. This chapter is concerned with the **criminalization of dissent**, which can be defined in a number of ways, including:

- "criminalizing the political" (Watts, 2020, p. 9), which includes "the policing of protest" (p. 1), and often involves the detainment of dissenters, the laying of criminal charges, and/or the use of state-sanctioned lethal force against individuals engaged in social protest;
- the surveillance monitoring of dissenters, critical journalists, and other social activists;
- the infiltration and disruption of social movements by undercover state agents;
- the unethical application of anti-terror security legislation to social activist demonstrations so as to classify environmental or animal rights protesters and other activists as terrorists;
- the professional persecution and legal prosecution of **whistleblowers**;
- the use of emergency decrees or ad hoc **martial laws** and other legal measures to detain protesters, disperse protesters, or impose curfews on civil populations; and
- the use of strategic lawsuits (SLAPP) to intimidate and silence critics and thus neutralize dissenting opposition (Malta Independent, 2018).

Thus, the criminalization of dissent involves a broad range of actions by the state that uses legal and extra-legal measures to silence civil dissent and political opposition (Shantz, 2011). In order to understand how dissent is treated as a crime, it is first necessary to understand what dissent is and who might want to stop it. If everything you knew about dissent came from the way protest was portrayed by police, the mainstream media, and many politicians, you might think that dissent was an unfortunate aberration and not something that was necessary and normal in a democracy. You might also think of protest not as a political intervention but as a random disruption, like a gang of people yelling in the street and blocking traffic for no reason. However, by demonstrating that protest is a fundamental part of a democracy and that it is all about challenging repressive aspects of the existing social order, this chapter illustrates why protest is repressed, according to critical scholarship: broadly, because it poses a challenge to those in power.

In the words of scholars ...

If there is no struggle, there is no progress. Those who profess to favor freedom, and yet depreciate agitation, are men who want crops without plowing up the ground. They want rain without thunder and lightning. They want the ocean without the awful roar of its many waters. This struggle may be a moral one; or it may be a physical one; or it may be both moral and physical; but it must be a struggle. Power concedes nothing without a demand. It never did and it never will.

Frederick Douglass, The significance of emancipation in the West Indies: An address delivered in Canandaigua, New York, on August 3, 1857. *The Frederick Douglass Papers.* 1857

THE CRIMINOLOGY OF DISSENT

The criminalization of dissent is the process of treating organized social disagreement and political opposition as if they were forms of deviant or criminal behaviour. The acts that come to mind when we hear the word *criminal* rarely include **social activism**, yet throughout modern history, acts of political dissent have commonly been treated as criminal and deviant despite the positive function such social actions play in the process of social and political progress. Recall that Chapter 2 refers to how legacy theorist Émile Durkheim wrote that some acts of crime and deviance serve positive and functional roles in society. For Durkheim, deviant behaviour is a necessary component of a healthy society. Durkheim's theory of deviance views unconventional and non-conformist forms of conduct that are designated as deviant are socially "useful" and serve to propel "the normal evolution of morality and law" (2010, p. 36). Organized public dissent as a significant form of non-conformity is the expression of a public will that pushes the boundaries of freedom and progress that creates the impetus for legal changes that reduce legal oppression and limitations on freedoms. The most significant recent Canadian example of deviant behaviour changing the law and the definition of normalcy is the case of the legalization of marijuana in October 2018. It took decades of pro-pot activism to finally get the Canadian government to recognize that laws criminalizing the possession and use of marijuana were unfair, unjust, and discriminatory and needed to be changed. Pushing back against that which is widely seen as unfair often means pushing forward for freedom.

Although it has an uneven history, organized social and political dissent is no longer as rare as it once was, nor is it perceived and represented as deviant as it was as recently as the 1960s, when popular social movements came to change the world irrevocably. Dissent and protest, in many forms, is today becoming popular once again. As Watts writes, "the resurgence of populism has been driven by anger about what some people see as the 'unfair' treatment of minorities like Indigenous people, gays and lesbians, or refugees and asylum seekers or as the toxic effects of economic globalization" (2020, p. 2). The paradoxical condition of global society in this early period of the 21st century is evident in the rise of political authoritarianism alongside the rise of progressive protest and justice movements worldwide. In order to understand the role that dissent plays in the present era, it makes sense to review the history of progressive dissent from the modern era, to which we shall now turn, if only briefly.

In the words of scholars ...

We get a first hint of [the essentially political] democratic tendency when we look at the genealogy of modern resistances, revolts, and revolution, which demonstrates a tendency toward increasingly democratic organization, from centralized forms of revolutionary dictatorship and command to network organizations that displace authority in collaborative relationships.

Michael Hardt and Antonio Negri, *Multitude: War and Democracy in the Age of Empire*. 2004

The historical progress that gave rise to the modern, secular world of increased freedoms and opportunities, the creation of public service institutions such as healthcare and education, the expansion of open economies with increased labour rights, voting rights, legal protections for women and children, criminal justice advances, and more have all been realized through coordinated collective struggles against traditional, often oppressive, forms of power that prevented people from living freer, fuller, and more prosperous lives. Such progressive developments did not materialize because they were freely granted to the people by ruling powers— they came into existence through collective resistance, struggle, and the often violent demand for egalitarian change. In the West, the philosophical and scientific Enlightenment, the Renaissance, the Reformation, the French Revolution, and political liberalism marked pivotal historic developments that promoted ideals of freedom and the rights of individuals to be included in the various walks of society, regardless of their birth status or cultural background. Such developments helped establish a break with the oppressive authority of various dominant institutions of the early modern era such as the Catholic Church, the monarchical states, and persistent dogmatic modes of thought preserved in traditional cultures. Social progresses led to successive historic developments. For example, after the atrocities of the 20th century, including the gross injustices of World War II, leaders from various regions of the world in 1948 created the *Universal Declaration of Human Rights*, a historical milestone of human freedom that begins as follows:

> Whereas recognition of the inherent dignity and of the equal and inalienable rights of all members of the human family is the foundation of freedom, justice and peace in the world.
>
> Whereas disregard and contempt for human rights have resulted in barbarous acts which have outraged the conscience of mankind, and the advent of a world in which human beings shall enjoy freedom of speech and belief and freedom from fear and want has been proclaimed as the highest aspiration of the common people. Whereas it is essential, if man is not to be compelled to have recourse, as a last resort, to rebellion against tyranny and oppression, that human rights should be protected by the rule of law (United Nations, n.d.).

The achievements of the modern age would not have been possible without substantial, organized protest and dissent against the oppressive conditions of life that benefitted the elites at the expense of virtually everyone else. One should not for a moment think that such progresses have fully eliminated the horrors and injustices of the past that persist into the present, such as enslavement, poverty, racism, sexism, war, and crime. Substantial social problems still exist, and human rights violations continue to occur in different ways across different nations. If we consider these problems inherited from the past along with many contemporary problems such as environmental destruction, ongoing poverty, and prejudicial discrimination on the basis of one's identity, the struggle for social progress remains an essential imperative, and organized dissent will continue to play a historic role in that struggle. Thus, the criminalization of dissent is a pressing social concern and that makes it central to the new directions in a 21st century criminology that raise questions about power and order rather than simply classifying types of crime.

The practice of questioning political authorities reached a critical point during the 1960s and gave rise to numerous progressive social movements such as the civil rights, anti-racism, anti-war, feminist, environmental, and organized labour movements that took place across the globe, peaking in 1968. Such monumental social developments did not go unnoticed by criminologists. Recall that the labelling theorists discussed in Chapter 2 stated that those with the power to do so often apply deviant designations or labels to the conduct of others in order to maintain the status quo, and the application of labels has significant legal and personal consequences for those who are stigmatized by such them. Thus, late 1960s labelling theorists introduced the concept of power squarely into criminological theory as they were influenced by the emerging critical social consciousness and political upheavals of the time, including protests for civil rights on university campuses (Pfohl, 1985). A popular slogan among progressive youth at the time was to *question authority* and that is exactly what labelling theory did, by asking the following questions:

- Who has the right to decide what is right and what is wrong, legal and illegal?
- How have the traditional values of previous generations maintained unequal gender roles, as well perpetuated sexual, racial, and other forms of discrimination?
- Why do war, poverty, and crime continue to exist?

A pivotal event that shaped the rise of labelling theory in criminology (discussed later in this chapter) occurred at Kent State University in 1970 when the "Ohio National Guard fired on Kent State University students as they protested against the Vietnam War. Four students were killed. Nine were injured.... It prompted a nationwide student strike that forced hundreds of colleges and universities to shut down" (Kaur, 2020).

Image 6.1: Kent State Shootings

Source: "National Guard personnel walking toward crowd near Taylor Hall, tear gas has been fired," *News Service May 4 photographs. Kent State University Libraries. Special Collections & Archives.* https://omeka .library.kent.edu/special-collections/items/show/1427.

Labelling theorists, among other critical thinkers, began to focus their analyses of crime and society on issues such as

- the use by state authorities of stigmatizing labels such as "enemy of the state" and "communist" to defame individuals targeted as a threat to those in power;
- the power of the law to designate an act as criminal;
- how the law reflects the economic and political interests of those in power;
- the right of people to challenge what they see as unjust or unfair practices, laws, regulations, and restrictions on their freedom; and
- the issue of the state's monopoly on the use of violent force, and the repressive use of military and police violence against citizens in the name fighting crime and protecting law and order.

Today, critical criminology remains concerned with the relation between the power of the law, social order maintenance, and the process of criminalization. As the world is faced with new and ongoing challenges such as the continued threat of terror attacks, the COVID-19 pandemic and other biological threats, the rise of political authoritarianism, the development of advanced computer-driven surveillance systems, and the crisis of homelessness, migration, and refugee emergencies, among others, dissent against wrongdoing remains an essential form of social action in the quest for a more just world.

Image 6.2: Hippie Image

Source: Question Authority by Rick McKee, The Augusta Chronicle, GA via politicalcartoons.com

TYPES OF DISSENT AND THEIR CRIMINALIZATION

The practice of dissent is a regular form of social action across the globe, as "sustained political protest has become a recurrent feature of our time" (Watts, 2020, p. 1). Thus, the *criminalization* of dissent is increasingly becoming a significant theme within contemporary criminology. In the simplest terms, dissent is saying "no" to some form of political power. Dissent is disagreement and opposition to laws, rules, official practices, or political decisions that are made or perpetuated by those in power. Dissent is often expressed in a publicly visible manner such as through various forms of social activism, civil disobedience, critical journalism, blogging, or public expression. Dissent refers to a variety of social and political activities that engage in critique for the purpose of achieving social change or challenging political corruption and abuses of power. The concept of dissent is invoked in this chapter in a broad and inclusive sense, from publicly marching for a just cause and critical journalism that reveals the hypocrisy of those in power, to creating works of art that provoke thought and social critique.

Social Movements

As indicated earlier in this chapter, social movements have made profound changes to global society throughout the modern era, and "the first two decades of the twenty-first century have been marked by near-global expressions of protest with significant political effects" (Watts, 2020, p. 2). A social movement is an organized, coordinated effort involving large numbers of people who are united in drawing attention to a particular social issue. This is accomplished through a variety of means including public gatherings, demonstrations, social activism, radical publishing, and promoting awareness of social issues through various communications media. The majority of sustained social movements are progressive and aim to create social change or draw attention to a significant concern that represents an issue of wrongdoing, oppression, or injustice. Some of the more historically recent and noteworthy social movements centered in North America include Occupy Wall Street, Idle No More, anti-war/US Invasion of Iraq, Dakota Access Pipeline protests, Black Lives Matter, the Maple Spring/ Quebec Student Movement, and #MeToo, just to name a few. Noteworthy movements that are global in scale or took place outside of North America include anti-globalization, the Arab Spring, environmental/global warming protests, the Hong Kong pro-democracy protests, and the Indian Farmers' protest. Many of these movements were met with significant resistance by police and other state agencies in attempts to suppress protest activities.

In the Canadian context, it is important to mention the historic and infamous anti-globalization G20 Summit demonstrations, which took place in Toronto in the summer of 2010—an occasion that represents "the largest mass arrests in Canadian history, [where] police arrested roughly 900 people in G20-related incidents [later estimated to be over 1,000 people] … The Canadian Civil Liberties Association [CCLA] denounced the mass arrests, saying they were illegal and unconstitutional because police did not have reasonable grounds to believe that everyone they detained had committed a crime or was about to do so. 'To us [in the CCLA], it's abhorrent that we would be arresting more than 900 people to find maybe 50 or 100 … vandals'" The civil protest groups in attendance ranged from workers' organizations, Indigenous rights groups, and anti-poverty groups to Oxfam and many more globally recognized progressive organizations, as well as thousands of individual conscientious citizens. In addition, there were a very few unruly groups who believed damaging corporate property represented a legitimate display of dissent. The media coverage at the time seemed obsessed with reproducing the stereotype of "violent protesters" as sensationalized coverage dominated the early reporting and virtually no coverage of the points of view of protest groups made the news. In stereotypical media sensationalist fashion, dissenters were silenced and caricatured as unwelcome troublemakers and "violent anarchists."

The hasty passage of last-minute legislation called *The Public Works Protection Act* by the Executive Council of Ontario gave police forces the power to bypass the normal protocols of detainment and arrest. Those arrested were kept in a detention centre under conditions and treatment tantamount to torture, including harassment and strip searches, confiscation of property, unlawful detainment, and numerous other civil rights abuses. Police seemed unfettered in their abuse of those arrested, believing that the new order increased their powers and gave them the authority to act as if under martial law, where individual rights are temporarily suspended and police powers are increased. At first denied by the police, it was later admitted that tear gas, **kettling**, rubber bullets, and pepper spray were used against protesters. The 2010 G20 summit protest in Toronto represents an example of how tyrannical spasms of authoritarianism can and do regularly occur within the official governance of democratic societies. Especially in the **post-9/11 era**, where numerous states have entered a *hypersecurity* mode of regulating populations, this intensification of state power has led to an increase of the criminalization of dissent.

Box 6.1: Media-Generated Myths That Criminalize Dissent

Source: *Maclean's*. July 19, 2010.

Look at the above image, which represents *Maclean's* view of the 2010 G20 summit in Toronto. Touted as the occasion for the largest mass arrests in Canadian history, this event saw many innocent bystanders detained under conditions that denied them basic rights and freedoms. This particular magazine cover image mystifies the complexity of the event, the diversity of groups in attendance, and in particular the gross human rights violations that occurred—all of which are completely overshadowed by a law and order-themed "lock them up" headline, which reduces all protesters to "thugs" who "don't deserve any leniency." The interpretation of complex events is narrowly framed for the reader as violence and disorder so as to reinforce dominant ideologies that portray democratic dissenters as criminals and police as enforcers of order and peace. Can you think of other democratic protests that were misrepresented and portrayed as criminal chaos?

(*Maclean's*. (2010). G20 thugs don't deserve a break. *Maclean's*, *124*(17), 4–5)

Political Protest and Opposition as Dissent

While the G20 summit protests represented a type of political protest insofar as an estimated 10,000 demonstrators assembled to voice concerns about the destructiveness of neoliberal capitalist globalization, in most cases political dissent is confined to protest against specific policies implemented by a ruling government in a given nation. A recent example of criminalized political protest is the Hong Kong–based Civil Human Rights Front (CHRF), a pro-democracy movement that resisted mainland China's numerous attempts to impose greater restrictions on the autonomy of Hong Kong. Although CHRF made substantial strides in drawing attention to Chinese restrictions on freedom and "galvanized millions to take part in street protests in 2019, it has disbanded in the latest blow to the opposition movement … [and] 'The police reiterated that for crimes committed by an organization and its members, the criminal responsibility will not be wiped out due to the disbandment or resignation of the members,' police said in a statement, adding they will continue to pursue any organization or person for violations of the Hong Kong National Security Law and others" (Reuters, 2021).

Another significant recent case of political opposition comes from Myanmar where "mass protests have been taking place across Myanmar since the military seized control on 1 February. Elected leader Aung San Suu Kyi and members of her National League for Democracy (NLD) party are among those detained. Hundreds of people, including children, have been killed" (Cuddy, 2021). The unauthorized government has been using anti-terrorist laws to criminalize citizens who want their democratically elected leader reinstated to office. "Even after six months [as of 14 August 2021] of horrifying news from Myanmar, it is an incident that's shocked the country—five people who chose to jump from a building they were hiding in, some to their deaths, rather than face arrest. The police have condemned the group as terrorists, but the husband of one victim tells the BBC she was a compassionate wife and mother who felt she was working to alleviate the people's suffering" (Head, 2021).

In Cuba in August 2021, the "government … spelled out its laws against using social media or the internet to stir up protests or insult the state—and offered people a form to report offenders. The decrees published in the Official Gazette follow the largest protests Cuba has seen in years, which broke out last month and apparently were fed in part by messages on social media applications" (Canadian Press, 2021). A Reuters report indicates "Hundreds of people, including dozens of **dissident** artists and opposition activists, remain detained in Communist-run Cuba a month after unprecedented anti-government protests, according to rights groups. Thousands took to the streets nationwide on July 11 to protest a dire economic crisis and curbs on civil rights. The government said the unrest was fomented by counter-revolutionaries exploiting hardship caused largely by U.S. sanctions" (Marsh, 2021).

Political dissent can be a dangerous activity, especially in authoritarian nations where dissenters and opposition figures are seen as a threat to those in power, are deemed enemies of the state, and are often incarcerated as **political prisoners**. Imprisoning people who disagree with or question those in power is a type of political neutralization that takes a number of forms, such as the illegal detainment, arrest, imprisonment, kidnapping, torture, and murder of political opponents and critics. An example of political neutralization is the case of the Lukashenko government in Belarus where, in September 2021,

> two leading opposition figures who challenged Belarus's discredited presidential polls have been jailed for trying to threaten national security and seize power. Protest organiser Maria Kolesnikova was jailed for 11 years while lawyer Maxim Znak received 10 years. They joined an opposition council after President Alexander Lukashenko claimed victory in 2020's disputed

election…. For months, Belarusians protested against the August 2020 vote, denounced by the EU, US, and UK as neither free nor fair. Tens of thousands of protesters were detained, and many were brutally beaten, as Mr. Lukashenko, who has been in power since 1994, tried to silence dissent. Independent journalists and activists have been arrested in a crackdown that continues a year later, with some 650 political prisoners in detention, activists say. (BBC News, 2021c)

In another recent case of political imprisonment,

a Thai woman has been jailed for 43 years for criticising the royal family, the country's harshest ever sentence for insulting the monarchy. The former civil servant, known only as Anchan, posted audio clips from a podcast on social media. The 63-year-old said she had simply shared the audio files and had not commented on the content. Thailand's lèse-majesté law, which forbids any insult to the monarchy, is among the strictest in the world. After a three-year break, Thailand revived the controversial law late last year in an attempt to curb months of anti-government protests, with demonstrators demanding changes to the monarchy. (BBC News, 2021a)

The Criminalization of Critical Journalists

Journalists who take their roles as reporters and representatives of the **fourth estate** seriously are regularly targeted for persecution by those with power whose acts of wrongdoing they report on. Journalists and other news media professionals whose reporting exposes injustice, crime, fraud, corruption, and the abuse of power by government officials and others are engaging in a unique and essential type of dissent insofar as they are *speaking truth to power*. It is not surprising then that "(o)n average, every five days a journalist is killed for bringing information to the public. Attacks on media professionals are often perpetrated in non-conflict situations by organised crime groups, militia, security personnel, and even local police, making local journalists among the most vulnerable. These attacks include murder, abductions, harassment, intimidation, illegal arrest, and arbitrary detention" (United Nations Educational, Scientific and Cultural Organization, n.d.). A disturbing 2017 case is that of "Daphne Caruana Galizia, the journalist who led the Panama Papers investigation into corruption in Malta was killed on Monday in a car bomb near her home. [She] died on Monday [October 16, 2017] when her car, a Peugeot 108, was destroyed by a powerful explosive device which blew the vehicle into several pieces and threw the debris into a nearby field" (Garside, 2017).

Another, more publicized case took place "on 2 October 2018, [when] Jamal Khashoggi, a US-based journalist and critic of Saudi Arabia's government, walked into the Saudi consulate in Istanbul, where he was murdered. In the months that followed, conflicting narratives emerged over how he died, what happened to his remains, and who was responsible. Saudi officials said the journalist was killed in a 'rogue operation' by a team of agents sent to persuade him to return to the kingdom, while Turkish officials said the agents acted on orders from the highest levels of the Saudi government" (BBC News, 2021b).

Fear of the truth and facts as reported by journalists is such a concern for those who abuse their positions of power that a new market has opened up for spying on journalists. A recent Associated Press article reads: "Hundreds of journalists, activists among firm's spyware targets, probe finds. [The spyware named Pegasus] 'is being used to spy on journalists, human rights activists and political dissidents … The number of journalists identified as targets vividly illustrates how Pegasus is used as a tool to intimidate critical media. It is about controlling public narrative, resisting scrutiny, and suppressing any dissenting voice,' Amnesty International quoted its secretary-general, Agnes Callamard, as saying" (2021).

Recognizing that the suppression of dissent is a growing global concern, in 2021 "journalists Maria Ressa [who was served ten arrest warrants by the Philippines government] and Dmitry Muratov won the Nobel Peace Prize for their fights to defend freedom of expression in the Philippines and Russia. The Nobel committee called the pair 'representatives of all journalists who stand up for this ideal.' They are known for investigations that have angered their countries' rulers, and have faced significant threats" (BBC News, 2021d).

Press freedom is also under threat in democratic North America:

In an ominous sign for press freedom, documentary filmmaker and journalist Deia Schlosberg was arrested and charged with felonies carrying a whopping maximum sentence of up to 45 years in prison—simply for reporting on the ongoing Indigenous protests against fossil fuel infrastructure. Schlosberg was arrested in Walhalla, North Dakota [in October 2016] for filming activists shutting down a tar sands pipeline, part of a nationwide solidarity action organized on behalf of those battling the Dakota Access Pipeline … [and] held without access to a lawyer for 48 hours, and her footage was confiscated by the police. Schlosberg was then charged with three felonies: "conspiracy to theft of property, conspiracy to theft of services, and conspiracy to tampering with or damaging a public service. Together, the charges carry 45 years in maximum prison sentences." (Knight, 2016)

In the words of scholars …

Throughout the Western liberal democracies new laws have given governments greater powers to eavesdrop on the population and the journalists whose job it is to keep them informed. Those laws which gave governments sweeping surveillance powers were introduced ostensibly to track terrorists and reduce the number of attacks. But detailed analysis suggests the so-called anti-terror surveillance laws have not achieved what governments promised. Instead they have often been more effectively used to track down whistle-blowers, and criminalise the work of journalists.

Andrew Fowler, *Shooting the Messenger: Criminalising Journalism.* 2018

Whistleblowing as Dissent

It is often the case that governments, their agencies and branches, and business corporations will engage in ongoing, significant unethical or illegal practices in relative secrecy. Individuals known as whistleblowers who work inside such organizations and are uncomfortable allowing secretive practices of wrongdoing to continue with impunity will expose them to public scrutiny in an effort to have them stopped. Whistleblowers are often former employees of the organization they are exposing, since people who are currently employed by such organizations risk losing their jobs or facing serious legal action if they engage in the exposure of organized wrongdoing. Some whistleblowers will expose wrongdoing anonymously while others will publicly reveal their identity. Each situation is different and carries different risks. Whistleblowing is a distinct form of dissent (Elliston et al., 1985). It carries significant risks because it is usually committed by an individual (and not by a collective), who is then vulnerable to reprisals. As one Council on Foreign Relations states,

murder of [a] South African whistleblower illustrates dangerous status quo…. The murder of Babita Deokaran on August 23 [2021] is one tragic example. Deokaran was a senior financial officer at the Gauteng Department of Health and an important witness in an investigation of corruption within the department; former colleagues believe she was helping authorities link senior political figures to irregular procurement deals and contracts in an organization that is supposed to be committed to public health, not elite enrichment. President Ramaphosa hailed the late whistleblower as "a hero and a patriot" and several individuals have been arrested, but it remains to be seen whether those ultimately responsible for ordering the assassination of a public servant acting with integrity will be exposed or held accountable. (Gavin, 2021)

Whistleblowers are both hailed as heroes and decried as traitors; nevertheless prominent acts of whistleblowing have changed the course of modern history, from the Pentagon Papers leak in 1971, which revealed egregious acts of military wrongdoing by the US government, to the creation of the WikiLeaks whistleblower site in 2006, which, in 2010, released video footage of collateral murder perpetrated by American military personnel against civilians, journalists, and children during the invasion of Iraq circa 2007, among many others exposés of wrongdoing worldwide (Ali & Kunstler, 2019). The case of WikiLeaks and its founder, Julian Assange, represents the most significant example of the criminalization of whistleblowing dissent because of the tremendous legal reaction inflicted upon Assange. Under pressure from a US espionage indictment, Sweden, on what has been decried as trumped-up charges, issued an arrest warrant (which was subsequently withdrawn) for Assange, who in 2010 had sought refuge in the Ecuadorian embassy in London. In 2019, he was arrested and placed in a maximum-security prison in London where he remains in a state of physical and mental deterioration. As Hedges writes,

> the arrest of Julian Assange eviscerates all pretense of the rule of law and the rights of a free press. The list of illegalities, embraced by Ecuadorian, British, and US governments, in the seizure of Assange are ominous. They presage a world where the internal workings, abuses, corruption, lies, and crimes, especially war crimes, carried out by corporate states and the global ruling elite will be masked from the public. They presage a world where those with the courage and integrity to expose the misuse of power will be hunted down, tortured, subjected to sham trials, and given lifetime prison terms in solitary confinement.

In the age of the internet and social media, public participation in media discourse such as blogging and whistleblowing has been made more openly available, and yet the same system of communication that is the internet and social media has given corporations like Facebook immense power over the control and dissemination of information. In this context, in October 2021, whistleblower Frances Haugen gained widespread international news coverage for disclosing thousands of internal Facebook documents to the media regarding how the company deliberately puts profits above human safety and well-being. Haugen revealed how the company's website algorithms are designed to increase user engagement through eliciting an addictive emotional response to often socially divisive and malicious content, such as hate speech, fake news, and misinformation (Hao, 2021).

The entire issue of whistleblowing raises the question of legal protections for freedom of speech. To what extent do people who do good deeds by spreading the truth about injustice, corruption, and wrongdoing receive protection under the law for doing so? In comparison to many other modernized democratic nations, Canada does not fare well. A *National Post* report states, "A report by Transparency International says, 'Canada's current legal framework for whistleblowing is outdated and out of step with international recognized best practices.' David Hutton, a whistleblower protection advocate working at the Centre for Free Expression (CFE), put it even more bluntly: 'Canada has the international reputation of being the Titanic [disaster] of whistleblower protection'" (Maddeaux, 2021).

Activist Dissent and Persecution

Social and political activism that draws attention to significant human issues has been a fundamental type of dissent that has long been a target of repression and criminalization. In Canada, activists involved in labour movements, Indigenous rights, racial injustice, and environmental activism have historically faced retribution from state authorities. Thus, state suspicion of those deemed a political threat to those in power is not confined to authoritarian nations. During the Cold War, Canada's Royal Canadian Mounted Police (RCMP) began collecting secret files on pro-labour activists through a campaign known as PROFUNC (Prominent Functionaries of the Communist Party), "believed to be one of the most draconian peace-time national security programs in Canadian history ... it proposed the RCMP spy on or even detain about 16,000 Communists and 50,000 sympathizers" (CBC News, 2010). More recently, in 2013, the Canadian government was revealed to be compiling a detailed dossier on the Indigenous education activist Cindy Blackstock, who had raised the issue that the education of Indigenous children was significantly underfunded in relation to other Canadian children. Blackstock "was allegedly being monitored through her social media profiles and at her speaking engagements. Cindy figured all of this out after requesting any and all information the government was keeping on her" (Irwin, 2013).

The case of Canadian-American animal rights activist Paul Watson is note-worthy example of criminalizing activist dissent. Watson's activism focuses on marine conservation. He was a founding member of Greenpeace and years later founded the Sea Shepherd Conservation Society, which engaged in direct action primarily against vessels engaged in illegal whaling operations. The harvesting and slaughter of whales and other marine mammals remains a controversial practice. The World Wildlife Organization reports,

> six out of the 13 great whale species are classified as endangered or vulnerable, even after decades of protection. An estimated minimum of 300,000 whales and dolphins are killed each year as a result of fisheries bycatch, while others succumb to a myriad of threats including shipping and habitat loss.... Despite a moratorium on commercial whaling and a band on international trade of whale products, three countries—Iceland, Japan, and Norway—continue their commercial whale hunts. Over 1,000 whales a year are killed for such commercial purposes. The blue whale, the largest animal ever known to have existed, was almost exterminated in the 20th century due to commercial whaling. (n.d.)

Whale parts used for food, oil, and in the cosmetics industry remain major commodities, so there is also an illegal market for whale parts. Although seen as a crime against nature, and part of the massive global trade in wildlife parts, the primary issue from an activist point of view is the lack of policing the illegal practice of whaling in international waters—this is where activists like Watson play a role. Over the years, Watson has on occasion deliberately rammed his vessel into the hulls of whaling ships to disrupt whaling action. As a result, he has been repeatedly charged, arrested, imprisoned, and otherwise been the target of enforcement activity by Japan, Costa Rica, Norway, Canada, and Interpol for his many direct actions in an attempt to save the lives of whales, dolphins, seals, sharks, and other sea creatures (Swift, 2021).

The criminalization, persecution, and murder of environmental activists remains a pressing justice issue. A BBC report reads,

> a record number of activists working to protect the environment and land rights were murdered last year, according to a report by a campaign group.

Two hundred and twenty-seven people were killed around the world in 2020, the highest number recorded for a second consecutive year, the report from Global Witness said. Almost a third of the murders were reportedly linked to resource exploitation—logging, mining, large-scale agribusiness, hydroelectric dams, and other infrastructure. The [Global Witness] report called the victims "environmental defenders" killed for protecting natural resources that need to be preserved, including forests, water supplies, and oceans.... Logging was the industry linked to the most murders with 23 cases—with attacks in Brazil, Nicaragua, Peru, and the Philippines. Indigenous peoples, most often on the frontline of climate change, accounted for a further one third of cases. Colombia had the highest recorded attacks, with 65 people killed last year. (Marshall, 2021)

Critical Art as Expressions of Dissent

Various artistic expressions in the form of painting, sculpture, film, cartoon, theatre, literature, and music have played a substantial role in critiquing injustice throughout history. Satire, mockery, and critical representations are modes of expression that constitute the socially transformative power of art. Many artists in modern times whose work expresses dissent and critique have thus been the targets of silencing, persecution, and criminalization. A 2017 World Economic Forum report reads, "in a time of political and economic uncertainty, the role of art and expression has never been more important. Cultural leaders—from filmmakers to cartoonists—bring new perspectives to tackle challenging issues and inspire people to fulfil their potential. But artists the world over are under threat, with many arrested or even killed for expressing their ideas and showing any signs of dissent" (Schulman, 2017).

One example of fine art as social critique is Pablo Picasso's 1937 mural titled *Guernica*, a graphic anti-war statement that depicts the violence and devastation caused by the aerial firebombing of the village of Guernica under the direction of the Spanish fascist regime just prior to World War II. Most of the men who lived in Guernica were off serving as anti-fascist resistance fighters; thus, the primary targets of the bombing were defenseless women and children as the bombing was timed to coincide with their being out at the market in the centre of town (Preston, 2007). Picasso escaped the persecution of Spain's fascist leader Francisco Franco because he was living in France. The artwork was celebrated worldwide upon its unveiling and to this day stands as a monumental indictment of the horror and injustice of war.

A more recent example of artistry as dissent can be found in the works of Chinese artist Ai Weiwei, once named the most powerful dissident artist in the world, who "'makes daring works unlike anything the world has ever seen,' and a long-time critic of the Chinese government's authoritarian policies and its denial of basic freedoms and human rights to citizens, [who] in 2011 was secretly detained by the Chinese government" (Stevens 2012). Labelled as a political dissident and the subject of regular surveillance by the Chinese government, his passport was returned to him in 2015, whereupon he fled China. In 2018, the Chinese government demolished Weiwei's Beijing art studio and works contained therein without warning (Van Sant, 2018). Although art exhibitions in China require the approval of the state and freedom of expression is heavily censored, artists continue to push the boundaries of creative expression and often engage in "subtle forms of criticism" that evade the scrutiny of authorities (Peschel, 2019).

The repression of artists is evident in most authoritarian regimes, including Cuba. A December 2020 report by The Human Rights Foundation "calls on the Cuban dictatorship to free all imprisoned artists ... on November 16, 2020, rapper Denis Solís was sentenced to eight months in prison after being arrested on November 9 for criticizing the police in one of his songs. He was charged with 'contempt of authority.'" Subsequently, fellow artists began to protest his arrest and then they were arrested in turn. "The Communist regime in Cuba has a long history of violently and relentlessly suppressing free speech, and in particular, any form of artistic expression that does not conform with the 'values of the revolution'" (Human Rights Foundation, 2020).

Image 6.3: Snake Ceiling (Ai Weiwei)
Source: Photo Credit Courtesy of Ai Weiwei Studio

THE ELEMENTS OF ACTIVIST PROTEST AND DISSENT

Understanding why protest and other forms of dissent are disruptive is key to under-standing why dissent is criminalized and repressed. Police often justify restricting protest by saying they are protecting the needs of others in the city who want to use that road or park. Indeed, anyone stuck in traffic waiting for a political march to pass might have wondered out of frustration why protest has to be so disruptive. There are many ways to make your views known, and you might have wondered why people would choose tactics that inconvenience others or provoke a violent reaction from police. It is true that there are many different protest "tactics" (ways to protest), but unfortunately they are not all equally accessible to everyone, they do not all work the same way or achieve the same goals, and many of them require disruption in order to work. Four of the main goals of protest tactics are as follows.

1. To *demonstrate support* for a position—to articulate a position on a social issue and to show those in power that people feel strongly about it.
2. To *make change directly*, often by directly challenging and disrupting an unjust process or proposing or creating a more just process that is desired.
3. To *convince members of the public* of a position on a social issue—to con-vince others that this position is important and in the best interest of society as a whole.
4. To *pressure authorities* by creating circumstances in which it is in their in-terest to take action on a social issue. In practice, many protest strategies combine the following goals:
   • convince the public of the importance of an issue
   • demonstrate support for the issue
   • make change directly when possible to do so
   • pressure authorities to act

Most social movements pursue each of these goals. For instance, while there is a common tendency to think that it is large marches and rallies that have changed the course of history, marches and rallies do not necessarily convince those in power to act. For example, many consider the March on Washington in 1963 and the rally at the Lincoln Memorial where Dr. Martin Luther King, Jr., gave his "I Have a Dream" speech to have been a key turning point in the American civil rights movement. However, it is important to remember that this march and rally were the result of years of organizing for change in local communities, which involved more militant tactics such as sit-ins, boycotts, and other forms of civil disobedi-ence and direct action that pressured authorities directly (Graeber, 2009, p. 363).

Simply demonstrating support for a position and presenting strong arguments on their own are rarely enough to convince authorities to act in favour of a just cause. There are several reasons for this. First, those in power often have interests that compete with the change being requested. Remember that those in power tend to benefit from the status quo and tend to be wary of making changes that might cause them to lose power. They might be happy to make more surface-level changes, but historically more than just good arguments have been needed to convince those in power to fundamentally change the current social order. Second, some tactics, such as lobbying governments or filing court challenges, require a considerable amount of money and contact with those in power, which are not accessible to everyone (Galanter, 1974). Third, some tactics, such as court challenges or waiting until the next election and electing a new government, also take a considerable amount of time, during which people's lives can be seriously affected if change is not made. Typically, a community group or social movement will begin by lobbying a government or business and trying to convince it to act more justly and fairly. However, if those in power have shown themselves to be indifferent to arguments and reason, community groups often try to build political pressure "by disrupting day-to-day economic and political routines and depleting authorities' resources" (Wood, 2014, p. 127). This approach aims not just to demonstrate support for a demand for social justice but also to create circumstances in which it is politically or economically difficult to ignore the community's demands for social justice.

Common Dissent Tactics That Depend on Disruption

In practice, most political actions pursue more than one of the goals listed above, as the following three examples illustrate. These are examples of tactics that (along with marches, increasingly) are most often targeted by police repression. Notice that some form of disruption is key to all three.

Civil Disobedience

Civil disobedience is a set of tactics that involve breaking the law deliberately to communicate a message to the public and lawmakers. It pursues all four of the goals outlined above but aims mainly to demonstrate support for a position and convince the public. Civil disobedience is a symbolic act that usually involves physical defiance but not physical confrontation. An act of civil disobedience is designed to appeal to the public's sense of fairness and justice, often by breaking an unjust law in order to draw the public's attention to the injustice of that law. Civil disobedience aims to create a dilemma wherein authorities can either accept the group's demands or arrest the group, both of which would help the group's cause by amplifying its public message. Those involved typically see it as their duty to break/resist an unjust law and are willing to accept the consequences of breaking that law (usually arrest)—even sometimes alerting police in advance (Kauffman, 2017, p. 10). The demonstrators' willingness to go to jail is seen to show the public their sincerity and seriousness by demonstrating their readiness to make sacrifices for what they believe in (Hughes, 2014, p. 242). This approach was a powerful tactic of the American civil rights movement and many other movements internationally.

Direct Action

Direct action is another tactic that is commonly repressed. Examples of direct action include blockades, pickets, sabotage, squatting, occupations, slow-downs (Graeber, 2009, p. 202), and wildcat strikes. Direct action includes all four of the goals outlined above but aims mainly to make change directly and pressure authorities. There is often overlap between direct action and civil disobedience. Unlike civil disobedience, direct action is less concerned with symbolic gestures and gaining public support than it is with shutting something down or directly stopping the process that is deemed to be unjust. Also, unlike civil disobedience, breaking the law is not central to direct action, although breaking the law often occurs (D'Arcy, 2014; Kauffman, 2017, pp. 11, 63). Like civil disobedience, direct action tactics are oriented towards creating a dilemma for those in power. Direct action often builds political pressure using the "logic of disruption." According to sociologist Frances Fox Piven (2006), social systems depend on the participation and compliance of those who are affected by those systems. For instance, workplaces depend on employees obeying their bosses, and schools depend on students listening to their teachers. According to Piven (2006), this is a strength of these institutions, but it is also a weakness: if people refuse to cooperate (if employees refuse to obey their bosses, for example), those institutions cannot function. There is a long tradition of using this idea in protest. If people protest by collectively refusing to cooperate in the activities of an institution, it is costly for those who benefit when that institution runs smoothly. This builds pressure on authorities until it becomes costlier for the authorities to ignore the protestors than to listen to them and at least partially address their concerns. D'Arcy (2014) has identified three types of direct action. The first is a "disruptive withdrawal," which occurs when people together withdraw their contribution to the normal functioning of an institution, for instance in a strike when workers collectively refuse to work until their concerns are addressed. The second is a "disruptive convergence," through which people gather in a place or manner that prevents the normal functioning of an institution, such as when Indigenous Idle No More protestors took over and shut down the Ambassador Bridge in Windsor in 2013 to protest the erosion of treaty rights (CBC News, 2013a). The third is a "disruptive outburst," through which people together disrupt the normal functioning of an institution in ways that make it unworkable, for instance showing up at a city council meeting and disrupting it with noisemakers and chants so that an unjust motion cannot be passed.

Riots

Riots are third type of protest that is commonly criminalized. It is important to note that riots typically are not planned but are often immediate responses to an action or inaction of authorities, so it is not exactly correct to call them a "tactic." Still, consciously or not, riots advance all four of the goals outlined above but mainly convince the public and build political pressure. Usually, we think of a riot as a random destruction of property, but historically riots have precipitated important social and political change. "Grievance rioting" occurs when a group of people "defies public order to press a grievance" or political concern (D'Arcy, 2014). Sometimes the political side of a grievance riot is not obvious. This is normal, because riots often occur in the very early stages of what later becomes a more coherent political movement and because there are often some people who engage in looting, which tends to become the focus of media coverage. Although certainly destructive, when anger and frustration with continued and overwhelming injustices have built up over some time, a grievance riot—which is often triggered by a further unjust event—draws public attention to concerns that have long been ignored. It creates public pressure for a discussion of those concerns, for further collective activism, and for authorities to address those concerns. Grievance riots often have served as the spark that ignites broader social change. In this way, riots can be seen as what Dr. Martin Luther King, Jr., called "the language of the unheard" (CBS News, 2013). The Stonewall Riots are a good example. Police have a long and ongoing history of involvement in the regulation of gender and sexuality norms, including targeting LGBTQ+ communities. From the 1960s through the 1980s (and beyond), police in Canada and elsewhere raided bars, parks, and bathhouses where queer people were known to frequent. In 1969, police raided a gay bar in New York City called the Stonewall Inn and began harassing and violently arresting patrons. The police harassment was not unusual, but this time the patrons of the bar fought back. The conflict that ensued became known as the Stonewall Riots. This was not a coherent or planned political action and might have appeared to outsiders to be random violence and destruction, but this act of resistance to police was deeply political and marked the beginning of the gay rights movement of the 1970s and 1980s as we know it. The annual pride parades that today celebrate queer communities in cities around the world began as commemorations of the Stonewall Riots. A further example is the rioting in Ferguson, Missouri, in 2014 following the killing of Mike Brown by police. The vastly disproportionate killing of young Black men by white police officers and broader issues of racialized injustice had been occurring for generations without redress and with minimal public attention. In the moment, the rioting was quickly dismissed in mainstream media reports as random acts of violence, but soon after, the militarized response of police to the protests was condemned by the UN Committee Against Torture, and the public discussion that took place following the riots led to the development of the Black Lives Matter movement and the broader movement for Black Lives, which have gone on to organize numerous successful actions and campaigns.

Note that all three of the above tactics—civil disobedience, direct action, and riots—are meant to be disruptive; in fact, the success of these tactics depends on their ability to disrupt the "business as usual" of the normal social order. The disruption is designed to create a minimal inconvenience for the public and a major inconvenience for those who benefit from an injustice. The use of these tactics in struggles for a more inclusive and just society is an important part of democratic dissent and participation. Yet these tactics typically are portrayed by police, media, and many politicians merely as dangerous, disorderly, and deviant. This portrayal allows the criminal justice system to treat these tactics as crimes, and this is a major way that the criminalization of dissent gains public support.

Modes of Policing Dissent and Repressive Police Tactics

Throughout the history of modern policing, the police have responded to protest as if it were criminal violence through the use of police counterviolence and other repressive tactics. Here are six common (often overlapping) examples.

The first is the use of *police violence*, sometimes referred to as police brutality, or the abuse of lethal force. This involves inflicting pain on protestors through physical violence, often using weapons and tear gas. The physical effects can be serious, even fatal, for protestors. Common examples include police striking demonstrators in the head with batons, shooting them with projectiles at close range and/or in the heads and upper torsos, and spraying them with chemical irritants such as pepper spray directly in the eyes, nose, and mouth (e.g., Onisko, 2006, p. 43). Police violence against demonstrators has the effect of demobilizing protestors in the moment and deterring them and others from participating in future protests. As mentioned earlier in this chapter, a well-known example is the Kent State shootings. On May 4, 1970, the Ohio National Guard opened fire on a protest against the Vietnam War by unarmed students at Kent State University in Ohio. Four students were killed and nine were wounded by the 67 rounds that were fired at the demonstrators (Hariman & Lucaites, 2001).

The second is *police intimidation*. Police intimidation includes intimidating appearances (such as riot gear), verbal threats, token arrests, and physical violence. The arbitrariness of violent police actions also can create feelings of fear or terror. Intimidation can create serious emotional stress for those involved in struggles for social change (Wilson, 1976, p. 477) and can deter them from participating in future protest activity.

The third is *police infiltration*. This involves undercover police pretending to be community members and joining in the activities of community groups under the pretense that they are not police officers. Police use this as a means of gathering intelligence, or spying, on the group. For instance, in the months prior to the 2010 G20 protests in Toronto, at least two OPP officers infiltrated and became active participants in groups organizing protest. In one case, a police officer moved in with organizers before disappearing "as the mobilization began, reappearing in court to provide quotes from casual conversations and late-night jokes as evidence" for the serious and unprecedented charges laid against activists, following their preemptive arrest (Robé, 2016, p. 181; Wood, 2014, p. 142). Police can also use infiltration as a means to sabotage a group or protest. For instance, police have used "**agents provocateurs**," who are often undercover police officers pretending to be community members, to join a community group, then try to convince the group to take illegal action or commit a violent act at a demonstration in order to justify a severe police response.

The fourth is *police cooptation*. This involves police convincing community groups to work with them to create a tamer (but also less disruptive, and therefore often less effective) protest. This includes, for instance, police pressuring community groups to work with police to plan the route of their march and to adjust their protest plans to suit police goals. This can be understood as part of a divide-and-conquer tactic through which police treat more and less radical parts of a movement differently and play them off each other.

The fifth is *removal of dissenters*. This has involved arresting demonstrators on real or bogus charges, including preemptive arrests and mass arrests. *Preemptive arrests* are used increasingly and involve arresting potential demonstrators prior to the demonstration or at the demonstration before they have engaged in any criminal activity, which is criticized for going against basic principles of the criminal justice system. *Mass arrests* involve a decision by police to arrest everybody within a given space. Critical research has shown that preemptive and mass arrests are often used not because police hold evidence of a threat but as a crowd control tactic (e.g., Robé, 2016, p. 173), which raises serious questions about protestors' rights to free assembly. Preemptive and mass arrests also are used to gather information about demonstrators or potential demonstrators, which can be entered into databases and shared with other law-enforcement agencies (Onisko, 2006, pp. 38, 40; Power, 2012, p. 417). Arrest also can be seen as a way to intimidate demonstrators as the process of being arrested can have serious consequences for demonstrators' physical and psychological well-being, as well as on the family members they care for, their job, and other aspects of their lives. Removal of demonstrators also includes physically restricting a demonstration, for instance by kettling, through which police forcibly detain a group of people inside a police cordon without actually laying charges against them, and without allowing them to leave to go home, use the washroom, or access food, water, or shelter. Police also physically restrict protest by forcing demonstrators to take a certain route or confining demonstrators to "free-speech zones" in a designated area far from the demonstrators' target audience (Starr et al., 2008, p. 253).

The sixth is monitoring of dissenters through *surveillance*. This can occur either with the knowledge of those being surveilled or without their knowledge. Surveillance gives police information about those being surveilled. When community members know they are being monitored, surveillance can also serve to intimidate those being surveilled. For example, police have used tactics such as walking down the block outside an organizing meeting and writing down the licence plate numbers of the organizers' parked cars (Starr et al., 2008, p. 265) or very obviously and continuously taking photos of all demonstrators at a demonstration. Police often have used these tactics in combination. A prominent example in the US is the FBI's counter-intelligence program COINTELPRO, which "was intended to 'expose, disrupt, misdirect, discredit, or otherwise neutralize'" various political organizations (Cunningham, 2004, p. 253). Through COINTELPRO, from 1956 until 1971, the FBI illegally surveilled social movements, including the civil rights movement, the Black Panthers, and the anti-war movement. The FBI tapped the phones of activists and community organizers and infiltrated, harassed, and disrupted leftist organizations. The FBI spied on Martin Luther King, Jr., and other prominent activists and politicians (Giroux, 2015, pp. 120, 125). The FBI used this information in attempts to assassinate organizers it decided were enemies (Giroux, 2015, p. 125; Goodman, 2014). For instance, in conjunction with Chicago police, the FBI created the conditions for the assassinations of Black Panthers Fred Hampton and Mark Clark (Giroux, 2015, p. 125). Hampton was 21 years old and was shot by police while asleep in his bed in the middle of the night. While COINTELPRO has ended, the FBI and other police agencies in the US, Canada, and beyond continue much of the same work, attempting to surveil, entrap, and otherwise sabotage activist groups (Cunningham, 2004; Giroux, 2015, p. 126; Greenwald, 2014; Starr et al., 2008, p. 253). Thus, for many people, the image of police as protecting the public from violence by repressing protestors is difficult to sustain given the violence in our society, including police violence towards certain communities and towards protestors.

The sorts of police activities described above are termed by Greenberg (2013) as forms of **political policing**. Political policing is one of the primary tasks of domestic security forces who engage in counterintelligence gathering activities most often conducted by the highest-level police agencies in a given nation. Greenberg's book entitled *The Dangers of Dissent* (2010) illustrates how government spying often violates civil liberties and human rights in the name of protecting national security at the expense of individual liberty. Thus, it is important to note that the criminalization of dissent involves policing activities at virtually all levels of law enforcement.

Box 6.2: Four Models of Public Order Policing

della Porta identifies four models of public order policing used to respond to protest:

- The first is "total control," which involves "combative policing" that violently represses protestors.
- The second involves a "ritualistic standoff" with demonstrators.
- The third is "negotiation," in which the police see themselves as mediating between the interests of demonstrators and the public and local business interests.
- The fourth is "cooperation," through which police see themselves as accommodating the demonstrators. (1998, as cited in King, 2006, p. 42)

It is crucial to note that all four of these approaches can be seen as attempts by police to contain and control the protest. For instance, negotiation with police is criticized for rarely leading to major concessions on the part of *police*. Instead, it encourages protestors to tame and dilute the forcefulness of their tactics and pits demonstrators who are willing to "play the game" (King, 2006, p. 43) by acquiescing to police demands against those who are not. At the same time, it allows police to appear accommodating as they gather intelligence on protestors through these interactions. Moreover, these approaches often work together as a carrot-or-stick tactic through which the "cooperation" and "negotiation" responses of the police (the "carrot") are always underpinned by the threat that police can change to a "standoff" or "total control" response (the "stick") at any time.

The Militarization of Policing

Since the events of September 11, 2001, police tactics in many democratic nations have become increasingly militarized (Kraska, 2001). The introduction of anti-terrorist security legislation across many nations has allowed for the expansion of the police use of force against those deemed a threat or enemy of the state. Identifying protesters as a threat to state and security allows police to justify anything they do as an effort to contain that threat, including an increasingly militarized response to protest (Robé, 2016, p. 164; Wood, 2014, pp. 126, 137). Intelligence-based policing often is combined with overt repressive tactics that represent the seeping of a war mentality into domestic policing. This includes, for example, using military-style weapons, no-go zones, and snatch squads to intimidate and arrest key community organizers. A good example of the scale of the increased militarization of protest policing is the police response to the protest against the Summit of the Americas, which met in Quebec City in 2001 to create the Free Trade Area of the Americas (FTAA). Police designed what was at the time the largest police operation in Canadian history. Canadian government officials mobilized 6,518 police officers plus additional army personnel. They built a 6.1-kilometre-long security perimeter around the meeting and surrounding area, which included a 3.8-kilometre-long, 3-metre-high wall in order to keep demonstrators far from the vicinity of the conference (King, 2006, p. 44; King & Waddington, 2005, p. 266; McNally, 2001, p. 2). Police were armed with sniper units, tear-gas, rifles, rubber bullets, shields, water cannons, stun guns, pepper spray, and concussion grenades, amongst other weapons. They used water cannons, batons, 903 plastic bullets, 5,148 canisters of tear gas, and lead-shot balls against the demonstrators and raided supplies from the informal medical centre that demonstrators had set up. There were roughly 493 arrests. One demonstrator was arrested and detained for 17 days for using a megaphone. Together, these measures were widely criticized as an attempt to silence opposition to the trade agreement (King, 2006, p. 45; McNally, 2001). Importantly, this criticism was not based on the argument that the protestors did not *do anything* but rather on arguments that the protestors' actions were within the scope of acceptable confrontational protest in a democracy and that the police response was vastly disproportionate, inappropriate, and politically motivated. The risk-management, intelligence, and militarized elements of this approach often are used together for what can be understood as *strategic incapacitation*: using surveillance, preemptive arrests, and cordoned-off protest zones to isolate and contain the "threat" of protest (Gillham, 2011). Again, the example of the G20 is instructive. During the demonstration, police arrested an estimated 1,100 people, making this the largest mass arrest in Canadian history.

The fact that only 330 of these people were charged (and 201 of those cases were subsequently dismissed) strongly suggests that the arrests were made not due to criminal behaviour but in order to remove demonstrators from the streets (Robé, 2016, p. 182) and intimidate them and others from attending future demonstrations. Further to this, police intelligence was used to arrest 17 people in pre-dawn raids prior to the protests even beginning (Wood, 2014). This police response to the demonstrations drew widespread criticism from within and outside Canada. For instance, Ontario Ombudsperson André Marin indicated that these actions were illegal and violated civil liberties (Renzi & Elmer, 2012; Robé, 2016, p. 182).

The (Ab)use of Anti-Terror Security Legislation to Criminalize Dissent

As indicated earlier in this chapter, not only police but also legislators have contributed to the recent addition of terrorism charges to the ways in which dissent is criminalized. As a response to the terrorist attacks of September 11, 2001, major anti-terrorism legislation has been passed in many countries in the global North. This legislation has been controversial for a number of reasons. Notably, the legislation typically has not enabled more effective detection and prevention of terrorist attacks than pre-existing legislation; it is often reinforced in ways that disproportionately target racialized communities; and the definition of terrorism is typically so broad that protest activity can easily be seen as "terrorist activity" and protestors punished as "terrorists." For instance, disruptions to "critical infrastructure" are commonly included in definitions of terrorism in anti-terrorism acts. This element of the definition is heavily criticized because "critical infrastructure" is often broad enough to include the functioning of businesses and government agencies, and much legitimate and worthy protest historically has disrupted business and government activity (Wood, 2014). Likewise, in the US, the 2001 *PATRIOT Act* included "violence against property" in the definition of terrorism, which enabled many kinds of direct action and civil disobedience to be legally considered terrorism (Robé, 2016, p. 164).

With each new piece of "security" legislation, the definition of a terrorism offence has broadened. After much struggle, Bill C-51, for instance, was amended to specifically exclude "advocacy, protest, dissent, and artistic expression," but it still includes interference with the Government of Canada, interference with critical infrastructure, and activities that cause serious harm to a person or their property because of that person's association with Canada. It has been argued that parts of Bill C-51 violate Section 2 of the *Charter of Rights and Freedoms*, but this has not yet been decided in court (PEN Canada, 2016). Usually, restricting protest in the name of "security" is justified by saying we have to "balance security and freedom." However, critical scholarship has pointed out that security and freedom do not exist on a continuum and that, if they did, it would be impossible to balance anything against an existential threat like terrorism. Thus, key questions become, is giving up freedom necessary, and is it effective? For instance, countries like France and Belgium that have given up significant political freedoms have not actually been more secure from terror threats. Moreover, according to increasing research, when governments reduce freedoms, this is useful to those who recruit terrorists, because it enables them to point to the hypocrisy of Western countries' claims to champion freedom while invading other countries in the name of freedom and restricting freedom at home. Furthermore, reducing people's ability to fight for social change assumes that those who would benefit from this social change do not actually need it—that their quality of life (and their certain, preventable daily suffering) is less important than other people's fear of death in the much less likely event of a terrorist attack.

Box 6.3: The "Terrorist" Label and the Repression of Indigenous Dissent

Racialized people and groups are particularly targeted by police in the repression of protest. The recent development of a risk-management, intelligence-led, militarized approach to the policing of protest has accentuated both the racialized repression of protest and the targeting of racialized communities by police that occurs on a daily basis. For instance, in Canada, political dissent and collective action by Indigenous peoples has long been repressed as part of ongoing processes of colonization. Indigenous land and resources were taken by settlers and by what became the Canadian government, and police forces in Canada developed in part to target Indigenous resistance to these processes. The Canadian government has accepted a mandate for reconciliation with Indigenous peoples, yet Canadian legislators continue to ignore treaty obligations, legal verdicts within Canada, and international legal mandates that require them to gain, for instance, prior and informed consent from Indigenous communities for the use of their land and resources (Proulx, 2014, p. 87). Instead, when Indigenous peoples have defended their land, they have been repressed with particular severity. For instance, the separation between police (who are to police within the borders of a country) and military (who are to police outside the borders of a country) is considered a fundamental feature of a democracy. However, Canada has taken both military action and lethal police or military action against Indigenous protestors far more regularly than against non-Indigenous protestors, including infamously at Oka, Gustafson Lake, and Ipperwash. Canadian police and security agencies continue to treat Indigenous protest as an external threat by framing Indigenous peoples who protest resource extraction that proceeds without their legally mandated consent as dangerous insurgents, grouping them together with Islamist terrorists (Government of Canada, 2011; McCarthy, 2012; Pasternak et al., 2013, p. 77; Proulx, 2014, p. 87). This is possible legally because recent anti-terrorism legislation includes in the vast definition of terrorism those actions that are deemed to be threats to the "national interest" and security of the country (Proulx, 2014, p. 87), including its critical infrastructure. However, what constitutes sabotage of "critical infrastructure" is increasingly broad. For instance, the RCMP Criminal Intelligence Aboriginal Joint Intelligence Group has defined "critical infrastructure" as "infrastructure, both tangible and intangible, that is essential to the health, safety, security, or economic well-being of Canadians and the effective functioning of government," particularly "the energy, transportation, and communications and information technology sectors" (RCMP Criminal Intelligence, 2009, as cited in Proulx, 2014, p. 90). One can imagine how resistance to any effort to develop energy or other economic resources on Indigenous land could be categorized as a threat to "critical infrastructure" and thus considered a security threat.

Characterizing Indigenous political organizing and protest as potential terrorism has enabled the measures used against terror threats to be levelled at Indigenous peoples, including extreme forms of surveillance. For instance, in 2007, the federal ministry of Indian and Northern Affairs Canada developed a Hot Spot Reporting System to identify Indigenous leaders, participants, and supporters and "to closely monitor their actions" (Diabo & Pasternak, 2011; Proulx, 2014, p. 88). The RCMP's Integrated Security Unit has a Joint Intelligence Group that collects and distributes information about "situations involving First Nations" (Groves & Lukacs, 2011; Proulx, 2014, p. 88). Both are part of integrated networks of government security groups that monitor external security threats but focus increasingly on domestic activist groups, Indigenous peoples, "and others who are publically [sic] critical of government policy" (Monaghan & Walby, 2011; Proulx, 2014, p. 88).

There are also examples of actors in the resource extraction industry collecting information on Indigenous peoples and giving this information to the RCMP, and examples of the RCMP and CSIS (Canadian Security Intelligence Service) providing private energy companies with classified information about potential protest actions that might be taken by Indigenous peoples, for example against the Northern Gateway pipeline (Proulx, 2014, p. 87). This has raised important questions about democracy in Canada since the government is effectively spending considerable public resources to spy on citizens and give the information to private companies so they can protect their profits at the expense of these citizens' urgent concerns (which arise from that same government's ongoing colonization of those communities) and at the expense of their right to protest for these concerns to be addressed. Palmater has argued that Indigenous peoples essentially are being treated as internal enemies of the Canadian state (2011; Proulx, 2014, p. 87). This police response to Indigenous protest is an example of how a risk-management approach can be used to frame protest as terrorism and legitimize the criminalization of dissent.

CONCLUSION: THE NEED FOR DISSENT

Dissent is an essential feature of open, inclusive, pluralist societies. Dissent takes a number of forms, from the grassroots mobilization of citizens for a just cause to the efforts of journalists, artists, whistleblowers, and activists across various realms of society to express alternative viewpoints and visions for a better world. In virtually all cases, the types of dissent that get criminalized are people engaging in their right to exercise their freedoms of speech, assembly, and expression. As Watts writes, "dissent involves speaking truth to power, it is a good and legitimate practice. This is because the pursuit of truth, however uncomfortable this is, helps to dispel ignorance in all of its many forms: dissent is something we all need" (2020, p. 221).

While the criminalization of dissent has not traditionally been a topic of study within formal criminology, the ongoing threats to freedoms gained and the attempts to use legal, quasi-legal, and illegal methods to repress dissent mean that 21st century criminology, if it is to be taken seriously, shall be compelled to include the criminalization of dissent as one its many fields of analysis. Dissent is also directly connected to social control and formal policing, thus further making it the terrain of criminological inquiry. Although the police serve a variety of complex functions in society, there is a substantial history of police brutality used against those engaged in legal forms of dissent and democratic expression. The ongoing imprisonment and murder of activists and journalists in both democratic and authoritarian countries remains a significant threat to social freedom and progress globally. This chapter has thus aimed to provide readers with the context required to understand why the criminalization of dissent is significant, what important issues it raises, and how it connects to key debates in critical criminology and in our society more broadly.

Contrary to popular, media-generated perceptions of activist dissent as disorder, violence, and terrorism, this chapter has attempted to address misconceptions about activist-inspired change and to remind the reader how major social movements and other types of social dissent lie at the foundation of modern progress. The criminalization of dissent is dangerous for democracy and for social progress more generally. Those who benefit from the criminalization of dissent have a stake in maintaining systems of power and order as they are, and thus dissent is to be understood part of a larger social struggle across space and time. Thus, the criminalization of dissent is not always a sudden and complete process, where protest is outlawed all at once; it can also happen gradually as freedoms gained are often at risk of being taken back. The gradual, "creeping criminalization of dissent" (Starr et al., 2008, p. 267) is often harder to notice and oppose, but it also provides many opportunities for study, debate, and resistance to injustice along the way.

REVIEW QUESTIONS

1. Why is dissent and social activism important for social progress?
2. Explain some of the social control processes, including policing tactics, involved in the criminalization of dissent.
3. What type of dissent do you find to be especially interesting and why?

GLOSSARY

agent provocateur: An undercover agent acting on behalf of law enforcement officials who induces someone to deliberately break the law so they can be apprehended.

authoritarian society: A society where individual rights are severely restricted and the state engages in the repression of political opponents, imposes limitations on social freedom, and gains support through the promotion of patriotism, propaganda, and the suppression of dissent.

civil disobedience: A type of dissent that involves the act of deliberately violating the law in order to prove a point, or make a statement, and otherwise draw attention to an unjust law.

criminalization of dissent: The use of criminal law and other governmental powers to persecute, harass, and legally charge those engaged in acts of dissent.

direct action: A type of social activism that involves taking action that stops or disrupts processes or practices deemed to be unjust.

dissent: The public expression of opposition to a particular practice or policy being upheld by an authority, usually the state.

dissident: An individual identified by state authorities as a vocal dissenter and who opposes state policy or practice.

fourth estate: That aspect of the free press whose task it is to monitor and keep in check those with political authority through responsible and truthful reporting of state activities.

human rights: The basic freedoms that uphold the dignity and equality of all people by virtue of their being human and thus deserving of respect and protection from oppression and persecution as guaranteed by law.

kettling: A police tactic of crowd control, mostly used against those engaged in street demonstrations, that involves the cordoning off of large groups of people into a single location to disrupt protest activities or to detain them.

martial law: The suspension of civil rights and the imposition of restrictive laws and conditions when a state of emergency is declared.

political policing: A type of police activity engaged in by domestic security forces involving counterintelligence gathering activities that is most often conducted by the highest-level police agencies in a given nation.

political prisoner: An individual who is imprisoned for political reasons, often those who disagree with, defame, challenge, or oppose political authorities in primarily authoritarian nations.

post-9/11 era: The span of time following the terrorist attacks of September 11, 2001, which compelled numerous nations globally to institute strict anti-terror legislation that emphasized security over liberty.

riot: The disruptive activity engaged in by a large crowd often as an unplanned, immediate reaction to an action by state authorities.

social activism: The process of attempting to achieve progressive social change through involvement in an activist organization or as an individual engaged in dissent.

social movement: Organized collectivities of individuals and organizations who sustain themselves over time to initiate social change directed at a particular cause or social issue.

whistleblower: An individual who works inside an organization who exposes wrongdoing taking place within the organization in an effort to have it stopped.

REFERENCES

Ali, T., & Kunstler, M. (Eds.). (2019). *In defense of Julian Assange*. OR Books.

Associated Press. (2021, July 19). Hundreds of journalists, activists among firm's spyware targets, probe finds. *CBC*. Retrieved from https://www.cbc.ca/news/world/spyware-journalists-activists-1.6108070

BBC News. (2021a, January 19). Thai woman jailed for record 43 years for criticising monarchy. *BBC*. Retrieved from https://www.bbc.com/news/world-asia-55723470

BBC News. (2021b, February 24). Jamal Khashoggi: All you need to know about Saudi journalist's death. *BBC*. Retrieved from https://www.bbc.com/news/world-europe-45812399

BBC News. (2021c, September 6). Belarus jail terms for opposition figures Kolesnikova and Znak. *BBC*. Retrieved from https://www.bbc.com/news/world-europe-58395120

BBC News. (2021d, October 8). Nobel Peace Prize: Journalists Maria Ressa and Dmitry Muratov share award. *BBC*. Retrieved from https://www.bbc.com/news/world-58841973

Canadian Press. (2021, August 17). Following protests, Cuba lays out laws on social media use. *Yahoo!news*. Retrieved from https://ca.finance.yahoo.com/news/following-protests-cuba-lays-laws-211250425.html

CBC News. (2010, October 15). Secret internment plan included Toronto landmark. *CBC*. Retrieved from https://www.cbc.ca/news/canada/secret-internment-plan-included-toronto-landmark-1.964079

CBC News. (2013, January 11). Idle No More draws hundreds to Ambassador Bridge. *CBC*. Retrieved from http://www.cbc.ca/news/canada/windsor/idle-no-more-draws-hundreds-to-ambassadorbridge-1.1302410

CBS News. (2013, August 25). MLK: A riot is the language of the unheard. *CBS*. Retrieved from https://www.cbsnews.com/news/mlk-a-riot-is-the-language-of-the-unheard/

Cuddy, A. (2021, April 1). Myanmar coup: What is happening and why? *BBC*. Retrieved from https://www.bbc.com/news/world-asia-55902070

Cunningham, D. (2004). *There's something happening here: The New Left, the Klan, and FBI*. University of California Press.

D'Arcy, S. (2014). *Languages of the unheard: Why militant protest is good for democracy*. Zed Books.

Diabo, R., & Pasternak, S. (2011). First Nations under surveillance. *The Media Co-op*. Retrieved from https://mediacoop.ca/story/first-nations-under-surveillance/7434

Douglass, F. (1857). The significance of emancipation in the West Indies: An address delivered in Canandaigua, New York, on 3 August 1857. *Frederick Douglass Papers*. Retrieved from http://frederickdouglass.infoset.io/islandora/object/islandora%3A1802#page/1/mode/1up

Durkheim, É. (2010). The normal and the pathological. In H. N. Pontell (Ed.), *Social deviance: Readings in theory and research* (5th ed.). Prentice Hall.

The Editors. (2020, September 20). What's driving the rise of authoritarianism and populism in Europe and beyond? *World Politics Review*. Retrieved from https://www.worldpoliticsreview.com/insights/27842/the-rise-of-authoritarianism-and-populism-europe-and-beyond

Elliston, F., Keenan, J. P., Lockhart, P., & van Schaick, J. (1985). *Whistleblowing: Managing dissent in the workplace*. Praeger Press.

Fowler, A. (2018). *Shooting the messenger: Criminalising journalism*. Routledge.

Galanter, M. (1974). Why the haves come out ahead: Speculations on the limits of legal change. *Law & Society Review, 9*(1), 95–160.

Garside, J. (2017, October 16). Malta car bomb kills Panama Papers journalist. *The Guardian*. Retrieved from https://www.theguardian.com/world/2017/oct/16/malta-car-bomb-kills-panama-papers-journalist

Gavin, M. (2021, September 10). *Murder of South African whistleblower illustrates dangerous status quo*. Council on Foreign Relations. Retrieved from https://www.cfr.org/blog/murder-south-african-whistleblower-illustrates-dangerous-status-quo

Gillham, P. F. (2011). Securitizing America: Strategic incapacitation and the policing of protest since the 11 September 2001 terrorist attacks. *Sociology Compass, 5*(7), 636–652.

Giroux, H. A. (2015). Totalitarian paranoia in the post-Orwellian surveillance state. *Cultural Studies, 29*(2), 108–140.

Goodman, A. (2014, January 8). From COINTELPRO to Snowden, the FBI burglars speak out after 43 years of silence (part 2). *Democracy Now!* Retrieved from https://www.democracynow.org/blog/2014/1/8/from_cointelpro_to_snowden_the_fbi

Government of Canada. (n.d.). *The Canadian Charter of Rights and Freedoms*. Retrieved from https://publications.gc.ca/collections/Collection/CH37-4-3-2002E.pdf

Government of Canada. (2011). *Building resilience against terrorism: Canada's counter-terrorism strategy*. Public Works and Government Services Canada. Retrieved from https://www.publicsafety.gc.ca/cnt/rsrcs/pblctns/rslnc-gnst-trrrsm/index-en.aspx

Graeber, D. (2009). *Direct action: An ethnography*. AK Press.

Greenberg, I. (2013). *The dangers of dissent: The FBI and civil liberties since 1965*. Lexington Books.

Greenwald, G. (2014, January 7). 4 points about the 1971 FBI break-in. *Common Dreams*. Retrieved from https://www.commondreams.org/views/2014/01/07/four-points-about-1971-fbi-break

Groves, T., & Lukacs, M. (2011, December 4). Mounties spied on native protest groups. *Toronto Star*. Retrieved from https://www.thestar.com/news/canada/2011/12/04/mounties_spied_on_native_protest_groups.html

Hao, K. (2021, October 5). The Facebook whistleblower says its algorithms are dangerous. Here's why. *MIT Technology Review*. Retrieved from https://www.technologyreview.com/2021/10/05/1036519/facebook-whistleblower-frances-haugen-algorithms/

Hardt, M., & Negri, A. (2004). *Multitude: War and democracy in the age of empire*. Penguin Books.

Hariman, R., & Lucaites, J. L. (2001). Dissent and emotional management in a liberal-democratic society: The Kent state iconic photograph. *Rhetoric Society Quarterly*, *31*(3), 5–31. https://doi.org/10.1080/02773940109391204

Head, J. (2021, August 14). Myanmar: The woman who jumped to her death while fleeing police. *BBC*. Retrieved from https://www.bbc.com/news/world-asia-58196465

Hedges, C. (2019, April 12). The martyrdom of Julian Assange. *Common Dreams*. Retrieved from https://www.commondreams.org/views/2019/04/12/martyrdom-julian-assange

Hughes, M. L. (2014). Civil disobedience in transnational perspective: American and West German anti-nuclear-power protesters, 1975–1982. *Historical Social Research*, *39*(1), 236–253.

Human Rights Foundation. (2020, December 3). *Cuba: Stop criminalizing freedom of speech and artistic expression*. Retrieved from https://hrf.org/cuba-stop-criminalizing-freedom-of-speech-and-artistic-expression

Irwin, N. (2013, May 30). Meet the Native activist who the Canadian government was spying on. *Vice*. Retrieved from https://www.vice.com/en/article/ava4gp/meet-the-native-activist-who-the-canadian-government-was-spying-on

Kauffman, L. A. (2017). *Direct action: Protest and the reinvention of American radicalism*. Verso Books.

Kaur, H. (2020, May 4). 50 years ago today, the shooting of 4 college students at Kent State changed America. *CNN.* Retrieved from https://www.cnn.com/2020/05/04/us/kent-state-shooting-50th-anniversary-trnd/index.html

King, M. (2006). From reactive police to crowd management?: Policing antiglobalization protest in Canada. *Jurisprudencija*, 79(1), 40–58.

King, M., & Waddington, D. (2005). Flashpoints revisited: A critical application to the policing of anti-globalization protest. *Policing and Society*, 15(3), 255–282.

Knight, N. (2016, October 17). Filmmaker faces 45 years in prison for reporting on Dakota Access protests. *Countercurrents.* Retrieved from https://countercurrents.org/2016/10/filmmaker-faces-45-years-in-prison-for-reporting-on-dakota-access-protests/

Kraska, P. B. (2001). *Militarizing the American criminal justice system: The changing roles of the armed forces and the police.* Northeastern University Press.

Maclean's. (2010, July 19). G20 thugs don't deserve a break. *Maclean's, 124*(17), 4–5.

Maddeaux, S. (2021, October 16). If Facebook whistleblower was Canadian, she may have never come forward. *National Post.* Retrieved from https://nationalpost.com/opinion/sabrina-maddeaux-if-facebook-whistleblower-was-canadian-she-may-never-have-come-forward

Mahoney, J., & Hui, A. (2010, June 28). G20-related mass arrests unique in Canadian history. *The Globe and Mail.* Retrieved from https://www.theglobeandmail.com/news/world/g20-related-mass-arrests-unique-in-canadian-history/article4323163/

Malta Independent. (2018, January 26). *SLAPP is an attempt to silence journalists—Francis Zammit Dimech.* Retrieved from https://www.independent.com.mt/articles/2018-01-26/local-news/SLAPP-is-an-attempt-to-silence-journalists-Francis-Zammit-Dimech-6736184075

Marsh, S. (2021 August 12). One month after Cuba protests, hundreds remain behind bars. *CTV.* Retrieved from https://www.ctvnews.ca/world/one-month-after-cuba-protests-hundreds-remain-behind-bars-1.5544611

Marshall, C. (2021, September 13). Record number of environmental activists murdered. *BBC.* Retrieved from https://www.bbc.com/news/science-environment-58508001

McCarthy, S. (2012, February 10). Ottawa's new anti-terrorism strategy lists eco-extremists as threats. *The Globe and Mail.* Retrieved from https://www.theglobeandmail.com/news/politics/ottawas-new-anti-terrorism-strategy-lists-eco-extremists-as-threats/article533522/

McNally, D. (2001). Mass protests in Quebec City: From anti-globalization to anti-capitalism. *New Politics, 8*(3), 76–86.

Monaghan, J., & Walby, K. (2011, August 23). Making up "terror identities": Security intelligence, Canada's Integrated Threat Assessment Centre and social movement suppression. *Policing and Society, 22*(2): 133–151. https://doi.org/10.1080/10439463. 2011.605131

Onisko, M. (2006). Criminalization of dissent in the United States: Obligations of the US under articles 19 and 21 of the ICCPR. *Guild Practitioner, 63*(1), 35–46.

Palmater, P. D. (2011). *Beyond blood: Rethinking Indigenous identity.* Purich Publishing.

Pasternak, S., Collis, S., & Dafnos, T. (2013). Criminalization at Tyendinaga: Securing Canada's colonial property regime through specific land claims. *Canadian Journal of Law and Society, 28*(1), 65–81.

PEN Canada. (2016, April 1). *Can I be arrested for protesting?* Retrieved from https:// pencanada.ca/blog/canadians-right-to-protest/

Peschel, S. (2019, June 2). Political art in China 30 years after the Tiananmen Square protests. *DW.* Retrieved from https://www.dw.com/en/ political-art-in-china-30-years-after-the-tiananmen-square-protests/a-49006585

Pfohl, S. J. (1985). *Images of deviance and social control: A sociological history.* McGraw-Hill Publishing.

Piven, F. F. (2006). *Challenging authority: How ordinary people change America.* Rowman & Littlefield Publishers.

Power, N. (2012). Dangerous subjects: UK students and the criminalization of protest. *The South Atlantic Quarterly, 111*(2), 412–420.

Preston, P. (2007). George Steer and Guernica. *History Today, 57*(5), 12–19.

Proulx, C. (2014). Colonizing surveillance: Canada constructs an Indigenous terror threat. *Anthropologica, 56*(1), 83–100.

Renzi, A., & Elmer, G. (2012). *Infrastructure critical: Sacrifice at Toronto's G8/G20 Summit.* Arbeiter Ring.

Reuters. (2021, August 15). Organizer of Hong Kong mass protests disbands in latest blow to democracy movement. Retrieved from https://www.reuters.com/world/ china/organizer-hong-kong-mass-protests-disbands-latest-blow-democracy-movement-2021-08-15/

Robé, C. (2016). Criminalizing dissent: Western state repression, video activism, and counter-summit protests. *Framework, 57*(2): 161–188.

Schulman, M. (2017, January 20). *The art of dissent.* World Economic Forum. Retrieved from https://www.weforum.org/agenda/2017/01/the-art-of-dissent/

Shantz, J. (Ed.). (2011). *Law against liberty: The criminalization of dissent.* Vandeplas Publishing.

Starr, A., Fernandez, L. A., Amster, R., Wood, L. J., & Caro, M. J. (2008). The impacts of state surveillance on political assembly and association: A socio-legal analysis. *Qualitative Sociology, 31*(3), 251–270.

Stevens, M. (2012, September). Is Ai Weiwei China's most dangerous man? *Smithsonian Magazine*. Retrieved from https://www.smithsonianmag.com/arts-culture/is-ai-weiwei-chinas-most-dangerous-man-17989316/

Swift, R. (2021, June 10). *Sea Shepherd Captain Paul Watson: "It's the radicals who are destroying the planet."* VipBoat. Retrieved from https://vipboat.es/sea-shepherd-captain-paul-watson-its-the-radicals-who-are-destroying-the-planet/

United Nations. (n.d.). *Universal Declaration of Human Rights*. Retrieved from https://www.un.org/en/about-us/universal-declaration-of-human-rights

United Nations Educational, Scientific and Cultural Organization. (n.d.). *Safety of journalists*. Retrieved from https://en.unesco.org/themes/safety-journalists

Van Sant, S. (2018, August 4). Ai Weiwei responds to Chinese authorities destroying his Beijing studio. *npr*. Retrieved from https://www.npr.org/2018/08/04/635654200/ai-wei-weis-beijing-studio-destroyed-by-chinese-authorities

Watts, R. (2020). *Criminalizing dissent: The liberal state and the problem of legitimacy*. Routledge.

Wilson, J. (1976). Social protest and social control. *Social Problems, 24*(4): 469–481.

Wood, L. J. (2014). Protest as threat. In *Crisis and control: The militarization of protest policing*. Pluto Press.

World Wildlife Fund. (n.d.). *Whale*. Retrieved from https://www.worldwildlife.org/species/whale

CHAPTER 7

Crime, Psychopathology, and the Idea of the Natural-Born Criminal

Stephanie Griffiths, Jarkko Jalava, and Claudio Colaguori

LEARNING OBJECTIVES

In this chapter, you will

- learn about the history of various biological and psychological theories of crime;
- discover how biological determinism is both relevant and problematic for understanding criminal and deviant behaviour;
- explore methods of studying the contributions of genes and environment to antisocial behaviour;
- examine relationships between brain abnormalities, mental illness, and antisocial behaviour; and
- look at case study examples that illustrate the difficulties that psychological and biological cases of crime pose for the criminal justice system.

INTRODUCTION

In 2009, Canadian crime rates had been declining sharply for almost two decades, with homicide rates steadily declining for an even longer period. One of the safest places in Canada was, and continues to be, Ontario (Keighley, 2017, p. 3). Around 2007, however, southeastern Ontario began to record a series of unusual crimes. First, a thief broke into several homes and took women's and girls' underwear, family photos, and other personal items, sometimes leaving taunting notes behind. Two years later, a woman was raped by an intruder in her home in Tweed, a small municipality 220 kilometres northeast of Toronto. Soon afterwards, the same type of sexual assault was reported by another Tweed resident. Then, on November 25, 2009, 38-year-old Marie-France Comeau, a corporal in the Canadian Air Force, was raped and murdered in her home in Brighton, an hour's drive from Tweed. Two months later, 27-year-old Jessica Lloyd disappeared in nearby Belleville.

Police soon had a suspect, 46-year-old Russell Williams, who was intercepted driving a car with tires that matched prints left outside Lloyd's residence. After a lengthy interrogation, Williams confessed to murdering Comeau and Lloyd and led police to Lloyd's body. In court, he also pleaded guilty to the rapes and break-ins. He confessed to 88 crimes in total and received 2 life sentences with no chance of parole for 25 years (Jalava et al., 2015).

The average violent offender is a young, relatively poor male with little educa-tion (Farrington, 2007; Miladinovic & Mulligan, 2015). Only one of these was true of Williams: he was male. But he was also married, well educated, financially stable, and employed. A decorated commander in the Canadian Forces stationed in Trenton, Ontario, Williams had consulted with senior government officials and piloted planes for foreign dignitaries, including the Queen of England. The fact that Williams did not fit the typical offender profile led many to wonder about his mental and neurological health. *The Globe and Mail* speculated that Williams was a psychopath because, as a group, such people "appear to have weaknesses in the inner recesses of the brain that make up the paralimbic system, which involves emo-tions and self-control" (McIlroy & Anderssen, 2010, p. F4). Others believed that Williams suffered from paraphilia, a diagnostic term covering various abnormal sexual behaviours: "Williams escalated and continued his crimes," explained one re-tired FBI criminal profiler, "because it was who he was and he couldn't do anything about it" (Klismet, as cited in Gibb, 2011, p. 499). In other words, the problem was with Russell Williams—or the brain of Russell Williams—not his circumstances.

Crime statistics seem to support this perspective, at least in part. The vast majority of young, low socioeconomic status men do not commit serious violent crimes, while men from higher socioeconomic classes—and women—sometimes do. Although most multiple murderers are not highly educated or particularly talented, they have included doctors, nurses, teachers, businessmen, and at least one PhD student in criminology (British serial murderer and cannibal Stephen Griffiths). Melvin Rees, who murdered at least five people in the 1950s, was a musi-cian. Harold Shipman, a British physician, was convicted of killing 15 patients be-tween the 1970s and 1990s, though an inquiry later found that the actual number of victims may have been more than 200. Amy Bishop was a biology professor at the University of Alabama in 2010 when she opened fire on her colleagues, killing three. What do these offenders have in common with drifters and petty thieves who also became multiple murderers? Are they individuals with *criminal minds*? Do their brains make them predisposed to homicide? Are they mentally ill?

The way we answer these questions has deep implications for criminal and social justice. For example, if some people are biologically or psychologically predisposed to crime through no fault of their own, would it be fair to hold them responsible for their actions? Should they be punished? If we could identify born criminals in infancy, would it be ethical to treat them or, failing that, to incarcerate them or banish them to a distant colony before they commit crimes? What about sterilizing those who might pass on criminal traits believed to run in families? On the other hand, would the families of a mass murderer's victims be within their rights to sue a government for not averting a potentially preventable act? While some of these questions are hypothetical, others are not. Biological theories of crime have sometimes informed decisions about guilt and innocence as well as appropriate punishments. They have also provided justifications for sterilizing and even exterminating members of populations considered to be dangerous or undesirable. These populations have included, in disproportionate numbers, visible and religious minorities.

BIOLOGY AND CRIME

The idea that criminals are biologically different from non-criminals is more than two centuries old. Theologians and physicians in the 18th and 19th centuries attempted to study the human body for overt signs of immorality. Franz Joseph Gall and Gaspar Spurzheim believed that the human brain was made up of different organs, or faculties, each with a different function. These faculties included such things as mechanical skill, verbal memory, parental love, and murder. The shape of a person's skull, Gall and Spurzheim argued, corresponded to the size of each faculty, and character could be determined by examining the shape of the skull, a process termed **phrenology**. Although phrenology would later be discredited for lack of evidence that skull shape had anything to do with character, the idea that different parts of the brain are responsible for different functions turned out to be mostly correct. Phrenology was also an early example of a new type of criminology that would become popular in the late 19th century and then again in the late 20th century: **biological criminology**. Biological criminology subscribed to two related approaches, **positivism,** and **biological determinism**. Positivism was first and foremost a method. It held no interest in unobservable or metaphysical phenomena—including free will—but instead concentrated only on what could be observed. Biological determinism proposed that human behaviour, including crime, was the product of biological forces such as genes, brain abnormalities, and neurotoxins.

Box 7.1: Geographic Variations in Crime Rates—A Challenge to Biological Theories

One problem with biological determinism is that while it can, at least theoretically, explain individual-level violence, it cannot readily account for the fact that even though human biology is largely consistent, crime rates vary greatly from country to country. Homicide rates in the Americas (North, Central, and South America, and the Caribbean), for example, are five to eight times higher than in Europe and Asia. The United Nations Office of Drugs and Crime (2013) attributes the difference mainly to political violence and organized crime, not to biological factors.

Nor are biological theories likely to have much to say about why crime rates differ *within* countries. Canada's overall crime rate has fluctuated significantly since reliable recordkeeping began in the 1960s. Different regions consistently show different levels of crime, yet there is little evidence that the biological makeup of Canadians has fluctuated accordingly.

The Idea of the "Born Criminal"

The first comprehensive biological theory of crime was developed by Cesare Lombroso. As outlined in Chapter 2, Lombroso, often touted as the father of criminology, worked as a physician in insane asylums in Italy, and he suggested that born criminals could be distinguished from regular criminals (whose offending could have social causes) by their physical, moral, and psychological makeup. **Born criminals**, according to Lombroso, had regressed to an earlier stage of human evolution, a process he called **atavism**. These offenders had distinct facial features and bodily peculiarities, used archaic language, had high pain tolerance, and felt no remorse. Lombroso published the first version of his theory in an 1876 book titled *L'uomo Delinquente* (*Criminal Man*) and led a movement to put criminology on a scientific footing. The movement, called the *positivist school of criminology*, aimed to replace the classical school by shifting attention from crime, which Beccaria thought was a matter of rational calculation, to a focus on the measurable identification of something biologically wrong with the criminal. The positivist school of criminology profoundly shaped the understanding of crime in the late 19th and early 20th centuries (see Gibson, 2002; Horn, 2003).

The positivist school of criminology is today mostly remembered for where it went wrong. Subsequent studies failed to confirm that the bodies of criminals were different from those of non-criminals or that they were evolutionary throw-backs. Lombroso misread the logic of Darwinian evolution in two ways. Species, Darwin pointed out, evolve, but not individuals within those species. So even if Lombroso's idea of reverse evolution had been correct (and it was not), he would still have been wrong about the ability of select *individuals* to devolve. However, the most significant problem with Lombroso's theory was that it was put into practice. For example, Lombroso and his colleagues frequently appeared in court to determine guilt or innocence on the basis of a defendant's physiology (Gould, 1996). Worse, fascists throughout Europe used Lombroso's ideas to intensify fears of *social degeneration*, a process they thought was caused by the presence of inferior races. In Nazi Germany, atavism provided a eugenicist rationale for exterminating millions of Jews, Slavs, "gypsies" (Roma), and other populations deemed undesirable (Pick, 1989).

In the words of scholars ...

It seems to me important ... to determine whether the criminal man belongs in the same category as the healthy man or the insane individual or in an entirely separate category. To do this and decide whether there is a force in nature that causes crime, we must abandon the sublime realms of philosophy and even the sensational facts of the crime itself and proceed instead to the direct physical and psychological study of the criminal, comparing results with information on the healthy and the insane.

Cesare Lombroso, *Criminal Man*. 1876

However, Lombroso made important contributions to criminology as well. He took precise measurements of the skulls, hairlines, and eyebrows of prison inmates and so laid the foundations for modern physiological research on profiling offenders. Furthermore, Lombroso advocated for many contemporary criminal justice practices. He argued that punishment should be made to fit the needs of the offender rather than as a deterrent to future crime. Moreover, he did not believe that born criminals should be held morally responsible for their behaviour as they were, after all, simply following their biological natures, a point made frequently by philosophers and legal scholars today about offenders with brain damage or mental illness (Nadelhoffer, 2013).

At around the same time that Lombroso was developing his theory, other biological theories of crime were being proposed as well, and these too would soon be put into practice. A popular theory held that crime was inherited in the same way as physical characteristics were. One line of evidence was that crime seemed to run in families. Richard Dugdale's (1841–1883) study of the "Juke" family and Henry H. Goddard's study of the "Kallikaks" (not their real names) appeared to show striking consistency across generations. Among the more than 1,000 "Juke" descendants, Dugdale identified scores of *murderers, thieves, beggars, bastards,* and *prostitutes*—all labels that denoted deviancy in that era. Goddard's "Kallikaks" appeared to show two distinct lineages. The "good" side consisted of upstanding citizens like doctors, lawyers, and landholders, while the "bad" side had a disproportionately large number of criminals and other unwanted types, many of whom were deemed *feeble-minded*. **Feeble-mindedness** is a problematic 19th-century label that was applied by practitioners to a wide range of people in prisons, asylums, and hospitals, which primarily referred to low intelligence and limited social functioning. The diagnosis was associated with crime and social disorder and often applied to socially marginalized persons such as the homeless; young, unwed mothers; the unemployed; the traumatized; and racialized immigrants. Feeble-mindedness, Goddard's data seemed to indicate, was an inherited trait.

In the words of scholars ...

The born criminal theory has always fundamentally rested on an empirical argument. Degenerationism was popular for over half a century not only because of its flexibility in explaining social and personal ills, but because it donned the mantle of science.... Degeneration was not seriously challenged until 1913 ... and the full realization that degenerationism was wild, pseudo Darwinian conjecture did not arrive until the middle of the twentieth century.

Jarkko Jalava, Stephanie Griffiths, and Michael Maraun, *The Myth of the Born Criminal: Psychopathy, Neurobiology, and the Creation of the Modern Degenerate.* 2015

For Goddard, feeble-mindedness was not only inherited but also eradicable. The best way to do this, he believed, was **negative eugenics**. As opposed to positive eugenics, which promoted selective breeding among the fit and intellectually superior, negative eugenics sought to discourage the unfit and intellectually deficient from reproducing. This was primarily achieved through surgical means or by prohibiting marriages. The first forced sterilizations of those deemed "mentally defective" were carried out in the US in the late 19th century. In 1907, Indiana became the first jurisdiction to make such surgical procedures mandatory.

With the help of Goddard and other leading intellectuals, 33 states passed sterilization laws in the early 20th century, resulting in roughly 65,000 sterilizations of the feeble-minded, criminals, prostitutes, epileptics, alcoholics, drug users, the physically deformed, and the "morally degenerate." US Congress also passed laws to restrict immigration from Southern and Eastern Europe based on the belief, drawing on data supplied by Goddard, that such populations were more likely than Northern and Western Europeans to be feeble-minded (NPR, 2016). Soon, eugenic laws were being passed around the world. British Columbia and Alberta carried out 3,000 sterilizations that disproportionately targeted women, Indigenous people, and the poor. Most horrifically, Nazi Germany used US-style eugenic laws as a basis for their own racial purification laws that ultimately led to the Holocaust (Hansen & King, 2013; Hothersall, 2003; Kevles, 1995; Leahey, 2004; Rafter, 1997).

Box 7.2: Selected Biological Theories of Crime: Evaluating the Evidence

In the 20th century, a number of biological theories of crime were proposed, with varying degrees of success. One popular theory, proposed by Ernst Kretschmer and William Sheldon, classified humans according to body types and corresponding temperaments. The endomorphic type was heavy-set and soft-skinned and tended to be extroverted and easy-going. The mesomorphic type was lean, muscular, assertive, and energetic, while the ectomorphic type was thin and pale, with an introverted, inactive personality. The mesmorphic type, Sheldon thought, was most likely to be delinquent. No convincing evidence has materialized to support this theory.

Another theory held that a rare chromosomal abnormality, in which a male has an extra Y chromosome (XYY), caused violence and a host of other characteristics such as tallness, learning disabilities, acne, and below-average IQ. Since the Y chromosome is a male chromosome and males tend to be more violent than females, XYY has been called the *super-male syndrome*. In 1966, soon after the discovery of the syndrome, a tall, pockmarked high school dropout named Richard Speck raped and murdered eight nursing students at knifepoint in a student dormitory in Chicago. One of his victims managed to survive by hiding under a bed and later identified him in a police line-up. Speck was charged for the murders, but shortly before his trial it was reported in the news that he was XYY. Despite intense media speculation about the implications for the case, chromosomal analysis soon proved Speck was in fact a "normal" XY male (Raine, 2013).

Case studies such as Speck's are attention-grabbing, but even if his genotype had indicated XYY, it would not establish that everyone with XYY syndrome is predisposed to crime. A large-scale study conducted in 1976 found that XYY is associated with crime, but not violent crime. Other studies have suggested that XYY boys may be more impulsive than XY boys (Ross et al., 2012). At best, XYY syndrome may be related to a personality trait that, in turn, is often related to crime.

Even though many theories have tried to link a person's biological makeup with criminality have been disproven, why do you think ideas about "born criminals" and criminal types continue to circulate in the popular imagination?

Quantitative Genetics

Was the idea of hereditary crime and feeble-mindedness wrong or simply misapplied? Goddard had begun to voice misgivings about his own research in the 1920s, and later scholarship suggested that many of his methods and assumptions were deeply flawed. Perhaps most importantly, neither Goddard nor Dugdale had been able to separate the relative contributions of heredity and environment in their subjects. In the late 19th century, Francis Galton, Charles Darwin's cousin and the man who coined the term *eugenics*, developed a method to identify the unique contributions of genes and environment. Galton gave questionnaires to parents to assess whether the development of twins born similar (identical or monozygotic, in contemporary terms) would diverge if they had differing life experiences, and whether twins dissimilar at birth (fraternal or dizygotic) would become more similar in similar environments (Burbridge, 2001). Galton's method is called the **twin study** and proceeds on the basis that dizygotic twins share 50 percent of their genetic material, while monozygotic twins share 100 percent of their genetic material. If monozygotic twins are behaviorally more like one another than dizygotic twins, genes should play a role in that behaviour. **Adoption studies** also examine degrees of similarity, but between adopted children and both their biological and adoptive parents. If adopted children are more like their biological parents than their adoptive parents with respect to a given trait, we assume the trait is at least somewhat genetically determined.

Based on twin and adoption studies, researchers calculate **heritability estimates**. These are reported as a proportion (between 0 and 1) or percentage (between 0% and 100%), and they are a snapshot of the relative contribution of genetic variations to variation in a behaviour or trait at the population level. The contribution of environmental factors is sometimes called an **environmentability estimate**. Generally, human behavioural traits have heritability estimates in the moderate range (0.30–0.60), and **antisocial behaviour** is no different: an analysis of 51 twin and adoption studies by Rhee and Waldman (2002) estimated the moderate heritability (0.41) and environmentability (0.59) of antisocial behaviour. If these estimates are accurate, then the reason why crime and disorder seemed to run in the Juke and Kallikak families may have been much more complex than either Dugdale or Goddard appreciated. Genes may have played a role, but so did the environment, as well as any number of interactions between genes and environment.

The Limitations of Heritability Estimates

Twin and adoption studies are useful but imperfect tools for estimating heritability and environmentability. How antisocial behaviour is defined (whether by self-reports or parent ratings) can generate inconsistency in heritability estimates. Also, accurate statistical estimates rely on the populations under investigation to show a broad range of characteristics. The heritability of the number of heads in humans, for example, would be near zero, not because head number is not genetically determined but because nearly everyone, save for conjoined twins, is born with one head. As the screening of adoptive parents aims to ensure that their family environments resemble each other much more than would those of randomly selected families, heritability estimates could be inflated in these groups. Also, heritability depends on the environment in which it is estimated. Heritability estimates are likely to be lower in aversive environments than in better-off conditions. This is because adversities can overwhelm or "wash out" any genetic influences. For these and other reasons, heritability estimates of traits like aggression vary widely from study to study (Rhee & Waldman, 2002).

Perhaps the most serious limitation of traditional heritability models involves how they assume genes and environments affect behaviour in a binary nature versus nature sort of way. Recent advances in genetics indicate that trying to distinguish between genetic and environmental influences may be much more difficult than previously thought. Studies suggest that personal experiences and cultural practices can alter how genes are expressed and that this gene expression may in turn affect behaviour and even change the course of species evolution (Richerson & Boyd, 2005). The study of the interplay between environment, culture, gene expression, and behaviour is called **behavioural epigenetics**.

In the words of scholars ...

Culture affects the success and survival of individuals and groups; as a result, some cultural variants spread and others diminish, leading to evolutionary processes that are every bit as real and important as those that shape genetic variation. These culturally evolved environments then affect which genes are favored by natural selection.

Peter J. Richerson and Robert Boyd, *Not by Genes Alone: How Culture Transformed Human Evolution.* 2005

Molecular Genetics

Quantitative genetics broadly estimate genetic and environmental influences on a trait at the population level. These studies cannot tell us which, if any, specific genes are involved in criminality, which in turn means that they cannot explain why any given *individual* commits crimes. That task falls to **molecular genetics**, or the study of single gene-behaviour relationships. The search for a gene that predisposes an individual to antisocial, violent, or criminal behaviour has proven futile thus far; however, one of the most promising contemporary candidate genes for antisocial behaviour is a gene coding for monoamine oxidase A (MAOA). MAOA is a gene that encodes an enzyme that breaks down monoamine neurotransmitters such as serotonin, dopamine, and norepinephrine.

A 1993 study described a Dutch family in which several of the males were violent and sexually deviant and had committed crimes including rape, assault, and arson. When the family was genotyped, the males turned out to have a rare point mutation in the MAOA gene, which completely deactivated the enzyme. This finding suggested that poorly controlled aggression might be related to atypical MAOA function (Brunner et al., 1993a, 1993b). However, in response to the ensuing interest in MAOA as a potential explanation for aggression, the lead author of the original study cautioned that affected males suffered other consequences of MAOA deficiency potentially relevant to aggression (for example, borderline mental retardation and sleep deprivation), and that environmental variables were not even evaluated (Brunner, 1996).

To address these limitations, researchers have examined MAOA gene variants, or alleles, commonly found in the normal population. The most consistent finding has been that, when combined with childhood maltreatment, a low-activity MAOA allele increases the risk for antisocial behaviour (Byrd & Manuck, 2014; Caspi et al., 2002; Jackson & Beaver, 2015). This is roughly what quantitative genetics predicted: both genetic and environmental influences play a role in behaviour. However, this childhood maltreatment–low-activity MAOA gene interaction effect appears to be relatively small, at 0.14 to 0.18 (Haberstick et al., 2014).

While a low-activity MAOA allele, in combination with childhood maltreatment, could increase a person's risk for antisocial behaviour, it is not a gene for crime or aggression. Nevertheless, the low-activity MAOA was christened the *warrior gene* in popular science writing. The gene began to appear in court as early as 1994 when the defence team for the convicted murderer Stephen Mobley requested—unsuccessfully—a genetic test for their client. In a 2009 Tennessee murder case, the defence argued that Bradley Waldroup, a man who admitted to killing one woman and attempting to kill another, had the low-activity MAOA gene variant and was abused as a child. Based on the evidence, the jury found Waldroup guilty of a lesser crime, because, as one juror put it, "a bad gene is a bad gene" (Hagerty, 2010).

Brain Structure and Function

If genes are related to antisocial behaviour (to whatever extent and in whatever complex ways) such a relationship would seem to focus on the structure and/or function of the brain. Much of the research into the relationship between the brain and crime has concentrated on the **prefrontal cortex**, the structures in the front half of the brain that are responsible for complex cognitive and emotional processes, such as impulse control. The prefrontal cortex has the longest developmental timeline of all brain regions, and this may partly explain why youth tend to be more impulsive than adults. Prefrontal cortex injuries have been associated (though imperfectly) with impulsive aggression (Brower & Price, 2001); at least 60 percent of prison inmates convicted of violent crimes have experienced traumatic brain injury (TBI), a much higher rate than in the general population (Farrer & Hedges, 2011). Such injuries are also a predictor of younger age at incarceration, psychiatric problems, and recidivism (Schofield et al., 2006; Williams et al., 2010).

Box: 7.3: The Complex Case of Phineas Gage

The best-known case of prefrontal brain injury occurred in 1848, when a construction foreman named Phineas Gage was laying explosives to clear a railbed in Vermont. Dynamite exploded unexpectedly, driving a long metal rod through the orbit of Gage's left eye and into his prefrontal cortex. Although bits of his brain lay 100 feet away, he remained conscious. His personality, however, changed noticeably. Previously a conscientious, morally upstanding man, he became impulsive and unreliable. The case of Phineas Gage quickly became famous for its apparent ability to illustrate the direct relationship between brain function and personality traits. Phrenologists believed that the injury had destroyed Gage's faculty of benevolence, the faculty responsible for morality (Macmillan, 2000). For others, the case illustrated the neural basis of antisocial behaviour (e.g., Damasio et al., 1994). For some contemporary neuroscientists, Gage's "story became a classic of neuroscience because it revealed that behavior, which seems a matter of personal will, is fundamentally biological" (Kiehl & Buckholtz, 2010, p. 26). While the injury apparently affected Gage's behaviour immediately following the accident, he still remained close to his family, worked hard at various jobs, and had no trouble with the law. Some have also suggested that Gage's personality changes may have been caused by his facial disfigurement and the social rejection it inspired, rather than his brain injury alone (Kotowicz, 2007).

As the case of Phineas Gage (box 7.3) demonstrates, prefrontal injuries can increase impulsivity and antisocial behaviour; neuroimaging studies have explored whether non-brain injured offenders might still show subtle abnormalities in their prefrontal regions. These studies consistently report that violent offenders have smaller and less active prefrontal areas than non-violent populations (Bannon et al., 2015; Yang & Raine, 2009); however, this does not necessarily mean that reduced prefrontal volume and activation cause violence. According to the principle of neuroplasticity, neurons can change the strength and nature of their connections in response to environmental demands. In other words, experiences can alter brain structure and function. Violent offenders' brain abnormalities may, therefore, be either the cause or the effect of their behaviour.

PSYCHOLOGY AND CRIME

Are offenders psychologically different from non-offenders? One thing is relatively clear: prison inmates are much more likely to suffer from mental disorders than the general population (Fazel et al., 2016). In addition, some (but not all) mental illnesses appear to increase a person's risk of committing different kinds of crimes, particularly violent offences (e.g., Arsenault et al., 2000; Vinkers et al., 2011). In Canada, a little less than 20 percent of homicides are committed by people suspected of having a mental disorder (Mulligan et al., 2016). The following disorders are most strongly related to crime and, unsurprisingly, many of them are related to impulsivity and prefrontal cortex abnormalities.

Schizophrenia

As indicated in Chapter 2, it is important to remember that just because a person may have psychological impairments does not mean that they will engage in crime. Nor do all types of criminality necessarily involve forms of mental incapacitation. The case of **schizophrenia** is noteworthy because it is often mentioned in relation to those deemed *criminally insane*. Schizophrenia and related psychoses can involve diverse symptoms, including *hallucinations* (a sensory perception such as a sight or sound that does not objectively exists but is experienced as real) and *delusions* (false but strongly held beliefs that are resistant to change). Individuals with untreated schizophrenia may also have blunted emotions, low motivation, and cognitive deficits (American Psychiatric Association [APA], 2013). Schizophrenia is a complex disorder that manifests in numerous ways in different people and does not always correlate with antisocial or criminal behaviour. In cases of schizophrenia that are associated with criminality, persecutory hallucinations involving threatening voices and paranoid delusions (beliefs that others are plotting harm or violence to oneself) are the presenting symptoms most commonly associated with violence (Douglas et al., 2009). The risk is particularly high when these symptoms are combined with substance use disorders (see below) and medical intervention is absent (Fazel et al., 2009). The central criminogenic feature of untreated schizophrenia appears to be impulsivity (Robertson et al., 2014). Impulse control problems may be related to the prefrontal abnormalities that, along with other neurological dysfunctions, are commonly observed in schizophrenics (Hoptman et al., 2014; Shenton et al., 2001).

Bipolar Disorder

Bipolar disorder involves profound instability in emotions and behaviour (APA, 2013). In most cases, bipolar disorder is effectively managed through a combination of medicine and therapy, and what is described here refers to cases that are correlated with antisocial behaviour and not *all* forms of bipolar disorder. Individuals with untreated bipolar disorder can have dramatic mood swings, alternating between severe depression and its opposite, mania. During manic episodes, individuals often feel infallible and invincible, and can engage in impulsive and risky behaviours. Having a bipolar disorder that is left untreated increases a person's likelihood of committing violent offences even more than schizophrenia (Robertson et al., 2014). Like schizophrenia, bipolar disorder is associated with abnormalities in the prefrontal cortex and other brain areas related to impulse control (Bearden et al., 2001; Lim et al., 2013).

Box 7.4: Intergroup Violence: Personality or Context?

Some theories propose that specific personality features increase the chances of participation in politically motivated aggression and violence. For instance, Adorno and colleagues (1950) have described what they call an *authoritarian personality*. An authoritarian personality is characterized by adherence to conventional morality, cynicism, superstitious black-and-white thinking, and endorsement of aggressive methods to enforce conformity, a set of traits the authors linked with fascist ideas and actions. Individuals with these traits would feel morally entitled to vilify and persecute minority groups and would be overrepresented in state-sanctioned intergroup violence (in other words, violence between different groups in society). American examples of intergroup violence in the 1950s included antisemitism and racism.

A counterpoint, articulated by Philip Zimbardo (2007), is that in a context permissive of punitive aggression, virtually anyone can become a perpetrator. Zimbardo's seminal Stanford Prison Experiment illustrated how, without instruction to do so, undergraduate students randomly assigned to be prison guards dehumanized and abused students randomly assigned to be prisoners.

Consider intergroup violence: Do you think that perpetrators of politically motivated violence are attracted to fascist groups due to an individual's personality structure, or do politically unstable regimes create morally bankrupt environments in which anyone can become a perpetrator? How might both "causes" interact with historical intergroup tensions to produce politically motivated violence?

Attention Deficit Hyperactivity Disorder

Attention deficit hyperactivity disorder (ADHD) is characterized by impulsivity and significant inattentiveness (APA, 2013). These symptoms are evident during childhood, and they may predict academic and social difficulties in adolescence and early adulthood (Loe & Feldman, 2007). While ADHD symptoms generally decrease in severity with age (Döpfner et al., 2015), a small subset of children with ADHD show persistent rule-breaking. While ADHD itself does not seem to increase the chances of committing crimes, it may be a precursor to other disorders that do lead to defiant behaviours (Mordre et al., 2011).

Box 7.5: Do Severe Psychological Disorders Cause Crime? Assessing Myths and Misperceptions

Which is the first cause of impulsive criminality: genes, environment, untreated mental illness, brain injury, or substance abuse? Imagine the following scenario: Simon has a biological predisposition towards paranoid schizophrenia. He grows up in a stressful environment and begins to develop delusions and persecutory hallucinations in his late teens. At 22, he is diagnosed with schizophrenia but refuses to take his medication because of the unpleasant side effects. He begins to drink heavily and, believing that his mother is conspiring to have him imprisoned, attempts to set the family home on fire. The intuitive first cause of the arson in Simon's case is his genetic predisposition to schizophrenia. Would your interpretation change if you knew that Simon lives below the poverty line and that conditions like schizophrenia and substance use disorder—as well as homicide—are more common in those from lower socioeconomic classes (Pridemore, 2011; Scott et al., 2014; Werner et al., 2007), due to constrained opportunities and historical patterns of marginalization? Does poverty increase the risk of mental health problems and create more encounters with the criminal justice system? What sorts of commonly held assumptions frame public understandings of people with severe psychological diagnoses? What is less commonly understood by the public is that people with schizophrenia are far more likely to harm themselves than someone else. Stereotypical representations of schizophrenia that circulate in the media contribute to widespread misunderstandings. The reality is that most people with schizophrenia who seek treatment lead productive lives. Such misperceptions feed into myths about "criminal minds" and "serial killer monsters" that receive disproportionate coverage in news and entertainment media in comparison to cases that exist in reality.

Oppositional Defiant Disorder, Conduct Disorder, and Antisocial Personality Disorder

Some, but not all, children with ADHD also show habitual anger, argumentativeness, and vindictive behaviour, in which case they may also be diagnosed with **oppositional defiant disorder (ODD**; APA, 2013). For some children with ADHD and ODD symptoms, behaviour can become increasingly antisocial over time (Van Lier et al., 2007) and severe enough to meet the diagnostic criteria for **conduct disorder (CD)**. Conduct disorder reflects persistent, willful violation of social norms, where behaviour is often aggressive, destructive, and cruel (APA, 2013). The antisocial behaviour seen in CD differs from the typical rule-breaking in childhood or adolescence in its severity, pervasiveness, and hostility. It is not surprising that youth with CD are often in conflict with the law; some research suggests that over half of incarcerated youth meet the diagnostic criteria for CD (Fazel et al., 2008).

In most cases, defiance and aggression in childhood and adolescence abates by adulthood. However, children with disruptive behaviours are difficult to parent, which puts them at risk of maltreatment and abuse (Moffitt & Caspi, 2001). Abuse, in turn, further increases the risk that these children will commit crimes (De Sanctis et al., 2012). ODD and CD are uncommon in the general population (their prevalence is less than 5%), but the particular combination of impulsivity and aggression can develop into persistent patterns of antisocial behaviour in adulthood (Fairchild et al., 2013). In such cases, once a person reaches the age of 18, he or she may be diagnosed with **antisocial personality disorder (APD)**. People with APD show pervasive disinhibition (impulsivity, irresponsibility, and risk-taking) and disregard for other people's feelings.

Substance Use Disorders

Offending is also strongly predicted by **substance use disorders (SUDs)** (Assink et al., 2015). SUDs involve physiological symptoms, such as tolerance and withdrawal; psychological symptoms, such as cravings and preoccupation with illicit drug use; and an inability to function at work, school, or home (APA, 2013). While consumption of illicit drugs is itself a crime, the relationship between drugs and other types of crime is relatively complex. Studies suggest that people with antisocial personality disorders are more likely to have SUDs than the general population, and the co-occurrence of the disorders probably stems from core deficits in impulse control (Szalavitz, 2015). From this perspective, impulsivity increases the chances of both antisocial behaviour and problematic drug use.

Prenatal Exposure to Toxins

Prenatal alcohol exposure, particularly through maternal alcohol consumption, can significantly affect neurodevelopment and can lead to a set of disorders known as **fetal alcohol spectrum disorders (FASDs)**. FASDs include three general symptom clusters: anomalies in facial features, persistently stunted growth, and central nervous system dysfunction. Central nervous system dysfunction most commonly involves deficits in attention, impulse control, and complex thinking. Children with FASD may show some or all of these symptoms, and their symptoms can vary considerably in severity. Youth with FASD are frequently impulsive, aggressive, and more likely to abuse substances than other youth (Streissguth et al., 2004). They also tend to be overrepresented in correctional facilities (Corrado & McGuish, 2015).

Other prenatal environmental factors have been studied as potential predictors of antisocial behaviour. These include prenatal nicotine exposure, although this may be due less to nicotine and more to poverty and mental or physical health problems that characterize parents who smoke (Tiesler & Heinrich, 2014), and maternal stress (Rice et al., 2010).

Box 7.6: Ashley Smith, Adam Capay, and the Treatment of Inmates with Psychological Disorders

Although most governments recognize mental illness as a health issue, the mentally ill are incarcerated at disproportionately high rates, with some countries housing more mentally ill people in prisons than in hospitals (Fazel et al., 2016). In Canada, inmates are up to three times more likely than the general population to be mentally ill and up to seven times more likely to commit suicide. These figures are roughly consistent across the Western hemisphere (Simpson et al., 2013). What should be done with mentally ill offenders? Correctional Service Canada (CSC), which runs correctional services for inmates serving a sentence of more than two years, has established five Regional Treatment Centres to care for the most seriously mentally ill inmates. However, the Office of the Correctional Investigator (Sapers, 2015) estimates that current psychiatric services on the federal level meet about half of the actual need. Moreover, there are no consistent mental health services for offenders on remand or in sentenced custody of less than two years, as these services are under provincial jurisdiction.

Recently, two high-profile cases have highlighted the shortcomings of mental health services in Canadian prisons. In 2007, 19-year-old Ashley Smith committed suicide in her cell in the Grand Valley Institution for Women. In her 11 months in federal custody, she was transferred 17 times between 8 different institutions. She had received a number of diagnoses, including for ADHD, borderline personality disorder, and a learning disorder. During her time in custody, Smith had frequently assaulted prison staff and attempted self-injury. She sometimes had to be restrained and spent long periods in segregation. On October 19, 2007, she choked herself to death while three correctional officers—having been told not to enter her cell—waited outside (*The Fifth Estate*, 2010). The Office of the Correctional Investigator described the response of Correctional Service Canada to a 2014 inquest into Smith's death as "frustrating."

On October 7, 2016, the former Chief Commissioner of the Ontario Human Rights Commission Renu Mandhane was given a tour of the Thunder Bay District Jail. Management arranged meetings with three inmates as well as prison staff. In a private meeting with a correctional officer, Mandhane asked whether there was anything else she should see, anything that prison management might want to keep from her. "Adam Capay," the correctional officer replied. Capay, a 24-year-old from Lac Seul First Nation who was charged with the murder of a fellow inmate in 2012, had been kept in administrative segregation for four years. Capay's plexiglass-covered cell in the basement of the jail measured about 5 × 10 feet and was lit 24 hours a day. He spoke slowly and haltingly and had self-inflicted wounds on his wrists and scalp (Patriquin, 2016). News of Capay's treatment provoked public outrage, and *The Globe and Mail* wrote, "Mr. Capay is arguably being tortured by the state" (2016). Capay was moved to a new cell shortly thereafter.

Considerations of cases like those discussed here concentrate on two issues: mental illness and segregation. While Smith had received mental health diagnoses before her death in custody, it was less clear what, if any, diagnoses fit Adam Capay. An earlier psychiatric evaluation had found him fit to stand trial, but his condition at the time of Mandhane's visit had deteriorated to a point where a new psychiatric evaluation was approved in November 2016. Is mental illness, then, a cause or effect of segregation, or are both related to other challenging behaviours? And what, exactly, is segregation?

According to CSC, segregation is different from solitary confinement. Administrative segregation may involve isolating inmates up to 23 hours a day, but unlike solitary confinement, it includes regular visits by prison staff and healthcare personnel. For critics of administrative segregation, the difference is trivial (White, 2016a). In 2012, the United Nations Committee Against Torture agreed, urging Canada to stop using administrative segregation for mentally ill offenders. (The UN mandates that inmates should be held in isolation for no more than 15 days.) In response to public pressure, CSC has recently begun to reduce the number of inmates in administrative segregation (White, 2016b) and in 2017 proposed new rules that would, among other things, prohibit the placement of mentally ill inmates into segregation (White, 2017). Separately, Ontario announced plans to alter its administrative segregation policies and to hire more than 200 new mental health staff in anticipation of a review into Adam Capay's treatment (White, 2016c).

Several studies have demonstrated that segregation can lead to serious mental health problems. These include anxiety, panic, insomnia, hypersensitivity, cognitive dysfunction, poor impulse control, paranoia, rage, depression, self-mutilation, and suicidal behaviour (Haney, 2012). While we may lack adequate treatment resources for inmates with mental illnesses, it is clear that administrative segregation does them no good and may contribute to additional psychological distress.

Psychopathy

Most studies on violence and aggression we have considered so far are about one type of aggression only: **impulsive aggression**. Impulsive aggression, also known as reactive or affective aggression, is spontaneous. It occurs in response to frustration or fear, and usually involves anger, exemplified by arguments that can escalate into assault or manslaughter. Real-life aggression, however, is not always impulsive. **Premeditated aggression** (also called instrumental or proactive aggression) is emotionless and directed towards goals such as possessions or status in a group. First- and second-degree murder, robbery, and bullying are examples of this type of aggression. What sets impulsive and premeditated aggression apart, then, is the *reason* for the behaviour, which suggests that individuals committing premeditated aggression may be psychologically different from impulsive individuals. While impulsive aggression is linked to conditions like schizophrenia, bipolar disorder, and ADHD, premeditated aggression is frequently observed in **psychopaths** (Glenn & Raine, 2009).

The rough description of psychopathy was proposed in the late 18th century by the American psychiatrist Benjamin Rush. Rush, like phrenologists before him, suggested that the mind was divided into faculties, including the moral faculty. Rush argued that the moral faculty could be damaged by such things as disease, diet, and alcohol, resulting in the inability to distinguish right from wrong. He called this condition *moral derangement*, a diagnosis eventually replaced by psychopathy. The term *psychopathy* derives from Greek and literally, though perhaps misleadingly, means "suffering soul." Today, the diagnosis of psychopathy is usually based on criteria developed by Robert Hare in the *Hare Psychopathy Checklist-Revised* (PCL-R; Hare, 2003). The PCL-R lists 20 symptoms concerning interpersonal style, (e.g., pathological lying, glibness/superficial charm), affect (e.g., lack of remorse or guilt), lifestyle (e.g., need for stimulation/ proneness to boredom, impulsivity), and antisocial behaviour (e.g., early behavioural problems, criminal versatility). Hare describes psychopathy as involving a "sense of entitlement ... [and] disparate understanding of behavior and socially acceptable behavior" among people who are "unremorseful, apathetic to others, unconscionable, blameful of others, manipulative and conning, affectively cold ... disregardful of social obligations, nonconforming to social norms, [and] irresponsible" (1996, p. 39).

Although psychopaths also engage in impulsive aggression, they are significantly more likely than non-psychopathic offenders to show premeditated aggression. One Canadian study suggested that, relative to non-psychopathic offenders, the homicides committed by psychopaths were twice as likely to be premeditated (Woodworth & Porter, 2002).

What causes psychopathy? Contemporary theories often refer to brain abnormalities. Researchers have focused on the prefrontal cortex, since prefrontal injuries can cause behaviour problems like impulsivity, problems in long-term planning, aggression, and lack of empathy. Prefrontal injury appears to result in only a partial manifestation of psychopathy, however, because while psychopaths commonly engage in premeditated aggression, frontal lobe injury patients do not (Kiehl, 2006). Psychopaths are also believed to have difficulty in fear conditioning (i.e., learning to associate a neutral stimulus with a painful outcome), in learning from punishment, and in recognizing emotion in others. These skills are mediated by the amygdalae—two almond-shaped structures deep within the brain— considered essential for fear conditioning (Blair, 2003).

Some neuroimaging studies describe abnormalities in the structure and function of the prefrontal cortex and amygdalae in psychopaths. Based on these findings, some psychologists, legal scholars, and philosophers have argued that psychopaths should not be held legally, or at least morally, responsible for their actions (e.g., Malatesti & McMillan, 2010). In 2009, neuroimaging studies of psychopaths were offered as mitigating evidence in the serial killer Brian Dugan's sentencing hearing (*People v. Dugan*, 2009), and US judges have admitted similar evidence in other cases (Aspinwall et al., 2012). Bioethicist Peter Singer has proposed that if a neurobiological test for psychopathy became available, potential psychopaths should be detained. As Singer explains, "we might think of it not so much as punishment in a sense that implies moral responsibility, but as detention to prevent the person from offending again, and to deter others from committing similar crimes" (Singer, cited in Hingston, 2012, p. 5).

Singer's scenario is highly unlikely, however, as review studies have found that neurobiological differences between psychopaths and non-psychopaths are not consistent, suggesting that psychopaths may not have distinctive patterns of brain dysfunction after all (Griffiths & Jalava, 2017; Koenigs et al., 2011; Pujara & Koenigs, 2014; Yang & Raine, 2009). Experimental evidence of psychopaths' emotional processing deficits, such as fear, also does not appear as conclusive as previously thought (Brook et al., 2013; Hoppenbrouwers et al., 2016). Furthermore, neither the World Health Organization nor the American Psychiatric Association recognizes psychopathy as a legitimate mental disorder. Nevertheless, psychopathy continues to figure prominently in the public imagination and some legal cases.

MENTAL ILLNESS AND THE LAW

What happens to a mentally ill person accused of a crime? The courts have two main ways to address the situation. First, if the person, because of their mental disorder, cannot participate in their own defence, they may be found **unfit to stand trial**. In that case, the person is usually either diverted to mental healthcare in the community or to a psychiatric hospital until such time that they are fit to stand trial. If they are unlikely to ever become fit to stand trial, proceedings against them may be stayed (discontinued) if they do not pose a danger to society.

Second, if it is determined that at the time of the offence the person did not understand what they were doing or that what they were doing was wrong, they may be found **not criminally responsible on account of mental disorder (NCRMD)**. Depending on the severity of the offence and the threat the person poses, they may be released into the community with or without conditions, or they may be detained in a psychiatric hospital. It is important to note that NCRMD does not mean a person is acquitted. Rather, NCRMD means that the person is found guilty but not criminally responsible, as they lacked the necessary *mens rea* (criminal intent) to be found responsible. Also, having a mental disorder does not mean that the person will be found NCRMD. Many mentally ill people are tried, convicted, and incarcerated in Canada, and as we discussed above, mental disorders are more common in incarcerated populations than in the general population.

Box 7.7: Public Reaction to Not Criminally Responsible on Account of Mental Disorder (NCRMD)

On July 30, 2008, 22-year-old Tim McLean was travelling home on the bus from his job at a carnival in Alberta. He was asleep outside Portage la Prairie, Manitoba, when the man sitting next to him suddenly pulled out a large knife and began stabbing him. The bus stopped, and the passengers ran out. Left alone with his victim, the assailant, 40-year-old Vince Li, cut off McLean's head and displayed it to the horrified passengers outside. Li was convicted of second-degree murder but was found not criminally responsible due the fact that he was suffering from untreated schizophrenia at the time of the offence and was hearing voices telling him to kill McLean. Li was detained at the Selkirk Mental Health Centre. In time, his hallucinations began to subside, and the Manitoba Review Board began the process of reintegrating him to society. In 2017, he was granted absolute discharge.

McLean's family and some conservative politicians found Li's release difficult to accept. Rona Ambrose, then interim leader of the Conservative Party of Canada, argued that "Justin Trudeau must put the rights of victims before the rights of criminals." McLean's mother began a petition to change Canada's NCRMD laws. Others disagreed. The national director of the Canadian Mental Health Association argued that the decision and the current NCRMD laws were reasonable. John Stefaniuk, the chair of the Manitoba Criminal Code Review Board, found that releasing low-risk NCRMD offenders like Li strikes a fair balance between the rights of the offenders and concerns for public safety (Malone, 2017). A 2015 Canadian study found that NCRMD offenders had significantly lower recidivism rates than other offenders, and NCRMD offenders who had committed the most serious offences were the least likely to re-offend. Only 0.6 percent of all NCRMD offenders committed a serious violent offence within three years of their release (Charette et al., 2015).

Serial and Mass Murder

If neurobiology and psychopathy are the root causes of crime, it would make sense that such causes would be most evident in people who commit the most serious crimes. These crimes, most would agree, are serial and mass murder. Generally, **serial murder** is defined as the killing of three or more people with a cooling-off period between each murder. **Mass murder** refers to the killing of three or more people in one place, without a cooling-off period (Holmes & Holmes, 2010). Do serial and mass murderers have a distinct psychological and/ or neurobiological profile?

Box 7.8: Charles Whitman: Neurobiology and Violence

Under exceedingly rare circumstances, abnormal neurobiology and psychology can be directly related to multiple murder. On the morning of August 1, 1966, Charles Whitman, a former marine and an engineering student, murdered his wife and his mother. He then took an elevator to the top floor of a tower at the University of Texas, beat a receptionist to death with his rifle, and began shooting at people below. He killed 16 people that day and wounded many more. Eventually, police entered the tower and shot Whitman dead.

The night before his attack, Whitman wrote a suicide note. It read:

I don't really understand myself these days. I am supposed to be an average reasonable and intelligent young man. However, lately (I can't recall when it started) I have been a victim of many unusual and irrational thoughts.... I talked with a doctor once for about two hours and tried to convey to him my fears that I felt [overcome by] overwhelming violent impulses. After one session I never saw the Doctor again, and since then I have been fighting my mental turmoil alone, and seemingly to no avail. (quoted in Eagleman, 2011)

A medical examiner opened Whitman's skull at the morgue and found a tumor pressing on the amygdala. The amygdala is responsible for emotional processing, and abnormalities in it have been linked to aggression and fearlessness (Eagleman, 2011).

Since serial murder tends to be premeditated, it is easy to assume that all serial murderers are therefore psychopathic. This, however, may not be the case. In a close analysis of five high-profile American serial murderers (Ted Bundy, Jeffrey Dahmer, John Wayne Gacy, Edmund Kemper, and Gary Ridgway), a team of researchers found that only one (Bundy) was classified as a psychopath (Hickey et al., 2018).

What then, if anything, is unique about serial murderers? For one, they are overwhelmingly male. According to some studies, serial murderers are also more likely to have suffered from neurodevelopmental disorders, brain injuries, and child abuse than the general population (Allely et al., 2014). As we saw earlier, however, this is roughly true of other violent criminals as well. Since no single thing appears to explain serial murder, theories of serial murder typically propose a number of interacting causes. According to one theory, for example, rejection, abuse, and other childhood traumas can lead to low self-esteem. If the individual (typically a male) lacks effective coping mechanisms, he may suppress any memory of the trauma, thereby leading to a state of dissociation from reality. When coupled with facilitators like alcohol, drugs, and violent pornography, he may become desensitized to violence, begin to fantasize about murder, and eventually commit murder itself (Hickey, 2006). Theories like these, however, are speculative at best. Compared to other types of violent criminals, there are not many serial murderers to study, and motives for serial murder vary widely.

In some ways, mass murderers are an even more difficult group to study than serial murderers. This is because mass murderers, more so than serial murderers, tend to die during or shortly after the murders. Even if an offender is caught alive, psychological evaluations may not always be conclusive. For example, Anders Breivik, who murdered 77 people in Norway in 2011, was variously diagnosed with paranoid schizophrenia, Asperger's syndrome (a label once used to indicate milder cases of autism), antisocial personality disorder, narcissistic personality disorder, Tourette's syndrome, and/or pseudologia fantastic, a form of pathological lying (Faccini & Allely, 2016). One small-scale study in 2016 examined neurocognitive abilities of 23 mass murderers. The results showed that the murderers' intelligence, memory, attention, and reasoning skills were not significantly different from those of the general population. But one interesting difference did emerge: mass murderers' neurocognitive abilities were on average higher than those of murderers with a single victim (Fox et al., 2016). If this finding holds in subsequent studies, it suggests a paradox: the worse the offence, the more intellectually normal the offender.

Box 7.9: Myth vs. Reality: Serial Killers and Their Victims

Serial murderers are often fictionalized as intelligent and fascinating. Striking examples are Hannibal Lecter in Thomas Harris's *The Silence of the Lambs* (and the subsequent film adaptation by Jonathan Demme), John Doe in David Fincher's *Seven* (2005), and Dexter Morgan in the book and TV series *Dexter*. Moreover, these killers are almost always white males. Are such portrayals realistic? According to Radford University's Serial Killer Database, the average IQ of serial killers—or at least those whose intelligence was measured—is 94.5, not significantly different from the population average of 100. Compiling data on a complex type of crime like serial killing is never a precise science; however, the Radford University study indicates some interesting statistics: the United States of America has 4.4 percent of the world's population but 66.7 percent of all recorded serial killers; serial killing peaked in the 1980s in North America and has dropped substantially since then; 92.5 percent of American serial killers are male; examining data from all decades as far back as the early 1900s, 52.4 percent of serial killers on average were white, and although whites comprised approximately 70 percent of serial killers from the 1940s to the 1970s, numbers began to change in the 1990s when gang-affiliated serial killing may have skewed statistics to include Black and Hispanic perpetrators into the total count (Aamodt, 2016).

What about motives? The FBI's early attempts to understand serial murder concentrated on sexually motivated offenders, a decision that shaped how popular media would portray the offenders as well (Schmid, 2005). Almost any discussion of American serial killers now references names like Ted Bundy, John Wayne Gacy, and Gary Ridgway, all sexually motivated offenders. The same goes for Canadian counterparts like Clifford Olson and Paul Bernardo. But are these offenders representative of serial murderers as a whole? According to Radford University's database, only 32 percent of American killers were motivated by enjoyment (thrill, lust, or power). About an equal number were motivated by money. Other common motives included anger and gang conflict. About 10 percent appeared to have multiple motives. Finally, serial murderers' victims show an almost even gender split, with 52 percent female and 48 percent male (Aamodt, 2016).

Perhaps the biggest problem in explaining multiple murder in individualistic terms is the fact that rates of multiple murder vary greatly across place and time. The United States has recorded more serial and mass murders than any other country (Aamodt, 2016; Lankford, 2016). Globally, serial murder rates rose quite steadily between 1900 and the 1990s, and then began to decrease (Aamodt, 2016), while mass murder in the US has recently shown the opposite trend (Cohen et al., 2014). What could this mean? Perhaps serial and mass murders are not entirely determined by what goes on inside a person's mind or brain but also by what goes on in society. Indeed, different periods in history seem to have their so-called signature murders. In the US, the 1850s were characterized by violent deaths in railway and mining camps. The 1920s saw murders by bootleggers, and the 1980s by gangs involved in the crack cocaine trade (Roth, 2009). The 1990s produced a spike in serial murder, while the 2010s saw a rise in religious terrorism and mass shootings. Even though we do not know what the next signature pattern of multiple murders will be, one thing is almost certain: contemporary biological and psychological theories will provide an imperfect explanation at best.

CONCLUSION

This chapter has provided the reader with an overview of some theories that explain the individual causes of criminal behaviour rooted in biological and psychological explanations. Since it is a popular belief that criminality is caused primarily by biological and psychological deficiencies, it is important to clarify both the usefulness and the misconceptions associated with such *naturalistic* explanations. Numerous crime-themed programs promote myths such as the "natural-born killer" and the "criminal mind," and yet most scientific research into the biological and psychological causes of criminal and deviant behaviour does not support such ideas. The relationship between criminality, biology, and psychology is more nuanced and complex than what is depicted in popular media. Furthermore, identifying the causes of problematic criminality in biological and psychological causes has historically been used to justify horrific human rights abuses such as eugenics and discrimination against people deemed different through their classification as degenerates. In light of these concerns, it is also important to recognize the scientifically valid ways that biology and psychology do relate to certain kinds of criminal and deviant behaviour.

Biological and psychological understandings of criminal behaviour were central to the formation of the discipline of criminology in its early days and, despite some shortcomings in the theories of Lombroso and others, continued efforts at studying the relation between biology, psychology, and neurobiology paved the way for important research into how such factors relate to criminality. The influence of prenatal exposure to toxins, brain injury, and brain development, among other factors, can be associated with a person's potential to lack impulse control and thus be predisposed to wrongdoing. Similarly, psychological conditions like antisocial personality disorder, schizophrenia, and bipolar disorder are not specifically causes of crime but can be correlated with criminal behaviour in some cases. Case study examples discussed in this chapter further illustrate the difficulties that psychological and biological cases of criminality pose for their treatment within the criminal justice system.

REVIEW QUESTIONS

1. Where does the idea of the *born criminal* come from? Why is it a problematic concept?
2. What is the relation between psychological disorders and crime? Discuss the myths versus the realities.
3. Choose a case study from the chapter and explain how some of the theories and concepts discussed are relevant to that case.

GLOSSARY

adoption study: A method for estimating the relative contributions of genes and environment on human traits or behaviours by comparing similarities between adopted children and their biological parents to those between adopted children and their adoptive parents.

antisocial behaviour: Behaviour characterized by a lack of respect or consideration for the dignity and rights of others that can range from the absence of a moral compass to perpetrating willful harm against others.

antisocial personality disorder (APD): A personality disorder, diagnosed in people 18 years or older, that involves a pattern of morally inconsiderate willful harm, including the violation of the rights of others.

atavism: A process by which some people, according to thinkers like Cesare Lombroso, became less evolved than the rest of humanity.

attention deficit hyperactivity disorder (ADHD): A neurodevelopmental disorder that involves hyperactivity, inattention, and impulsivity.

behavioural epigenetics: The study of how environments can affect gene expression and how that gene can in turn affect behaviour.

biological criminology: The study of biological causes of crime.

biological determinism: A theory according to which behaviour is caused by biological events, such as genes and neurobiology.

bipolar disorder: A mental disorder that involves dramatic mood swings between depression and mania.

born criminals: A group of offenders who, according to Cesare Lombroso, could be distinguished by bodily signs, such as unusual and distinct facial features.

conduct disorder (CD): A mental disorder usually diagnosed in childhood or adolescence that involves aggression and persistent violation of social norms as well as the rights of others.

environmentability estimate: A quantitative estimate of the relative contribution of environment on a trait or behaviour, usually expressed either as a proportion (0–1) or percentage (0–100%).

feeble-mindedness: A problematic 19th-century label applied by practitioners to a wide range of people in prisons, asylums, and hospitals, which primarily referred to low intelligence and limited social functioning. The diagnosis was associated with crime and social disorder and often applied to socially marginalized persons.

fetal alcohol spectrum disorders (FASDs): A set of neurodevelopmental disorders caused by excessive drinking by the mother that involves anomalies in facial features, stunted growth, and central nervous system dysfunction.

heritablity estimate: A quantitative estimate of the relative contribution of genes on a trait or behaviour, usually expressed either as a proportion (0–1) or percentage (0–100%).

impulsive aggression: Spontaneous aggression that occurs in response to frustration or fear.

mass murder: The killing of three or more people in one place, without a cooling-off period.

molecular genetics: The study of genes at the molecular level.

negative eugenics: An attempt to improve the characteristics of a population by preventing unwanted populations from procreating, usually by prohibiting marriages or by surgical sterilization.

not criminally responsible on account of mental disorder (NCRMD): A legal designation for a person who, at the time of the offence, did not understand what they were doing or that what they were doing was wrong.

oppositional defiant disorder (ODD): A mental disorder usually diagnosed in childhood or adolescence that involves anger, argumentativeness, and vindictive behaviour.

phrenology: The idea that a person's personality can be inferred from examining the shape of his or her skull.

positivism: The idea only observable phenomena should be the objects of scientific study.

prefrontal cortex: The part of the brain located at the front, which is responsible for complex cognitive and emotional processes as well as impulse control.

premeditated aggression: Goal-directed aggression with an aim to personal gain.

psychopathy: A personality disorder that involves antisocial behaviour, dishonesty, and impulsivity.

schizophrenia: A psychotic disorder that involves symptoms such as delusions and hallucinations.

serial murder: The killing of three or more people, with a cooling-off period between each murder.

substance use disorders (SUDs): A mental disorder that involves withdrawal symptoms, preoccupation with substance use, and an inability to function in daily life.

twin study: A method for estimating the relative contributions of genes and environment on human traits or behaviours by comparing similarities between monozygotic twins to those between dizygotic twins.

unfit to stand trial: A legal designation for a person who cannot participate in his or her own defence.

REFERENCES

Aamodt, M. G. (2016, September 4). *Serial killer statistics.* Radford University. Retrieved from http://maamodt.asp.radford.edu/serial%20killer%20information%20center/project%20description.htm

Adorno, T. W., Frenkel-Brunswik, E., Levinson, D. J., & Nevitt Sanford, R. (1950). *The authoritarian personality.* Harper & Brothers.

Allely, C. S., Minnis, H., Thompson, L., Wilson, P., & Gillberg, C. (2014). Neurodevelopmental and psychosocial risk factors in serial killers and mass murderers. *Aggression and Violent Behavior, 19*(3), 288–301.

American Psychiatric Association (APA). (2013). *Diagnostic and statistical manual of mental disorders* (5th ed.) APA.

Arseneault, L., Moffitt, T. E., Caspi, A., Taylor, P. J., & Silva, P. A. (2000). Mental disorders and violence in a total birth cohort: Results from the Dunedin Study. *Archives of General Psychiatry, 57*(10), 979–986.

Aspinwall, L. G., Brown, T. R., & Tabery, J. (2012). The double-edged sword: Does biomechanism increase or decrease judges' sentencing of psychopaths? *Science, 337*(6096), 846–849.

Assink, M., van der Put, C. E., Hoeve, M., de Vries, S. L. A., Stams, G. J. J., & Oort, F. J. (2015). Risk factors for persistent delinquent behavior among juveniles: A meta-analytic review. *Clinical Psychology Review, 42*, 47–61.

Bannon, S. M., Salis, K. L., & O'Leary, K. D. (2015). Structural brain abnormalities in aggression and violent behavior. *Aggression and Violent Behavior, 25*(Part B), 323–331.

Bearden, C. E., Hoffman, K. M., & Cannon, T. D. (2001). The neuropsychology and neuroanatomy of bipolar affective disorder: A critical review. *Bipolar Disorders, 3*(3), 106–150.

Blair, R. J. R. (2003). Neurobiological basis of psychopathy. *British Journal of Psychiatry, 182*(1), 5–7.

Brook, M., Brieman, C. L., & Kosson, D. S. (2013). Emotion processing in Psychopathy Checklist—assessed psychopathy: A review of the literature. *Clinical Psychology Review, 33*(8), 979–995.

Brower, M. C., & Price, B. H. (2001). Neuropsychiatry of frontal lobe dysfunction in violent and criminal behaviour: A critical review. *Journal of Neurology, Neurosurgery & Psychiatry, 71*(6), 720–726.

Brunner, H. G. (1996). MAOA deficiency and abnormal behaviour: Perspectives on an association. In CIBA Foundation 194, *Genetics of Criminal and Antisocial Behaviour* (pp. 155–164). John Wiley & Sons.

Brunner, H. G., Nelen, M. R., van Zandvoort, P., Abeling, N. G., van Gennip, A. H., Wolters, E. C., Kuiper, M. A., Ropers, H. H., & van Oost, B. A. (1993a). X-linked borderline mental retardation with prominent behavioral disturbance: Phenotype, genetic localization, and evidence for disturbed monoamine metabolism. *American Journal of Human Genetics, 52*(6), 1032–1039.

Brunner, H. G., Nelen, M., Breakefield, X. O., Ropers, H. H., & van Oost, B. A. (1993b). Abnormal behavior associated with a point mutation in the structural gene for monoamine oxidase A. *Science, 262*(5133), 578–580.

Burbridge, D. (2001). Francis Galton on twins, heredity, and social class. *The British Journal for the History of Science, 34*(3), 323–340.

Byrd, A. L., & Manuck, S. B. (2014). MAOA, childhood maltreatment, and antisocial behavior: Meta-analysis of a gene-environment interaction. *Biological Psychiatry, 75*(1), 9–17.

Caspi, A., McClay, J., Moffitt, T. E., Mill, J., Martin, J., Craig, I. W., Taylor, A., & Poulton, R. (2002). Role of genotype in the cycle of violence in maltreated children. *Science, 297*(5582), 851–854.

Charette, Y., Crocker, A. G., Seto, M. C., Salem, L., Nicholls, T. L., & Caulet, M. (2015). The National Trajectory Project of individuals found not criminally responsible on account of mental disorder in Canada. Part 4: Criminal recidivism. *The Canadian Journal of Psychiatry, 60*(3), 127–134.

Cohen, A. P., Azrael, D., & Miller, M. (2014, October 15). Rate of mass shootings has tripled since 2011, Harvard research shows. *Mother Jones.* Retrieved from http://www.motherjones.com/politics/2014/10/mass-shootings-increasing-harvard-research

Corrado, R. R., & McCuish, E. C. (2015). The development of early onset, chronic, and versatile offending: The role of fetal alcohol spectrum disorder and mediating factors. *International Journal of Child and Adolescent Health, 8*(2), 241–250.

Damasio, H., Grabowski, T., Frank, R., Galaburda, A. M., & Damasio, A. R. (1994). The return of Phineas Gage: Clues about the brain from the skull of a famous patient. *Science, 264*(5162), 1102–1105.

De Sanctis, V. A., Nomura, Y., Newcorn, J. H., & Halperin, J. M. (2012). Childhood maltreatment and conduct disorder: Independent predictors of criminal outcomes in ADHD youth. *Child Abuse & Neglect, 36*(11–12), 782–789.

Döpfner, M., Hautmann, C., Görtz-Dorten, A., Klasen, F., Ravens-Sieberer, U., & BELLA Study Group. (2015). Long-term course of ADHD symptoms from childhood to early adulthood in a community sample. *European Child & Adolescent Psychiatry, 24*(6), 665–673.

Douglas, K. S., Guy, L. S., & Hart, S. D. (2009). Psychosis as a risk factor for violence to others: A meta-analysis. *Psychological Bulletin, 135*(5), 679–706.

Eagleman, D. (2011, July/August). The brain on trial. *The Atlantic.* Retrieved from https://www.theatlantic.com/magazine/archive/2011/07/the-brain-on-trial/308520/

Faccini, L., & Allely, C. (2016). Mass violence in individuals with autism spectrum disorder and narcissistic personality disorder: A case analysis of Anders Breivik using the "Path to Intended and Terroristic Violence" model. *Aggression and Violent Behavior, 31,* 229–236.

Fairchild, G., van Goozen, S. H. M., Calder, A. J., & Goodyer, I. M. (2013). Research review: Evaluating and reformulating the developmental taxonomic theory of antisocial behaviour. *Journal of Child Psychology and Psychiatry, 54*(9), 924–940.

Farrer, T. J., & Hedges, D. W. (2011). Prevalence of traumatic brain injury in incarcerated groups compared to the general population: A meta-analysis. *Progress in Neuro-Psychopharmacology and Biological Psychiatry, 35*(2), 390–394.

Farrington, D. (2007). Origins of violent behavior over the life span. In D. J. Flannery, A. T. Vazsonyi, & I. D. Waldman (Eds.), *The Cambridge handbook of violent behavior and aggression* (pp. 19–48). Cambridge University Press.

Fazel, S., Doll, H., & Långström, N. (2008). Mental disorders among adolescents in juvenile detention and correctional facilities: A systematic review and metaregression analysis of 25 surveys. *Journal of the American Academy of Child & Adolescent Psychiatry, 47*(9), 1010–1019.

Fazel, S., Gulati, G., Linsell, L., Geddes, J. R., & Grann, M. (2009). Schizophrenia and violence: Systematic review and meta-analysis. *PLoS Med, 6*(8), e1000120.

Fazel, S., Hayes, A. J., Bartellas, K., Clerici, M., & Trestman, R. (2016). Mental health of prisoners: Prevalence, adverse outcomes, and interventions. *The Lancet Psychiatry, 3*(9), 871–881.

The Fifth Estate. (2010, November 12). Timeline: The life & death of Ashley Smith. *CBC.*

Fox, J. M., Brook, M., Stratton, J., & Hanlon, R. E. (2016). Neuropsychological profiles and descriptive classifications of mass murderers. *Aggression and Violent Behavior, 30,* 94–104.

Gibb, D. A. (2011). *Camouflaged killer: The shocking double life of Canadian Air Force Colonel Russell Williams.* The Berkley Publishing Group.

Gibson, M. (2002). *Born to crime: Cesare Lombroso and the origins of biological criminology.* Praeger.

Glenn, A. L., & Raine, A. (2009). Psychopathy and instrumental aggression: Evolutionary, neurobiological, and legal perspectives. *International Journal of Law and Psychiatry, 32*(4), 253–258.

Globe Editorial: Ontario's sickening mistreatment of Adam Capay. (2016, October 24). *The Globe and Mail.* Retrieved from http://www.theglobeandmail.com/opinion/editorials/ontarios-sickening-mistreatment-of-adam-capay/article32498319/

Gould, S. J. (1996). *The mismeasure of man.* W. W. Norton & Company.

Griffiths, S. Y., & Jalava, J. V. (2017). A comprehensive neuroimaging review of PCL-R defined psychopathy. *Aggression and Violent Behavior, 36,* 60–75.

Haberstick, B. C., Lessem, J. M., Hewitt, J. K., Smolen, A., Hopfer, C. J., Halpern, C. T., Killeya-Jones, L. A., Boardman, J. D., Tabor J., Siegler, I. C., Williams, R. B., & Mullan Harris K. (2014). MAOA genotype, childhood maltreatment, and their interaction in the etiology of adult antisocial behaviors. *Biological Psychiatry, 75*(1), 25–30.

Hagerty, B. B. (2010, July 1). Can your genes make you murder? *npr.* Retrieved from http://www.npr.org/templates/story/story.php?storyId=128043329

Haney, C. (2012). Prison effects in the era of mass incarceration. *The Prison Journal,* 1–24.

Hansen, R., & King, D. (2013). *Sterilized by the state: Eugenics, race, and the population scare in twentieth-century North America*. Cambridge University Press.

Hare, R. D. (1996). Psychopathy and antisocial personality disorder: A case of diagnostic confusion. *Psychiatric Times, 13*(2), 39–40.

Hare, R. D. (2003). *Hare psychopathy checklist-revised (PCL-R)* (2nd ed.). Multi-Health Systems.

Hickey, E. W. (2006). *Serial murderers and their victims* (4th ed.). Thomson/Wadsworth.

Hickey, E. W., Walters, B. K., Drislane, L. E., Palumbo, I. M., & Patrick, C. J. (2018). Deviance at its darkest: Serial murder and psychopathy. In C. J. Patrick (Ed.), *Handbook of psychopathy* (2nd ed., pp. 570–584). The Guilford Press.

Hingston, S. (2012, June 28). The psychopath test. *Philadelphia Magazine*. Retrieved from https://www.phillymag.com/news/2012/06/28/kids-psychopath-test/

Holmes, R. M., & Holmes, S. T. (2010). *Serial murder* (3rd ed.). SAGE Publications.

Hoppenbrouwers, S. S., Bulten, B. H., & Brazil, I. A. (2016). Parsing fear: A reassessment of the evidence for fear deficits in psychopathy. *Psychological Bulletin, 142*(2), 573–600. http://dx.doi.org/10.1037/bul0000040

Hoptman, M. J., Antonius, D., Mauro, C. J., Parker, E. M., & Javitt, D. C. (2014). Cortical thinning, functional connectivity, and mood-related impulsivity in schizophrenia: Relationship to aggressive attitudes and behavior. *American Journal of Psychiatry, 171*(9), 939–948.

Horn, D. G. (2003). *The criminal body: Lombroso and the anatomy of deviance*. Routledge.

Hothersall, D. (2003). *History of psychology* (4th ed.). McGraw-Hill Education.

Jackson, D. B., & Beaver, K. M. (2015). The influence of nutritional factors on verbal deficits and psychopathic personality traits: Evidence of the moderating role of the MAOA genotype. *International Journal of Environmental Research and Public Health, 12*(12), 15739–15755.

Jalava, J., Griffiths, S., & Maraun, M. (2015). *The myth of the born criminal: Psychopathy, neurobiology, and the creation of the modern degenerate*. University of Toronto Press.

Keighley, K. (2017). *Police-reported crime statistics in Canada, 2016* (Catalogue no. 85-002X). Canadian Centre for Justice Statistics. Retrieved from http://www.statcan.gc.ca/pub/85-002-x/2017001/article/54842-eng.pdf

Kevles, D. J. (1995). *In the name of eugenics: Genetics and the uses of human heredity*. Harvard University Press.

Kiehl, K. A. (2006). A cognitive neuroscience perspective on psychopathy: Evidence for paralimbic system dysfunction. *Psychiatry Research, 142*(2), 107–128.

Kiehl, K. A., & Buckholtz, J. W. (2010). Inside the mind of a psychopath. *Scientific American Mind, 21*(4), 22–29.

Koenigs, M., Baskin-Sommers, A., Zeier, J., & Newman, J. P. (2011). Investigating the neural correlates of psychopathy: A critical review. *Molecular Psychiatry, 16*(8), 792–799.

Kotowicz, Z. (2007). The strange case of Phineas Gage. *History of Human Sciences, 20*(1), 115–131.

Lankford, A. (2016). Public mass shooters and firearms: A cross-national study of 171 countries. *Violence and Victims, 31*(2), 187–199.

Leahey, T. H. (2004). *A history of psychology: Main currents in psychological thought* (6th ed.). Pearson/Prentice Hall.

Lim, C. S., Baldessarini, R. J., Vieta, E., Yucel, M., Bora, E., & Sim, K. (2013). Longitudinal neuroimaging and neuropsychological changes in bipolar disorder patients: Review of the evidence. *Neuroscience & Biobehavioral Reviews, 37*(3), 418–435.

Loe, I. M., & Feldman, H. M. (2007). Academic and educational outcomes of children with ADHD. *Journal of Pediatric Psychology, 32*(6), 643–654.

Lombroso, C. (2006). *Criminal man.* (M. Gibson & N. H. Rafter, Trans.). Duke University Press. (Original work published 1884)

Macmillan, M. (2000). *An odd kind of fame: Stories of Phineas Gage.* MIT Press.

Malatesti, L., & McMillan, J. (Eds.). (2010). *Responsibility and psychopathy: Interfacing law, psychiatry, and philosophy.* Oxford University Press.

Malone, K. (2017, February 11). Victim's family disappointed by Vince Li's discharge. *CBC News Manitoba.* Retrieved from http://www.cbc.ca/news/canada/manitoba/ambrose-vince-li-concerns-rona-ambrose-1.3978761

McIlroy, A., & Anderssen, E. (2010, October 22). How a psychopath is made. *The Globe and Mail*, F1, F4.

Miladinovic, Z., & Mulligan, L. (2015). *Homicide in Canada, 2014* (Catalogue no. 85-002-X). Canadian Centre for Justice Statistics. Retrieved from http://www.statcan.gc.ca/pub/85-002-x/2015001/article/14244-eng.htm?fpv=2693

Moffitt, T. E., & Caspi, A. (2001). Childhood predictors differentiate life-course persistent and adolescence-limited antisocial pathways among males and females. *Development and Psychopathology, 13*(2), 355–375.

Mordre, M., Groholt, B., Kjelsberg, E., Sandstad, B., & Myhre, A. M. (2011). The impact of ADHD and conduct disorder in childhood on adult delinquency: A 30 years follow-up study using official crime records. *BMC Psychiatry, 11*(1), 57.

Mulligan, L., Axford, M., & Solecki, A. (2016). *Homicide in Canada, 2015* (Catalogue no. 85-002-X). Canadian Centre for Justice Statistics. Retrieved from http://www.statcan.gc.ca/pub/85-002-x/2016001/article/14668-eng.htm?fpv=2693

Nadelhoffer, T. A. (Ed.). (2013). *The future of punishment.* Oxford University Press.

NPR. (2016, March 7). The Supreme Court ruling that led to 70,000 forced sterilizations. https://www.npr.org/sections/health-shots/2016/03/07/469478098/the-supreme-court-ruling-that-led-to-70-000-forced-sterilizations

Patriquin, M. (2016, November 2). Why Adam Capay spent 1,560 days in solitary. *Maclean's*. Retrieved from http://www.macleans.ca/news/why-adam-capay-has-spent-1560-days-in-solitary/

The People of the State of Illinois v. Brian J. Dugan (2009). 05 CF 3491. (US).

Pick, D. (1989). *Faces of degeneration: A European disorder, c. 1848–c. 1918.* Cambridge University Press.

Pridemore, W. A. (2011). Poverty matters: A reassessment of the inequality–homicide relationship in cross-national studies. *British Journal of Criminology, 51*(5), 739–772.

Pujara, M., & Koenigs, M. (2014). Neuroimaging studies of psychopathy. In R. A. J. O. Dierckx, A. Otte, E. F. J. de Vries, A. van Waarde, & J. A. den Boer (Eds.), *PET and SPECT in psychiatry* (pp. 657–674). Springer-Verlag.

Rafter, N. H. (1997). *Creating born criminals.* University of Illinois Press.

Raine, A. (2013). *The anatomy of violence: The biological roots of crime.* Pantheon Books.

Rhee, S. H., & Waldman, I. D. (2002). Genetic and environmental influences on antisocial behavior: A meta-analysis of twin and adoption studies. *Psychological Bulletin, 128*(3), 490–529.

Rice, F., Harold, G. T., Boivin, J., van den Bree, M., Hay, D. F., & Thapar, A. (2010). The links between prenatal stress and offspring development and psychopathology: Disentangling environmental and inherited influences. *Psychological Medicine, 40*(02), 335–345.

Richerson, P. J., & Boyd, R. (2005). *Not by genes alone: How culture transformed human evolution.* University of Chicago Press.

Robertson, A. G., Swanson, J. W., Frisman, L. K., Lin, H., & Swartz, M. S. (2014). Patterns of justice involvement among adults with schizophrenia and bipolar disorder: Key risk factors. *Psychiatric Services, 65*(7), 931–938.

Ross, J. L., Roeltgen, D. P., Kushner, H., Zinn, A. R., Reiss, A., Bardsley, M. Z., McCauley, E., & Tartaglia, N. (2012). Behavioral and social phenotypes in boys with 47,XYY syndrome or 47,XXY Klinefelter syndrome. *Pediatrics, 129*(4), 769–778.

Roth, R. (2009). *American homicide.* The Belknap Press.

Sapers, H. (2015). *Annual report of the Office of the Correctional Investigator 2014–2015.* The Correctional Officer Canada. Retrieved from http://www.oci-bec.gc.ca/cnt/rpt/pdf/annrpt/annrpt20142015-eng.pdf

Schmid, D. (2005). *Natural born celebrities: Serial killers in American culture*. University of Chicago Press.

Schofield, P. W., Butler, T. G., Hollis, S. J., Smith, N. E., Lee, S. J., & Kelso, W. M. (2006). Traumatic brain injury among Australian prisoners: Rates, recurrence and sequelae. *Brain Injury, 20*(5), 499–506. https://doi.org/10.1080/02699050600664749

Scott, K. M., Al-Hamzawi, A. O., Andrade, L. H., Borges, G., Caldas-de-Almeida, J. M., Fiestas, F., Gureje, O., Hu, C., Karam, E. G., Kawakami, N., Lee, S., Levinson, D., Lim, C. C. W., Navarro-Mateu, F., Okoliyski, M., Posada-Villa, J., Torres, Y., Williams, D. R., Zakhozha, V., & Kessler, R. C. (2014). Associations between subjective social status and DSM-IV mental disorders: Results from the World Mental Health surveys. *JAMA psychiatry, 71*(12), 1400–1408.

Shenton, M. E., Dickey, C. C., Frumin, M., & McCarley, R. W. (2001). A review of MRI findings in schizophrenia. *Schizophrenia Research, 49*(1–2), 1–52.

Simpson, A. I. F., McMaster, J. J., & Cohen, S. N. (2013). Challenges for Canada in meeting the needs of persons with serious mental illness in prison. *Journal of the American Academy of Psychiatry and the Law, 41*(4), 501–509.

Streissguth, A. P., Bookstein, F. L., Barr, H. M., Sampson, P. D., O'Malley, K., & Young, J. K. (2004). Risk factors for adverse life outcomes in fetal alcohol syndrome and fetal alcohol effects. *Journal of Developmental & Behavioral Pediatrics, 25*(4), 228–238.

Szalavitz, M. (2015). Genetics: No more addictive personality. *Nature, 522*(7557), S48–S49.

Tiesler, C. M. T., & Heinrich, J. (2014). Prenatal nicotine exposure and child behavioural problems. *European Child & Adolescent Psychiatry, 23*(10), 913–929.

United Nations Office of Drugs and Crime. (2013). *Global Study on Homicide 2013*. Retrieved from http://www.unodc.org/documents/gsh/pdfs/2014_GLOBAL_HOMICIDE_BOOK_web.pdf

van Lier, P. A. C., van Der Ende, J., Koot, H. M., & Verhulst, F. C. (2007). Which better predicts conduct problems? The relationship of trajectories of conduct problems with ODD and ADHD symptoms from childhood into adolescence. *Journal of Child Psychology and Psychiatry, 48*(6), 601–608. https://doi.org/10.1111/j.1469-7610.2006.01724.x

Vinkers, D. J., de Beurs, E., Barendregt, M., Rinne, T., & Hoek, H. W. (2011). The relationship between mental disorders and different types of crime. *Criminal Behaviour and Mental Health, 21*(5), 307–320.

Werner, S., Malaspina, D., & Rabinowitz, J. (2007). Socioeconomic status at birth is associated with risk of schizophrenia: Population-based multilevel study. *Schizophrenia Bulletin, 33*(6), 1373–1378.

White, P. (2016a, December 12). Prison agency argues segregation doesn't affect inmates' health. *The Globe and Mail*, A1, A13.

White, P. (2016b, December 13). Judge certifies inmates' class action. *The Globe and Mail*, A3.

White, P. (2016c, December 16). Ontario to tackle inmates' mental health, segregation. *The Globe and Mail*, A4.

White, P. (2017, May 24). Canada's prison agency closes in on segregation overhaul. *The Globe and Mail*, A1, A12.

Williams, H. W., Cordan, G., Mewse, A. J., Tonks, J., & Burgess, C. N. W. (2010). Self-reported traumatic brain injury in male young offenders: A risk factor for re-offending, poor mental health and violence? *Neuropsychological Rehabilitation, 20*(6), 801–812, https://doi.org/10.1080/09602011.2010.519613

Woodworth, M., & Porter, S. (2002). In cold blood: Characteristics of criminal homicides as a function of psychopathy. *Journal of Abnormal Psychology, 111*(3), 436–445.

Yang, Y., & Raine, A. (2009). Prefrontal structural and functional brain imaging findings in antisocial, violent, and psychopathic individuals: A meta-analysis. *Psychiatry Research: Neuroimaging, 174*(2), 81–88.

Zimbardo, P. G. (2007). *The Lucifer effect: Understanding how good people turn evil*. Random House Publishing Group.

CHAPTER 8

Violence, Violent Crime, and State Violence

Claudio Colaguori

LEARNING OBJECTIVES

In this chapter, you will

- learn how a wide range of actions, behaviours, and types of conduct may constitute violence;
- explore how violence is deployed as a basic form of social control;
- examine different definitions and theories of violence, revealing that violence is a complex and contested concept;
- understand general parameters that frame the criminological understanding of violent crime; and
- learn how the political state has perpetrated some of the worst forms of violence in human history, including genocide, war crimes, and mass atrocities.

INTRODUCTION

On April 18, 2020, in the province of Nova Scotia, a 51-year-old male named Gabriel Wortman, while impersonating a police officer, began a campaign of murderous **violence** that involved **arson** and the shooting deaths of 22 people in 16 locations. This criminal event was the deadliest act of mass killing perpetrated by a single individual in Canadian history (Mercer, 2020). When such heinous acts of violence occur, it is reasonable for citizens to ask the question "why?" How could a successful businessman with no ties to any criminal organization turn into a murderous maniac with no regard for the lives of innocent strangers? Did he have a hidden history of aggressive behaviour? How was he able to continue killing for 13 hours before finally being shot dead by the RCMP? If he was a psychologically disturbed man, why did he choose to act against others with violence instead of seeking help? These are all valid questions, and they raise a more general question: Why do acts of destructive violence persist in our society? Why is violence such a difficult problem to address? The *question* of violence is a profound and important one; it raises issues about human nature, culture, and power (Ray, 2011, p. 7). Violence is also fundamentally related to issues involving social control, warfare, and crime.

In the words of scholars ...

Since violence is intimately interconnected with the body, pain, and vulnerability, its discussion evokes fundamental issues of security, embodiment culture, and power.

Larry Ray, *Violence and Society*. 2011

Violence is a behaviour that is endemic to human social life, and yet there is little consensus among scholars about how to properly explain it or control it. There is not even a dedicated discipline of study that focuses specifically on violence. Most scholars "relegate violence to the domain of criminology and deviance" (Jackman, 2002, p. 387), even though it takes many forms beyond criminality. Violence is *normalized* and woven into the fabric of everyday life through adversarial social interactions and through sensationalized representations in the entertainment and news media.

Violence can take a number of different forms. It can be physical, emotional, direct, indirect, political, domestic, collective, symbolic, or even self-inflicted. Violence can be understood as an expression of the power to control others through destructive force (Colaguori, 2010); alternatively, it can also be understood as an expression of insecurity, weakness, and powerlessness (Arendt, 1969). The typical, common sense understanding of violence is that it is a force behind physical destruction, as in the case of violent damage inflicted on bodies or property. Understanding violence is also confusing because it is a contradictory phenomenon. For example, violence is destructive, but it is also a thrilling component of competitive sports, action movies, crime dramas, and many video games. Is violence to be understood as something deviant and abnormal or as something common and normal? Contradictions and uncertainties concerning violence are also evident in the fact that people tend to claim that violence is morally wrong, and yet people regularly engage in acts of psychological violence and **aggression** in their interactions with others. Violence also has a special allure: many people who claim to be against violence will nevertheless happily consume forms of entertainment that feature excessive violence.

Scholarly literature on violence reveals that it is indeed a complex phenomenon and complicated topic of research that spans disciplines from sociology and psychology to criminology, political science, philosophy, and sociobiology. As Ferguson writes, "violence is complex, multifaceted, and best understood from a multivariate perspective" (2009, p. 7). There are many varying definitions covering the many varieties of violence, and thus numerous theories are offered to explain the social phenomenon of violence. This chapter offers an overview of various perspectives on violence, including an overview of definitions of violence, types of criminal violence, and the forms of violence perpetrated by the political state.

In the words of scholars ...

Quite apart from the damaged and destroyed lives it leaves in its wake, violence represents a couple of problems: it can be such terrible fun, and it looks useful. Of course, in conventional economics, utility and enjoyment go together. But violence is unusual and complex for all that it aims to simplify.

James Brown, *Other Means: On the Political Economies of Violence*. 2000

DEFINING VIOLENCE

Although the term *violence* is commonly used in everyday language, when it is examined closely as a concept, it is not easy or simple to define. As Holmes writes, "physical violence, which is what we most often have in mind when we speak about violence, is the use of physical force to cause harm, death, or destruction, as in rape, murder, or warfare. But some forms of mental or psychological harm are so severe as to warrant being called violence as well" (1990, p. 1). If violence refers to something more than physical, destructive force, then can we speak of an essence of violence? For Bufacchi (2007) and Brown (2000), violence is understood broadly to be something that *violates*, especially since the root word of *violence* is violation. Thus, its effects are coercive and disruptive in a moral sense as well as a physical one. Defining violence is complicated for other reasons, partly because it is common for the word *violence* to be used metaphorically, as when someone refers to such things as "violent weather." However, from a sociological perspective, it is important to emphasize that violence is an activity directed by humans against other persons primarily as a way of exercising *repressive social control* over them. Violence is the most extreme form of attempt to control others. Whether we are talking about warfare, criminal violence, **domestic violence**, or emotional violence, we see that violence is a type of *instrumental action* employed as a strategy to control others, generally with the aim of getting them to submit to the will of the violator. Sometimes, a violent action seems to have no clear purpose or intent, in which case it is referred to as *senseless violence*.

Discussions about the human capacity for violence often tend to revert to universalist claims about inherent destructive impulses that form part of human nature. It is important to recognize (as shall be discussed below) that violence is best understood not as mere instinctual aggression endemic to all humans, but rather as an action that emerges from conscious human will and individual determination. Whether the violence is criminal, interpersonal, or political, it is, with few exceptions, the product of conscious human intention—in other words, an action that someone made a deliberate decision to engage in.

How violence is defined in scholarly work depends largely on the disciplinary framework of the person doing the defining and on the type of violence being defined. Consider these additional definitions of violence.

Narrow Definitions of Violence

- "Behaviour by persons against persons that intentionally threatens, attempts, or actually inflicts physical harm. [This definition] is based on psychosocial research on aggressive behaviours" (Reiss & Roth, 1993, p. 35).
- "The unwanted physical interference by groups and/or individuals with the bodies of others, which are consequentially made to suffer a series of effects ranging from shock, bruises, scratches, swelling, or headaches to broken bones, heart attack, loss of limbs, or even death" (Keane, 1996, pp. 66–67).

Broad Definitions of Violence

- "Violence is the threatened or actual use of physical force or power against another person, against oneself, or against a group or community that either results in, or has a high likelihood of resulting in, injury, death, or deprivation" (Rosenberg, as cited in Jackman, 2002, p. 391).
- Structural or institutional violence occurs when "violence is built into the [social] structure and shows up as unequal power and consequently as

unequal life chances.... There may not be any person who directly harms another person in the structure ... [and yet violence is evident when] resources are unevenly distributed, as when income distributions are heavily skewed, literacy/education unevenly distributed, medical services [exist] in some districts and for some groups only, and so on" (Galtung, 1969, p. 171).

Types of Violence

As Collins writes, "there is a vast array of types of violence. It is short and episodic as a slap in the face; or massive and organized as a war. It can be passionate and angry as a quarrel; or callous and impersonal as the bureaucratic administration of gas chambers" (2008, p. 1). As indicated in the various definitions of violence listed above, violence is complex and takes different forms. Adding to its complexity are the ways it is woven into the fabric of social life at various levels. Research on violence is organized around a variety of categories in the attempt to classify it. For analytic purposes, violence can be divided into:

Microsocial violence: The physical assaults, violations, and conflicts that occur between individuals and within small groups, including murder, bullying, rape, sexual assault, domestic violence or intimate partner abuse, child abuse, and elder abuse, as well as self-inflicted physical bodily damage and suicide;

and

Macrosocial violence: The conflicts that occur on a larger scale by organized collectivities of people or states, including social protest violence, political violence, **genocide**, **terrorism**, militarized warfare, and large-scale bombings with weapons of mass destruction or chemical weapon attacks.

There are also types of violence that fall into both the micro and macro categories, as well as those that do not fit easily into either category, as follows:

media violence: The depiction of violent acts, physical destruction, gun violence, victimization, and other lethal actions such as militaristic violence on television, in movies, and in other forms of entertainment such as video games, competitive sports, numerous internet sites, and some social media content. Stahl (2010) calls this type of violence **militainment**.

criminal violence: Criminal acts that are violent by their very nature and are also violations of criminal law, such as **homicide**, physical assault, sexual assault/rape, robbery, car-jacking, the destruction of property, and home invasion. This type of violence also includes the unauthorized use of lethal force with the intent to inflict deadly or potentially deadly harm against another person through destructive acts including weaponized violence, arson, and other forms of lethal action that result in injury, damage, or death.

political violence: The use of violent force such as non-peaceful revolutionary action or terrorism perpetrated by individuals and groups who aim to achieve political change that serves their own interests. This type of violence may also be carried out by those who use violent tactics against state authorities, institutions, private property, and those deemed "enemies of the cause" as part of political protest. It may involve murder, kidnapping, or property damage.

state violence: The use of violent force by government authorities and their agents perpetrated against citizens or foreigners deemed "enemies of the state" that may include police brutality, extra-judicial killings, imprisonment of political opponents and journalists, or unlawful detainment. It also describes state engagement in unlawful and unjust wars of aggression, including foreign invasion, **war crimes**, state-sponsored genocide, and the indiscriminate use of weaponry, such as the use of land mines, missiles, drone strikes, arial bombings, and chemical weapons that target civilian populations.

As you may have gathered so far reading this chapter, violence is not a straightforward topic to explain or define, and many professional researchers have differing and sometimes conflicting conceptions of violence. Mainstream thinkers such as Pinker (2002) often subscribe to **biological determinist** views, arguing that the capacity for violence in humans is part of the natural order of things and emerges from the evolutionary forces that have shaped human nature. Researchers such as Burstyn (1999) and Colaguori (2012) emphasize how violent behaviour is reinforced by sociocultural influences. There is no doubt that humans have the natural propensity for violence and conflict, just as they have the potential for peacefulness and cooperation. Multiple perspectives that take into consideration both human behaviour and human nature more broadly are best understood from a multifactorial perspective. Such a perspective takes into consideration cultural, individual/psychological, and biological factors. Different theories of violence emphasize these factors to varying degrees.

In the words of scholars ...

VIOLENCE:
>   Actions that inflict, threaten, or cause injury.
>   Actions may be corporal, written, or verbal.
>   Injuries may be corporal, psychological, material, or social.

Mary R. Jackman, *Violence in Social Life.* 2002

THEORIES OF VIOLENCE

Students and researchers studying violence often ask the question: "Where does violence come from?" Such a question is motivated by the assumption that if we can understand the origins of violence and identify its specific causes, then we may be better able to control it or even stop it altogether. However, the more one explores violence, the more one realizes it is not really a *thing in itself* that has some elusive origin. Rather, violence emerges as part of complex social relations and has multiple causes, motivations, and contexts. As Ray (2011), among others, has indicated, *violence is socially organized.* Violence most often emerges from an arrangement of social relations that leads to violent outcomes. Despite scholars' general acceptance of this finding, early researchers, such as Sigmund Freud, did try to identify the singular root causes of violence in humans. Freud suggested that violence and human destructiveness result from the expression of an innate *death drive* inherent in human consciousness, and that warfare is the outward expression of the death drive unleashed on a mass scale. He later recanted this view, but the idea that violence is some sort of instinctual, primordial urge inherent in human nature remains a popular, albeit highly problematic, belief.

Modern theories concerning the origins and causes of violence are often reflective of a particular discipline of thought. A biologist may emphasize the physiological, hormonal, or biochemical factors that stimulate the potential for violence; a psychologist would identify the emotional and cognitive factors, as well as the social learning processes, that stimulate an individual to behave violently, or explore the ways in which traumatic personal experience may be causative factors motivating the violent behaviour of the criminal offender. A sociologist would emphasize the role of social circumstances, life chances, and affiliations a person develops, or the role of institutional powers, along with the real or perceived deprivations that push or pull a person towards violence across their life course. A criminologist's view on violence, however, is generally explained through the following theories.

Violence as an Instrumental Force

Violence is an instrumental force. It is often used as a *means to an end*; in other words, it is a technique that is utilized to achieve a desired goal through coercion. For example, the armed robber who holds up a convenience store is not necessarily interested in shooting the store clerk (although that reckless dimension of criminal violence certainly exists), but the robber may do so if the clerk fails to comply with the demand to hand over the money in the cash register. In this example, violence is the *instrument* used to compel the behaviour of another into submission. In criminal violence, domestic violence, and violence perpetrated by the state against its adversaries, violence is the instrument or means utilized to force others to submit.

Social Thrill Violence

Social thrill violence, which is engaging in violence for the sake of fun, excitement, and the thrill of recklessness, is also a dimension of criminal violence because of the intrinsic pleasure that some people get from engaging in risky acts of wanton destruction, whether it be property damage, throwing objects off bridges onto passing vehicles, sabotage, arson, or torturing animals (Burt & Simons, 2013; Katz, 1988). This explanation of violent crime is also relevant to understanding the commission of crimes by youths who are more likely to engage in criminality for which there is no external reward except for the thrill of the act itself, a type of reckless thrill referred to in Chapter 4 as *transgression*.

Violence as Aggression

Violence is often understood in terms of aggression, and while the two concepts are sometimes used interchangeably, they are distinct from one another. When a military general gives an order to his soldiers to launch an attack against enemy forces, that general is clearly unleashing a type of violence, but the general is not likely in an *aggressive* state of mind. It is more likely that the general is in a rational and calculating state of mind rather than one that is emotionally charged, angry, or out of control. Aggression, which can lead to violence, is also a complex concept. What distinguishes aggression from violence is that aggression is a hostile emotional response characterized by anger and impulsive rage, often used as a threat to inflict violence.

Aggression is highly correlated with criminal behaviour. Research on criminal aggression seems to indicate that persistent patterns of childhood aggression that are not corrected through proper socialization or effective treatment are a strong predictor of adolescent delinquency and violent behaviour in adulthood (Beaver, 2009). Individuals whose temperaments are characterized by an inability to control aggressive impulses often find themselves socially isolated and in regular conflict with law enforcement agencies.

Criminal violence among persistent offenders has been theorized to result from *low impulse control* or low self-control (Gottfredson & Hirschi, 1990). This explanation of criminal violence can be understood as an extension of the **frustration–aggression hypothesis** (Dollard et al., 1939), which proposes that some individuals fail to develop healthy, prosocial coping strategies for dealing with stressful situations, and their frustration is then expressed through displays of aggression, often directed at others.

A dubious concept often mentioned in relation to aggression is **catharsis**, the idea that if a person has an alternative (usually recreational) avenue for releasing pent-up anger and aggression, it will reduce their overall capacity for expressing actual aggression against others. The catharsis hypothesis suggests that aggressive forms of sport and rough play activities serve a useful social function insofar as they allow for the *cathartic release* of stress, frustration, and anger that would otherwise be expressed by people in socially unacceptable ways. We might hear people say, "I like to throw my fists at a punching bag after work to blow off steam and vent my frustrations." Such views are often invoked to promote the social utility of competitive sports, gaming, and other adversarial social rituals. However, as Aronson writes, "the weight of evidence does not support the catharsis hypothesis … when somebody angers us, venting our hostility against that person does indeed seem to make us feel better. However, it does not reduce our hostility…. Aggressing the first time can reduce your inhibitions against committing other such actions; the aggression is legitimized, and it becomes easier to carry out such assaults" (1984, p. 195). Although frustration leading to aggression is a factor in some violent crimes, it does not fully explain the vast range of violent crimes that require careful planning, coordination, and execution on the part of the perpetrator.

TWO GENERAL PARAMETERS OF VIOLENT CRIME: THE INDIVIDUAL AND CULTURE

In the public perception, crime is almost synonymous with violence. The word *crime* usually evokes an act of physical destruction. Among all types of crime, it is violent crime that produces the greatest emotional response, as well as the strongest sense of injustice. Violent crime comes the closest to pure violation. Although many crimes do not involve direct physical violence, the most sensational crimes do. Violent crimes also tend to provoke public fears and panics more than other types of crime, because their destructive effects are immediate and visible and victimization is clear and self-evident. Violent killers gain notoriety in the news and on crime shows, and their names are publicly known. Some violent criminals deliberately choose new names to glamorize their identity. In Canada, there is Paul Bernardo (born as Paul Jason Teale) also known as the Scarborough Rapist, and Luka Rocco Magnotta (once again, not his birth name, which is Eric Clinton Kirk Newman). Both fake names problematically invoke Italian heritage. Many people instantly recognize the names of notorious American serial killers who gain further popularity through their sensationalized nicknames, such as Ted Kaczynski, "the Unabomber"; John Wayne Gacy, Jr., "the Killer Clown"; Richard Ramirez, "Night Stalker"; and David Berkowitz, "the Son of Sam." Most violent criminals, from serial killers to tyrannical dictators, are marked in the annals of history, while many non-violent criminals who have perpetrated great harm tend to be forgotten.

Thus far, this chapter has examined various definitions, theories, and types of violence as a prelude to examining violent crime and state crime. The amount of detailed research on violent crime is vast and cannot be fully summarized here; however, attempts to understand the causes and motivations for violent crime have given rise to two general areas of research:

Characteristics of the Individual Offender

- <u>Neurological and biochemical deficits</u>, which, as Beaver indicates, are often evident in "the making of criminals [as] a sequential process that begins at conception and continues throughout the rest of life course" (2009, p. 36). As Ferguson recounts, "there is no gene for violence"; however, one might refer to biological causes of violent behaviour as *soft determinism* insofar as they may act as factors that predispose some individuals to persistent patterns of violent behaviour (Ferguson, 2009, pp. 7–8). These soft determinants may include the potential for malformation of brain components due to prenatal exposure to toxins such as tobacco, alcohol, and synthetic chemicals. Brain injury, toxicity damage, or genetic defects can, in some individuals, lead to a severely hampered ability to control aggressive impulses. As discussed above, individuals who have low self-control, either through biosocial or psychosocial factors, and who respond with anger and violence to certain social situations may be more likely to have numerous encounters with the criminal justice system.

- <u>Persistent patterns of childhood aggression</u> that appear in early childhood and fail to be corrected with age and socialization are often correlated with adult criminal violence. As Beaver writes, "one of the best predictors of future criminal behaviour is a history of aggressive behaviour in childhood and adolescence" (2009, p. 38). However, Moffit (1993) distinguishes between *life-course persistent* offenders and *adolescent-limited* offenders. Thus, it seems that some individuals who engage in excessive violence and/or interpersonal aggression during adolescence may abandon such behaviours as they become adults. Self-correction of antisocial behaviour often occurs because such behaviour conflicts with the pursuit of other significant adult life goals that require social conformity, such as romantic attachments, raising children, the demands of securing housing and associated living costs, stable employment, and planning for the future.

Cultural Norms that Directly Influence and Encourage Patterns of Criminal Behaviour

- <u>Individual membership in subcultures of violence,</u> where members internalize the norms and values of the group, as well as learn the behaviours and skills ("tricks of the trade"), including the use of violence to execute criminal objectives and maintain group solidarity. Wolfgang and Ferracuti's seminal study on the *subculture of violence* suggested that in "groups with the highest rates of homicide, we should find in the most intense degree subcultures of violence" (1967/1982, p. 153).
- <u>Cultures that are characterized by a strong sense of honour, reputation, pride, and respect,</u> where actual or perceived threats to one's personal, family, or group honour is met with violent retaliations. This "culture of honour" (Nisbett & Cohen, 1996) is evident in many places worldwide from urban criminal gangs of North and Central America, where a "code of the streets" (Anderson, 2000) operates, to the village cultures of Italy, Greece,

and Turkey, for example, where those whose honour is disrespected feel justified in retaliating through a vendetta against those who disrespected them in order to restore honour and reputation. Within prison subcultures, for example, inmates learn patterns of adaptation and must follow a code of respect by earning a reputation for being tough, known as gaining *a hard name*, that comes from reacting against others with violent retributions for any verbal or physical assaults perpetrated against them (Zweig, 2009). Prison inmates often form ideological or ethnic subcultural gangs as a way of creating group solidarity and collective defense against threats from other prison gangs.

- The broader patriarchal culture of hypermasculinity or machismo (Burstyn, 1999; Katz, 2006; Messerschmidt, 1993) that prevails as a dominant cultural norm among boys and men and is reflected in stereotypically violent media representations of male identity. This factor is also apparent in the rates of homicide where the majority of perpetrators and victims are male, usually in their mid- to late twenties.

Masculinity within patriarchal cultures is defined by an identity based on toughness, brawn, and aggression, and a reputation for brutality and excess based on participation in status elevation rituals such as competitive sports, hard drinking, crime, and unruly behaviour, as evidenced in sports hooliganism and other forms of aggressive or adversarial conduct (Burstyn, 1999). The spectrum of masculine rituals contributes to the formation of a hegemonic masculinity that is celebrated as a masculine ideal in popular media stereotypes of violent male iconic figures such as Dirty Harry, Rambo, the Terminator, and Iron Man, among many others (Boggs & Pollard, 2007; Renzetti, 2004).

In the words of scholars ...

Violent crime is a deeply emotive topic, and graphic illustrations of it abound on television and cinema screens and in newspapers, colouring the political and criminal justice responses not just to violence but to crime in general. Yet despite its prominence in both fiction and the news, the attention it has received from criminologists has been patchy, focused mainly on a few specific forms of offending

Michael Levi and Mike Maguire, "Violent Crime." In *The Oxford Handbook of Criminology*, edited by Maguire et al. 2002

THE RANGE OF VIOLENT CRIMES

Homicide and Assault

Homicide is the preeminent type of violent crime because it results in the taking of another life, in some cases as a gruesome murder. In Canada, homicide includes both murder and manslaughter, with each having two categories. Murder is classified as first or second degree and refers to causing a deliberate, intentional death, while manslaughter refers to an act that causes an unintentional death through reckless disregard (*Criminal Code*, C-46). The more prevalent type of physical violence is assault, which is one of the most common types of charged offences; it is defined as any unwanted application of force (or even the threat thereof) without consent, and can include strikes, pushes, punches or kicks, grabbing, holding, and spitting (*Criminal Code*, s. 266). Crime statistics in North America consistently indicate that the majority of homicide victims are males in their mid- to late twenties, and most perpetrators of violence are also male.

Domestic Violence

The problem of homicidal deaths and violent assaults continues to remain a fundamental challenge for justice systems worldwide. Such forms of violence occur across the social spectrum to include family violence or domestic violence, partner violence and abuse, as well as child and elder abuse. A report by Walby indicates, "a fifth of all violent crime occurs in the course of, or at the end of, a long-term relationship between two people. One in four women will experience this kind of violence during their adult lives. [In the United Kingdom] one hundred and fifty people are killed each year by a current or former partner; thousands of people turn up each year in … hospital casualty departments … with injuries inflicted by a current or former partner" (2004, p. 7). A 2021 Statistics Canada report indicates that "rates of police-reported family violence against children and youth, intimate partners, and seniors all rose in 2019. The overall rate of police-reported family violence increased for the third consecutive year, rising 13% over this period. This follows a long span of decline, with the rate falling by almost one-fifth (-19%) from 2009 to 2016" (Statistics Canada, 2021). An April 2021 report indicates how, in times of crisis, intimate partner violence can increase:

> The COVID-19 pandemic led to an exacerbation of pre-existing hardships and disparities in many vulnerable populations, including individuals affected

by intimate partner violence. Pre-pandemic statistics showed that 30% of women are victims of sexual or physical Intimate Partner Violence in their lifetime, and numerous reports have shown that the incidence and severity of intimate partner and family violence increased substantially after the pandemic began. (Rodriguez, 2021)

Box 8.1: Family Violence in Canada

Family violence is an important public health issue. Its impacts on health go beyond direct physical injury, are widespread and long-lasting, and can be severe, particularly for mental health. Even less severe forms of family violence can affect health.

Some Canadian families are experiencing unhealthy conflict, abuse, and violence that have the potential to affect their health. Known collectively as family violence, it takes many forms, ranges in severity, and includes neglect as well as physical, sexual, emotional, and financial abuse. People who experience family violence need to be supported, while people who are abusive or violent need to be held accountable. Family violence is a complex issue that can happen at any point in a lifetime.

In Canada,

- an average of 172 homicides are committed every year by a family member.
- for approximately 85,000 victims of violent crimes, the person responsible for the crime was a family member.
- just under 9 million, or about one in three Canadians, said they had experienced abuse before the age of 15 years.
- just under 760,000 Canadians said they had experienced unhealthy spousal conflict, abuse, or violence in the previous five years.
- more than 766,000 older Canadians said they had experienced abuse or neglect in the previous year.

Women, children, Indigenous peoples, people with disabilities, and people who identify as lesbian, gay, bisexual, trans, or questioning are at greater risk of experiencing family violence and its impacts. Women are more likely than men to be killed by an intimate partner and more likely to experience sexual abuse, more severe and chronic forms of intimate partner violence, particularly forms that include threats and force to gain control. Women are also more likely to experience health impacts.

Violence against women and children is a public health issue of global importance. Global data show that one out of every three women will experience physical or sexual abuse in their lifetime. Approximately 18% of women and almost 8% of men say they have been victims of sexual abuse as children.

Family violence is complicated—no single factor can accurately predict when it will happen. Different combinations of factors at the individual, family, relationship, community, and societal level affect the risk for family violence. Examples of factors include beliefs about gender and violence, and relationship characteristics such as power and control.

People are reluctant to talk about family violence, meaning it often goes unreported. Reasons for not reporting family violence include fear and concerns about safety, stigma, and not being believed. In some cases, people believe it is a personal matter or not important enough. They may also be dependent on the person who is being abusive or violent.

Using what we know about the social determinants of health can help prevent family violence and build effective ways to address it. Approaches to prevention include changing beliefs and attitudes, building safe and supportive communities, supporting our youth, healthy families, and relationships and promoting good health and well-being.

More knowledge is needed about the effectiveness of prevention strategies and interventions in different situations.

Excerpt from Taylor, G. (2016). *The Chief Public Health Officer's Report on the state of public health in Canada 2016: A focus on family violence in Canada.* Public Health Agency of Canada, p. 3.

Violence against Children

Violence against children can also occur in the context of domestic violence. This is illustrated in a disturbing 2016 Canadian example reported by the *Toronto Star*:

Everton Biddersingh, accused of torturing his daughter Melonie for four years, then killing her by drowning or by starving until her 17-year-old body weighed the same as an 8-year-old, has been found guilty of first-degree murder after seven hours of jury deliberations. The verdict comes twenty-one years after Melonie Biddersingh's unidentified body was found in a smouldering suitcase in an industrial parking lot on Sept. 1, 1994. An autopsy revealed 21 healing fractures, severe malnourishment, a contusion to the skull and evidence that she may have drowned in fresh water. (Hasham, 2016)

Violence against children takes numerous other forms, including child molestation, as well as through victimization by pedophilia. One example is outlined in a 2016 CBC report:

> Thirteen men are in custody after police busted an alleged online pedophile ring in six Quebec cities and Toronto following a three-year investigation. Police were executing warrants Wednesday morning at homes in Montreal, Quebec City, Lévis, Trois-Rivières, Saint-Eustache, Richelieu-Saint-Laurent, Toronto. The men in custody are between 27 and 74 years old and could face charges linked to the sexual exploitation of children. (CBC News, 2016)

The sexual exploitation of children is one of the most disturbing human rights abuse issues worldwide, and yet it receives very little attention and activist response in relation to other categories of injustice. Child sex tourism and pedophile crime networks continue to operate globally, targeting the most vulnerable members of the population, as indicated in news reports such as a June 2020 BBC report that reads, "Germany Investigates 30,000 Suspects over Paedophile Network" (BBC News, 2020a). In some regions, child sex tourism, also referred to as the extraterritorial sexual exploitation of children, is on the rise. Maria Fernanda Felix de la Luz writes of the damage done by sex tourism:

> Sex tourism is increasing worldwide but its rise has been particularly high in Latin American countries…. Even though in recent years Latin American countries have made significant efforts to combat sexual exploitation, including passing anti-slavery laws, granting resources for special programmes and creating partnerships with NGOs, the problem is still present, and it endangers thousands of lives. According to the 2017 Trafficking in Persons Report, the majority of countries in Latin America do not fully satisfy the standards for combating this crime…. In sex tourism, the perpetrator tends to be a foreigner who leaves the country after committing the crime. This represents a major difficulty for the investigation and the prosecution. (2018)

Female Infanticide and Feticide

Violence against children also extends to the murder of newborn infants and fetuses, predominantly females. Ansari writes, "female feticide is perhaps one of the worst forms of violence against women where a woman is denied her most basic and fundamental right i.e. 'the right to life'" (2018, p. 1154). The phenomenon of gender-selective infanticide (also known as feticide) is a cultural practice endemic to extreme patriarchal cultures, where the preference for male offspring is driven by a gendered honour code so strong that female offspring are often killed, and women who repeatedly give birth to female offspring are often abandoned by their husbands. Gender-selective infanticide is in part responsible for an imbalance in the male–female birth ratio in the East. For example, a June 2020 *ThePrint* news report headline reads, "India accounts for 45.8 million of world's missing females over last 50 years: UN report. Citing data by experts, the report said China and India together account for about 90–95% of the estimated 1.5 million missing female births annually worldwide" (PTI, 2020).

Violence against Women

Violence against women is a pernicious, recurrent category of violent crime, and it takes a number of forms depending on the culture. Some patriarchal cultures generate highly misogynistic crimes, including bride burning, gang rape, and in-the-face acid attacks against females. Sexual assault, stalking, and murder, committed predominantly but not exclusively by male perpetrators, are more common forms of violence that occur in virtually every culture.

The deliberate murder of females because of their gender is termed **femicide**, and in some nations, it is exacerbated by the lack of a serious formal response from law enforcement, which enables impunity for perpetrators. Femicidal violence is a global problem that also exists in relation to organized crime activity, the fate of women in war zones, sexual orientation hate crime, and honour killings. Femicide is especially prevalent in areas such as Afghanistan, France, Turkey, Latin America, and South Asia. There has been some attention to the issue of femicide by human rights organizations and other governing bodies. For example, as reported by Leffert,

> By an overwhelming margin, the European Parliament has voted to condemn the murders of women in Central America and Mexico.... Lawmakers gathered in Brussels officially criticized both the killings and the widespread impunity which has surrounded the crimes. The European deputies called on governments to take meaningful actions aimed at eradicating discrimination and violence against women, punishing killers and strengthening legal systems. (2007, p. 1)

As of 2017, the situation of gender violence in Central America and Mexico remained dire: "A culture of machismo, combined with judicial corruption, has led to widespread impunity for perpetrators, with the vast majority of killings going unsolved" (Oxford Analytica, 2017).

Canada is no exception to femicidal violence. Three notorious cases are as follows:

- The event known as the Montreal Massacre, where, "late in the afternoon on 6 December 1989, a young man walked into Montreal's Polytechnique engineering school with a semi-automatic rifle and killed 14 women, injured 14 others (including four men), then killed himself. Marc Lépine's page-long suicide note, written in French, made his motivations clear: 'Feminists have always enraged me,' he wrote. 'I have decided to send the feminists, who have always ruined my life, to their Maker'" (Lépine, as cited in Lindeman, 2019).
- In April 2018, "a man named Alek Minassian drove a van on to a Toronto sidewalk and killed 10 people, eight of them women. The sexually frustrated young man behind the van's wheel—a self-described incel, or 'involuntary celibate'—saw his act as retribution against women who had starved him of the affection he felt he was rightfully owed. Minassian said he was inspired by Elliot Rodger, an incel and wannabe pickup artist who shot 20 people in 2014" (Lindeman, 2019).
- The third example refers to the case of Robert Pickton, described as the "'worst serial killer in history,' who fed prostitutes to pigs" (Miller, 2016). "Between 1978 and 2001, at least 65 women disappeared from Vancouver's Downtown Eastside. Robert Pickton, who operated a pig farm in nearby Port Coquitlam, was charged with murdering 26 of the women. He was convicted on six charges and sentenced to life in prison. In a jail cell conversation with an undercover police officer, Pickton claimed to have murdered 49 women. The murders led to the largest serial killer investigation in Canadian history, and Pickton's farm became the largest crime scene in Canadian history. The case became a flash point in the wider issue of missing and murdered Indigenous women and girls in Canada" (Butts, 2017).

Gun Violence

Firearms are directly involved in numerous types of violent crime, including homicide, gang-related shootings, armed robbery, home invasions, school shootings, and carjacking. The availability of guns varies from country to country, and, despite restrictive gun laws, guns are readily accessible to those who aim to acquire them for criminal purposes. The increasing proliferation of guns resulting from both legal ownership and illegal possession complicates the relation between guns and violent crime. Kleck (2009) points out that victims also use guns defensively and thus gun ownership has the measurable effect of reducing homicide rates. Kleck further writes, "understanding the connection between guns and crime requires appreciating three fundamental facts:

1. Whereas gun ownership affects crime in various ways, crime also affects gun ownership.
2. The possession and use of guns have both violence-reducing and violence-increasing effects.
3. The kinds of effects that possession and use of guns have on crime depend on who possesses and uses them. The effects of victims using guns for self-protection are predominantly violence-reducing, whereas the effects of criminals using guns for aggressive purposes are a mixture of violence-increasing and, more surprisingly, violence-reducing effects" (2009, p. 86).

Scholars, as well as politicians and citizen groups, disagree on the point that legal gun ownership and gun availability may tend to reduce violence due to deterrence and self-defence. The gun-as-deterrence argument does not consider the extra-criminal situations where guns cause death by accident, such as toddlers finding guns in their surroundings and inadvertently firing them at siblings. For example, a 2021 Associated Press news article reads, "Florida authorities say a 3-year-old boy accidentally shot his 2-year-old sister after finding a gun that had been hidden between sofa cushions by a family friend" (Associated Press, 2021b). Further, Cukier and Eagen argue that "there is ample international research that suggests the availability of guns increases the risk of lethal violence. When guns are present suicide attempts are more likely to succeed and assaults are more likely to become homicides" (2018, p. 109).

In places where handgun ownership is heavily restricted by law, as is the case in Canada, criminals who possess and use handguns in the commission of crime have an advantage over victims who have restricted access to handguns and are unarmed. Gun-related homicide is a phenomenon that feeds into and is informed by themes of hypermasculinity in popular culture, because it reinforces the idea that the capacity to wield lethal gun violence is an expression of manhood. Related to the aforementioned, Sheptycki (2009) refers to the phenomenon of the *pistolization* of crime:

> When it comes to guns, crime, and social order, one process stands out and that is the process of pistolization. It is not a question of the number of guns in a society, or the ratio of guns-to-adult members of the population, it is a question of the meaning of the weapons. The evidence ... suggests that Canada is not, on the whole, a very weaponized society. There are some worrisome indications that some segments of criminalized youth sub-culture may be becoming pistolized and this is reflected in both official crime statistics and artefacts from popular culture (pp. 331–332).

The Government of Canada reports that 1 in 3 homicides in Canada are firearm related, and there has been an 81 percent increase in violent offences involving guns from 2009 to 2019 (Public Safety Canada, 2021). Various factors are contributing to the current increase of gun-related violent crime across many large cities in both Canada and the US. One factor might be the legalization of marijuana in Canada. Although this has removed some portion of the cannabis drug trade from gangs and other organized crime groups, it has also contributed to the liberalization and proliferation of illegal marijuana growth and sale across the country. This illegal growth is sold by criminals, who often engage in drug territory turf wars that escalate to include gun-related shootings (Canadian Press, 2021).

Although the phenomenon of gun and weapons crime is often presented in the media alongside images of gangs and street-level shootings, it is merely one dimension of a larger global issue concerning the weaponization of conflict and crime fuelled by the arms trade. The availability of guns remains part of both the legitimate economy and the underground economy, as a substantial number of guns and weapons are illegally obtained. For example, a BBC News report, titled "US Warship Seizes Huge Weapons Shipment in Arabian Sea," discusses the global proliferation of weaponry: "In a statement, the navy said the source and intended destination of the weapons were under investigation.... 'The cache of weapons included dozens of advanced Russian-made anti-tank guided missiles, thousands of Chinese Type 56 assault rifles, and hundreds of PKM machine guns, sniper rifles, and rocket-propelled grenade launchers. Other weapon components included advanced optical sights,' the US Navy's Fifth Fleet, which is based in Bahrain, said in the statement" (2021).

Hate Crime Violence

Hate crimes are "crimes in which the offender is motivated by a characteristic of the victim that identifies the victim as a member of a group towards which the offender feels some animosity" (Roberts, 1995). These are considered very serious crimes because the malice is directed both against the individual *and* against the group they represent. In Canada, three sections of the *Criminal Code* deal with what have colloquially come to be known as "hate crimes."

- Section 318(1) makes it a crime to advocate or promote genocide.
- Section 319(1) makes it a criminal offence to communicate statements in any public place that would incite "hatred against any identifiable group where such incitement is likely to lead to a breach of the peace."
- Section 319(2) makes it a criminal offence to "willfully [promote] hatred against any identifiable group."

Any offence (for instance, assault or vandalism) can be considered a hate crime if it can be determined that hate was the motivating factor. If this can be successfully proven in court, stiffer penalties may apply at sentencing (Yang, 2017). These conditions mean that hate crimes can be difficult to prosecute. Another factor preventing the swift and easy prosecution of hate crimes is that police must secure the permission of the provincial Attorney General for the first two types of hate crimes (advocating or promoting genocide and inciting hatred against an identifiable group).

Hate crime activity has not always been prohibited in Canada. Blatantly discriminatory laws existed in North American societies for much of the 20th century in the form of anti-miscegenation laws, restrictive covenants blocking certain groups from home purchases, head taxes on immigrants, anti-homosexuality laws, the Canadian residential school system that targeted Indigenous children, and many more examples which serve to illustrate how racial and ethnic exclusion institutionalized as hatred of the *other* has been officially sanctioned by governments.

The public promotion of hatred has, in many nations, had the direct effect of emboldening individuals to engage in hate-based violence. For example, "On July 22, 2011, right-wing extremist Anders Behring Breivik infiltrated the camp on Utoya Island [Norway] and opened fire, killing 69 people, the deadliest mass shooting by a lone gunman in modern history. He killed eight others in a car bomb that same day" (CBC Radio, 2021). Breivik, a self-proclaimed Islamophobe, fascist, and anti-feminist, precisely represents the extremes of hate-based criminal violence.

The relationship between hatred and criminal violence is well established in history. On the basis of individual or group identity (be it ethnic, racial, sexual, gendered, or religious), marginalized people designated as "other" have suffered some of the worst forms of violence. Hate-based violence ranges from the beating, lynching, and murder of targeted individuals to the desecration of religious buildings and symbolic monuments. The worst forms of hate crime coincide with mass-scale, historically significant atrocities that recount the slaughter of innocents. The lynching of Blacks in the United States for much of the early 20th century, the **Holocaust** against Jews during World War II, the ethnic cleansing of Bosniaks in the early 1990s, the slaughter of hundreds of thousands of minority Tutsis during the 1994 Rwandan **civil war**, and numerous other atrocities stem, in part, from the promotion of hatred. Preventing the open expression of hatred in a public forum is one of the primary reasons that anti-hate legislation has been put in place in many nations.

Hate crimes stem directly from racism and other forms of prejudicial discrimination. The effort to prevent the normalization of hate-based acts in contemporary society also takes the form of modifying everyday language to discourage the promotion of racial and ethnic stereotypes, thus rendering racist and sexist discourse as socially taboo. There is an unequivocal relationship between the promotion of hatred against an identifiable group and the subsequent victimization of members of that group. Miller and Kim write, "in general a hate crime is considered to be an illegal act against a person, institution, or property that is motivated (in whole or in part) by the offender's prejudice against the victim's group membership status" (2009, p. 490). Miller and Kim further point out that hate-crime laws have a symbolic function in that they declare the victimization of people of difference from the dominant group is not tolerable in modern society. Yet some argue that hate-crime laws are problematic because they can be used to protect the rights of some identifiable groups over others and are thus susceptible to abuse and preferential application. Further, hate-crime laws shift the focus of prosecution onto *bias* and *motive* of the perpetrator instead of the criminal act itself, and thus some claim that existing laws against criminal violence are sufficient to prosecute offenders (Gerstenfeld, 2010; Miller & Kim, 2009). As with many other issues involving crime and justice, scholarly and legal debate remains part of the ongoing development of more effective crime control policies.

Terrorist Violence

Terrorism is both a disruptive and destructive type of violence that impacts social life in many nations of the world. Terrorism can be defined as the illegitimate use of violence by fringe groups operating outside of conventional political processes to achieve a political or revolutionary goal. One aspect that distinguishes terrorism from other types of violence is its intended goal: to strike fear and terror into the population at large as part of a broader strategy to destabilize the ruling powers and force them to submit to the demands of the terrorists. Since the terrorist attacks on American soil on September 11, 2001, the issue of terrorist violence has become a prominent global concern, one that spawned the US-led "war on terror." Official responses to the threat of terrorism have substantially modified social control policies and social life in the 21st century. From the implementation of anti-terrorist legislation to new rules for travel, intensified border patrol, and invasive surveillance systems, anti-terrorist measures implemented in many nations have created a post-9/11 era of hypersecurity, in which substantial resources are expended to implement anti-terrorist policing measures. Many anti-terror measures have met with considerable criticism insofar as they infringe upon the ideal of liberty and restrict social freedoms (Colaguori & Torres, 2012). Although a profoundly political issue, terrorism and the range of counter-terrorist responses are a typically criminological concern. As Deflem writes, "it is the unique province of criminology to focus on terrorism as a form of criminal or deviant behaviour and on counter-terrorism as social control" (2009, p. 533).

Terrorist violence has been employed as a strategy among both political and religious revolutionaries and has a history that long predates the events of September 11, 2001 (Chaliand & Blin, 2016). Political terrorism in early modern Europe was directed primarily at state authorities, whereas in the current era, terrorist violence often targets civilians and in some cases workers and security officers in an effort to demoralize the population into subservience. A news report from early 2021 reads, "Islamic State claims responsibility for attack on Pakistan's Shi'ite Hazara minority that kills 11…. 'The throats of all coal miners have been slit, after their hands were tied behind their backs and (they were) blind folded,' a security official told Reuters, requesting anonymity as he is not allowed to speak to media" (Yousafzai, 2021). As this headline indicates, different conceptions of terrorism exist, including that of the "lone wolf" terrorist who does not act on behalf of a particular group but acts alone, often with explicit ideological intent. A BBC news report on the Christchurch Mosque shootings that took place on March 15, 2019, states, "a white supremacist who killed 51 people at two mosques in New Zealand will serve life in jail without parole—the first person in the country's history to receive the sentence. Australian Brenton Tarrant, 29, admitted to the murder of 51 people, attempted murder of another 40 people and one charge of terrorism. The judge called Tarrant's actions 'inhuman,' saying he 'showed no mercy.' The attack … which was livestreamed, shocked the world. Tarrant's sentencing also marks the first terrorism conviction in New Zealand's history" (BBC News, 2020b). With no group affiliations expressed, Tarrant was considered to be a "lone wolf," acting on his own to commit his violence.

Another conception sees terrorism as a type of unconventional, illegal warfare. In this view, terrorism is a type of *asymmetrical* military conflict insofar as it does not conform to traditional rules of combat, where fighting generally occurs on a clearly defined field of battle between state-legitimated soldiers (Colaguori & Torres, 2012). Yet another conception of terrorism aims to minimize the negative stigma of barbaric irrationality associated with terrorist violence, suggesting that it can be justified as part of a successful revolutionary strategy used to overturn repressive governments and is therefore a legitimate form of political revolt (Price, 1977).

Discussions of terrorist violence as a matter of global concern often revolve around the claim that, despite wide media coverage, it is not a significant cause of death globally. Ritchie et al. (2019) note that "media coverage of terrorism is disproportionate to its frequency and share of deaths" and further, that there is "much larger coverage if the perpetrator was Muslim" (section 6). The authors break down the number of deaths by terrorism worldwide:

> In 2017, an estimated 26,445 people died from terrorism globally. Over the previous decade the average number of annual deaths was 21,000. However, there can be significant year-to-year variability. Over this decade [from 2007 to 2017] the global death toll ranged from its lowest of 7,827 in 2010 to the highest year of 44,940 in 2014. (Ritchie et al., 2019, summary point 3)

Although these figures may be seen as numerically low in comparison to other causes of death, it is important to recognize that where terrorism is a regular part of life in a given nation, it becomes virtually impossible to establish a civil society with a modern infrastructure, peace, and social prosperity.

Box 8.2: The Ethics of Violence

Is the use of violent physical force always wrong or unethical? Consider the use of violent force by a police officer who is attempting to detain and subdue a dangerous criminal who poses a threat to others. In such a case, would most people agree that the use of violent force is justified? What about when the state uses military and police violence to quash peaceful public protest? How do we decide what crosses the fine line between the legitimate versus illegitimate use of violent force? Sociologist Max Weber asserted that the political state maintains a monopoly on the use of violent force and that power is an essential part of its legitimacy and sovereignty. The state needs to control the means of violence (largely through its police, military, and criminal punishment mechanisms) so it can ensure public order and civil rule with the backing of force. In the United States of America, this ethic is challenged to some extent by the 2nd amendment to the constitution, which allows citizens the right to bear arms and therefore enact violence as well. Thus, societies sometimes sustain inherent contradictions about who can legitimately wield the power of violence. According to the anarchist theorist R. P. Wolff, the meaning of a physical act of violence is defined by the ethics underlying its intended purpose. For Wolff, violence is only problematic when it is abused as "the illegitimate or unauthorized use of force to effect decisions against the will or desire of others" (1999, p. 15). Is violence justifiable in the name of a higher cause, such as fighting a ruthless invader, or to achieve progressive revolutionary social change against a despotic ruler? Or is violence a failed measure that inevitably unleashes an unending cycle of violence and thus perpetuates the absence of peace? While those who espouse the moral values of peace often see violence as an ill-fated strategy in all cases, the matter of the utility and ethics of violence remains the subject of much debate.

In the words of scholars ...

Violence has played an enormous role in human affairs.

Hannah Arendt, *On Violence*. 1969

VIOLENCE AND CRIME COMMITTED BY THE STATE

Throughout history, political leaders and state officials have committed a wide range of serious crimes, ranging from **corruption** to the overt violence of war crimes, foreign invasions, and mass atrocities. **State crimes** (also known as governmental crimes) continue to occur, yet they are less frequently featured in media coverage of crime, and despite being named "the crime of all crimes" (Rothe, 2009), "state criminality is not generally a topic of everyday life" (Kramer, 2009, p. x). The discipline of criminology, with its traditional, biased focus on street crime, perpetuates this mystification. Michalowski et al. write, "criminology has served as an extension of state power," and "states and their crimes did not form part of the founding consciousness of the discipline. Simply put, the criminological canon excludes from its catalogue of concerns most harms against human, animal, and environmental well-being committed by states" (2010, pp. 1–2). Mainstream criminology has thus historically served the interests of state power by focusing heavily on the crimes of the marginalized and on the illegal acts of individual criminals instead of focusing on large-scale crimes of the state. Critical criminology examines crimes by state actors and governmental authorities to reveal the unjust abuse of power by state officials in both democratic and authoritarian countries, and it thus raises questions regarding the legitimacy of state authority.

Issues concerning state-sponsored mass atrocities, human rights abuses, and political violence have generally been covered in an interdisciplinary realm of study that includes history, political science, sociology, and sociolegal studies. Critical criminology has also made substantial contributions to the analysis of state crime since William Chambliss's 1988 address to the American Criminology Society, entitled *State-Organized Crime* (Chambliss, 1989; Rothe & Mullins, 2011). Given the extent of the serious crimes and violent atrocities perpetrated by states in the modern era, it is likely that state-sponsored crime and injustice will continue to develop as an important area of focus within criminological inquiry.

In the words of scholars ...

Critical theorists hold that *it is the modern state that is most instrumental in creating and sustaining a violent social environment.* Because violence is no longer a rare event but rather an integral part of our everyday lives, we tend to ignore it, as simply part of the nature of things. Its very normalcy and routine nature make it commonplace. Automobile accidents, homicides, terrorist attacks on abortion clinics, airplane hijacking and bombings, military and secret police raids on helpless civilians are all documented in the daily press. After the dictatorships of Stalin and Hitler, we have grown accustomed to horror, atrocities, and state-managed mass murders. In critical sociologists' terms, the *routinization of evil* dominates our century [emphasis original].

Nannette Davis and Clarice Stasz, *Social Control of Deviance: A Critical Perspective.* 1990

State crime is criminal conduct committed by governments and state officials. The 21st century is defined by various disruptive sociopolitical forces, including neoliberal globalization, transnational crime and corruption, and ongoing warfare, which combine to create a geopolitical context that increases the potential for state crime. There are many different types of state crime, ranging from political wrongdoing to acts of mass violence. Some of them are:

- political corruption, political manipulation, and grand theft of public monies by state officials;
- wars of invasion and aggression, war crimes, genocide, and **crimes against humanity**;
- wrongfully accusing, convicting, and imprisoning individuals who are factually innocent;
- state-sponsored use of lethal force including torture, extra-judicial killings, assassinations, and wrongdoing by national security personnel, and abuses of force by police and military personnel; and
- the state-sponsored "disappearance" of those deemed enemies of the state, and the theft of the children of political opponents.

Political Crimes

Political crimes and wrongdoings occur in nations under authoritarian rule, as well as in nations where presumably democratic political systems are in place. In the course of attempting to attain political office by any means, political officials often attempt to secure or retain power by engaging in rule-breaking conduct involving "dirty tricks" such as election fraud, vote tampering, campaign finance violations, political corruption, and **bribery** of election officials. Egregious political crimes tend to occur in authoritarian regimes where those who rule refuse to give up the power of political office in their attempts to rule-for-life by neutralizing or eliminating political adversaries. The neutralization of political opposition takes a number of forms, such as the illegal detainment, arrest, imprisonment, and murder of political opponents and critics. An example of such neutralization is the February 2021 case of Russian opposition figure Alexei Navalny, a prominent critic of Russian leader Vladimir Putin, who was tried in court and subsequently sentenced "to prison for 3½ years for violating the terms of his probation while he was recuperating in Germany from nerve-agent poisoning" (Associated Press, 2021a).

Political wrongdoing is often systemically maintained by backroom deal-making that involves the corruption of political allies and others who hold positions of power and influence within political and economic spheres. Corrupted state officials will exchange political favours for personal and material gain through widespread wrongdoing known as bribery. When political rivalry escalates to egregious acts against opponents, governments will often justify their ruthlessness by resorting to excuses. Sometimes, the ruling power will claim that its opponents have committed crimes *against* the state such as **treason**, terrorism, or **sedition**, among other trumped-up charges. In such instances, state officials who are empowered to apply the law originally designed for purposes of justice and national security openly abuse it for self-serving ends. Such abuses of law represent the descent into **tyranny**, which is a social condition created when the state itself becomes a fully criminal enterprise where despotic leaders rule through fear and violence. Tyrannical states are characterized by the imposition of excessive restrictions over the lives of their citizens and a significant absence of any basic human rights and freedoms, especially freedoms of speech, expression, and assembly. Such regimes are often maintained by intrusive surveillance monitoring and repressive policing. Tyrannical states also impose significant restrictions on the freedom of their citizens to travel beyond national borders. By doing so, these states contribute to the creation of migration and refugee crises, which unfortunately opens criminal opportunities for organized crime groups engaged in illegal smuggling operations.

In the words of scholars ...

That one has to go on killing in order to go on living, has become the principle that defines the strategy of states.

Michel Foucault, *The History of Sexuality Volume 1: An Introduction.* 1980

The Violence of War and Genocide

Warfare represents the highest form of violence. During the conduct of war, atrocities, acts of injustice, and criminal activities increase substantially. Bassiouni writes, "throughout history, abuses of power by tyrannical rulers and ruling-regime elites, which are carried out under their direction by state actors, have occasioned significant human, social, and economic harm to their respective national societies and those of others. Under the guise of war, large-scale human depredations have taken place, as well as in the colonization context and in other contexts manifesting oppression or repression by states that victimize groups in other states or territories" (2011, p. 1). Thus, war, which is itself a type of violence, gives rise to numerous other gross violations.

In the 20th century and into the present, over 220 million people have perished in the violence of warfare, and approximately 170 million were killed by their own government (Rummel, 1994). Death caused by war and other types of armed conflict remains a persistent problem in the 21st century. The World Bank Group reports that "in the 21st century, conflicts have increased sharply since 2010" (Marc, 2016). Thus, contrary to ideologies that claim human society progresses with the advance of time, the persistence of state-sponsored violent conflict indicates that some things worsen.

Violence and crime also occur in violent conflicts that take place outside of official declarations of war. They include acts of genocide, massacres, mass kidnappings, and other crimes. In some conflicts, insurrectionist and rebel groups engage in armed conflict with the government of a given territory, and some of the worst armed conflicts have been those perpetrated by states against their own citizens. In what is known as civil war, citizens of the same country will take up arms against each other.

The conduct of warfare is supposed to observe humane rules of combat as outlined in the Geneva Conventions and additional protocols that have been ratified by all member states of the United Nations (United Nations, n.d.). The Geneva Conventions set out ethical rules governing warfare, which aim to limit civilian casualties and keep armed combat limited to battle between soldiers, among other protocols. Nevertheless, the official rules of warfare are rarely followed by states engaged in military action. Aside from unintentional casualties caused by collateral damage, unarmed civilians have been the target of genocides, "ethnic cleansings," detention camps, direct killing, indiscriminate bombing, rape, famine, forced displacement, and the loss of livelihood and property (Slim, 2008). As Slim (2008) emphasizes, unarmed, innocent civilians are often the primary victims of war violence. Even more problematic is that they are also often the direct *target* of war violence, which gives rise to large-scale atrocities known as crimes against humanity and war crimes. One recent example is the Yemen War, where "children made up a quarter of civilian casualties [since 2019] … especially children, continue to pay the heaviest price of the conflict as it enters its seventh year.… In a new report, [Save the Children] said there had been 2,341 confirmed deaths and injuries of children in Yemen between 2018 and 2020, though they added the true figure was likely much higher" (MEE Staff, 2021). Another disturbing example is chronicled in an African Union report of 2015:

> The cruelty to civilians during South Sudan's war shocked the AU commission, which spared few details in describing the crimes. People were beaten and forced to jump into fires. Bodies were drained of blood and other victims were forced to drink the blood or eat human flesh. Women, old and young, were gang-raped and left bleeding and unconscious. Children were forced to fight or were enslaved by militias. (Dixon, 2015)

Killing in warfare that takes the form of state-sponsored violence against domestic populations often involves mass atrocities against specifically targeted, identifiable ethnic groups. The most historically noteworthy case of a short-duration mass genocide, outside of settler colonialism, is the Holocaust, perpetrated against Jewish people by the Nazi regime during World War II. Within the context of settler colonialism, genocides against Indigenous peoples in the Americas have arguably destroyed more lives than any other genocide occurring over extended periods of time (Smith, 2017). However, official responses to the violence against Indigenous peoples did not give rise to tribunals that would become the basis of international law because the violence of settler colonialism was so protracted, spanning centuries. Thus, some claim that the Holocaust is the *crime of the century* (Friedrichs, 2011), whereas the genocide of Indigenous peoples worldwide could be named the *crime of modernity* if one considers "the role of diseases, wars, genocidal violence, enslavement, forced relocations, the destruction of food sources, the devastation of ways of life, declining birthrates, and other factors in the Indigenous Holocaust" (Smith, 2017, p. 7). Writing on how atrocity is integral to modernity, Bauman states, "The Holocaust was indeed a Jewish tragedy. Though Jews were not the only population subjected to a 'special treatment' by the Nazi regime (six million Jews were among more than 20 million people annihilated at Hitler's behest), only the Jews had been marked for total destruction, and allotted no place in the New Order that Hitler intended to install" (1989, p. x).

In the 20th century and up to the present, numerous genocides, mass atrocities, and crimes against humanity have contributed substantially to what Theodor Adorno called the "horror of our world" (1998, p. 196). A partial list of such horrors would include:

- The Belgian Congo: an estimated 15 million deaths in the Congo, beginning in the 1870s into the 1920s, perpetrated by Belgian colonizers capitalizing on the trade in rubber and ivory at the expense of African lives;
- The Ottoman Turks: the atrocities (circa 1915) perpetrated by the Ottoman empire against Assyrians, Armenians, and Greeks that targeted upwards of 3 million people through death marches, forced religious conversions, and expulsion from ancestral lands;
- The Soviet Union: the estimated 20 million who died under the tyranny of Soviet dictator Joseph Stalin, who ruled from 1924 to 1953, by execution, starvation, and detainment in forced labour camps;
- China: from 1958 to 1962, Chinese dictator Mao Zedong enacted policies that "led to the deaths of up to 45 million people—easily making it the biggest episode of mass murder ever recorded" (Somin, 2016);
- Cambodia: upwards of 2.5 million people were murdered by the Khmer Rouge under the rule of Pol Pot that occurred from 1975 to 1979 following a 5-year civil war. The state-sponsored violence targeted a wide range of ethnic minorities, including Thais, Chinese, Vietnamese, Christians, and Buddhist monks, as well as former officials, teachers, and administrators from the previous government;
- Rwanda: in the context of the early 1990s civil war, upwards of 1 million mostly minority ethnic Tutsis were slaughtered by mostly ethnic Hutu perpetrators in a genocide that was noteworthy for its high rate of sexual violence against women and girls, as well as the virtual absence of outside intervention to halt the killing;
- The Balkan wars: in the 1990s, a number of interconnected ethnic and religious conflicts that resulted in the breakup of Yugoslavia, which included Bosnia, Slovenia, Serbia, Montenegro, and Croatia, led to atrocities including war crimes, rape, genocide, and ethnic cleansing. The escalation and scale of violence was remarkable insofar as it took place in a part of Europe that was relatively free of conflict; only a few years earlier, in 1984, the city of Sarajevo, the current capital of Bosnia and Herzegovina, had hosted the Winter Olympic games.

Image 8.1: Syrian girl "surrendering" to a photographer

Source: Rene Schulthoff

A full mention of violent conflicts that have occurred and/or are ongoing is too extensive to include in this brief overview. However, in the past few decades, regions where significant loss of life due to warfare, state-sponsored killing, and social disruption has occurred include Iraq, Libya, Mexico, Kashmir, Chechnya, Sudan, Syria, Yemen, Somalia, Ethiopia, Myanmar, Afghanistan, and Ukraine. Despite the efforts of peace activists, diplomats, non-governmental organizations, aid organizations, and other international groups who attempt to intervene to cease hostilities in numerous nations, armed conflicts remain an ongoing reality of the global political order (Joxe, 2002).

Controlling State Crime

Controlling state crime and violence represents a significant challenge for many reasons, but especially because the political state is a paradoxical institution with two distinct and sometimes conflicting dimensions:

1. The civil state maintains order and aims to ensure justice by protecting citizens against threats through its sovereign authority and its monopoly on the use of violence, and,
2. The authoritarian state, backed by its military and police forces, may on occasion use the power of violence for repression against citizens, dissenters, and other nations.

Thus, outside of a few exceptions, the state generally does not police itself very well and "governments [see themselves as being] above the law because by their very nature they are lawmaking not lawbreaking institutions" (Ross, 2011, p. 189). Further, when a state commits crimes against other, less powerful states or against its own citizens, there is rarely a reliable, authoritative global governance system in place to sanction the transgression. Even when there is an official, external response to state crimes and wrongdoings, these responses are often long and complex and may not necessarily produce formidable results. Nevertheless, one famous historical example of a coordinated response to the war crimes of the German state was the Nuremberg Trials (1945–1949), which came after World War II, where prominent members of the Nazi regime were tried for atrocities. The trials were among the earliest 20th-century legal endeavours aimed at installing international measures to ensure that atrocities such as the Holocaust could never be repeated. As Mullins writes, "the 20th century saw a number of attempts to create a permanent court to adjudicate cases involving the worst sorts of crimes people commit—genocide or crimes against humanity ... while [such attempts] are indeed meaningful and important components of international justice there are far more instances that require tribunals than have received them" (2011, p. 275). The development of an internationally binding legal framework to address war crimes in modern times has been an ongoing process, beginning with "The Hague Conventions adopted in 1899 and 1907 [which] focus on the prohibition to warring parties to use certain means and methods of warfare" (United Nations, n.d.). By 2002, the Rome Statute of the International Criminal Court (ICC) went into force, and as of 2010, 111 countries are party to it (Mullins, 2011, p. 275).

Bassiouni reiterates the difficulty of enforcement of the rule of international humanitarian law in cases of war crimes and other state crimes. In many cases, perpetrators are offered immunity and amnesty in exchange for the cessation of violence (2011, p. 17). Further, the level of atrocity committed is substantially higher in **failed states** than it is in states that maintain a high level of democratization that, for the most part, uphold the rule of law (p. 18). Democratic states are also complicit in war crimes, often committed against citizens of other nations rather than against their own citizens, thus further complicating efforts at prosecuting state-sponsored war crimes (Encarnación, 2005).

CONCLUSION

Violence is an aspect of life that confronts us in various ways. On an almost daily basis, we are faced with images and reports of violence in the news, in our entertainment programs, and, more painfully for some, through traumatic personal experiences with violence. Violence is generally understood to be among the most extreme of all social problems, affecting human lives in virtually all societies around the world with devastating effects on individuals, families, communities, and nations. The problem of violence certainly presents significant challenges for institutions that are tasked with controlling it, such as the criminal justice system and other departments of the state, as well as global governance institutions such as the ICC. Furthermore, at the existential level, violence is a complex phenomenon that presents us with difficulties in our ability to understand it. Nevertheless, understanding the causes and complexities of violence is a fundamental aspect of the overall strategy to curb it.

The problem of violent crime also consists of a complex set of factors. It involves interconnected factors such as the violence of the perpetrator, the harm inflicted on the victim, the context of the occurrence, and the response of state and legal authorities to address and control violent crime. As this chapter has indicated, the complexity of violence, the way it is woven into the fabric of social relations, and its variety of forms, from murder and femicide to warfare and genocide, all combine to make the problem of violence one of the most fundamental issues obstructing the quest for justice in the world today. If we recognize that violence, along with most of the other problems in society, are products of our own human-generated social realities, then we will be much more able to do something to keep violence to a bare minimum, insofar as that is humanly possible.

REVIEW QUESTIONS

1. Why is the concept of violence difficult to define in simple terms?
2. What are the parameters that criminology uses to understand violent crime?
3. Explain how various political states have used violence to maintain power and control. List some examples.

GLOSSARY

aggression: A type of hostile behaviour characterized by emotional anger and impulsive rage, often used as a threat that may lead to violence.

arson: The criminal act of intentionally or recklessly setting fire to property or woodlands without legal authorization.

biological determinism: The theory that human behaviour is primarily determined by biological factors.

bribery: When a person voluntarily solicits or accepts any benefit, financial or otherwise, in exchange for influencing an official act so as to afford the provider preferential treatment.

catharsis: The idea that if a person has an alternative (usually recreational) avenue for releasing pent-up anger and aggression, it will reduce their overall capacity for expressing actual aggression in real-life circumstances.

civil war: Warfare that occurs between groups and/or citizens belonging to the same country.

corruption: Unethical conduct by a person in a position of power who violates their authority of office by facilitating wrongdoing, usually for personal gain.

crimes against humanity: Large-scale criminal acts committed by states that persecute civilians in the course of implementing specific state policies or campaigns that lead to massive suffering, displacement, and death.

domestic violence (also known as *family violence*): Emotional abuse, aggression, or physical violence directed at someone living in a family, intimate relation, or cohabitation setting.

failed state: A political state that has failed to maintain power, legitimacy, or sovereignty because the government has collapsed.

femicide: The deliberate murder of females because of their biological sex, usually committed by males.

frustration–aggression hypothesis: The theory that aggression against others is primarily a response to frustration in individuals who fail to develop prosocial coping strategies for dealing with stressful situations.

genocide: The deliberate and targeted killing of people, often by mass slaughter, who are members of an identifiable ethnic, racial, or national group for the purposes of their elimination.

Holocaust: The genocide of an estimated 6 million European Jews in World War II by the German Nazi regime.

homicide: The legal term referring to causing the death of one person, directly or indirectly, by another person.

militainment: Television, films, video games, and other forms of entertainment that celebrate militarism and armed violence.

sedition: An act, in words or in deeds, that incites rebellion against a state or other political authority.

state crime: Criminal conduct committed by state officials and governments, ranging from political corruption to war crimes.

terrorism: The illegitimate use of indiscriminate violence by fringe groups operating outside of conventional political processes to achieve a political or revolutionary goal.

treason: The criminal act of betraying one's own sovereign nation by using violent force to overthrow the government or to conspire with and/or offer assistance to foreign entities or enemies of the government.

tyranny: An oppressive condition created when a despotic leader rules through fear and violence and engages in the arbitrary use and abuse of political power against citizens.

violence: A force, action, or type of conduct that violates, harms, or destroys.

war crime: An action or conduct that initiates an illegal war of aggression or invasion against a sovereign entity, or one that violates the internationally mandated humanitarian rules and norms that govern combat action during the conduct of war.

REFERENCES

Adorno, T. (1998). Education after Auschwitz. In H. W. Pickford (Trans.), *Critical models: Interventions and catchwords*. Columbia University Press.

Anderson, E. (2000). *Code of the street: Decency, violence, and the moral life of the inner city*. W. W. Norton & Company.

Ansari, S. N. (2018). Born to die: Female infanticide and feticide: An analysis of India. *International Journal of Social Science and Economic Research, 3*(4), 1154–1159.

Arendt, H. (1969). *On violence*. Harcourt Brace & Company.

Aronson, E. (1984). *The social animal* (4th ed.). W. H. Freeman.

Associated Press. (2021a, February 2). Alexei Navalny sentenced to prison term for violating probation as protesters detained. *CBC*. Retrieved from https://www.cbc.ca/news/world/russia-navalny-court-1.5897347

Associated Press. (2021b, May 22). Toddler finds gun in sofa, accidentally shoots young sister. *ABC News*. Retrieved from https://apnews.com/article/fl-state-wire-accidents-ce131ae5fe745785704aadd7cbf2f295

Bassiouni, M. C. (2011). Introduction: Crimes of state and other forms of collective group violence by nonstate actors. In D. L. Rothe & C. W. Mullins (Eds.), *State crime: Current perspectives*. Rutgers University Press.

Bauman, Z. (1989). *Modernity and the Holocaust*. Cornell University Press.

BBC News. (2020a, June 29). Germany investigates 30,000 suspects over paedophile network. *BBC*. Retrieved from https://www.bbc.com/news/world-europe-53224444

BBC News. (2020b, August 27). Christchurch mosque attack: Brenton Tarrant sentenced to life without parole. *BBC*. Retrieved from https://www.bbc.com/news/world-asia-53919624

BBC News. (2021, May 10). US warship seizes huge weapons shipment in Arabian Sea. *BBC*. Retrieved from https://www.bbc.co.uk/news/world-middle-east-57065894

Beaver, K. M. (2009). Aggression and crime. In J. M. Miller (Ed.), *21st century criminology: A reference handbook* (pp. 36–43). SAGE Publications.

Boggs, C., & Pollard, T. (2007). *The Hollywood war machine: U.S. militarism and popular culture*. Paradigm Publishers.

Brown, J. (2000). Other means: On the political economies of violence. *Third Text, 14*(51) 91–96. https://doi.org/10.1080/09528820008576857

Bufacchi, V. (2007). *Violence and social justice*. Palgrave Macmillan.

Burstyn, V. (1999). *The rites of men: Manhood, politics and the culture of sport*. University of Toronto Press.

Burt, C. H., & Simons, R. L. (2013). Self-control, thrill seeking, and crime: Motivation matters. *Criminal Justice and Behaviour, 40*(11), 1326–1348. https://doi.org/10.1177/0093854813485575

Butts, E. (2017, April 24). Robert Pickton case. In *The Canadian Encyclopedia*. Retrieved from https://www.thecanadianencyclopedia.ca/en/article/robert-pickton-case

Canadian Press. (2021, May 20). "We will do everything we can," B.C. police say to reassure public amid gang violence. *Times Colonist*. Retrieved from https://www.timescolonist.com/we-will-do-everything-we-can-b-c-police-say-to-reassure-public-amid-gang-violence-1.24317214

CBC News. (2016, January 27). Alleged pedophile ring busted by police in Quebec, Toronto. *CBC*. Retrieved from http://www.cbc.ca/news/canada/montreal/pedophile-ring-quebec-1.3421648

CBC Radio. (2021, April 30). They survived a mass shooting meant to silence them. But these Norwegian women are louder than ever. *CBC*. Retrieved from https://www.cbc.ca/radio/asithappens/as-it-happens-friday-edition-1.6009143/they-survived-a-mass-shooting-meant-to-silence-them-but-these-norwegian-women-are-louder-than-ever-1.6009150

Chaliand, G., & Blin, A. (Eds.). (2016). *The history of terrorism: From antiquity to ISIS*. University of California Press.

Chambliss, W. J. (1989). State-organized crime—the American society of criminology, 1988 presidential address. *Criminology, 27*(2), 183–208.

Colaguori, C. (2010). Symbolic violence and the violation of human rights: Continuing the sociological critique of domination. *International Journal of Criminology and Sociological Theory, 3*(2), 388–400.

Colaguori, C. (2012). *Agon culture: Competition, conflict and the problem of domination*. de Sitter Publications.

Colaguori, C., & Torres, C. (2012). Policing terrorism in the post 9/11 era: Critical challenges and concerns. In L. Tepperman & A. Kalyta (Eds.), *Reading sociology: Canadian perspectives* (2nd ed., pp. 291–294). Oxford University Press.

Collins, R. (2008). *Violence: A micro-sociological theory.* Princeton University Press.

Cukier, W., & Eagen, S. A. (2018). Gun violence. *Current Opinion in Psychology, 19,* 109–112.

Davis, N. J., & Stasz, C. (1990). *Social control of deviance: A critical perspective.* McGraw-Hill Publishing Company.

de la Luz, M. F. F. (2018, March 9). *Child sex tourism and exploitation are on the rise. Companies can help fight it.* World Economic Forum. Retrieved from https://www.weforum.org/agenda/2018/03/changing-corporate-culture-can-help-fight-child-sex-tourism-heres-how/

Deflem, M. (2009). Terrorism. In J. M. Miller (Ed.), *21st century criminology: A reference handbook* (pp. 533–540). SAGE Publications.

Dixon, R. (2015, October 29). Child slaves, gang rapes, forced cannibalism: The shocking truths of South Sudan. *The Sydney Morning Herald.* Retrieved from https://www.smh.com.au/world/child-slaves-gang-rapes-forced-cannibalism-the-shocking-truths-of-south-sudan-20151029-gklcag.html

Dollard, J., Miller, N. E., Doob, L. W., Mowrer, O. H., & Sears, R. R. (1939). *Frustration and aggression.* Yale University Press.

Encarnación, O. G. (2005). The follies of democratic imperialism. *World Policy Journal, 22*(1), 47–60. Retrieved from http://www.jstor.org/stable/40209949

Ferguson, C. J. (2009). Violent crime research: An introduction. In C. J. Ferguson (Ed.), *Violent crime: Clinical and social implications* (pp. 3–18). SAGE Publications.

Foucault, M. (1980). *The history of sexuality: Volume 1: An introduction.* Vintage.

Friedrichs, D. O. (2011). The crime of the last century—and of this century? In D. L. Rothe & C. W. Mullins (Eds.), *State crime: Current perspectives* (pp. 49–67). Rutgers University Press.

Galtung, J. (1969). Violence, peace, and peace research. *Journal of Peace Research, 6*(3), 167–191.

Gerstenfeld, P. B. (2010). Hate crimes. In C. J. Ferguson (Ed.), *Violent crime: Clinical and social implications* (pp. 257–275). SAGE Publications.

Gottfredson, M. R., & Hirschi, T. (1990). *A general theory of crime.* Stanford University Press.

Hasham, A. (2016, January 7). Everton Biddersingh found guilty in daughter Melonie's death. *Toronto Star.* Retrieved from https://www.thestar.com/news/crime/2016/01/07/everton-biddersingh-found-guilty-in-daughter-melonies-death.html

Holmes, R. L. (Ed.). (1990). *Nonviolence in theory and practice.* Wadsworth.

Jackman, M. R. (2002). Violence in social life. *Annual Review of Sociology, 28*, 387–415.

Joxe, A. (2002). *The empire of disorder.* MIT Press.

Katz, J. (1988). *Seductions of crime: Moral and sensual attractions in doing evil.* Basic Books.

Katz, J. (2006). *The macho paradox: Why some men hurt women and how all men can help.* Sourcebooks.

Keane, J. (1996). *Reflections on violence.* Verso.

Kleck, G. (2009). Guns and crime. In J. M. Miller (Ed.), *21st century criminology: A reference handbook* (pp. 85–92). SAGE Publications.

Kramer, R. C. (2009). Foreword. In D. L. Rothe (Ed.), *State criminality: The crime of all crimes* (pp. xi–xii). Lexington Books.

Leffert, M. (2007). *European Union blasts Central America femicides.* Latin America Data Base. Retrieved from https://digitalrepository.unm.edu/cgi/viewcontent.cgi?article=10553&context=noticen

Levi, M., & Maguire, M. (2002). Violent crime. In M. Maguire, R. Morgan, & R. Reiner (Eds.), *The Oxford handbook of criminology* (3rd ed., pp. 795–843). Oxford University Press.

Lindeman, T. (2019, December 4). "Hate is infectious": How the 1989 mass shooting of 14 women echoes today. *The Guardian.* Retrieved from https://www.theguardian.com/world/2019/dec/04/mass-shooting-1989-montreal-14-women-killed

Marc, A. (2016, October 1). *Conflict and violence in the 21st century: Current trends as observed in empirical research and statistics.* World Bank Group. Retrieved from https://www.un.org/pga/70/wp-content/uploads/sites/10/2016/01/Conflict-and-violence-in-the-21st-century-Current-trends-as-observed-in-empirical-research-and-statistics-Mr.-Alexandre-Marc-Chief-Specialist-Fragility-Conflict-and-Violence-World-Bank-Group.pdf

MEE Staff. (2021, March 23). Yemen war: Children made up quarter of civilian casualties in last two years. *Middle East Eye.* Retrieved from https://www.middleeasteye.net/news/yemen-war-children-quarter-dead-and-injured-civilians

Mercer, G. (2020, July 5). "I was scared to death of him": How red flags were raised over the Nova Scotia killer before April's massacre. *The Globe and Mail.* Retrieved from https://www.theglobeandmail.com/canada/article-i-was-scared-to-death-of-him-how-the-nova-scotia-gunman-raised-red/

Messerschmidt, J. W. (1993). *Masculinities and crime: Critique and reconceptualization of theory.* Rowman and Littlefield Publishers.

Michalowski, R., Chambliss, W. J., & Kramer, R. C. (2010). Introduction. In W. J. Chambliss, R. Michalowski, & R. C. Kramer (Eds.), *State crime in the global age* (pp. 1–11). Willan Publishing.

Miller, H. A., & Kim, B. (2009). Hate crime. In J. M. Miller (Ed.), *21st century criminology: A reference handbook* (pp. 490–498). SAGE Publications.

Miller, M. E. (2016, February 23). "Worst serial killer in history," who fed prostitutes to pigs, sparks rage by publishing book. *The Washington Post*. Retrieved from https://www.washingtonpost.com/news/morning-mix/wp/2016/02/23/worst-serial-killer-in-history-who-fed-prostitutes-to-pigs-sparks-rage-by-publishing-book/

Moffitt, T. E. (1993). Adolescence-limited and life-course persistent antisocial behavior: A developmental taxonomy. *Psychological Review, 100*(4), 674–701.

Mullins, C. W. (2011). The current status and role of the international criminal court. In D. L. Rothe & C. W. Mullins (Eds.), *State crime: Current perspectives* (pp. 275–292). Rutgers University Press.

Nisbett, R. E., & Cohen, D. (1996). *Culture of honor: The psychology of violence in the South*. Westview Press.

Oxford Analytica. (2017). *Gender crime ups Mexico and Central America migration*. Emerald Publishing. Retrieved from https://doi.org/10.1108/OXAN-DB220777

Pinker, S. (2002). *The blank slate: The modern denial of human nature*. Penguin Books.

Price, Jr., H. E. (1977). The strategy and tactics of revolutionary terrorism. *Comparative Studies in Society and History, 19*(1), 52–66. Retrieved from http://www.jstor.org/stable/177984.

PTI. (2020, June 30). India accounts for 45.8 million of world's missing females over last 50 years: UN report. *ThePrint*. Retrieved from https://theprint.in/india/india-accounts-for-45-8-million-of-worlds-missing-females-over-last-50-years-un-report/451545/

Public Safety Canada. (2021, July 26). *Taking action to reduce gun violence*. Government of Canada. Retrieved from https://www.canada.ca/en/public-safety-canada/campaigns/firearms.html?utm_campaign=not-applicable&utm_medium=vanity-url&utm_source=canada-ca_firearms

Ray, L. (2011). *Violence and society*. SAGE Publications.

Reiss, Jr., A. J., & Roth, J. A. (Eds.). (1993). *Understanding and preventing violence* (Vol. 1). National Academies Press.

Renzetti, C. M. (2004). Feminist theories of violent behaviour. In M. A. Zahn, H. H. Brownstein, & S. L. Jackson (Eds.), *Violence: From theory to research* (pp. 131–143). Anderson Publishing.

Ritchie, H., Hasell, J., Appel, C., & Roser, M. (2019, November). Terrorism. *Our World in Data*. Retrieved from https://ourworldindata.org/terrorism

Roberts, J. V. (1995). *Disproportionate harm: Hate crime in Canada*. Department of Justice, Canada. Retrieved from https://justice.gc.ca/eng/rp-pr/csj-sjc/crime/wd95_11-dt95_11/toc-tdm.html

Rodriguez, T. (2021, April 23). Expert roundtable: Intimate partner violence and COVID-19. *Psychiatry Advisor.* Retrieved from https://www.psychiatryadvisor.com/home/topics/violence-and-aggression/expert-roundtable-intimate-partner-violence-and-covid-19/

Ross, J. I. (2011). Reinventing controlling state crime and varieties of state crime and its control: What I would have done differently. In D. L. Rothe & C. W. Mullins (Eds.), *State crime: Current perspectives* (pp. 185–197). Rutgers University Press.

Rothe, D. L. (Ed.). (2009). *State criminality: The crime of all crimes.* Lexington Books.

Rothe, D. L., & Mullins, C. W. (Eds.). (2011). *State crime: Current perspectives.* Rutgers University Press.

Rummel, R. J. (1994). *Death by government.* Transaction Publishers.

Sheptycki, J. (2009). Guns, crime and social order: A Canadian perspective. *Criminology & Criminal Justice, 9*(3), 307–336.

Slim, H. (2008). *Killing civilians: Method, madness, and morality in war.* Columbia University Press.

Smith, D. M. (2017, November 3). *Counting the dead: Estimating the loss of life in the Indigenous Holocaust, 1492–present.* 2017 Native American Symposium, Durant, OK. Retrieved from https://www.se.edu/native-american/wp-content/uploads/sites/49/2019/09/A-NAS-2017-Proceedings-Smith.pdf

Somin, I. (2016, August 3). Remembering the biggest mass murder in the history of the world. *The Washington Post.* Retrieved from https://www.washingtonpost.com/news/volokh-conspiracy/wp/2016/08/03/giving-historys-greatest-mass-murderer-his-due/

Stahl, R. (2010). *Militainment Inc.: War, media, and popular culture.* Routledge.

Statistics Canada. (2021). Family violence in Canada: A statistical profile, 2019. *The Daily.* https://www150.statcan.gc.ca/n1/daily-quotidien/210302/dq210302d-eng.htm

Taylor, G. (2016). *The Chief Public Health Officer's Report on the State of Public Health in Canada 2016: A focus on family violence in Canada.* Public Health Agency of Canada. Retrieved from https://www.canada.ca/content/dam/canada/public-health/migration/publications/department-ministere/state-public-health-family-violence-2016-etat-sante-publique-violence-familiale/alt/pdf-eng.pdf

United Nations. (n.d.). *War crimes.* Retrieved from https://www.un.org/en/genocideprevention/war-crimes.shtml

Walby, S. (2004). *The cost of domestic violence.* Women and Equality Unit. Retrieved from https://eprints.lancs.ac.uk/id/eprint/55255/1/cost_of_dv_report_sept04.pdf

Wolff, R. P. (1999). On violence. In M. B. Steger & N. S. Lind (Eds.), *Violence and its alternatives: An interdisciplinary reader.* Palgrave Macmillan.

Wolfgang, M. E., & Ferracuti, F. (1982). *The subculture of violence: Towards an integrated in criminology.* SAGE Publications. (Original work published 1967)

Yang, J. (2017, February 27). Why hate crimes are so hard to prosecute. *Toronto Star*. Retrieved from https://www.thestar.com/news/gta/2017/02/27/why-hate-crimes-are-hard-to-prosecute.html

Yousafzai, G. (2021, January 3). Islamic State claims responsibility for attack on Pakistan's Shi'ite Hazara minority that kills 11. *Reuters*. Retrieved from https://www.reuters.com/article/pakistan-killings-minority-idUSKBN2980HH

Zweig, A. (Director). (2009). *A Hard Name* [Film]. Primitive Entertainment.

Legislation

Criminal Code of Canada, RSC, 1985, c. C-46.

Criminal Code of Canada, RSC, 1985, c. C-46, s. 266.

Criminal Code of Canada, RSC, 1985, c. C-46, s. 319.

CHAPTER 9

Corporate Crime and Wrongdoing and White-Collar Crime

Dan Antonowicz and Claudio Colaguori

LEARNING OBJECTIVES

In this chapter, you will

- understand how the crimes of powerful individuals and business corporations represent substantial harm to people and to the planet;
- learn the difference between corporate crime and white-collar crime and review various examples of each;
- develop an understanding of some of the main causes of corporate crime and wrongdoing;
- develop critical thinking skills that help you understand how criminal activities are woven into the fabric of elite society and the global economic system; and
- develop an understanding of the difficulties of prosecuting elite and corporate crimes.

INTRODUCTION

Despite the major harm caused, discussion of crimes committed by people with power and privilege were virtually absent from early criminology. The primary focus was on traditional theories of criminality, which developed predominantly on the basis of clinical explanations of those deemed to be "degenerate" members of the "dangerous classes," who were associated with conventional "street crimes" such as loitering, homicide, robbery, and assault. Thus, traditional criminology has long neglected to adequately consider and conceptualize crimes committed by economically privileged, high-status, *elite* individuals, whose wrongdoings eventually came to be known as **white-collar crime**, and by powerful corporate business enterprises in what is now referred to as **corporate crime**. Up to the present, public conceptions of crime have tended to focus on crimes committed by less powerful and often marginalized members of society. Such skewed, media-generated views of the reality of crime obscure the fact that crimes of the powerful represent a substantial level of harm to individuals and to planetary ecology. The scale and scope of the crimes and wrongdoings committed by the professional elites of society and by **business corporations** is extensive and ranges from wholesale financial **fraud** to species extinction. Thus, critical criminologists often remark how corporate crime and wrongdoing is responsible for substantially more death, destruction, and injustice on a global scale than all other types of crime combined (Clinard & Yeager, 2006).

Elite professionals and the corporate business enterprises that are directly involved in the economic organization of society possess a substantial amount of power and privilege, which make their crimes particularly complex, troubling, and difficult to control. Even though the amount of criminal harm perpetrated by powerful business corporations and elite members of society *vastly* exceeds the damage, victimization, and harms committed by so-called street criminals, mainstream criminology had, for a long time, ignored the *crimes of the powerful*. Early criticisms of criminology overlooking the crimes of the powerful from pioneers in the field, such as Edwin Sutherland and William Chambliss among others, has prompted many 21st-century criminologists to focus on the scale and scope of the crimes and wrongdoings perpetrated by powerful corporations and elites. The expanding scope of criminological inquiry includes new subfields of study such as crimes against consumers (Rosoff et al., 2020) and **green criminology**, which focuses on crimes against the ecological environment (Lynch et al., 2017).

In today's increasingly globalized world, it is virtually impossible to ignore the vast scale and scope of the criminal harms and wrongdoings perpetrated by elite individuals and business corporations. These acts often have such widespread, disastrous effects that they now form part of public awareness and civic activism. The crimes of the wealthy, of corporations, and crimes against the environment, once relegated to the margins, are also becoming more prominent in the news media and within criminology.

Corporate crime is defined as *organized* criminal activity engaged in by the executives of business corporations in the course of conducting business and may include forms of wrongdoing such as the violation of labour laws, polluting the ecological environment, and manipulating the norms of fair and responsible business practices. Clinard and Yeager (2006) outline and describe types of legal violations by corporations and their executives in various industries including oil, pharmaceutical, and financial accounting. Some of the more noteworthy examples of corporate crime and wrongdoing include:

- The release of pollutants and toxins into waterways, on land, or into the air. There have been notorious cases such as the pollution of approximately 1,000 kilometres of the Ok Tedi and Fly rivers in Papua New Guinea for 30 years, caused by uncontrolled leakage of billions of tons of effluent waste from mining operations into the waterways. Another disaster is the collapse of a tailings dam in Brumadinho, Brazil, in 2019 that killed 272 people (London Mining Network, 2020).

- The negligent practices of extractive industries that result in ecological catastrophe, such as the Deepwater Horizon oil spill of 2010 that spewed 5 million barrels of oil into the Gulf of Mexico and is considered to be the largest oil spill in history (Dodd, 2021).

- The banking and mortgage fraud that led to the 2008 global financial crisis, caused by willful negligence and misrepresentation by a number of major financial institutions, which resulted in extensive economic damage virtually worldwide and forced the governments of many nations to bail out numerous large companies (Pontell et al., 2014).

- The negligent operation of machinery that leads to loss of life, as in the Lac-Mégantic rail disaster of July 2013. Forty-seven people lost their lives in eastern Quebec when "an unattended runaway train carrying 7.7m litres of petroleum crude oil barrelled into Lac-Mégantic at 104 km/h and jumped the tracks near the centre of town. It slammed to a stop and erupted in flames. The ensuing inferno destroyed most of the lakeside town's downtown core. Twenty-seven children lost parents, over 2,000 people were evacuated, and dozens of homes were destroyed. Over 40 buildings were razed—including the public library—and millions of litres of oil seeped into the soil and the nearby Chaudiere river" (Murphy, 2018).

- The negligent decisions of auto manufacturers that fail to protect consumer safety, as evidenced in the example of General Motors failing to recall faulty ignition switches that shut off vehicles and caused drivers to lose control and crash to their deaths. "GM engineers knew about the faulty switch at least as far back as 2004 but failed to address it until 2006—possibly because it would have been too expensive to fix. And the defective vehicles themselves didn't get recalled until 2014" (Plumer, 2015).

- The negligent decisions of auto manufacturers that fail to protect the environment through deliberate attempts to bypass environmental regulations, as evidenced in the Volkswagen emissions scandal, known as *Dieselgate*, where the company installed "defeat devices" to enable "cheating on diesel-emissions tests" so that the toxic emissions of their diesel engines they touted as "clean diesel" could pollute substantially more than the legal limits of tailpipe emissions undetected (Atiyeh, 2019).

- Aircraft manufacturer Boeing's complicity in the loss of 346 lives due to "two fatal crashes of Boeing 737 Max aircraft [that] were partly due to the plane-maker's unwillingness to share technical details" of their new computerized flying system that led to pilot loss of control of the planes. A 250-page report on the tragedy cites company policies aimed at "Cost-cutting … that jeopardized the safety of the flying public," a "culture of concealment" over issues with the aircraft, and "troubling mismanagement misjudgments" (BBC News, 2020).

In the words of scholars …

Corporate lawbreaking covers a very wide range of misbehaviour, much of it serious: among these violations are accounting malpractices, including false statements of corporate assets and profits; occupational safety and health hazards; unfair labour practices; the manufacture and sale of hazardous products and misleading packaging of products; abuses of competition that restrain trade such as antitrust and agreements among corporations to allocate markets; false and misleading advertising; environmental violations of air and water pollution, and illegal dumping of hazardous materials; illegal domestic political contributions and bribery of foreign officials for corporate benefits.

Marshall B. Clinard and Peter C. Yeager, *Corporate Crime*. 2006

Although it is related to corporate crime, white-collar crime is a distinct type of criminal wrongdoing that often (but not always) involves strategies to acquire money. It is committed by high-status or seemingly well-to-do individuals, who are generally trusted by others because they occupy positions of privilege, social status, and influence. Some of the more noteworthy examples of white-collar crime reported in the news media include:

- The infamous 2008 case of fraudulent American investor Bernie Madoff, who, for years, took money from individuals with the promise of returning profits, but instead used the money to perpetuate an elaborate **Ponzi scheme** that amounted to billions of dollars in losses for his clients (Thomson Reuters, 2021).
- In 2019, the Hollywood "tuition scandal" made headlines because it revealed how some rich celebrities abused their economic power and social influence by paying large sums of money to guarantee that their children gained acceptance into their preferred American universities (Friedman, 2019).
- Another disturbing case in what is referred to as professional **malpractice**, which can be classified as white-collar crime, is wrongdoing by medical practitioners. For example, each year in Canada, hundreds of objects such as medical instruments and gauze are negligently left inside the bodies of surgical patients, creating serious medical debilitation and potential death (Canadian Press, 2019; Marchitelli, 2020). There is also the odd case of a British surgeon who violated basic medical ethics when he deliberately branded his initials onto the livers of his transplant patients (Domonoske, 2017)!
- Professional misconduct by lawyers is an ongoing problem in Canada. "An analysis of public records over six years shows law societies sanctioned 220 members for taking or mishandling money from clients or overcharging them, either negligently or intentionally.... More than 200 Canadian lawyers who were disciplined by their law societies between 2010 and 2015 misappropriated about $160 million of their clients' funds, a CBC News investigation has found. But most of those lawyers were never charged with crimes. CBC could find evidence of criminal prosecutions involving fewer than 10 per cent of the total number of disciplined lawyers in that time frame" (Pederson et al., 2017).

As public awareness of the economic disparities between the wealthy and the working classes grows, criminological researchers with an active interest in progressive social change are becoming more likely to emphasize the harms and wrongdoings committed by the powerful as opposed to researching traditional criminological categories such as murder and robbery. One would hope that with increased awareness of crimes of the powerful, there would be a corresponding effort to police such crimes. However, such a task is fraught with difficulty for numerous reasons, not the least of which is how business corporations occupy a paradoxical position in the modern global economic system. The corporate sector is relied upon by many as provider of jobs, and corporate economic growth establishes the general economic prosperity of a nation, while at the same time corporate wrongdoing and unfair practices are often a normal component in the pursuit of profit and shareholder value—all of which raise questions: Do we as citizens of a nation benefit financially by the ongoing commission of corporate crime? What sort of a *citizen* should the business corporation be?

Aside from the questions of power, privilege, and justice, the problem of corporate crime is further complicated by the historic inadequacy of the legal system to properly *define*, *prosecute*, and *punish* it. Corporate and white-collar crimes are generally more *elaborate* and *concealed* than typical street crimes, thus posing further challenges to policing and control (Yeager, 2016). In addition to addressing such issues, this chapter provides an overview of this important area of criminology by examining various types of corporate and white-collar crime, including economic crime, crimes against consumers, crimes against employees and workers, and crimes against the ecological environment through the use of examples.

Box 9.1: Edwin Sutherland and White-Collar Crime, and C. Wright Mills and The Power Elite

Academic criminology has long minimized the crimes of the powerful; however, there is one significant early exception from a pioneer in the field. In his 1939 address to the American Sociological Association, Edwin H. Sutherland sought to expose some commonly held misconceptions about crime and its causes. Sutherland suggested the types of crime based on data gathered from criminal justice statistics and explanatory theories that link crime with "poverty, feeble-mindedness, psychopathic deviations, slum neighbourhoods, and deteriorated families ... are misleading and incorrect [since they neglect] the criminal behaviour of business and professional men [sic]" (1940, p. 1). Sutherland's work indicated there is a *vast array* of criminal wrongdoing that goes underreported and undertheorized that is regularly committed by high-status, "white-collar" (i.e., well-dressed and seemingly respectable) individuals who are well placed within the echelons of business society and use their positions of economic privilege for personal gain.

Sutherland defined *white-collar crime* as "a crime committed by a person of respectability and high status in the course of his [sic] occupation" (1949, p. 9). Sutherland emphasized the relation between crime and economic power in a manner that varies in significant ways from how Marxist-oriented criminologists (see Chapter 3) approached the issue at that time. Sutherland aimed to reorient criminologists to the fact that possessing the professional privilege of upper-class social status *does not preclude* a person from committing serious crimes and can actually shield elites from legal scrutiny and prosecution. As Simon writes, "elite deviance, in all its forms, now constitutes a major problem for ... much of the world.... Notions of elite wrongdoing, white-collar crime, and related concepts are now the focus of intense debate in the social sciences" (2006, pp. 12–13). In 1956, C. Wright Mills also wrote about how those deemed *the power elite* occupied positions of political and economic influence that demanded greater critical scrutiny from social scientists.

Criminal behaviours that can be classified as *white-collar* include money laundering to hide proceeds gained from illicit sources or to evade income taxes; the theft of intellectual property such as patent infringement, reverse engineering, and copyright violations; financial accounting fraud; **bribery** of public officials and business associates for the purpose of securing lucrative business contracts; fraudulent investment schemes; and the many sorts of professional wrongdoings that violate the ethical codes of conduct that aim to govern practitioners within professions such as law, engineering, and medicine, among others.

In the words of scholars ...

The power elite is composed of men [sic] whose positions enable them to transcend the ordinary environments of ordinary men and women; they are in positions to make decisions having major consequences. Whether they do or do not make such decisions is less important than the fact they do occupy such pivotal positions: their failure to act, their failure to make decisions, is itself an act of greater consequence than the decisions they do make. For they are in command of the major hierarchies and organizations of modern society. They rule the big corporations. They run the machinery of the state and claim its prerogatives. They direct the military establishment. They occupy the strategic command posts of the social structure, in which are now centered the effective means of the power and the wealth and the celebrity which they enjoy.

C. Wright Mills, *The Power Elite.* 1956

THE GLOBALIZATION OF CORPORATE POWER AND INFLUENCE

Despite early criminology overlooking the fact, the commission of illegal acts, gross harms, and deliberate wrongdoings by corporate business enterprises and professional elites, it is by no means a new phenomenon. The modern global capitalist system itself was founded upon the unjust exploitation of millions of enslaved African people who were literally stolen from their homelands, many of them worked to death in the Americas—a criminal legacy whose effects remain with us up to the present. As Glasbeek writes, "In relatively recent history, wealth-seekers, supported by European nations such as England, France, Germany, Spain, Portugal, and the Netherlands, as well as, even more recently, the United States, have enslaved populations and bought and sold human beings as if they were baubles" (2002, p. 2). The exploitation of people by those with the power to do so in the course of doing business is but one example of how wealth and profit is generated in the modern global economy where human rights are superseded by corporate rights. Of central importance to this system of exploitation as a means of profit generation is the invention of the legal entity known as the *corporation*. Once an entity whose power was restricted by law in both the USA and Canada, the corporation has now become, as some have argued, the *most dominant* institution of the modern world order (Glasbeek, 2002; Korten, 2015; Rowland, 2005; Wood, 2013).

The business corporation is a coordinated administrative business enterprise whose aim is to generate wealth for those who own it or own shares in it. It has exceptional powers granted under law, especially the power to claim **limited liability**, meaning that, to a large extent, persons who own or work for a business corporation cannot generally be held personally responsible or *liable* for wrongdoings committed in the course of operating their business. This legal protection power has given many corporations special privileges that often make corporate executives unaccountable for certain criminal actions they may have undertaken. This point alone makes corporate crime a matter of serious concern, because limited liability protection hampers attempts at controlling acts of corporate crime through the criminal justice system.

Since the 1980s, the status of business corporations has undergone some historically significant developments that have substantially expanded corporate power, especially **globalization** and **corporate personhood**. The first development, *globalization*, refers to the *free trade* process. This involves the removal of trade barriers such as import and export taxes and tariffs to allow goods and services to move more freely beyond the national borders of a country and expand globally into previously restricted foreign markets. Corporate globalization has increased the size of many corporations, so they are better poised to dominate specific sectors of the economy. For example, Nestlé, the largest food company in the world, owns over 8,000 brands in more than 80 countries throughout the world, including baby food, pet food, bottled water, cereal, coffee, chocolate, ice cream, and more (Nestlé, n.d.). The global scope of such business organizations makes them **multinational corporations**, which is a business enterprise that has production facilities, administrative offices, and sales forces spread out across various nations to increase market share, to take advantage of cheaper foreign labour and production costs, and to benefit from tax incentives wherever such advantages are possible.

The second development, that of *corporate personhood*, relates to the status of a corporation to be deemed a *legal person* granted individual rights and freedoms, as if that corporation was a living person with legally granted entitlements (Totenberg, 2014). This aspect of corporate power allows corporations to make substantial rights claims when pursuing profits; when facing obstacles in doing so, it will vigorously protect those claims through legal court challenges and appeals. Virtually all large corporations have in-house legal departments and spend substantial amounts of money protecting and defending their business interests in the legal system. In Canada, a corporation that is called out for its misleading advertising claims, for example, may appeal to the courts under the *Charter of Rights and Freedoms* on the basis that the challenge violates their freedom of expression rights. In 2012, the Canadian telecommunications company Rogers faced a lawsuit from the Competition Bureau for allegedly engaging in false advertising in one of their marketing campaigns. According to the Competition Bureau, the company did not conduct adequate tests on its product or have sufficient evidence to make certain claims. Rogers claimed that this violated their freedom of expression rights under the Charter (da Silva, 2012).

Through globalization and free trade agreements, there has been a significant increase in the power and influence of multinational corporations in particular.

They have risen to become dominant players on the global political stage. The rise of corporate power has had many negative outcomes on the wages and rights of workers, environmental protections, and on issues such as food safety, among others. Placing profits over people and safety in order to remain globally competitive has become commonplace in business practice.

TYPES OF CORPORATE CRIME

The phrase *corporate crime* refers to a wide variety of wrongdoings, and they often overlap with other categories of illegal activity. For the sake of clarity of organization, this section will outline and describe four major types of corporate crime and wrongdoing: economic and financial crime, crimes against consumers, crimes against employees and workers, and crimes against the ecological environment.

Economic and Financial Crime

Economic or financial crimes are one of the major forms of corporate crime. They may include misrepresentations in financial statements, bribery, anti-competitive activities such as **price-fixing**, and monopolization of markets and stock market manipulation such as **pump and dump schemes**. An example of the latter is the infamous case of Bre-X gold mining company, where stock investors lost billions in the late 1990s (CBC Digital Archives, n.d.). Economic crime and wrongdoing accounts for enormous financial losses to private individuals while serving to protect the business interests of powerful corporations and economic elites.

Misrepresentation in the Financial Statements of Corporations

The misrepresentation of values on financial statements involves deliberate falsifications of monetary amounts on the accounting records of a company with the intent to deceive investors and shareholders. One of the most highly publicized examples of financial misrepresentation involved the publicly traded energy company Enron (McLean & Elkind, 2003). The company was betting on the future price of commodities such as natural gas and electricity. Ultimately, Enron's success was based on its exploitation of the existing accounting regulations. As a result of their apparent success, Enron became the seventh largest company in the United States in terms of sales. Enron executives also used illegal financial measures to make it appear as if profits were increasing when, in fact, the company had been hiding billions of dollars in debt via various accounting loopholes and inflating profits in financial statements. The company collapsed after revelations of systemic accounting fraud and then declared bankruptcy. At the time, it was the largest corporate bankruptcy in American history. Why didn't the auditors pick up on the accounting irregularities? Investigations revealed that the accounting firm Arthur Andersen helped facilitate the accounting coverup. This accounting firm was performing both auditing and consulting work for Enron. Others that facilitated this fraud included large banks on Wall Street and brokerage firms, members of Enron's board of directors, auditors, and lawyers. Unfortunately, Enron was not an isolated incident or anomaly. Other cases such as WorldCom, a telecommunications company whose less-sophisticated accounting fraud led to a larger restatement of earnings, followed. During this same period, numerous other corporations experienced accounting scandals as well. This included an American national drugstore chain named Rite Aid; Halliburton, one of the world's largest providers of products and services to the energy industry; and Adelphia, the fifth largest cable company in the US at the time. Europe also witnessed the Parmalat financial reporting scandal in 2003. Parmalat is a dairy company based in Italy. More recently, the company Wirecard in Germany was involved in an accounting scandal in 2020. This is a payments processor company that has been referred to as the "Enron of Germany" (Browne, 2020).

Price-Fixing

In a fair, competitive market, companies attract consumers by holding prices down while at the same time maintaining product quality. When competitors conspire to fix prices, however, consumers pay higher prices for these goods and services. Those individuals in a company whose salary/compensation are tied to the financial performance of the business have an incentive to engage in price-fixing in order to increase profits. These violations are widespread across industries. Over a 14-year period, a number of Canada's leading bread makers and bread sellers conspired to fix the price of bread (Russell, 2018). This included Loblaws, Sobeys, Walmart, and Metro. As part of their agreement, these companies agreed to not lower their prices in order to maximize profits for mutual gain. Furthermore, these companies would raise their prices at about the same time. The competition watchdog in Canada has also investigated price-fixing schemes in the country's chocolate industry and Quebec's gasoline industry.

One other notable case was the Archer Daniels Midland (ADM) lysine case (Walsh, 1996). Lysine is an amino acid used in animal feed. ADM and several other companies in the 1990s conspired to increase the price of lysine and were uncovered after an inquiry by the American Federal Bureau of Investigation (FBI).

The informant was a one-time ADM executive. The case was made into a Hollywood movie based on a book about the ADM scheme (Russell, 2018).

The Monopolization of Markets

Economic competition is touted as being the wellspring of market dynamics that benefits consumers, yet many corporations seek to eliminate free competition by attempting to secure a **monopoly** or **oligopoly** over a particular industry. In Canada, for example, a very small group of corporations have come to dominate key sectors of our economy such as technology platforms, telecommunications, and banks. With increased market concentration, and without essential competition, concerns have been raised by anti-monopoly experts (Dayen, 2020; Teachout, 2020). Through market dominance, corporations come to yield considerable power over the economy. The loss of competition means that consumers pay higher prices for lower-quality items. Over the last several decades, nearly every single industry has become more concentrated (Dayen, 2020; Teachout, 2020). With less competition, these corporate giants are able to take advantage of consumers, suppliers, stifle innovation, drive down workers' wages, and even influence the outcome of elections with their tremendous economic power and political clout. In Canada, Bell, Telus, and Rogers control 91 percent of the wireless telecom industry based on both revenue and subscribers (Hearn, 2020). This places them in a position whereby they can resist access into their industry from competitors. Hearn (2020) also points out that high degrees of concentration also exist in other industries like funeral services, beer and alcohol, pharmacies, eyeglasses, and grocers. The COVID-19 pandemic further worsened concentration, with many larger companies able to purchase financially distressed companies at much lower prices.

Banking and Mortgage Finance Crime

Wrongdoing in the financial sector is among the most economically damaging of all forms of corporate crime. Financial losses to individuals and their investments have been in the hundreds of billions of dollars and have disrupted job creation, home ownership, pensions, investments, and the quality of life of masses of populations on a global scale. In addition to the Great Depression of the 1930s, when many banks went bankrupt and unemployment and poverty levels were at an all-time high, one of the costliest of all financial failures is the crime known as the US Savings and Loan crisis of the 1980s and 1990s. As Calavita and colleagues write, "the estimated cost to taxpayers, not counting the interest payments on government bonds sold to finance the industry's bailout, is $150 to

$175 billion … economists and financial experts have attributed the disaster to faulty business decisions or business risks gone awry. We argue instead that deliberate insider fraud was at the very centre of the disaster" (1997, p. 1). Contrary to the widely held idea that financial market fluctuations are the result of a naturally occurring, wavering, and hidden economic logic, if there is a *hidden hand* orchestrating economic ups and downs, it is controlled by those who, in their positions of economic privilege, put personal economic gain above the economic well-being of the society as a whole.

The global financial crisis of 2008 has come to be known as the world's largest financial crisis since the Great Depression. Although it is referred to as a "crisis," which seems to imply that it happened by accident due to causes beyond human control, that is not the case. It was caused by reckless risk-taking by banking and lending institutions who, among other unethical activities, engaged in lending mortgage monies to homeowners with deceptive terms and conditions that would eventually lead to inability to pay by borrowers, and the subsequent collapse of a substantial part of the mortgage market along with other sectors of the global economy.

Morgan Stanley, an American multinational investment bank, was one of the organizations that misrepresented the risks of mortgage-backed securities leading up to the 2008 housing and financial crisis. Bankers in the US had developed a lucrative business of buying up the US mortgages of low-income Americans (known as "subprime"), packaging them together with better quality mortgages, and selling them on as essentially risk-free assets known as mortgage-backed securities. "Morgan Stanley knew that it was selling securities backed by residential mortgages with 'material defects'—such as loans that were 'underwater,' where the loan was larger than the value of the house.… [Eventually] Morgan Stanley reached a $3.2 billion settlement with state and federal authorities, the New York attorney general's office announced Thursday. In the deal, the investment bank acknowledges that it misrepresented the risks of mortgage-backed securities leading up to the 2008 housing and financial crisis" (Domonoske, 2016).

Box 9.2: Tax Evasion, Legal Malpractice, and Money Laundering

Wealthy and powerful individuals as well as criminals all over the globe will often shift their money to other countries to avoid paying taxes on their money or to conceal the purposes of transactions. In order to *evade taxes* or conceal the *proceeds of crime*, these individuals or businesses require the expertise of legal and financial organizations that promote or sell such tax arrangements and financial *tax haven* schemes (Fitzgibbon & Hallman, 2020). These "experts" deliberately misrepresent or make false statements involving tax shelters or arrangements to assist clients in exchange for obtaining a financial benefit. According to Bernstein (2017), this network conceals the identities of the individuals who benefit from these activities and is assisted by bankers, lawyers, and auditors. Clients have included wealthy individuals, corrupt politicians, and organized crime groups. Some are evading taxes while others are trying to conceal the money generated by criminal activities such as drug trafficking. The process of making large amounts of money generated by criminal activities appear legitimate is referred to as *money laundering* and is an illegal practice (Chen, 2021).

When the International Consortium of Investigative Journalists (ICIJ) released the Panama Papers in 2016, millions of leaked documents and hundreds of thousands of secret **tax shelter** companies revealed an illicit money laundering network that served to financially benefit the global elite (Bernstein, 2017). The Panama Papers leak focused on millions of financial and legal documents from the files of the Panamanian law firm Mossack Fonseca that set up secret tax shelter companies for the global elite in various tax haven locations such as the British Virgin Islands—an event that was satirized in the 2019 film *The Laundromat* (Fitzgibbon & Hallman, 2020).

The Panama Papers revealed how the rich and powerful hid billions of dollars in complex financial networks. The anonymous disclosure of files from Mossack Fonseca, one of the world's largest offshore law firms, further revealed how the wealthy exploit tax havens through various forms of legal manoeuvring and trickery. "The Panama Papers exposed the wealthy's— including 12 national leaders, 131 politicians, and others—exploitation of offshore tax havens" (Green, 2021).

In 2017, another trove of document leaks from the offshore law firm Appleby and other corporate services providers highlighted even more financial and tax shelter schemes. These document leaks, known as the Paradise Papers, consisted of 13.4 million documents and 1.4 terabytes of data documenting the deceptive offshore activities of national leaders, wealthy individuals, and numerous companies. The Paradise Papers leak shows how deeply the offshore financial system is entangled with the overlapping worlds of political players, private wealth, and corporate giants, including Apple, Nike, Uber, and other global companies that avoid taxes through increasingly imaginative bookkeeping manoeuvres (Green, 2021).

The Paradise Papers expand on the revelations from the leak of offshore documents that produced the 2016 Panama Papers. The new files shine a light on a different cast of underexplored island havens, including some with cleaner reputations and higher price tags, such as the Cayman Islands and Bermuda.

The Paradise Papers exposed a series of links that connected the offshore financial industry with organized crime and large-scale financial wrongdoing. Also exposed were public officials and high-powered executives who used this secretive financial system for personal gain. These leaked documents show how the offshore financial system is connected with the overlapping worlds of political players, private wealth, and corporations.

The promise of tax havens is secrecy—offshore locales create and oversee companies that often are difficult, or impossible, to trace back to their owners. While having an offshore entity is often technically legal, the built-in secrecy attracts money launderers, drug traffickers, kleptocrats, and others who want to conceal their finances. Offshore companies, often "shells" with no employees or office space, are also used in complex tax-avoidance structures that drain billions from national treasuries.

Addressing tax evasion and other financial crimes is important because the taxes owed help fund important programs and services such as healthcare, childcare, education, scientific research, and infrastructure projects (e.g., public transportation)—all of which are essential to the functioning of modern society. Canadian elites are also complicit in the practice of tax evasion. A 2020 *National Post* article states, "Canada Revenue Agency [is] claiming $4.4 billion from Canadian companies and individuals suspected of tax evasion" (Nardi, 2020).

Bribery

Bribery, the act of offering someone money or other incentive to compel them to return a favour, is considered by some to be an acceptable way of doing business. It is often associated with conducting business involving public officials in foreign countries, although bribery in some form or another takes place in virtually all contexts. The practice of bribery gives an unfair advantage to those who wish to compete for services and contracts in a fair and transparent manner and is often the major component in the corruption of corporate officials.

In Canada, the *Corruption of Foreign Officials Act* (Government of Canada, 2017) outlines in detail the legal prohibition against bribery by Canadian companies and their employees from bribing foreign officials to gain an advantage while doing business abroad. It helps to ensure that Canadian companies act in good faith and aims to create a level playing field for international business. Nevertheless, internationally recognized Canadian engineering and construction firm SNC Lavalin engaged in bribery in order to be awarded lucrative government contracts for construction and infrastructure projects overseas. The Montreal-based firm faced charges of fraud and corruption in connection with nearly $48 million in payments made to Libyan government officials between 2001 and 2011. If convicted, the company could have been blocked from competing for federal government contracts for a decade. Reports are that SNC Lavalin settled criminal charges in 2019 related to business dealings in Libya, with its construction division pleading guilty to a single count of fraud that helped tie off a long-standing scandal that tarnished its reputation and involved the highest office of the Canadian government (Reynolds, 2019).

CRIMES AND WRONGDOINGS AGAINST CONSUMERS

Many people are familiar with the open deceptions that were part of the early days of consumer society, where so-called snake oil salesmen would offer bogus cure-all concoctions often made from dangerous substances that had no medicinal value at all. With the passage of time, such products, for the most part, fell out of favour or were restricted from sale and replaced by more scientifically proven health remedies. Nowadays consumers expect that the products they purchase are safe, reasonably priced, and authentic. They trust the companies that manufacture and sell products largely because they assume that government regulators perform their duties in the enforcement of **consumer protection laws**. Yet consumers continue to suffer the consequences of crimes and wrongdoings perpetrated against them. On a regular basis, people encounter fake online product reviews; they consume tainted and adulterated foods; they overpay for staple goods because manufacturers have engaged in market manipulation and price-fixing; people are deceived by false and misleading advertising, marketing, and promotion; people are prescribed pharmaceutical drugs that pose serious health risks; people are sold so-called health foods that have questionable health value; people buy automobiles that are sold by their manufacturers despite known safety issues; people are sold counterfeit products, from fake designer handbags and shoes to toxic cosmetics—the list goes on. In this context, consumers are often the victims of various types of consumer crimes (Croall, 2009).

Each year, numerous individuals are injured or die as a result of unsafe products: "Everyday products are associated with at least 15.5 million injuries and 8,000 deaths per year" (Consumer Reports, n.d.). They may include injury, poisoning, or death from faulty airbags in automobiles, children's car seats, baby formula, laundry detergent pods, pharmaceutical products, household chemicals, leaded gasoline, breast implants, and tobacco, among other items. Although governments have become more active in regulating consumer products for safety reasons, unsafe products continue to cause injury and death. Not only do individuals become victims of consumer crime but the United Nations also reports that "unsafe consumer products cost the US economy [alone] $1 trillion each year" (UNCTAD, 2018).

One case of consumer product wrongdoing involved a company that manufactures children's car seats (Porat & Callahan, 2020). It is alleged that Evenflo Company, one of the largest sellers of booster seats, falsely marketed and advertised its car booster seat as "side-impact tested" and safe for children as small as 30 pounds. However, internal company documents revealed that the company's side-impact safety tests were not stringent whatsoever. Nevertheless, Evenflo continued to market its products as being safe.

As a result of the ongoing problem of crimes against consumers, the concept of consumer rights has arisen. A Canadian example of consumer rights can be found in the legislation regarding air passenger rights. In 2019, the Canadian Transportation Agency finalized *Air Passenger Protection Regulations*: "The regulations provide for clearer and more consistent air passenger rights by imposing certain minimum airline requirements in air travel—including standards of treatment and, in some situations, compensation for passengers. The regulations set out airlines' obligations to passengers in the following areas: delayed or cancelled flights [and] lost or damaged baggage [among others]" (Canadian Transportation Agency, 2019).

In some cases, there are significant legal and financial consequences for those organizations that perpetrate crimes against consumers. A few cases worth mentioning are as follows:

- As of a spring 2020 report, the Apple corporation "will pay up to 500 million US to settle [a] slow iPhone lawsuit … [the] proposed class-action suit accused Apple of quietly slowing down older iPhones as it launched new models" (Thomson Reuters, 2020).
- The BBC reported how "A French drug maker has been found guilty of aggravated deceit and involuntary manslaughter over a weight loss pill at the centre of a major health scandal. The drug Mediator was developed

for use in overweight diabetics and was on the market for 33 years. It was eventually withdrawn in 2009 over concerns it could cause serious heart problems. Hundreds of people are believed to have died as a result of the drug" (BBC News, 2021b).

- General Motors (GM) had to recall millions of cars because of a faulty ignition switch. The company had known about the problem for years but did not warn car owners and regulators. The *Detroit Free Press* reported, "the faulty ignition switches led to at least 124 fatalities and 274 injuries nationwide. The defect also resulted in the recall of more than nine million vehicles in 2014—one of the biggest recalls in the nation's history—from the largest U.S. automaker because the switches sometimes caused the sudden termination of electrical systems, including power steering and power brakes." "In 2015, GM agreed to pay a $900 million settlement to end a U.S. Department of Justice criminal probe, as well as $1 million in 2017 to the U.S. Securities and Exchange Commission for an accounting case. Later that year, the automaker settled with dozens of states for $120 million" (Associated Press, 2021).

- For many decades, the tobacco industry concealed evidence that cigarettes cause cancer (WHO, 2019). They employed deceptive tactics to keep generations of smokers addicted to cigarettes. Furthermore, they denied that smoking/nicotine was highly addictive. The industry hired "independent" scientists to support results from studies conducted by the tobacco industry and to question smoke-free policies. They marketed their products as being safe and posing little or no health risk to the public. Thousands of internal tobacco industry documents released through litigation and **whistleblowers** have revealed systemic corporate deceit. Many documents reveal the companies' focus on teenagers and younger children and the lengths they have gone to in order to influence smoking behaviour in these age groups.

Although changes have been made to consumer protection laws over the years, there is still a continued effort needed to protect the rights of consumers. As indicated earlier in this book, the ground between crime, wrongdoing, and willful manipulation is shifty. Some cases of wrongdoing against consumers are blurrier, such as the case of clothing retailers who operate designer outlet malls that sell inauthentic designer goods that are of lower quality than the real thing (Mancini, 2018). Food is another market segment where crime and deception is rampant. From "dishonest labeling, such as presenting a food as 'organic' when it is not, or something as 'free range' or 'farmed' ... [to] the use of horsemeat in beef products ... [to] food or drink containing things which it shouldn't ...," one estimate is that food crimes reach $50 billion per year (Sandle, 2016).

In Canada, consumer protection legislation does not necessarily form part of the *Criminal Code*; instead, the *Canada Consumer Product Safety Act* (CCPSA) regulates the safety of a wide variety of consumer products. Anti-competitive practices in the marketplace, such as price-fixing and misleading advertising, are regulated by the *Competition Act*. Other acts regulate the packaging, labelling, sale, importation, and advertising of prepackaged products, vehicle safety, food, meat, fish, and agricultural products (Government of Canada, 2020). Despite consumer protection laws, many fraudulent or adulterated consumer items continue to appear on the market, and the practice of individuals reselling products on internet marketplaces is also complicated by fraud and wrongdoing.

CRIMES AGAINST EMPLOYEES AND WORKERS

Another type of corporate crime involves crimes against employees and workers. This typically includes union-busting and occupational health and safety. Other noteworthy cases of harms and crimes against workers (that are covered in other areas of this book) involve enslavement and abuse of in-home workers and workers abroad, and violence, sexual harassment, and racial and gender discrimination in the workplace.

Union-Busting

From a worker's perspective, the ability to engage in collective bargaining with employers is very important in seeing wages, benefits, and working conditions improve. On the other hand, employers and corporations generally perceive unions and collective bargaining as an impediment to generating profits. As a result, some employers will engage in activities that are considered "union-busting." **Union-busting** is typically referred to as the process where employers attempt to prevent employees from forming or joining a labour union, or to do away with unions that already exist (McNicholas et al., 2019). Some corporations have gone to great lengths to interfere in employees' efforts to unionize. The Economic Policy Institute in the United States published a report showing that in more than 40 percent of union election campaigns, employers were charged with unfair labour practices (2019). This included companies firing, disciplining, or retaliating against workers who were attempting to form a union. In 2019, concerns were raised about alleged union-busting in oilsands company firings in

Alberta (Malbeuf, 2019). It is alleged that six workers at a Canadian Natural Resources Limited site south of Fort McMurray were fired for trying to organize a union through Unifor Canada. Unifor is Canada's largest private-sector union. In another example, a judge ruled that the Chief Executive Officer (CEO) of the electric car maker Tesla and other company executives were illegally sabotaging employee efforts to form a union (Fernández Campbell, 2019). The company was repeatedly questioning union organizers and later fired one of them. Amazon and Walmart are two other large corporations that have a history of union-busting or aggressive anti-union activities (Greenhouse, 2015; Kopytoff, 2014). A number of efforts have been made by employees in these two corporations to organize union activities but with limited success. These companies have gone so far as to produce training videos to discourage employees from union activities (Greenhouse, 2015). According to Greenhouse (2015), Walmart requires new employees to view a video intended to suppress employee organizing. A number of these large corporations hire anti-union consultants to assist them. In total, employers spend approximately $340 million annually on "union avoidance" consultants to help them combat efforts to organize labour (McNicholas et al., 2019).

Occupational Health and Safety Violations

Another type of crime against employees and workers involves unsafe working conditions and exposure to health hazards in the workplace. Throughout the history of industrial society, many corporations have aggressively pursued profits with a callous disregard for the health, safety, and the lives of their workers (Rosner & Markowitz, 2020). In some cases, the harm done to workers is immediate and clearly visible, but in most other cases the harm inflicted on workers takes a longer time to inflict damage or death. Two well-known examples of immediate harm are McWane Corporation in the US and Westray in Nova Scotia. McWane is a cast-iron pipe manufacturer with operations in the United States and Canada. This company has a reputation as being one of the most dangerous workplaces in America. Workers at their plants have been injured on many occasions, and there have been deaths as well. As a *Frontline* report indicates, some of the injuries have resulted from the company allowing its employees to work on conveyor belts that did not have a safety guard, and it "has amassed more workplace violations than all of its major competitors combined" (n.d.).

The example of the 1992 Westray coal mine disaster in Nova Scotia is historically significant, as it represents a clear example of putting corporate profits before worker safety. The owner of the mine, Curragh Incorporated of Toronto, failed to comply with numerous safety regulations, which led to a lethal explosion at this mine. A deadly combination of methane gas and coal dust ignited, sending a huge fireball through the tunnels of the mine (Bittle, 2012). As a result of the explosion, 26 miners working at the time were instantly killed. Unfortunately, various government departments in Nova Scotia tolerated poor safety practices. It was later revealed that there was little safety training at the mine, ventilation was poor, and the mine's methane detectors were often broken.

On the other end of the spectrum, a number of corporations have exposed workers to hazardous chemicals and products. In these cases, workers may develop respiratory diseases and/or cancer many years after their initial exposure. The long latency periods between occupational exposures and a cancer diagnosis can result in difficulty linking a cancer to work exposures. One well-known example is the exposure to asbestos. Many worksites across North America depended on products containing asbestos for decades. Mining, shipbuilding, manufacturing, and construction were some industries that were impacted. At particular risk of occupational asbestos exposure were workers who needed to remove, repair, or destroy asbestos materials (such as damaged insulation or pipe coverings). These actions could release asbestos particles into the air, causing construction workers to inhale them and become ill with mesothelioma cancer later on. Exposure to chemical toxins is often the cause of unsafe working conditions. Take note of the following examples.

- Workers in the General Electric (GE) plant in Peterborough, Ontario, which operated from 1891 to 2018, built everything from household appliances to diesel locomotive engines and had long-term exposure to more than 3,000 toxic chemicals, of which at least 40 were known or suspected to cause cancer, at levels hundreds of times higher than what is now considered safe (DeMatteo & DeMatteo, 2017).
- Workers suffered toxic chemical exposures while employed by Algoma Steel, which operates a plant on the Canada–U.S. border in Sault Ste. Marie, Ontario. The company produces steel for construction and military vehicles and other uses, with the majority of sales to US customers. The workers at this plant are being exposed to chemicals such as benzene and asbestos, which cause cancer, and hydrogen cyanide, a poisonous chemical used in death row executions (Beaumont, 2020). Many Algoma Steel workers have reported occupational illnesses and disease.

Although governments in modern, industrialized societies have legal provisions in place to protect the health and safety of workers, such provisions cannot guarantee unforeseen accidents, management neglect, and violations of safety protocols do not take place. In Canada, the Association of Workers' Compensation Boards of Canada (AWCBC) "produces an annual publication that contains statistical data on the number of accepted time-loss injuries and diseases, and the number of fatalities" that occur (Canadian Centre for Occupational Health & Safety [CCHOS], 2017). In developing countries, the challenge to curb the occurrence of workplace accidents and death remains an ongoing struggle due to difficulties faced creating and enforcing regulations to protect workers. In a global context, the International Labour Organization (ILO) estimates that "over one million work-related deaths occur annually … and hundreds of millions of workers suffer from workplace accidents and occupational exposure to hazardous substances worldwide" (ILO, 1999).

CRIMES AGAINST THE ECOLOGICAL ENVIRONMENT

Criminal justice has traditionally focused on crimes perpetrated by people against other people; however, that *anthropocentric* conception of justice is being challenged by a rights-based framework of thought and action that focuses on destructive acts against the ecology of nature itself. Most people are familiar with the concept of human rights but are less familiar with the concept of the *rights of nature*. Due to ongoing efforts of critical scholars and environmental activists, some significant developments involving environmental justice have transpired in various places around the world. For example, in 2021, the Magpie River in Quebec was granted legal rights as part of a global "personhood" movement in an effort to protect it from future threats, such as hydro development (Lowrie, 2021). Furthermore, "more than 100 constitutions across the world have adopted a human rights approach to a healthy environment, often serving as a powerful tool to protect the natural world" (Zimmer, 2021). If rivers and animals and the natural environment can be granted legal rights, this expands the sphere of justice to include environmental protection against the occurrence of what criminologists call *green crimes* (Beirne, 2007; Lynch 2020). *Green crime* refers to crimes, destruction, and wrongdoings against the natural environment, as well as the flora and fauna that inhabit it, including humans. Since the scope of green crimes is vast, has many subcategories, and cannot be fully explained in this brief subsection, our discussion shall be limited to a few examples.

Environmental or green crimes represent a persistent threat to the interconnected living systems that make up the planet and of which humans are a part. The rights of nature intersect with the *biocultural* rights of people and communities who live off the land and are directly affected by poisoned rivers, such as the Ok Tedi and Fly River disaster—where 50,000 people were impacted by the discharge of billions of gallons of chemical waste into the rivers—or mining and other resource extraction activities that threaten the lives of people living in the immediate areas of such activities (Toscano, 2019).

Green crimes are extensive and include animal poaching and trafficking in animal parts such as ivory, bear paws, and organs; shark finning; illegal hunting; illegal fishing and overfishing; illegal whaling; rainforest depletion and unlicensed clear cutting; the release or dumping of toxic chemicals and waste into waterways, into the air, and on land; oil spills and leaks; and nuclear radiation disasters such as Chernobyl and Fukushima Daiichi.

In the words of scholars ...

Although three decades old, green criminology is marginalized within criminology, treated as if it were a curiosity rather than a field of research focusing on a tremendously important set of global concerns. For example, there is significant scientific research suggesting that Earth has entered an era of global ecosystem collapse (Sato & Lindenmayer, 2018) caused by adverse human activities (i.e., excessive ecological consumption, pollution; York et al., 2003). Given such assessments, green crimes—like corporate and state crimes—can be shown to produce more harm and victimization than street crime.

Michael J. Lynch, "Green Criminology and Environmental Crime: Criminology That Matters in the Age of Global Ecological Collapse." 2020

Crimes against the environment, animals, and nature are a regular occurrence and can be illustrated through a brief sample of news headlines.

- "Galápagos Tortoises: 185 Babies Seized from Smugglers": "Customs officials in Ecuador discovered 185 baby tortoises packed inside a suitcase that was being sent from the Galápagos Islands to the mainland on Sunday. The reptiles had been wrapped in plastic and were found during a routine inspection at the main airport on the island of Baltra. Ten of them had died, officials said. One of the biggest threats to Galápagos tortoises is illegal trading for animal collectors and exotic pet markets" (BBC, 2021a).

- "Extinction: Elephants Driven to the Brink by Poaching": "The ivory trade, loss of vital habitat and a deeper understanding of elephant biology have all combined to reveal a previously underestimated threat to Africa's elephants. African forest elephants are now critically endangered, an update from the International Union for the Conservation of Nature (IUCN) reveals. Savanna elephants are also endangered. And 'declines over decades' have driven the species into the two highest categories of extinction threat" (Gill, 2021).

- "S$1.2 million worth of rhinoceros horns seized at Changi airport, largest seizure in Singapore ever" (Tan, 2022). The illegal wildlife trade is a particularly disturbing practice that not only targets "iconic species, such as the tiger, the elephant, and the rhinoceros" (van Uhm, 2016), it now includes wild animals taken as exotic food, such as the shark; numerous species found in the wild known as bushmeat, which includes chimpanzees, bonobos, and gorillas (Goodall, n.d.); and the pangolin—"the world's most trafficked wild mammal" (Environmental Investigation Agency, n.d.).

- "Judge Threatens to Stop Carnival Ships from Docking in U.S.": "Miami-based Carnival has been on probation for two years as part of a $40 million settlement for illegally dumping oil into the ocean from its Princess Cruises ships and lying about the scheme, according to court filings. Despite this, prosecutors say ships have dumped grey water into Alaska's Glacier Bay National Park, prepared ships in advance of court-ordered audits to avoid unfavourable findings, falsified records and dumped plastic garbage into the ocean. The company has acknowledged these incidents in court filings" (Associated Press, 2019).

- "Plastic Trash Flowing into the Seas Will Nearly Triple by 2040 without Drastic Action": "No one knows for certain how much plastic, which is virtually indestructible, has accumulated in the seas. The best guess, made in 2015, was about 150 million metric tons. Assuming things remain the same, the study estimates that accumulation will become 600 million metric tons by 2040" (Parker, 2020).

Green Crimes and the Chemical Industry

The modern age could rightly be called the chemical age. The introduction into society of pesticides, herbicides, household cleaners and solvents, and numerous other modern chemicals "has provided enormous material benefits, equally the costs have been enormous, even catastrophic" (Pearce & Tombs, 1999, p. 1).

Since the 1900s, humans have created a vast number of synthetic chemical compounds, and these are now persistent in the environment. The *bioaccumulation* of chemical compounds is found in virtually all living tissue, in soil, and in waterways around the world: "The European Chemicals agency estimates there are more than 144,000 man-made chemicals in existence. The US Department of Health estimates 2000 new chemicals are being released every year. The UN Environment Program warns most of these have never been screened for human health safety" (SciNews, 2017). From chemicals used in industry to everyday household chemicals found in body products, cleaners, and detergents; flame retardants in beds and sofas; and plastic bottled water, and soda—such vast bodily exposure to chemical toxins has created hormone disruptions, leading to birth defects and increasing rates of cancer and numerous other diseases. While known toxins such as arsenic, lead, and mercury have been substantially reduced in consumer products, such restrictions were a long time in the making as corporations vigorously resisted the cessation of their sale and use. A few examples serve to illustrate how chemical poisonings were a regular part of life for much of the 20th century and, in some cases, still continue.

- The use of tetraethyllead in vehicle fuel, known as leaded gasoline, has been associated with a disturbing history of public deception, the abuse of corporate legal power, and mass poisoning (Eschner, 2016). The health hazards of lead were covered up and denied by the petrochemical and automotive industries for decades. Lead was introduced into gasoline fuel in the 1920s to enable the use of pollution emissions–reducing catalytic converters in cars (Kitman, 2000). The US banned tetraethyllead in 1986, and Canada phased out leaded gasoline in 1990, although a controversial amendment allowed it to be used in race cars until 2010 (McIntosh, 2019).

  Some researchers also suggested that crime rates increased alongside leaded gasoline use and subsequently dropped sharply when lead was phased out (Reyes, 2007). This was based on the notion that children born without exposure to lead were less likely to have symptoms such as higher aggression and poor decision-making. This product was finally removed from the market not solely because of the health concerns but because it actually harmed automobiles and growing public awareness of lead poisoning created mounting pressure on governments to act.

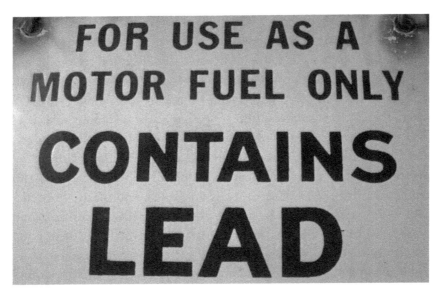

Image 9.1: Toxic Emissions in Petroleum Fuels

Source: iStock/jganser

- In 2012, a panel of experts working for the World Health Organization (WHO) concluded that exhaust fumes from diesel engines are a class-one carcinogen causing lung cancer and may also cause tumours in the bladder (Gallagher, 2012). Their findings were based on research in high-risk workers such as miners, railway workers, and truck drivers. Diesel is a type of fuel derived from crude oil. This fuel is used in most large engines, including those used in many trucks, buses, trains, construction and farm equipment, generators, ocean liners and ships, and in some cars (Kelland, 2012).

Box 9.3: Environmental Racism: Grassy Narrows First Nation and Toxic Mercury Poisoning

The concept of environmental racism refers to how racialized communities are disproportionately impacted by chemical and other toxic exposures that threaten their lives to a greater extent than other communities. Grassy Narrows, an Anishinaabe community in Northwestern Ontario, has lived with the consequences of one of the worst environmental disasters in Canadian history.

The pulp and paper mill operated by Dryden Chemicals Ltd. spilled untreated mercury into the nearby river system that connected to Grassy

Narrows. "For over half a century, the Grassy Narrows First Nation of Northwestern Ontario has been plagued by this odious chemical intruder in their water, fish, and bloodstreams, with appallingly flaccid government responses. From 1962 to 1970, a now defunct Dryden paper mill poured 10 tonnes of mercury into the Wabigoon-English River system. Though the contamination of the river and the Grassy Narrows community has been long-known and well-documented, the perduring poisoning, and apparently the leaching of mercury, continues" (Scharper, 2016). The area still maintains high levels of mercury in the river system and its fish.

There are other examples of environmental racism in Canada, mostly affecting Indigenous communities and African Nova Scotian communities. Environmental racism is a global phenomenon. From the ship-breaking industry in Bangladesh to the poisoning of the water supply in Flint, Michigan, environmental racism represents a disturbing example of how crime, discrimination, and environmental justice are intersecting issues (Taylor, 2014).

SOME GENERAL CAUSES OF CORPORATE CRIME AND WRONGDOING

Corporate business enterprises do not operate in a vacuum. Understanding the imperatives of how economic systems have historically operated gives us insight into the forces, which, up to today, continue to stimulate illegal activity on the part of corporations. In the course of "doing business in the marketplace," with the primary aim of generating monetary profits, business corporations operate under certain restrictive conditions and face obstacles that often interfere with that aim. The pressure of such obstacles can often compel directors, managers, and others within the corporation to commit wrongdoing. The restrictive arena of business has thus been described as a **criminogenic market structure**, where the imposition of specific pressures and policies by corporate officials "sets in motion a downward spiral of illegal activities" by employees and managers who are thus compelled to achieve corporate goals at high risk (Farberman, 1975, p. 1). Needleman and Needleman also propose a "crime-facilitative" system. A second model of criminogenesis, [where] members are not forced to break the law, but rather are presented with extremely tempting structural conditions—high incentives and opportunities coupled with low risks—that encourage and facilitate crime, both by system members and by outsiders who seek to enter or use the system for criminal purposes" (1979, p.1). A criminogenic market structure also includes general factors such as:

- *Complying with the pressures of competition in the open marketplace*: While competition is a major aspect of capitalist economies and is said to be good for the consumer, it is not necessarily good for businesses that wish for consumers to buy their products instead of what is being sold by competitors. Competition also compels some companies to sell their commodities for a cheaper price. This can compel businesses to collude with competitors to engage in price-fixing. Competition can also compel some companies to cut costs and reduce timelines in the manufacturing of their products, thereby making them more unsafe or of inferior quality. One example of this is the Boeing 737 Max airplane. Boeing's bestselling plane was grounded in 2019 after 2 air disasters that killed 346 people (Nader, 2019). The crashes were attributed to malfunctioning software that was designed to prevent the plane from stalling. Boeing should have developed a brand-new aircraft design, but the company was focused on getting the plane to the market as soon as possible in order to compete with its rival, Airbus. As a result, Boeing modified an older plane design and added larger engines, sensors, and problematic software that impacted the aerodynamics of the 737 Max. Companies also cut costs by laying off workers, using automation, outsourcing to low-paid foreign workers, and interfering with the right of workers to form labour unions. Over the years, many powerful companies such as Amazon and Walmart have aggressively fought attempts by their employees to unionize (Rosenberg, 2019).

- *Maintaining the business imperative towards expansion and market dominance*: The larger the corporation, the greater its market share and the more likely it is to dominate and control the market and thereby secure greater revenues. Corporate businesses, especially those that are shareholder driven, seek perpetual expansion and often do so by acquiring smaller companies or merging with their competition to achieve growth. However, the tendency towards market domination (that benefits the business) violates the principle of free-market open competition (that benefits consumers) to result in control of the market sector. In such cases, the interests of large corporations are in conflict with the interests of consumers who prefer greater choice. Furthermore, dominance of any one sector of the economy means corporations have greater power to act in their own interests and may be more likely to engage in unethical practices and wrongdoing. Recent examples include "Big Tech" companies such as Google, Amazon, Apple, and Facebook. In total, these companies have acquired more than 436 companies and startups in the past decade (Hearn, 2019). However, there are countless other industries that operate by the same strategy. The chemical industry has witnessed several mergers and acquisitions in the past few years. DuPont and Dow Chemical merged and then de-merged while Bayer acquired Monsanto. Dayen's study highlights a number of industries in the United States that are "monopolized" (Dayen, 2020). They range from the airline industry to the banking industry. In Canada, the telecom industry is dominated by a few corporations that combine to create an oligopoly.

- *Engaging in accumulation by dispossession and economic imperialism*: Corporations involved in the natural resources sector of the global economy often secure lucrative contracts with governments in generally underdeveloped, "business friendly" nations, where they may be able to avoid legal restrictions to business operations. In such contexts, legal obstacles (such as environmental regulations and labour laws) are less evident or poorly enforced, so that corporations can engage in the over-extraction of natural resources (e.g., in mining and harvesting), and economic elites can more easily amass wealth through their connections in law, banking, and finance. Such practices are less easily achieved in countries with a stricter and enforceable rule of law that operates on democratic principles of transparency.

A number of the practices mentioned earlier in this chapter, such as bribery and corruption, help to facilitate corporate involvement in what Harvey (2012) refers to as *accumulation by dispossession*, whereby the wealth of a nation becomes concentrated in the hands of elites through a complex process of dispossessing— meaning depriving people in a manner akin to legalized theft. Harvey (2012) identifies the processes of privatization, financial hegemony, and taking advantage of economic crises as the basis of **economic imperialism**, in which globalized corporations are often directly involved. In this context, corporations are complicit in creating disparities of wealth and poverty, as well as corporate crimes and human rights violations abroad. Gordon gives examples of how Canadian corporations and banks are complicit in coups, invasions, occupations of foreign countries, and eco-disasters, often on Indigenous lands, and argues that "Canada is an imperialist country—not a superpower, but a power that nevertheless benefits from and actively participates in the global system of domination in which the wealth and resources of the Third World are systematically plundered by capital of the global North" (2010, p. 9).

One example of the complexity of colluding interests that result in corporations profiting from human rights abuses is also found in the example of a former Canadian mining company called Nevsun Resources. This company is accused of human rights abuses in the African country of Eritrea. This included colluding with a repressive regime in order to mine precious metals with slave labour (AFP Ottawa, 2020). Nevsun's primary partner was Eritrea's repressive state government itself, which owns 40 percent of the operations and has earned more than $1 billion USD in taxes and revenues from the mine since 2011. The Vancouver-based mining firm isn't Canadian-owned any longer—it was purchased by the Chinese outfit Zijin Mining in 2018 for $1.9 billion.

Mine workers from Eritrea are suing Nevsun in the Canadian court system over allegations of forced labour, slavery, and torture. The Supreme Court of Canada ruled that a lawsuit by three former Eritrean workers against Nevsun for alleged violations of human rights overseas could go forward. This court ruling clears the way for cases to be brought in Canadian courts against Canadian companies accused of human rights abuses abroad. The case will have a large global effect, as Canada is home to almost half the world's publicly listed mining and exploration companies and Canadian mining companies operate in more than 100 countries (Poplak, 2020).

Box 9.4: Business-to-Business Crime and Wrongdoing

Business corporations regularly engage in wrongdoing against other businesses. This area of corporate crime ranges from financial losses from non-payment or unethical bankruptcy to theft of intellectual property and copyright infringement, to unscrupulous practices that defraud insurance companies and other creditors from unpaid monies owed. The following are examples.

- A January 2020 news report on Canadian-founded La Senza lingerie retailer reads, "Companies that supply garments for retailer La Senza are trying to push the company into bankruptcy because they say the lingerie chain isn't paying its bills. According to court documents, U.S. apparel manufacturer MGF Sourcing is seeking an involuntary petition against the owner of La Senza under Chapter 7 of the U.S. bankruptcy code.... MGF says La Senza now owes them almost $42 million for goods that have already been sent off to La Senza to sell" (Evans, 2020).

- The business interactions between insurance companies, auto body repair shops, and towing companies has long been rife with unethical business practices. A CBC report from March 2018 reads, "Workers at auto body shops deliberately damaged cars, installed used parts but billed for new ones, or invoiced for phantom repairs, according to an investigation by a Canadian insurer that is calling on the government to help in curbing the problem. Aviva Canada found about half the total expenses submitted for repairs to crashed vehicles during its investigation in Ontario were bogus—an amount the company estimates adds up to hundreds of millions of dollars a year" (Canadian Press, 2018).

- The theft of business secrets and intellectual property by competitors, especially foreign entities, is a major type of business crime that, in at least one infamous case, has led to the destruction of a major Canadian tech company: Nortel Networks Corporation. A July 2020 BNN headline reads, "Did a Chinese Hack Kill Canada's Greatest Tech Company?" (Pearson, 2020). The *National Post*, reporting on this case, claims, "For at least 10 years, it was revealed in 2012, the company was invaded by hackers based in China who stole hundreds of sensitive internal documents from under the noses of its top executives" (Blackwell, 2020).

These few examples of predatory business to businesses crimes give some indication of how such wrongdoings represent yet another type of challenge posed by corporate crime, as they entail the loss of economic prosperity that would otherwise benefit citizens and workers in the form of jobs and national productivity.

CONCLUSION: CONTROLLING CORPORATE CRIME

Perhaps no other type of injustice reveals hypocrisy more than the vast disparities of wealth and power inherent in the global capitalist system, where corporations and economic elites prosper despite a historical record of crime and wrongdoing and **impunity**. When harmful crimes committed by economic elites go unpunished, public faith in democratic capitalism and in the rule of law is severely diminished. The public sees elites getting away with robbery as a reflection of the privileges of elite class and power. Public outrage to elite crimes is evident in the reaction to the 2008 financial crisis, expressed in news headlines such as "How Wall Street's Bankers Stayed Out of Jail: The Probes into Bank Fraud Leading Up to the Financial Industry's Crash Have Been Quietly Closed. Is This Justice?" (Cohan, 2015) and "Fed Up: The Impunity of Central Banks" (Jackson, 2019).

A review of the literature on corporate crimes reveals that deterring and policing corporate crime is difficult, and, further, discourses about crime prevention generally do not include consideration of corporate crime (Alvesalo et al., 2006). For better or worse, the criminal justice system does not always get involved in the prosecution of corporate crimes. Instead, there are a number of regulatory bodies that are involved in the attempt to control corporate crime. These range from environmental protection to anti-competitive legislation, to name a few. Nevertheless, the enforcement and prosecution of corporate criminality in Canada continues to be a challenge despite the introduction of progressive legislation over time. Bittle writes, "In March 2004, the Canadian government introduced Bill C-45, *An Act to Amend the Criminal Code* (Criminal Liability of Organizations), thereby creating a legal duty for 'all persons directing work to take reasonable steps to ensure the safety of workers and the public' and attributing criminal liability to an 'organisation' if a senior officer knew or ought to have known about the offence. Commonly referred to as the 'Westray Bill,' the law's enactment followed the deaths of 26 workers in an explosion at the Westray mine in Pictou County, Nova Scotia, in 1992, a disaster caused by dangerous and illegal working conditions" and further that "the law has fallen into a state of virtual disuse" but "provides a potentially important foundation for ensuring workers' safety" (2013, p. 45).

Despite efforts to regulate corporate crime, it remains difficult to control and prosecute individual offenders. Not only is corporate crime difficult to control from a legal perspective but corporations also utilize a number of strategies to avoid prosecution for wrongdoing. Often times wrongdoers will agree to pay fines in conjunction with legal assertions that prevent them from admitting liability. In other cases, those with the power to do so will lobby politicians to change laws to weaken existing protections, as in the infamous American "hot coffee" case, where a woman was severely burned by a cup of scalding hot coffee from McDonald's. In that case, laws were changed so as to weaken consumer protections and protect corporations from lawsuits brought against them. The changes were justified by the claim that there is an abundance of frivolous lawsuits (Mayyasi, 2016). The manipulation of the law is also one of the primary strategies that some small companies and white-collar criminals use to avoid penalties for wrongdoing through the abuse of bankruptcy laws. The case of Canadian Earl Jones, who "swindled at least 50 investors out of at least \$30 million in a possible Ponzi scheme," is one example of how a fraudster can benefit from bankruptcy laws (CBC News, 2009).

Another remedy to address corporate and white-collar wrongdoing are **deferred prosecution agreements (DPAs)** that "were introduced under Canadian law in September 2018 as part of a broader effort by the federal government to enhance its toolkit in the fight against corruption and other white-collar crime. DPAs are voluntary agreements that are negotiated between an accused and the Crown to resolve corporate wrongdoing as an alternative to long and costly prosecutions. The effect of a DPA is that the outstanding investigation or prosecution is suspended, in exchange for certain undertakings that the corporation must fulfil in order to have the charges dropped. DPAs often require full co-operation with the relevant law enforcement authority and an admission of guilt, fines, and governance reform" (Ritchie & Pavic, 2020).

Do corporations have a responsibility to shareholders and directors, or do they have an obligation to the social community and nation where they are located? Pressure on corporations to become more socially responsible as citizens who must take into consideration other responsibilities besides shareholder profits has given rise to an ethics movement termed **corporate social responsibility (CSR)**. In the early 2000s, many of the largest publicly traded corporations realized that practising CSR was becoming more important than ever before (Bakan, 2020). They were concerned that governments might intervene to rein in corporations in response to the growing public distrust of large corporations (Reich, 2019). However, these corporations were not completely sincere in their commitment to CSR. Bakan (2020) writes that, ultimately, corporations are responsible to shareholders and maximizing profits. Reich (2019) alleges that CSR is thus a *sham* or a *con*. He asserted that the only way to make corporations socially responsible is through laws requiring them to give workers a larger say in corporate decision-making, raising corporate taxes, and breaking up monopolies.

Despite the extensive history of corporate wrongdoing, it is important to emphasize that not all corporate business activity is nefarious in nature. The profit-generating activities of corporate businesses add a substantial amount of monetary revenue to the national economy that governments use to build roads, schools, militaries, hospitals, and other essential services. Furthermore, many people rely on the corporate business sector for their income and for their pensions and other investments. Corporate innovations are an integral part of modern society and have contributed substantially to progress in medicine, engineering, communications, food production, and many other areas. The interdependent relationship between corporate business activities, economic exchange, and social prosperity is yet another factor that limits possibilities for quick and straightforward punishments for wrongdoings in the corporate sector.

REVIEW QUESTIONS

1. What are the differences between white-collar crime and corporate crime?
2. What types of corporate crimes do you think do the most significant harm, and why?
3. What roles do the power of law and social status play in the commission of corporate crime and attempts to control it?

GLOSSARY

bribery: The act of offering someone money or other incentives to compel them to return a favour.

business corporation: A company that is legally registered as an incorporated entity for the purposes of conducting business.

consumer protection laws: A set of laws (legislation) designed to protect the rights of consumers, consumer safety, and consumer transactions.

corporate crime: Criminal activities, including ethical wrongdoings and harm, committed by business corporations or by persons acting on behalf of a corporation.

corporate personhood: A type of legal status granted to a corporation to be deemed a *legal person* that entitles the corporation to individual rights and freedoms akin to a living person seeking their own self-interest.

corporate social responsibility (CSR): A type of ethical self-regulation engaged in by business corporations who endeavour to behave in a socially responsible manner as citizens by voluntarily seeking to limit the harms they may contribute to society, as well as contributing to humanitarian social causes unrelated to their core business activities.

criminogenic market structure: A set of behavioural arrangements within a particular business market that structurally compels employees and managers to engage in risk-taking and wrongdoing in their attempts to achieve corporate goals.

deferred prosecution agreements (DPAs): Voluntary agreements negotiated between a corporation accused of wrongdoing and prosecuting legal officials as an alternative to long and costly prosecutions, which may compel the corporation to fulfill certain obligations in order to have legal charges dropped.

economic imperialism: A type of foreign domination over a territory and its population through control of the economic system.

fraud: A form of wrongdoing with the aim of deceiving another for the purpose of material gain that is prohibited by criminal law.

globalization: The process of interconnecting economic markets on a global scale through the reduction of trade barriers, which also has effects at the levels of political integration and shared cultures.

green criminology: A branch of criminology that focuses on crimes against the ecological environment, including animals, plants, air, land, and waterways, and takes a rights-based approach.

impunity: To be exempted from consequential action or punishment after having perpetrated crime, harm, or wrongdoing.

limited liability: A type of legal status afforded to incorporated persons or companies that protects them by imposing limits on the requirement to pay damages in case of law breaking, bankruptcy, or other malfeasance.

malpractice: Negligent, unethical, or illegal actions engaged in by licensed professionals in the course of practising their profession.

monopoly: A type of market dominance that occurs when one business entity maintains exclusive control over the sale or supply of a particular commodity or service, thus dominating the market against the principle of free competition.

multinational corporation: A corporate business enterprise that has production facilities, administrative offices, and sales forces spread out across various nations and markets.

oligopoly: A type of market dominance that occurs when a relatively small number of companies control the sale or supply of a particular commodity or service, thus dominating the market and imposing limits on the principle of free competition.

Ponzi scheme: A type of economic fraud involving the use of investors' money to pay returns on the investments of previous investors, based on no authentic financial investments that generate a monetary return for any investors.

price-fixing: A type of conspiracy to maintain an agreed-upon sale price for a commodity among competitors in a given market, which results in higher consumer prices and violates the principle of free and open competition.

pump and dump scheme: A type of securities fraud where the value of a company's stock is artificially raised through false, misleading, and manipulative promotion, and where initial investors will sell off, or dump, their stock holdings once it is raised, knowing the inflated stock value is not based on actual market conditions.

tax shelter: A type of financial accounting designed to minimize or avoid the payment of taxes owed that often, but not exclusively, involves the violation or manipulation or tax laws.

union-busting: A process whereby employers attempt to prevent employees from forming or joining a labour union, or to do away with unions that already exists.

whistleblower: An insider who works for a company or organization who leaks or reveals information to the public about crime or wrongdoing taking place inside of or by that organization.

white-collar crime: A type of criminal wrongdoing that often (but not always) involves strategies to acquire money, committed by high-status or seemingly well-to-do individuals who are generally trusted by others because they occupy positions of privilege, social status, and influence.

REFERENCES

AFP Ottawa. (2020, February 28). Canada mining firm accused of slavery abroad can be sued at home, Supreme Court rules. *The Guardian*. Retrieved from https://www.theguardian.com/world/2020/feb/28/canada-nevsun-eritrea-lawsuit-human-rights-slavery

Alvesalo, A., Tombs, S., Virta, E., & Whyte, D. (2006). Re-imagining crime prevention: Controlling corporate crime? *Crime, Law and Social Change, 45*(1), 1–25. https://doi.org/10.1007/s10611-005-9004-2

Associated Press. (2019, April 11). Judge threatens to stop Carnival ships from docking in U.S. *CTV News*. Retrieved from https://www.ctvnews.ca/business/judge-threatens-to-stop-carnival-ships-from-docking-in-u-s-1.4375257

Associated Press. (2021, February 12). General Motors settles with California for $5.75M over ignition switches. *Detroit Free Press*. Retrieved from https://www.freep.com/story/money/cars/general-motors/2021/02/12/gm-ignition-switches-settlement-california/4469385001/

Atiyeh, C. (2019, December 4). Everything you need to know about the VW diesel-emissions scandal. *Car and Driver*. Retrieved from https://www.caranddriver.com/news/a15339250/everything-you-need-to-know-about-the-vw-diesel-emissions-scandal/

Bakan, J. (2020). *The new corporation: How "good" corporations are bad for democracy*. Allen Lane.

BBC News. (2020, September 16). Boeing's "culture of concealment" to blame for 737 crashes. *BBC*. Retrieved from https://www.bbc.com/news/business-54174223

BBC News. (2021a, March 29). Galápagos tortoises: 185 babies seized from smugglers. *BBC*. Retrieved from https://www.bbc.com/news/world-latin-america-56564326

BBC News. (2021b, March 29). Mediator drug: French pharmaceutical firm fined over weight loss pill. *BBC*. Retrieved from https://www.bbc.co.uk/news/world-europe-56562909

Beaumont, H. (2020, September 17). Algoma Steel workers allege company had "full knowledge" of exposure to lethal, cancer-causing chemicals. *Environmental Health News*. Retrieved from https://www.ehn.org/algoma-steel-worker-health-2647660541.html

Beirne, P. (2007). Animal rights, animal abuse and green criminology. In P. Beirne & N. South (Eds.), *Issues in green criminology: Confronting harms against environments, humanity and other animals* (pp. 55–86). Willan Publishing.

Bernstein, J. (2017). *Secrecy world: Inside the Panama Papers investigation of illicit money networks and the global elite*. Henry Holt and Company.

Bittle, S. (2012). *Still dying for a living: Corporate criminal liability after the Westray Mine disaster*. UBC Press.

Bittle, S. (2013). Cracking down on corporate crime? The disappearance of corporate criminal liability legislation in Canada. *Policy and Practice in Health and Safety, 11*(2), 45–62. https://doi.org/10.1080/14774003.2013.11667789

Blackwell, T. (2020, February 24). Exclusive: Did Huawei bring down Nortel? Corporate espionage, theft, and the parallel rise and fall of two telecom giants. *National Post*. Retrieved from https://nationalpost.com/news/exclusive-did-huawei-bring-down-nortel-corporate-espionage-theft-and-the-parallel-rise-and-fall-of-two-telecom-giants

Browne, R. (2020, June 29). "The Enron of Germany:" Wirecard scandal casts a shadow on corporate governance. *CNBC*. Retrieved from https://www.cnbc.com/2020/06/29/enron-of-germany-wirecard-scandal-casts-a-shadow-on-governance.html

Calavita, K., Pontell, H. N., & Tillman, R. H. (1997). *Big money crime: Fraud and politics in the savings and loan crisis*. University of California Press.

Canadian Centre for Occupational Health & Safety (CCHOS). (2017, May 4). *Work injury statistics*. Government of Canada. Retrieved from https://www.ccohs.ca/oshanswers/information/injury_statistics.html

Canadian Press. (2018, March 11). Insurance company uncovers "pervasive" auto body shop scams in Ontario, urges action. *CBC*. Retrieved from https://www.cbc.ca/news/canada/toronto/insurance-company-uncovers-pervasive-auto-body-shop-scams-in-ontario-urges-action-1.4571582

Canadian Press. (2019, November 7). Surgical objects being left inside more patients in Canada. *CBC*. Retrieved from https://www.cbc.ca/news/health/surgical-objects-1.5351173

Canadian Transportation Agency. (2019, July 8). *Air passenger protection regulations highlights*. Retrieved from https://otc-cta.gc.ca/eng/air-passenger-protection-regulations-highlights

CBC Digital Archives. (n.d.). Stranger than fiction: The Bre-X gold scandal. *CBC*.

CBC News. (2009, July 29). Earl Jones's company declared bankrupt. *CBC*. Retrieved from https://www.cbc.ca/news/canada/montreal/earl-jones-s-company-declared-bankrupt-1.806531

Chen, J. (2021, March 16). *Money laundering*. Investopedia. Retrieved from https://www.investopedia.com/terms/m/moneylaundering.asp

Clinard, M. B., & Yeager, P. C. (2006). *Corporate crime*. Transaction Publishers.

Cohan, W. D. (2015, September). How Wall Street's bankers stayed out of jail. *The Atlantic*. Retrieved from https://www.theatlantic.com/magazine/archive/2015/09/how-wall-streets-bankers-stayed-out-of-jail/399368/

Consumer Reports. (n.d.). *Safe products for our everyday lives*. Retrieved from https://advocacy.consumerreports.org/issue/product-safety/

Croall, H. (2009). White collar crime, consumers and victimization. *Crime, Law and Social Change, 51*(1), 127–146.

da Silva, M. (2012, August 7). Rogers Communications challenges false advertising lawsuit with freedom of expression. *Georgia Straight*. Retrieved from https://www.straight.com/news/rogers-communications-challenges-false-advertising-lawsuit-freedom-expression

Dayen, D. (2020). *Monopolized: Life in the age of corporate power*. The New Press.

DeMatteo, R., & DeMatteo, D. (2017). *The report of the Advisory Committee on Retrospective Exposure Profiling of the production processes at the General Electric Production Facility in Peterborough, Ontario 1945–2000*. Unifor National Health and Safety Department.

Dodd, C. (2021, May 29). Oil spill disasters. *WorldAtlas*. Retrieved from https://www.worldatlas.com/articles/oil-spill-disasters.html

Domonoske, C. (2016, February 11). Morgan Stanley will pay $3.2 billion for contributing to mortgage crisis. *npr*. Retrieved from https://www.npr.org/sections/thetwo-way/2016/02/11/466399992/morgan-stanley-will-pay-3-2-billion-for-contributing-to-mortgage-crisis

Domonoske, C. (2017, December 13). We regret to inform you that a British surgeon was branding his initials on livers. *npr*. Retrieved from https://www.npr.org/sections/thetwo-way/2017/12/13/570624311/we-regret-to-inform-you-that-a-british-surgeon-was-branding-his-initials-on-live

Environmental Investigation Agency. (n.d.). *Saving pangolins from extinction.* Retrieved from https://eia-international.org/wildlife/helping-pangolins/saving-pangolins-from-extinction/

Eschner, K. (2016, December 9). Leaded gas was a known poison the day it was invented. *Smithsonian Magazine.* Retrieved from https://www.smithsonianmag.com/smart-news/leaded-gas-poison-invented-180961368/

Evans, P. (2020, January 30). Suppliers seeking to push Canadian lingerie chain La Senza into bankruptcy for unpaid bills. *CBC.* Retrieved from https://www.cbc.ca/news/business/la-senza-bankruptcy-1.5445693

Farberman, H. A. (1975). A criminogenic market structure: The automobile industry. *The Sociological Quarterly, 16*(4): 438–457.

Fernández Campbell, A. (2019, September 30). Elon Musk broke US labor laws on Twitter. *Vox.* Retrieved from https://www.vox.com/identities/2019/9/30/20891314/elon-musk-tesla-labor-violation-nlrb

Fitzgibbon, W., & Hallman, B. (2020, April 6). What is a tax haven? Offshore finance, explained. *International Consortium of Investigative Journalists.* Retrieved from https://www.icij.org/investigations/panama-papers/what-is-a-tax-haven-offshore-finance-explained/

Friedman, Z. (2019, March 12). Hollywood celebrities charged in major college admissions scandal. *Forbes.* Retrieved from https://www.forbes.com/sites/zackfriedman/2019/03/12/hollywood-celebrities-charged-in-major-college-admissions-scandal/?sh=29134a301dc5

Frontline. (n.d.). The McWane story. *PBS.* https://www.pbs.org/wgbh/pages/frontline/shows/workplace/mcwane/

Gallagher, J. (2012, June 12). Diesel exhausts do cause cancer, says WHO. *BBC.* Retrieved from https://www.bbc.com/news/health-18415532

Gill, V. (2021, March 25). Extinction: Elephants driven to the brink by poaching. *BBC.* Retrieved from https://www.bbc.com/news/science-environment-56510593

Glasbeek, H. (2002). *Wealth by stealth: Corporate crime, corporate law, and the perversion of democracy.* Between the Lines.

Goodall, J. (n.d.). *The illegal commercial bushmeat trade in Central and West Africa.* United Nations. Retrieved from https://www.un.org/en/chronicle/article/illegal-commercial-bushmeat-trade-central-and-west-africa

Gordon, T. (2010). *Imperialist Canada.* Arbeiter Ring Publishing.

Government of Canada. (2017, October 31). *Corruption of Foreign Public Officials Act.* Retrieved from https://laws-lois.justice.gc.ca/eng/acts/c-45.2/page-1.html

Government of Canada. (2020, May 12). Federal consumer protection legislation in Canada. Retrieved from http://www.ic.gc.ca/eic/site/oca-bc.nsf/eng/ca03084.html

Green, L. (2021, January 1). *Paradise Papers*. Investopedia. https://www.investopedia
.com/terms/p/paradise-papers.asp

Greenhouse, S. (2015, June 8). How Walmart persuades its workers not to unionize. *The
Atlantic*. Retrieved from https://www.theatlantic.com/business/archive/2015/06/
how-walmart-convinces-its-employees-not-to-unionize/395051/

Harvey, D. (2012). The "new" imperialism: Accumulation by dispossession. In
B. Ollman & K. B. Anderson (Eds.), *Karl Marx*. Routledge.

Hearn, D. (2019, February 25). Canadian, U.S. regulators asleep at the switch as monopolies
thrive. *The Globe and Mail*. Retrieved from https://www.theglobeandmail.com/business/
commentary/article-canadian-us-regulators-asleep-at-the-switch-as-monopolies-thrive/

Hearn, D. (2020, August 3). Canadian lawmakers have a choice: Defend corporate
interests or competitive markets. *The Hill Times*. Retrieved from https://www
.hilltimes.com/2020/08/03/hearn/258692

International Labour Organization (ILO). (1999, April 12). ILO estimates over
1 million work-related fatalities each year. Retrieved from https://www.ilo.org/
global/about-the-ilo/newsroom/news/WCMS_007969/lang--en/index.htm

Jackson, T. (2019). Fed up: The impunity of central banks. *Dissent Magazine*. Retrieved
from https://www.dissentmagazine.org/article/fed-up-the-impunity-of-central-banks

Kelland, K. (2012, June 12). Diesel exhaust fumes can cause cancer, WHO says.
Reuters.

Kitman, J. L. (2000, March 2). The secret history of lead. *The Nation*. Retrieved from
https://www.thenation.com/article/archive/secret-history-lead/

Kopytoff, V. (2014, January 16). How Amazon crushed the union movement. *Time*.
Retrieved from https://time.com/956/how-amazon-crushed-the-union-movement/

Korten, D. C. (2015). *When corporations rule the world*. Berrett-Koehler Publishers.

London Mining Network. (2020, February 19). *New report names top British companies
responsible for toxic mining legacies*. Retrieved from https://londonminingnetwork
.org/2020/02/press-release-new-report-names-top-british-companies-responsible-
for-toxic-mining-legacies/

Lowrie, M. (2021, February 28). Quebec river granted legal rights as part of global
"personhood" movement. *CBC*. Retrieved from https://www.cbc.ca/news/canada/
montreal/magpie-river-quebec-canada-personhood-1.5931067

Lynch, M. J. (2020). Green criminology and environmental crime: Criminology that
matters in the age of global ecological collapse. *Journal of White Collar and Corporate
Crime, 1*(1), 50–61.

Lynch, M. J., Long, M. A., Stretesky, P. B., & Barrett, K. L. (2017). *Green criminology:
Crime, justice, and the environment*. University of California Press.

Malbeuf, J. (2019, November 1). Unifor looks into alleged union-busting in oilsands company firings. *CBC*. Retrieved from https://www.cbc.ca/news/canada/edmonton/union-busting-cnrl-1.5342808

Mancini, M. (2018, January 7). Mythbusting: Outlet stores might not be as good a deal as you think. *CBC*. Retrieved from https://www.cbc.ca/news/business/outlet-stores-quality-1.3392279

Marchitelli, R. (2020, October 2). Ontario woman finds needle in her spine 16 years after giving birth. *CBC*. Retrieved from https://www.cbc.ca/news/health/needle-spine-patient-hospital-1.5743567

Mayyasi, A. (2016, November 18). How a lawsuit over hot coffee helped erode the 7th amendment. *CBC*. Retrieved from https://priceonomics.com/how-a-lawsuit-over-hot-coffee-helped-erode-the-7th/

McIntosh, J. (2019, June 14). The unexpected reason we stopped using leaded gasoline. *AutoTrader*. Retrieved from https://www.autotrader.ca/newsfeatures/20190614/the-unexpected-reason-we-stopped-using-leaded-gasoline/

McLean, B., & Elkind, P. (2003). *The smartest guys in the room: The amazing rise and scandalous fall of Enron*. Penguin Books.

McNicholas, C., Poydock, M., Wolfe, J., Zipperer, B., Lafer, G., & Loustaunau, L. (2019, December 11). Unlawful: U.S. employers are charged with violating federal law in 41.5% of all union election campaigns. *Economic Policy Institute*. Retrieved from www.epi.org/publication/unlawful-employer-opposition-to-union-election-campaigns/

Mills, C. W. (1956). *The power elite*. Oxford University Press.

Murphy, J. (2018, January 19). Lac-Megantic: The runaway train that destroyed a town. *BBC*. Retrieved from https://www.bbc.com/news/world-us-canada-42548824

Nader, R. (2019). *Greedy Boeing's avoidable design and software time bombs* [Blog]. Ralph Nader. Retrieved from https://nader.org/2019/03/21/greedy-boeings-avoidable-design-and-software-time-bombs/

Nardi, C. (2020, May 11). CRA claiming $4.4B from Canadian companies and individuals suspected of tax evasion. *National Post*. Retrieved from https://nationalpost.com/news/politics/cra-claiming-4-4-billion-from-canadian-companies-and-individuals-suspected-of-offshore-tax-evasion

Needleman, M. L., & Needleman, C. (1979). Organizational crime: Two models of criminogenesis. *The Sociological Quarterly, 20*(4), 517–528. https://doi.org/10.1111/j.1533-8525.1979.tb01232.x

Nestlé. (n.d.). About us. Retrieved from https://www.nestle.com/aboutus

Parker, L. (2020, July 23). Plastic trash flowing into the seas will nearly triple by 2040 without drastic action. *National Geographic*. Retrieved from https://www.nationalgeographic.com/science/article/plastic-trash-in-seas-will-nearly-triple-by-2040-if-nothing-done

Pearce, F., & Tombs, S. (1999). *Toxic capitalism: Corporate crime and the chemical industry*. Canadian Scholars.

Pearson, N. O. (2020, July 1). Did a Chinese hack kill Canada's greatest tech company? *BNN Bloomberg*. Retrieved from https://www.bnnbloomberg.ca/did-a-chinese-hack-kill-canada-s-greatest-tech-company-1.1459269

Pedersen, K., Nicholson, K., & Marcoux, J. (2017, February 16). Lawyers misappropriated millions from clients' funds but few faced criminal charges. *CBC*. Retrieved from https://www.cbc.ca/news/canada/lawyers-misappropriated-millions-1.3981266

Plummer, B. (2015, May 11). The GM recall scandal of 2014. *Vox*. Retrieved from https://www.vox.com/2014/10/3/18073458/gm-car-recall

Pontell, H. N., Black, W. K., & Geis, G. (2014). Too big to fail, too powerful to jail? On the absence of criminal prosecutions after the 2008 financial meltdown. *Crime Law and Social Change, 61*, 1–13. https://doi.org/10.1007/s10611-013-9476-4

Poplak, R. (2020, March 6). Canadian mining companies better start behaving, thanks to Nevsun. *The Globe and Mail*. Retrieved from https://www.theglobeandmail.com/opinion/article-canadian-mining-companies-better-start-behaving-thanks-to-nevsun/

Porat, D., & Callahan, P. (2020, February 6). Evenflo, maker of the "big kid" booster seat, put profits over child safety. *ProPublica*. Retrieved from https://www.propublica.org/article/evenflo-maker-of-the-big-kid-booster-seat-put-profits-over-child-safety

Reich, R. (2019, December 29). The biggest business con of 2019: Fleecing workers while bosses get rich. *The Guardian*. Retrieved from https://www.theguardian.com/commentisfree/2019/dec/29/boeing-amazon-business-ethics-robert-reich

Reyes, J. W. (2007). Environmental policy as social policy? The impact of childhood lead exposure on crime. *The B.E. Journal of Economic Analysis & Policy, 7*(1), Article 51.

Reynolds, C. (2019, December 18). SNC-Lavalin settles Libya charges, pleads guilty to single count of fraud. *Toronto Star*. Retrieved from https://www.thestar.com/business/2019/12/18/snc-lavalin-back-in-court-in-shadow-of-former-executives-conviction.html

Ritchie, L. E., & Pavic, S. (2020, December 11). *Canada's deferred prosecution agreements: Still waiting for takeoff*. Osler. Retrieved from https://www.osler.com/en/resources/regulations/2020/canada-s-deferred-prosecution-agreements-still-waiting-for-takeoff

Rosenberg, J. (2019, December 11). How much are your favorite companies spending on union-busting consultants? *Mother Jones*. Retrieved from https://www.motherjones.com/politics/2019/12/how-much-are-your-favorite-companies-spending-on-union-busting-consultants/

Rosner D., & Markowitz, G. (2020). A short history of occupational safety and health in the United States. *American Journal of Public Health, 110*(5), 622–628. https://doi.org/10.2105/AJPH.2020.305581

Rosoff, S., Pontell, H., & Tillman, R. (2020). *Profit without honor: White collar crime and the looting of America* (7th ed.). Pearson Education.

Rowland, W. (2005). *Greed, Inc: Why corporations rule our world and how we let it happen*. Thomas Allen Publishers.

Russell, A. (2018, January 31). 7 Canadian companies committed indictable offences in bread-price fixing scandal: Competition bureau. *Global News*. Retrieved from https://globalnews.ca/news/3998023/bread-price-fixing-scandal-competition-act-crimes/

Sandle, T. (2016, July). Food crime reaches $50 billion per year. *Digital Journal*. Retrieved from http://www.digitaljournal.com/news/crime/food-crime-reaches-50-billion-per-year/article/469668

Sato, C. F., & Lindenmayer, D. B. (2018). Meeting the global ecosystem collapse challenge. *Conservation Letters: A Journal for the Society of Conservation Biology, 11*(1), e12348.

Scharper, S. B. (2016, June 29). Grassy Narrows mercury disaster a form of environmental racism. *Toronto Star*. Retrieved from https://www.thestar.com/opinion/commentary/2016/06/29/grassy-narrows-mercury-disaster-a-form-of-environmental-racism.html

SciNews. (2017, February 7). Scientists categorize Earth as a "toxic planet." *Phys.org*. Retrieved from https://phys.org/news/2017-02-scientists-categorize-earth-toxic-planet.html

Simon, D. R. (2006). *Elite deviance* (8th ed.). Pearson Education.

Sutherland, E. H. (1940). White-collar criminality. *American Sociological Review, 5*(1), 1–12.

Sutherland, E. H. (1949). *White collar crime*. Dryden Press.

Tan, A. (2022, October 5). "S$1.2 million worth of rhinoceros horns seized at Changi airport, largest seizure in Singapore ever." *Mothership*. https://mothership.sg/2022/10/rhinoceros-horn-seized-changi-airport/

Taylor, D. E. (2014). *Toxic communities: Environmental racism, industrial pollution, and residential mobility*. New York University Press.

Teachout, Z. (2020). *Break 'em up: Recovering our freedom from big AG, big tech, and big money*. All Points Books.

Thomson Reuters. (2020, March 2). Apple will pay up to $500 million US to settle slow iPhone lawsuit. *CBC*. Retrieved from https://www.cbc.ca/news/business/apple-will-pay-up-to-500-million-us-to-settle-slow-iphone-lawsuit-1.5482313

Thomson Reuters. (2021, April 14). Bernie Madoff, who orchestrated largest known Ponzi scheme in history, dead at 82. *CBC*. Retrieved from https://www.cbc.ca/news/world/bernie-madoff-obit-1.5986763

Toscano, N. (2019, November 3). PNG's Ok Tedi mine disaster money locked in new legal fight. *Sydney Morning Herald*. Retrieved from https://www.smh.com.au/business/companies/png-s-ok-tedi-mine-disaster-money-locked-in-new-legal-fight-20191102-p536s7.html

Totenberg, N. (2014, July 28). When did companies become people? Excavating the legal evolution. *npr*. Retrieved from https://www.npr.org/2014/07/28/335288388/when-did-companies-become-people-excavating-the-legal-evolution

UNCTAD. (2018, July 11). *Unsafe consumer products cost the US economy $1 trillion each year*. Retrieved from https://unctad.org/news/unsafe-consumer-products-cost-us-economy-1-trillion-each-year

van Uhm, D. P. (2016). *The illegal wildlife trade: Inside the world of poachers, smugglers and traders*. Springer International Publishing.

Walsh, S. (1996, October 15). ADM to pay 100 million to settle price-fixing case. *The Washington Post*. Retrieved from https://www.washingtonpost.com/archive/politics/1996/10/15/adm-to-pay-100-million-to-settle-price-fixing-case/95671342-94e0-492f-a439-4e8c19a74398/

Wood, R. J. (2013, December 16). Corporation law. In *The Canadian Encyclopedia*. Retrieved from https://www.thecanadianencyclopedia.ca/en/article/corporation-law

World Health Organization (WHO). (2019). *Tobacco industry: Decades of deception and duplicity*. Retrieved from https://untobaccocontrol.org/impldb/wp-content/uploads/FS-TFI-198-2019-EN.pdf

Yeager, P. C. (2016). The practical challenges of responding to corporate crime. In S. R. Van Slyke, M. L. Benson, & F. T. Cullen (Eds.), *The Oxford handbook of white-collar crime* (pp. 643–661). Oxford University Press.

York, R., Rosa, E. A., & Dietz, T. (2003). A rift in modernity? Assessing the anthropogenic sources of global climate change with the STIRPAT model. *International Journal of Sociology and Social Policy, 23*(10), 31–51.

Zimmer, K. (2021, March 16). More than 100 constitutions across the world have adopted a human right to a healthy environment, often serving as a powerful tool to protect the natural world. *BBC*. Retrieved from https://www.bbc.com/future/article/20210316-how-the-human-right-to-a-healthy-environment-helps-nature

CHAPTER 10

Canadian Criminal Law: Policing, Prosecution, and Corrections

Frances E. Chapman and Claudio Colaguori

LEARNING OBJECTIVES

In this chapter, you will

- examine the institutional elements of the criminal justice system, which includes courts of law, policing, prisons and corrections, and criminal law;
- explore the fundamental concepts that legally define a criminal act and learn to differentiate between types of criminal offences;
- observe how the ideals of legal justice such as the rights of the accused are not always upheld, such that *miscarriages of justice* can occur;
- examine the role of policing, including its challenges and some of the injustices that arise from police practices; and
- learn about prisons, sentencing, and issues surrounding corrections in Canada today.

INTRODUCTION

Understanding the basics of criminal law is essential to criminology because criminal acts are defined as such by law. The criminal law is a complex set of principles and procedures that constitutes just one part of the overall institution of law and forms the basis of the criminal justice system. Criminal law differs from country to country, but in most of Canada a **common law** system is in place (which is also used in most of the United States, England, New Zealand, and Australia). Canadian law is also based on the **civil law** system. Most of Western Europe (as well as Scotland, Louisiana in the United States, and the

Province of Quebec) have adopted the Roman system of law, which eventually became known as the civil code system. Legal actors within the justice system are obligated to uphold the **letter of the law** and in doing so maintain a system of legal equity and fairness that forms the basis of a civil society. Canada is also a nation that has **legal pluralism** insofar as it includes Indigenous legal traditions, which has relevance for the criminal law system mostly at sentencing, especially with restorative justice initiatives, but also with respect to Gladue courts, also known as Indigenous Peoples Court (Department of Justice, 2018; Macklem, 2014).

State law as an instrument of justice and order aims to protect individuals from harm, uphold human rights, and maintain public security, among other civil obligations, yet state agents of the criminal justice system have also been responsible for **miscarriages of justice** such as **wrongful convictions**. The development and enforcement of law presents a number of challenges that compel the justice system to constantly revise itself. Those who create and practise law regularly deal with some fundamental questions: Is the current state of law adequate to address contemporary social problems involving crime and punishment? How is it that some state agents of the law become corrupt, abusing their power and violating their own rules despite the many checks and balances that are built into the modern legal system? How do legal theorists decide which persistent, unjust social realities (e.g., systemic discrimination on the basis of race, class, and gender) are addressed in the creation of new or revised laws?

Among a basic overview of Canadian criminal law and the institutions of the criminal justice system, this chapter explores how the system of law (often referred to as jurisprudence) operates as one of the most powerful institutions in a society undergoing constant change. Understanding the nature and operation of the state institutions that form the criminal justice system, which includes criminal law, policing, and corrections, is essential for students of criminology.

In the words of scholars ...

Canadian criminal law derives from a mixture of statutory enactments and common law, a combination that has evolved over time in a slightly spasmodic and haphazard manner.

Morris Manning and Peter Sankoff, *Criminal Law.* 2015

THE LEGAL DEFINITION OF CRIME

Canadian criminal law has, in fact, developed in a random and piecemeal manner because the *Criminal Code* came originally from a drafted (but unused) code developed in England. Regardless of the patchwork code that we use, our conception of crime (as discussed in Chapter 1) is defined in a number of different ways. This chapter is concerned with the *legal definition* of crime as an act or behaviour that is prohibited by criminal law and enforced through punishment. Earlier chapters explored crime as a conception wherein a range of acts are classified as wrong, criminal, or illegal in a certain time or place by those in power. But defining something as illegal does not mean it is inherently wrong or unjust. Today, a crime is considered a *public wrong* because it is a wrong against the totality of society. Criminal law categorizes what society deems unacceptable deviance; it is arguably the most invasive form of law in the Canadian justice system because an individual's freedom is in jeopardy. Criminal law is not like civil law, where money may be exchanged as a means of resolving disputes or restitution for wrongdoing; criminal law sanctions putting a person in prison to punish them for their acts. As such, the focus of critical inquiry should be on whether the state is properly wielding this particularly important power and questioning who defines what is criminal.

From a macro perspective, crime is defined broadly as a distinction between what is, in Latin, *mala in se* and *mala prohibita*. These are two categories of wrongdoing; there is an act that is *evil in itself* or, conversely, an *evil which is prohibited* because the law says it is wrong. *Mala in se* are crimes are considered inherently immoral, such as murder, arson, or sexual assault, while *mala prohibita* are crimes prohibited by law, such as unlawful assembly, recreational drug use, or regulatory offences (e.g., driving offences). As we have seen in other chapters, what society may consider wrong in itself and something that is a prohibited wrong does not remain constant through time, and the penalties for such crimes may also change (e.g., marijuana use).

Today in criminal law, the opposing sides are the state, represented by the Crown Attorney, and the individual accused, who is usually represented by a defence lawyer. The Crown has the burden of proving that the individual committed the crime. Our adversarial system (discussed below) places a great deal of emphasis on playing by the rules. This is something that we call **due process** or, according to the *Canadian Bill of Rights*, the court system must act "according to the legal processes recognized by Parliament and the Courts in Canada." Our system emphasizes and prioritizes this procedural fairness, because *how* guilt is established is arguably just as important as establishing the truth.

The Requisite Elements of a Crime: *Actus Reus* and *Mens Rea*

A crime has two requisite elements: *actus reus* and *mens rea*. *Actus reus* is the Latin term for the physical action that constitutes a crime, while *mens rea* is the term for a guilty mind. A crime has to have both an act of doing something (*actus reus*) *and* the will or intent to commit the crime (*mens rea*). It is necessary to establish some threshold of transgression that triggers the criminal justice system to intervene. It is not enough for a criminal to simply think about acting; an external act must have taken place in order for the justice system to engage. We need *actus reus* because it is impossible to prove a purely mental state. We need something that is outwardly visible because it is not a crime to contemplate doing something illegal.

For example, the *mens rea* of the crime of forcible entry would be the *intent* to forcibly enter a property that belongs to someone else, while the *actus reus* of forcible entry is committed (according to s. 72 of the *Criminal Code*) "when that person enters real property that is in the actual and peaceable possession of another." So, if security cameras show that someone came to your house and broke the window and crawled in, they have committed the *actus reus* of forcible entry. The Crown Attorney attempts to prove that the *actus reus* occurred beyond a reasonable doubt.

Remember that there is also a requirement that a guilty mind or *mens rea* accompany the act that constitutes a crime. That being said, there is no single type of fault that is applicable in all circumstances, and there may also be more than one mental element in an individual crime. In addition, the guilty mind does not necessarily mean that the accused had a malicious intention. The first step in analyzing the *mens rea* of any particular offence is to go to the *Criminal Code* and read the very specific *mens rea* requirements for the particular crime.

It is important to note that the Crown must prove all mental elements required in order to obtain a conviction of a criminal offence. Persons are assumed to intend the natural consequences of actions; one cannot always say that they did not anticipate that something would happen. The court will look at the circumstances surrounding the act to see if they can conclude that there was *mens rea*. Some people may question why the criminal law has this mental element. The answer is that the system must make sure that only those who are morally blameworthy are convicted of true crimes. The *actus reus* and the *mens rea* must also occur at the same time.

Box 10.1: *Actus Reus* and *Mens Rea* in Action: *Fagan v Commissioner of Metropolitan Police*, [1969] 1 QB 439

In this classic British example of *actus reus* and *mens rea* occurring at the same time, Mr. Fagan parked his car on a city street. Constable Vickers, who was close by, told him to park closer to the curb and guided him into the space. When Mr. Fagan parked the car, one of the rear wheels came to rest on top of the Constable's foot. At that moment, the car engine stopped (but the evidence does not make it clear whether this was because the engine stalled or because Mr. Fagan switched off the ignition). Constable Vickers said, very politely but with a few more expletives, "get off, you are on my foot." Mr. Fagan made a snide remark and left the car on the Constable's foot for a period of time until he again turned on the ignition and moved the car off his foot. Mr. Fagan was charged with assaulting a police officer in the execution of his duty.

Mr. Fagan's lawyer argued that, when the car wheel came to rest on the constable's foot, Mr. Fagan performed the *actus reus* of an offence of assault but at the time he had no *mens rea*. When he had the *mens rea*—that is, when he finally decided to leave the wheel on the constable's foot—he was not committing any *actus reus* as it was merely an omission and not an act. Mr. Fagan did not *act*; instead he *failed* to act. The defence contended that there was no coincidence of *mens rea* and *actus reus* as they did not occur simultaneously. The defence further argued that criminal liability would have been more feasible if Mr. Fagan's foot had been the method of harm because that would have required a continuing willed pressure. The pressure of the car was not an act.

The Court of Appeal did not accept this defence and convicted Mr. Fagan on the basis that the *actus reus* was an ongoing one. When Mr. Fagan decided that he would not immediately accede to the policeman's request, he committed *mens rea* as well. The court said that the act was continuing from the time the car came to rest on the foot until the time that the wheel was removed. Thus, there was concurrence between the *actus reus* and the *mens rea*.

CANADIAN CRIMINAL LAW AND THE FUNDAMENTAL PRINCIPLES OF JUSTICE

Canadian criminal law has a unique history that is rooted in British common law and defined by our Canadian constitution. The constitution encompasses the fundamental laws of our system because it governs how the state can act at the most basic level. A constitution is a body of law that establishes a framework for a government and is the supreme law of the country. Constitutional law is the system of written (and unwritten) principles that defines what power we give to our government while still protecting individuals and certain groups. Constitutional law is formed from statutes and court decisions (among other sources). Canadian law was built on the British parliamentary model but is federally united by a single document called the *Constitution Act, 1867*. In 1982, the constitutionally enshrined *Charter of Rights* was added to the Canadian constitution, so that while **parliamentary supremacy** was preserved, there were limits placed on the exercise of government power.

Constitutional law and the fundamental values of the *Charter* override all other laws in Canada. Laws are enacted and repealed, but a constitution also looks to the future and puts limits on the power of government while allowing for legitimate forms of state power. As such, a constitution can and will grow over time, sometimes in ways that were not necessarily foreseen. Each level of government is assigned duties in the constitution, and neither is able to control the activities of the others. There are certain *Charter* values that are particularly important in criminal law, and many times these are described in terms of human rights.

However, the laws of the land only tell part of the story. In Canada, a nuanced understanding of criminal law is not possible without discussing human rights in the *Charter*, including section 2 which outlines fundamental freedoms, including "(a) freedom of conscience and religion; (b) freedom of thought, belief, opinion, and expression, including freedom of the press and other media of communication; (c) freedom of peaceful assembly; and (d) freedom of association." Section 7 provides that "everyone has the right to life, liberty, and security of the person and the right not to be deprived thereof except in accordance with the principles of fundamental justice," and section 8 provides that "everyone has the right to be secure against unreasonable search or seizure," in addition to sections 9 and 10, which provide rights upon arrest and detention and the right not to be arbitrarily detained (*Charter*, sections 2–10). These rights will be explored further below.

However, the history of Canadian criminal law is not complete without discussing the fundamental and systemic racism inherent in our system. Criminal law was used by colonial settlers to "extend and consolidate power over a territory with which Indigenous peoples had a relationship far deeper than Western concepts of ownership, and on which Indigenous nations had administered systems of law and justice long before the arrival of European law" (Roach et al., 2020, p. 17). One must remember that the history of Canadian criminal law is filled with injustices for those who are most vulnerable, and we must study settler laws that affect Indigenous peoples as well as Indigenous legal systems in the context of discussing the power of the Canadian state. We must also recognize the overwhelming importance of the treaties negotiated between Indigenous nations and the British Crown. While, in many instances, these have not been honoured by settlers, they are nevertheless "foundational constitutional document[s] that provide … a basis for governing with consent, respect and harmony, as opposed to coercion, force and polarization" (Roach et al., 2020, p. 17).

State power and the rights of free and independent persons are central issues in criminal law. The state needs to justify the use of this power to determine whether individuals deserve punishment or what is referred to as a *just desert*. In 1882, Samuel Robinson Clarke and Henry Pigott Sheppard said that a "crime is the violation of a right when considered in reference to the evil tendency of such violation as regards the community at large" (p. 49). Thus, this complex system of rights (which also includes responsibilities) makes Canada unique not only in our history, our geography, and the treatment of Indigenous peoples but also in our conception of the *moral blameworthiness* or disregard of the offender.

In the words of scholars …

Rule of law is another elusive phrase that is apt to be used in support of many different arguments. In one sense it describes an ordered society as opposed to one where the person with the gun always gets his own way. It conjures up the vision of stability and tranquillity that the framers of the Canadian confederation had in mind when they spoke of the "Peace, Order, and Good Government of Canada." A similar view underlies the mottos: "Freedom under the law," and "Equal justice under the law."

Stephen M. Waddams, *Introduction to the Study of Law.* 1997

The Rule of Law

One of the fundamental principles that establishes the fairness and legitimacy of law is the concept of the **rule of law**. In order for the system of law to be respected, it must appear fair and equal in the eyes of the public. It has to apply to all people regardless of their identity or social status; nevertheless, as Waddams (1997) noted, the phrase *rule of law* is elusive. The goal of the Canadian justice system is not to deem the powerful party the victor but rather to emphasize basic principles including a measured government, freedom, and equality. Rule of law can also refer to the role of judges to make impartial decisions according to the law of the jurisdiction and not through arbitrary power. However, the common law system used in Canada is based on preventing arbitrary power. In historical terms, it refers to the monarch not interfering with the course of justice. It also refers to the concept that the government cannot make law, it can simply use the powers conferred upon it by law; moreover, the law should not be governed by the whims of human decision-making.

Box 10.2: Case Study: Rule of Law and the Sexual Assault of Children—*R v KRJ*, [2016] SCJ No 31

In the Supreme Court of Canada case *R v KRJ*, the court had to make the difficult determination of allowing a sentence to accord with the rule of law. In this case, the defendant pleaded guilty to charges of incest involving his preschool-aged daughter and the creation of child pornography between the years of 2008 and 2011. The government, induced by such cases, felt that there should be more protection of the victims of such crimes and introduced the *Safe Streets and Communities Act*, which came into force on August 9, 2012. The *Act* included a new section of the *Criminal Code* that would prohibit all contact with the young persons involved, no matter the means, and also introduced a new internet prohibition. This case is illustrative of the principles of Canadian law in modern times and how difficult the principles may be to uphold. Section 11(i) of the *Charter* states that "if found guilty of the offence and if the punishment for the offence has been varied between the time of commission and the time of sentencing, [the person charged has the right] to the benefit of the lesser punishment." Thus, following through on the principle of the rule of law, even for a crime as horrendous as child sexual abuse, the court must give a lesser sentence if that was the law at the time the offence was committed. The crimes took place from 2008 to 2011 but the law changed in 2012. We cannot have a retrospective law apply to this offender, although many would agree that he probably should have no contact with young persons and should be prohibited from using the internet. The rule of law establishes the principle that we must not do this. Laws change over time, but the rule of law ideally ensures that offenders realize the sentencing consequences they face at the time a crime is committed.

In this case, the court surveyed principles of the rule of law and noted that Lord Diplock in *Black-Clawson International Ltd v Papierwerke Waldhof-Aschaffenburg AG* said that "acceptance of the rule of law as a constitutional principle requires that a citizen, before committing himself to any course of action, should be able to know in advance what are the legal consequences that will flow from it." Even with this important law drafted in protection of children, the court found that, subject to section 11(i) of the Charter, the law must not have retrospective operation of the no-contact provision. Thus, even when it means that an important provision such as a just punishment would not be applied to a convicted child sex offender, the rule of law is paramount.

The rule of law also holds that laws should not be retroactive; this accords with the legal maxim ***nulla poena sine lege***, which means that there should be no punishment unless it is in accordance with an unambiguous and non-retroactive law. The rule of law can mean various things to various people. Hogg and Zwibel note that views on the rule of law range from those who say that it is purely "lawyers' rhetoric that means nothing" to those who argue that "the rule of law means almost everything" (2005, p. 717). Thus, the phrase *rule of law* is both a fundamental concept and one that remains the subject of controversy and debate. In theory, it is easy to say that we should adhere to the rule of law, but in practice, the law must fulfill the difficult promise that, for example, everyone is equal under the law. Even if we believe someone is guilty, this adherence to the rule of law must be preserved to the point of allowing an offender to go free (even if we find them morally reprehensible).

Box 10.3: Crime Control and Due Process Models of Justice

As discussed briefly in Chapter 1, Herbert Packer famously distinguished between a *crime control model* and a *due process model* of justice. In 1968, Packer wrote, in his seminal text *The Limits of the Criminal Sanction*, that the most important function of the crime control model is to repress crime and maximize social freedom through the proper screening of suspects to determine their guilt and punishment as quickly and efficiently as possible. This model hinges on the presumption of guilt and the timely disposition of the criminal in an "assembly line" model of justice (Packer, 1964, p. 14). This model validates the authority of the state through the criminal system and the maintenance of social order.

Conversely, the due process model can be described as an "obstacle course" where there are various stages of investigation and prosecution that recognize the possibilities of human error (Packer, 1964, p. 14). Packer makes it clear that the due process model also recognizes the social benefits in repressing crime but differentiates between a formal process and *non-adjudicative fact-finding* that recognizes the real possibility of human error. This model stresses the competitive process within the **adversarial system** and is based on a legal contest whereby two parties compete for victory granted by an impartial tribunal with the full ability of the accused to answer the case against them. This adversarial tradition has evolved over time to include antagonistic parties who are arguing over the guilt or lack of guilt of the accused. In medieval Europe, the parties would physically fight one another to determine the winner through trial by battle. Today, the due process model recognizes that criminal justice procedures are very important because (for example) witnesses are notoriously inaccurate with their observations, confessions may be induced by the police, and witnesses may have personal biases towards the parties. The due process model is a rejection of the crime control model's reliance on police fact-finding as determinative of guilt and relies on the evidence that is formally adjudicated.

Packer's work is the subject of criticism, and he himself acknowledges that the two models are not opposites. Legal theorist Kent Roach has been critical of Packer's two models and has suggested instead four models. Although Roach admits that Packer's typology was "remarkably durable" (1999, p. 674) over the years, the models do not necessarily add clarity to debates on issues like hate speech, discrimination against minority groups, or the influence of theories like feminism or critical race theory. Roach notes that the role of victim is absent from Packer's model and so adds a punitive model of victim's rights (the "roller coaster") and a non-punitive model of victim's rights (the "circle") to Packer's original formulation (p. 699). Ironically, Roach has the same criticisms for his own models as those he levies upon Packer but notes that recognizing victims is essential in today's world of criminal law.

Factual Guilt and Legal Guilt

In the criminal law sphere, there is a difference between *factual guilt* and *legal guilt*. A person can fully commit a crime and yet be found not guilty in a court of law if that person's due process rights were violated. For example, if an arresting officer does not follow proper procedure in collecting evidence (e.g., drugs), that evidence may be eliminated from the trial because of the breach of an individual's fundamental rights. If there is no longer evidence of drugs at the crime scene, the accused must be found not guilty or the charges must be dropped by the Crown. So, although the person is factually guilty, they are not legally guilty.

Box 10.4: The Virtues of Lady Justice

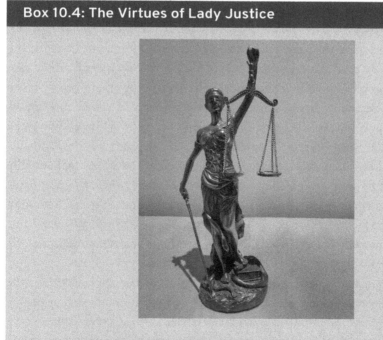

The image of Justitia, the Roman goddess of justice (also known as Lady Justice), is noteworthy for how she symbolizes the main principles of legal justice. The scale she holds signifies that the formal process of pursuing legal justice should be balanced and fair insofar as the perspectives of both sides of a dispute need to be considered in weighing the judgment. The blindfold indicates that justice should not be biased in favour of one type of person over another. Justice is to be dispensed equally, regardless of the individual characteristics of the parties involved. The sword symbolizes the power of force. For legal judgments to have authority, they must be backed up by a sanction or punitive action, such as a fine or imprisonment, and also by a reward, such as monetary damages to the party that has been unjustly wronged. The snake at her feet represents how Lady Justice presides over the evil of wrongdoing. Does the justice system in Canada reflect the virtues embodied in the figure of Lady Justice?

For an accused to be found criminally responsible and for legal guilt to be established, the Crown must prove all the elements of the offence **beyond a reasonable doubt**. This means that the Crown discharged the **burden of proof** (which is the duty to prove the charge against the accused). The standard of proof in a criminal matter is almost always beyond a reasonable doubt using all the permitted (admissible) evidence. *Beyond a reasonable doubt* was defined in the criminal case *R v Lachance* as the burden on the Crown to prove the elements of a crime "'outside the limit or sphere of' or 'past' a reasonable doubt" (*Lachance*, 1963, para 6). Thus, the Crown does not have to prove that the evidence is certain and there is no chance of error; rather, the evidence is so complete and convincing that reasonable doubts are erased from the minds of the judge or jury. This means that the Crown must prove *all* elements of the crime to this standard of *actus reus* and *mens rea* coinciding with one another. In contrast, factual guilt is whether the individual actually committed the crime with which they are charged. *Factual guilt*, or *factual innocence*, are not terms that are usually used in the criminal justice system. Although the accused may be factually guilty, if they are not also legally guilty, it would be improper to take away their freedom. If legal guilt cannot be determined, the evidence is excluded and the accused person will walk free.

Until an accused is proven legally guilty according to the applicable law, the courts have an obligation under section 11(d) of the *Charter* to presume that person innocent. Of course, we all know of individuals, or perhaps we know that we ourselves, have committed illegal acts but have not been caught by the state. Are we any less guilty because we were not apprehended? We may be factually guilty, but because we did not engage with the criminal justice system, we cannot be held legally guilty.

THE *CRIMINAL CODE OF CANADA*

In Canada, criminal law is the purview of the federal government through the en-actment of the *Criminal Code*. The *Criminal Code* is a statute that applies whether the offender is in Quebec, Nunavut, or any province or territory in between. An act is only criminal if the Canadian government has deemed it criminal. Some crimes have been prohibited for hundreds of years, like murder and treason, while newer crimes like cyberbullying are captured under the criminal harassment sec-tions of the *Criminal Code*. Many observers argue, however, that updated defin-itions and understandings of new types of crime are needed.

THE CANADIAN *CHARTER OF RIGHTS AND FREEDOMS* AS A SOURCE OF THE LAW

As mentioned above, a discussion of the sources of criminal law begins with the **division of powers** between the federal and provincial government through the *Constitution Act, 1982*, and the *Charter*, which is the first 34 sections of the constitution. Many constitutional issues arise outside of the *Charter*, but the *Charter* is of utmost importance in criminal law because of the latter's potential to take away an offender's liberty. The introduction of the *Charter* in 1982 had a huge impact on Canadian law as the development empowered judges to declare a piece of legislation invalid if it infringed on an individual's rights. Contrary to public assumptions, it should be noted that *Charter* challenges are primar-ily about challenging the government's purported power in any given area of legislation, rather than a citizen's right to challenge issues like their neighbour's racist behaviour.

A constitution can be thought of as a list of rules for lawmakers. It defines the roles of different laws and how they work together and provides mechanisms for how they can be changed. The purpose of a constitution is to provide limits on state power. Canada's system was adapted from the British system through the *Constitution Act, 1867* (and before that, the *British North America Act*). Before the Charter, parliamentary supremacy dictated that parliament and statute law was above all law made by judges (called common law or case law). In Canada, parlia-mentary supremacy has always been limited by the *Constitution Act, 1867*, but since the inception of the Charter, the court has taken on a more important role by put-ting certain entrenched individual and group rights beyond the power of federal or provincial governments. The courts are powerful in that they can declare that the federal or provincial government acted outside of its power, with the result that a law can be declared to have no force or effect.

A variety of criminal law rights are provided for in the *Charter*, such as the rights under section 10 to be informed on arrest or detention of the reason why one is stopped, and also to retain and instruct counsel without delay. All of these principles have been interpreted by subsequent case law (many times); thus, the *Charter* is about structuring a relationship between the state and individuals. The courts must be careful not to alter anything that would contravene the intention of the Parliament of Canada or of the province or territory. Some say that adding words or meaning that were not intended by the legislators is not the proper purview of courts. Others note that it is not the role of courts to interpret a statute so narrowly that it does something that the government did not intend. This constant push and pull of the courts and legislature is what makes constitutional law interesting because no rights are absolute under section 33 (the notwithstanding clause) of the *Charter*.

SOURCES OF CRIMINAL LAW: STATUTE AND CASE LAW

The criminal justice system derives its power to prosecute criminal matters through the division of powers in the *Constitution Act*. Section 91 provides that lawmaking is the responsibility of the federal government, while the provinces' powers are delegated under section 92. The *Criminal Code* is a federal document, and only the federal government has the power to enact criminal legislation. The provincial and territorial governments also have the authority to make legislation when it comes to certain matters. For example, provincial governments can legislate driving offences, such as driving while your licence is suspended, and other provincial offences which are sometimes called **quasi-criminal** matters.

All Canadian citizens are presumed to be versed in the provisions of the *Criminal Code* as ignorance of the law is not an excuse. However, as discussed above, only crimes that exist at the time of the act can be prosecuted; retroactive crimes are not permitted. It is important to remember that through the rule of law, all people are equal, and no one is above the law. The law must be certain and not vague. If it is too vague, a court can say that it is void because people could not tell if their actions were criminal, and the accused person is accorded the benefit of the doubt if this is in question.

In Canadian criminal law, the *Criminal Code* is the most important document, but there are other provisions like the *Controlled Drugs and Substances Act* that function in conjunction with the criminal law. There are two primary sources of criminal law in Canada: legislation (like the *Criminal Code*) and judge-made case law that interprets legislation. Our system is based on law interpreted by appointed judges, which may lead to the accusation of **judicial activism**. An activist court is one that has engaged in making the law (perhaps for policy reasons) rather than simply interpreting the law and applying it to the case. Some observers are wary of judicial activism, believing that policy development is reserved for the politicians and not unelected judges (as we have in Canada). Some say that judicial activism is needed in cases we agree with and is something to be reviled when we do not agree with the decision. The bottom line is that the legal system is a human system defined by human actors, whether at the political or judicial level.

Substantive and Procedural Law

There is also a difference between substantive and procedural criminal law that aids in the administration of justice. A crime may be classified as such by the state, but the state also devised a series of rules to govern the prosecution and adjudication of any breach of the criminal law. Section 91(27) of the *Constitution Act, 1867* dictates that the federal government has authority over "Procedure on Criminal Matters."

It is important to note that a person can only be found liable by a properly comprised and charged judge and/or panel of one's peers (jury) by a court exercising the given power provided under the *Criminal Code*. Often, these rules are very technical and narrowly applied, but other stipulations may be extremely broad, such as the doctrine of due process, which dictates that one receives a fair hearing, or double jeopardy, which dictates that an accused must not be tried twice for the same crime. The rules and principles of criminal justice have only been bolstered since the inception of the Canadian *Charter*. Through the *Criminal Code* and these procedural rules, the Crown Attorney must prove all elements of an offence.

TYPES OF CRIMINAL CONVICTIONS IN CANADA: SUMMARY OFFENCES/INDICTABLE OFFENCES/HYBRID OFFENCES

Historically, crimes were divided into treason, felonies, and misdemeanors, and these terms are still used in the United States. Felonies were originally punishable by death and forfeiture of property, while misdemeanors were less serious. Today, Canadian criminal offences are divided into **summary**, **indictable**, and **hybrid offences**. Summary offences are those crimes that are considered less serious than indictable offences and are tried before a provincial or territorial judge. Under the *Criminal Code*, summary offences are punished by a fine of no more than $5,000 or a term of imprisonment of not more than two years less a day. In some instances, both types of punishment may apply.

Indictable offences have more serious consequences, up to and including life in prison. Life in prison refers to the time required for the offender to be eligible for parole. For a crime like first-degree murder, the individual must serve 25 years of the sentence before being eligible for parole. The location where an offender serves this sentence is also important, as those given a sentence of two years or more must serve their time in a federal penitentiary while those with a sentence of less than two years do so in a provincial institution.

Under section 718 of the *Criminal Code*, the court must consider the fundamental purposes of sentencing, which includes the protection of society and crime prevention (as noted by Herbert Packer; see above), respect for the law, and the "maintenance of a just peaceful and safe society" while considering denunciation, deterrence, separation, rehabilitation, reparations, and the responsibility of the offender.

Those charged with an indictable offence may have a choice of court, including a trial in the Provincial Court of Justice or the Superior Court of Justice, and a choice of whether one wishes to be tried by judge alone or judge and jury. The most serious offences are in the exclusive jurisdiction of the Superior Court of Justice in the province. Some individuals who are charged with an indictable offence elect to proceed with a preliminary hearing, but these rights have been curtailed in recent years. The matter begins with an **indictment**, a legal document that sets out the charges that the accused is facing.

The *Criminal Code* also has hybrid offences, which may be tried either as an indictable or summary offence at the choice of the Crown. The classification of an offence may depend on factors such as future plea negotiations and whether the Crown has a reasonable prospect of conviction. Until the Crown elects that a hybrid offence will be tried as an indictable or summary offence, it proceeds as an indictable offence in accordance with the *Interpretation Act* s. 34(1). Hybrid offences are sometimes also referred to as dual procedure offences or Crown option offences, as the prosecutor is solely in control of how the offence proceeds. In recent years, Parliament has allowed the maximum penalty for some hybrid offences that are tried summarily to be increased to 18 months incarceration.

ADMINISTRATIVE LAW AND REGULATORY OFFENCES

Outside of the traditional criminal law system are those wrongs that we call **regulatory offences**. The term *regulatory offence* describes a wide variety of wrongs established by statute to regulate in the areas of health, convenience, safety, and the general welfare of the public. These charges are non-criminal and are dealt with at administrative tribunals and not in a traditional courtroom setting. In a regulatory offence, the Crown is not required to fully prove the element of *mens rea* as they would an offence in the *Criminal Code*. Many statutes make room for external bodies to administer these areas of law. Administrative tribunals may look as if they are courts, but they are really part of the executive branch and not the judicial branch of the government. Even though these tribunals are not in a formal court system, their decisions are binding on the parties. These tribunals are not permitted to go beyond their jurisdiction, and the rules of due process must be followed.

Each of these tribunals have specific legislation that governs their jurisdiction and the powers delegated to them by government. These bodies often have significant authority and can levy fines, send people back to prison, de-certify professionals, revoke licences, terminate people from jobs, deport individuals, and impose a wide variety of punishments. Ideally, administrative tribunals provide an impartial body that ensures the government's authority is exercised in a fair and non-discriminatory way.

Typically, members of these tribunals have specialized knowledge, training, education, and/or experience. The goal is that tribunals should have autonomy and not be unduly influenced by authorities. The job of administrative tribunals is to hear complaints and grievances by citizens against government departments and resolve these conflicts according to certain principles, remaining consistent with the law.

In the words of scholars ...

For the law holds, that it is better that ten guilty persons escape, than that one innocent suffer.

Sir William Blackstone, *Commentaries on the Laws of England.* 1836

THE MAIN ELEMENTS OF THE CRIMINAL JUSTICE SYSTEM

The criminal justice system has a unique structure. A criminal law case is heard by a provincially or federally appointed judge with or without a jury, and the case is brought in the name of the state, which is why the **style of cause** reads *Regina v Smith* (which often gets shortened to *R v Smith*). "Regina" refers to the Queen of England; in a constitutional monarchy like Canada, this individual is the symbolic head of state. If a man is the sitting monarch in Britain, the style of cause in Canada would read "Rex v Smith." The style of cause indicates that the wrong was committed against the state (not just the victim). The Crown Attorney is employed by the state to prepare a case and the accused will plead "guilty" or "not guilty." The victim has little control and, in most cases, gets no personal benefit other than a period of separation from the offender, restitution, and perhaps formal recognition that they were criminally wronged if the offender is found guilty beyond a reasonable doubt.

If the accused in a criminal trial is found guilty, they will be convicted and, to varying extents, punished. The maxim that it is better to let ten guilty persons go free than convict one innocent person is a cornerstone of the criminal system. If the wrong judgment is given in a civil trial, only a few individuals will be impacted, but in a criminal trial, the fundamental basis of our system is brought into question for all if an innocent person is found guilty.

The Structure of the Courts

There is a distinct hierarchy to the courts involved in the criminal justice system. Canadian courts have four general levels that hear all types of criminal hearings. At the first level are the provincial courts, or what are called **inferior courts**, followed by the **superior courts** for each province (which deal with more serious matters), courts of appeal, and finally the Supreme Court of Canada.

Inferior Courts

The provincial and territorial courts that are commonly referred to as the lower courts are established by each territorial or provincial government. These courts handle the majority of cases before the courts. Examples include the Ontario Court of Justice, the Provincial Court of Manitoba, and the Territorial Court of the Northwest Territories. The one exception to this structure is the Nunavut Court of Justice, which is Canada's only single-level trial court with both the powers of the territorial court and the superior trial court so that all judges can hear all cases that arise in the territory.

These lower courts are usually presided over by a Justice of the Peace who follows the authority the *Justices of the Peace Act*. They make decisions at almost all bail hearings in the province and also set dates for criminal matters. A Justice of the Peace receives the Crown's first documents in a hearing (called an **information**), which starts a criminal matter, and can issue summons or warrants, including search warrants. A Justice of the Peace may also preside at some trials.

Youth courts are also at this level and govern young offenders from 12 to 17 years old who are charged with an offence under federal youth justice laws. Youth courts attempt to protect the privacy of the young person, and any court at either the provincial/territorial or superior court level can be designated a youth court. Inferior courts also deal with traffic and bylaw violations and provincial/territorial regulatory offences.

Superior Courts

The next level of courts are the provincial and territorial superior courts, which are established under the *Constitution Act, 1867*. These courts deal with more serious matters, as well as appeals from the lower courts. There are also federal courts at this level that deal with matters like immigration and intellectual property law. Each province and territory has a superior court; this level of court is said to have inherent jurisdiction, which allows the adjudication of cases except where legislation curtails that authority. Superior courts try the most serious criminal cases and include courts like the Supreme Court of British Columbia, the Alberta Court of Queen's Bench, and the Supreme Court of Yukon. The provinces and territories operate the superior courts, but the federal government appoints and compensates the judges that preside over these courts.

Courts of Appeal

Each province and territory has an appeal court, including the Court of Appeal for Saskatchewan, the Nova Scotia Court of Appeal, and the Court of Appeal of Newfoundland and Labrador. Above each provincial and territorial appeal court is the Supreme Court of Canada, which has been the final court of appeal for Canada since 1949.

Appeal courts are responsible for reviewing the decisions of the lower courts when they are empowered to do so. Appeal courts do not hear witnesses, but rather they take into account material provided by the lawyers describing what happened at trial while following strict rules about what evidence can be discussed. The goal is to ensure that the trial judge followed the rules of evidence and that the accused had a fair trial. Appeal judges often defer to the trial judge, because trial judges were in the unique position to hear witnesses directly, while appeals courts hear no witness testimony. However, there might be situations where the law was clearly used in an incorrect way, and the court of appeal may substitute its own decision in place of the trial judge. With a few exceptions, the provincial courts of appeal generally sit in panels of three judges.

While trial courts resolve individual arguments based on facts, the appeal court applies legal rules and makes sure that the law is applied evenly from case to case. For a case to be heard by the Supreme Court, the appellate must first ask the Supreme Court for leave (permission) to appeal. The Supreme Court only gives leave to appeal to select cases that have particular significance to the population. The court is comprised of eight justices and one chief justice, and it may hear a case in panels of three, five, seven, or all nine members. Appeals to the Supreme Court of Canada must follow the rules set out in the *Supreme Court Act*.

Canada also has a Federal Court of Appeal. The Federal Court of Appeal has jurisdiction to hear appeals from judgments of the Federal Court and the Tax Court of Canada, and it may also hear judicial review applications for over a dozen federal boards and tribunals listed under section 28 of the *Federal Courts Act*. This court also hears appeals regarding other federal legislation.

The Courts and Procedural Justice

Procedure is of utmost importance in the criminal law system. Since all of the power of the state comes to bear on one individual—the accused—the scales must be balanced between the parties to allow the rule of law to operate. As discussed, all people are equal and no one is above the law, but the law must also be certain and not vague. If it is too vague, the benefit of the doubt is given to the defendant, because the state has all of the power to draft a law in any way seen fit. If a citizen cannot determine if actions are criminal, there would be no way to ensure compliance with the law. Although defendants may represent themselves, often lawyers represent the parties.

The Parties in a Criminal Case

In most jurisdictions in Canada today, criminal cases are prosecuted by Crown counsel. Crown counsel are provincially appointed lawyers who act as agent for the Attorney General of the Province. Prosecutorial authority is not only addressed by legislation and common law, it is also controlled through the Attorney General's delegation of authority to their agents. While the Attorney General is a member of the cabinet, who presides at the pleasure of the government of the day, the exercise of the prosecutorial function in individual cases is carried out by permanent, appointed civil servants who act as the Attorney General's agents. These agents include the individual Crown counsel who appear in the criminal courts on a daily basis. These individual Crowns must exercise their judgment and discretion in a manner that is independent of political influence or interference. Generally, the Attorney General's control over their agents is not exercised in individual cases but rather is expressed in formal written directives or policies that guide the exercise of prosecutorial discretion in all cases.

On the other side of the adversarial relationship, a criminal defence lawyer must represent the individuals who are being prosecuted by the Crown. It is the obligation of the defence lawyer to represent every one of their clients to the best of their abilities, regardless of the charge. Defence counsel must be conscious of their responsibilities to their clients, the justice system, and the community. An accused can represent themselves at the lower court hearings, but many individuals hire a lawyer if they have the means to do so.

The Rights of the Accused, the Presumption of Innocence, and Equality before the Law

The accused person has many rights, but one of the most fundamental is that a person is considered innocent until proven guilty. This right is protected through section 6(1) of the *Charter*, which states that a "person shall be deemed not to be guilty of the offence until he is convicted or discharged," and section 11(d) which provides that "any person charged with an offence has the right ... to be presumed innocent until proven guilty according to law in a fair and public hearing by an independent and impartial tribunal." Thus, no person is to be considered guilty of an offence unless convicted of that offence at a proper trial, and the person must be convicted on every element of the charge beyond a reasonable doubt. The rationale for this standard is that it protects an accused from all of the massive powers of the state and its resources.

It is also important to remember that each individual is presumed to be equal under the law. Section 15 of the *Charter* provides that "every individual is equal before and under the law and has the right to the equal protection and equal benefit of the law without discrimination and in particular without discrimination based on race, national or ethnic origin, colour, religion, sex, age, mental or physical disability." The accused also has a right to silence, a right to counsel, and other fundamental rights. Theoretically, the power imbalance between the state and the accused is addressed with these provisions, but whether these rights are respected in practice is the question we all need to ask ourselves.

Box 10.5: Case Study of a Miscarriage of Justice: *R v Mullins-Johnson*, 2007 ONCA 720

Mr. William Mullins-Johnson was wrongfully convicted of sexually assaulting and murdering his four-year-old niece in Sault Ste. Marie, Ontario. The evidence against him was based on the testimony of disgraced child pathologist Dr. Charles Smith, who was called as an expert witness. Dr. Smith was eventually found to be complicit in manufacturing, misplacing, and misrepresenting the evidence in dozens of cases. Mr. Mullins-Johnson received $4.25 million in compensation for this wrongful conviction and for the 12 years that he spent in prison after he was found guilty in 1994. It was later determined that there was no evidence that his niece was sodomized and asphyxiated, and, in fact, experts concluded that she died of natural causes.

Mr. Mullins-Johnson was acquitted by the Ontario Court of Appeal in 2007, and the appeal court used this as an example of factual and legal guilt or innocence. It was acknowledged by all parties that there was no evidence that Mr. Mullins-Johnson was guilty of any crime, and the court went as far as to say that his conviction was the result of a rushed judgment based on flawed scientific opinion. Mr. Mullins-Johnson asked the court to declare him innocent of the crimes alleged against him. The court declined to do so, saying that the courts get their jurisdiction from statutes (like the *Criminal Code*) and lacked jurisdiction to make a formal declaration of factual innocence. The court adopted the prior reasoning of Chief Justice Lamer who, in a previous inquiry, said that "a criminal trial does not address *factual innocence*. The criminal trial is to determine whether the Crown proved its case beyond a reasonable doubt. If so, the accused is guilty. If not, the accused is found not guilty. There is no finding of factual innocence since it would not fall within the ambit or purpose of criminal law" (*Mullins-Johnson*, para 23). Thus, even in a situation where the system failed an individual who was clearly wrongfully convicted, the only action that may be taken by the courts is to enter an acquittal. Courts at all levels have declined to find an individual accused *innocent*.

The problem of wrongful convictions is a longstanding systemic issue within the justice system. The issue has, however, begun to receive more attention in recent years due to increased representation of wrongfully convicted persons in the news and entertainment media. Contrary to popular belief that wrongful convictions are the result of unintended human error and honest mistakes, Anderson and Anderson argue that such convictions arise from deliberate professional and bureaucratic wrongdoing (2009, p. 10). Official forms of professional misconduct include biased use of discretion among judges, prosecutors, and police; defence counsel misconduct; coerced witness testimony; flawed or biased expert witness testimony; poor legal representation for the accused; jury tampering; false confessions obtained under duress; and the falsification of evidence. Colaguori (2016) discusses how the Mullins-Johnson case reveals structural biases in the adversarial system of criminal law that disadvantage marginalized defendants, as well as gross power imbalances between the legal power of the prosecution and the accused that can produce unjust outcomes such as wrongful convictions.

Sentencing

Sentencing is the process that the court engages in after a finding of criminal guilt (beyond a reasonable doubt) in order to establish a just and principled punishment for the offender. The court must take into account the offender's needs in addition to the impact of the crime on the victim and society as a whole. Historically, **retribution** has been seen as the primary purpose of a criminal sanction through the concept of *lex talionis*, or retaliation in kind by the state (an eye for an eye, a tooth for a tooth). A retributive sentence was believed to restore and repay the offender's debt to society. Today, section 12 of the *Charter of Rights* states that "everyone has the right not to be subjected to any **cruel and unusual** treatment or **punishment**," or a punishment that is grossly inappropriate and shocking to the community.

In September 1996, the *Criminal Code* was amended to give judges more guidance on the principles to adhere to when sentencing an offender. These principles became section 718 of the *Criminal Code*, which states that:

> The fundamental purpose of sentencing is to protect society and to contribute, along with crime prevention initiatives, to respect for the law and the maintenance of a just, peaceful, and safe society by imposing just sanctions that have one or more of the following objectives:
>
> a. to denounce unlawful conduct and the harm done to victims or to the community that is caused by unlawful conduct;
> b. to deter the offender and other persons from committing offences;
> c. to separate offenders from society, where necessary;
> d. to assist in rehabilitating offenders;
> e. to provide reparations for harm done to victims or to the community; and
> f. to promote a sense of responsibility in offenders, and acknowledgment of the harm done to victims or to the community. (*Criminal Code*, s. 718)

Judges are given great flexibility on the application of these principles. Section 718.3 allows for the "discretion of the court" when offenders are sentenced, and appeal courts tend to show great deference to sentencing judges who may exercise this discretion. Judges rely on **precedent** to determine the sentences for like offenders in like crimes. The judge may also hear **victim impact statements** from the victim or others impacted by the crime. This in-court statement gives an opportunity for a victim to describe the ongoing physical, social, emotional, psychological, or financial damage to those involved.

If the offender has multiple offences, the judge may rule that they can serve their sentence concurrently (at the same time) or consecutively (one sentence after the other). In Canada it is most common for sentences to be served concurrently. Under section 719.3, a sentence may also be reduced for time served pre-trial. Those deemed a dangerous offender may be kept indefinitely in a federal penitentiary, while other dangerous offenders can be designated long-term offenders under the *Criminal Code* and can face additional supervision for up to 10 years when they are released into the community.

Plea Bargaining

Plea bargaining is a deal between the Crown and defence attorney for a sentencing reduction or a certain form of punishment, in return for a guilty plea. While a plea bargain can occur at any stage in the process, it often happens after the charge but before trial. Plea bargain negotiations can range from a simple and informal discussion to an actual agreement between the parties. Plea bargaining discussions are also referred to as pre-trial negotiations, resolution discussions, plea negotiations, and plea agreements.

Plea bargaining is made possible by the accused's right to plead guilty or not guilty and the Crown's discretionary powers regarding the charges laid. In a plea bargain, the accused person relinquishes their right to a trial by pleading guilty in exchange for concessions by the Crown. There may be several things that the parties can negotiate through a plea agreement including, but not limited to, reducing the number of charges, withdrawal or stay of some of the charges and promise not to pursue other charges, reducing the charge to a lesser charge, and an agreement to withdraw the charge for the defendant who promises to keep the peace, among others.

The accused's motive for plea bargaining is usually to obtain a lesser sentence, but the judge in the case is still permitted to impose a wide range of sentences *regardless* of the deal reached between the Crown and the defence counsel. The sentence negotiated is not guaranteed. With this in mind, it is important to look to the source of the charges and the power that is bestowed upon the police. There are many who oppose plea bargaining because of the potential problems inherent in the process. Some critics argue that the process of making deals with criminals that result in more lenient sentences brings the administration of justice into disrepute, but it is important to remember that the accused person also gives up the right to a trial because of this process. Others see plea bargaining as unjust for the accused as it is an infringement on the right to due process that the individual is guaranteed under the *Charter*.

Some also see plea bargaining as secretive *deal-making* because the deals often happen between the Crown and defence lawyer behind closed doors, which could result in an unjust outcome. Although there is efficiency in avoiding a cost-prohibitive trial, plea bargaining is also criticized as being an informal and hurried affair that can compromise justice for marginalized defendants. In such situations, the defendant may not be made fully aware of what is happening, what their rights are, or what the legal repercussions of a guilty plea may include. Plea bargaining, in short, may victimize those that the system is charged with protecting.

From a social justice standpoint, there is a real risk of false confessions and false pleas from those individuals who are simply afraid to go through the trial process. Critics also accuse the police and the Crown of overcharging in order to have a negotiation tool later in the process. Some defence lawyers will put a great deal of pressure on their clients to accept a deal that may not be in the accused's best interests for the sake of efficiency or because of the risk involved in a trial. There is also a risk that lawyers who do not believe their clients, who are inexperienced, or who are being underpaid (especially through legal aid) may resort to unfair deals simply to keep the system functioning.

THE *YOUTH CRIMINAL JUSTICE ACT*

When a person who is not legally considered an adult commits a crime, they are treated as a special case. Historically, youths were seen as not having the same level of responsibility and accountability as adults, and thus the Canadian legal system devised a specific body of laws to deal with youth offenders. The *Youth Criminal Justice Act* (*YCJA*) evolved from the *Juvenile Delinquents Act* (*JDA*), which was introduced in Canada in 1908, and the *Young Offenders Act* (*YOA*), which replaced the JDA in 1984. Today, the youth criminal justice system is based upon the principles of accountability, rehabilitation, and crime prevention, as outlined in section 3 of the *Youth Criminal Justice Act*:

3 (1) The following principles apply in this Act:

a. the youth criminal justice system is intended to protect the public by
   i. holding young persons accountable through measures that are proportionate to the seriousness of the offence and the degree of responsibility of the young person,
   ii. promoting the rehabilitation and reintegration of young persons who have committed offences, and
   iii. supporting the prevention of crime by referring young persons to programs or agencies in the community to address the circumstances underlying their offending behaviour.

The *YCJA* applies to young Canadians between 12 and 17 years of age and connects with the *Criminal Code of Canada* through section 140 of the *YCJA*, which states that:

> Except to the extent that it is inconsistent with or excluded by this *Act*, the provisions of the *Criminal Code* apply, with any modifications that the circumstances require, in respect of offences alleged to have been committed by young persons.

A separate system is set up for young offenders because they have different needs than adult offenders. This age requirement is also important for sentencing as section 76(2) of the *YCJA* states that "[no] young person who is under the age of 18 years is to serve any portion of the imprisonment in a provincial correctional facility for adults or a penitentiary." The *YCJA* maintains that all matters including those under the age of 18 years should be disposed of in a special system of youth court, and sentences should be served with other young people. This includes crimes committed while the offender was under the age of 18 even if the individual turns 18 years of age during the proceeding.

Provincial court judges in youth court have the same powers as judges hearing summary matters under the *Criminal Code*, and a superior court judge has the same powers as a superior court of criminal jurisdiction. Many rights are the same as in an adult criminal court as the young person has the right to retain and instruct counsel without delay. However, young persons also have the right to speak with an adult before making a statement to the police and to have that adult (and counsel) present when their statement is made or while they are in court. Statements cannot be used against the young person unless the ramifications of giving that statement were explained in language appropriate to the young person's age and understanding.

Under the *YCJA*, the goal is to reduce the incarceration of young people before trial. A judge is presumed to release the young person into the community, and incarceration before trial should be the exception (unless the youth committed a particularly violent offence). The government (in Ontario through the Ministry of Children, Community and Social Services) provides resources for families dealing with a youth in conflict with the law.

Box 10.6: Youth Justice Denied: The Case of Ashley Smith

Even though there are multiple protections for young people, there are many young people who are not served by the justice system. One of these young persons was Ashley Smith, who died from asphyxiation at the Grand Valley Institute (GVI) for Women in Kitchener, Ontario. She was only 19 years old at the time of her death in 2007, and the inquest that followed showed that guards watched and recorded her last moments as she lay dying for 45 minutes.

Ms. Smith received a relatively short sentence as a young offender, but because of disciplinary infractions that she incurred during her stay, she remained in custody. On her 18th birthday, the Crown Attorney applied to transfer her to an adult facility; she was ultimately transferred 17 times between 8 institutions over 11 months. Ms. Smith was strip-searched, cavity-searched, pepper-sprayed, and tasered during her time in incarceration. Ms. Smith spent more than 1,000 days in **segregation** away from other inmates. She was forced to take medication and was only permitted to talk to mental health practitioners through the food slot in her door.

Although healthcare officials said that Ms. Smith had various mental illnesses, some believe that she was not properly diagnosed. While her sentence was for just one month, she was accused of participating in over 800 incidents while she was in foster homes, and she continued to be charged with new offences. Ms. Smith tried to harm herself more than 150 times, but these events were also subject to discipline. Her one-month sentence turned into four years before her death.

Ms. Smith's family sued Corrections Canada for $11 million dollars in 2011 and settled the action for an undisclosed sum. The warden at her last facility was fired, leading to two inquests by the Ontario Coroner, raising doubts about the warden's competence. Although the first inquest ended with a mistrial, the second inquest concluded in 2013 with a verdict of homicide. As of the time of writing, no individual or institution was found responsible; however, Ms. Smith's death did result in discussions about how to help other mentally ill young people in the justice system.

Although there have been recent attempts at legislation through Bill C-83 (*An Act to amend the Corrections and Conditional Release Act and another Act*) to end "indefinite segregation," Ms. Smith's family maintains that renaming segregation as "structured intervention" is simply segregation with another name (and provides no more mental health supports). Bill C-83 received royal assent in June 2019, but *Global News* reported that Ashley's Smith's family was said to be "furious" over the new bill and continues to call for justice for Ms. Smith (Wright, 2019).

POLICING IN CANADA

Policing is the most publicly visible component of the criminal justice system. Police officers patrol the streets of the communities in which we live, and police activity is often in the news. The role played by police in responding to public calls for assistance, attending to emergencies, and engaging in patrols is fundamental to the process of crime control, law enforcement, and keeping the peace (Banton, 2005). Policing takes numerous forms, from street patrols to detective work on unsolved cases that usually involve serious crimes, to preventative efforts targeting online pedophile activity, for example, to policing threats to national security, which in Canada is operated by the Canadian Security Intelligence Service (CSIS). Yet policing remains one of the most controversial and divisive practices in our society. Since police officers are endowed with extraordinary powers to conduct searches, detain, and arrest people; carry weapons; and use lethal force, they play a uniquely challenging and often troubling role in society. The police also perform a variety of social service–type activities beyond dealing with criminal matters, such as being called to traffic accidents, attending to noise violations, dealing with teenage unruliness, and addressing public drunkenness, among others. The police also attend to matters of a sensitive and complex nature such as domestic violence, drug overdose cases, and mental health calls where individuals are engaging in self-harm or attempting suicide.

Is policing merely the enforcement of law for the purposes of crime control, or do police forces engage in a type of order maintenance that benefits the lives of certain people and disadvantages others? Does policing activity actually result in lowering crime rates and creating safer communities? Are policing practices on the cusp of change or will the traditional paramilitary structure of policing remain the same as it has been for the past 100 years? Insofar as the very institution of policing has come under greater scrutiny in the early 21st century such questions are essential for a critical understanding of current and future policing.

In the words of scholars ...

Some modern nations have been police states: all, however, are policed so-cieties.... The policed society is unique in that central power exercises pot-entially violent supervision over the population by bureaucratic means widely diffused throughout civil society in small and discretionary operations that are capable of rapid concentration.

Allan Silver, "The Demand for Order in Civil Society." 2005

A Brief History of Policing in Canada

Since ancient times, those who ruled have attempted to establish public order through the enforcement of laws, codes of conduct, and punishments. Policing in Canada is based on the English policing system, which originally was actual community responsibility where able-bodied men would respond to those who disrupted public order, in a system known as **hue and cry**. In the absence of state-funded police forces, it was the role of individual members of the community to be responsible for neighbourhood safety in what was known as the **frankpledge system**. Organized police forces that we know today emerged in England with the rise of the Industrial Revolution. Increasing wealth and private property meant that increased tax revenue could be used to fund police forces, many of which were used to quell dissent and protests among workers and others who were disadvantaged by the inequalities emerging in the industrial society. The formation of early police forces was initially resisted by members of the public but supported by the wealthy class who welcomed the protection of their private property offered by police forces.

Box 10.7: Public Backlash against Lethal Force: Black Lives Matter and the Quest to Modernize Policing

Police officers are empowered by law and by training to use lethal force in the course of fulfilling their duties as enforcers of the law (Miller, 2015). The use of force when apprehending a suspect is a normal part of police practice. The type and level of force used is based on a combination of police training methods of apprehension and techniques of incapacitation, along with officer discretion. In numerous cases across North America and around the world, police officers have often abused this discretionary power in numerous ways including detaining and harassing members of the public, racial profiling, over-policing certain areas, carding racialized individuals, and using lethal force. In May 2020, in numerous cities across the globe, public demonstrations protested police killings of Black men. While the uprising was sparked by the killing of George Floyd by Minneapolis police, racialized violence at the hands of the police has a long history. The protests that ensued following the death of George Floyd were led by the Black Lives Matter (BLM) movement. BLM arose circa 2013 in the United States of America as a response to the racist bias inherent in policing practices that have led to numerous killings of Black men.

There have been several notorious cases of police killings of Black men involving the unjust use of lethal force. The 1991 case of Rodney King, who was brutally beaten by police following a high-speed chase by the Los Angeles Police Department, serves as the hallmark example of how public outrage against police brutality has become an almost regular event following cases of police violence. In the book *Policing the Planet*, the authors link the increase of zero-tolerance type police patrols to the problem of mass incarceration of Black youth and the increasing level of racial profiling and lethal policing tactics. The authors argue that "broken windows policing has become the political expression of neoliberalism at the urban scale ... [and, the authors also] ... consider the struggle against racism, militarism and capital—the policing of the planet—as a central political challenge of our times" (Camp & Heatherton, 2016, p. 2). The spring 2020 protest movement against anti-Black police brutality drew connections between the increase of militarized policing practices and the ongoing problem of racism in society. Since policing is an expression of order maintenance, many social justice activists see police practices as the continuation of injustice associated with slavery and colonialism. These activists argue that the quest to correct racial injustices for a better future requires raising public awareness about the history of racial discrimination by institutional authorities, as well as a radical reformulation of police use-of-force practices, a redirection of police funding towards social services, and a more inclusive form of police engagement with the communities they aim to serve.

The establishment of policing in Canada was largely influenced by the geographical expansiveness of the country and the impact of European settlement. While Indigenous communities "already had systems of social control as well as mechanisms for sanctioning against violations of customary law ... these systems were gradually displaced by British law" (Griffiths, 2007, p. 12). In addition, sparsely populated settler outposts far from major cities were difficult to police. Many regions in Quebec and Ontario were policed by haphazard forces composed of night watchmen and other, often corrupt, poorly paid, disorganized law enforcers. In 1873, a national force, what we now know as the Royal Canadian Mounted Police (RCMP), was formed to establish state presence in remote places far from the range of urban police forces. By the early 1900s, the organization and structure of policing that we have today was becoming more established. Some provinces and territories still use the services of the RCMP while Newfoundland and Labrador, Quebec, and Ontario have their own provincial forces, and most cities have their own police force.

Box 10.8: Understanding Policing—Binary Thinking versus Constellation Thinking

The theorist Michel Foucault pointed out how systems of power maintain social order by organizing the world into simple *binary* categories such as good/evil, right/wrong, nature/nurture. Such binaries simplify the complexity of the social world and influence how people perceive it. Social phenomena are far more complex than is indicated by the false dichotomies inherent in binary forms of thinking. In contrast to a limited binary perspective, a constellation perspective allows us to understand matters relating to crime, deviance, and social control more comprehensively as phenomena with multiple factors that exist in a dynamic interrelation. Let us take the controversial example of policing to explain. Policing is often understood in two basic ways:

1. as the basis of law enforcement necessary for public safety and the maintenance of law and order; or
2. as the expression of the repressive power of the state resulting in racial and class oppression.

While both of these views have some degree of validity, they do not convey the full reality of factors that are part of the complexity of policing. For example:

*   media reports often fail to explain policing from the standpoint of police officers who deal with violent, traumatized, deceptive, disturbed, and often difficult people on a regular basis;

- policing is a profession with very high levels of stress that leads to high rates of post-traumatic stress and suicide among officers;
- policing today goes beyond dealing with crime and traffic control and increasingly involves cybercrime, surveillance, and counter-terrorism;
- the police are under constant pressure by the public to maintain order and safety, and they are criticized both when they fail to apprehend criminals and also when they go too far in their attempts to do so;
- within the police force itself, there is a strong subculture that officers are compelled to obey and it is one that is often resistant to change, which further exerts pressure on officers;
- policing is a historically patriarchal institution aiming to be more inclusive by hiring more women and culturally diverse people, but recruiting from these groups has been difficult;
- sexual harassment, homophobia, and racism are ongoing problems experienced by police officers themselves;
- the police use and abuse of lethal force comprises a small percentage of police activity; and
- fighting crime is only one dimension of overall police activity, as administrative tasks and tedious "paperwork" have increased substantially in the past few decades.

These points do not invalidate the claim that the abuse of police powers and the killing of innocents is a serious problem; nor do they negate the reality that law enforcement officers do substantial, important work maintaining public order and safety. The points serve to illustrate that a full understanding of any phenomena having to do with crime and society has many sides to it. A *critical understanding* of matters relating to crime and control involves much more than subjective alignment with emotionally charged and limited categories of judgment; it involves seeing such matters in their multifaceted complexity. Rather than being detached observers of social life, social researchers are encouraged by sociologists such as Max Weber to employ the practice of *verstehen*, which asks one to try to identify with the position of the people one is studying through empathetic understanding. In the case of police powers, that means empathetic understanding towards both police officers and the civilians they interact with.

Police Practices and the Maintenance of Order

While early policing was largely focused on enforcement efforts against labour un-rest, property crimes, harassment of immigrants, petty offences such as vagrancy, and moral violations and vice crimes perpetrated by the so-called dangerous classes, eventually police forces had to turn their attention towards more serious crime control. Troubling rates of violent crime in many cities compelled citizens to demand order and civility within their communities (Silver, 1992). While the *enforcement of law* and the *maintenance of order* have long been key mandates as-sociated with policing, some have asked, "whose law" and "what type of order"? Ericson asks: "How do the police spend their time? What do they concentrate on and what do they ignore?... Whose interests are served by these outcomes?... What wider functions of the police can be theorized from this? (Ericson, 1992, p. 165). Critical studies of policing indicate that the police, when engaging in the discretionary process of selective crime control, also engage in a larger social order maintenance function: they function to secure the boundaries of existing power structures in society, thereby maintaining economic and political hierarchies, as well as social divisions of race, class, and gender, often through repressive means. In the post-9/11 era, policing in many parts of the world has become increasingly militarized and has extended into matters of national security (Kraska, 2001). Re-cently, as in the virtually worldwide public protests against police abuse of lethal force in the spring of 2020, the repressive aspect of police activity has come under unprecedented levels of public scrutiny, so much so that changes in the nature and structure of policing are being demanded.

Box 10.9: Policing beyond the Streets: The Security State and International Espionage

Thoughts of policing generally bring to mind street-level patrols; however, policing practices also take place at higher levels in terms of securing against domestic and foreign threats to security. Security and other high-level threats policed by the Canadian Security Intelligence Service (CSIS), the Communications Security Establishment (CSE), and affiliated authorities include the funding of terrorist groups and the risk of terrorist attacks; the theft of state and military secrets; the impact of monies gained from criminal activity (known as the *proceeds of crime*); foreign threats to industry and cybercrime; and threats to government authorities, among others. Such threats are policed in a preventative manner by the gathering of secret information known as intelligence that state agents will collect covertly, often through espionage, otherwise known as spy activities.

The state has an obligation to protect its citizens from harm. In the post-9/11 era the matter of *securitization* has become a primary concern because it raises the debate about liberty versus security. Should citizens be asked to sacrifice some of their basic liberties and freedoms in order to secure against threats to life? What measures should be adopted to safeguard human lives in the name of security? Beyond criminal law, the political state creates law designed to protect against security threats from foreign and domestic adversaries. For example, following the attacks of September 11, 2001, the Canadian government enacted

> the *Anti-terrorism Act* (*ATA*), [which] amended the *Criminal Code*, the *Official Secrets Act*, the *Canada Evidence Act*, the *Proceeds of Crime (Money Laundering) Act* and a number of other Acts. It also enacted the *Charities Registration (Security Information) Act*. It was not a stand-alone Act, but rather an amending statute. The *ATA* formed a key component of the Government's Anti-terrorism Plan, which had four objectives:
>
> • to prevent terrorists from getting into Canada and protect Canadians from terrorist acts;
> • to activate tools to identify, prosecute, convict, and punish terrorists;
> • to keep the Canada–U.S. border secure and a contributor to economic security; and
> • to work with the international community to bring terrorists to justice and address the root causes of violence. (Department of Justice, 2017)

Anti-terrorist and security protections have become substantial components of high-level policing, so much so that the Canadian government has spent approximately $1 billion on a "spy palace" (Weston, 2013). This state-of-the-art facility is touted as "the largest repository of top-secret information in Canada" and serves as headquarters for both CSE and CSIS (CSE, 2014). Such developments are evidence of the security focus of government and policing in the post-9/11 era, which has contributed to the transformation of the traditional political state into a **hypersecurity state**. Increased levels of surveillance and heightened security measures at airports, borders, and numerous other public spaces are signs of securitization. These measures place the practice of policing closer to that of the military insofar as state agents are now engaged in a new form of asymmetrical war with clandestine enemies (Colaguori & Torres, 2011). Policing terrorism is "controversial and divisive" insofar as it raises concerns about the use of torture, extraordinary rendition, racial profiling, arbitrary detention of those deemed to be suspects, and the compiling of no-fly lists—all of which have contributed to substantial human rights violations on a global scale (Colaguori & Torres, 2011, p. 291).

The Challenges and the Future of Policing

As long as there is criminal activity, violent interactions among people, and threats to peaceful order, there will be an argument for maintaining policing. Along with crime prevention techniques and informal social controls, policing remains a structural component of societal efforts to maintain public safety and respond to emergencies. As indicated above, the institution of policing is complex, contradictory, and controversial. At one level, the police are mandated to serve and protect the public, but historically policing is "an exercise of control, [that] fundamentally consists of privilege" (McCormick & Visano, 1992, p. xi). Police forces have served the interests of those with power and property, and in many instances (such as the criminalization of dissent) continue to function in the service of the repressive power of the state.

Police officers are drawn from the ranks of the public, require specialized training, and face special challenges in performing their duties and responsibilities with care. The job of policing is difficult, and many police officers suffer from mental and psychological problems, including post-traumatic stress disorder and suicide. Policing, like law, is compelled to adapt to reflect new social realities and new priorities. The growth of cybercrime and the sexual trafficking of minors, for example, has prompted police forces to develop new crime prevention strategies. Maintaining the rules of due process means that police officers need to be especially diligent with paperwork and the note-taking that is part of the administrative side of the job. Many police forces are now having officers wear body cameras to ensure accountability and to record video evidence of public encounters. There are also suggestions to deputize social workers to assist police officers with sensitive matters such as dealing with disruptions involving individuals who are mentally ill.

Policing has evolved substantially from its early inception in Canada and more changes lie ahead. Contemporary policing no longer exclusively consists of government-funded public policing. Private police and security firms have become increasingly common. Police efforts to control crime and create safe communities are most effective when they include the "willing participation of the public, therefore police should transform communities from being passive consumers of police protection to active co-producers of public safety" (Bayley & Shearing, 2005, pp. 716–717). With this in mind, next-generation police forces would do well to swear in officers from within the communities they serve, including women, LGBTQ+ individuals, and people who represent the racial and cultural diversity of those same communities.

THE PRISON SYSTEM IN CANADA: CORRECTIONS

A custodial sentence is imposed to physically separate an offender from society as punishment for their proven crimes. Incarceration is expensive and the highest form of coercive punishment, but it seeks to prevent the offender from re-offending for the time they are incapacitated. A sentence of less than 30 days is often served in a local detention centre, while a sentence of less than two years' imprisonment will be served at a provincial correctional facility or jail. A sentence of two years plus a day usually means a sentence at a federal penitentiary. Multiple sentences may be served concurrently (at the same time, and the most common option) or consecutively (one sentence after the other).

Individuals awaiting trial without bail and those serving sentences in provincial institutions are spread throughout the provinces' correctional facilities. For example, in Ontario, the provincial institutions include the Algoma Treatment and Remand Centre in Sault Ste. Marie; the Central East Correctional Centre in Lindsay; the Central North Correctional Centre in Penetanguishene; Maplehurst Correctional Complex in Milton; Monteith Correctional Complex in Monteith; the Ontario Correctional Institute in Brampton; the St. Lawrence Valley Correctional and Treatment Centre in Brockville; the Thunder Bay Correctional Centre in Thunder Bay; and the Vanier Centre for Women in Milton. Having so few institutions over a large geographical area means hardships for families who may have to engage in significant travel to see loved ones.

Today, there are relatively few federal penitentiaries spread throughout Canada, which can cause even more geographical problems for families of those serving a federal sentence. In 2020, there were approximately 58 federal institutions spread across Canada in the Atlantic, Quebec, Ontario, Prairies, and Pacific regions. These prisons include six maximum security institutions; four facilities for women at various levels of security (the notorious Prison for Women in Kingston Penitentiary closed on July 6, 2000); eight multi-level institutions; seven traditional Healing Lodges and Centres; and two maximum-/medium-, fifteen medium-, three medium-/minimum-, and thirteen minimum-security prisons.

Racial disparities in the offender population in federal and provincial institutions is a matter of pressing concern. As of 2016, Statistics Canada identified that almost 1.7 million people identified as Aboriginal (First Nations Peoples, Métis, or Inuit), which is a 4.9 percent share of the total population in Canada (Statistics Canada, n.d.). However, Indigenous offenders represented 24 percent of the 2017–2018 total federal offender population. From 2008–2009 to 2017–2018, the in-custody Indigenous offender population increased by 43.3 percent, while the total Indigenous offender population increased by 45.7 percent in the same period. The number of in-custody Indigenous women offenders increased from 168 in 2008–2009 to 270 in 2017–2018, for an increase of 60.7 percent in 10 years (Public Safety Canada Portfolio Corrections Statistics Committee, 2018). Clark's 2019 report to the Department of Justice Canada asks, "Why are Indigenous people so vastly overrepresented as offenders and victims? The Royal Commission on Aboriginal Peoples (RCAP) identified three viable explanations, each of which has currency in government thinking and academic literature: colonialism, socio-economic marginalization, and culture clash. Systemic discrimination against Indigenous people in the criminal justice system is also a serious problem. These factors have acted together over many years" (p. 16).

The Impact of Imprisonment

Offenders deal with extremely serious repercussions of imprisonment, including increased risk of violence, homicide, and infectious diseases. In addition, society, families, employment, and economic and social interactions change over time while the offender is segregated. Evolving gender and social roles impact offenders when they are released back into society. Prison overcrowding and psychological impacts may increase the harm caused in incarceration, not to mention the social stigma and practical limitations imposed when one is released. It is important to remember that, with few exceptions, almost everyone is released. For this reason, judges are urged to consider incarceration as a last resort among sentencing tools.

Cruel and Unusual Punishment: The Issue of Prisoners' Rights

The writer Fyodor Dostoyevsky famously said that a society can be judged by the way it treats its prisoners. That ethical stance is directly relevant to the issue of prisoners' rights and the administrative operation of correctional institutions. Inhumane prison conditions are a problem in Canada, as evidenced at the maximum-security Correctional Facility in Edmonton, Alberta. An *Edmonton Journal* report reads, "In 2018, Correctional Service Canada (CSC) said 11 Edmonton Institution staffers had been fired, suspended or quit voluntarily following workplace misconduct allegations ranging from harassment to alleged sexual assault against colleagues ..." and further, "In recent years, the Edmonton Max has had the highest number of inmate-on-inmate assaults of Canada's maximum security prisons, in addition to the highest number of use of force incidents involving guards and the highest number of inmates engaging in self-harm" (Wakefield, 2020). The appalling conditions for inmates and staff at the Edmonton Institution was most recently exposed in a report by Dr. Ivan Zinger (2019), a Correctional Investigator for Correctional Service Canada.

First among Zinger's conclusions was that the "protected status inmates," or inmates who were to be segregated from other members of the population, were treated to inhumane living conditions including having things thrown at them (food, liquids, and bodily substances) when the individual would walk through the institution. Prison staff were told to ignore the "assaultive and intimidating behaviour" and did not intervene to stop the assailants (Zinger, 2019, p. 36). The report found that even though senior management knew of this behaviour, they did nothing, thus allowing the inmates to continue to assault others with impunity (Zinger, 2019).

Ultimately, 24 inmates were charged with attacking vulnerable others using "assaultive, degrading and humiliating behaviour," leading the investigator to conclude that no "human being, regardless of their status or crime, deserves to be treated in such a cruel and unusual manner" (p. 37). The report found that the Edmonton Institution had the "highest number of inmate-on-inmate assaults, the highest number of uses of force (including firearms) and the highest number of incidents and individual inmates engaged in self-injurious behaviour" (p. 38). One of the most disturbing allegations was that guards were forcing inmates to assault one another in what became known as a "fight club."

The example of the Edmonton Institution also shines a light on programs that are available to inmates while incarcerated. Members of the public often note how "easy" prison is, and that individuals have more benefits than others in society. However, the stark conditions at this institution were noted in its annual report.

Inmates ate all meals in their cells (which are described as the size of a parking space), group classes were offered once a week for a cell block, and the classrooms were not used because there were no overhead catwalks to provide gun coverage in classrooms. There was no library or librarian. Vocational studies were no longer provided after the closure of the metal fabrication shop in 2015, and confinement to the cells was the norm. The Correctional Investigator concluded that, in failing to provide work and living conditions that are "safe and free of practices that undermine human dignity, the Service is in breach of *Charter* protections and other statutory human rights obligations" and that the recurrent nature of these allegations "required immediate intervention" (p. 39).

In addition to the treatment of the inmates, there were also issues with how the staff treated each other. It was found that 96 percent of employees had experienced conflict in their workplace; 17 current employees had been sexually assaulted by a co-worker, while 23 percent reported being sexually harassed by a co-worker. More than half of those surveyed said they worked in a culture of fear, and 60 percent of employees had experienced violence in the workplace (p. 34). The report warned that a workplace that "runs on fear, reprisal, and intimidation is highly dysfunctional; it is the antithesis of modeling appropriate offender behaviour.... If staff disrespect, [or] humiliate ... each other one can only imagine how they might treat prisoners" (p. 33).

Box 10.10: Is Solitary Confinement Over?

On April 20, 2020, the Office of Public Safety and the Attorney General announced that, after five years of litigation, the government would be abandoning an appeal to the Supreme Court of Canada about solitary confinement. The appeal sought to overturn lower court decisions seeking to end solitary confinement, a practice that had been revealed to last months or even years for some inmates. The government filed documents to wholly discontinue the appeal.

Since 2015, groups have been pushing to show the psychological damage caused by long periods of solitary confinement. Documented trauma includes "paranoia, psychosis, heart palpitations, eating disorders, permanent difficulty coping with social interaction, self-harm, and suicide" (White, 2020). The death of Ashley Smith was mentioned as an impetus for this sizable shift in policy; Smith died following more than 1,000 days in solitary confinement (see box 10.6). It is recommended that solitary confinement be for no more than 15 days, and that it not be used at all with certain vulnerable populations. The government said that the new "structured intervention" outlined in Bill C-83 (discussed above), which called for at least four hours outside of a cell and two hours of "meaningful human interaction," was no longer akin to solitary confinement (White, 2020). Critics wish to ascertain whether these guidelines and the alleged prohibition of extended solitary confinement are honoured in Canada's prisons.

MISCARRIAGES OF JUSTICE: THE PROBLEM OF WRONGFUL CONVICTIONS

Public faith in the Canadian justice system is generally strong, yet many people fail to recognize that the justice system itself can be an instrument of grave injustice, especially when it punishes those who are innocent of any wrongdoing. It has been estimated in Canada that approximately 20 percent of all DNA-based exonerations involve false confessions. These numbers likely fall short of capturing the full numbers of false confessions as it is difficult to determine conclusively that a confessor is innocent. Interrogations are inherently stressful, and the potential for abuse involved in breaking down the will of another in interrogations is well documented. Since the 1966 case of *Miranda v Arizona*, the US Supreme Court has recognized that "even without employing brutality, [or] the 'third degree' ... the very fact of custodial interrogation exacts a heavy toll on individual liberty and trades on the weakness of individuals" (*Miranda*, 1966, p. 455).

The techniques used by police in the course of interrogations, and the methods used by officers when questioning a suspect, are the focal point for an analysis of false confessions. Police officers try to persuade a suspect to confess because the denial of the crime is considered undesirable, while a confession is considered successful. The pressure on officers to obtain confessions from suspects sometimes leads officers to resort to coercive interrogation tactics, which have the potential to lead to false confessions. The impact on vulnerable populations is potentially catastrophic. Research shows that having a confession (false or otherwise) causes police to investigate less. Additionally, if a suspect confesses, crown attorneys are more likely to charge the maximum number of offences, prosecutors are less willing to offer or accept a plea bargain, and bail is more difficult to obtain. A confession decreases the likelihood of an acquittal, defence lawyers are less likely to advise their clients to plead not guilty, and juries overwhelmingly convict where there is a confession (Kassin & Neumann, 1997). In a study of 125 wrongful conviction cases by Steven Drizin and Richard Leo, "more than four-fifths (81%) of the innocent defendants who chose to take their case to trial were wrongfully convicted 'beyond a reasonable doubt' even though their confession was ultimately demonstrated to be false" (2004, pp. 922–923).

One of the main catalysts for a false confession arises from the use of the "Reid Technique" method of interrogation, a widely used and highly coercive police technique. The literature notes bias from the outset as the method assumes that the subject of the interrogation is guilty, and the method can produce "false confessions [which are] one of the leading causes of wrongful convictions" (Moore & Fitzsimmons, 2011, p. 509). The techniques taught to state interrogators are often flawed, and the basis of these interrogations has been proven faulty by empirical evidence.

The potentially damaging effects of police interrogation techniques serve to exacerbate institutional injustices that are a part of the colonial legacy forming the foundation of law in Canada. When coercive policing techniques are used on marginalized and disempowered suspects in the criminal law context, cultural groups, such as Indigenous people, are disproportionately affected. Little is published on this important topic, but with the over-incarceration of Indigenous offenders in Canada, it is a subject that needs further study (Clark, 2019). Suspects who are vulnerable due to a lack of adequate legal representation as a result of systemic injustice need extra accommodations in the interrogation process. Addressing systemic discrimination within Canadian jurisprudence and case law is an issue that continues to demand attention in both sociolegal research and practice.

CONCLUSION

The criminal justice system is one of the most important institutions in our society. It is designed to ensure justice as well as to protect citizens from criminal harm, but it does not always accomplish these aims. As a result of ongoing attempts at improving the efficiency and accuracy of the justice system, the system of law that furnishes its order of operations is constantly revisited. While some fundamental concepts, such as the rule of law, remain intact, other legal concepts and procedures will undergo changes. Among the social forces that influence the evolution of criminal law is the activist quest for social justice and equity among marginalized and disadvantaged members of society. The increasing focus, on a global scale, of the value of human rights is also a prominent factor that exerts force on the direction and application of law and the operation of the justice system.

Understanding how criminal law defines crime, and operates to control criminal behaviour, is essential for criminologists. Criminology as a discipline also needs to keep abreast of changes in criminal law and policy, as well as the larger world of rights-based activism that points to the future of a more just society.

REVIEW QUESTIONS

1. What are the institutional elements of the criminal justice system in Canada and what are their primary functions?
2. What are the legal elements of a crime? Explain with definitions of the main concepts.
3. What are some of the ongoing controversies that exist within the operation of criminal law and the criminal justice system? Explain with examples.

GLOSSARY

adversarial system: A system where disputes between parties are decided by an impartial individual after hearing the evidence presented to the court by a representative of each of the parties.

beyond a reasonable doubt: The standard of proof required in criminal law. The Crown must prove all elements of a crime to this standard (*mens rea*, *actus reus*, etc.).

burden of proof: The duty, usually of the state, to prove the charge against the accused.

civil law: A system of law based on the Roman tradition.

common law: The law that comes from the decisions of the court recorded in law reporters. Often called "judge-made" law, it is often a written decision where the judge explains their reasoning in the case. Also refers to the body of law derived from judicial decision.

cruel and unusual punishment: Punishment that is degrading, torturous, disproportional, or shocking to the community, making it inappropriate.

division of powers: Provisions of the *Constitution Act* that dictate that the criminal law is under the jurisdiction of the federal government.

due process: The principle that the court system must act according to the legal processes recognized by Parliament and the Courts in Canada.

frankpledge system: A type of community policing that existed in medieval Britain, under which individual members of the community were responsible for crime control and the apprehension of offenders to ensure neighbourhood safety.

hue and cry: The act of calling out publicly for the immediate assistance of others to apprehend someone caught in the act of committing a crime or fleeing a crime scene.

hybrid offence: A crime that is tried either summarily or by indictment at the option of the prosecution.

hypersecurity state: The shift in the priorities of the political state away from liberty to that of security, which takes place through an increase in the use of surveillance, the coercive monitoring of those deemed security threats, new interpretations of the rules of warfare, and an erosion of citizenship rights.

indictable offence: A crime that is tried by way of "indictment," which is considered more serious than a summary offence and can have punishments up to and including life in prison.

indictment: A legal document that sets out the formal charges the accused is facing.

inferior courts (also called *lower courts*): Courts that are established by provincial and territorial governments.

information: A document that alleges an accused person committed a criminal offence.

judicial activism: The accusation that a court has engaged in making the law (perhaps for policy reasons) rather than simply interpreting the law and applying it to the case.

legal pluralism: The existence of a plurality of legal systems within a particular national jurisdiction, which usually consists of pre- and postcolonial systems of law.

letter of the law: The literal interpretation of how a law is written and what it actually says, as opposed to interpretations and applications of the law that violate the original intention of the law, or the *spirit of the law.*

lex talionis: "an eye for an eye, a tooth for a tooth"; otherwise known as the *law of retaliation*, which comes from the Code of Hammurabi. It forms the basis of many of the attempts to create an ordered and just society using the power of legal authority.

miscarriage of justice: A grossly unfair result in a judicial matter that produces a conviction despite an absence of evidence on an essential elements of a crime.

nulla poena sine lege: A Latin phrase that translates as "there is no punishment without a law."

parliamentary supremacy: The doctrine that Parliament is the lawmaker, and this ability cannot be overridden, even by the courts.

precedent: Deciding like cases in similar ways as a method of predictability.

quasi criminal: An offence created by provincial law, which carries a penalty similar to criminal law.

regulatory offence: A term that describes a wide variety of wrongs established by statute to regulate in the areas of health, convenience, safety, and the general welfare of the public. The Crown is not required to fully prove the element of *mens rea* as they would an offence in the *Criminal Code*.

retribution: A sanction (historically physical punishment) representing the moral blameworthiness of the offender.

rule of law: The doctrine that no person is above the law. The supremacy of law over arbitrary power.

segregation: Isolating a prisoner away from the general population. This type of punishment is considered more restrictive and deprives the individual of liberty, as many "privileges" can be taken from the individual while segregated.

style of cause: The name of the case, which includes all parties involved (including the state who is represented by the Crown).

summary offence: A crime that is tried "summarily," which is considered less serious and has a less punitive sentence (under $5,000 fine and/or two years less a day incarceration).

superior courts: Courts established under section 96 of the *Constitution Act, 1867* that deal with more serious crime.

victim impact statement: A written statement from the victim describing harm done and losses (physical, emotional, mental) suffered by the victim because of the offence.

wrongful conviction: A conviction that did not properly come from a judicial determination of guilt (because of a coerced statement, fabrication of evidence, improper use of the justice system, etc.).

REFERENCES

Anderson, D., & Anderson, B. (2009). *Manufacturing guilt: Wrongful convictions in Canada* (2nd ed.). Fernwood Publishing.

Banton, W. (2005). The police as peace officers. In T. Newburn (Ed.), *Policing: Key readings* (pp. 132–140). Routledge.

Bayley, D. H., & Shearing, C. D. (2005). The future of policing. In T. Newburn (Ed.), *Policing: Key readings* (pp. 715–732). Routledge.

Blackstone, W. (1836). *Commentaries on the laws of England.* Sweet, Maxwell, and Stevens & Sons. (Original work published 1753)

Camp, J. T., & Heatherton, C. (2016). *Policing the planet: Why the policing crisis led to Black Lives Matter.* Verso.

Clark, S. (2019). *Overrepresentation of Indigenous people in the Canadian criminal justice system: Causes and responses.* Research and Statistics Division, Department of Justice Canada. Retrieved from https://www.justice.gc.ca/eng/rp-pr/jr/oip-cjs/oip-cjs-en.pdf

Clarke, S. R., & Sheppard, H. P. (1882). *A treatise on the criminal law of Canada.* Hart & Company.

Colaguori, C. (2016). The agony of injustice: The adversarial trial, wrongful convictions and the agon of law. *International Journal of Criminology and Sociological Theory, 9*(2), 1–10.

Colaguori, C., & Torres, C. (2011). Policing terrorism in the post 9/11 era: Critical challenges and concerns. In L. Tepperman & A. Kalyta (Eds.), *Reading sociology: Canadian perspectives* (2nd ed.). Oxford University Press.

Communications Security Establishment [CSE]. (2014, September 4). *New CSE headquarters.* Government of Canada. Retrieved from https://www.cse-cst.gc.ca/en/careers-carrieres/csec-cstc/headquarters-installation

Department of Justice. (2017, July 26). *About the Anti-terrorism Act.* Government of Canada. Retrieved from https://www.justice.gc.ca/eng/cj-jp/ns-sn/act-loi.html

Department of Justice. (2018, October 16). *Spotlight on* Gladue*: Challenges, experiences, and possibilities in Canada's criminal justice system.* Government of Canada. Retrieved from https://www.justice.gc.ca/eng/rp-pr/jr/gladue/p4.html

Drizin, S. A., & Leo, R. A. (2004). The problem of false confessions in the post-DNA world. *North Carolina Law Review, 82,* 891–1007.

Ericson, R. V. (1992). The police as reproducers of order. In K. R. E. McCormick & L. A. Visano (Eds.), *Understanding policing* (pp. 163–208). Canadian Scholars.

Griffiths, C. T. (2007). *Canadian police work* (3rd ed.). Nelson.

Hogg, P. W., & Zwibel, C. F. (2005). The rule of law in the Supreme Court of Canada. *University of Toronto Law Journal, 55*(3), 715–732.

Kassin, S. M., & Neumann, K. (1997). On the power of confession evidence: An experimental test of the fundamental difference hypothesis. *Law and Human Behavior, 21*(5), 469–484. https://doi.org/10.1023/A:1024871622490

Kraska, P. B. (Ed.). (2001). *Militarizing the American criminal justice system: The changing roles of the armed forces and the police.* Northeastern University Press.

Macklem, P. (2014). Indigenous Peoples and the ethos of legal pluralism in Canada. SSRN. https://dx.doi.org/10.2139/ssrn.2403909

Manning, M., & Sankoff, P. (2015). *Criminal law* (5th ed.). LexisNexis Canada.

McCormick, K. R. E., & Visano, L. A. (Eds.). (1992). *Understanding policing.* Canadian Scholars.

Miller, L. (2015). Why cops kill: The psychology of police deadly force encounters. In *Aggression and Violent Behaviour* (pp. 97–111). Elsevier Science.

Moore, T. E., & Fitzsimmons, L. C. (2011). Justice imperiled: False confessions and the Reid technique. *Criminal Law Quarterly, 57*(4), 509–542. https://www.researchgate .net/publication/255686705_Justice_Imperiled_False_confessions_and_the_Reid_ technique

Packer, H. L. (1964). Two models of the criminal process. *University of Pennsylvania Law Review, 113*(1), 1–68.

Packer, H. L. (1968). *The limits of the criminal sanction*. Stanford University Press.

Public Safety Canada Portfolio Corrections Statistics Committee. (2018). *2018 corrections and conditional release statistical overview*. Public Works and Government Services Canada. Retrieved from https://www.publicsafety.gc.ca/cnt/rsrcs/pblctns/ ccrso-2018/index-en.aspx#sectionc1

Roach, K. (1999). Four models of the criminal process. *The Journal of Criminal Law and Criminology, 89*(2), 671–684.

Roach, K., Berger, B. L., Cunliffe, E., & Kiyani, A. G. (2020). *Criminal law and procedure: Cases and materials* (12th ed.). Emond Montgomery Publications.

Silver, A. (1992). The demand for order in civil society. In K. R. E. McCormick & L. A. Visano (Eds.), *Understanding policing* (pp. 72–84). Canadian Scholars.

Silver, A. (2005). The demand for order in civil society. In T. Newburn (Ed.), *Policing: Key readings* (pp. 7–24). Routledge.

Statistics Canada. (n.d.). *Statistics on Indigenous peoples*. Retrieved from https://www .statcan.gc.ca/eng/subjects-start/indigenous_peoples

Waddams, S. M. (1997). *Introduction to the study of law*. Carswell.

Wakefield, J. (2020, February 18). "Feared one another more than inmates": Workplace toxicity persists at Edmonton prison, report finds. *Edmonton Journal*. Retrieved from https://edmontonjournal.com/news/local-news/feared-one-another-more-than- inmates-workplace-toxicity-persists-at-edmonton-prison-report-finds

Weston, G. (2013, October 8). Inside Canada's top-secret billion-dollar spy palace. *CBC News*. Retrieved from https://www.cbc.ca/news/politics/inside-canada-s-top- secret-billion-dollar-spy-palace-1.1930322

White, P. (2020, April 21). Canada abandons solitary confinement appeal to Supreme Court. *The Globe and Mail*. Retrieved from https://www.theglobeandmail.com/ canada/article-canada-abandons-solitary-confinement-appeal-to-supreme-court/

Wright, T. (2019, May 30). Ashley Smith died in solitary confinement. Her family is "furious" over the new segregation bill. *Global News*. Retrieved from https:// globalnews.ca/news/5336592/ashley-smith-solitary-confinement-family/

Zinger, I. (2019). *Annual report 2018–2019*. Office of the Correctional Investigator. Retrieved from https://www.oci-bec.gc.ca/cnt/rpt/pdf/annrpt/annrpt20182019- eng.pdf

Cases

Black-Clawson International Ltd v Papierwerke Waldhof-Aschaffenburg AG, [1975] AC 591.

Fagan v Commissioner of Metropolitan Police, [1969] 1 QB 439.

R v KRJ, [2016] SCJ No 31.

R v Lachance, [1963] 2 CCC 14 (ONCA).

R v Mullins-Johnson, 2007 ONCA 720.

Miranda v Arizona, 84 US 436, 455 (1966).

Legislation

Charter of Rights and Freedoms, Part 1 of the Constitution Act, 1982, being Schedule B to the *Canada Act 1982* (UK), c. 11.

Constitution Act, 1867, 30 & 31 Victoria, c. 3 (U.K.) reprinted in RSC 1985, App II, No 5.

Constitution Act, 1982, Schedule B to the *Canada Act 1982* (UK), 1982, c. 11.

Controlled Drugs and Substances Act, S.C. 1996, c. 19.

Criminal Code of Canada, RSC, 1985, c. C-46.

Federal Courts Act, RSC, 1985, c. F-7.

Interpretation Act, RSC, 1985, c. I-21.

Justices of the Peace Act, RSO 1990, C J4.

Safe Streets and Communities Act, SC 2012, c. 1.

Supreme Court Act, RSC, 1985, c. S-26.

Youth Criminal Justice Act, SC, 2002, c. 1.

CHAPTER 11

Scams, Fraud, and Cybercrime in a Globalized Society

Michael Adorjan and Claudio Colaguori

LEARNING OBJECTIVES

In this chapter, you will learn

- about the varieties of scams and fraudulent activities perpetrated against victims, and how these types of crimes have proliferated to pose major risks for citizens and organizations;
- how the computerization of social life and communications networks have become venues for the commission of various types of criminal activity, creating new criminal opportunities that previously did not exist;
- about traditional types of scams, frauds, and new types of cybercrimes;
- about specific noteworthy cases and examples of fraud, scams, and cybercrimes;
- how cybercrime poses special challenges for law enforcement authorities; and
- how the computerization of global society has created a virtual battleground for nations in conflict with each other.

INTRODUCTION: CRIMINAL SCAMS, FRAUDS, AND THE INTERNET

We live in a **global village**, an interconnected world of instant communication where communicative networks created in **cyberspace** enable social interactions and community building on a global scale. Many of us have become *digital citizens* within this **cyber** global village, yet inter-networks have also greatly facilitated the extent to which criminal activity can occur. Computer scammers can prey on victims in both local and distant contexts. News reports tell us, on an almost daily basis, about the **frauds** and **scams** that have become a normal part of life in the age of the **internet** and **social media**.

Many of us are familiar with being *scammed*, *ripped off*, *swindled*, or *defrauded*. Perhaps you have received an email asking you to assist in acquiring a large monetary inheritance from a foreign stranger, or you may have been deceived into sending a sum of money in advance in order for you to get a portion of a promised substantial inheritance. Perhaps you have been asked to join a **pyramid scheme**, where you give someone a sum of money and are promised a much larger sum of money when new members are recruited for a big pay-out in a promised future. Hopefully you did not get lured in by such emails. People with *malintent* have often devised clever ways of deceiving and taking advantage of others for personal gain. Most often, these types of behaviours are prohibited by law and considered crimes. Deceptions of these sorts have been happening for a long time. In the early 1600s, Zhang Yingyu (1573–1620) published *The Book of Swindles*, outlining tales of scams and deception. Scamming people through manipulation and taking advantage of their vulnerabilities is a pernicious type of wrongdoing that ranges from everyday, seemingly minor acts of deception to serious legal infractions listed in the *Criminal Code* as acts of fraud. In Canada, it is a crime to engage, "by deceit, falsehood, or fraudulent means … [to] defraud the public or any person … of any property, money, or valuable security or any service" (Government of Canada, 2021). Scams and frauds often involve predatory criminality, and they may take the form of financial crimes, such as the attempt to **extort** money from people by pretending to be a government official; violent forms of criminal harassment, such as **cyberbullying**; or significant life disruptions such as **identity theft**. The following examples serve to illustrate examples of predatory scams and frauds.

- In 2015, "Canada's Top 10 Scams Earned Crooks $1.2B Says BBB": "Fear of the taxman and offers of love are two of the top tricks used by scammers to separate unsuspecting victims from more than a billion dollars last year" (Laanela, 2016).
- "Montreal Woman Terrified Her Personal Info Was Posted in Escort Ads. Did Police Do Enough?": "When Melissa started receiving a flurry of texts asking her availability for sex, she thought it was strange but brushed it off as spam. Hours later, when a strange man knocked on the doors of all the apartments in the Montreal building where she lives, she thought maybe he was lost. A day and a half later, her nonchalance turned to horror when an acquaintance sent her a link to an escort website. She clicked on the link and was taken to an ad for an escort—featuring her face, name, phone number and address" (McKenna, 2017).

- "B.C. Couple Told They Owe $100K after Identity Thieves Buy SUV with Fraudulent Loan": "An Abbotsford couple is speaking out about what they call an identity theft nightmare. Scotiabank has been sending Joey Abra and his wife letters to start paying a $99,378.80 loan that was taken out to purchase a 2016 Range Rover. It turns out Joey Abra's wife was the victim of identity theft" (Ke, 2019).

While frauds, scams, and other criminal deceptions are not new practices, it is important to note that, with the advent of electronic communication technologies that connect people across space and time, criminals can take advantage of the many ways that interactive technologies allow for the *innovative* commission of crimes. Personal handheld devices with internet connectivity offer modern conveniences that enable the instant social interactions we have come to take for granted in our daily routines; they also provide new *criminal opportunities* for deceptions, scams, and harassments that were not as easily perpetrated when face-to-face social interactions were the norm in human communication (Grabosky et al., 2001). Thus,

- traditional forms of scams and frauds that have existed prior to the establishment of the world wide web have taken on an intensified dimension in our modern, interconnected technological communication society, as they are transformed into computer-assisted crimes; and

- the rise of technologically mediated modes of communication, information storage, computer delivery and control systems, and social media have created new categories of criminal activity and new forms of victimization that are endemic to cyberspace.

Internet crimes, otherwise known as **cybercrime** or computer-mediated crime, often take the form of traditional scams and fraud that target individuals through **extortion** and identity theft, but they also target institutions, organizations, and governments. There has been an increasing proliferation of internet crimes that have large-scale impacts, such as the illegal installation of **ransomware** and **malware** onto *mainframe* computers that disrupt the operation of institutions and infrastructure systems, as well as content piracy attacks that take hostage private data and proprietary information. In addition, **distributed denial-of-service (DDoS) attacks** disrupt computer-operated systems and crash websites. The following examples give some idea of the extent to which computer-mediated crime can have large-scale consequences:

- "Winners Security Breach Hits Canadian Cardholders": "Fraudulent activity has been confirmed on the accounts of thousands of Canadian credit-card holders who had their information stolen during a security breach at the U.S. parent company of Winners and Home Sense" (CTVNews.ca Staff, 2007).
- "US Fuel Pipeline Hackers 'Didn't Mean to Create Problems'": "A cyber-criminal gang that took a major US fuel pipeline offline over the weekend has acknowledged the incident in a public statement. 'Our goal is to make money and not creating problems for society,' DarkSide wrote on its website. The US issued emergency legislation on Sunday after Colonial Pipeline was hit by a ransomware cyber-attack. The pipeline carries 2.5 million barrels a day—45% of the East Coast's supply of diesel, petrol and jet fuel" (Russon, 2021).
- "An Unprecedented Look at Stuxnet, the World's First Digital Weapon": "In January 2010 inspectors with the International Atomic Energy Agency visiting the Natanz uranium enrichment plant in Iran noticed that centrifuges used to enrich uranium gas were failing at an unprecedented rate. The cause was a complete mystery—that is, until the researchers found a handful of malicious files on one of the systems and discovered the world's first digital weapon. Stuxnet, as it came to be known, was unlike any other virus or worm that came before. Rather than simply hijacking targeted computers or stealing information from them, it escaped the digital realm to wreak physical destruction on equipment the computers controlled" (Zetter, 2014).

THEORIZING CYBERCRIME

Cybercrime and international frauds and scams have become such a major form of criminal activity that their impact on people and organizations worldwide can no longer be taken lightly. Computer-mediated crime, from incessant **robocalls** to your cell phone to service disruptions against websites you need to access for work and school, are a regular occurrence. This category of criminality has compelled criminologists to develop novel theories and research into the nature and scope of this significant type of 21st-century wrongdoing. New criminological theories must therefore consider how the growth of technologically mediated communication systems have created a unique terrain for social interaction that transcends traditional geographical barriers. Social interactions in cyberspace take place at a distance across national borders, and this can give perpetrators of cybercrime a sense of anonymity and embolden some in the belief that they are immune from detection. Such *social distance* also gives cybercrime another one of its distinctive features—as a type of crime whose effects are felt on a global scale. Cybercrime may be perpetrated by lone individuals or by criminal organizations operating in countries other than where their victims reside. Criminologists have developed particular theories related to this *victimization from a distance*. Not only are criminals and victims often geographically separated, but cyberspace serves as a virtual platform enabling opportunities to commit crimes that are not always possible in conventional physical spaces. Criminological theorist Jaishankar (2008) proposes a **space transition theory** of cybercrime. He postulates that existing theories of criminal behaviour are inadequate to the study of cybercrime since they do not take into account how people behave differently when they move from conventional social spaces to cyberspace. The anonymity offered by cyberspace removes the typical social deterrents to criminal behaviour and can cause repressed criminal tendencies to emerge.

Brown (2006) proposes that cybercrimes pose a challenge to traditional criminology, which usually frames the problem of crime in binary terms (such as criminal and victim), and that theorizing cyberspace creates novel "technosocial networks that compel researchers to understand actors within cyberspace through a 'hybrid' framework." Computer users are now so connected to their technology that they are virtual "cyborgs," and the simplistic binary distinction between criminal and victim is blurred when we consider that generally law-abiding computer users can behave as online trolls, **spammers, hackers,** or cyberbullies who thus have the capacity to display significant deviance when engaged in some online activities (Brown, 2006).

In a similar vein of inquiry, Stalans and Donner (2018) also draw attention to the unique interplay that exists in the blending of cyberspace with social reality. They indicate that explaining cybercrime involves a blending of insights from traditional criminological theories such as social learning theory, self-control theory, neutralization, and subcultural theories, with novel perspectives that explore how the virtual world of cyberspace alters social interactions in ways that have consequences for the real world.

Most of the existing theoretical literature on technologically enabled crime can be categorized under Wall's (2001) typology, as follows:

1. Cyber-trespass: Refers to the trespassing (hacking) of barriers and private boundaries online such as accessing someone else's private computer and downloading files without permission (malware, viruses, etc.).
2. Cyber-deception and theft: Refers to the theft of data, personal files, and proprietary information from personal or institutional computing systems.
3. Cyber-porn and obscenity: Refers to the distribution through computer networks of explicit, illegal sexualized materials such as child pornography, and the use of the internet to engage in the sale or purchase of sexual services in locations where they are prohibited by law.
4. Cyberviolence: Refers to the use of the internet to harm others in various ways such as **bullying**, harassment, stalking, threatening, or publicly defaming someone's character or reputation (Holt & Bossler, 2014; Wall, 2001).

Despite this typology, computer-assisted crime and deviance is difficult to categorize since communications media and digital technology represent a fast-changing realm of modern society with new crimes regularly emerging across social media platforms alongside increased hardware capacities and personal device innovations being developed at a rapid pace. Such rapid innovation "creates myriad opportunities for individuals to misuse these devices to engage in acts of deviance and crime" (Holt & Bossler, 2014, p. 21).

Box 11.1: Leaving Personal Information in Places Where Perhaps It Shouldn't Be

One day I (C.C.) was at the checkout counter in a store paying for some clothes I bought, and the cashier asked me for my phone number and email address to enter into their computer system. I politely responded that I would prefer to not provide such personal information—a remark that was met with a smirk and some rolling eyes on her part. I said, "Why do you get upset that I don't want to have my personal information stored in your database? Can you guarantee that my information will be protected against theft by criminals and not sold to other criminals who may want to steal my identity and rack up my credit card?" She said, "Wow, you sound like a very paranoid person." I said, "No, I'm just a criminologist."

How many times have you given out or entered personal information without considering the potential consequences? Has your credit card ever been compromised? Do you know someone who has had their identity stolen and then had to do years of legal repair work to clear their name and restore their credit rating? Do you do a lot of online shopping that requires you to enter your address, email, and credit card information, and if so, does that worry you? One of the things about our computerized society is that the very actions we are compelled to take in order to participate in that society also makes us vulnerable to predation and victimization.

Is it the responsibility of each individual to be vigilant in protecting themselves from cybercrime? Should the responsibility for consumer information protection be with the retailers whose products we buy or with the institutions we bank with or with law enforcement agencies? How many retailers and organizations in the past decade have had massive *data breaches* where the personal information of millions of people was stolen by cybercriminals? These sorts of questions ask us to reflect on the complex nature of cybercrime and its control in an interconnected world, and, as mentioned in Chapter 1, the extent to which criminality is increasingly interwoven into the fabric of everyday life.

TRADITIONAL SCAMS, FRAUDS, AND CONS

A fool and his money are soon parted.
If it sounds too good to be true then it probably is!
There's a sucker born every minute.

What are the conditions that favour someone becoming the victim of a scam? Who is more likely to fall victim to a scam? As with most types of victimization, it is generally those with the least power and protections that are disproportionately affected. The typical victims of scams in Canada include the elderly, children, minors, immigrants or temporary residents of the country, and those who aren't fluent in English or French. Cybercriminals and scammers will target those who are vulnerable, are fearful of authority, or those who do not exercise diligence in their online activities and may inadvertently download malicious software, such as minors or those who lack computer literacy.

In the practice of scamming, the criminal seeks a willing or intended victim known as a **mark** who becomes the target of the scam. Scammers are sometimes referred to as **con artists** because they gain the trust and *confidence* of those they target. People can become the target of a scam in various ways. Specific types of scams will come and go, as once they are revealed they are replaced by newer, cleverer scams of which the public is unaware. Large-scale scams that spread across communities are often revealed through public alerts and media reports that raise awareness about them. In 2018, the Canada Revenue Agency (CRA) phone scam had become a growing public concern, as vulnerable Canadians lost millions to scammers pretending to be from the CRA or the police, and it continued to run for years. "The scammers, who often call from clandestine call centres in India, typically operate by telling their victims that they owe back taxes and should pay up immediately if they want to avoid serious consequences including imprisonment" (Kalvapalle, 2019).

The following sections outline merely a few of the many traditional types of frauds and scams.

Pyramid Scheme

A pyramid scheme is a type of get-rich-quick scheme that involves the constant recruitment of new paying members into a network of people shaped like a pyramidal hierarchy, where the person at the top receives the monies paid by the new recruits entering at the lower rungs of the pyramid. The entire concept is fundamentally flawed, because the constant recruitment of new paying members becomes unsustainable as individual members' social networks run dry and participants quickly lose their initial investments. Pyramid schemes are usually perpetrated by laypersons and not by those registered as investment professionals. Pyramid schemes are illegal in Canada, the US, and in numerous other countries, and they are no longer as widespread as they once were.

Ponzi Scheme

A **Ponzi scheme** is another type of get-rich-quick scheme and a type of economic fraud involving the use of investors' money to pay returns on the investments of previous investors. In most cases, no authentic financial investments are made to generate true monetary returns for the investors. The basic premise rests on money taken from one investor being used to pay off debts from former investors; that is, "borrowing from Peter to pay Paul" (Darby, 1998). New investors are lured by the appeal of high rates of return on their investment early on, but they end up losing their initial large monetary investment. The Ponzi schemer gets rich by living off the income created by a steady stream of investors, and their usually lavish lifestyles act as a lure for a constant stream of new investors.

Ponzi schemes have been around since the early 1900s. The scheme is named after Charles Ponzi, who, in 1920, scammed tens of thousands of people living in Boston for an estimated total of $15 million (around $190 million today; Darby, 1998). Ponzi set up a company named Securities Exchange Company to trick investors into thinking he was a real investor who would generate returns for his clients using legitimate means. Eventually the scheme collapsed, and investors lost millions. Nevertheless, the practice of Ponzi scheming still continues. A recent notorious case is that of American Bernard (Bernie) Madoff, whose illegal activities were for many years integrated into legitimate investments; Madoff ran the largest Ponzi scheme known to date. Fairly recent Canadian cases include that of Earl Jones, who cost his victims over $51 million, and Gary Sorenson and Milowe Brost, who cost their victims upwards of $400 million (Grant, 2017).

In some cases, Ponzi-type scammers gather money from investors under the false pretense of raising capital for a business venture. One Canadian case involves Rashida Samji, who was banned "for life from participating in B.C.'s capital markets after a panel ruled she defrauded 200 investors of at least $100 million between 2003 and 2012. Ms. Samji told investors their money was being used to raise financing for a winery in Kelowna. However, the Mission Hill Family Estate winery knew nothing about Ms. Samji's scheme and said it had no business arrangement with her.... The regulator ordered Ms. Samji to pay $33 million in fines and $10.8 million as an additional penalty" (McFarland, 2015).

Another notorious case involves American Silicon Valley fraudster Elizabeth Holmes, who raised over $700 million from private investors and venture capitalists for her company Theranos, which falsely claimed to have developed innovative blood testing technology that would revolutionize laboratory processes, despite having no new technology or innovative intellectual property to accomplish their business goals. The Theranos case was the subject of a telling HBO documentary entitled *The Inventor: Out for Blood in Silicon Valley*. In January 2022, Holmes was found guilty of defrauding investors, and her former business partner Ramesh Balwani was also found guilty a few months later (Campoamor, 2021; Khorram, 2022; Paul, 2022).

Advance Fee Scam—419/Nigerian Scam

Similar to many other scams, the particular content of advance fee scams varies. The central form of this mail-by-letter or fax scam (that became a **phishing scam** with the advent of email) is that a person is promised a substantial reward of money if an advance of money is sent to a party, who is eventually revealed to be a fraudster. You "pay a little, get a lot" (Newman, 2018). The "Nigerian fraud" scams (sometimes called 419 scams) are sent often by a (fictitious) prince, king, or other high-ranking government official and declare that a fortune has been discovered, but due to particularly dangerous circumstances, such as war, the official seeks a trustworthy person living abroad who is to hold the fortune securely for a period of time. Other versions highlight the plight of someone who has been wrongfully imprisoned or kidnapped. Before the fortune can be sent, the receiver of the email must forward a smaller amount of money, based on particular banking circumstances that vary by the particular email sent. The number 419 refers to the part of the Nigerian *Criminal Code* that centres on this form of fraudulent activity (Yar & Steinmetz, 2019, p. 135). It is important to note that while many of these scams originated in Nigeria, they now originate from numerous parts of the world. Recent evidence suggests not an abatement but increase in these types of scams, including from Nigeria. Nigerian groups such as the "yahoo boys" are increasingly targeting small businesses, with the FBI estimating that businesses worldwide reported over 40,000 compromised emails linked to $5.3 billion of losses (Newman, 2018). Scammers may not be as sophisticated as others, such as **black hat hackers,** but the damages to individuals and businesses is significant.

Grandparent Scam

The invention of the telephone enabled the **grandparent scam**—which involves the scammers' use of the telephone to fool an unsuspecting grandparent into believing their teenage or young adult grandchild is in desperate need of money because they are stranded somewhere else in the world and in an emergency situation. The scammers pretend to be the grandchild by impersonating their voice and plea for the transfer of monies to an account in that distant place. To some extent, this scam is a modern example because it involves the use of money transfer systems, and increasingly it can involve the use of other messaging systems other than the traditional home telephone line (AARP, 2020).

Identity Theft and Identity Fraud

Identity theft or fraud is a long-standing form of fraud that involves assuming the identity and name of another person for the purposes of committing various forms of wrongdoing, monetary gain, or to evade the law. The Canadian Anti-Fraud Centre (2021) states, "Identity theft refers to criminals stealing someone else's personal information for criminal purposes [and] ... happens when criminals use stolen personal information ... to commit another crime" (para. 1). Identity theft is a type of traditional fraud and has been accomplished using stolen or fabricated identification documents such as a passport or social insurance number. However, identity theft is also an example of a crime that has become more easily achieved in the digital age, where identities can be stolen by accessing personal information stored in computer databases. Identity thieves will use the stolen identity to access credit or take monies from the legitimate accounts of the person they are pretending to be. In some cases, identity fraudsters will assume multiple identities (stolen or fabricated) in an attempt to cover up a longstanding pattern of crimes across different regions, as a way of avoiding law enforcement. One example of the latter is "Notorious Australian con artist Samantha Azzopardi, [who] has been sentenced to prison in Melbourne for child stealing. Having created a trail of false identities around the world, she has a history that runs deep. Emily Peet, Lindsay Coughlin, Dakota Johnson, Georgia McAuliffe, Harper Hernandez, Harper Hart. Behind all these names—and many more—was just one woman: serial fraudster Azzopardi, 32, from Sydney. Over the past decade, she has been caught under assumed names in Ireland, Canada and various states within her home nation" (Baker, 2021). In another case, "A con woman who was jailed for financial crimes while posing as a wealthy New York socialite has been detained by US immigration authorities. Anna Sorokin, who created a fake persona as Anna Delvey, was taken into custody on 25 March. The 30-year-old is facing deportation to her home country Germany after her release from prison in February. She was found guilty in April 2020 of stealing from banks and hotels, having scammed more than $200,000" (BBC News, 2021b).

Fortune Teller/Psychics Scam

In Canada, it is a criminal offence to fraudulently pretend to practise witchcraft, sorcery, enchantment or conjuration, to tell fortunes for money, and/or to pretend to discover through the use of the occult—yet many people remain convinced of the power of supernatural occult forces, and that makes them vulnerable to being scammed by psychics, fortune tellers, and mediums. As mentioned in Chapter 2, in 2018, a Toronto woman was "charged with fraud and pretending to practice witchcraft after she allegedly convinced a man that ... in order to get rid of evil spirits in his home, he had to sell the house and transfer the money to her account, where it would remain until the spirits were gone.... The man sold his car and home and lost more than \$600,000 in the alleged scheme, police said" (CTVNews.ca Staff, 2018). This type of fraud remains persistent. It is difficult for law enforcement to police and prosecute, and it seems to have increased substantially in the US. The American Association of Retired Persons (AARP) reports that "psychic scams rose during COVID-19 pandemic" as people feeling especially vulnerable are more likely to fall victim to psychic scams (Skiba, 2020).

Petty scams and frauds are a global phenomenon. In addition to some of the longstanding types of scams listed above, others include distraction theft/pickpocketing, insurance fraud, travel scams, and fake diploma and degree scams, to name a few. New types of scams and frauds will emerge with changing social conditions, which create new opportunities for criminal activity. For example, the real estate rental scam that preys upon tenants desperately trying to find housing in a market with low housing availability is not likely to happen when rental properties are widely available. Regardless of how these scams may change, including the technologically mediated scams we turn to next, their success is often based on preying on the vulnerable when emotions are high and impulsive decisions are made.

In the words of scholars ...

"Cyber-terrorism," "information warfare," "phishing spams," "denial of service attacks," "hacktivism," "hate crime," "identity thefts," "online gambling," plus the criminal exploitation of a new generation of pornographic peccadilloes, comprise the new language that describes the criminal and harmful behaviours that are conspiring to degrade the overall quality of life online and beyond. In so doing they pose significant threats to public safety that are tempering commercial and governmental ambitions to develop the information society.

David S. Wall, *Crime and Deviance in Cyberspace.* 2017.

MODERN CYBERCRIMES

In the age of the internet and social media, crimes increasingly have some sort of digital component to them, and cybercrime has become a pernicious aspect of everyday life. On an almost daily basis we see news headlines such as "Attacks on the Internet Getting Bigger and Nastier"—"Could millions of connected cameras, thermostats and kids' toys bring the internet to its knees? It's beginning to look that way" (Fowler, 2016). The internet and the cyber-connected world it has created have become an open field of deviance and crime, disruption, and harassment, from ex-lover revenge websites to online **trolling** and hate speech, to the rise of the **Internet of Things,** which promises convenience but is also a potential mechanism for someone who wishes to cause people harm. For instance, one's "smart," internet-connected house thermostat can be hacked, with the heat fully increased in the middle of summer; or one's "smart" fridge can be hacked in order to have food spoil, among other, more criminal goals! In 2013, a "refrigerator-based botnet was used to attack businesses" (Grau, 2019). Computers offer users a sense of anonymity and encourage forms of wrongdoing that would not be possible in the open and visible public realm. The internet has created a new type of cyberoutlaw: the hacker, who may engage in disruptive activity known as a **cyberattack.** As you shall read in what follows, hackers can be criminal disruptors, computer system hostage-takers, and thieves, as well as progressive social change **hacktivists** who use computer systems in an attempt to create awareness about social issues and bring about social change.

Cybercrime may be categorized into *pure computer crimes* and *computer-supported crimes.*

- *Pure computer crimes* are "where a computer is the object of the crime" and includes "offences that target computer systems and networks." Hacking, DDoS attacks, and dissemination of computer viruses are some examples of pure computer crimes.
- *Computer-supported crimes* involve a computer as "the instrument used in perpetrating the crime." Using the computer to disseminate and/or produce child pornography, engage in harassment or fraud, or traffic drugs are examples of computer-supported crimes (Valiquet, 2011, p. 1).

The following sections represent some of the more significant cybercrimes and techniques for perpetrating them.

Distributed Denial-of-Service (DDoS) Attacks

Whereas an electronically mediated denial of service disrupts services and access online (Esen, 2002), a *distributed denial-of-service attack* often involves numerous computers, which coordinate to "flood" a computer system (i.e., a targeted website) to overwhelm the servers and render it inaccessible to other users, thus making it crash (Yar & Steinmetz, 2019, pp. 62–63).

In 2000, high school student Michael Calce, known by the online handle Mafiaboy, singlehandedly shut down a number of major websites, including Amazon, CNN, Dell, E*Trade, eBay, and Yahoo!. Damages from the attack totalled $1.7 billion (Edwards, 2017). A recent interview, however, reveals that money was not the primary, or even secondary, objective. "The overall purpose was to intimidate other hacker groups," Calce discloses (Hersher, 2015). This motive aligns with the *hacker ethic*, which values freedom of information and optimism about technology's potential to positively affect lives, social change, and democracy, but also distrusts authorities, governmental authorities in particular (Levy, 1984; Yar & Steinmetz, 2019). Calce argues that this ethic has shifted among hacking subcultures. Whereas in the past "the whole of the hacking community was all about notoriety and exploration," today the emphasis among hackers is "all about monetization" (Hersher, 2015).

One of the largest DDoS attacks on record occurred in October 2016, with internet services disrupted throughout both the US and Europe. Servers owned by the company Dyn, which "controls much of the internet's domain name system (DNS) infrastructure," was the target of a **botnet**, called Mirai (Woolf, 2016). Mirai shut down major websites including Twitter, Netflix, Reddit, CNN, and others in Europe and the US. In this case, Mirai took advantage of common household devices with internet connectivity (i.e., the Internet of Things). This greatly amplified the attack's reach, involving "100,000 malicious endpoints," ranking it about twice as powerful as any existing DDoS attack on record. Such botnet attacks, powerful as they are, are often deployed by non-state actors (e.g., lone "black hat" hackers). However, some observers express concern that state-based DDoS attacks, which take advantage of Internet of Things devices, may do exponentially more damage (Woolf, 2016).

Botnets

Botnets are "a collection of software robots, or 'bots,' that creates an army of infected computers (known as 'zombies') that are remotely controlled by the originator" (known as a "botherder") (Get Cyber Safe, n.d.; Yar & Steinmetz, 2019, p. 60). "Yours may be one of them and you may not even know it" (Get Cyber Safe, n.d.). Botnets "[use] the computing power and bandwidth of other people's devices for their own purposes" (Yar & Steinmetz, 2019, p. 60). Other computer systems attacked by botnets are compromised by malicious code and may be harnessed to deploy attacks on other computer systems, including spreading harmful software, "leeching" of bandwidth from others' internet service, and in relation to other scams like identity theft, phishing, engaging in DDoS attacks, and so on (Yar & Steinmetz, 2019).

Phishing, Spoofing, Trojans, Malware, and Ransomware

Compared to casting a fishing hook into waters populated with large amounts of fish, with the aim of catching a small number of fish, phishing scams "involve the mass distribution of emails, casting a wide net to capture potential marks" (Yar & Steinmetz, 2019, p. 137). Phishing scams often involve fraudsters posing as financial institutions, such as banks and credit card companies, requesting that targeted users (marks) release secure information about themselves, such as social insurance numbers, credit card information, addresses, and so on (James, 2005). These scams are often convincing based on their mimicking the appearance of official communications from financial institutions. Users are often directed to click on hyperlinks, which, if clicked, send the user to a *spoof* website, mimicking the appearance of the institution or organization. It is on these spoof (fake duplicate) sites that users are often asked to provide further identifying information (Yar & Steinmetz, 2019, p. 137).

Ransomware is a form of malicious software, or malware (Berghel, 2001), sent by a computer hacker that *holds hostage* or restricts access to a computer or files, typically until money, or *ransom*, is paid. An estimated 91 percent originate from a "spear phishing" email (Morgan, 2017). Spear phishing emails are an increasingly common form of phishing that makes use of information about a target to make attacks more specific and "personal." These attacks may, for instance, refer to their targets by their specific name or job position, instead of using generic titles, as seen in broader phishing campaigns (Sjouwerman, 2020). Usually the condition involves paying a ransom fee to regain access; the fee is often paid using a **crypto-currency** such as Bitcoin (Elliott, 2016). Cryptocurrency is becoming the legal tender of choice for cybercriminals because it is easier to hide and launder. A 2018 BBC report states, "Criminals hide 'billions' in crypto-cash—Three to four billion pounds of criminal money in Europe is being laundered through cryptocurrencies, according to Europol" (Silva, 2018).

Ransomware demands are growing in frequency and sophistication but are usually relatively small, targeting individuals for on average a few hundred dollars; those targeting corporations and other organizations tend to range in the tens of thousands of dollars to millions of dollars. Two versions of ransomware are most frequently encountered. Lockscreen ransomware shows a full-screen message that prevents access to one's computer until money is paid. Encryption ransomware encrypts a user's files so they can't open them until a ransom is paid (Microsoft, 2009). Similar to "phishing" email scams, ransomware adopts a "spray and pray mentality" (Elliott, 2016).

Ransomware seems to work based on the expectation that marks will pay the ransom so long as it is calibrated to be an optimal amount; a demand too high, and users may opt to simply erase their hard drive contents. With a "reasonably low" ransom, at least some targeted users will be willing to pay, rather than risk their data being wiped. This principle may also be applied to larger organizations. Hospitals and universities, for instance, have been targeted for tens of thousands of dollars (Elliott, 2016; McKenzie, 2019), though here too this amount of money is arguably "attuned" to an amount organizations are likely to pay, especially with sensitive and critical data to protect. While a ransom of, say, $2 million is certainly nothing to scoff at, it is an amount that criminals likely feel larger organizations are willing to pay. On a global scale, however, one projection from 2017 estimated ransomware attacks to be $11.5 billion by 2019 (up from $325 million in 2015; Morgan, 2017).

As of 2021, ransomware attacks have become a significant concern, as a BBC report shows: "A global coalition of technology companies and law enforcement bodies is calling for 'aggressive and urgent' action against ransomware. Microsoft, Amazon, the FBI, and the UK's National Crime Agency have joined the Ransomware Task Force (RTF) in giving governments nearly 50 recommendations. Ransomware gangs are now routinely targeting schools and hospitals" (Tidy, 2021). Further, "The world's largest meat processing company has been targeted by a sophisticated cyber-attack. Computer networks at JBS were hacked, temporarily shutting down some operations in Australia, Canada, and the US, with thousands of workers affected. The company believes the ransomware attack originated from a criminal group likely based in Russia, the White House said" (BBC News, 2021c). More significantly, "The federal government is working with the Georgia-based company that shut down a major pipeline transporting fuel across the East Coast after a ransomware attack, the White House says" (Associated Press, 2021).

Hacktivism, Black Hat, and White Hat Hacking

Hacking is defined as the unauthorized access and subsequent use of other people's computer systems (Taylor, 1999). They may be considered electronic intruders, but this is a definition that often reflects the standpoint of law enforcement (Yar & Steinmetz, 2019). It is near impossible to be certain about the number of hackers worldwide or extent of hacking—indeed, much lies in how hacking is perceived. Twist estimated 900 distinct hacking groups, and 11,000 individuals operating in the early 2000s: "The underground network is vast, with thousands of individuals and groups, ranging from lurkers who are intrigued by hacker chat to 'script kiddies' who try out hacker tools for a laugh" (Twist, 2003). Early media depictions of hackers, including movies such as *Hackers* (1995) and *Die Hard 2* (1990), influenced not only public conceptions of hackers but governments as well. The

US senate, for instance, compared the threat hackers pose with that of a virtual equivalent of Pearl Harbor (Taylor, 1999), and, as of June 2021, elevated ransomware hacks to the highest level of threats to national security, given the same priority as terrorism (Bing, 2021).

While hacking need not take up political motivations (i.e., hacking for the sake of hacking), *hacktivism*, or political hacking, which emerged during the mid-1990s, involves the mobilization of hacking in the service of political activism, human rights, and protest (Yar & Steinmetz, 2019). Hacktivism may take the form of virtual sit-ins and blockades (i.e., an electronically mediated civil disobedience, such as DDoS attacks, or website defacements [one estimate is that 30% of website defacements are politically motivated]; Yar and Steinmetz, 2019).

The label "hacker" is ambiguous, given the blurring of a wide spectrum of motivations, dispositions, and political beliefs held among those who self-identify as hackers. Invitations to "hackathons" are popular and are even encouraged by governments and institutions such as the Catholic Church as a way to promote education of youth in science, technology, engineering, and mathematics (STEM; Valdez, 2018). Hackers often self-identify as either *black hat* or *white hat*. Black hat hackers are those who engage in crimes such as theft, sabotage, and other malicious attacks with criminal intent. **White hat hackers** are those, often former black hats who have been charged and served a sentence through the justice system, who hack with the intention of identifying and stopping black hat hackers. "White hats are authorized to access systems and try to compromise them, in contrast to the black hats who exploit systems with unauthorized access" (Jelen, 2018). The actions of white hat hackers may be seen as part of a wider shift to "ethical hacking." Examples of white hat hackers include Michael Calce, aka Mafiaboy, who ended up working as a security consultant for companies aiming to protect vulnerabilities, particularly undiscovered vulnerabilities or sensitive code exploits called "zero day" vulnerabilities (Hersher, 2015, Hutchins, 2014). In an interview, Calce refers to these zero day vulnerabilities: "You've got to understand that, when hackers have this type of sensitive code, they are going to keep it private for as long as they can. When it's kept private, it's called 'zero-day.' 'In the wild' means it has become public" (Hutchins, 2014). One impactful vulnerability that went "in the wild" was the "heartbleed bug" in Canada, which was a serious flaw in Secure Socket Layer (SSL) encryption software that allowed access to previously secured websites (Hutchins, 2014).

As mentioned above, the motivations for hacking are complex. Law enforcement, it may be expected, often highlights the actions of black hat hackers as criminals, but among hacking subcultures, criminal motives are often concomitant to the hacker ethic, which emphasizes curiosity and "hacking for the sake of hacking" (Hawn, 1996). There is, from this perspective, a beauty and art to crafting "perfect" code and observing its implementation. Moreover, there is in public discourses a *hacker mystique*, with hackers viewed more with admiration and fascination, especially by youth (Friedman, 2005). This allure is often braided to the risks and dangers associated with hacking and broader anxieties related to technology and fear of crime (Shelley, 1891).

Box 11.2: Examples of Significant Hacks and Cyberattacks

The Equifax Hack

It is often the case that hackers want to access personal information, such as social insurance and credit card numbers, and offer them on the black market to criminals who will use or resell identifying information to others to commit crime. When a person has their identity stolen and the thief racks up financial debt, this can ruin someone's credit score; rectifying that score can be extremely difficult. Credit rating agencies and banks have some obligation to protect the information of their customers, so when Equifax, one of the three largest consumer credit reporting agencies, was hacked, this was a major breach of data. When even financial security systems themselves are successfully targeted by criminals, this is a grave concern. In the 2017 hack of Equifax, the hackers gained access to customer names, social security numbers, and credit card numbers (Hadi & Logan, 2017). A *Wired* news article reports,

> In September 2017 credit reporting giant Equifax came clean: It had been hacked, and the sensitive personal information of 143 million US (as below) citizens had been compromised—a number the company later revised up to 147.9 million. Names, birth dates, Social Security numbers, all gone in an unprecedented heist. [In January 2020], the Department of Justice identified the alleged culprit: China. In a sweeping nine-count indictment, the DOJ alleged that four members of China's People's Liberation Army were behind the Equifax hack, the culmination of a years-long investigation. In terms of the number of US citizens affected, it's one of the biggest state-sponsored thefts of personally identifiable information on record. It also further escalates already tense relations with China on multiple fronts. (Barrett, 2020)

The Fruitfly Malware

Malware used for spying—known as **spyware**—is a type of malicious software that has been downloaded onto a computer without the user's consent to monitor or *spy* on their online activity and gather private information, thus representing a gross violation of privacy and potential harm. As reported in *Cleveland Scene*, "In early 2017, computer security experts noticed a particularly malicious and nearly undetectable strain of malware infecting computers across America, specifically Macs. Dubbed 'Fruitfly,' the malware collected keystrokes and spied on users' screens, webcams and microphones … a 28-year-old North Royalton man named Phillip R. Durachinsky was federally indicted on 16 counts for creating malware—specifically Fruitfly—which he used to infect computers, steal identities, log keystrokes, turn on webcams and microphones to spy on users, and produce child pornography, among other things, all over the course of 13 years" (Grzegorek, 2018).

The Ashley Madison Hack

Ashley Madison is a popular dating site for people wishing to have extra-marital affairs. The site popularized itself at launch by advertising itself as different from other dating websites, which ostensibly had outdated valuations of monogamy: "when monogamy becomes monotony" was the initial catchphrase of Ashley Madison (Hancock, 2007). Ashley Madison's website itself was defaced by hackers who dubbed themselves Impact Team, who demanded that the site be "shut down immediately." The defacement itself was a mashup of a stock image of a woman holding her fingers to her lips in the "shhh" motion combined with what appears to be a screen capture of a scene from the movie *Scanners* (1981) involving a graphic head explosion (Pearl, 2015). Included in the website defacement was the following text:

> Shutting down [Ashley Madison] … will cost you, but non-compliance will cost you more: We will release all customer records, profiles with all the customers' secret sexual fantasies, nude pictures, and conversations and matching credit card transactions, real names and addresses, and employee documents and emails. (Pearl, 2015)

By non-compliance, Impact Team referred to a window of 30 days, after which they threatened to **doxx** users (i.e., reveal their personal details publicly online) if the site was not shut down. The 30 days passed, but the website was not shut down and Impact Team hackers followed through with their threat, releasing almost ten gigabytes of user email addresses (Lord, 2017). An additional 20 gigabytes of internal data from the parent company of Ashley Madison, Avid Life Media, was subsequently released by Impact Team. A third leak only a few days after the initial one included governmental emails used to sign up for accounts and lists of users in several US states. Several serious consequences followed, including two suicides in Toronto by Ashley Madison users who had their identities revealed in the hack. Other users faced threats of blackmail and further identity theft (Lord, 2017).

The Ashley Madison hack illustrates not only the general threat hackers impose on users, including financial and interpersonal risk, but a particular *morality* directing selection of appropriate targets for hacking. As discussed in this chapter, there are a variety of types of hackers, and their personal motivations often range beyond economic incentives or even personal glory. In the case of Impact Team, this group of hackers presumably saw Ashley Madison's existence, and its users, as morally repugnant and therefore a justifiable target. Of course, their actions are still criminal, and the negative consequences highlighted above testify to the—at best—unintended consequences of crimes such as doxxing and identity theft.

The Beef Hack

Cybercriminals have become so sophisticated that they are able to exploit vulnerabilities in the computer operation systems of numerous large-scale organizations, from government to infrastructure and businesses. Organizations often do not have the technical or administrative ability to recover from attacks that hold them hostage, and in many cases company executives agree to pay the ransom in the hopes that the criminals will follow through on their promise to release the stolen data they are holding hostage. An NBC news report states,

> Beef supplier JBS paid ransomware hackers $11 million. The company was hacked in May [2021] by a Russian-speaking hacker gang, which led meat plants across the U.S. and Australia to shut down

for at least a day ... JBS, the largest beef supplier in the world, paid the ransomware hackers who breached its computer networks.... The company was hacked in May by REvil ... [who] has made millions in recent years by hacking organizations, encrypting their files and demanding fees, often large bitcoin payments, in exchange for a decryptor program and a promise not to leak the files to the public. (Collier, 2021)

CYBERBULLYING, CYBERSTALKING, AND ONLINE SEXTORTION

The violent act of bullying has long been a disturbing aspect of interactional dynamics, especially among youth, who may use aggression as a way of establishing dominance over others. Bullying has now also become a type of technologically intensified form of aggression that has a number of variants that involve disparaging someone's reputation over social media with the intent to cause them harm and/or emotional suffering. Online or social media bullying, known as cyberbullying, is a type of aggressive harassment that aims to intimidate, coerce, or harm someone, or to break their spirit or tarnish their reputation. Often there is the threat of retaliation if the victim fails to comply with demands of the aggressor, in which case the bullying is classified as a type of crime known as extortion.

Box 11.3: Cybercrime and Romantic Relationships—When Love Turns to Hate

Cyberspace can amplify pre-existing forms of romantic and partner-based violence by allowing abusers to use the internet, social media, and other platforms to take revenge on ex-lovers. Sites such as myex.com, which was a revenge porn website that allowed people to post nude images of their former sex partners as a form of retaliation or humiliation, serves as one example of the brazen acts of violation that occur in such contexts. A case in point is revealed in a CBC report:

A Burnaby, B.C., man convicted of harassing his ex-wife with a vulgar website and torrent of threatening emails is heading back to jail for continually refusing to pull the site down. Patrick Fox, 47, was sentenced in Vancouver on Monday to one year and four months in jail for breaching his probation. He was charged after leaving the website up and running, despite multiple court orders to take it down after his original jail term. After credit for time served, Fox has six more months left in his new sentence. Fox was first sentenced to four years in prison in 2017 for an online harassment campaign tormenting his ex-wife. The website falsely labelled his ex-wife, Desiree Capuano, as a white supremacist, child abuser and drug addict. The site, which has now been up for seven years, calls Capuano a "horrible, lying, sociopathic monster" and also contained intimate photos. Fox used Google ads to direct internet traffic from workplaces and neighbourhoods near Capuano's home in Arizona to his website. After credit for time served, Fox was released after spending two years in prison. He was supposed to remove the website and remain on probation for three years. Last August, after another run-in with authorities, Fox said he would never deactivate the site. "They can lock me up for the rest of my life, but I will never take down the website," he said in a post.... Authorities have been unable to remove the revenge website because it's operated through a server in a foreign country. (CBC News, 2021)

The internet is also quickly becoming a place for people to meet potential romantic partners, and dating sites and apps have grown substantially since the advent of the internet. While this creates unique opportunities to meet people one might normally never encounter, it has also created the potential for harm and abuse of trust, as in the case of **catfishing** and other romance/relationship scams where fraud artists lure others into their trust under false pretenses in order to gain money.

Young users of the internet are often the primary victims of a type of extortion known as **sextortion**—which preys upon the sexual vulnerabilities of primarily female internet users. *Sextortion* can involve the posting or sharing of intimate images without consent with the intention of obtaining something (usually money or illicit images) by threatening to harm the target if they do not comply with the demands. The troubling cases of Amanda Todd and Rehtaeh Parsons made international headlines on the unpleasant consequences of cyberbullying and sextortion and highlighted this growing problem alongside the inadequacy of the criminal justice system to police such crimes. In a CBC documentary, *The Sextortion of Amanda Todd* (2013), it was revealed that the RCMP in British Columbia were alerted at least five times over the course of two years about the ongoing sexual extortion that was occurring before she committed suicide (Kelley & Weinstein, 2013).

Box 11.4: Cyberdeviance: Internet Trolls, Conspiracy Theories, and Fake News

In addition to cybercrimes that are technically classified as illegal, the presence of the internet in our everyday lives also allows for various other types of problematic behaviours and forms of wrongdoing that aren't technically crimes but qualify as forms of cyberdeviance. For example, internet trolling, malvertising, clickbaiting, online hoaxes, conspiracy theories, the spread of fake news, *bad* influencers, education cheating websites, fake online product reviews, false videos, and fabricated photo images—all of these serve as forms of mass deception that interfere with the integrity of knowledge and democracy in civil society.

Special interest groups will often attempt to manipulate information to serve their own ends. An example of this is the attempt to eliminate actual events from history, such as was the case with the Sandy Hook Hoax. The 2012 mass shooting at Sandy Hook Elementary School in Connecticut, saw 26 people, 20 of whom were children, killed by a lone gunman in yet another case of the kind of mass gun violence that happens with relative frequency in the US. In an attempt to obfuscate the reality of this tragedy, a conspiracy theory, promoted by pro-gun activists among other self-proclaimed "truthers," went viral on the internet, claiming the tragedy never happened. Some parents of the dead children became targets of online hatred and threats, accused of promoting lies. One report writes, "a 30-minute YouTube video, titled 'The Sandy Hook Shooting—Fully Exposed' which asked questions like 'Wouldn't frantic kids be a difficult target to hit?' had been viewed more than 10 million times," indicating the overwhelming currency of the hoax (Wiedeman, 2016).

The COVID-19 pandemic was yet another grand occasion for the dissemination of falsehoods, fears, paranoia, and hatred. One Reuters news report writes, "Several French social media sites say they have been approached by a communications agency that offered them money to spread negative publicity about the Pfizer COVID-19 vaccine,

a ploy the health minister described as dangerous and irresponsible....
In April, a European Union report said Russian and Chinese media
were systematically seeking to sow mistrust in Western COVID-19
vaccines through their disinformation campaigns aimed at the West"
(Reuters, 2021).

Fake product reviews are another pressing concern that can be
classified as wrongdoing against consumers and businesses. One BBC
report states, "Google is failing to do enough to combat fake reviews
within its business listings and must be held to account by a UK watchdog,
according to which the consumer group set up a fake company and bought
bogus five-star reviews as part of an investigation. In doing so, it was able
to tie its sham 'customers' to dozens of other highly rated British firms,
including a dentist and a stockbroker. Google says it has 'significantly'
invested in tech to tackle the issue" (BBC News, 2021a).

Another form of online bullying that has an interpersonal dimension to it is
cyberstalking, which involves the ongoing harassment of the target victim by following them online in order to make them live in fear of impending harm. Cyberstalking is not exclusive to online youth as it also affects adults who seek revenge or retaliation against former romantic partners. Cyberstalking can be accompanied by online trolling and doxxing, both of which involve posting identifying defamatory comments on publicly visible communication platforms with the intent to harass the target victim. **Revenge porn**, which involves a number of interconnected forms of online bullying, refers to someone seeking revenge by posting fake or actual nude pictures of their target victim online in order to slander their reputation and cause them distress.

Box 11.5: The Dark Web: A Playground for Cybercriminals

The invention and global reach of the world wide web, also known as
the internet, created an innovative global communications forum that
facilitated dynamic group formation and interactions based on shared
social interests, as well as *subcultural communities*, some of which
engage in criminal activity. While most internet users access mainstream
websites relating to shopping, leisure, hobbies, banking, and work, there

exists another dimension to the internet that is the exclusive space of non-conforming online activities known as the **dark web**—which is private content on the web that requires specialized software applications, specific user skillsets, and by-invitation-only authorization codes to gain access. The web has many layers: distinctions need to be drawn between the "surface web," "dark web," and "deep web." The surface web refers to online content that is indexable, searchable, and not secured behind paywalls or subscriptions (e.g., accessed through the Google search engine; BrightPlanet, 2014). The deep web is much vaster compared with the surface web and contains information not searchable through standard search engines. This content is contained behind password-protected sites, firewalls, and internal servers, including library databases and internet accounts. The dark web is a subset of the deep web, including content more directly associated with crime and deviance. These sites are accessed through a special web protocol known as The Onion Router, or TOR, which is a type of internet browser that can disguise the user's Internet Protocol (IP) address. This software contains a high degree of encryption and security, which can be used for both licit and illicit purposes (BrightPlanet, 2014). TOR-based, secure drop sites, such as the one used by *The Globe and Mail* (n.d.), offer **whistleblowers** and other activists an opportunity to anonymously upload content. However, TOR also enables access to sites on the dark web that range from illegal drug markets, such as Silk Road (which has been shut down, but many comparable and competitive marketplaces remain and continue to emerge), to sites distributing and soliciting child pornography and sites that offer "services" such as targeted assassinations.

Hackers who have stolen identifying information from websites, including credit card information, real names and addresses, social insurance numbers, and so on, may take advantage of the dark web to sell this information to hacking subnetworks for profit (sometimes for very little profit; one report found complete stolen ID records, including name, address, online passwords, and banking info were being sold for as little as £10 [$17.00 CAD] worth of bitcoin; Cuthbertson, 2018). The ongoing presence of these sites as a whole greatly complicates law enforcement efforts, which need to be continually up-to-date on technological developments (Martin, 2014).

In the words of scholars …

The concept of cyber warfare has now become a regular part of public discourse. It dominates the content of popular technical outlets such as *Wired* and *SlashDot*; it often appears in the more general media such as CNN, it has become a political priority in the United States, and a major concern for militaries around the world.

Sushil Jajodia, Preface. In Shakarian et al. (Eds.), *Introduction to Cyber Warfare: A Multidisciplinary Approach.* 2013

INTERGOVERNMENTAL CYBERWARFARE AND THE COMPUTERIZATION OF POLITICAL ANTAGONISMS

The computerization of society via the internet and its connection to millions of digital networks has led to the computerization of political antagonisms, creating a new type of virtual warfare among geopolitical opponents. Infrastructure systems have become vulnerable targets for governments who seek to destabilize enemy or "unfriendly" foreign governments without having to rely on the use of conventional weaponry to inflict damage. **Cyberwarfare**, as it is called, refers to the infiltration, disruption, and attacks by foreign agents against primary computerized systems that form part of the governmental and/or military infrastructure of a nation. There is much debate over whether computer attacks can be considered acts of warfare or terrorism, and differing definitions will emphasize the character of the perpetrator of attacks, while others will emphasize the importance of the target. Shakarian et al.'s definition is useful: "Cyber war is an extension of policy by actions taken in cyberspace by state actors or non-state actors that either constitute a serious threat to a nation's security or are conducted in response to a perceived threat against a nation's security" (Shakarian et al., 2013, p. 2). What is becoming clearer is that global antagonisms between nation-states have not abated in the 21st century, and cyberspace is becoming established as a new type of battlefield of the future. The advent of cyberwarfare and cyber terrorism have added yet another layer of concern to the quest for **cybersecurity**.

The Stuxnet case perhaps remains the hallmark example of a cyberattack that retains many characteristics of inter-state warfare. Perhaps one of the most complex computer malware programs ever developed, Stuxnet deployed in two "phases"—delivery and payload. Primarily spread by infected USB drives, the malware would search systems for the presence of a particular device—a programmable logic controller designed by Siemens (Yar & Steinmetz, 2019). Without the target hardware detected, the malware would move to other systems, not affecting its original host. The key system the malware searched for, and was designed to deliver its "payload" to, was in Iran, specifically, the site of its nuclear enrichment facility in Natanz (Yar & Steinmetz, 2019). What Stuxnet was designed to do was disrupt centrifuges used to enrich uranium; that is, it "varied the spin speed of the centrifuges, wearing them out"; in addition, signals were sent to falsely indicate that the centrifuge spin speeds were operating normally (Real Human Stories, 2011; Winer, 2019). Stuxnet thus became the first well-known, if not the first, instance of computer malware that affected physical systems linked to the computers it infected (Zetter, 2014). Up to 1,000 centrifuges of a total of 5,000 were damaged over time (Winer, 2019). More recent reports allege that joint US and Israeli intelligence services recruited an Iranian engineer to "implant the virus program into Iran's Natanz enrichment facility.… The mole gained entry to the site by posing as a technician for a front company, created by the US and Israel for the purpose of infiltrating the site" (Winer, 2019). Currently Stuxnet has morphed into an "open-source weapon," with videos publicly available on YouTube where people are analyzing the code and redesigning it. Code that can "crash power grids" or "destroy oil pipelines" has been developed. This raises important questions regarding the sources of malware and the processes through which it is deployed. Categorizing developers of malicious code as state versus non-state actors may once have been appropriate, but these lines are quickly blurring (Real Human Stories, 2011). Cyberwarfare, too, may soon be simply deemed modern warfare which incorporates affordances of digital and connective technologies (Dyer-Witheford & Matviyenko, 2019).

Cyberwarfare can also be understood in terms of global interstate **espionage** as nation-states regularly maintain spy networks and dedicate substantial resources to taking down competing governmental agencies and/or stealing intellectual property from foreign corporations. A CBC report writes, "Canada's spy agency says 2020 saw the highest level of foreign espionage and foreign interference directed at Canadian targets since the end of the Cold War" (Tunney, 2021).

Adversarial nation-states are increasingly engaging in the practice of gaining illegal entry into databases containing classified information. A December 2020 *Guardian* report writes,

A vast trove of US government emails has been targeted in a hack thought to have been carried out by Russia, American officials revealed on Monday. The stunningly large and sophisticated operation reportedly targeted federal government networks and marks the biggest cyber-raid against US officials in years. The treasury and commerce departments were both affected, and others may have been breached. Hackers gained entry into networks by getting more than 18,000 private and government users to download a tainted software update. Once inside, they were able to monitor internal emails at some of the top agencies in the US. (Paul, 2020)

Another *Guardian* report from 2017 outlines a case of cyberattack retaliation:

The US and UK may be engaged in cyber-offensives against North Korea in retaliation for attacks such as WannaCry, which caused widespread disruption to public services, companies, and homes around the world in May. Neither the UK nor the US government will confirm whether they have already mounted revenge cyber-attacks against North Korea. However, a hint that action was already being taken was offered on Tuesday when Facebook said it had recently deleted accounts linked to the Lazarus Group, a hacking entity associated with North Korea that both the US and UK blame for the WannaCry attacks. (MacAskill & Hern, 2017)

Cyberwarfare is clearly recognized as a major concern for global peace and security. Insofar as infrastructure systems, and data storage and retrieval systems, remain computerized, they are vulnerable to being breached, hacked, or compromised in various ways by those who seek to inflict damage. Beyond data systems themselves, there is also the computerized control of aircraft and weaponry, such as missiles and drones, making them vulnerable to being compromised. The future of cyberwarfare remains uncertain as virtually all computer systems are at risk in the tit-for-tat cycle of security versus criminal innovations that eventually breach security protections. Herrington and Aldrich refer to the challenge of achieving cyber security vis-à-vis the persistent security threats as *cyber-resilience*; they write, "The only way to protect against cyber-warfare will be to retain a certain proportion of national infrastructure that is under dual control. In other words, cyber-resilience may require the ability for a residual proportion of water supplies, power, and other key utilities to be controlled by analogue systems, or even by humble human beings turning wheels and pulling levers" (2013, pp. 305–306).

In the words of scholars ...

Organized crime groups have established themselves as early adopters of technology. Criminals embraced the online world long before the police ever contemplated it, and they have outpaced authorities ever since.

Mark Goodman, *Future Crimes: How Our Radical Dependence on Technology Threatens Us All.* 2015

POLICING CYBERCRIME AND THE RISE OF CYBERSECURITY

Law enforcement agencies are increasingly challenged by the overwhelming occurrence of the many new cybercrimes and technologically enhanced forms of fraud and deception. The difficulty of policing cybercrime has transformed many traditional policing practices and given rise to the relatively new area of crime control that forms part of overall attempts at cybersecurity. Often, the perpetrators of cybercrime (including telephone fraudsters, for example) evade law enforcement, or they outsmart existing cybersecurity technologies by finding loopholes in current software platforms. Cybercriminals benefit from both anonymity and the jurisdictional restrictions faced by law enforcement agencies, and yet efforts at staying one step ahead of criminal organizations continue: "In 2014, the Government of Canada enacted the *Protecting Canadians from Online Crime Act* (Bill C13). Considered by some as Canada's response to implement obligations to *The Budapest Convention on Cybercrime* (2001), Bill C13 was adopted to increase the power of law enforcement in their investigation of online activity" (Thomson et al., 2017)—and yet new challenges continue to arise.

The Canadian Anti-Fraud Centre reports that, in 2017, CA $110 million was lost due to fraudulent activities, based on 71,793 complaints, which are increasingly being perpetuated online (Yar & Steinmetz, 2019, p. 130). Online threats are perceived as fairly commonplace for Canadians today. Forty-three percent of Canadians in one survey felt that online threats are "very common," and one in three believe they will "likely ... be affected by an online threat in the near future" (EKOS Research Associates Inc., 2018, p. x). The FBI's 2020 *Internet Crime Report* indicates escalating trends in fraud and cybercrime, facilitated by the COVID-19 pandemic. The report indicates that the FBI's Internet Crime Complaint Center "received a record number of complaints from the American public in 2020: 791,790, with reported losses exceeding $4.1 billion. This represents a

69% increase in total complaints from 2019. Business E-mail Compromise (BEC) schemes continued to be the costliest: 19,369 complaints with an adjusted loss of approximately $1.8 billion. Phishing scams were also prominent: 241,342 complaints, with adjusted losses of over $54 million. The number of ransomware incidents also continues to rise, with 2,474 incidents reported in 2020" (Internet Crime Complaint Center [IC3], 2020, p. 3). Rising trends in both total complaints and total losses are indicated in the report. Between 2016 and 2020, total complaints to the FBI's Crime Complaint Center rose from 298,728 to 791,790; losses during this time rose from $1.5 billion to $4.2 billion (IC3, 2020, p. 5).

The computerization of contemporary society makes criminal apprehension and police work very different than in the pre-computer age. The computerization of crime has had such an enormous impact on crime commission and on crime control that it marks a new paradigm of policing and criminal investigation that requires specialist experts on cybercrime. New innovations in computing, such as the rise of cloud-based information and operation systems continue to complicate policing efforts. Future innovations in computerization such as **artificial intelligence (AI)** and **quantum computing** may further complicate policing the internet than is the case with conventional digital systems.

Despite the difficulties of policing cybercrime, police forces have substantially expanded their resources to deal with this complicated task—often through the use of innovative policing techniques, task forces, and *special operations* designed to lure, foil, and apprehend cybercriminals. One noteworthy example is highlighted in a CTV world report as follows:

> When the FBI dismantled an encrypted messaging service based in Canada in 2018, agents noticed users moving to other networks. Instead of following their tracks to rivals, investigators decided on a new tactic: creating their own service. ANOM, a secure-messaging service built by the FBI and other law enforcement agencies, launched in October 2019 and solidified its following after authorities took down another rival. Popularity spread by word of mouth. When ANOM was taken down Monday, authorities had collected more than 27 million messages from about 12,000 devices in 45 languages—a vast body of evidence that fueled a global sting operation. Authorities on Tuesday revealed the operation known as Trojan Shield and announced that it had dealt an "unprecedented blow" to organized crime around the world. "Each and every device in this case was used to further criminal activity," said Suzanne Turner, the agent in charge of the FBI in San Diego, where the investigation began in 2016. Users were "upper-echelon, command-and-control" figures in more than 300 criminal organizations. (Corder, 2021)

Policing cybercrime is not solely the responsibility of public police forces. Wall (2007/2011) suggests that the police play a role as actors in a broader *network* of control measures that include internet users and user groups, virtual environment managers, network infrastructure providers, corporate security organizations, and non-governmental organizations, among others. There is also increasing pressure on "Big Tech" companies, such as Google, Facebook, Microsoft, Apple, and Amazon, to play a larger role and take greater responsibility for the cyberspaces they control (CB Insights, 2019). Calls are being made for internet regulations that would help foster a legal framework of accountability for corporations who possess dominance in terms of worldwide use (e.g., Facebook). In April 2019, for instance, the British government introduced an "Online Harms" white paper, which "proposes an arm's-length regulator that would be responsible for setting and enforcing rules prohibiting speech that is illegal (think: child porn and hate crimes) or socially damaging (think: cyberbullying and intimidation)" (Haggart & Tusikov, 2019). Critics, however, argue that while necessary, such legislation is not sufficient in addressing the wider "systemic conditions that have made commercial online platforms so problematic," including the "personalized-advertising, algorithm-fuelled, maximized-engagement-at-any-cost business model" that has "played a large role in creating a poisonous online environment" (2019).

CONCLUSION: THE COSTS OF CYBERCRIME

The costs of cybercrime are very high. From damaged lives and businesses to disrupted infrastructure systems, as well as huge financial losses, the problem seems to be growing larger year after year. The McAfee report *The Hidden Costs of Cybercrime* states, "Since 2018, we estimated that the cost of global cybercrime reached over $1 trillion. We estimated the monetary loss from cybercrime at approximately $945 billion. Added to this was global spending on cybersecurity, which was expected to exceed $145 billion in 2020. Today, this is a $1 trillion dollar drag on the global economy" (Smith & Lostri, 2020).

The US Department of Justice, highlighting a report by Cybersecurity Ventures, projected a doubling annual cost of cybercrime between 2015 ($3 trillion) and 2021 ($6 trillion; Rosenstein, 2017). Small businesses may declare bankruptcy after a hacking breach, with larger corporations often paying damages of hundreds of millions of dollars; private reports indicate the average cost of a data breach to be about $3.5 million (Rosenstein, 2017). In 2015, Canadians reported losing $61 million due to scams, though the Better Business Bureau estimates the total figure is closer to $1.2 billion (Laanela, 2016). Online attacks targeting Canadians may be on the rise. One survey indicates that 56 percent reporting being victimized through a virus attack, spyware, or malware attack on devices used to go online for personal use. "Between 5 and 12 per cent have experienced identity theft and financial loss as a result of online activity," and one in five report the attacks as having a "significant impact" (EKOS Research Associates Inc., 2018, p. 8). Given such statistics, it is striking to consider that Canadians' risky behaviours online are "prevalent," with "nearly half report[ing] using the same passwords for multiple accounts, and four in ten allow[ing] their browsers to store their passwords" (EKOS Research Associates Inc., 2018, p. 8).

The figures listed in the preceding examples remain speculative insofar as the actual cost of cybercrime is difficult to quantify with precision. What remains clear is that scams, frauds, and cybercrime represent a substantial portion of *illegal economic activity* otherwise known as the underground economy (which will be discussed in Chapter 13), as they also pose a real concern to public safety and well-being. The extent to which such wrongdoings can be effectively controlled remains to be seen. Beyond the economic damage, which is also reportedly on the rise due to advantages cybercriminals took during the COVID-19 pandemic, the personal costs from revenge porn, phishing, identity theft, and related crimes are pernicious and debilitating not only for individual victims but for their communities and society as well.

REVIEW QUESTIONS

1. Compare traditional scams and frauds to contemporary cybercrime. How are they related and how do they differ?
2. List three different examples of a scam, fraud, or cybercrime and explain why you think they pose a significant risk to society.
3. What makes policing cybercrime a difficult challenge? Can you think of ways that cyber criminality can be more effectively controlled?

GLOSSARY

artificial intelligence (AI): The attempt to make complex computerized machines achieve or approximate the cognitive capacities of human beings.

black hat hackers: Computer hackers who engage in crimes such as theft, sabotage, and other malicious attacks with criminal intent.

botnets: Networks of personal computers that have been infected by malicious software in order for cyber criminals to commandeer them for nefarious activities rather than using their own.

bullying: Intimidating, threatening, or inflicting physical violence upon a person in a position of vulnerability.

catfishing: A type of online fraud or deception where the perpetrator creates a fake identity, often using someone else's flattering personal image to lure another into a romantic involvement.

con artist: A person skilled at gaining the trust and confidence of their intended victim for the purposes of deceiving or defrauding them.

cryptocurrency: A type of digital money or currency that is not controlled by centralized banks that is difficult to restrict or control, which is thus often the preferred currency of criminal organizations but is still subject to value fluctuations.

cyber: Having to do with computerization or technological modes of information storage and delivery.

cyberattack: A deliberate and unauthorized attempt to compromise, disable, withhold, or destroy a computer or computer system and the information contained therein.

cyberbullying: Intimidating, threatening, or inflicting emotional suffering on a person through the use of electronic communication systems such as email, the internet, or social media.

cybercrime: Criminal activity perpetrated or mediated by means of computer systems and/or electronic communication devices.

cybersecurity: Electronic security systems, user protocols, and procedures implemented to prevent unauthorized access to computer systems.

cyberspace: The information sharing, communications, and interaction environment created by a vast interconnected network of computers that is enabled by human participants.

cyberstalking: An ongoing pattern of harassment aimed at the target victim usually by following them online in order to make them live in fear of impending harm.

cyberwarfare: The use of computers and electronic code to infiltrate, disrupt, or attack the governmental and/or military infrastructure of a nation by foreign agents.

dark web: The cyberspace of generally non-conforming online activities that exists on the internet but requires specific software applications and user authorization to access, which contains activity that is difficult to trace or monitor.

distributed denial-of-service (DDoS) attack: A type of cyberattack that disables a website or computer system by involving numerous coordinated devices to flood and overwhelm the target computer server, making it crash and thus rendering it inaccessible to other users.

doxxing: Posting private, personal, or confidential information about a person or organization on the internet with malicious intent.

espionage: The secretive practice of spying by covert government agents, usually to obtain secretive military and state-classified information from a foreign government.

extort/extortion: The practice of obtaining something, such as money, contracts, special treatment, or sexual favours, from someone through threats or some other form of coercion.

fraud: A person or item deliberately manipulating someone through the presentation of false, deceptive, or misleading information with the intention of personal or monetary gain.

global village: The idea that the vastness of the world is virtually compressed into a small village due to the instantaneous communication systems that allows people to connect with each other as if they were neighbours.

grandparent scam: A telephone or Facebook scam that targets unsuspecting grandparents and tricks them into sending money by convincing them that their teenage or young adult grandchild is in desperate need of money, because they are stranded somewhere else in the world and in an emergency situation.

hacker: An individual who uses high-level computer skills to gain unauthorized access into computer systems.

hacktivist: A computer hacker who gains unauthorized access to computing systems in order to engage in some sort of social activism or protest.

identity theft: A form of fraud that involves assuming the identity and name of another person for the purposes of committing various forms of wrongdoing, monetary gain, or to evade the law.

internet: The globally connected network of computers, devices, and information systems that initializes the world wide web, including websites, email, and numerous other connected devices.

Internet of Things: Household objects connected to the internet, including "smart" thermostats and fridges, smartwatches, musical devices, and automobiles, which have computer processors that can be remotely accessed.

malware: A type of malicious software that is secretly or inadvertently downloaded onto computers in order to allow someone to commandeer them, gain access to personal information stored on the computer, or hold its content hostage.

mark: The victim chosen to be the target of a scam or fraud.

phishing scam: A type of email, text message, or clickbait scam in which someone is deceived into entering confidential information, which is then apprehended by the scammer who uses it to access bank accounts or steal other personal information.

Ponzi scheme: A type of economic fraud involving the use of new investors' money to pay returns on the investments of previous investors; in most cases, no authentic financial investments are made to generate an authentic monetary return for the investors, which causes the scheme to fail all investors except for the primary perpetrator, who retains investors' money for themselves.

pyramid scheme: A type of illegal get-rich-quick scheme that involves the constant recruitment of new paying members into a network of people with a pyramidal hierarchy, where the person at the top receives the monies paid by the new recruits entering at the lower rungs of the pyramid. It eventually fails because there are no longer enough new members to sustain the process.

quantum computing: An advanced, extremely fast, and sophisticated type of computing system; quantum technology that surpasses the capabilities of current binary code computers.

ransomware: A type of malicious software that blocks a user's access to a computer system until a sum of money, known as a ransom, is paid.

revenge porn: Sexually explicit images of someone posted on the internet or social media without their consent for the purpose of retaliation.

robocall: An unwelcome, pre-recorded phone message generated by an automatic system that is sent to large numbers of people, usually by scammers or telemarketers.

scam: An unfair exchange of some sort that defrauds or swindles an unsuspecting person.

sextortion: A type of extortion where the perpetrator threatens to reveal sexual images of the victim over the internet if they fail to comply with their demands.

social media: Electronic communication forums located on websites and hand-held device applications that allow for and facilitate social networking.

space transition theory: The theory that social behaviour in conventional social spaces changes when people occupy cyberspace, as the anonymity it offers removes the typical social deterrents of criminal behaviour and can cause repressed criminal tendencies to emerge.

spammer: Someone who uses computer systems to send unsolicited or unauthorized *spam* messages to large number of email recipients.

spyware: A type of malicious program that is used to *spy* on the activities performed with or data stored on a computer system.

trolling: Engaging in unwelcome, disruptive, or inflammatory online behaviour, usually by deliberately posting offensive or inappropriate content on a Web forum or comment section.

whistleblower: Someone who releases information, often anonymously, regarding the unethical conduct of an individual or an organization with the intent of having them called to account.

white hat hackers: An ethical hacker who uses their computer security expertise to combat black hat hackers, often is hired to improve the cybersecurity of computer systems by attempting remote firewall penetration exercises.

REFERENCES

AARP. (2020, June 30). Grandparent scam. Retrieved from https://www.aarp.org/money/scams-fraud/info-2019/grandparent.html

Associated Press. (2021, May 9). Cyberattack on U.S. pipeline is linked to criminal gang. *NBC News*. Retrieved from https://www.nbcnews.com/politics/white-house/cyberattack-u-s-pipeline-linked-criminal-gang-n1266791

Baker, V. (2021, May 30). Samantha Azzopardi: Australia's notorious con artist sentenced for child theft. *BBC*. Retrieved from https://www.bbc.com/news/world-australia-57284621

Barrett, B. (2020, October 2). How 4 Chinese hackers allegedly took down Equifax. *Wired*. Retrieved from https://www.wired.com/story/equifax-hack-china/

BBC News. (2021a, March 9). UK businesses caught buying five-star Google reviews. *BBC*. Retrieved from https://www.bbc.co.uk/news/technology-56321576

BBC News. (2021b, April 2). Anna Sorokin: Fake heiress detained by US immigration authorities. *BBC*. Retrieved from https://www.bbc.com/news/world-us-canada-56614021

BBC News. (2021c, June 2). JBS: Cyber-attack hits world's largest meat supplier. *BBC*. Retrieved from https://www.bbc.com/news/world-us-canada-57318965

Berghel, H. (2001). The code red worm. *Communications of the ACM, 44*(12), 15–19.

Bing, C. (2021, June 3). Exclusive: U.S. to give ransomware hacks similar priority as terrorism. *Reuters*. Retrieved from https://www.reuters.com/technology/exclusive-us-give-ransomware-hacks-similar-priority-terrorism-official-says-2021-06-03/

BrightPlanet. (2014, March 27). *Clearing up confusion—deep web vs. dark web*. Retrieved from https://brightplanet.com/2014/03/27/clearing-confusion-deep-web-vs-dark-web/

Brown, S. (2006). The criminology of hybrids: Rethinking crime and law in technosocial networks. *Theoretical Criminology, 10*(2), 223–244.

Campoamor, D. (2021, May 24). From private jets to luxury hotels, the "lavish lifestyle" of Elizabeth Holmes will also be put on trial. *Refinery29*. Retrieved from https://www.refinery29.com/en-us/2021/05/10487562/elizabeth-holmes-lavish-lifestyle-criminal-trial

Canadian Anti-Fraud Centre. (2021, May 17). *Identity theft and fraud*. Government of Canada. Retrieved from https://www.antifraudcentre-centreantifraude.ca/scams-fraudes/identity-identite-eng.htm

CB Insights. (2019, March 27). How big tech is finally tackling cybersecurity. Retrieved from https://www.cbinsights.com/research/facebook-amazon-microsoft-google-apple-cybersecurity/

CBC News. (2021, April 12). B.C. man jailed again for refusing to remove revenge website targeting ex-wife. *CBC*. Retrieved from https://www.cbc.ca/news/canada/british-columbia/patrick-fox-revenge-website-sentenced-breach-of-probation-1.5984329

Collier, K. (2021, June 9). Beef supplier JBS paid ransomware hackers $11 million. *NBC News*. Retrieved from https://www.nbcnews.com/tech/security/meat-supplier-jbs-paid-ransomware-hackers-11-million-n1270271

Corder, M., Perry, N., & Spagat, E. (2021, June 8). FBI-run messaging app deals "unprecedented blow" to organized crime around the world. *CTV*. Retrieved from https://www.ctvnews.ca/world/fbi-run-messaging-app-deals-unprecedented-blow-to-organized-crime-around-the-world-1.5460685

CTVNews.ca Staff. (2007, January 25). Winners security breach hits Canadian cardholders. *CTV*. Retrieved from https://www.ctvnews.ca/winners-security-breach-hits-canadian-cardholders-1.226180

CTVNews.ca Staff. (2018, October 25). Woman charged with pretending to practice witchcraft after allegedly bilking man out of $600K. *CTV News*. Retrieved from https://www.ctvnews.ca/canada/woman-charged-with-pretending-to-practice-witchcraft-after-allegedly-bilking-man-out-of-600k-1.4149336

Cuthbertson, A. (2018, December 25). Stolen UK identities selling for as little as £10 on the dark web. *Independent*. Retrieved from https://www.independent.co.uk/life-style/gadgets-and-tech/news/dark-web-id-value-hackers-cyber-crime-a8683821.html

Darby, M. (1998, December 1). In Ponzi we trust. *Smithsonian Magazine*. Retrieved from https://www.smithsonianmag.com/history/in-ponzi-we-trust-64016168/

Dyer-Witheford, N., & Matviyenko, S. (2019). *Cyberwar and revolution: Digital subterfuge in global capitalism*. University of Minnesota Press.

Edwards, E. (2017, April 13). IT security faces huge challenge, says hacker "Mafiaboy." *The Irish Times*. Retrieved from https://www.irishtimes.com/business/technology/it-security-faces-huge-challenge-says-hacker-mafiaboy-1.3046238

EKOS Research Associates, Inc. (2018, September 30). *Survey of internet users regarding cyber security: Summary*. Public Safety Canada. Retrieved from https://publications.gc.ca/collections/collection_2018/sp-ps/PS4-245-2018-1-eng.pdf

Elliott, N. (2016, October 27). Ransomware is booming and companies are paying up. *The Wall Street Journal*. Retrieved from https://blogs.wsj.com/riskandcompliance/2016/10/27/ransomware-is-booming-and-companies-are-paying-up/

Esen, R. (2002). Cyber crime: A growing problem. *The Journal of Criminal Law, 66*(3), 269–283.

Fowler, B. (2016, October 22). Attacks on the internet getting bigger and nastier. *CTV*. Retrieved from https://www.ctvnews.ca/sci-tech/attacks-on-the-internet-getting-bigger-and-nastier-1.3127001

Friedman, T. (2005). *Electric dreams: Computers in American culture*. New York University Press.

Get Cyber Safe. (n.d.). *Glossary*. Government of Canada. Retrieved from https://www.getcybersafe.gc.ca/en/glossary

The Globe and Mail. (n.d.). SecureDrop at *The Globe and Mail*. Retrieved from https://sec.theglobeandmail.com/securedrop/

Goodman, M. (2015). *Future crimes: How our radical dependence on technology threatens us all*. Doubleday Canada.

Government of Canada. (2021, July 12). *Criminal Code (R.S.C., 1985, c. C-46)*. Retrieved from https://laws-lois.justice.gc.ca/eng/acts/c-46/section-380.html

Grabosky, P., Smith, R. G., & Dempsey, G. (2001). *Electronic theft: Unlawful acquisition in cyberspace*. Cambridge University Press.

Grant, M. (2017, November 1). Con artists who orchestrated Canada's largest Ponzi scam spend only 2 of 12 years in prison. *CBC*. Retrieved from https://www.cbc.ca/news/canada/calgary/brost-sorenson-parole-fraud-ponzi-1.4382289

Grau, A. (2019, August 12). When refrigerators attack—how cyber criminals infect appliances, and how manufacturers can stop them. *IOT Business News*. Retrieved from https://iotbusinessnews.com/2019/08/12/00939-when-refrigerators-attack-how-cyber-criminals-infect-appliances-and-how-manufacturers-can-stop-them/

Grzegorek, V. (2018, January 10). Federal indictment alleges 28-year-old Cleveland man created "Fruitfly" malware, spied on thousands of computers over 13 years. *Cleveland Scene*. Retrieved from https://www.clevescene.com/scene-and-heard/archives/2018/01/10/

federal-indictment-alleges-28-year-old-cleveland-man-is-creator-of-fruitfly-malware-spied-on-thousands-of-computers-over-13-years

Hadi, M., & Logan, B. (2017, September 7). Equifax: Hackers may have the personal details of 143 million US customers. *Business Insider*. Retrieved from https://www .businessinsider.com/equifax-hackers-may-have-accessed-personal-details-143-million-us-customers-2017-9

Haggart, B., & Tusikov, N. (2019, April 26). White paper sets blueprint for internet regulation. *Winnipeg Free Press*. Retrieved from https://www.winnipegfreepress.com/ opinion/analysis/white-paper-sets-blueprint-for-internet-regulation-509101772.html

Hancock, T. (2007, March 13). When monogamy becomes monotony. *The Times*. Retrieved from https://www.thetimes.co.uk/article/when-monogamy-becomes-monotony-mdj3qz2fc8d

Hawn, M. (1996). Fear of a hack planet: The strange metamorphosis of the computer hacker. *ZDNet*.

Herrington, L., & Aldrich, R. (2013). The future of cyber-resilience in an age of global complexity. *Politics, 33*(4), 299–310.

Hersher, R. (2015, February 7). Meet Mafiaboy, the "bratty kid" who took down the internet. *npr*. Retrieved from https://www.npr.org/sections/alltechconsidered/ 2015/02/07/384567322/meet-mafiaboy-the-bratty-kid-who-took-down-the-internet

Holt, T. J., & Bossler, A. M. (2014). An assessment of the current state of cybercrime scholarship. *Deviant Behavior, 35*(1), 20–40.

Hutchins, A. (2014, April 17). The interview: "MafiaBoy" speaks up. *Maclean's*. Retrieved from https://www.macleans.ca/society/technology/the-interview-4/

Internet Crime Complaint Center (IC3). (2020). *Internet Crime Report 2020*. Federal Bureau of Investigation. Retrieved from https://www.ic3.gov/Media/PDF/ AnnualReport/2020_IC3Report.pdf

Jaishankar, K. (2008). Space transition theory of cyber crimes. In F. Schmallager & M. Pittaro (Eds.), *Crimes of the internet* (pp. 283–301). Prentice Hall.

Jajodia, S. (2013). Preface. In P. Shakarian, J. Shakarian, & A. Ruef (Eds.), *Introduction to cyber-warfare: A multidisciplinary approach* (pp. xi–xii). Elsevier/Syngress.

James, L. (2005). *Phishing exposed*. Syngress.

Jelen, S. (2018, November 6). An ode to white hats: What is ethical hacking? [Blog]. *SecurityTrails*. Retrieved from https://securitytrails.com/blog/ode-white-hats-ethical-hacking

Kalvapalle, R. (2019, January 30). Here's how to tell between a genuine CRA phone call and a scammer. *Global News*. Retrieved from https://globalnews.ca/news/4907961/ cra-phone-scams/

Ke, G. (2019, March 12). B.C. couple told they owe $100K after identity thieves buy SUV with fraudulent loan. *Global News.* Retrieved from https://globalnews.ca/news/5050298/bc-couple-identity-theft-nightmare/

Kelley, M. (Writer), & Weinstein, T. (Director). (2013, November 15). The sextortion of Amanda Todd (Season 39, Episode 7) [TV Series episode]. In J. Williamson (Executive Producer), *The Fifth Estate.* Canadian Broadcasting Corporation. Retrieved from https://www.cbc.ca/player/play/2418622078

Khorram, Y. (2022, July 7). Theranos ex-COO Sunny Balwani found guilty on all 12 fraud charges 6 months after founder Holmes' conviction. *CNBC.* Retrieved from https://www.cnbc.com/2022/07/07/theranos-ex-coo-sunny-balwani-found-guilty-in-all-12-charges-6-months-after-founder-holmes-conviction.html

Laanela, M. (2016, March 1). Canada's top 10 scams earned crooks $1.2B last year, says BBB. *CBC.* Retrieved from https://www.cbc.ca/news/canada/british-columbia/canada-s-top-10-scams-earned-crooks-1-2b-last-year-says-bbb-1.3471279

Levy, S. (1984). *Hackers: Heroes of the computer revolution.* Doubleday.

Lord, N. (2017, July 27). A timeline of the Ashley Madison hack. *Digital Guardian.* Retrieved from https://digitalguardian.com/blog/timeline-ashley-madison-hack

MacAskill, E., & Hern, A. (2017, December 19). Facebook action hints at western retaliation over WannaCry attack. *The Guardian.* Retrieved from https://www.theguardian.com/technology/2017/dec/19/wannacry-cyberattack-us-says-it-has-evidence-north-korea-was-directly-responsible

Martin, J. (2014). *Drugs on the dark net: How cryptomarkets are transforming the global trade in illicit drugs.* Palgrave Macmillan.

McFarland, J. (2015, January 21). BCSC fines woman $33-million for operating Ponzi scheme. *The Globe and Mail.* Retrieved from https://www.theglobeandmail.com/report-on-business/industry-news/the-law-page/bcsc-fines-woman-33-million-for-operating-ponzi-scheme/article22552636/

McKenna, K. (2017, September 7). Montreal woman terrified her personal info was posted in escort ads. Did police do enough? *CBC.* Retrieved from https://www.cbc.ca/news/canada/montreal/montreal-woman-terrified-her-personal-info-was-posted-in-escort-ads-did-police-do-enough-1.4276602

McKenzie, L. (2019, July 15). Hackers demand $2 million from Monroe. *Inside Higher Ed.* Retrieved from https://www.insidehighered.com/news/2019/07/15/hackers-demand-2-million-monroe-college-ransomware-attack

Microsoft. (2009, September 10). *Ransomware.* Retrieved from https://docs.microsoft.com/en-ca/windows/security/threat-protection/intelligence/ransomware-malware

Morgan, S. (2017, November 14). Global ransomware damage costs predicted to hit $11.5 billion by 2019. *Cybercrime Magazine*. Retrieved from https://cybersecurityventures.com/ransomware-damage-report-2017-part-2/

Newman, L. H. (2018, May 3). Nigerian email scammers are more effective than ever. *Wired*. Retrieved from https://www.wired.com/story/nigerian-email-scammers-more-effective-than-ever/

Paul, K. (2020, December 15). What you need to know about the biggest hack of the US government in years. *The Guardian*. Retrieved from https://www.theguardian.com/technology/2020/dec/15/orion-hack-solar-winds-explained-us-treasury-commerce-department

Paul, K. (2022, January 14). Elizabeth Holmes to be sentenced nine months after guilty verdict. *The Guardian*. Retrieved from https://www.theguardian.com/technology/2022/jan/13/elizabeth-holmes-sentence-september-fraud

Pearl, M. (2015, July 21). Everything we know so far about the Ashley Madison hack. *Vice*. Retrieved from https://www.vice.com/en_us/article/yvxwdy/everything-we-know-so-far-about-the-ashley-madison-hack-265

Real Human Stories. (2011, June 8). STUXNET: The virus that almost started WW3. [Video]. YouTube. Retrieved from https://www.youtube.com/watch?v=7g0pi4J8auQ

Reuters. (2021, May 26). "Dangerous" mystery campaign seeks influencers to discredit Pfizer vaccine. *National Post*. Retrieved from https://nationalpost.com/news/world/pathetic-dangerous-mystery-campaign-sought-influencers-to-discredit-pfizer-vaccine

Rosenstein, R. J. (2017, October 4). Deputy Attorney General Rod J. Rosenstein delivers remarks at the Cambridge Cyber Summit. *United States Department of Justice*. Retrieved from https://www.justice.gov/opa/speech/deputy-attorney-general-rod-j-rosenstein-delivers-remarks-cambridge-cyber-summit

Russon, M.-A. (2021, May 10). US fuel pipeline hackers "didn't mean to create problems." *BBC*. Retrieved from https://www.bbc.com/news/business-57050690

Shakarian, P., Shakarian, J., & Ruef, A. (2013). *Introduction to cyber-warfare: A multidisciplinary approach*. Elsevier/Syngress.

Shelley, M. (1891). *Frankenstein or the modern Prometheus*. George Routledge and Sons.

Silva, S. (2018, February 12). Criminals hide "billions" in crypto-cash—Europol. *BBC*. Retrieved from https://www.bbc.com/news/technology-43025787

Sjouwerman, S. (2020, November 29). *91% of cyberattacks begin with spear phishing email* [Blog]. KnowBe4. Retrieved from https://blog.knowbe4.com/bid/252429/91-of-cyberattacks-begin-with-spear-phishing-email

Skiba, K. (2020, September 25). Psychic scams rise during COVID-19 pandemic. *AARP*. Retrieved from https://www.aarp.org/money/scams-fraud/info-2020/psychic-scams-coronavirus.html

Smith, Z. M., & Lostri, E. (2020). *The hidden costs of cybercrime*. Center for Strategic and International Studies. Retrieved from https://www.mcafee.com/enterprise/en-us/assets/reports/rp-hidden-costs-of-cybercrime.pdf

Stalans, L. J., & Donner, C. M. (2018). Explaining why cybercrime occurs: Criminological and psychological theories. In H. Jahankhani (Ed.), *Cyber criminology* (pp. 25–45). Springer.

Taylor, P. (1999). *Hackers: Crime and the digital sublime*. Routledge.

Thomson, J., Adam, J., & Pang, B. (2017). Panel discussion: What's the greatest challenge in policing cybercrime? *Gazette, 79*(3), 12–13. Retrieved from https://www.rcmp-grc.gc.ca/en/gazette/whats-the-greatest-challenge-policing-cybercrime

Tidy, J. (2021, April 30). The ransomware surge ruining lives. *BBC*. Retrieved from https://www.bbc.com/news/technology-56933733

Tunney, C. (2021, April 12). CSIS says 2020 was a banner year for espionage operations targeting Canada. *CBC*. Retrieved from https://www.cbc.ca/news/politics/nsicop-espionage-pandemic-1.5983612

Twist, J. (2003, November 14). Cracking the hacker underground. *BBC*. Retrieved from http://news.bbc.co.uk/2/hi/technology/3246375.stm

Valdez, A. (2018, March 12). Inside the Vatican's first-ever hackathon. *Wired*. Retrieved from https://www.wired.com/story/inside-vhacks-first-ever-vatican-hackathon/

Valiquet, D. (2011). *Cybercrime: Issues* [Background Paper]. Government of Canada, Library of Parliament. Retrieved from https://publications.gc.ca/collections/collection_2011/bdp-lop/bp/2011-36-eng.pdf

Wall, D. (2001). *Crime and the internet: Cybercrimes and cyberfears*. Routledge.

Wall, D. S. (2011). Policing cybercrimes: Situating the public police in networks of security within cyberspace. *Police Practice & Research: An International Journal, 8*(2): 183–205. (Original work published 2007)

Wall, D. S. (Ed.). (2017). *Crime and deviance in cyberspace*. Routledge.

Wiedeman, R. (2016, September 5). The Sandy Hook hoax. *Intelligencer*. Retrieved from https://nymag.com/intelligencer/2016/09/the-sandy-hook-hoax.html

Winer, S. (2019, September 3). "Dutch mole" planted Stuxnet virus in Iran nuclear site on behalf of CIA, Mossad. *The Times of Israel*. Retrieved from https://www.timesofisrael.com/dutch-mole-planted-infamous-stuxnet-virus-in-iran-nuclear-site-report/

Woolf, N. (2016, October 26). DDoS attack that disrupted internet was largest of its kind in history, experts say. *The Guardian*. Retrieved from https://www.theguardian .com/technology/2016/oct/26/ddos-attack-dyn-mirai-botnet#img-1

Yar, M., & Steinmetz, K. (2019). *Cybercrime and society* (3rd ed.). SAGE Publications.

Zetter, K. (2014, November 3). An unprecedented look at Stuxnet, the world's first digital weapon. *Wired*. Retrieved from https://www.wired.com/2014/11/ countdown-to-zero-day-stuxnet/

CHAPTER 12

Indigenous Justice and Colonial Injustice: Remembering the Past to Change the Future

Lisa Monchalin

LEARNING OBJECTIVES

In this chapter, you will

- reflect on various Indigenous worldviews, concepts of justice, and methods of addressing wrongdoings;
- learn about government policies of assimilation and residential schools and recognize the violence against, and incarceration of, Indigenous peoples by the colonial state; and
- consider the importance of Elder knowledge as a strategy for countering colonialism.

INTRODUCTION

This chapter examines Indigenous conceptions of justice by looking at various worldviews, laws, and examples of addressing wrongdoings. It also discusses colonialism, displacement, imprisonment, and abuse in residential schools, and the resulting intergenerational trauma. Finally, the chapter scrutinizes the ways in which Indigenous peoples in Canada face unique challenges in relation to the criminal justice system, arguing that Canada's early colonial goals remain largely unchanged. The continued rise of Indigenous overrepresentation in prisons, as well as the crisis of missing and murdered Indigenous women and girls, is a direct reflection of colonialism and its continuation. Moving forward, Indigenous peoples' resistance to the colonial project remains strong. Cultures, traditions, and teachings from Elders, who reinforce a remembrance of who we are, remain a driving force for positive change and countering colonialism and its impacts.

WORLDVIEWS AND CONCEPTS OF JUSTICE

There are many different Indigenous languages, cultures, and traditions across Turtle Island (North America). Thus, so too are there various concepts and notions of "justice." To assume there is only one "Indigenous worldview" or one definition of "Indigenous justice" that applies to all Indigenous peoples is incorrect. This would be taking a **pan-Indian** approach, which is very limiting, as it lumps all Indigenous peoples into a category that incorrectly assumes all are the same. As Stó:lō scholar Wenona Victor has explained, "it is important to avoid and be aware of the colonial habit to pan-Indianize all things Indigenous, including how we practice and experience justice" (2007, p. 15). At the same time, she also states that, "along with this diversity there are also similarities and philosophical beliefs that unite all Indigenous peoples of Turtle Island" (p. 15). So, while it is important to note that not all Indigenous peoples are one in the same, it is also important to note that they do have some shared commonalities. Citizen of Fisher River Cree Nation Michael Anthony Hart (Kaskitémahikan) states, "as Indigenous peoples of Turtle Island we have our own worldviews. Our worldviews have divergences from one another, but they also share commonalities that are distinguishable from an Amer-European 'Enlightened' worldview" (2009, p. 154). Therefore, while Indigenous worldviews and views of justice are different, there are shared commonalties, and these commonalties tend to be in stark contrast to those informing Euro-Canadian or American western worldviews.

The dominant way to achieve so-called justice in Canada today is through a reliance on police, court, and corrections systems. Justice is realized by arresting, convicting, and imposing sanctions. Such a system relies largely on deterrence, a fear-based strategy whereby the apprehension and threat of punishment is assumed to curb behaviour. The worldview informing this "justice" system is one largely rooted in a capitalist and economic development ideology, one that has a drive for greed, a thirst for rising to the top, and a willingness to conquer all to achieve.

For Indigenous peoples, forms of doing "justice" would stem from the specific community's worldviews and value systems. As Professor Leroy Little Bear, Blood Tribe of the Blackfoot Confederacy, explained, "Aboriginal traditions, laws, and customs are the practical application of the philosophy and values of the group"

(2009, p. 79). Depending on the community, people, or person, there are many different worldviews, which inform notions of justice. What might be considered "justice" would be built into Indigenous forms of governance and everyday life. Wenona Victor explains that "Indigenous forms of justice tend to guide almost all aspects of one's life from the basis of good governance and leadership to the guidance of daily interactions between neighbors" (2007, p. 14). Ojibwe grandmother Shirley O'Connor taught Mohawk scholar Patricia Monture-Angus that, for Ojibwe peoples, children learn how to live through stories passed down by grandparents. They are taught about respect and how to live in an honest way. O'Connor explained, "justice was a part of everyday living and how you were good to yourself" and further explained, "justice is teaching about life" (Monture-Angus, 1995, pp. 241–242). Chantal Fiola describes her Métis Anishinaabe-Kwe worldview as coming from Creation Stories that have been passed down "through the generations orally and through writing systems which include *wiigwas* (birchbark) scrolls, petroglyphs and petroforms, wampum belts, and 'Medicine Wheels' made of stones and boulders" (2015, p. 76). She explains how these Creation Stories teach one how to live and pursue ***mino-bimaadiziwin***, meaning the "good life, good relations" (p. 76). Discussing his Ojibway traditions in the 1800s, Mississaugas Ojibway writer Kah-ge-ga-gah-bowh stated, "customs handed down from generation to generation have been the only laws to guide them" (Copway, 1851, p. 141). Thus, ways to live have been passed down through generations through various forms, including through the passing down of stories, oral teachings, and through various types of writings, signs, and symbols.

For some, ways of living passed down through generations have also acknowledged a sacred link between all things on the planet, recognizing humans as being part of a web or circle of life. Larry McDermott (Algonquin) and Peigi Wilson (Métis) explain that Algonquin Law outlines the sacred responsibilities between people and the earth. This is law that comes directly from the Creator, to which a key principle is ***ginawaydaganuk***, a concept that takes into consideration the "physical, emotional, mental, and spiritual connections to all of life" (2010, p. 206). This includes all of the life-givers, such as "the plants, animals, water, air, earth, and fire" (p. 206). All of these aspects are recognized as sacred gifts that must be honoured to make sure these gifts flourish. This is both a collective and individual responsibility of the people. All action taken must be considered in relation to the impact it will have on the next seven generations. As McDermott and Wilson further state, "Algonquin law requires consideration of the cumulative impacts of actions on the entire web of life" (p. 206). Russell Means (Lakotah) and Bayard Johnson state, "we understand, like all indigenous people, that we are intrinsically part of a system that is not above or outside or separate from the natural world and natural law, we are part of a mosaic or web of life" (2013, p. 5). Huron-Wendat scholar and historian Georges Sioui has described a similar notion when outlining traditional Huron-Wendat social principles. He illustrates the universe as a great chain of relationships, whereby all things on the planet are equal, and human beings are not more or less important than any other life forms. He refers to this as the "Sacred Circle of Life" (1999, p. 114). Métis scholar Brenda Macdougall explains the Cree concept of *wahkootowin*, which is "itself a worldview linking land, family, and identity in one interconnected web of being" (2010, p. 242). It conveys ideas and family values about how to live, such as "reciprocity, mutual support, decency, and order" which in turn shape "the behaviours, actions, and decision-making processes" of the community (p. 8). In addition to serving as a guide for mediating interactions between humans, it also extends beyond humans to include guiding interactions between all things human and non-human within the environment. Thus, within various Indigenous worldviews, peoples strive to live their lives in a good way, guided by a knowledge that all is connected.

Macdougall (2010) further maintains that language both shapes and expresses worldviews. Similarly, Fred Kelly from the Ojibways of Onigaming First Nation, and a member of Midewewin, the Sacred Law and Medicine Society of the Anishinaabe, explains that "the very meaning of world views and traditional lifeways are understandable in their original languages" (2008, p. 36). Thus, looking to Indigenous languages for notions of "justice" and "crime" may provide further insight into these concepts, as well as the worldviews that frame them. At the same time, this will never be a total replacement for fully understanding such concepts, because, as Kelly further explains, "the cultural nuances and intricacies of Indigenous constitutions, laws, and governance structures must be explained and understood in the language of origin" (p. 37). In other words, learning about these concepts and ideologies using English as the primary language from which to understand will never provide a fully accurate account and appreciation of Indigenous worldviews, laws, and concepts of justice. For instance, Monture-Angus states that many First Nations languages do not have a word to express the concept of "justice" (1995, p. 243). When she queried Professor Leroy Little Bear about the term *justice* in the Blackfoot language, he told her there was no word for it in his language. Rather, he stated, "Justice is not a concept but a process" (p. 238). She also came to learn from Ojibwe Grandmother Shirley O'Connor that the word for "justice" in Ojibwe was a word created after contact with Europeans, as their word *ti-baq-nee-qwa-win* means "to come before a system for something that has already been done wrong," and this "system" is in reference to the Euro-Canadian system of law (p. 238). Thus, Indigenous forms of "justice" are not something separate; instead, justice is a process embedded within communities' ways of living and being. To fully comprehend such systems, one must be speaking the language of their origin. On the other hand, within Euro-Canadian systems, "justice" is typically associated with the Canadian criminal justice system, not something embedded as part of everyday life. Given that value systems are embedded within Indigenous governance structures, prevention of injustices or harms would also thereby be built into the structures of society.

Indigenous Forms of Justice and Methods of Addressing Wrongdoings

Within the Euro-Canadian system, laws guiding behaviours are not "truths" until they are written down. Once new legislation is passed, it is recorded and transcribed into case law, and once bills are passed, they are written into legislation. Indigenous laws on the other hand do not require transcription in books or on paper to be truth. For instance, Victor (2007) explains that "for the Stó:lō our laws are found 'written' throughout our territory in the form of sxwoxwiyám and transformer sites" (p. 9) They are also "found within the hearts and minds" of the grandmothers (p. 9). So, while they may not be written in a "criminal code" they are still "vibrant living laws" (p. 9).

Means and Johnson explain that once a language comes to be written down, it becomes easier to misrepresent, because once a language is put onto paper, distributed, or published, it comes to be seen by many as an accepted version of "truth" to some extent (2013, p. 4). On the other hand, in oral tradition, lying is much more difficult, as people have to remember what they said and "the only way to be sure is to tell the truth" (p. 4). Stories all have to align, and if one person's story is inconsistent with other people's accounts, it becomes obvious. Thus, lying is not consistent with oral tradition; it is not part of the structure of the custom (p. 4). In reference to his Lakota ways, John Fire Lame Deer states: "We had no written law, no attorneys or politicians, therefore we couldn't cheat" (Lame Deer & Erdoes, 1972, p. 75).

Mi'kmaq Elder Daniel N. Paul notes that in traditional Mi'kmaq societies, there was no torture equipment or instruments of death used to control populations. Yet in European societies, there were. In fact, you can go to museums and see the many types of torture equipment used in European societies (2006, p. 28). Means and Johnson also discuss how in the English language "there are numerous words for killing—murder, slaughter, torture, evisceration, disembowelment, decapitation, strangulation, genocide, patricide, fratricide, matricide—the list goes on and on," yet, in the Lakotah language, these words never existed, and such concepts never existed until the arrival of the colonizers (2013, p. 6). The idea of getting "revenge" on someone is also not part of Lakotah language or tradition (p. 37). Rather, if someone does something that harms another person, or if they steal, it affects not just the individual to whom they caused harm but also their whole family, so restitution must satisfy both the individual and their family (Means & Johnson, 2013).

In Blackfoot tradition, if a crime is committed, the perpetrator must take some sort of action that would please all parties harmed, and focus is on restoring balance back to the relationships (Peat, 1997). Maintaining harmony and balance is at the core of many Indigenous ways of living and being, and thus, many actions to address wrongs are rooted in this philosophy. Sociologist John G. Hansen (member of the Opaskwayak Cree Nation) explains how, in Cree traditions, importance is also placed on repairing harm when a wrong is committed (2012). He states that the Cree word *Poonā 'yétum* "describes the ability to heal from wrongdoing by utilizing the processes of accountability, repairing harm and reconciliation" (p. 2). Hansen conducted interviews with six Omushkegowuk (Swampy Cree) Elders and found that a "response to wrongdoing encourages accountability, repairs harm, restores relationships, forgives wrongdoers, and advocates peace" (p. 15). In Omushkegowuk law, reparation is encouraged and seen as a way to restore balance from harm caused (p. 13).

Rupert Ross, a former Crown Attorney in Northern Ontario, recalls a conversation he had with Charlie Fisher, Ontario's first full-time Indigenous justice of the peace. He asked Fisher how his home community dealt with crimes of violence in traditional times, which Fisher explained to Ross as being to "restore people to peace and harmony" by means of Elders counselling victims and offenders (Ross, 2014, p. 19). Fisher further explained to Ross that the Elders who do the counselling rarely speak of the violence that occurred. Rather, the conversation focuses on why people have a duty to live in harmony, and what it means to live in harmony. Then, every so often, Elders would gather to assess whether this goal of harmony was achieved. If they felt it was, Elders would place their pipes in the circle together to indicate that they were satisfied. For the community, this would be an indication that the process of justice had ended. In terms of offering restitution, compensation, or apologies, Ross notes that this was entirely left up to the peoples involved (p. 19).

Box 12.1: The Indigenous Bar Association's Accessing Justice and Reconciliation Project

While concepts of "healing, reconciliation, harmony, and forgiveness" are often commonly associated with Indigenous forms of justice and addressing crime, it is important not to assume that all Indigenous legal traditions implement these concepts in the same ways (Friedland, 2014, p. 8). This was a key finding of a 2014 research study that examined various Indigenous legal traditions through an analysis of various print materials and through oral knowledge shared with the researchers from Elders and other knowledge keepers. One of the two major overall themes identified in the project was that there is "no 'one size fits all' approach within or among Indigenous legal traditions"; rather, there "are a wide variety of principled legal responses and resolutions to harm and conflict available within each legal tradition" (p. 3). For instance, in the Mi'kmaq legal tradition, offenders are encouraged to take responsibility for the harm they have caused through providing restitution to victims and practising empathy (p. 8). For Cree peoples, healing is a central response to wrongdoings, but risks of harm are still taken into consideration; if someone needs to be kept safe from an offender, they are. Sometimes, temporary separations, or avoidance, are employed for safety reasons (p. 9). In extreme cases of harm, incapacitation is also used. For Tsilhqot'in peoples, both individual and community safety is also central. Responses to conflict and harm include temporary separation, and in certain exceptional cases, permanent separation is employed as well (p. 10). Some Elders observed that temporary separation provided an opportunity for people to heal themselves. Elder Catherine Haller explained how those who have committed a harm might be "locked in a pit house" in the mountains temporarily to allow time for their anger to decrease (p. 10).

Victor explains that Indigenous forms of justice have been overshadowed and marginalized by colonial systems of "justice," but this does not mean that they cease to exist. If Elders are in communities, then Indigenous forms of justice are most likely being practised (2007, p. 13). We even see the influence of Indigenous forms of justice on the Canadian and American criminal justice systems. Recognizing the ineffectiveness of the current mainstream structures, some colonial justice practitioners have looked to Indigenous traditional forms of addressing crime for solutions, borrowing various ideas and concepts. These include numerous forms of mediation, victim compensation, and restorative justice circles.

Box 12.2: Land Protectors at Standing Rock Sioux Reservation

Worldviews influence notions of what is "just" and "unjust." In many ways, we can see how these worldviews are still influencing people today. Consider the gathering of **Land Protectors** at Standing Rock Sioux Reservation in the United States. These individuals advocated to have their land protected against the proposed Dakota Access Pipeline, a 1,172-mile crude oil pipeline that would cut straight through sacred land sites, including travelling right beneath the Standing Rock Sioux Reservation's primary water source. Governments and the Dakota Access Limited Liability Company (LLC) argued that this pipeline is not on Standing Rock Sioux land; however, this is not the reality. The original route of this pipeline was to go through Bismarck, a community that is 90 percent white. After residents complained that they did not want this pipeline to go near their water, it was rerouted to go straight through Sioux traditional and ancestral Sioux territories, putting Standing Rock's water source at risk of contamination instead. What's more is that it is constructed right next to the gravesite of historian and Standing Rock Sioux Tribe member Ladonna Allard's son—only 500 yards away.

Although members of the Standing Rock Sioux Tribe have been opposing and resisting this pipeline since initially learning about its plan in 2014, the major gathering of organizers against the pipeline began in the summer of 2016. This followed the Standing Rock Sioux Tribe's first legal action against the US Army Corps of Engineers, after the US Army Corps of Engineers granted permits for this pipeline in their territories. The Tribe reached out to the United States federal government, to Congress, and to the State. They were ignored, and, rather, the government sided with the project developers. In September 2016, Dakota Access hired private security who used pepper spray and aggressive dogs on the men, women, and children who were protecting the sacred sites. In November 2016, the police sprayed people with mace, fired rubber bullets, and used water cannons in subfreezing temperatures in an attempt to get the Land Protectors to leave the sites they were protecting. During this attack, a North Dakota law enforcement officer shot a concussion grenade at a 21-year-old Water Protector, Sophia Wilansky, who was handing out water, badly injuring her. Just four days after assuming office, President Donald Trump signed an executive order in January 2017, which ordered the US Army Corps of Engineers to go ahead with the pipeline, and, by the following June the flowing of oil through the pipelines began.

Despite these recent advances, however, the systems of "justice" brought over by the colonizers were the ones that became dominant in these lands. Filled with fear, some Europeans arrived in the Americas evading their own religious persecution and political degradation; many were running from oppressors who had taken over their lives and their lands (Hill, 1995, p. 8). Although escaping their own persecutions, "they were not above using the same modes of oppression under which they themselves had suffered" (Smith, 2004, pp. 119–120).

Box 12.3: Mainstream Media Representation of Land and Water Protectors at Standing Rock

Mainstream media did not cover the organizing efforts of the Land and Water Protectors at Standing Rock to any large extent. When they did give the protection efforts news coverage, media referred to those at the gathering at Standing Rock as "protestors" or many times cast people in a negative light. This is why many people who gathered were speaking out and asking to be referred to as "protectors" and not "protestors." Many times, the word *protest* is linked with aggression. People who resist state or corporate actions come to be portrayed as militant or as those who are insinuating violence. According to Mohawk scholar Taiaiake Alfred and Lana Lowe (from Fort Nelson First Nation), the media portrayal of Indigenous resistances to injustice has changed very little since the 1970s. Key themes have remained, such as those that "build upon the colonial mythology" and strive to "demonize" Indigenous people (2007, p. 25). They further explain that the media spin typically emphasizes armed resistance and violence, even if this is not present. Very rarely is armed resistance cast as self-defence. Instead, Indigenous peoples are criminalized, and the media sends out a message that peoples are just partaking in "violence for violence's sake" (p. 25).

Looking through the eyes of some Land Protectors, many are there to protect Mother Earth from harm. Ponder the worldviews informing what is "just" and "unjust" in regard to this situation. The Dakota Access LLC is driven by monetary means rooted in a capitalist and economic development ideology. The environment and the earth are not seen as part of the web of life or great chain of relationships. On the Dakota Access LLC website, the company states its goals of investments "into the US economy" and cites the "millions in sales" the pipeline would produce (Dakota Access, 2016). On the other hand, for the Land Protectors, the Stand with Standing Rock website states the following: "In honor of our future generations, we fight this pipeline to protect our water, our sacred places, and all living beings" (Standing Rock Sioux Tribe, 2016). On December 9, 2016, various Tribal Leaders appeared before the Inter-American Commission on Human Rights, asking for protection against the abuses by law enforcement officers. Spotted Eagle of the Yankton Sioux Tribe reminded the commission of the excessive force used against women by law enforcement officers and stated, "the rape of Mother Earth is the rape of women" (Funes, 2016).

FROM PEACE AND FRIENDSHIP TO SETTLER SOCIETIES' SICKNESS OF EXPLOITATION

It must be recognized that before the arrival of Europeans, Indigenous peoples had advanced ways of governance and laws; many communities still do and still practise them. Yet, upon the arrival of European colonists, ways of living and being were disrupted due to settlers' genocidal policies and their colonization efforts to eliminate Indigenous peoples. The disparate impacts of this violence are still felt today. Moreover, with colonization still ongoing, impacts will continue to be felt. At the same time, however, early relations between Indigenous peoples and European colonists also included sharing traditions and knowledges. In some parts of Canada, colonists relied on Indigenous peoples to teach them how to survive through harsh winters and sub-zero temperatures. Europeans were also introduced to corn and taught how to plant and harvest the vegetable, in addition to many other local native agricultural crops. European colonists also looked to Indigenous peoples to teach them how to navigate the territories and terrain to which they were unfamiliar (Rice & Snyder, 2008, p. 49).

Peace and friendship treaties that spoke of how to live together in harmony were also put forward and agreed to by both Indigenous and non-Indigenous peoples. Some of these treaty agreements are represented and codified in Wampum

Belts (belts made with shell and clam beads). This includes the *Kaswentha*, or Two-Row Wampum, a treaty agreement between the Haudenosaunee and Dutch peoples that dates back to 1613 (King, 2007, pp. 459–460; Lyons 1997, p. 308). The "two-row" is in reference to the Haudenosaunee peoples and the peoples of the Netherlands travelling down the river of life together but in their own respective vessels (King 2007, p. 460). As Mohawk legal scholar Joyce Tekahnawiiaks King explains:

> In the Two Row Wampum, there are two parallel rows of purple beads, to symbolize the two paths for two vessels: one for the Haudenosaunee canoe and one for the Dutch ship. The two vessels are forever parallel, never meeting, but, by agreement, the vessels were intended to pursue parallel paths, not interfering with each other. Between the two paths of purple were three rows of white beads to symbolize the River of Life and three words to show the continued relationship of the two peoples: peace, respect, and friendship. This metaphor explains how the two nations would agree to exist, living side by side, but never interfere in each other's government or way of life. So water is both the "river of life" and, importantly, the medium or backdrop of the *Kaswentha*. (2007, p. 460)

This agreement of non-interference rooted in peace, respect, and friendship continued to be relayed throughout the years, and still is to this day. Since the initial Two-Row Wampum treaty in 1613, this agreement specifically has continued to be presented to the colonizers. For instance, in July and August 1764, as a way to cement or ratify the Royal Proclamation of 1763, the Two-Row Wampum was presented by more than 24 nations to the British colonial government (Gehl, 2014, p. 33; Saul, 2008, p. 69). The superintendent of Indian Affairs at the time, Sir William Johnson, accepted and reaffirmed this relationship with about 2,000 Indigenous leaders present in what is referred to as the Treaty of Niagara (Borrows, 2002, p. 163).

In the early 1700s, the Three Figure Welcoming/Sharing Wampum Belt agreement was also negotiated. According to McDermott and Wilson, this belt portrays three figures who are holding hands. These three figures are representative of "the French and English flanking the Algonquin" and the cross shows that a representative of the Vatican witnessed the agreement (2010, p. 206). Algonquin Elder Grandfather William Commanda was the carrier of this belt until his passing in 2011. Upon his appointment to Officer of the Order of Canada, he wrote that this belt represented the agreement "to share the grand natural resources of our land and our values in three equal parts," which, at the time, was with the French and the English (Commanda, 2009).

For Indigenous peoples, these agreements continued to be voiced, but unfortunately, the colonizers started to ignore their commitments. Near the end of the 1700s, European goals centred on gaining Indigenous land, thus displacing Indigenous peoples from their territories (Gehl, 2014, p. 55). A central focus of the colonizers also became eradication. Greed took over, and perhaps what Jack D. Forbes (Powhatan-Renape, Delaware-Lenape) refers to as the **wétiko** psychosis took hold. According to Forbes (2008), the *wétiko* psychosis is a sickness of exploitation. *Wétiko* is a Cree term denoting a "cannibal," whereby people consume other beings in order to gain profit. Those with *wétiko* psychosis do not consume the actual flesh of another; rather, they will cause destruction to anything that gets in their way. Thus, colonizers wanted land and would do anything to get it. Forbes explains that Christopher Columbus had the *wétiko* psychosis upon arriving in the Americas in 1492; he was literally insane, suffering from this psychological disease. Forbes further explains that *wétiko* psychosis is very contagious, and it has since spread like wildfire across the lands.

This sickness of exploitation entered the collective conscience, whereby Canadian and American perceptions of "justice" came to be driven by this *wétiko* psychosis. Rather than upholding peaceful relations, settlers have fallen into greed and exploitation and a fear-driven desire for power. For instance, upon Columbus's first contact with Indigenous peoples in the Caribbean, he wrote that peoples suffered from a "fault" in that they were so "peaceful" and "generous"; Means and Johnson question: "Generosity and peacefulness a fault? What kind of world do you suppose he was coming from?", further contending, "if you live in a world where everything you need is freely available, greed looks like a form of insanity" (Means & Johnson, 2013, p.16). Thus, what came to be a central motivator for the colonizers is this thirst for rising to the top and conquering all to achieve.

Driven by greed, the colonizers wanted more and more. In order to get more, they started to rewrite history in a way that suited their interests and advanced their goals. Indigenous peoples were deemed by the colonizers as "savage and untutored, wretched creatures in need of the civilizing influences of the settlers from Europe" (Elsey, 2013, p. 30). These viewpoints were pushed as part of a self-serving agenda to take the land Indigenous peoples had been living and thriving on since time immemorial. This is a key component of advancing the agenda of colonialism. According to Tsalagi scholar Jeff Corntassel, "colonialism is all about distorting Indigenous histories and destroying our collective and individual confidence" (2012, p. 86). Driven by greediness in an attempt to achieve "progress," colonizers went to great lengths to rewrite history in a way that benefits themselves and maintains their positions of privilege.

Barbara Perry states that "whether by violence or assimilationist policy, whites have consistently exerted their energies in the ongoing effort to physically or culturally annihilate Native peoples" (2008, p. 26). Seneca leader Cornplanter referred to the colonizers as the "town destroyers" (Dunbar-Ortiz, 2014, p. 82). Colonists set out to lay claim to as much land as they could. Lands were depicted as *terra nullius*, meaning "empty" or "vacant" land, or "a wilderness to be settled and turned to more productive pursuits by the presumed superior civilization of the new arrivals" (Elsey, 2013, pp. 29–30). Colonizers were under the assumption that they had a God-given right to claim any land that was inhabited by non-Christians (Smith, 2004, p. 118). As Maureen E. Smith (Oneida Tribe of Wisconsin) explained, "colonists often believed they were destined by God to conquer the new land" (p. 119).

Europeans also brought germs and diseases, causing massive devastation. For some nations, an estimated 50, 70 to 90 percent of the population was lost to diseases, and some communities were completely devastated (Calloway, 1994, p. 2; Ross, 2014, p. 76). For example, Calvin Martin (1987) explains that from 1781 to 1782, an estimated 60 percent of Indigenous peoples from the Upper Great Lakes and northern Plains died of smallpox alone (as cited in Wesley-Esquimaux & Smolewski, 2004, p. 19). Colonizers attributed these circumstances to "divine providence" that "God has cleared the land of the 'heathen' to make way for His chosen people" (Calloway, 1994, p. 4).

Recognizing the devastation and impact affecting Indigenous peoples, some of the British decided to use this as a stratagem to advance their goals. They started to implement germ warfare, whereby the British purposely gave blankets infected with smallpox to Indigenous peoples (Calloway, 1994, p. 4). In 1763, Lord Jeffrey Amherst, Governor General of British North America, wrote in a letter that his stated goal was to infect "the Indians by means of blankets as well as to try every method that can be served to extirpate this exorable race." Similarly, a United States captain wrote in his journal "we gave them two blankets and a handkerchief out of the smallpox hospital. I hope it will have the desired effect" (Cook as cited in Perry, 2008, p. 26; Stannard, 1992; Stiffarm & Lane, 1992, p. 32). As Indigenous peoples succumbed to these horrible diseases, and the European populations boomed, the missionaries advocated that this was a due to the European God being more powerful and divine (Smith, 2004, p. 120). Europeans set out to indoctrinate Indigenous peoples with their belief systems. Christian missionaries travelled across the lands with the intended goal to convert Indigenous peoples to Christianity.

By the 1860s and 1870s, the central view held by colonizers was one that saw Indigenous peoples as an "obstacle" to the establishment of "a Euro-Canadian civilization" (Rice & Snyder, 2008, p. 49). First Nations peoples were subsumed under white man's "Indian" legislation, put into place to eliminate the "Indian" and rid Canada of its professed "Indian problem." Some of the first pieces of "Indian" legislation were passed in the 1850s and 1860s, but in 1876, all "Indian" legislation was brought together under one umbrella and named the *Indian Act*, which has since undergone amendments and is still in force today (Monchalin, 2016, pp. 106–108). This act has enforced many laws to keep First Nations peoples controlled. For instance, beginning in the 1880s, restrictions were placed on "Indians'" ability to sell agricultural products. This continued until 1951 (Monchalin, 2016, p. 105), even though governments made the argument that "Indians" were being "moved" to reserves in order to implement agriculture. Settler laws contradicted their own claims and lies.

In 1884, First Nations ceremonies were legally prohibited; this included the Potlatch, which is a very significant ceremony for some First Nations on the West Coast. People found to be practising their cultures could face imprisonment. Such provisions relating to culture, dancing, and the ability to practise ceremonies remained in force until 1951. Many more restrictive laws were put in place since the first piece of "Indian" legislation rolled out. For instance, First Nations people were not allowed to drink alcohol or enter pool halls. People caught doing so could face fines or imprisonment, and pool hall owners who allowed First Nations people in their establishments could face sanctions (Monchalin, 2016, p. 116). Between 1927 and 1951, the *Indian Act* forbid First Nations people from hiring lawyers to pursue land claims; anyone found trying to do so could face imprisonment, including non-First Nations people supporting First Nations people. There were major amendments to the act in 1951, when some of the most coercive restrictions were lifted; however, even with these changes, the act as it stands today has "retained much of its regulatory demand for assimilation and for the expansion of Euro-Canadian goals" (p. 110).

Among these *Indian Act* laws was the forced policy for "Indian" children to be put into residential schools. In 1920, this was policy as per the *Indian Act*; parents could not withhold their children from the schools and had no legal recourse against this policy because "Indians" were not "persons" under Canadian law but rather "wards of the government" (Kelly, 2008, pp. 23–24). The colonizers believed that Indigenous peoples must become Christians in order to be "saved." So began this horrible government strategy of Christian indoctrination through residential schools.

Imprisonment in Residential Schools

In the early 1600s and 1700s, there were some boarding schools set up to "civil-ize" and "Christianise" Indigenous children in Canada (TRC, 2015, p. 50). The majority of the residential schools started to open throughout the 1800s, with the last federally run residential school remaining open until 1996. At least 150,000 Indigenous children went through the residential school system (p. 3). The Euro-Canadian histories taught in school systems and promoted by mainstream institu-tions and media tried to hide the truth about these schools and their long histories of abuse. In the 1990s, more and more survivors started legal challenges against the government and the churches for the horrific abuses that went on within the walls of these residential schools. Survivors from coast to coast came forward with their testimonies on the truth of what went on. This was something that could no longer continue to be pushed under the rug by governments, churches, and the many Canadians who were refusing to face the truths. On May 10, 2006, a landmark, historic agreement took place, and it confirmed that a comprehensive resolution to the legacy of residential schools would be set into motion, known as the Indian Residential Schools Settlement Agreement. This agreement is the largest class-action settlement in Canada. It included several measures, such as fi-nancial compensation for survivors and monies for healing projects to help address residential school legacies, including commemorative initiatives to honour and educate. Monies for public awareness included the establishment of the Truth and Reconciliation Commission (TRC). This commission travelled across Canada, collecting testimonies from survivors and their families and anyone impacted by the residential schools. The TRC heard testimonies from over 6,000 people, most of whom were Survivors (TRC, 2015, p. v). On June 2, 2015, the TRC released 94 calls to action, and on December 15, 2015, they released their final report. This report has over 2 million words and spans 6 volumes.

The TRC (2015) outlined how the government purposely wanted to separate children from their families in order to break the connection to their identity and culture. It cited the first prime minister of Canada, Sir John A. Macdonald, who in 1883 stated to the House of Commons,

> When the school is on the reserve the child lives with its parents, who are savages; he is surrounded by savages, and though he may learn to read and write, his habits and training and mode of thought are Indian. He is simply a savage who can read and write. It has been strongly pressed on myself, as the head of the Department, that Indian children should be withdrawn as much as possible from the parental influence, and the only way to do that would be

to put them in central training industrial schools where they will acquire the habits and modes of thought of white men. (TRC, 2015, p. 2)

This policy of assimilation and the goal of cultural destruction on the part of the government were reiterated throughout the years. For instance, in 1920, Deputy Minister of Indian Affairs Duncan Campbell Scott stated, "our object is to continue until there is not a single Indian in Canada that has not been absorbed into the body politic" (TRC, 2015, p. 3).

Children were torn from their homes and placed into these institutions that were modelled on prisons. Ross explains that it is crucial to acknowledge that the children in these schools were not simply "students." They were prisoners, and many became imprisoned as early as five years old. Thus, today, adults who went to residential schools are referred to as "Survivors" and not "former students," as they are survivors of compulsory government imprisonment in these institutions as children (2014, p. 92). As Monture-Angus has stated, for "anyone who has studied criminology and the development of the prison system, the parallels between residential school and the early penitentiary are obvious" (1995, p. 94).

Upon arrival, children had their hair cut short or shaved off. Some schools doused children in chemicals, and school nuns or administrators would scrub children's skin sometimes almost raw. Children would be renamed by administrators, who gave them anglicized names and numbers (Kelly, 2008, p. 24). Clothing was confiscated and instead children were forced to wear school-issued uniforms. Murray Crowe, who attended a residential school in northwestern Ontario, had his clothes from home taken and burned (TRC, 2015, pp. 39–40). Lorna Morgan, who attended the Presbyterian school in Kenora, Ontario, explained that she was wearing "these nice little beaded moccasins that my grandma had made me to wear for school, and I was very proud of them." However, she had these moccasins taken away upon her arrival, and they were thrown into the garbage (p. 40).

Children were forbidden to speak their traditional languages and could receive severe punishments for doing so. This ranged from "beatings to the shaving of one's head" (Dion Stout & Kipling, 2003, p. 31). In some cases, needles were pushed through children's tongues and left for extended periods as punishment (Chrisjohn, Young, & Maraun, 2006, p. 49). Physical, emotional, and sexual abuse was persistent throughout the residential schools. As residential school survivor Fred Kelly (from Ojibways of Onigaming First Nation) stated, "Many of us were physically beaten, sexually fondled, molested, and raped" (2008, p. 24).

In 1990, the Special Advisor to the Minister of National Health and Welfare on Child Sexual Abuse declared that "closer scrutiny of past treatment of

Native children at Indian residential schools would show 100% of children at some schools were sexually abused" (Milloy, 1999, p. 298). However, during the schools' operation, when children came forward telling of their abuses, they would be dismissed. Officials would sometimes cover up victimizations. This was the case with several boys at Kuper Island School in 1939. The TRC revealed that the police confirmed that these boys had run away because they were being sexually abused. However, the official from Indian Affairs was concerned about the reputation of the residential schools, so rather than face prosecution, the abusers were sent out of the province. In terms of the boys who had been abused, nothing was done. This story is not an exceptional circumstance; in fact, the TRC identified that such patterns "persisted into the late twentieth century. Officials continued to dismiss Aboriginal reports of abuse. In some cases, staff members were not fired" even after they were convicted of assaults against children and youth (TRC, 2015, pp. 105–106).

At the St. Anne's Residential School in Fort Albany, Ontario, there was a homemade electric chair used to punish children. Edmund Metatawabin, a survivor of St. Anne's, was put in this chair when he was seven years old. He explained how when he was put in the chair, his feet couldn't even reach the floor, and "there was a metal handle on both sides you have to hold on to," further stating that "there were brothers and sisters sitting around in the boys' room. And of course, the boys were all lined up. And somebody turned the power on and you can't let go once the power goes on. You can't let go." He also explained how the school administrators would be watching and laughing—that this was entertainment for them. As he stated, "my feet were flying in front of me and I heard laughter. The nuns and the brothers were all laughing. Thought it was funny that my feet were flying around, I guess" (Roman, 2013).

Nutritional experiments were also conducted on children in residential schools and in First Nation communities in the 1940s and 1950s. According to food historian Ian Mosby, Indigenous bodies were used "as experimental materials" and residential schools and Aboriginal communities as kinds of "laboratories" (2013, p. 148). For instance, several schools were given nutritional supplements as experiments. At St. Mary's Indian Residential School in Kenora Ontario, for example, residential school students were used to test "Newfoundland Flour Mix" (p. 162). This was a product that was not allowed to be legally sold under Canadian law but was given to residential school students as an "experiment" to test the whether the "added thiamine, riboflavin, niacin, and bonemeal" was nutritionally effective (p. 162). In addition to the schools who were receiving these added test products, there were also control groups. In fact, the St. Paul's Indian Residential School, in

Cardston, Alberta, was chosen as an entire "control" group. Thus, at this school, children were purposely fed food "that provided inadequate intakes of vitamins A, B, and C as well as iron and iodine" (p. 162). Furthermore, in the residential schools that were part of the nutritional studies, children were cut off from dental care, as the researchers stated that providing dental care would interfere with their study results (p. 163).

Residential schools were also often in poor structural condition, including not having proper ventilation. Government inspectors would report the deplorable conditions in the schools, yet no action would be taken to address these issues, so many times, conditions would worsen. Residential schools were also often overcrowded. Poor ventilation combined with overcrowded conditions exacerbated and fuelled the tuberculosis epidemics that plagued the residential schools, causing many to fall ill and die. Peter Henderson Bryce, Chief Medical Officer for the Departments of the Interior and Indian Affairs, released a report in 1907 that outlined the high disease and death rates of children attending residential schools, as well as the horrible sanitary conditions that fuelled them. His report declared that "the defective sanitary condition of many schools, especially in the matter of ventilation, have been the *foci* from which disease, especially tubercular, has spread, whether through direct infection, from person to person, or indirectly through the infected dust of floors, school-rooms and dormitories" (Bryce, 1907, p. 17). He noted how children were kept in dormitory rooms without proper ventilation and exposed to tuberculosis for 10 continuous hours (p. 18). Of the 1,537 residential school students he reported on, he identified that almost 25 percent died, and, at one school 69 percent of children died, citing tuberculosis as the most likely cause of death (p. 18). The response by the government to Bryce's report was to do nothing, making no changes at all. In fact, in 1918 Duncan Campbell Scott, Deputy Superintendent of Indian Affairs from 1913 to 1932, wrote:

> It is readily acknowledged that Indian children lose their natural resistance to illness by habituating so closely in the residential schools, and that they die at a much higher rate than in their villages. But this alone does not justify a change in the policy of this Department, which is geared towards a final solution of our Indian Problem (Department of Indian Affairs Superintendent D. C. Scott to B. C. Indian Agent-General Major D. McKay, DIA Archives, RG 1-Series 12 April 1910).

The government disallowed Dr. Bryce from presenting his findings at academic conferences. Although qualified, he was refused any further civil service positions and eventually was forced out of the federal public service (Wattam, 2016).

So many children died before they were able to make it back home. For many of the children who survived, traumatic impacts were endured. This includes Survivors, their families, and communities suffering from post-traumatic stress disorder (PTSD; Kelly, 2008). The intergenerational impacts and trauma of residential schools are still felt today in many forms. As stated by Madeleine Dion Stout (Cree) and Gregory Kipling,

> Like a pebble dropped in a pond, the effects of trauma tend to ripple outwards from victims to touch all those who surround them, whether parents, spouses, children, or friends. There is ample evidence to support this view among residential school Survivors, where the consequences of emotional, physical and sexual abuse continue to be felt in each subsequent generation. (2003, p. 33)

Some peoples denied their Indigenous identity after getting out of the schools and, in some cases, developed internalized hatred for themselves and their identity as an Indigenous person. As this testimonial from Susie, who was in residential school from the age of 10 to 16, explains:

> When I came out of residential school, I didn't know who I really was. I knew my colour was brown, but I really didn't belong to either society. I didn't belong to the Indian society because people knew I had gone to residential school and other kids did not want to associate with me. I just didn't belong, and I didn't understand their way any more. And when I went to the white society, I didn't belong there either because I was looked upon as a savage or Indian squaw or a drunken Indian woman. In order to pass through and be accepted into the white society, you had to hide your identity. So, I began to dress like the white people dressed and I put lots of powder on my face because I thought I would be more accepted in the white society if my skin were not so brown. (The Canadian Council on Social Development and Native Women's Association of Canada, 1991, pp. 19–20)

Internalized hatred, racism, and colonization is a legacy of residential schools. These institutions aimed to indoctrinate children with false notions about their identities and families, including the mistaken idea that Indigenous peoples were "lesser" or not as "civilized." Some people started to believe these false notions as truth, viewing their own identities and cultures through this colonizing lens. Others developed hatred or shame for who they are or where they come from because of the years and years of being told that they are less by institutions that had a central aim to indoctrinate these notions into children. In turn, even though the schools have closed, these internalized notions continue to be passed down through families and communities. According to Chantal Fiola (Métis Anishinaabe-Kwe), "internalized colonization occurs when colonized peoples believe in the superiority of the dominant culture while criticizing their own culture and (sometimes forcefully) encouraging other colonized peoples to adopt these values" (2015, pp. 29–30). Sto:lō nation scholar and writer Lee Maracle states that "the result of being colonized is the internalization of the need to remain invisible. The colonizers erase you, not easily, but with shame and brutality" (1996, p. 8). Thus, colonizers tried very hard to instill shame and notions claiming that the white man is more superior, which, in turn, has in some cases been passed down through families generationally.

STRATAGEMS OF COLONIALISM: CONTINUED CRIMINALIZATION, IMPRISONMENT, AND VICTIMIZATION

The harm, violence, and imprisonment of Indigenous peoples has, horribly, not yet come to an end in Canada. Indigenous peoples experience the highest rates of violence in Canada as compared to any other group. Statistics gathered in 2014 show that the rate of violent victimization among Indigenous peoples is double that of non-Indigenous peoples (Boyce, 2016, p. 3). For Indigenous females, rates of violent victimization are double as compared to Indigenous men, almost triple compared to non-Indigenous females, and more than triple as compared to non-Indigenous men (p. 3).

The Office of the Correctional Investigator of Canada has identified that as of 2018, Indigenous peoples represent 28 percent of the total federal prison population, a staggering number given that Indigenous peoples make up 4.3 percent of the total population in Canada (2018, p. 61). Indigenous women in federal prisons now encompass over 40 percent of the in-custody female prison population (p. 61). These numbers have continued to increase, and at rates much faster than the general prison population. In response to this, the government has made very few changes to its criminal justice system operations. The Office of the Correctional Investigator made this clear when it stated that Correctional Service Canada

> has made little discernible or meaningful progress in narrowing the gap in key areas and outcomes that matter to Aboriginal offenders and Canadians.

This commitment goes to corporate focus and establishing some political direction for federal corrections in light of the year-on-year increases in the national rate of incarceration of Canada's Indigenous Peoples. (2016, p. 44)

Howard Sapers, the Correctional Investigator of Canada for 12 years, continued to call the government to account for these grave injustices, but again, there is little to no government action. The current Correctional Investigator, Ivan Zinger, continues to do the same, yet still with little to no action. This sounds like a similar story to what happened during residential schools, whereby we have someone in a paid position by government who is in place to provide oversight. They release their findings, expose injustices, and call for change, yet no action ensues. Thus, not surprisingly, there are many Indigenous people who do not bother looking to the Canadian criminal justice system for action or assistance. For some, this is a system of oppression and a system set up to eliminate Indigenous peoples, so why trust it?

Box 12.4: The Wrongful Conviction of Indigenous People: The Case of William Mullins-Johnson

Some people have given up on a system that ignores or discriminates against them, their family, and their friends. This includes William Mullins-Johnson (from Batchewana First Nation), who in 1994 was wrongfully convicted of a murder and rape that never happened. He spent 12 years in prison after a court incorrectly ruled him guilty of strangling and sodomizing his four-year-old niece—who, in fact, died of natural causes. The now-disgraced pathologist Charles Smith, along with other witnesses, came to conclusions that were far from the truth. As a result, Mullins-Johnson's life was forever changed. Grieving the loss of his beloved niece, he was thrown in prison and given the label of a convicted sex offender. In prison, he received death threats; he feared for his life. He was put into solitary confinement for four months because of the threats he faced inside prison. In addition, his family relationships and reputation in the community would never be the same.

With the help of Innocence Canada (formerly the Association in Defence of the Wrongly Convicted), a non-profit organization dedicated to assisting people wrongfully convicted of crimes, Mullins-Johnson was exonerated and later received $4.25 million in compensation. In April 2016, Innocence Canada noted that, of the 80 cases they had under review at the time, 20 of those were First Nations applicants (Fontaine, 2016). Amanda Carling (Métis), who works for Innocence Canada, stated, "after you've been wrongfully convicted of something, why would you turn to a system that you already don't trust and look for a remedy from that system?" She identified that "Indigenous people are not only more vulnerable to being wrongfully convicted, but also less likely to get help after they've been wrongfully convicted" (Fontaine, 2016). Consider for a moment some reasons for why you think this might be. Why do you think Indigenous peoples are more vulnerable to being wrongfully convicted and less likely to get help afterwards? In what ways does colonialism play a role in this reality?

The colonial criminal justice system has a history of denying help to Indigenous people and families. This includes outright ignoring Indigenous families' pleas to help solve cases of loved ones who have become victims of abduction or murder. There is a crisis of missing and murdered Indigenous women and girls in Canada. Although this tragedy has been going on for decades, it took until 2015 for a National Inquiry to finally be initiated. In June 2019, the report of the National Inquiry into Missing and Murdered Indigenous Women and Girls was released. The introduction to the report states that

> Indigenous women, girls, and 2SLGBTQQIA people in Canada have been the targets of violence for far too long. This truth is undeniable. The fact that this National Inquiry is happening now doesn't mean that Indigenous Peoples waited this long to speak up; it means it took this long for Canada to listen. (National Inquiry into Missing and Murdered Indigenous Women and Girls, 2019, p. 49)

Countless family members who have had loved ones murdered or go missing, as well as Indigenous communities, organizations, artists, and advocates, tirelessly raised awareness and called for this inquiry and action into the investigation of this ongoing national tragedy. Before government cut funding in 2010, the Sisters in Spirit Initiative recorded 582 cases of missing and murdered Indigenous women in Canada that had occurred between the 1960s and 2010 (Native Women's Association of Canada, 2010). As part of her doctoral dissertation,

Maryanne Pearce (2013) created a database of missing and murdered women in Canada covering 1946 to 2013, citing 824 cases of missing and murdered Indigenous women. In 2014, the Royal Canadian Mounted Police released a report that identified 1,181 missing and or murdered Indigenous women between 1980 and 2012. This includes 1,017 women who were murdered and 164 who were still missing (RCMP, 2014, p. 7). In 2005, Gladys Radek (Gitxsan/Wet'suwet'en) had her 22-year-old niece Tamara Lynn Chipman go missing from Prince George, BC. In 2008, Gladys founded the Walk 4 Justice, a walk from Vancouver to Ottawa that brings awareness to the tragedy of missing and murdered Indigenous women. On her journey to raise awareness, she has collected names of over 4,200 women who are missing or murdered in Canada, and at least 3,000 of those names are Indigenous women (Chartrand, 2014, pp. 120–123).

Indigenous peoples have also been subjected to abuse at the hands of criminal justice officials. For instance, in Northern British Columbia, Human Rights Watch has documented extreme violence, including sexualized violence, against Indigenous women and girls at the hands of police officials. In half of the 10 towns the researchers investigated, they identified cases of rape and sexual assault by police officers (2013, p. 59). For instance, one testimony described how, in July 2012, a group of four police officers took a woman outside of town to rape her, then threatened to kill her if she told anyone. As she stated, "they threatened that if I told anybody they would take me out to the mountains and kill me and make it look like an accident" (p. 59). This was not an isolated incident; even during the course of the Human Rights Watch investigation, this woman experienced further rapes by police. She also noted that the police confiscated her underwear after the rape. This practice is so common in the area that a community worker in the town has begun to distribute underwear, knowing that women routinely have them confiscated after being sexually assaulted by police officers.

Researchers also noted how struck they were at the high levels of fear the women they interviewed displayed, levels of fear they explained as being that which they find "in communities in post-conflict or post-transition countries such as Iraq" (p. 34). The incidents of police abuse, violence, and neglect cited in this report are multiple. This ranges from "young girls pepper-sprayed and Tasered; a 12-year-old girl attacked by a police dog; a 17-year-old punched repeatedly by an officer who had been called to help her; women strip-searched by male officers; and women injured due to excessive force used during arrest," and more (pp. 7–8).

Indigenous peoples face violence and incarceration at the hands of the colonial state. From imprisonment and violence in residential schools, to imprisonment and violence by Canada's criminal justice system, colonial abuses endure. Historically, Indigenous peoples lived freely in their communities, without the continuing threat of discrimination, violence, and criminalization that many face in today's colonized society. Women are sacred in Indigenous societies, viewed as the life givers, and in many cases are leaders. As explained by Nishnawbe spiritual teacher Arthur Solomon, women are the "foundations on which nations are built. She is the heart of her nation. If that heart is weak, the people are weak ... the woman is the centre of everything" (1990, p. 35). The imposed oppressive patriarchal systems that now dominate in these lands have displaced women-centred societies. Violence, and the threat of violence, is a stratagem to oppress and control Indigenous peoples.

The criminalization and oppression of Indigenous peoples and the targeting of Indigenous women and girls directly connects to Canada's colonizing past and present. Colonialism and patriarchy are intrinsically linked. A fundamental aspect of colonialism is its desire to alter and falsify Indigenous histories—histories in which women are never left out, pushed to the outskirts, or placed in subordinate positions. Colonialism serves to erase and alter these key roles of women, completely flipping the narrative. These altered and falsified histories are then reflected in actions and are played out on women's bodies. Rather than respecting and honouring the life givers, those who are sacred, it is the complete reverse. The heart of communities are attacked, a purposeful stratagem of colonialism. Women, the leaders, are broken down, through rewritten histories, physical force, and sexual violence. This is not a coincidence; it is a deliberate strategy taken by the colonizers to attack the heart of the communities. In the words of Tsistsistas (Cheyenne), "a nation is not conquered until the hearts of its women are on the ground" (Brant Castellano, 2009, p. 203).

Colonialism is ongoing and continues to be reproduced through society's dominant institutions and discourses. The overrepresentation and continued growth of the number of Indigenous people in prison is a direct reflection of colonialism and its continuance. A central aim of colonialism is to dominate and keep the racialized "other" in a lower subordinate societal position. Imprisonment does exactly that. As the incarceration of Indigenous peoples continues, so too does the colonial agenda to supress, break down, and hide away the fabricated narrative of so-called criminals.

Box 12.5: Indigenous Resistance and Resiliency and the Idle No More Movement

The ability to survive through Canada's deplorable past and present is a marker of Indigenous peoples' resiliency and strength. Indigenous peoples are not a conquered people—that idea is a false colonial narrative. Indigenous peoples have continued to resist the onslaught of this colonial project since the initial arrival of Europeans to Turtle Island. One way Indigenous peoples have done this is through the **Idle No More** movement. This arose from objection to omnibus bills such as Bill C-45: *The Jobs and Growth Act* and Bill C-38: *The Jobs, Growth and Long-term Prosperity Act*. Each over 400 pages in length, these bills were fast-tracked through parliament and contained several amendments that threaten lands and waters. Many of the amendments were a large-scale attack on Indigenous rights, lands, and resources, including the right to self-government.

So began Idle No More, a peaceful, grassroots movement taking a stand against centuries of ongoing occupation and colonialism perpetrated by the settler society in Canada. Hundreds of rallies, flash-mobs, and teach-ins were held across Canada, as well as internationally. The concept of "Idle No More" began with four women in Saskatchewan, Sylvia McAdam, Sheelah McLean, Jessica Gordon, and Nina Wilson, when they started sharing their concerns about Bill C-45. Jessica Gordon decided on the name "Idle No More" to act as a reminder for people "to get off the couch and start working" (Woo, 2013, p. 5). The women began teach-ins, petitions, and rallies, with the original goal of stopping this bill from being passed. According to Sheelah McLean, "when we started the rallies and the petitions, the central goal was to stop Bill C-45. Since our first rally in Saskatoon on November 10, 2012, we have framed that goal within a long-standing history of colonial attacks on Indigenous lands and bodies" (Lilley & Shantz, 2013, p. 115). Events were advertised and shared through Facebook and Twitter. On November 30, 2012, Tanya Kappo (from Edmonton) was the first person to Tweet the hashtag #idlenomore, which spread rapidly through social media (Kinew, 2012). While Idle No More did not stop these bills from passing, the movement brought many Indigenous peoples (and allies) together towards a common goal of taking a stand against the ongoing colonial project.

Some Indigenous leaders and peoples went on hunger strikes in support of the Idle No More movement and to call attention to the unequal treatment Indigenous peoples face. Attawapiskat Chief Theresa Spence went on a six-week-long hunger strike on Victoria Island (across the water from Parliament), beginning on December 11, 2012, and ending January 23, 2013. On March 1, 2013, Shelley Young of Eskasoni First Nation and Jean Sock of the Elsipogtog First Nation also went on hunger strikes for 10 days. They were taking a stand against government efforts to extinguish treaties through the passing of Bill C-45. Idle No More has since expanded beyond Bill C-45 and Bill C-38 to focus on Indigenous human rights, the equal treatment of Indigenous peoples, treaty relationships, Indigenous sovereignty, and the importance of protecting the land, water, and resources. It is a movement against the ongoing colonial project.

CONCLUSION: "WHEN YOU KNOW, THAT YOU KNOW, THAT YOU KNOW": REMEMBERING WHO WE ARE, INNATE KNOWING, AND FOLLOWING THE WISDOM OF THE ELDERS

My Grandma Monchalin (Citizen of the Métis Nation of Ontario) shared with me stories of her father. She spoke of how he was violent, but also how he was a hunter and trapper. He would bring home animals such as fox that he would regularly trap to feed the family and use the fur on coats for her and her siblings to keep them warm. She tells of the bad and the good. As she advises, we share the negative aspects of the stories, so we know what not to repeat. At the same time, we also must share the positive stories, so we remember what to pass on and replicate.

Professor Raven Sinclair (Ótiskewápíwskew) from Gordon First Nation states that "our Elders remind us that in order to know where we are going, we have to know where we have been" (2009, p. 19). While the recent history must be recognized, we must also look to the ancient teachings and rich cultures that helped us thrive since time immemorial. The worldviews, traditional modes of governance, and ideologies that emphasized living in a good way, which takes into consideration all peoples, beings, and aspects of life, must be recognized. All peoples must collectively acknowledge the sacredness and importance of women. Indigenous peoples on Turtle Island have continued to resist the extended attacks on women and nations. Many Indigenous peoples continue to teach about the negotiated relations of peace and friendship in an effort to remind settlers that these histories are not so distant.

Countering colonialism through remembering and acting on ancient knowledge is also key. Elders still have the ancient wisdom. As Cynthia Wesley-Esquimaux (a member of Chippewas of Georgina Island First Nation) and Magdalena Smolewski state, "the Elders are here to help with their wisdom, experience, and healing force" (2004, p. 93). My Grandma has always taught me about the importance of love, compassion, and being positive, even when confronted with the opposite. She taught me to be aware of the signs and signals related to violence, and to surround myself with positive people. As Wesley-Esquimaux and Smolewski further contend, "today's Elders know that, although some aspects of the Aboriginal social self were deeply hurt and damaged, there is yet another side of the Aboriginal psyche: the Aboriginal spiritual self that is full of positive energy, waiting to be revealed and used in the right way" (2004, p. 92). We must shift our collective consciousness to one of love and compassion and draw on our positive energy to guide us.

We must open our hearts and let them guide us as well. My Grandma speaks of this innate inner knowing, and the need to trust it. For example, she told me of when her sister gave birth to a baby girl. While she was not physically present, nobody had to tell her—she knew, right when it was happening. She refers to this innate knowing as: "when you know, that you know, that you know." She speaks of looking inside ourselves and trusting our inner sense of knowing, as it too can guide us in positive directions. We can feel inside if a decision is wrong or not in alignment with harmony, love, and compassion. Many times, people put so much focus on searching for answers in places such as books, spinning their wheels, when many answers are found within. Thus, Elders can guide us and help us to remember, just as my Grandma has done for me. Sometimes, they will remind you that the answers are not so complicated, prompting us to remember the bad and the good, open our hearts, and follow our inner guidance. Thus, rather than looking for "justice," perhaps *this* is justice—following the prompts and guidance from our Elders on how to live in a good way. As Patricia Monture-Angus contends, rather than seeking "justice," we should strive for "harmony," as that is a "higher standard than mere justice" (1995, p. 243).

REVIEW QUESTIONS

1. Consider the peace and friendship treaties that have been agreed upon. What do you think are some of the main reasons the government chooses to ignore these agreements?

2. Even though residential schools are now closed, legacies of these institutions are still felt today. What, if anything, has the government done since the closing of the residential schools to address these legacies? What other current government-imposed policies impact Indigenous children and families?

3. Compare and contrast Indigenous approaches to justice and Euro-Canadian approaches to justice. Note both similarities and differences. What changes do you think should be made today to reduce the criminalization, imprisonment, and victimization of Indigenous peoples by the criminal justice system?

GLOSSARY

ginawaydaganuk: An Algonquin principle that takes into consideration the "physical, emotional, mental, and spiritual connections to all of life." This includes all of the life givers, such as "the plants, animals, water, air, earth, and fire" (McDermott & Wilson, 2010, p. 206).

Idle No More: A peaceful, grassroots movement taking a stand against centuries of ongoing occupation and colonialism from the settler society.

Land Protectors: People gathering at Standing Rock to protect their sacred water and lands. Peoples gathered noted how they preferred the terms *Land Protectors* or *Water Protectors* rather than being referred to as "protestors." Many times the word *protest* is linked with aggression, and people gathering at Standing Rock are not aggressive; rather, they are acting peacefully to protect Mother Earth for future generations.

mino-bimaadiziwin: An Anishinaabe concept referring to living life in a good way. Chantal Fiola describes this as the "good life, good relations" (2015, p. 76).

pan-Indian: An approach that lumps all Indigenous peoples into one category, incorrectly assuming that all are the same.

peace and friendship treaties: Nation-to-nation agreements agreed to by both Indigenous and non-Indigenous peoples in North America. Some of these treaty agreements are represented and codified in Wampum Belts, many of which speak of how to live together in harmony, peace, friendship, share the lands, and not interfere with each other's ways of life.

Poonā 'yétum: A Cree term that John G. Hansen describes as "the ability to heal from wrongdoing by utilizing the processes of accountability, repairing harm and reconciliation" (2012, p. 2).

wahkootowin: A Cree concept that Brenda Macdougall explains as "a worldview linking land, family, and identity in one interconnected web of being" (2010, p. 242).

wétiko: A Cree term denoting a "cannibal," whereby people "consume" other beings in order to gain profit (Forbes, 2008).

REFERENCES

Alfred, T., & Lowe, L. (2007). *Warrior societies in contemporary Indigenous communities.* Research Paper Commissioned by the Ipperwash Inquiry.

Borrows, J. (2002). Wampum at Niagara: The Royal Proclamation, Canadian legal history, and self-government. In M. Asch (Ed.), *Aboriginal treaty rights in Canada* (pp. 155–172). UBC Press.

Boyce, J. (2016). Victimization of Aboriginal people in Canada, 2014. *Juristat.* Catalogue no. 85-002-X ISSN 1209-6393, pp. 1–44. Canadian Centre for Justice Statistics, Statistics Canada.

Brant Castellano, M. (2009). Heart of the Nations: Women's contribution to community healing. In G. G. Valaskakis, M. Dion Stout, & E. Guimond (Eds.), *Restoring the balance: First Nations women, community, and culture* (pp. 203–235). University of Manitoba Press.

Bryce, P. H. (1907). *Report on the Indian schools of Manitoba and the North-West Territories.* Government Printing Bureau.

Calloway, C. (Ed.). (1994). *The world turned upside down: Indian voices form early America.* Bedford Books of St. Martin's Press.

Canadian Council on Social Development and Native Women's Association of Canada. (1991). *Voices of Aboriginal women: Aboriginal women speak out about violence.* Canadian Council on Social Development.

Chartrand, V. (2014). Tears 4 Justice and the missing and murdered women and children across Canada: An interview with Gladys Radek. *Radical Criminology, 3*(Winter), 113–126.

Chrisjohn, R., & Young, S., with Maraun, M. (2006). *The circle game: Shadows and substance in the Indian Residential School experience in Canada.* Theytus Books.

Commanda, W. (2009). *Re: Appointment to Officer of the Order of Canada and my work.*

Copway, G. (1851). *Traditional history and characteristic sketches of the Ojibway Nation.* C. Gilpin.

Corntassel, J. (2012). Re-envisioning resurgence: Indigenous pathways to decolonization and sustainable self-determination. *Decolonization: Indigenity, Education & Society, 1*(1), 86–101.

Dakota Access. (2016). *Dakota Access Pipeline facts: The Dakota Access Pipeline will keep America moving efficiently and in an environmentally safe manner.*

Department of Indian Affairs Superintendent D. C. Scott to B. C. Indian Agent-General Major D. McKay, DIA Archives, RG 1-Series 12 April 1910.

Dion Stout, M., & Kipling, G. (2003). *Aboriginal People, resilience and the Residential School legacy.* The Aboriginal Healing Foundation.

Dunbar-Ortiz, Roxanne. (2014). *An Indigenous Peoples' history of the United States.* Beacon Press.

Elsey, C. J. (2013). *The poetics of land & identity among British Columbia Indigenous Peoples.* Fernwood Publishing.

Fiola, C. (2015). *Rekindling the sacred fire: Métis ancestry and Anishinaabe spirituality.* University of Manitoba Press.

Fontaine, T. (2016, April 30). Justice denied: 5 times Indigenous people were wrongfully convicted in Canada. *CBC.* Retrieved from http://www.cbc.ca/news/indigenous/justice-denied-5-times-indigenous-people-wrongfully-convicted-canada-1.3559644

Forbes, J. D. (2008). *Columbus and other cannibals: The wétiko disease of exploitation, imperialism, and terrorism* (rev. ed). Seven Stories Press.

Friedland, H. (2014, February 4). *Accessing justice and reconciliation: IBA Accessing Justice and Reconciliation Project: Final report.* The University of Victoria's Indigenous Research Clinic, the Indigenous Bar Association, and the Truth and Reconciliation Commission, funded by the Ontario Law Foundation.

Funes, Y. (2016). #NoDAPL tribal leaders testify before International Human Rights commission on abuses. *Colorlines.* Retrieved from http://www.colorlines.com/articles/nodapl-tribal-leaders-testify-international-human-rights-commission-abuses

Gehl, L. (2014). *The truth that Wampum tells: My Debwewin on the Algonquin land claims process.* Fernwood Publishing.

Hart, M. A. (Kaskitémahikan). (2009). For Indigenous People, by Indigenous People, with Indigenous People: Towards an Indigenist research paradigm. In R. Sinclair (Ótiskewápíwskew), M. A. Hart (Kaskitémahikan), & G. Bruyere (Amawaajibitang) (Eds.), *Wicihitowain: Aboriginal social work in Canada* (pp. 153–169). Fernwood Publishing.

Hill, B. (1995). *Shaking the rattle: Healing the trauma of colonization.* Theytus Books.

Human Rights Watch. (2013). *Those who take us away: Abusive policing and failures in protection of Indigenous women and girls in northern British Columbia, Canada.* Retrieved from https://www.hrw.org/report/2013/02/13/those-who-take-us-away/abusive-policing-and-failures-protection-indigenous-women

Kelly, F. (2008). Confession of a born again pagan. In M. Brant Castellano, L. Archibald, & M. DeGagné (Eds.), *From truth to reconciliation: Transforming the legacy of residential schools* (pp. 11–40). The Aboriginal Healing Foundation.

Kinew, W. (2012, December 6). From grassroots hashtag to real opportunity for change. *Winnipeg Free Press.* Retrieved from http://www.winnipegfreepress.com/opinion/columnists/from-a-grassroots-hashtag-to-a-real-opportunity-for-change-kinewview-182324221.html

King, J. T. (2007). The value of water and the meaning of water law for the Native Americans known as the Haudenosaunee. *Cornell Journal of Law and Public Policy, 16*(3), 449–472.

Lame Deer, J. (Fire), & Erdoes, R. (1972). *Lame Deer, seeker of visions.* Simon & Schuster.

Lilley, P. J., & Shantz, J. (2013). From Idle No More to Indigenous Nationhood. *Upping the Anti: A Journal of Theory and Action, 15,* 113–127.

Little Bear, L. (2009). Jagged worldviews colliding. In M. Battiste (Ed.), *Reclaiming Indigenous voices and vision* (pp. 77–85). UBC Press.

Lyons, O. (1997). Epilogue: The year of the Indigenous Peoples: Oka revisited (with extracts of the 1991 proceedings of the Standing Committee on Aboriginal Affairs). In A. P. Morrison (Ed.), *Justice for Natives: Searching for common ground* (pp. 299–314). Aboriginal Law Association of McGill University.

Macdougall, B. (2010). *One of the family: Metis culture in nineteenth-century Northwestern Saskatchewan.* UBC Press.

Maracle, L. (1996). *I am woman: A Native perspective on sociology and feminism.* Press Gang Publishers.

McDermott, L., & Wilson, P. (2010). "Ginawaydaganuk": Algonquin law on access and benefit sharing (pp. 205–214). In *Policy Matters 17: Exploring the right to diversity in conservation law, policy, and practice.* IUCN-CEESP: International Union for the Conservation of Native-Commission on Environmental, Economic and Social Policy.

Means, R., & Johnson, B. (2013). *If you've forgotten the names of the clouds, you've lost your way: An introduction to American Indian thought and philosophy.* Treaty Publications.

Milloy, J. S. (1999). *A national crime: The Canadian government and the residential school system, 1879 to 1986.* University of Manitoba Press.

Mosby, I. (2013). Administering colonial science: Nutrition research and human biomedical experimentation in Aboriginal communities and residential schools, 1942–1952. *Social History, 46*(91), 145–172.

Monchalin, L. (2016). *The colonial problem: An Indigenous perspective on crime and injustice in Canada.* University of Toronto Press.

Monture-Angus, P. (1995). *Thunder in my soul: A Mohawk woman speaks.* Fernwood Publishing.

National Inquiry into Missing and Murdered Indigenous Women and Girls. (2019). *Reclaiming power and place: The final report of the National Inquiry into Missing and Murdered Indigenous Women and Girls, Volume 1a.* Retrieved from https://www. mmiwg-ffada.ca/wp-content/uploads/2019/06/Final_Report_Vol_1a-1.pdf

Native Women's Association of Canada. (2010). *What their stories tell us: Research findings from the Sisters in Spirit Initiative.* Native Women's Association of Canada.

Office of the Correctional Investigator. (2016). *Annual report: Office of the Correctional Investigator 2015–2016.* Her Majesty the Queen in Right of Canada.

Office of the Correctional Investigator. (2018). *Office of the Correctional Investigator annual report 2017–2018.* Her Majesty the Queen in Right of Canada.

Paul, D. N. (2006). *First Nations history: We were not the savages: Collision between European and Native American civilization* (3rd ed.). Fernwood Publishing.

Pearce, M. (2013). An awkward silence: Missing and murdered vulnerable women and the Canadian justice system [Unpublished doctoral dissertation]. University of Ottawa.

Peat, F. D. (1997). Blackfoot physics and European minds. *Future, 29,* 563–573.

Perry, B. (2008). *Silent victims: Hate crimes against Native Americans.* University of Arizona Press.

Rice, B., & Snyder, A. (2008). Reconciliation in the context of a settler society: Healing the legacy of colonialism in Canada. In M. Brant Castellano, L. Archibald, & M. DeGagné (Eds.), *From truth to reconciliation: Transforming the legacy of residential schools* (pp. 45–61). The Aboriginal Healing Foundation.

Roman, K. (2013, December 18). St. Anne's Residential School: One survivor's story. *CBC News.* Retrieved January 8, 2017, from http://www.cbc.ca/news/politics/st-anne-s-residential-school-one-survivor-s-story-1.2467924

Ross, R. (2014). *Indigenous healing: Exploring traditional paths.* Penguin Canada Books.

Royal Canadian Mounted Police (RCMP). (2014). *Missing and murdered Aboriginal women: A national operational overview.* Her Majesty the Queen in Right of Canada.

Saul, J. R. (2008). *A fair country: Telling truths about Canada.* Viking Canada.

Sinclair, R. (Ótiskewápíwskew). (2009). Bridging the past and the future: An introduction to Indigenous social work issues. In R. Sinclair (Ótiskewápíwskew), M. A. Hart (Kaskitémahikan), & G. Bruyere (Amawaajibitang) (Eds.), *Wicihitowain: Aboriginal social work in Canada* (pp. 19–24). Fernwood Publishing.

Sioui, G. E. (1999). *Huron Wendat: The heritage of the circle.* UBC Press.

Smith, M. E. (2004). Crippling the spirit, wounding the soul: Native American spiritual and religious suppression. In A. Waters (Ed.), *American Indian thought: Philosophical essays* (pp. 116–129). Blackwell Publishing.

Solomon, A. (1990). *Songs for the people: Teachings on the natural way.* NC Press Limited.

Standing Rock Sioux Tribe. (2016). *Stand with Standing Rock*. Retrieved December 28, 2016, from http://standwithstandingrock.net/

Stannard, D. E. (1992). *American holocaust: The conquest of the new world*. Oxford University Press.

Stiffarm, L. A. & Lane, P. J. (1992) "The demography of native North America: A question of American Indian survival" in M. A. Jaimes (1992). *The state of Native America: genocide, colonization, and resistance*. South End Press.

Truth and Reconciliation Commission of Canada (TRC). (2015). *Honouring the truth, reconciling for the future: Summary of the final report of the Truth and Reconciliation Commission of Canada*. Retrieved from http://www.trc.ca/assets/pdf/Honouring_the_Truth_Reconciling_for_the_Future_July_23_2015.pdf

Victor, W. (2007). *Indigenous justice: Clearing space and place for Indigenous epistemologies*. Research Paper for the National Centre for First Nations Governance. Retrieved from http://fngovernance.org/ncfng_research/wenona_victor.pdf

Wattam, J. (2016). *Dr. Peter Henderson Bryce: A story of courage*. First Nations Child & Family Caring Society of Canada. Retrieved from https://fncaringsociety.com/sites/default/files/Dr.%20Peter%20Henderson%20Bryce%20Information%20Sheet.pdf

Wesley-Esquimaux, C. C., & Smolewski, M. (2004). *Historic trauma and Aboriginal healing*. The Aboriginal Healing Foundation.

Woo, G. L. X. (2013). Canada's democratic deficit and Idle No More. *Lawyers Rights Watch Canada*. Retrieved from http://www.lrwc.org/ws/wp-content/uploads/2013/04/Arctic-Review-LRWC2.pdf

CHAPTER 13

Transnational and Organized Crime in the Age of Globalization

Kenneth Dowler and Claudio Colaguori

LEARNING OBJECTIVES

In this chapter, you will

- learn how criminologists define and classify the different types of organized crime, and how organized criminal activity is connected to larger networks of transnational crime;
- learn how the globalization of society has led to an increase in the spread of organized criminal activity and contributes to the formation of an underground economy;
- learn about the specific types of crimes that criminal organizations tend to commit, including money laundering, human smuggling and trafficking, and the sale of illicit drugs and weapons;
- understand how the growing size and power of transnational criminal cartels pose a threat to political stability; and
- understand the difficulties involved in policing and controlling organized and transnational criminal organizations in a globalized society.

INTRODUCTION

The globalization of society has brought with it the proliferation of illicit markets and internationally organized criminality. Insofar as globalization can be understood as a type of political, economic, and cultural reorganization of society that creates a more deeply interconnected global society, it is not surprising that criminal activity which was once local is now an international phenomenon. This global spread of criminal activity is especially evident in the activities of **organized crime** groups. Street-level gang crime and *clandestine* organized crime run by groups such as the mafia, the **yakuza**, the Hell's Angels, the Triads, and MS-13 among others is now undertaken as a part of an interconnected network or **cartel** of criminal actors who cooperate with other criminal organizations internationally to coordinate their activities in what criminologists refer to as **transnational organized crime**. Organized criminal activity has traditionally involved the sale of goods and services that are prohibited by law, especially illicit drugs and weapons, gambling, and prostitution. In the current transnational context, these criminal activities have expanded to include trade in sexual trafficking, labour enslavement, human smuggling, money laundering, the sale of illegally harvested animals and their body parts (such as ivory and shark fins), firearms and weapons, stolen antiquities and fraudulent art, intellectual property theft, and cybercrime. When the law prohibits the sale of goods and services for which there nevertheless remains strong public demand, this creates criminal opportunity, and organized crime directly capitalizes on such financially lucrative demand.

So vast in dollar value are the combined earnings of organized crime groups worldwide that we are currently witnessing the formation of a massive **underground economy** (known colloquially as "the black market"), which consists of the total amount of financial activities that do not form a part of the *legitimate* capitalist consumer economy but are generated by a variety of illicit economic exchanges. The vast scope of underground criminal activity, which nevertheless is interwoven with the legitimate, *legal* economy through money laundering and other types of illicit exchange, makes transnational criminal organizations extremely powerful on the world economic and political stage—so powerful that the social philosopher Jacques Derrida (1930–2004) referred to the "mafia and drug cartels [operating] on every continent" as "phantom-States" that "invade not only the socio-economic fabric, the general circulation of capital, but also statist or inter-statist institutions" (1994, p. 83). Schönenberg and von Schönfeld (2013) write that the growth in scale and scope of organized crime is an essential feature of economic globalization itself. In the 21st century, organized crime is indeed a global phenomenon, and its harmful influence on social life demands both critical analysis and official response. Naím's analysis of the globalization of crime is specific in its brutal depiction of what is transpiring in the name of commerce: "virtually anything of value is offered for sale in today's global marketplace—including illegal drugs, endangered species, human chattel for sex slavery and sweatshops, human cadavers and live organs for transplant, machine guns and rocket launchers, and centrifuges and precursor chemicals used in nuclear weapons development.... Illicit trade is highly disruptive, of course, to legitimate businesses—except when it isn't.... There is an enormous gray area between legal and illegal transactions, a gray area that the illicit traders have turned to great advantage" (2006, p. 2).

This chapter introduces the reader to some of the basic definitions of organized crime and transnational organized crime, as well as discusses their emergence, development, and the various types of organized criminal activities engaged in. The chapter also addresses the challenges of controlling and policing organized and transnational crime.

In the words of scholars ...

How can one ignore the growing and undelimitable, that is, worldwide power of those super-efficient and properly capitalist phantom-States that are the mafia and drug cartels on every continent, including in the former so-called socialist States of Eastern Europe? These phantom-States have infiltrated and banalized themselves everywhere, to the point where they can no longer be strictly identified.

Jacques Derrida, *Spectres of Marx.* 1994

THE EMERGENCE AND DEVELOPMENT OF TRANSNATIONAL ORGANIZED CRIME

Transnational organized crime (TOC) is a type of broadly coordinated, organized criminal activity that extends beyond national boundaries and involves individuals acting in various administrative capacities to perpetrate and benefit from generally large-scale criminal activity. TOC can be understood as the evolution of traditional organized crime in the context of globalization. However, transnational organized crime is not a new phenomenon. Historically, TOC was largely regional in scope and hierarchically structured. Since the end of the Cold War (circa 1991), however, TOC has expanded dramatically in size, scope, and influence. At present, criminal networks are more fluid, creating new alliances with other networks in various regions of the world and engaging in a wide range of illicit activities, including the penetration of political states which gives TOC groups immense power. As such, TOC presents a significant threat to national and international security. The following section will briefly outline several factors that have contributed to the proliferation and evolution of TOC.

In the words of scholars ...

Today, transnational organized crime is an inherent feature of economic globalization and represents more than just the dark side of that development path. It is increasingly difficult to distinguish light from shadow in this context, and the fine line between legal and illegal forms of economic exchange is becoming increasingly blurred

Regine Schönenberg and Annette von Schönfeld, *Transnational Organized Crime: Analyses of a Global Challenge to Democracy.* 2013

The End of the Cold War and the Rise of Bribery and Corruption

On December 3rd, 1989, the Cold War officially ended when Soviet leader Mikhail Gorbachev met with US President George H. Bush aboard a Soviet ship docked at Malta's Marsaxlokk harbour. Earlier in that year, East and West Germans were tearing down the Berlin Wall, and by December 1991, the Soviet Union was dissolved. The end of the Cold War opened borders across Eastern Europe, resulting in freer trade, but also increased opportunities for criminal entrepreneurs. The rapid globalization of the 1990s helped criminal organizations expand their activities and gain global reach, especially with more porous borders. These same criminal networks also benefitted from the weakening of government institutions, allowing for increased levels of **corruption** and **bribery**. Described as the lubricant for organized crime, bribery is when a person voluntarily solicits or accepts any benefit in exchange for influencing an official act so as to afford the provider better than fair treatment. For example, transnational organized groups may do illicit favours or pay judges, police, or other public officials to "look the other way." For instance, in the Western Balkans, roughly 1 in 10 businesses (10.2%) that had contact with a public official in 12 months paid a bribe (Arsovska, 2019). In Nigeria, it is estimated that Nigerians pay six bribes per year, with approximately $4.6 billion in bribes paid to public officials. Although corruption was prevalent among many government agencies, Nigerian police officers were the most likely to solicit and collect bribes. According to a National Bureau of Statistics (NBS) survey, of all adult Nigerians who had direct contact with a police officer in the 12 months prior to the survey, almost half (46.4%) paid that officer at least one bribe. The same survey found that prosecutors and judges were also on the take, at 33 percent and 31.5 percent respectively. It is within this type of corrupt environment that organized crime groups are able to flourish, as authorities are unable to enforce the rule of law (Salihu & Gholami, 2018).

Failed States and Crime

Transnational organized crime tends to develop in nations where law enforcement institutions are weak or unstable. Fragile or **failed states** tend to exhibit high-capacity deficits, weak government institutions, and a substantial reliance on nongovernmental and traditional support structures and processes (Locke, 2012). Across the world, governmental corruption and illicit trade fuel and sustain each other. Traditionally, states that are weak or failing or those within conflict regions are considered as crime-facilitative environments. Transnational organized crime develops out of the power vacuum that is formed by the absence or lack of enforcement and good governance.

Failed states have weak institutions and high levels of corruption that can both cause and accelerate organized crime activities. Corrupt and ineffective state institutions allow criminal organizations to operate freely and with impunity. This institutional corruption is cyclical and is very difficult to eliminate, as those in power continually block reform. As such, organized crime groups take advantage of the state to further their interests, exploiting governance void, lack of law and order and institutional corruption. For example, Nagle (2010) argues that Mexico is a failing state, suffering from a deeply entrenched system of political corruption that destabilizes the three branches of government and undermines Mexico's law enforcement and national security. Mexican drug cartels corrupt local and state authorities, where they control entire towns and regions. In some Mexican provinces, the police, military, and government officials are on the cartel's payroll. Corrupt politicians and government officials depend on illicit funds to finance election campaigns and bribe supporters. The cartels are protected from prosecution and receive a virtual immunity from the justice system. This culture of corruption pervades Mexico, allowing political elites, the judiciary, military, and police officials to welcome corruption as a path for career advancement and personal wealth. The system itself is dependent on corruption to function, with immense financial, social, and personal costs. In 2019 alone, 35,588 Mexicans were victims of homicides, while nearly 5,000 people disappeared. Although not all are related to organized crime, much of the violence is attributed to organized crime diversification, with organized-crime groups fragmenting into warring cells. Organized crime is so powerful that the Sinaloa cartel gunmen virtually seized control of the city of Culiacan, forcing the government to release Ovidio Guzman, the son of cartel leader, Joaquin "El Chapo" Guzman. In December 2019, dozens of cartel gunmen attacked a townhall in Villa Union, 40 miles southwest of US border, resulting in a 2-day battle with security forces, leaving 19 dead (Sheridan, 2020).

Transnational organized crime also thrives in regions in which citizens have limited economic alternatives. For example, opium poppy cultivation occurs at high levels in Myanmar and Lao People's Democratic Republic, with estimates between 73.1 to 82.3 metric tonnes of street-grade heroin for regional and global drug markets. The 2015 Southeast Asian Opium Survey reveals that Myanmar remains the region's top opium producer, and second largest in the world after Afghanistan. In northern Myanmar, Shan state is a high-conflict region that accounts for 90 percent of opium poppy cultivation in the Golden Triangle. Due to food insecurity, poverty, and threats, farmers have little choice but to rely on the revenue from illicit drug trade. This upsets well-intentioned development plans and fuels large profits for transnational organized crime groups. Moreover, economic instability leads some citizens to seek work abroad, where they may fall victim to **human trafficking** rings (United Nations Office on Drugs and Crime [UNODC], 2015).

Crime in Conflict-Affected Regions

Criminal and illicit networks span the globe, infiltrating both developed and developing countries. They prosper, however, in conflict-affected and post-conflict states, where they take advantage of illicit opportunities to cement their economic and political influence through corruption, bribery, and violence. Further, **conflict-affected states** have significant social divisions, depleted infrastructure, large amounts of firearms, and crippling poverty rates. Coupled with religious or ideological division, this creates an ideal environment for trafficking and other illegal activity, which nets massive profits for organized crime groups. More recently, illicit exploitation of gold, oil, and other natural resources have overtaken traditional criminal activity, such as kidnapping for ransom and drug trafficking in these regions. The actual combatants, however, receive a small fraction of the illicit funds. It is estimated that $31.5 billion goes to politicians and transnational criminal networks, who remain the main beneficiaries from instability and violence. Thus, peacekeeping efforts are thwarted, as there is little motivation for ending conflict, as corrupt politicians at all levels are raking in massive profits (UN News, 2018).

One of the enduring legacies of the fall of the former Soviet Union was the resurgence of ethnic and regional conflicts. During the 1990s, gangsterism was on the rise, with an estimated 150 gangs roaming the streets of Moscow. Under the dictatorship of Putin and his strongarm tactics, the violence of the 1990s has dissipated considerably. However, corruption is an ongoing problem, with organized crime inextricably linked to corrupt governance. As a result of regional conflicts, there are several ethnic-based gangs, including ethnic Russians, Slavs, Georgians, and, most notably, the Chechen Mafia. In fact, the Chechen Mafia is the largest ethnic organized crime group operating in the former Soviet Union and engages in several illicit activities, including smuggling and arms trafficking to help fund the Chechen separatist movement (Hahn, 2012; Ross, 2011).

Aside from the former Soviet Union, there are several global examples of conflict zones that are breeding grounds for illicit networks, including Afghanistan, the Balkans, Syria, Iraq, and Nigeria. The Democratic Republic of the Congo (DRC) provides a prominent example of how conflict, fragility, and transnational organized crime bolster each other with lethal and long-lasting effects. In the mid-to-late 1990s, the DRC (formerly known as Zaire) encountered a surge of violence, triggered by the fall of the Mobutu regime and the 1994 genocide in neighbouring Rwanda. The convergence of events resulted in the First Congo War (1996–1997), which is also referred to the "African First World War" as the conflict spilled over to neighbouring states, including Sudan and Uganda. Although the conflict ended in 2002, the DRC continues to be extremely fragile. The state has limited control over its vast territory and multiple rebel groups, armed actors, and criminal organizations fight to control the country's exhaustive mineral resources. As such, state fragility is intertwined with a complex history of domestic and regional violence, thus allowing criminal entrepreneurs to flourish with little to no impunity (Kemp et al., 2013).

The Expansion of Financial Markets and Technological Development

Trade liberalization has vastly increased global commerce, which has resulted in the opening of borders, allowing criminal organizations unprecedented access to a globally interconnected transportation network. For instance, between 1980 and 2018, world container traffic has increased exponentially, from 39 million 20-foot equivalent united (TEU) to 793 million TEU. It is estimated that world merchandise and commercial services trade have increased by an average of 7 percent per year on average, with the global trade value of goods at approximately

US $19.5 trillion in 2018, up from US $6.45 trillion in 2000 (United Nations Conference on Trade and Development [UNCTAD], 2019). This remarkable expansion in trade reflects the vast changes in international trade, globalization, and advances in technology. The most important factor is the decline of trade barriers, which includes lower transportation costs; the reduction of policy barriers (tariffs, etc.); and the removal of internal trade processes (legal and regulatory costs, custom clearance procedures, administrative red tape, etc.). The incredible rise of global supply chains and just-in-time delivery of goods and services has greatly increased the pressure to keep commerce moving through ports of entry, which decreases the amount of time for the inspection of goods. As a result, illicit entrepreneurs take advantage of the open global markets to supply illicit goods and services to consumers. The success of criminal networks is based not only on their international mobility but also their capacity to take advantage of international boundaries. As a result, the increase in trade flows along border regions brought an absolute explosion of illegal activities. Moreover, the growing middle class in developing countries has fuelled new markets for a variety of goods such as drugs and counterfeit products (Naím, 2006).

This explosion of illegal trade has been facilitated by the growth of cutting-edge technology in both transportation and communication networks. Technological advances have allowed organized criminals to traverse previously inaccessible regions, expanding their scope of operation and their profits. Digital technology has transformed everyday life as developments in communications, information storage, and retrieval have greatly enhanced the efficiency with which legitimate organizations operate. Of course, the benefits are not lost on organized criminals, who exploit digital technology to enhance the efficiency and effectiveness of their operations. Digital technology has also transformed how criminal actors organize themselves, cultivating looser and more fluid organizational structures. The so-called *dark web* allows illicit entrepreneurs to sell illicit goods and services, easily establishing new markets and partnerships within in new territories. For example, the online marketplace Silk Road offered buyers access to drugs, stolen IDs, hacking tools, and other illicit products (Minnaar, 2017).

These technological advances are particularly prominent in the realm of money laundering and counterfeiting. The deregulation of global finance has allowed transnational criminals with an additional mechanism to launder illicit funds. **Money laundering** is the process of making funds generated by an illicit activity, such as drug trafficking or gambling, appear to have come from a legitimate source. The revenues from the illicit activity are considered "dirty," and the money is "laundered" to make it look "clean." The United Nations estimates that 2 to 5 percent of the global GDP, or $800 to $2 trillion US, are laundered globally (UNODC, 2020). In Canada, it is estimated that $46.7 billion was laundered through the Canadian economy in 2018, with British Columbia accounting for $7.4 billion, with BC's real estate market accounting for 72 percent of that figure (Comeau, 2019). The Hong Kong and Shanghai Banking Corporation (HSBC) was complicit in a money laundering scandal within its Mexico unit and agreed to a pay a $1.9 billion fine (Viswanatha & Wolf, 2012). Banking deregulation has exacerbated the problem, allowing organized criminals to easily launder their money. For example, in the former Soviet Union, the banking industry is a haven of corruption, with the Russian mafia controlling many banking executives. Similarly, the yakuza in Japan have had a long and scandalous history with the Japanese banking industry. Described as "Goldman Sachs with guns," the yakuza utilize blackmail, political connections, and threats of violence to manipulate bank executives into providing them with favourable loans, as well as launder illicit revenue (Webb, 2013). Most recently, Denmark's largest lender, the Danske Bank, was embroiled in the largest money laundering scandal in European history. Between 2007 and 2015, over $200 billion of non-resident funds flowed through Danske's Estonia branch, with more than 58 percent coming from Russia, Estonia, and Latvia (Bjerregaard & Kirchmaier, 2019).

THE COSTS OF TRANSNATIONAL ORGANIZED CRIME

The economic and social costs of transnational crime and corruption are immense. Although the negative effects of corruption, illicit trade, organized crime, and fragility are easy to characterize, the costs are difficult to quantify. Global illicit activity is hard to measure, primarily due to its clandestine nature. By the most conservative estimates, criminal proceeds comprise between 2 and 5 percent of global gross domestic product (GDP). Illicit trade is believed to represent between 7 and 10 percent of the global economy, while in some countries, illicit trade is the largest source of revenue. According to the United Nations, TOC is an US $870 billion a year business. Drug trafficking is the most lucrative form of business for organized criminals, with an estimated value of $320 billion per year. Counterfeiting and human trafficking are also high earners for TOC, with annual values of $250 and $32 billion, respectively. The exploitation of the environment is also a major revenue stream for TOC, with trafficking in timber generating $3.5 billion in Southeast Asia, while elephant ivory, rhino, and tiger parts from Africa and Asia produce approximately $75 million. In the health sector, counterfeit drugs represent almost 10 percent of the international pharmaceuticals market, equivalent to US $35 billion in revenue, causing millions of deaths per year. The World Bank estimates about $1 trillion is spent each year on bribery of public officials. This can cause an array of damage to legitimate economic activity, while severely undermining legitimate competition and innovation (UNODC, n.d.). Moreover, TOC can cause significant damage to the world financial system through its subversion, exploitation, and distortion of legitimate markets and economic activity. For example, in markets in which the rule of law is less reliable, legitimate business is at a competitive disadvantage as they must pay for additional security and transportation costs. In some regions, TOC organizations leverage their relationships with state-owned entities, industries, or state-allied actors and gain influence over crucial commodities markets such as gas, oil, and precious metals, which further exacerbates fair market practices. Moreover, illicit trade is also linked to the legitimate economy. For example, both human trafficking and forced labour have widely penetrated the legitimate economy. Corporations are most at risk, as their increasingly complex supply chains and vast distribution networks make them more vulnerable to counterfeiting, intellectual property infringement, and corruption. In some instances, corporations align themselves with organized crime entities in an attempt to recoup the potential of lost profits from the black market. For example, tobacco company executives at BAT, Philip Morris, and R.J. Reynolds have worked closely with individuals directly linked to organized crime in Hong Kong, Canada, Colombia, Italy, and the United States. The corporations actively supply the black market in what internal documents refer to as "duty not paid," "parallel" markets, "general trade," or "transit." Essentially, brand-name cigarettes are sold on the black market, undercutting government taxes and duties, gaining an unfair advantage against competitors and resulting in massive tax evasion, which depletes government treasuries in developing countries (Corpwatch, 2001).

THE CRITICAL ROLE OF THE FACILITATORS OF CRIME

Scholars have increasingly recognized the important role that the facilitators of crime play within TOC networks. **Facilitators** are semi-legitimate actors such as accountants, attorneys, notaries, bankers, and real estate brokers, who traverse both the licit and illicit worlds. These facilitators provide services to legitimate customers, criminals, and terrorists. The scope of licit–illicit relationships is wide-ranging. TOC networks use the public reputations of licit actors to maintain facades of legitimacy of their operations. TOC networks use industry experts to facilitate corrupt transactions and to create the essential infrastructure to carry out their illicit schemes (Abt Associates, 2020). For example, facilitators can create shell corporations, open offshore bank accounts, and create front businesses for illegal activity and money laundering. TOC networks enlist legitimate business owners and their employees to conceal smuggling operations. These networks depend on secure transportation networks and safe locations to allow massive amounts of cash, narcotics, or other smuggled goods to flow through. Smuggling networks also require fraudulently created or obtained documents, including passports and visas to facilitate the movement of people across borders. TOC networks also utilize legitimate businesses to "launder" or convert illicit profits into legitimate funds. Cash-intensive and high-volume businesses such as casinos are especially attractive for money laundering. This is even more pronounced in jurisdictions that lack regulatory oversight and where corruption within government or law enforcement is common.

The threat of TOC crosses borders and undermines the stability of nations, subverting government institutions through corruption and harming citizens worldwide. Transnational crime and corruption are highly interconnected with many dangers, ranging from geopolitical risks such as terrorism, political instability, and nuclear proliferation, to biodiversity loss and threats to critical information infrastructure. Criminal organizations can destabilize countries and entire regions, undermining development assistance and increasing corruption, extortion, racketeering, and violence. In turn, economic disparity provides an enabling environment for illicit trade, corruption, and organized crime to grow in advanced and emerging economies. In turn, the proceeds reinforce the power of the privileged, while undermining economic development by raising the costs of doing legitimate business, thereby increasing inequalities both within and between countries. Similarly, while global governance failures have created a growing space for illegal activities, these activities tend to undermine efficient global governance. Although this nexus of risks is often seen as more pervasive in emerging economies, a significant proportion of the demand for illicit goods is generated in advanced economies. Illegal networks also use the international banking and real estate systems to facilitate their financial management, laundering money and hiding profits from tax authorities. The human cost associated with TOC is also a major concern, with thousands of deaths caused by illegal firearms, **human smuggling**, and drug-related health problems and violence.

In the words of scholars ...

In defiance of regulations and taxes, treaties, and laws, virtually anything of value is offered for sale in today's global marketplace—including illegal drugs, endangered species, human chattel for sex slavery and sweatshops, human cadavers and live organs for transplant, machine guns and rocket launchers, and centrifuges and precursor chemicals used in nuclear weapons development.... This trade is illicit trade. It is trade that breaks the rules—the laws, regulations, taxes, embargos, and all the procedures that nations employ to organize commerce, protect their citizens, raise revenues, and enforce moral codes.

Moisés Naím, *Illicit: How Smugglers, Traffickers and Copycats Are Hijacking the Global Economy.* 2006

DEFINING TRADITIONAL ORGANIZED CRIME

Organized crime (OC), as Beare writes, "has always brought with it a mystique" (2015, p. xiii). People are especially fascinated with the myriad characters that represent the mythology of organized criminal gangsters as transgressive anti-heroes who are simultaneously admonished and admired. Media representations of notorious individuals like Al Capone (the Mobster), Pablo Emilio Escobar (the Narco), The Hell's Angels, and many others have shaped the way people generally think of organized crime figures. Organized crime is, however, more difficult to define than the mere illegal activities of such notorious figures. Defining organized crime is a challenge because "there is no one definition of organized crime, and authors wrestle with trying to determine what activities and which criminal individuals fit under that concept" (p. 3). As such, there are multiple definitions of traditional organized crime. These definitions are often developed by law enforcement agencies, political organizations, or by academic scholars.

Most definitions of organized crime emphasize the following characteristics:

- it is conducted through a clandestine network of conspirators who form a hierarchical command structure based on trust and mutual obligations;
- it is carefully planned and executed and often involves cooperative relations with corrupted members of society who are not necessarily members of the crime group;

- OC groups traditionally consist of members who are of the same ethnic culture to reinforce group solidarity, kinship, and codes of honour;
- involvement in OC crime constitutes a consistent lifestyle for its members.

Further, definitions of *transnational* organized crime usually include criminal offences that traverse international borders and involve more than one country or region. Nonetheless, there are considerable academic efforts to define organized crime, resulting in many debates and divisions. One of the leading experts, Klaus von Lampe (2015), found that there were over 150 definitions of organized crime, ranging from crime types and criminal activities to the constitution and composition of organized crime groups. Nonetheless, there is consensus among scholars about several issues that permeate the concept of organized crime, including the ethnicity trap; the terror-organized crime nexus; the criminal gang; traditional versus modern networks; and narco-terrorism.

Box 13.1: The MS-13 Gang

Described as the "world's most dangerous gang," Mara Salvatrucha (MS-13) was founded in Los Angeles in the 1980s by Salvadoran immigrant youth and expanded outwards. The gang is considered one of the largest street gangs in North and Central America, with a reputation for extreme brutality and a fast-expanding, transnational organized crime network. MS-13 received media attention when the Trump administration claimed to be *at war* against MS-13 because the gang was exploiting weak immigration laws to enter the United States on a mission of violent crime. Some researchers argue that the gang is not the largest, most violent, or fastest-growing gang in the United States. For instance, it is estimated that MS-13 has between 30,000 and 50,000 members worldwide, with approximately 10,000 gang members in the United States, accounting for 1 percent of total gang membership in the United States (Lind, 2019). The gang is not as large as urban gangs such as the Crips, Bloods, and the Latin Kings. It is even smaller than the Gangster Disciples, a notorious Chicago street gang responsible for thousands of murders in Chicago. Conversely, MS-13 is responsible for an average of 35 murders per year, a far cry from the Gangster Disciples (Lind, 2019).

In 2012, the US Department of Treasury officially designated MS-13 as a transnational criminal organization joining the Camorra, Russian gangsters, Mexican cartels, and the Yakuza. However, most experts suggest that MS-13 does not have the power, wealth, organizational structure, and sophistication of global syndicates. The Drug Enforcement Agency (DEA) categorized MS-13 as a "national gang" rather than a TCO (Lind, 2019). Nonetheless, the gang does have a reputation for gruesome violence and preys on immigrant youth and their families. Unfortunately, the gang's real victims often get lost in the anti-immigrant rhetoric used to serve political narratives (Dreier, 2018).

Source: "Inmates of the penal de Ciudad Barrios," Adam Hinton.

The Ethnicity Trap—Cultural Stereotypes and Crime

The roots of OC lie in economic, social, and political causes. These groups, however, are often defined in ethnic and national terms. This phenomenon has led to what criminologist Jay Albanese calls the **ethnicity trap**, which occurs when organized crime is described "in terms of the nature of the groups that engage in it," as opposed to the "nature of the organized crime activity itself, and how and why various groups specialize in certain activities (or fail to specialize)" (2011, p. 5).

The ethnicity trap is rooted in the **Alien Conspiracy theory**, which was at one time the most widely held theories of organized crime. Now debunked, the Alien Conspiracy theory blames immigrants and outsiders for the prevalence of organized crime within society. The theory posits that the Italian mafia are responsible for the foundations of organized crime in the United States and Canada. The theory was born out of hysteria created by the media, creating the myth of the Italian gangster as a *supercriminal* who dominated organized criminal activities. The reality, however, is that this theory gained support from law enforcement, public officials, and even some academics. Law enforcement had self-serving reasons for promoting the theory, using it to receive more resources and explain their inability to eradicate organized crime. The problem is that the theory lends itself to blaming immigrants for crime, which facilitates stereotypes, racist ideologies, and repressive crime control policies.

Of course, there is evidence to suggest that many organized crime groups are ethnically based. This is one of the problematic aspects of researching organized crime and gang subcultures, in that they are most often aggregated along ethnic, racial, and subcultural lines. This reality has the tendency to create the misperception that certain ethnic or racial groups are more *criminal* than others. As any honest criminologist will tell you, crime is endemic to all human groups. The reason we see some criminal groups organized according to ethnic and racial identity has more to do with the troubled political histories of these groups than any single group's natural inclination towards criminality. Furthermore, organized and gang-related crime is often *tribalistic*, meaning that members tend to only trust those they see as members of their own group and to exclude and be suspicious of those who do not form part of that group. This is especially important when we consider that bonds of trust are essential when groups of people plot to undertake illegal activities who are in direct competition with other opportunistic groups interested in their own criminal pursuits. We also see ethnic and racial *tribalism* occurring in many maximum-security prisons where groups of identical ethnic and racial people form alliances with one another and to protect themselves from reprisals from other gangs or groups.

Many scholars argue that we should not classify OC groups by nationality, race, or ethnicity. For example, Woodiwiss (2003), claims that governments have often defined organized crime as something outside of society, beyond the sphere of the normal and acceptable. He suggests that organized and transnational organized crime is, in fact, ingrained in society. Though his analysis focuses on the United States, Canadians often think of the threat as being, at the very least, foreign based, from the Italian or Russian mafia to street gangs of Latino or Asian origin. Even the Hell's Angels, of course, though well established in Quebec and across the country, originates from California.

Similarly, Sheptycki, commenting on the racialization of TOC groups, claims that the "seemingly technical language [about transnational organized crime] is infused with a rich set of connotative meanings ... [and] these connotative meanings are encapsulated in the reports of international policing and security agencies, which give pride of place to an exotic collection of ethnically based criminal organizations: Jamaican Yardies, **Chinese Triads**, Japanese Yakuza, the Russian Mafiya, Albanians, Iranians, Nigerians, Syrians, and Colombians" (2007, p. 5). These scholars further argue that a precise description of particular economic, social, and political conditions, opportunities, and influences are more useful in explaining organized crime than demographic attributes such as race or ethnicity. Currently, contemporary versions of TOC allow for increased cooperation amongst various racial/ethnic variants of TOC, which further enriches these criminal organizations.

The Street Gang/Organized Crime Dichotomy

Street-level criminal gangs are distinctly different than formal organized crime groups insofar as they tend not to operate secretively in the background of society, nor do they necessarily operate with well-organized, long-term plans. Street gangs are generally more fragmented, opportunistic, and based within specific regions or territories in inner cities. In some instances, street gangs are affiliated with and work under the direction of more powerful organized crime groups in various capacities, such as selling drugs and guns at the street level. Street gangs nevertheless maintain a hierarchical organizational structure, a division of labour, operate in more than one criminal activity, and in some cases maintain international operations. For example, research finds that street gangs are evolving into transnational organized criminal groups, including overlapping crimes such as drug and human trafficking. As such, there is growing concern that gangs are becoming more complex and organized and integrated into TOC.

Since 1980, the proliferation of youth gangs has fuelled public fear and magnified misconceptions about youth. Street gangs are most prevalent in the central cities of large urban areas. Historically, members of street gangs were primarily young adult males from homogeneous lower-class, inner-city neighbourhoods. Generally, these gangs were racially/ethnically segregated and active in a variety of criminal activities, including drug trafficking. Throughout the 1980s and 1990s, gangs spread beyond large urban regions to small cities, towns, suburban, and even rural areas. Most of the theoretical knowledge and empirical work on street gangs has come from the United States. However, in Canada, gang members account for a large amount of criminal behaviour, and there has been increased attention given to the scope and nature of street gangs in the Canadian context (Dunbar, 2017).

The vast literature suggests that gang membership sometimes provides psychological, social, and economic benefits. Members may seek affiliation with a gang to meet an unfulfilled need. There are several motivations to join a gang, including as a source of protection; to acquire material goods or resources; to serve a social function, in that members may find excitement, entertainment, or status associated with the gang; the ready access to drugs and alcohol; and gangs may provide a sense of belonging (a substitute family), as members receive empathy and emotional support from other members, which may also serve as a boost to self-esteem and identity. Finally, gangs may be an attractive option for youth who face difficult social and economic conditions, such as poverty, lower educational performance, lack of job skills, and high-conflict family situations (Dunbar, 2017).

Gangs also tend to form in areas in which disadvantages are high, including areas with poor economic indicators, poor infrastructure, underfunded education systems, lack of job opportunities, family disruption, and racial discrimination. Vigil (2002) calls this **multiple marginality**, defined as breakdowns of social and economic factors that lead to a "street socialization," in which at-risk youth populate street gangs as a mechanism to adapt to the perceived lack of life chances or choices. Simply put, this street socialization may form into a street subculture, otherwise known as a gang. Many gangs are organized with the intent of committing criminal activity for financial gain and acquisition of material goods. Gangs are hierarchically structured with an established leadership and a formal chain of command. Generally, gangs require expansion to meet needs and employ initiation rituals to screen new recruits based on their loyalty to the group. Nevertheless, some scholars argue that street gangs do not necessarily fit the criteria to be defined as an organized crime entity (Kelly & Caputo, 2005).

The Nexus between Transnational Organized Crime and Terrorism/Insurgency

In some instances, illicit activities fund so-called terrorist groups and their ideological and/or political goals. As such, the nexus between transnational organized crime and terrorism is complex and intricate. The definitions of organized crime and terrorism often overlap, as they both employ similar methods to acquire capital to achieve their objectives. Both groups operate in decentralized cells and structures and tend to target civilians. However, many experts distinguish the groups by motive. Generally, criminals are driven by financial gain while terrorists are motivated by political, ideological, or religious goals. Yet identifying groups' motives can be challenging, especially as terrorists often support their activities through crime. The definitions merge as extremists justify their criminal activities on the grounds that such acts enable them to meet their ideological goals. Terrorists and insurgents employ TOC to produce funding and acquire logistical support to carry out their violent acts. The US Department of Justice found a linkage between significant international drug trafficking organizations (DTOs) and terrorist groups (Kassab & Rosen, 2019). For example, the Taliban in Afghanistan and the Revolutionary Armed Forces of Colombia (FARC) both employed the drug trade to fund their terrorist activities. Moreover, the terrorist organization al-Shabaab has engaged in organized crime activities such as kidnapping for ransom and extortion of pirates to fund their operations. Still, the crime-terror nexus is mostly opportunistic rather than based in ideological motivations. However, the nexus is vital, as national security may be compromised with the possibility of terrorists/insurgents smuggling weapons of mass destruction or penetrating human trafficking networks as a means of illegally entering target countries.

Traditional versus Modern Crime Networks

A key feature in the definition of transnational organized crime is the differentiation between traditional crime organizations and more modern criminal networks. Traditional groups have a hierarchal structure that operates continuously or for an extended period. In contrast, modern networks are more decentralized, often with a cell-like structure. As such, law enforcement faces increasing challenges of infiltrating and investigating the modern networks (Schneider, 2017). Moreover, the relation to the state provides a key difference between modern and traditional networks. Scholars argue that traditional organizations have interests that are often aligned with the state. Simply, they rely heavily on the state, either through bribery and corruption, for contracts and services. These traditional organizations also tend to launder their illegitimate gains through legitimate businesses. Conversely, modern networks are less likely to launder large sums of money and profit from state contracts. These modern organizations thrive on the absence of effective governance. Mexico, with corruption at all levels of government, provides an excellent example of this phenomenon.

Narco-Terrorism

In the early 1980s, the term **narco-terrorism** was first used by former Peruvian president Belaúnde Terry to describe terrorist-like tactics used against Peruvian law enforcement by Shining Path Marxist rebels. Currently, *narco-terrorism* is broadly defined as terrorism financed by profits obtained from illegal drug trafficking. The

DEA argues that it is a "subset of terrorism," in which individuals or organizations directly or indirectly partake in the "cultivation, manufacture, transportation, or distribution of controlled substances and money derived from these activities" (cited in Shanty, 2011, p. 18). The DEA further estimates that 17 of the 41 designated foreign terrorist organizations engage in narco-terrorism (Björnehed, 2004). Many scholars, however, argue that the definition of *narco-terrorism* is too broad, as it could be applied to a wide range of organizations, from paramilitary groups such as FARC, whose profits exceed millions of dollars from the cocaine trade, to small terrorist cells. Further, some scholars argue that the term has lost "clarity" as it implies a symbiotic relationship between drug traffickers and terrorists, which is seldom verified by evidence. For instance, Gomis argues that the term "is a red herring as it diverts attention away from other important issues, such as corruption, state abuses, arms trafficking, human trafficking and other types of organized crime and violence ... [while] overestimating the importance of the drug trade in funding terrorism, and the use of terrorist tactics by drug traffickers" (Gomis, 2015, p. 1). As such, utilizing the term *narco-terrorism* to explain the complex nexus between terrorism and organized crime can lead to ineffective and counterproductive policies, which may be politically motivated rather than derived from evidence-based categorical distinctions.

THE ONGOING GLOBAL THREAT OF TRANSNATIONAL ORGANIZED CRIME

There is little doubt that TOC poses a significant and growing threat to international security. There are serious global implications for public safety, public health, democratic institutions, and economic stability. The United Nations (UN) has identified 18 categories of transnational criminal offences, which include:

- money laundering;
- theft of intellectual property;
- theft and sale of art and cultural artifacts;
- illicit arms trafficking;
- aircraft hijacking;
- sea piracy;
- insurance fraud;
- computer crime;
- environmental crime;
- trafficking in persons and human body parts;

- illicit drug trafficking;
- fraudulent bankruptcy;
- infiltration of legal business; and
- corruption and bribery of public or party officials.

Criminal networks continue to expand and diversify their activities, posing a threat to governments and citizens across the globe. It is vital to recognize that TOC groups are very malleable. They constantly adjust their modus operandi, seizing opportunities for criminal profit and adjusting their business model to changing markets and the prohibition of goods of services. These criminal organizations engage in ever-evolving types of criminal innovation that work around restrictive laws and vulnerabilities. Nonetheless, there is consensus that the threats posed by TOC are substantial and involve a wide range of illegal activities as listed below.

Penetration of State Institutions, Corruption, and Threats to Governance

The connections between TOC organizations, politicians, legal institutions, and high-level business figures signify a considerable threat to economic growth and democratic governance. TOC networks threaten stability and undermine free markets as they develop partnerships with political leaders, financial institutions, law enforcement, foreign intelligence, and security agencies. TOC saturation of states is expanding, resulting in increasing levels of corruption and the further weakening of governance. Developing countries that suffer from a weak rule of law are acutely vulnerable to TOC infiltration. In these countries, corrupt officials ignore TOC activity and TOC networks subvert the political process in a variety of ways. These can include direct bribery; having members successfully run for political office; setting up shadow economies; infiltrating financial and security sectors through coercion or corruption; and placing themselves as alternate providers of governance, security, services, and employment. The TOC penetration of governments is a double-edged sword, as it contributes to greater levels of corruption, which undermines political institutions, the rule of law, free press, and transparency. Absent significant political reforms (or even revolution), it is almost impossible for developing countries to rid themselves of TOC infestation of governmental and legal institutions.

Expansion of Drug Trafficking

The trade in illicit drugs is a serious threat to health, safety, and global security. The continuing demand for illicit drugs allows criminal organizations around the globe to operate with impunity, as well as fuelling violence and corruption.

Mexican cartels escalate their violence to consolidate and protect market interests within North America. Latin American cartels have partnered with West African criminal organizations to transport cocaine to Western Europe and the Middle East. Even well-established criminal organizations, including those in Russia, China, Italy, and the Balkans have established ties to drug producers, in order to develop their own distribution networks and markets. The growth of drug trafficking is often supplemented by steady increases in local crime and corruption. The so-called "war on drugs" has become an unwinnable battle, as demand for illicit drugs, coupled with high levels of governmental corruption, provides an uneven playing field in law enforcement's attempt to take down large-scale drug trafficking organizations.

Human Smuggling

The development of new markets and growing income inequality has triggered an increase in people willing to migrate, providing an expanding market for human smuggling networks. The UN estimates 272 million migrants in 2019, up from 154 million in 1990 (United Nations, 2019). The majority of these migrants came from developing countries and sought work in developed economies such as the United States and Europe. *Human smuggling* is the facilitation, transportation, or illegal entry of a person or persons across an international border. Smuggling violates one or more countries' laws, either covertly or through deception. For example, TOC groups can either use fraudulent documents or help facilitate the circumvention of legitimate border controls. The vast majority of illegal entries are smuggled, rather than trafficked. Human smuggling is an illicit commercial transaction between willing parties who end their relationship after illegal entry has been secured. That considered, many human smuggling rings are connected to other transnational crimes, including drug trafficking and the corruption of government officials. These rings can transport criminals, fugitives, terrorists, trafficking victims, and economic migrants. Human smuggling networks weaken the sovereignty of nations and often endanger the lives of those being smuggled. According to the first Global Study on Smuggling of Migrants, 2.5 million migrants were smuggled in 2016, with revenues of up to US $7 billion per year. The study found that worldwide there were 30 major smuggling routes and smuggling involved many complex schemes, including arranging fake marriages and fictitious employment, counterfeiting travel documents, or bribery of senior officials. Smuggling networks participated in systemic corruption at almost every level of government (UNODC, 2018a). The International Organization for Migration (IOM) report thousands of deaths due to migrant smuggling, with many deaths attributed to drowning or extreme terrain or weather conditions. The Mediterranean has the highest percentage of deaths, representing approximately 50 percent of the fatalities. Systemic murders of migrants also take place along human smuggling routes. However, smuggled migrants are also susceptible to other crimes such as violence, rape, theft, kidnapping, extortion, and trafficking in persons. Most illegal migrants are young males, yet along South-East Asia routes, women account for most of the smuggled migrants (IOM, 2014). Moreover, in 2016, almost 34,000 unaccompanied and separated children arrived in Europe (in Greece, Italy, Bulgaria, and Spain). Of note, children and women are particularly vulnerable to deception and abuse by smugglers and their associates (UNODC, 2018a).

Trafficking in Persons

Trafficking in Persons (TIP), also known as *human trafficking*, is when one person obtains or holds another person in forced service, such as involuntary servitude, slavery, **debt bondage**, and forced labour. TIP involves the crossing of international borders and within nation-states. Victims are transported between various locations, bought, and sold by trafficking organizations to engage in forced labour, sexual exploitation, and/or forced marriage. Unlike human smuggling, where persons consent to migration, trafficked persons are objects of criminal exploitation and are frequently physically, psychologically, and sexually abused. Experts argue that is difficult to quantify the actual number of persons that are trafficked each year. In many instances, the statistics represent arbitrary or best guess estimates. In 2009, the UN estimated that approximately 2.5 million people were victims of human trafficking, with many from Asia, East Europe, and South America. The report also estimated that human traffickers collected US $2.5 billion annually (UNODC, 2009).

The Global Data Hub on Human Trafficking estimates that 40 million people were victims of modern slavery in 2016, with 25 million enduring forced labour and 15 million in forced marriages. In terms of sex trafficking, the International Labour Organization (ILO) estimates that globally, 3.8 million adults and 1 million children were victims of forced sexual exploitation in 2016. The ILO also found that the vast majority (99%) of victims were female and that 70 percent of the victims originated from Asia Pacific, compared with 14 percent in Europe and Central Asia and 4 percent in the Americas. In a 2014 report, the ILO also found that profits for forced sexual labour is approximately $99 billion, accounting for the highest profits per victim in comparison to other types of forced labour, such as domestic work (ILO & Walk Free Foundation, 2017). In the United States, many victims of sex trafficking work at 9,000 illicit massage parlors. Illegal entrepreneurs pay approximately US $80,000 per victim, with the industry reaching profits of $2.8 billion annually (Keyhan et al., 2018).

Weapons Trafficking

TOC groups work with illicit arms dealers to help supply the black markets in which terrorists and drug traffickers obtain some of their weapons. The illicit trade in arms occurs globally, but it is concentrated where demand is highest, in regions afflicted by conflict, violence, and crime. The trade in illicit arms propels violence and undermines security, development, and justice across the globe. Each year, law enforcement intercepts large numbers of weapons or related items smuggled into various regions each year. In a 2010 report, the UNODC found that the global trade in illicit arms was valued about approximately $100 million, at about 10 to 20 percent of the licit market (UNODC, 2010).

The illegal trade in weapons is impacted by two interconnected phenomena, including the so-called "Ant Trade" and the dark web. Evidence suggests that arms trafficking takes place at the regional or local level, with multi-ton, intercontinental shipments accounting for a small percentage of illicit transfers. The Ant Trade refers to frequent deliveries of small numbers of weapons that, over time, result in in the accumulation of large numbers of illicit weapons that enter the black market. For example, according to the Small Arms Survey in 2013, thousands of firearms seized in Mexico are traced back to the United States. These weapons are bought from gun shops in small numbers and then smuggled across the border. While the individual transactions occur on a small scale, the sum total of firearms trafficked into Mexico is large (Small Arms Survey, 2013).

Further, the "dark web" has played an increasing, albeit smaller, role in the illegal trade of weapons. The dark web enables the movement of illegal weapons on the black market, allowing buyers better-performing, more recent firearms at lower prices than those available on the street. The US is the most common source for arms that for sale, with almost 60 percent of listings originating from the US, followed by European countries (25%) and unspecified locations (12%). Europe, however, accounts for the largest market, with revenues five times higher than the US. The value of the arms trade is approximately $80,000 per month, which is very small scale compared to more traditional arms trafficking, and not the option utilized in large conflict zones, where massive amounts of arms are required. Yet the dark web does provide a platform for individuals (e.g., lone-wolf terrorists) and small groups (gangs) to procure weapons and ammunition. Although small scale, the dark web offers another avenue for the marketing and sale of illicit weapons (Paoli et al., 2017).

Intellectual Property Theft

TOC groups participate in the theft of intellectual property, including through encroachment into corporate and proprietary computer networks. There are many types of intellectual theft, ranging from copyright infringement of movies, music, and video games to forged imitations of popular and trusted brand names, to trade-marked designs of high-tech devices and manufacturing processes. Intellectual property theft triggers significant revenue losses for legitimate business, erodes marketplace competitiveness, and can also threaten public health and safety. For example, fake medical supplies, counterfeit automobile and aircraft parts, toxic toys and cosmetics, and unapproved electrical goods can be dangerous for unwitting consumers.

There has been a marked increase in the number of intellectual property rights (IPR) violations over the last decade. In 2016, it was estimated that IPR infringement accounted for 3.3 percent of world trade. According to the *Trends in Trade in Counterfeit and Pirated Goods* report, it is estimated that the value of imported fake or pirated goods is now worth around US $509 billion (Organisation for Economic Co-operation and Development [OECD], 2019). Most fake goods originate in mainland China and Hong Kong, although some originate from the United Arab Emirates, Turkey, Singapore, Thailand, and India. Small parcels sent by post or express courier are a growing concern, as there is inadequate screening of smaller parcels by custom officials. Aside from insufficient inspections of small parcels, freer trade—with reduced taxes, custom controls, and lighter regulation—has accelerated the counterfeit trade. The illicit trade of fake or pirated goods generates large profits for transnational organized groups. Lenient sentences and high profit margins make IPR violations an enticing option for criminal entrepreneurs, who take advantage of more complex technology, expanded distribution channels and increased demand for pirated goods (OECD, 2019).

Global Cybercrime

Cybercrime costs consumers billions of dollars per year, threatens corporate and government computer networks, and destabilizes confidence in the international economy. TOC networks are increasingly involved in online frauds targeting the banking industry, stock markets, credit card networks, and digital currency. Estimates reveal that cybercrime costs between US $70 billion to $140 billion per year

(Council of Economic Advisers [CEA], 2018). Moreover, widespread criminal activity in cyberspace can jeopardize both citizens' and businesses' faith in digital systems, which are critical to our society and the economy. Society is dependent on personal computers and mobile devices, all of which are targets of TOC networks. However, these devices leave a trail of digital criminal evidence, which requires highly trained personnel to detect. Unfortunately, there is a critical shortage of investigators with this highly technical skill, providing even more opportunities for cybercriminals to profit with impunity.

MAJOR TRANSNATIONAL ORGANIZED CRIME GROUPS

Organized crime groups appear in every country and region in the world and include African, Asian, Balkan, Eurasian, Italian, Middle Eastern, and Western Hemisphere transnational organized crime groups.

African Transnational Organized Crime Groups

Since the 1980s, African TOC groups have developed rapidly due to globalization and advances in communications technology. African TOC groups have branched out from local and regional crime networks to pursue international victims and partner with other criminal networks in more economically affluent countries. The economic, political, and social conditions in African countries such as Nigeria, Ghana, and Liberia facilitate the expansion of criminal networks globally. Nigerian criminal networks are the most significant African TOC group. They operate in 80 countries and are primarily engaged in drug trafficking and financial frauds. They are notorious for various fraudulent schemes that target individuals, businesses, and government offices. The Nigerian scam, also known as advance-fee fraud or 419 fraud, is a scam in which a sender overseas offers a share in a large sum of money or a payment on the condition that you help them transfer money out of their country. Targets are lured by seemingly "easy" money and are tricked into paying the "costs" associated with the transfer. After the "costs" are paid by the victim, the scammers will disappear or ask for more money be sent to continue with the transfer. In the 1990s, Nigerians were heavily involved in this type of fraud, and advance-fee fraud was named "419" after the Nigerian criminal code clause that outlaws it (Shaw & Reitano, 2019). Currently, advance-fee fraud is a worldwide phenomenon, with a wide variety of criminal entrepreneurs from numerous countries engaging in the crime. It is also more complex, as fraudsters use fake emails, text messages, telecommunications, and variants such as employment offers, online sales/rentals, pet sales, and online dating scams to trick victims.

Asian Transnational Organized Crime

Asian criminal networks have flourished as a result of globalization and have influence in every continent in the world. The two major categories of Asian TOC are traditional and non-traditional criminal enterprises. Traditional criminal enterprises include Chinese Triads and the Japanese Yakuza or Boryokudan. Chinese Triads or underground societies are based in Hong Kong, Taiwan, and Macau. However, they are truly a global entity, worth billions of dollars. It estimated that they have more than 250,000 members, with almost 100,000 in Hong Kong alone (Pubrick, 2019). The yakuza has over 22 designated separate organized crime groups, which operate out of office buildings, use corporate logos, and even have pension plans. As a result of economic recession and law enforcement crackdowns, the yakuza's influence has steadily decreased since 2011, with membership falling from 184,000 in the early 1960s to just 30,500 in 2017. Still, the yakuza continue to earn billions in profits, even collecting 5 percent of all revenue from construction work (Adelstein, 2017). The yakuza operate several front companies that are involved in waste disposal, entertainment, and labour dispatch. The yakuza operate in corporate-style acquisitions with relatively lower levels of violence. They also benefit from a romantic image, as they wear expensive suits, have distinctive tattoos called *irezumi*, and engage in *yubitsume*, or finger-shortening, in which they cut off pinky fingers to show remorse or apologize for a mistake.

Non-traditional Asian criminal enterprises include Chinese criminally influenced Tongs, Triad affiliates, and ethnic street gangs found in several countries with sizable Asian communities. Asian TOC depends on vast networks of national and international criminal associates that are fluid and very mobile. They have highly sophisticated operations and advanced financial expertise, hiding their criminal interests in "legitimate" business, ranging from small family-run operations to large corporations. Asian criminal networks have partnerships with several TOC groups that cross ethnic and racial lines and have become truly global phenomena that engage in the gamut of criminal activities, from murder and kidnapping to sophisticated white-collar crimes (Schneider, 2017).

Balkan Transnational Organized Crime

Balkan TOC groups originate from Albania, Bosnia-Herzegovina, Croatia, Kosovo, Serbia, North Macedonia, Montenegro, Bulgaria, Greece, and Romania. The origins of Balkan groups are based in traditional clan structures in largely rural regions. They were guided by kanun, an ethical code that values loyalty and secrecy. The clans would provide members with shared protection and support, which sometimes led to violence between the clans. The structure of the clans became a pillar for modern-day Balkan organized crime. However, in the late 1980s and early 1990s, the collapse of communism facilitated the expansion of a thriving black market, expanding the Balkan criminal influence globally, with Balkan organized groups using large profits to co-opt newly democratic governments (Stojarová, 2007).

Modern Balkan TOC groups do not operate under a traditional hierarchy and are more flexible and project based. These groups are formed around ethnic associations and friendship connections. Modern Balkan TOC groups are proficient at implementing new technologies such as cyber-fraud, which further expands their criminal markets. Nonetheless, they also engage in multiple criminal activities including passport fraud, identify theft, healthcare fraud, real estate fraud, insurance fraud, money laundering, extortion, human smuggling, prostitution, and drug trafficking (Tarantini, 2016).

Middle Eastern Transnational Organized Crime

After 9/11, Middle Eastern TOC groups have received more attention, often being mistaken for terrorist groups. However, the primary goal of many Middle Eastern TOC groups is to make money through illicit activities. These organizations typically take part in high-end automobile theft, financial fraud, money laundering, drug trafficking, counterfeiting, cigarette smuggling, and various types of fraud. They are active in several regions, including Egypt, Iran, Iraq, Israel, Jordan, Lebanon, Oman, United Arab Emirates, Yemen, and Turkey. For example, Israel has 16 crime families, while Turkish mafia has strong influence throughout Western Europe. They are increasingly sophisticated and work with TOC groups to increase revenues and global status (Schneider, 2017; Viano, 2020).

Eurasian Transnational Organized Crime

Originating from the former Soviet Union or Central Europe, Eurasian TOC groups are profitable entities that have strong political connections and cross international borders They do not conform to the typical hierarchal structure of organized crime, operating in cell-like networks that have specific functions. This structure lets cells work autonomously, reducing their interaction with members of the larger organization, which gives immunity to higher-level OC figures. Eurasian TOC groups engage in several criminal activities but are adept at financial-based frauds, as well as the exploitation of state natural resources, such as gas, oil, and forestry (Schneider, 2017; Viano, 2020).

The Russian mafiya is the most well-known of the Eurasian TOC groups, with approximately 300,000 members and some 450 organizations. Some of these groups are linked to Russian oligarchs, who have connections to the highest levels of government. Russian crime lords have moved out of the black market and into "legitimate" operations such as chemical factories, ports, and banks. The expertise is in money laundering, where they export billions of dollars per year through legitimate banks through bribery, corruption, and violence. Russian mobsters are also involved in the killing of journalists, political rivals, and law enforcement officials (Galeotti, 2017).

Western Hemisphere Transnational Organized Crime

Western hemisphere TOC is of particular concern, as these groups account for a large portion of drug trafficking in the world. Criminal activity is categorized into three areas, which include the source zone, transit zone, and retail zone. The source zone is where the activity originates and includes countries such as Colombia, Peru, and Bolivia, where the world's coca is harvested, enabling the global distribution of cocaine. Aside from the large-scale production of narcotics, TOC participates in money laundering, human smuggling, weapons trafficking, and trafficking in persons within the source countries. In many of these regions, enormous profits from drug trafficking have enabled TOC to bribe public officials and co-opt justice. Moreover, some regions have experienced large amounts of violence, with murders at very high levels (Vilalta, 2020). The transit zone are regions in which activity passes through, including Mexico and Central American countries. Mexico serves a dual function, as both a source and transit country, as Mexican drug lords are the primary producers of meth, heroin, and marijuana in the western hemisphere, while also moving large shipments of cocaine that originate from South America. Central American TOC organizations, predominately within Panama, Nicaragua, Honduras, and El Salvador, are not only involved transport of illicit drugs but also involved in migrant smuggling and human and firearms trafficking. These regions have experienced increasing levels of violence as a result of illicit market competition. The retail zone is the ultimate destination of the illicit drugs and encompasses the United States and Canada. The United States is the leading drug consumption marketplace in the western hemisphere, while Canada serves two functions, as a destination country and transit country where drug and human smuggling are facilitated. The ports of Vancouver and Montreal are vulnerable to the smuggling of illegal drugs and counterfeit goods. For example, the BC

Hell's Angels have partnered with the Colombian and Mexican drug cartels to supply cocaine across Canada, while Mexican cartels utilize Canada as a trans-shipment port for European and Australia-bound cocaine shipments (Avilés, 2017; Schneider, 2017).

Italian Transnational Organized Crime

Italian organized crime is a huge money-making enterprise, with estimates of revenues that exceed $50 billion per year. In North America, Italian organized crime is referred to as traditional organized crime, the Mafia and La Cosa Nostra (LCN). In the 1950s, Meyer Lansky claimed that the Mafia was "bigger than U.S. Steel," generating profits larger than many corporations. Until the 1990s, the Italian mafia dominated organized crime in North America, losing some control to other groups after intense prosecution. Nonetheless, in certain pockets in both the US and Canada, such as New York, Montreal, and Hamilton, the Italian Mafia are still players in organized crime, continuing their involvement in illicit activities (Ruggiero, 2019; Schneider, 2017).

Italian transnational organized crime is a global phenomenon, with their influence extending beyond Italy into Europe, South America, and North America. There are four major Italian organized crime groups, including the Sicilian Mafia; 'Ndrangheta (Calabrian Mafia); Camorra (Neapolitan Mafia); and Sacra Corona Unita. The Sicilian Mafia is the second largest group in Italy and specializes in heroin trafficking. The Sicilians have a long and deadly history of violence, including the high-profile murders of judges, police officers, and politicians. The term *excellent cadaver* is used to describe the killing of high-ranking public officials. The 'Ndrangheta originates in the Calabria region and has emerged as a truly global presence, worth $55 billion per annum. It has an estimated 10,000 members and is at the centre of drug-trafficking networks linking Colombia and the European market (Lister, 2018). They make large amounts of money from cigarette smuggling bypassing European tariffs. They also have a strong presence in Canada, specifically the Greater Toronto Region, where they are known as the Siderno Group. Originating from the Naples region, the Camorra also has a global presence focused on drug trafficking and counterfeit goods market, taking advantage of their control of the Naples port, which is the one the largest ports in Europe. Based out of the Puglia region, the Sacra Corona Unita specializes in smuggling cigarettes, drugs, arms, and people. They control the southeast coast of Italy, which is a transit point for the smuggling of goods from Croatia, Albania, and the former Yugoslavia (Schneider, 2017).

CONCLUSION: POLICING AND CONTROLLING TRANSNATIONAL ORGANIZED CRIME—CHALLENGES AND LIMITATIONS

The control of transnational organized crime is a daunting task. This section will briefly outline 1) law enforcement responses and tools, 2) prosecution strategies, and 3) international cooperation.

Law Enforcement Responses and Tools

There are many strategies that law enforcement employs to fight transnational organized crime. Depending on the jurisdiction, some agencies have specialized enforcement units that focus on organized crime; others have no specialized units. Regardless, the investigation of organized crime can be complex and necessitate some degree of specialization and expertise. For example, financial crimes such as money laundering require investigators with very specialized knowledge and capabilities. Moreover, successful investigations require multiagency cooperation as crimes such as human trafficking, drug trafficking, and cybercrime cross international boundaries (Walker, 2011).

Law enforcement uses several specific strategies to combat TOC, which include controlled delivery, physical and electronic surveillance, undercover operations, financial analysis, and use of informants. According to article 2(i) of the United Nations organized crime convention, **controlled delivery** is "the technique of allowing illicit or suspect consignments to pass out of, through, or into the territory of one or more States, with the knowledge and under the supervision of their competent authorities, with a view to the investigation of an offence and the identification of persons involved in the commission of the offence" (UNODC, 2004, p. 6).

Controlled deliveries help to track the movement of illicit goods to uncover their source, transit routes, and destinations. This allows investigators to ascertain the magnitude of the criminal conspiracy, the structure of the organization, and the role of individual actors involved in the illicit activity. *Physical* and *electronic surveillance* are important investigative tools for law enforcement. However, citizens' rights to privacy, especially within their own homes, places limits on law enforcement agencies' actions. In most jurisdictions, law enforcement agencies require probable cause, reasonable suspicion, reasonable/probable grounds, and judicial authorization. Similarly, electronic surveillance entails strict judicial control and legal protections to prevent abuse and limit invasion of privacy

(UNODC, 2010). Electronic surveillance is the ideal investigative technique when organized crime group cannot be infiltrated or where access or surveillance would be too risky for investigators. There are several methods of electronic surveillance, including audio surveillance (phone tapping, voice over internet protocol, listening devices or "bugs"), visual surveillance (hidden video, in-car video, body-worn video, thermal imaging, CCTV), tracking surveillance (global positioning system, mobile phones, radio frequency identification devices, biometric info technology), and data surveillance (computer/internet, mobile phones, keystroke monitoring). **Undercover operations** involve the infiltration of criminal networks by undercover investigators who pose as offenders. The undercover agent is limited in their actions as they are not allowed to commit or provide opportunities for the commission of crime. Undercover agents that encourage targets to commit crime are termed **agents provocateurs** and most jurisdictions have rules against the **entrapment** of suspects. Undercover operations are expensive, time-consuming, and dangerous, and they are not frequently used by law enforcement. Nonetheless, undercover operations can lead to numerous convictions and can provide invaluable information about the nature and scope of organized crime activities. **Sting operations** are a type of undercover police activity that use deceptive *fronts* or agents to infiltrate criminal activity involving trade in stolen property, counterfeit goods, or money laundering. Although expensive to fund, *sting operations* can catch many offenders and disrupt criminal markets. **Financial analysis** is the evaluation of personal or business revenue, expenditures, and financial networks to uncover unexplained income. Organized crime groups employ several fraudulent schemes to conceal illicit profits, such as creating fictitious companies to launder funds, the overpayment of employees, and the overpayment of subcontractors for kickback. Financial analysis is an integral part in the investigation and prosecution of organized crime activities. However, they require specialized expertise on the part of investigators. The use of informants is vital in the fight against organized crime. Also known as *justice collaborators* or *cooperating witnesses*, informants can either be a member of the public or a victim of crime. However, most informants are criminals that cooperate with authorities to receive a reduced charge, reduced sentence, immunity from prosecution, or compensation from authorities. Informants can be helpful in providing inside knowledge, which helps build criminal cases against organized crime groups. A major limitation in the use of criminal informants is the issue of credibility, as juries may not believe the testimony of criminal informants who may have incentives to perjure themselves to receive immunity or compensation.

Prosecution Strategies

Although their role varies by country, prosecutors play an important role in the investigation of transnational organized crime groups. Prosecutors supervise and provide recommendations to police investigators. Prosecutors utilize several strategies in the fight against organized crime, the most important being **witness immunity** and **witness protection**. *Witness immunity* provides cooperating witnesses with legal protection from being prosecuted for criminal activities. This allows prosecutors to use lower-level organized crime actors to prosecute on higher-level organized criminals. Legal safeguards ensure that due process is followed, such as the cross-examination of witnesses, corroboration of evidence, and sanctions for perjured testimony. Nevertheless, immunity from prosecution has been criticized due to the potential of prosecutorial misuse or coercion, which can lead to wrongful convictions. Nonetheless, witness immunity is beneficial in the fight against TOC, as there are few alternatives to gathering evidence against organized criminals, in which illicit activities are secretive and dangerous for both investigators and potential witnesses. *Witness protection* is critical to the successful investigation, the prosecution of organized criminals, and the rule of law. The goal of witness protection is to ensure that witnesses are safeguarded from retaliation or intimidation. Witnesses who testify against organized criminals can be provided with physical protection, the closing of the court, sealing records of the trial, use of voice distortion, or video conferencing for testimony. In more extreme cases, witnesses may be given a temporary residence in a safe house or relocation and new identify after the conclusion of the trial.

International Cooperation

Policing TOC is very difficult and requires consistent and meaningful cooperation between law enforcement agencies. Globally, law enforcement agencies exchange information on a reciprocal basis. This cooperation, however, can be undermined by conflicting agendas, reduced communication and information-sharing, mistrust, and differences in resource allocation for law enforcement in various countries. Further, in some countries, bribery and corruption are rampant, and the legitimacy of the institutions are undermined. This makes it difficult for coordinated international responses to TOC, as these rogue states become safe havens for the criminal organizations. Global law enforcement efforts require compatible laws and legal protocols. Nonetheless, there are significant practical problems with investigative cooperation at the international level. Jurisdictional issues are a major issue, as many countries have multiple agencies that have enforcement authority including national/federal police services, local/regional police, specialized organized crime units, and customs. International cooperation also is beset with operational and bureaucratic problems, including differences in information technology, access to resources and specialized equipment, language barriers, and differing legal systems and procedures. Aside from these challenges, the threat of TOC forces states to work together to investigate, prosecute, and convict organized criminals (Schneider, 2017; Walker, 2011).

There are several initiatives that help expand law enforcement agencies global effort, including law enforcement liaison officers who establish communications channels between their agency and its counterpart in a foreign country. The largest institution for global police cooperation is **Interpol**, which allocates considerable effort to combat TOC. Interpol includes 192 member states and functions under international law. However, it does not have investigative powers or the ability to make arrests. The mandate of Interpol is the exchange of police information through a range of criminal databases and communication channels that distribute information about crimes, criminals, and threats (Interpol, 2018). Moreover, there are several regional organizations that have a similar mandate and structure as Interpol. Europol is the law enforcement agency of the European Union that combats serious international organized crime and terrorism. Similarly, ASEANAPOL, Afripol, and Ameripol are law enforcement organizations in Asia, Africa, and the Americas, respectively. International cooperation in TOC also includes mutual legal assistance, extradition, and transfer of criminal proceedings and sentenced persons. Overall, there has been a considerable global effort to design international treaties, model treaties, and laws that improve the effectiveness of TOC (Walker, 2011).

REVIEW QUESTIONS

1. What are the primary differences between traditional organized crime and transnational organized crime?
2. List three examples of organized or transnational organized crime that capture your attention and explain why they represent significant concerns for safety and security.
3. In what ways does transnational organized crime pose a threat to economic and political stability?

GLOSSARY

agents provocateurs: Undercover law enforcement agents or their operatives that create the conditions to induce targets to commit crime.

Alien Conspiracy theory: A debunked theory that blames immigrants, outsiders, and external influences for the prevalence of organized crime within society.

bribery: Described as the lubricant for organized crime, bribery is when a person voluntarily solicits or accepts any benefit, financial or otherwise, in exchange for influencing an official act so as to afford the provider preferential treatment.

cartel: An interconnected network of criminal actors who cooperate with other criminal organizations to coordinate their activities.

Chinese Triads: Underground criminal societies based in Hong Kong, Taiwan, and Macau that operate as a global entity whose criminal enterprises generate billions of dollars in revenues.

conflict-affected states: Political states that have significant social divisions, depleted infrastructure, large amounts of firearms, and crippling poverty rates, often coupled with religious or ideological division, which creates the conditions for human trafficking and other forms of illegal activity.

controlled delivery: According to the UN, it is "The technique of allowing illicit or suspect consignments to pass out of, through, or into the territory of one or more states, with the knowledge and under the supervision of their competent authorities, with a view to the investigation of an offence and the identification of persons involved in the commission of the offence." (United Nations Office on Drugs and Crime, 2018)

corruption: Unethical conduct by a person in a position of power who violates their authority of office by facilitating wrongdoing, usually for personal gain.

debt bondage: A technique used by captors to further the enslavement of individual victims who are denied freedom until such time as an onerous financial debt that is imposed on them is paid.

entrapment: The use of deliberate and deceptive methods to set a trap that compels a target of crime control to get caught in the act, so as to gain a criminal conviction.

ethnicity trap: The tendency to understand organized crime on the basis of the ethnicity of the groups that engage in it, instead of focusing on the type of organized criminal activity itself.

facilitators: Semi-legitimate actors such as accountants, attorneys, notaries, bankers, and real estate brokers who traverse both the licit and illicit worlds.

failed state: A political state characterized by a weak or non-existent government, high levels of military dominance, weak law enforcement, and poor infrastructure and social services—all of which create the conditions for organized crime and corruption to flourish.

financial analysis: The evaluation of personal or business revenue, expenditures, and financial networks to uncover unexplained income undertaken to investigate the proceeds of crime.

human smuggling: The facilitation, transportation, or illegal entry of a person or persons across an international border.

human trafficking: When one person obtains or holds another person in forced service, such as involuntary servitude, slavery, debt bondage, or forced labour.

Interpol: The largest institution for global police cooperation, which allocates considerable effort to combat organized crime and includes 192 member states and functions under international law.

money laundering: The process of making funds that are generated by an illicit activity, such as drug trafficking or gambling, appear to have come from a legitimate source.

multiple marginality: A type of social marginalization in which at-risk youth may be compelled to join street gangs as a way of adapting to the social and economic limitations imposed on their life chances, and which tend to occur in areas with poor economic indicators, poor infrastructure, underfunded education systems, lack of job opportunities, family disruption, and racial discrimination.

narco-terrorism: Terrorism financed by profits obtained from illegal drug trafficking.

organized crime: A criminal organization that operates through a clandestine network of conspirators who form a hierarchical command structure and who operate criminal enterprises across the long term, and traditionally consist of members who are of the same ethnic culture or are engaged in the same type of criminal activity.

sting operations: A type of undercover police activity that use deceptive *fronts* or agents to infiltrate criminal activity involving trade in stolen property, counterfeit goods, or money laundering.

transnational organized crime (TOC): An interconnected network or *cartel* of criminal actors who cooperate with other criminal organizations internationally to coordinate their criminal activities.

undercover operations: The infiltration of criminal networks by undercover investigators who pose as offenders.

underground economy: The total amount of financial activities that *do not* form a part of the *legitimate* capitalist consumer economy but are generated by illicit economic exchange.

witness immunity: Providing cooperating witnesses with legal protection from being prosecuted for criminal activities.

witness protection: Protecting witnesses in a criminal prosecution against organized criminals to ensure the witnesses are safeguarded from retaliation or intimidation.

yakuza: A well-organized Japanese crime group with over 22 designated separate groups that operate out of office buildings, have corporate logos, and operate at an international level.

REFERENCES

Abt Associates. (2020). *Research on facilitators of transnational organized crime: Understanding crime networks' logistical support.* US Department of Justice.

Adelstein, J. (2017, October 2). Why one of Japan's largest organized crime groups is looking for legitimate work. *Forbes.* Retrieved from https://www.forbes.com/sites/adelsteinjake/2017/10/02/why-one-of-japans-largest-organized-crime-groups-is-looking-for-legitimate-work/#12880abb321f

Albanese, J. S. (2011). *Transnational crime and the 21st century: Criminal enterprise, corruption, and opportunity.* Oxford University Press.

Arsovska, J. (2019). Western Balkans: Organised crime, political corruption and oligarchs. In F. Allum & S. Gilmour (Eds.), *Handbook of organised crime and politics* (pp. 86–104). Edward Elgar Publishing.

Avilés, W. (2017). *The drug war in Latin America: Hegemony and global capitalism.* Routledge.

Beare, M. E. (2015). *Criminal conspiracies: Organized crime in Canada.* Oxford University Press.

Bjerregaard, E., & Kirchmaier, T. (2019). *The Danske Bank money laundering scandal: A case study.* Copenhagen Business School. http://dx.doi.org/10.2139/ssrn.3446636

Björnehed, E. (2004). Narco-terrorism: The merger of the war on drugs and the war on terror. *Global Crime, 6*(3–4), 305–324.

Comeau, K. (2019, May 28). Why Canada's money-laundering problem is far bigger than we think. *Financial Post.* Retrieved from https://financialpost.com/opinion/why-canadas-money-laundering-problem-is-far-bigger-than-we-think

Corpwatch. (2001, March 3). *Tobacco companies linked to criminal organizations in lucrative cigarette smuggling.* Retrieved from https://corpwatch.org/article/tobacco-companies-linked-criminal-organizations-lucrative-cigarette-smuggling

Council of Economic Advisers. (2018). *The cost of malicious cyber activity to the U.S. economy.* The White House. Retrieved from https://trumpwhitehouse.archives.gov/articles/cea-report-cost-malicious-cyber-activity-u-s-economy/

Derrida, J. (1994). *Specters of Marx: The state of the debt, the work of mourning and the new international*. Routledge.

Dreier, H. (2018, June 25). I've been reporting on MS-13 for a year. Here are the 5 things Trump gets most wrong. *ProPublica*. Retrieved from https://www.propublica.org/article/ms-13-immigration-facts-what-trump-administration-gets-wrong

Dunbar, L. K. (2017). *Youth gangs in Canada: A review of current topics and issues*. Public Safety Canada.

Galeotti, M. (Ed.). (2017). *Russian and post-Soviet organized crime*. Routledge.

Gomis, B. (2015). *Demystifying "narcoterrorism."* Global Drug Policy Observatory.

Hahn, G. (2012). The Caucasus Emirate Jihadists: The security and strategic implications. In S. J. Blank (Ed.), *Russia's homegrown insurgency: Jihad in North Caucasus* (pp. 1–97). Strategic Studies Institute.

International Labour Organization (ILO) & Walk Free Foundation. (2017). *Global estimates of modern slavery: Forced labour and forced marriage*. Retrieved from https://www.ilo.org/wcmsp5/groups/public/@dgreports/@dcomm/documents/publication/wcms_575479.pdf

International Organization for Migration. (2014). *Fatal journeys: Tracking lives lost during migration*.

Interpol. (2018). What is Interpol. Retrieved from https://www.interpol.int/en/Who-we-are/What-is-INTERPOL

Kassab, H. S., & Rosen, J. D. (2019). General trends in drug trafficking and organized crime on a global scale. In *Illicit markets, organized crime, and global security* (pp. 87–109). Palgrave Macmillan.

Kelly, K., & Caputo, T. (2005). Linkages between street gangs and organized crime: The Canadian experience. *Journal of Gang Research, 13*(1), 17–32.

Kemp, W., Shaw, M., & Boutellis, A. (2013). Haiti. In *The elephant in the room: How can peace operations deal with organized crime?* (pp. 32–45). International Peace Institute.

Lind, D. (2019, February 5). MS-13, explained: President Trump has turned the Salvadoran-American street gang into public enemy no. 1. *Vox*. Retrieved from https://www.vox.com/policy-and-politics/2018/2/26/16955936/ms-13-trump-immigrants-crime

Lister, T. (2018, December 10). Inside Europe's most powerful mafia: The 'Ndrangheta. *CNN* Retrieved from https://www.cnn.com/2018/12/08/europe/ndrangheta-mafia-raids-analysis-intl/index.html

Locke, R. (2012). Introduction. In *Organized crime, conflict, and fragility: A new approach* (p. 1). International Peace Institute.

Minnaar, A. (2017). Online "underground" marketplaces for illicit drugs: The prototype case of the dark web website *"Silk Road." Acta Criminologica: African Journal of Criminology & Victimology, 30*(1), 23–47.

Nagle, L. E. (2010). Corruption of politicians, law enforcement, and the judiciary in Mexico and complicity across the border. *Small Wars & Insurgencies, 21*(1), 95–122.

Naím, M. (2006). *Illicit: How smugglers traffickers and copycats are hijacking the global economy.* Anchor Books.

Organisation for Economic Co-operation and Development (OECD). (2019, March 18). *Trade in fake goods is now 3.3% of world trade and rising.* Retrieved from https://www.oecd.org/newsroom/trade-in-fake-goods-is-now-33-of-world-trade-and-rising.htm

Paoli, G. P., Aldridge, J., Ryan, N., & Warnes, R. (2017). *Behind the curtain: The illicit trade of firearms, explosives and ammunition on the dark web.* RAND Corporation.

Polaris. (2018). *Human trafficking in illicit massage businesses.* Retrieved from https://polarisproject.org/resources/human-trafficking-in-illicit-massage-businesses/

Purbrick, M. (2019). Patriotic Chinese triads and secret societies: From the imperial dynasties, to nationalism, and communism. *Asian Affairs, 50*(3), 305–322.

Ross, T. M. (2011). *Wolves in wolves' clothing: The role of the Chechen mafia in the formation of an independent Chechen Republic* [Thesis]. Naval Postgraduate School: Department of National Security Affairs.

Ruggiero, V. (2019). Italian organized crime. In M. Natarajan (Ed.), *International and transnational crime and justice* (2nd ed., pp. 181–185). Cambridge University Press.

Salihu, H. A., & Gholami, H. (2018). Mob justice, corrupt and unproductive justice system in Nigeria: An empirical analysis. *International Journal of Law, Crime and Justice, 55*, 40–51.

Schneider, S. (2017). *Canadian organized crime.* Canadian Scholars'.

Schönenberg, R., & von Schönfeld, A. (2013). Introduction. In H.-Böll-Stiftung & R. Schönenberg (Eds.), *Transnational organized crime: Analyses of a global challenge to democracy* (pp. 11–16). transcript Verlag.

Shanty, F. (2011). *The nexus: International terrorism and drug trafficking from Afghanistan.* ABC-CLIO.

Shaw, M., & Reitano, T. (2019). Organized crime and criminal networks in Africa. In W. R. Thompson (Ed.), *Oxford research encyclopedia: Politics.* Oxford University Press.

Sheptycki, J. W. E. (2007). Transnational crime and transnational policing. *Sociology Compass, 1*(2), 485–498.

Sheridan, M. B. (2020, January 21). Mexico's homicide count in 2019 among its highest. *The Washington Post.* Retrieved from https://www.washingtonpost.com/world/the_americas/homicides-in-mexico-hit-record-highs-in-2019/2020/01/21/a9c5276a-3c5e-11ea-afe2-090eb37b60b1_story.html

Small Arms Survey. (2013). *Small arms survey 2013*. Cambridge University Press.

Stojarová, V. (2007). Organized crime in the Western Balkans. *HUMSEC Journal, 1*(1), 91–114.

Tarantini, G. (2016). *The Balkan route: Organized crime in South-Eastern Europe—root causes, current developments and future prospects*. United Nations University.

UN News. (2018, November 7). *International crime gangs amass "staggering" profits in conflict zones, expert tells Security Council*. Retrieved from https://news.un.org/en/story/2018/11/1025141

United Nations. (2019, September 17). *The number of international migrants reaches 272 million, continuing an upward trend in all world regions, says UN*. Retrieved from https://www.un.org/development/desa/en/news/population/international-migrant-stock-2019.html

United Nations Conference on Trade and Development (UNCTAD). (2019). *Review of maritime transport 2019*. Retrieved from https://unctad.org/en/PublicationsLibrary/rmt2019_en.pdf

United Nations Office on Drugs and Crime. (2004). *Legislative guides for the implementation of the United Nations Convention against Transnational Organized Crime and the protocols thereto*. United Nations Publications. https://www.unodc.org/unodc/en/treaties/CTOC/legislative-guide.html

United Nations Office on Drugs and Crime. (2009, February). *Global report on trafficking in persons*. Retrieved from https://www.unodc.org/documents/Global_Report_on_TIP.pdf

United Nations Office on Drugs and Crime. (2010). *The globalization of crime: A transnational organized crime threat assessment*. Retrieved from https://www.unodc.org/documents/data-and-analysis/tocta/TOCTA_Report_2010_low_res.pdf

United Nations Office on Drugs and Crime. (2015, December 15). *Opium production in Myanmar and Lao PDR stabilizes at high levels*. Retrieved from https://www.unodc.org/southeastasiaandpacific/en/2015/12/opium-survey-report/story.html

United Nations Office on Drugs and Crime. (2018a). *Global study on smuggling of migrants, 2018*. United Nations Publications. Retrieved from https://www.unodc.org/documents/data-and-analysis/glosom/GLOSOM_2018_web_small.pdf

United Nations Office on Drugs and Crime. (2018b). Controlled delivery. Retreived from https://www.unodc.org/e4j/zh/organized-crime/module-8/key-issues/special-investigative-techniques/controlled-deliveries.html

United Nations Office on Drugs and Crime. (2020). Money laundering. Retrieved from https://www.unodc.org/unodc/en/money-laundering/overview.html

United Nations Office on Drugs and Crime. (n.d.). Transnational organized crime: The globalized illegal economy. Retrieved from https://www.unodc.org/toc/en/crimes/organized-crime.html

Viano, E. C. (Ed.). (2020). *Global organized crime and international security*. Routledge.

Vigil, D. (2002). Community dynamics and the rise of street gangs. In M. M. Suárez-Orozco & M. M. Páez (Eds.), *Latinos: Remaking America* (pp. 97–109). University of California Press.

Vilalta, C. (2020). Violence in Latin America: An overview of research and issues. *Annual Review of Sociology, 46*, 693–706. https://doi.org/10.1146/annurev-soc-073018-022657

Viswanatha, A., & Wolf, B. (2012, December 11). HSBC to pay $1.9 billion U.S. fine in money-laundering case. *Reuters*. Retrieved from https://www.reuters.com/article/us-hsbc-probe/hsbc-to-pay-1-9-billion-u-s-fine-in-money-laundering-case-idUSBRE8BA05M20121211

von Lampe, K. (2015). *Organized crime: Analyzing illegal activities, criminal structures, and extra-legal governance*. SAGE Publications.

Walker, N. (2011). The pattern of transnational policing. In T. Newburn (Ed.), *Handbook of policing* (2nd ed., pp. 147–174). Taylor & Francis.

Webb, S. (2013, December 1). Japanese mobsters becoming "Goldman Sachs with guns": Executives at Japanese banks apologise for lending millions to underworld figures. *Daily Mail*. Retrieved from https://www.dailymail.co.uk/news/article-2516479/Japanese-mobsters-Goldman-Sachs-guns-Executives-Japanese-banks-apologise-lending-millions-underworld-figures.html

Woodiwiss, M. (2003). Transnational organised crime: The strange career of an American concept. In M. Beare (Ed.), *Critical reflections on transnational organised crime, money laundering, and corruption* (pp. 3–34). University of Toronto Press.

Copyright Acknowledgements

Index

FARC. *See* Revolutionary Armed Forces of
Colombia
fascism, 43, 212, 239, 248
Federal Bureau of Investigation (FBI), 122,
220, 259, 325; COINTELPRO, 220;
Internet Crime Complaint Center, 435–436
Federal Court of Appeal, 378
federal penitentiaries, 382, 394–395
feeble-mindedness, 240, 242, 262
female genital mutilation, 99, 170, 183
femicide, 41, 68, 171, 289–290, 307
feminism, 199, 368; radical, 164; second-wave,
162–163, 184; third-wave, 163, 185
feminist criminology, 97–100, 108
Ferri, Enrico, 44–45
fetal alcohol spectrum disorders (FASDs), 251,
262
feticide, 288–289
films: about crime and justice, 91, 116, 122,
135, 137, 140, 145–146
financial analysis, 515, 519
financial crime. *See* economic crime
financial crisis (2008), 4, 63, 66, 317,
327, 346
financial markets: expansion of, 491–493
financial statements: misrepresentation in,
324–325
Fiola, Chantal, 453, 470
firearms, 3, 24, 290, 486, 490, 507–508, 512;
illegal, 94, 495
Fisher, Charlie, 456
Floyd, George, 388
folk devils, 136–138
Forbes, Jack D., 462
forced labour, 5, 344, 494, 506
fortune teller scams, 417–418
Foucault, Michel, 3, 49, 92–94, 99, 157–158,
171, 389; *Discipline and Punish*, 93
fourth estate, 206, 228
Frankfurt School, 127–129
frankpledge system, 387, 400

fraud, 316, 349, 407–438, 440; traditional,
413–418
freedom, 193–196, 198; boundaries of, 197;
individual, 21; law as impediment to, 155;
legal, 42
Freud, Sigmund, 52, 133, 279
frustration–aggression hypothesis, 56, 68,
281, 307

Gacy, John Wayne, 258, 259, 282
Gage, Phineas, 246
Galizia, Daphne Caruana, 206–207
Galton, Francis, 46, 242
gambling, 100, 155, 156, 173–177; government
monopoly on, 175; as moral sin, 173;
problem, 176, 184
gangs, 120, 283–284, 292, 491, 507; criminal,
8, 61, 62; outlaw biker, 63; street, 63–64,
497, 499–501, 510; youth, 63–64, 136, 500
Gangster Disciples, 497
gay conversion therapy, 156, 183
gender, 391; and crime, 39, 97–99, 103;
difference and, 17; discrimination on basis
of, 27, 333, 360; ideologies of in crime-
themed media, 132–135; moral attitudes on,
170; regulation of, 217; rights and freedoms,
76, 171; and serial murderers, 55, 259;
stereotypes of, 98; stratification of, 99
gender identity, 100, 163; discrimination
on basis of, 25; non-conforming, 156;
persecution on basis of, 41
gender relations, 86, 166, 170
General Motors (GM), 5, 317, 332
genocide, 41, 47, 68, 277, 278, 299, 301–302,
307; cultural, 86; settler, 460
Gerbner, George, 96, 129
Germany: Nazi, 239, 241; sex workers in, 166
Ghomeshi, Jian, 168–169
ginawaydaganuk, 453, 478
girls: control over lives and bodies of, 171;
criminality of, 98; exclusion of from